United States of America by
obal
ess Science Reference (an imprint of IGI Global)
E. Chocolate Avenue
shey PA, USA 17033
: 717-533-8845
x: 717-533-8661
mail: cust@igi-global.com
Veb site: http://www.igi-global.com

Library of Congress Cataloging-in-Publication Data

es: Okur Dinçsoy, Meltem, 1974- editor. | Can, Hamit, 1988- editor.
: Optimizing energy efficiency during a global energy crisis / edited
y Meltem Okur Dinçsoy, Hamit Can.
scription: Hershey, PA : Business Science Reference, [2023] | Includes
bibliographical references and index. | Summary: "This book tries to
determine the factors affecting economic development and raise awareness
about the effects and consequences of these factors"-- Provided by
publisher.
Identifiers: LCCN 2023034626 (print) | LCCN 2023034627 (ebook) | ISBN
9798369304006 (hardcover) | ISBN 9798369304044 (paperback) | ISBN
9798369304013 (ebook)
Subjects: LCSH: Energy consumption. | Energy policy. | Economic
development--Environmental aspects.
Classification: LCC HD9502.A2 O678 2023 (print) | LCC HD9502.A2 (ebook) |
DDC 333.79--dc23/eng/20230811
LC record available at https://lccn.loc.gov/2023034626
LC ebook record available at https://lccn.loc.gov/2023034627

This book is published in the IGI Global book series Advances in Finance, Accounting, and Economics (AFAE) (ISSN: 2327-5677; eISSN: 2327-5685)

British Cataloguing in Publication Data
A Cataloguing in Publication record for this book is available from the British Library.

Optimizing E
Efficiency Dur
Energy Crisis

Meltem Okur Dinçsoy
Trakya University, Turkey

Hamit Can
Trakya University, Turkey

A volume in the Advances in Finance, Accounting, and Economics (AFAE) Book Series

IGI Global
PUBLISHER of TIMELY KNOWLEDGE

Advances in Finance, Accounting, and Economics (AFAE) Book Series

Ahmed Driouchi
Al Akhawayn University, Morocco

ISSN:2327-5677
EISSN:2327-5685

Mission

In our changing economic and business environment, it is important to consider the financial changes occurring internationally as well as within individual organizations and business environments. Understanding these changes as well as the factors that influence them is crucial in preparing for our financial future and ensuring economic sustainability and growth.

The **Advances in Finance, Accounting, and Economics (AFAE)** book series aims to publish comprehensive and informative titles in all areas of economics and economic theory, finance, and accounting to assist in advancing the available knowledge and providing for further research development in these dynamic fields.

Coverage

- Finance
- Economic Policy
- Ethics in Accounting and Finance
- Field Research
- Applied Finance
- Accounting Standards
- Accounting information systems
- E-Finance
- E-Accounting
- Stock Market

IGI Global is currently accepting manuscripts for publication within this series. To submit a proposal for a volume in this series, please contact our Acquisition Editors at Acquisitions@igi-global.com or visit: http://www.igi-global.com/publish/.

The Advances in Finance, Accounting, and Economics (AFAE) Book Series (ISSN 2327-5677) is published by IGI Global, 701 E. Chocolate Avenue, Hershey, PA 17033-1240, USA, www.igi-global.com. This series is composed of titles available for purchase individually; each title is edited to be contextually exclusive from any other title within the series. For pricing and ordering information please visit http://www.igi-global.com/book-series/advances-finance-accounting-economics/73685. Postmaster: Send all address changes to above address.

Titles in this Series

For a list of additional titles in this series, please visit: www.igi-global.com/book-series

Theory and Practice of Illegitimate Finance
Abdul Rafay (University of Management and Technology, Pakstan)
Business Science Reference • © 2023 • 390pp • H/C (ISBN: 9798369311905) • US $295.00

Sustainable Growth and Global Social Development in Competitive Economies
Andrei Jean Vasile (Petroleum-Gas University of Ploiesti, Romania & Romanian Academy, National Institute for Economic Research "Costin C. Kiriţescu", Romania) Mile Vasić (European Marketing and Management Association, Banja Luka, Bosnia and Herzegovina) and Predrag Vukovic (Institute of Agricultural Economics, Belgrade, Srbia)
Business Science Reference • © 2023 • 331pp • H/C (ISBN: 9781668488102) • US $250.00

The Impact of AI Innovation on Financial Sectors in the Era of Industry 5.0
Mohammad Irfan (NSB Academy Business School, India) Mohammed Elmogy (Information Technology Department, Faculty of Computers and Information, Mansoura University, Egypt) M. Shabri Abd. Majid (Faculty of Economics and Business, Syiah Kuala University, Banda Aceh, Indonesia) and Shaker El-Sappagh (Department of Artificial Intelligence and Machine learning, Sungkyunkwan University, South Korea)
Business Science Reference • © 2023 • 320pp • H/C (ISBN: 9798369300824) • US $275.00

Concepts and Cases of Illicit Finance
Abdul Rafay (University of Management and Technology, Pakistan)
Business Science Reference • © 2023 • 273pp • H/C (ISBN: 9781668485873) • US $250.00

The Importance of Entrepreneurship in Fostering Economic Progress
Mohammed El Amine Abdelli (University of Western Brittany, France) Naima Bentouir (Ain Temouchent University, Algeria) and Esra Sipahi Döngül (Aksaray University, Turkey)
Business Science Reference • © 2024 • 300pp • H/C (ISBN: 9781668471272) • US $240.00

Perspectives on the Transition Toward Green and Climate Neutral Economies in Asia
Patricia Ordóñez de Pablos (The University of Oviedo, Spain) Mohammad Nabil Almunawar (Universiti Brunei Darussalam, Brunei) and Muhammad Anshari (Universiti Brunei Darussalam, Brunei)
Business Science Reference • © 2023 • 465pp • H/C (ISBN: 9781668486139) • US $325.00

Revolutionizing Financial Services and Markets Through FinTech and Blockchain
Kiran Mehta (Chitkara Business School, Chitkara University, India) Renuka Sharma (Chitkara Business School, Chitkara University, India) and Poshan Yu (Soochow University, China & Australian Studies Centre, Shanghai University, China)
Business Science Reference • © 2023 • 340pp • H/C (ISBN: 9781668486245) • US $265.00

IGI Global
PUBLISHER of TIMELY KNOWLEDGE

701 East Chocolate Avenue, Hershey, PA 17033, USA
Tel: 717-533-8845 x100 • Fax: 717-533-8661
E-Mail: cust@igi-global.com • www.igi-global.com

Table of Contents

Advances in Finance, Accounting, and Economics (AFAE) Book Series

Ahmed Driouchi
Al Akhawayn University, Morocco

ISSN:2327-5677
EISSN:2327-5685

Mission

In our changing economic and business environment, it is important to consider the financial changes occurring internationally as well as within individual organizations and business environments. Understanding these changes as well as the factors that influence them is crucial in preparing for our financial future and ensuring economic sustainability and growth.

The **Advances in Finance, Accounting, and Economics (AFAE)** book series aims to publish comprehensive and informative titles in all areas of economics and economic theory, finance, and accounting to assist in advancing the available knowledge and providing for further research development in these dynamic fields.

Coverage

- Finance
- Economic Policy
- Ethics in Accounting and Finance
- Field Research
- Applied Finance
- Accounting Standards
- Accounting information systems
- E-Finance
- E-Accounting
- Stock Market

IGI Global is currently accepting manuscripts for publication within this series. To submit a proposal for a volume in this series, please contact our Acquisition Editors at Acquisitions@igi-global.com or visit: http://www.igi-global.com/publish/.

The Advances in Finance, Accounting, and Economics (AFAE) Book Series (ISSN 2327-5677) is published by IGI Global, 701 E. Chocolate Avenue, Hershey, PA 17033-1240, USA, www.igi-global.com. This series is composed of titles available for purchase individually; each title is edited to be contextually exclusive from any other title within the series. For pricing and ordering information please visit http://www.igi-global.com/book-series/advances-finance-accounting-economics/73685. Postmaster: Send all address changes to above address.

Titles in this Series

For a list of additional titles in this series, please visit: www.igi-global.com/book-series

Theory and Practice of Illegitimate Finance
Abdul Rafay (University of Management and Technology, Pakstan)
Business Science Reference • © 2023 • 390pp • H/C (ISBN: 9798369311905) • US $295.00

Sustainable Growth and Global Social Development in Competitive Economies
Andrei Jean Vasile (Petroleum-Gas University of Ploiesti, Romania & Romanian Academy, National Institute for Economic Research "Costin C. Kiriţescu", Romania) Mile Vasić (European Marketing and Management Association, Banja Luka, Bosnia and Herzegovina) and Predrag Vukovic (Institute of Agricultural Economics, Belgrade, Srbia)
Business Science Reference • © 2023 • 331pp • H/C (ISBN: 9781668488102) • US $250.00

The Impact of AI Innovation on Financial Sectors in the Era of Industry 5.0
Mohammad Irfan (NSB Academy Business School, India) Mohammed Elmogy (Information Technology Department, Faculty of Computers and Information, Mansoura University, Egypt) M. Shabri Abd. Majid (Faculty of Economics and Business, Syiah Kuala University, Banda Aceh, Indonesia) and Shaker El-Sappagh (Department of Artificial Intelligence and Machine learning, Sungkyunkwan University, South Korea)
Business Science Reference • © 2023 • 320pp • H/C (ISBN: 9798369300824) • US $275.00

Concepts and Cases of Illicit Finance
Abdul Rafay (University of Management and Technology, Pakistan)
Business Science Reference • © 2023 • 273pp • H/C (ISBN: 9781668485873) • US $250.00

The Importance of Entrepreneurship in Fostering Economic Progress
Mohammed El Amine Abdelli (University of Western Brittany, France) Naima Bentouir (Ain Temouchent University, Algeria) and Esra Sipahi Döngül (Aksaray University, Turkey)
Business Science Reference • © 2024 • 300pp • H/C (ISBN: 9781668471272) • US $240.00

Perspectives on the Transition Toward Green and Climate Neutral Economies in Asia
Patricia Ordóñez de Pablos (The University of Oviedo, Spain) Mohammad Nabil Almunawar (Universiti Brunei Darussalam, Brunei) and Muhammad Anshari (Universiti Brunei Darussalam, Brunei)
Business Science Reference • © 2023 • 465pp • H/C (ISBN: 9781668486139) • US $325.00

Revolutionizing Financial Services and Markets Through FinTech and Blockchain
Kiran Mehta (Chitkara Business School, Chitkara University, India) Renuka Sharma (Chitkara Business School, Chitkara University, India) and Poshan Yu (Soochow University, China & Australian Studies Centre, Shanghai University, China)
Business Science Reference • © 2023 • 340pp • H/C (ISBN: 9781668486245) • US $265.00

IGI Global
PUBLISHER of TIMELY KNOWLEDGE

701 East Chocolate Avenue, Hershey, PA 17033, USA
Tel: 717-533-8845 x100 • Fax: 717-533-8661
E-Mail: cust@igi-global.com • www.igi-global.com

Table of Contents

Detailed Table of Contents

The unwise use of natural resources has led to a global increase in greenhouse gases and widespread environmental pollution with a wide variety of wastes. The inefficient consumption of energy sources, the global energy crisis, and military actions in Ukraine have led to a drastic increase in the cost of energy sources and an increase in the prices of all goods and services worldwide. Countries around the world, and Bulgaria in particular, are solving tasks for improving energy, energy efficiency, and security and improving the energy sector. As part of the solution to this problem is the use of both renewable and alternative sources, more and more people are talking about this new generation of nuclear energy, and now nuclear energy according to a decision of the European Commission refers to green energy.

The chapter explores the principal dimensions of energy transformations and their repercussions for specific shifts in the economic and political realms. The research showcases the main vectors in the development of the energy sector with emphasis on contemporary metamorphoses in the context of the impact of the 2020 pandemic crisis, the 2021 energy crisis, and the continuing war in Ukraine, resulting in a redrawing of the world energy map. The author discusses explicit aspects of energy policy from the perspective of the evolutions in the last years, outlining the conceptual frame of the diversification efforts of different players in the energy chain, and their attempts to resolve energy dilemmas. Special attention is paid to the significant focus on global plans, launched with the goal of achieving "sustainable recovery," so as to take advantage of the opportunities generated by the current crises to switch to a new energy model.

Chapter 6

Paul Adjei Kwakwa, University of Energy and Natural Resources, Ghana
Solomon Aboagye, University of Cape Town, South Africa & Lancaster University Ghana, Ghana

The rising levels of carbon dioxide (CO2) emissions on the African continent has been an issue of concern. Consequently, this study analyses the mitigating role of renewable energy and mobile technology in the effect of industrial sector growth on carbon dioxide emissions. Using data from 32 African countries for the period 2002-2021, the study finds that expansion in industrial sector increases CO2 emissions for the region, while renewable energy consumption and mobile technology reduce carbon emissions. Also, renewable energy and mobile phone technology are found to moderate the effect of industrial growth on CO2 emissions. Other findings are that trade openness, urbanization, and income increase carbon dioxide emissions. The study recommends the removal of financial impediments in the way of industrial firms to enhance their acquisition of efficient technologies for operations to reduce carbon dioxide emissions. Also, governments in the region should increase financial support for the development and adoption of renewable energy.

Chapter 7

Fatma Dila Taşdemir, Independent Researcher, Turkey

Energy is an important input for economic growth and development of countries. The concepts of energy and economic growth have been prominent topics for economics literature and policy makers for many years. In this note, the existence and the direction of causality between primary energy supply (PES) and gross domestic products (GDP) for Türkiye's economy is examined using data for the period 1970-2021. The variables are subjected to augmented Dickey-Fuller and Phillips-Perron unit root tests, and then the Toda-Yamamoto causality test is performed to determine the direction of causality. Based on the causality test, bidirectional causality is observed between the primary energy supply variable and the GDP variable.

Chapter 8

Adjera Alitoska Kazaz, Trakya University, Turkey
Davut Kazaz, Trakya University, Turkey

This study aims to examine the long-run causal relationship between CO2 emissions, renewable energy consumption, GDP growth, and oil prices in Türkiye. The study covers the period 1990-2020. Toda-Yamamoto's causality test is used to avoid some of the problems faced by Granger's causality test. Furthermore, the study also utilizes variance decomposition and impulse-response function methods. The Toda-Yamamoto causality test indicates a two-way causal relationship between renewable energy and economic growth and between renewable energy and oil prices. The study revealed an undeniable and evident causality relationship in only one direction, from economic growth towards CO2 emissions and oil prices. Also, a unidirectional causal relationship between CO2 emissions and both oil prices and renewable energy was found. In order to achieve sustainable development and protect the environment, Türkiye requires renewable energy. Solar, wind, and hydropower can lessen the dependency on fossil fuels, generate employment opportunities and stimulate economic progress.

The Global Development Initiative, announced by China's President Xi Jinping in 2021, demonstrates China's ambition not only to strongly contribute to global development but also to have its voice in designing the dominant narrative when it comes to global development as well as to international order. This further enhances the strategic competition between China and the United States. Hence, the aim of the chapter is to study China's alternative approach to global development as an integral element of the transformation of the international order. It will analyze in comparative perspective the specific Chinese approach, key ideas, underlying values, and understanding of global development. The study will also examine China's economic, political, and geopolitical interests and motives that drive the country's approach to global development. Methodologically, the chapter will move away from the strict framework of Western theories on international development. It will rather look for better understanding of Chinese views on global development.

This study examines the interplay between energy consumption, environmental impact, and economic development by analyzing the relationship between GDP per capita and electric power consumption, energy use, renewable energy consumption, and research and development expenditure. The study uses panel ARDL methodology, analyzing data from OECD countries covering the period from 1996 to 2020. The results suggest that electric power consumption and energy use have a positive long-run relationship with GDP per capita, while renewable energy consumption and research and development expenditure have a negative relationship. The findings of this study provide valuable insights for policymakers seeking to promote sustainable economic growth while mitigating environmental degradation. The chapter concludes by highlighting the need for a holistic approach that takes into account the complex interplay between these variables and promotes policies that foster sustainable economic growth and environmental sustainability.

The chapter is focused on the study of the effect of the processes caused by the global COVID-19 pandemic on the health insurance market in Bulgaria – a field of business with a high return on investment and an exceptional public benefit, while at the same time suffering from a deficit of research, which necessitates the need for more in-depth and up-to-date scientific analysis and studies. In this regard, referring to the official statistical data of the Financial Supervision Commission, an analysis is made of the key indicators for the development of the insurance market in Bulgaria during the period 2017-2022, indicating the factors that influence the main processes taking place in it. The main result is expressed in confirmation of the thesis, that there is high market concentration in the current health insurance market, in favor of a few insurance companies performing a key role in it, and on the market, there is growth in terms of gross written premium income, also provoked by COVID-19.

Global renewable power capacity is growing. The intermittent nature of wind and solar, in particular, and the difficulty in forecasting generation lead to fluctuations and sometimes sudden increases in electricity prices. This leads to the need for more energy to balance the grid power. Through energy storage, the effect of these uncertainties can be partially eliminated, and potential price fluctuations can be prevented. Electricity generation from renewable sources has been increasing in Türkiye in recent years. In addition, recent legal regulations have paved the way for the installation of large-scale energy storage facilities. This chapter highlights the recent global and domestic developments in renewable energy policies and their potential reflections. The future of energy storage in Türkiye is also discussed.

The aim of this study is to discuss China's role in the development process in the current world order. This chapter elucidates how China's Belt and Road Initiative (BRI) connects countries from all over the world in the context of economic and trade prosperity. Thus, the revival of the China's old silk road by President Xi Jinping has initiated a global development programme on all the continents. Since 2013, China has been delivering through the successful launch of the BRI projects and dominate on their counterpart in the new world order. Now, the theory of globalisation is being pioneered by Chinese diplomacy in world politics. The concept of soft and hard power is applied to explain the main research problems of this study. The chapter relies on qualitative analysis and an empirical approach to discussion to investigate the goal of this research.

Energy crises have emerged as one of the most pressing and complex global challenges. As the world becomes increasingly interconnected and reliant on energy for its day-to-day operations, the repercussions of these crises are felt across societies, economies, and the natural environment. Disruptions in energy supply, fluctuating prices, and overreliance on finite and non-renewable resources demand urgent and proactive measures. In this context, strategic adaptive responses play a pivotal role in enabling organizations to navigate these challenges successfully and enhance their overall resilience. Effective crisis management constitutes a cornerstone of strategic adaptive responses to energy crises.

The study comes as a result and in response to the identified priorities of the social policy in Bulgaria and logically outlines the actions for an effective management of the social processes tailored to the dynamic social environment. The essential characteristics of the social policy, its relations with the social management, and the opportunities for it to become a way of realization of important public tasks gives the chance to fit in it more delicate and important problems and the associated solutions. For this reason, the achievement of an active labor market is perceived as an objective of the social management, reachable in the conduct of relevant social policies, reflecting the registered interests of interested parties and society's need for an appropriate and irreversible change. The actually active social programs, interpreted as a system of social projects with direct feedback of social interaction, define the possibilities for adaptation of their components to the coming changes.

The study presents the mechanisms influencing the development of innovations in industrial business organizations in the Republic of Belarus, emphasizing the stimulation of the innovative development of organizations from the real sector of the economy, research, and education sector. The innovation policy plays an important role in the development of country`s competitiveness, creating favourable conditions for the increase of financial potential, development of intellectual resources, modernization of scientific and innovation infrastructure. Some basic economic theories, such as the cluster theory, network theory, and integration theory describe the process of increasing the efficiency of an enterprise through collaborative partnership by combining functional advantages of each partner. These theories focus on achieving synergy in the form of developed and put into practice innovative product due to shared use of resource potential of the members of such associations.

The world economy and its energy sector are going through tough period of simultaneous imposition of the evolutionary processes of global transformation, digitalization, and green transition on the one hand, and global innovation challenges, geopolitical, and geostrategic upheavals on the other hand. Digitalization, climate mitigation programs, and the green transition contributed to the intensification of the globalization of production and services, and hence the expansion of distributed forms of multi-subject business activities—global value chains (GVC), global production networks (GPN), and global innovation networks (GIN)—and, at the same time, decentralization of green energy advancing the development of distributed generation and consumption of energy resources, as well as the widespread introduction of energy efficient technologies.

Different digital transformation applications have been developed in order to provide more qualified and higher quality services to the local people by using the internet, information, and communication technologies in local governments. This study has examined which applications they have implemented by using information technology in order to respond to the needs of local people in a shorter and faster time thanks to the digital transformation applications put into practice by local governments. Suggestions have been developed in order to provide the expected benefit from digital transformation in local governments. The problems encountered in the digital transformation transition and the predictions that will be encountered if these problems are not resolved are stated. In addition, energy efficiency and the applicability of European projects with digital transformation in local governments and their effects on the economic crisis and economic development in the country are mentioned.

Nutrition is the most basic need for human well-being. It also develops human capital. Foods are very important to all of us, and proper nutrition is essential for a healthy, active life. However, although the issues of access to food and healthy sustainable nutrition are very important for a healthy life, their effects on the economy cannot be ignored. There is a growing belief by many scientists that applications developed to improve the nutritional status of people, in addition to their nutritional content, have significant value in terms of economic outcomes. According to results from studies that integrate insights from nutrition and economics, many investments in nutrition are actually very good economic investments. It is thought that this study, which deals with the economic effects of nutrition in addition to a healthy lifestyle, will also have important benefits in terms of the improved design of programs and policies that aim to benefit the results related to nutrition.

The study comes as a result and in response to the identified priorities of the social policy in Bulgaria and logically outlines the actions for an effective management of the social processes tailored to the dynamic social environment. The essential characteristics of the social policy, its relations with the social management, and the opportunities for it to become a way of realization of important public tasks gives the chance to fit in it more delicate and important problems and the associated solutions. For this reason, the achievement of an active labor market is perceived as an objective of the social management, reachable in the conduct of relevant social policies, reflecting the registered interests of interested parties and society's need for an appropriate and irreversible change. The actually active social programs, interpreted as a system of social projects with direct feedback of social interaction, define the possibilities for adaptation of their components to the coming changes.

The study presents the mechanisms influencing the development of innovations in industrial business organizations in the Republic of Belarus, emphasizing the stimulation of the innovative development of organizations from the real sector of the economy, research, and education sector. The innovation policy plays an important role in the development of country`s competitiveness, creating favourable conditions for the increase of financial potential, development of intellectual resources, modernization of scientific and innovation infrastructure. Some basic economic theories, such as the cluster theory, network theory, and integration theory describe the process of increasing the efficiency of an enterprise through collaborative partnership by combining functional advantages of each partner. These theories focus on achieving synergy in the form of developed and put into practice innovative product due to shared use of resource potential of the members of such associations.

The world economy and its energy sector are going through tough period of simultaneous imposition of the evolutionary processes of global transformation, digitalization, and green transition on the one hand, and global innovation challenges, geopolitical, and geostrategic upheavals on the other hand. Digitalization, climate mitigation programs, and the green transition contributed to the intensification of the globalization of production and services, and hence the expansion of distributed forms of multi-subject business activities—global value chains (GVC), global production networks (GPN), and global innovation networks (GIN)—and, at the same time, decentralization of green energy advancing the development of distributed generation and consumption of energy resources, as well as the widespread introduction of energy efficient technologies.

Different digital transformation applications have been developed in order to provide more qualified and higher quality services to the local people by using the internet, information, and communication technologies in local governments. This study has examined which applications they have implemented by using information technology in order to respond to the needs of local people in a shorter and faster time thanks to the digital transformation applications put into practice by local governments. Suggestions have been developed in order to provide the expected benefit from digital transformation in local governments. The problems encountered in the digital transformation transition and the predictions that will be encountered if these problems are not resolved are stated. In addition, energy efficiency and the applicability of European projects with digital transformation in local governments and their effects on the economic crisis and economic development in the country are mentioned.

Nutrition is the most basic need for human well-being. It also develops human capital. Foods are very important to all of us, and proper nutrition is essential for a healthy, active life. However, although the issues of access to food and healthy sustainable nutrition are very important for a healthy life, their effects on the economy cannot be ignored. There is a growing belief by many scientists that applications developed to improve the nutritional status of people, in addition to their nutritional content, have significant value in terms of economic outcomes. According to results from studies that integrate insights from nutrition and economics, many investments in nutrition are actually very good economic investments. It is thought that this study, which deals with the economic effects of nutrition in addition to a healthy lifestyle, will also have important benefits in terms of the improved design of programs and policies that aim to benefit the results related to nutrition.

Preface

Economic development refers to the development of countries in many ways, such as social, political, and cultural, as well as economic growth. The level of development of countries; affects the living conditions and welfare levels of citizens. In this book, it has been tried to determine the factors affecting economic development. It is aimed to raise awareness about the effects and consequences of these factors. In this study, various factors affecting economic development are discussed in general terms. In addition, digital transformation, energy efficiency, energy crises, climate change, and the effects of nutrition on development have been examined in sections and their possible effects on development and other issues with economic effects have been tried to be determined.

It aims to contribute to the literature through different topics and various methods in the fields of economy, development, informatics, and policy. It is thought that the gaps in the missing and unexplored parts of these topics will be filled by using original methods and research on the topics covered.

Potential contexts in which this book will be used are economics, finance, and development strategies. Suitable for markets related to these scopes.

CHAPTER OVERVIEW

Chapter 1 delves into the challenges posed by the global energy crisis and its impact on the cost of energy sources worldwide. It discusses how inefficient energy consumption has led to environmental problems and rising energy prices. Moreover, it explores the role of nuclear energy, now considered a part of green energy according to the European Commission. The chapter emphasizes the need for improved energy efficiency and sustainable energy sources in Bulgaria and globally.

Chapter 2 offers an exploration of the intricate relationship between energy transformations and their multifaceted consequences on economic and political developments. It highlights the impact of the 2020 pandemic crisis, the 2021 energy crisis, and the ongoing conflict in Ukraine on global energy dynamics. The chapter also discusses various energy policies and efforts to attain "sustainable recovery" in the context of these crises, ultimately reshaping the global energy landscape.

Chapter 3 presents a comprehensive analysis of the relationship between Gross Domestic Product per Capita (GPC), Airport Activity Index (AAI), Electricity Consumption per Person (EPP), Physicians per 1,000 people (PPT), and Credit Volume (CRE) in Turkish cities with airports. It demonstrates that increased airport activity correlates positively with economic output, while electricity consumption and access to healthcare contribute significantly to regional economic development. Interestingly, higher credit volumes appear to have an inverse relationship with economic output.

Chapter 4 delves deep into China's economic development, exploring the multifaceted factors that have played pivotal roles. We shine a spotlight on the transformative impact of digital technologies, which have been driving China's economy at an astonishing pace. However, we also shed light on the challenges faced by local governments as they grapple with the complexities of adapting to these digital transformations.

Furthermore, we conduct a comprehensive analysis of China's response to the global energy crisis, dissecting the strategies and policies that the nation has implemented. This examination extends to the far-reaching implications of China's energy transitions on its overall development trajectory, underlining the critical role energy plays in its economic growth.

As climate change becomes an increasingly urgent global concern, we empirically investigate how it affects the Chinese economy and, in turn, how China is actively working to adapt to these environmental shifts. The empirical evidence presented here illuminates the real-world consequences of climate change on China's economic landscape.

Beyond the realms of technology and climate, this chapter takes a unique perspective by delving into the crucial role of nutrition in a nation's economy. We examine how nutrition impacts productivity and literacy rates, shedding light on a less-explored facet of economic development.

In sum, this chapter contributes fresh insights to the literature on economic growth and policy, providing a nuanced understanding of China's intricate economic ascent. Through a comprehensive examination of digital transformation, energy efficiency, climate change, and nutrition, we offer a holistic perspective on the multifaceted factors driving China's complex economic rise.

Chapter 5 examines the intricate relationship between renewable energy generation, consumption, and economic growth in Türkiye. It employs various analytical methods, including the vector autoregression model (VAR) and Granger Causality, to analyze data spanning from 1990 to 2020. The findings suggest a causal relationship between renewable energy consumption to economic growth in the long run, emphasizing the importance of renewable energy sources for Türkiye's economic development.

Chapter 6 explores the rising carbon dioxide emissions in Africa and assesses the moderating influence of renewable energy and mobile technology on the impact of industrial sector growth. Using data from 32 African countries from 2002 to 2021, the study reveals that industrial sector growth increases CO2 emissions while renewable energy consumption and mobile technology adoption reduce emissions. It recommends removing financial barriers for industrial firms to acquire efficient technologies and increasing support for renewable energy development.

Chapter 7 investigates the causal relationship between primary energy supply (PES) and gross domestic product (GDP) in Türkiye's economy using data from 1970 to 2021. Augmented Dickey-Fuller and Phillips-Perron unit root tests are conducted, followed by the Toda-Yamamoto causality test. The results reveal a bidirectional causal relationship between PES and GDP, underscoring the significance of energy as a driver of economic growth in Türkiye.

Chapter 8 embarks on an in-depth exploration of the intricate dynamics between key factors crucial to Türkiye's economic and environmental landscape. Over a three-decade span, from 1990 to 2020, the study employs Toda-Yamamoto's causality test, a method that offers valuable insights into causal relationships while addressing some of the limitations of earlier Granger's causality test.

The primary objective of this study is to unravel the long-term causal links between CO2 emissions, renewable energy consumption, GDP growth, and oil prices in Türkiye. To achieve this, the chapter employs not only Toda-Yamamoto's causality test but also employs variance decomposition and impulse-response function methods, allowing for a robust analysis of these interwoven factors.

The findings of this study are enlightening. The Toda-Yamamoto causality test reveals a bidirectional causal relationship between renewable energy and economic growth, indicating a mutually reinforcing connection between the two. Furthermore, it identifies a unidirectional causal relationship between economic growth towards CO_2 emissions and oil prices, underlining the pivotal role of economic growth in influencing these variables.

Moreover, this chapter emphasizes the urgency of Türkiye's transition towards sustainable development and environmental preservation. The study underscores the indispensable need for renewable energy sources such as solar, wind, and hydropower, which not only reduce dependency on fossil fuels but also hold the potential to generate employment opportunities and propel economic progress.

In essence, this chapter provides essential insights into Türkiye's sustainable development journey, highlighting the intricate web of relationships between CO_2 emissions, renewable energy, GDP growth, and oil prices. It offers valuable recommendations for steering Türkiye towards a more environmentally friendly and economically prosperous future.

Chapter 9 delves into China's Global Development Initiative and its ambition to shape global development and international order. It explores China's unique approach, values, and interests in global development, highlighting its strategic competition with the United States. This chapter adopts a comparative perspective, focusing on Chinese views and actions in the realm of global development, thereby offering fresh insights beyond Western theories on international development.

Chapter 10 examines the complex relationship between energy consumption, environmental impact, and economic development in OECD countries. Utilizing panel ARDL methodology and data spanning from 1996 to 2020, it reveals the long-run positive relationship between electric power consumption and energy use with GDP per capita. Conversely, renewable energy consumption and research and development expenditure exhibit negative relationships with economic growth. These findings hold implications for sustainable economic growth and environmental sustainability.

Chapter 11 investigates the impact of the COVID-19 pandemic on Bulgaria's health insurance market. Drawing from data provided by the Financial Supervision Commission, it assesses key indicators and market concentration in the health insurance sector from 2017 to 2022. The findings highlight a high level of market concentration, with a few insurance companies dominating the market. Additionally, the chapter underscores the growth in gross written premium income, partly driven by the pandemic's effects.

Chapter 12 explores the growth of global renewable power capacity and its impact on electricity price fluctuations. It underscores the need for energy storage to mitigate the intermittent nature of renewable energy sources. The chapter discusses recent developments in renewable energy policies in Türkiye and their implications for energy storage, shedding light on the future of energy storage in the country.

Chapter 13 examines China's role in global development and international order through the lens of the Belt and Road Initiative (BRI). It explores how the BRI connects countries worldwide, promoting economic and trade prosperity and reshaping the world order. The chapter analyzes China's use of soft and hard power in this context, providing insights into its global leadership and the evolution of globalization.

Chapter 14 delves into the challenges posed by energy crises in an interconnected world and the role of strategic adaptive responses in enhancing organizational resilience. It emphasizes the importance of crisis management in navigating energy-related challenges and promoting resilience in organizations.

Chapter 15 addresses the social policy priorities in Bulgaria and outlines actions to manage social processes effectively in a dynamic social environment. It emphasizes the importance of an active labor market as a means of achieving social development. The chapter discusses social programs and their adaptability to societal changes, offering insights into labor market policies in Bulgaria.

Chapter 16 delves into the intricate mechanisms that drive innovation within industrial business organizations in the Republic of Belarus. Our focus extends to stimulating and fostering innovative development, encompassing organizations from both the real sector of the economy and the research and education sector.

At the heart of our exploration lies the critical role of innovation policy in shaping the nation's competitiveness. Belarus recognizes that fostering innovation is vital to creating a conducive environment for increasing financial potential, nurturing intellectual resources, and modernizing its scientific and innovation infrastructure. These elements collectively contribute to the nation's ability to thrive in a rapidly evolving global economic landscape.

To illuminate the strategies behind fostering innovation, this chapter draws upon fundamental economic theories. The cluster theory, network theory, and integration theory are employed to describe the process through which enterprise efficiency is enhanced via collaborative partnerships. These theories underscore the significance of combining the functional advantages of each partner within these associations, ultimately leading to the achievement of synergy. This synergy manifests in the form of developed and practical innovative products, a direct result of shared resource potential among the association's members.

In summary, this chapter offers a comprehensive insight into the mechanisms that drive innovation within industrial business organizations in Belarus. By emphasizing the crucial role of innovation policy and applying essential economic theories, it provides a holistic understanding of how Belarus is actively fostering innovation. This, in turn, contributes to the nation's competitiveness, economic growth, and modernization efforts.

Chapter 17 presents a comprehensive exploration of the evolving landscape of global economics and the challenges and opportunities it brings. The world economy and its energy sector find themselves navigating a complex terrain marked by the simultaneous emergence of global transformation processes, including digitalization and the green transition, alongside global innovation challenges, geopolitical shifts, and geostrategic upheavals.

The chapter delves into the profound impact of digitalization, climate mitigation programs, and the green transition on global economic dynamics. These transformative forces have intensified the globalization of production and services, leading to the expansion of distributed multi-subject business activities, such as Global Value Chains (GVCs), Global Production Networks (GPNs), and Global Innovation Networks (GINs). Simultaneously, they have fueled the decentralization of green energy, fostering the development of distributed generation and consumption of energy resources, and facilitating the widespread adoption of energy-efficient technologies.

In essence, this chapter offers an insightful exploration of the challenges and opportunities that the modern firm faces in a rapidly evolving global economic landscape. By addressing the intricate interplay between digitalization, green transition, innovation challenges, and geopolitical shifts, it provides a nuanced understanding of the forces shaping the contemporary world economy.

Chapter 18 explores the challenges and opportunities presented by digital transformation in local governments. It examines the applications of information technology in providing faster and more efficient services to local communities. Additionally, the chapter discusses the role of digital transformation in energy efficiency, European projects, and its effects on economic development.

Chapter 19 underscores the importance of nutrition as a fundamental human need and its role in developing human capital. It explores the economic effects of nutrition, emphasizing its value in improving economic outcomes. The chapter highlights the economic benefits of investments in nutrition, contributing to a healthier lifestyle and societal well-being.

Meltem Okur Dinçsoy
Trakya University, Turkey

Hamit Can
Trakya University, Turkey

Chapter 1
Optimizing Energy Efficiency in the Conditions of a Global Energy Crisis

Nikolay Todorov Dolchinkov
https://orcid.org/0000-0002-6171-6083
National Military University "Vasil Levski", Veliko Tarnovo, Bulgaria

ABSTRACT

The unwise use of natural resources has led to a global increase in greenhouse gases and widespread environmental pollution with a wide variety of wastes. The inefficient consumption of energy sources, the global energy crisis, and military actions in Ukraine have led to a drastic increase in the cost of energy sources and an increase in the prices of all goods and services worldwide. Countries around the world, and Bulgaria in particular, are solving tasks for improving energy, energy efficiency, and security and improving the energy sector. As part of the solution to this problem is the use of both renewable and alternative sources, more and more people are talking about this new generation of nuclear energy, and now nuclear energy according to a decision of the European Commission refers to green energy.

INTRODUCTION

In connection with the global energy crisis of the last 2-3 years, the topic of energy resources and sources on a global scale is extremely relevant and is discussed at numerous high-level meetings between the heads of state of countries from all continents. This crisis did not pass by Europe and it can even be argued that the countries of Europe are one of the most affected by the energy and accompanying financial and resource crisis. This problem did not arise suddenly, and the leaders of the countries of Europe and the world started discussing the optimization of energy resources several decades ago (Mitev 2021). Since the beginning of this century, most countries in the world have followed a policy to limit harmful emissions of greenhouse gases and replace coal and other polluting plants with alternative and renewable sources, as well as ecological ones that do not pollute the environment. Unfortunately, many

DOI: 10.4018/979-8-3693-0400-6.ch001

of the world's leading economic powers and economically developed countries refuse to comply with international agreements and norms and do not even participate in the implementation of the agreements. The European Union (EU), as one of the main political players, aims to be one of the world leaders in the fight against climate change and, in this regard, strives to achieve the goals of the agreement of the United Nations Conference of the Parties, the Framework Convention on Climate Change of the climate in Paris while providing clean energy to the entire continent. Bulgaria, as a member of the union, adheres to the set norms and even the requirements for us are higher than for the more economically developed countries from the western part of the continent (Dolchinkov & Karaivanova-Dolchinkova, 2021). To meet this commitment, the EU has set the following binding climate and energy targets by 2030, namely:

1. Reduction of greenhouse gas emissions by at least 40% compared to 1990;
2. Increasing energy efficiency to at least 32.5%, as Bulgaria has a lot to catch up on here;
3. Increasing the share of energy from renewable sources to at least 32% of the gross final energy consumption in the EU. An evaluation of the energy efficiency of the alternative sources should also be made here, since a large part of them are energy-intensive and the consumed electricity is comparable to the produced;
4. Ensuring a minimum 15% level of intersystem electricity connectivity between member countries. Bulgaria is energetically connected with its neighbors in terms of electricity, but the connections are not at the necessary operational level.

To ensure a coordinated and coherent approach across the EU and to implement the Energy Union Strategy, each Member State had to submit to the European Commission a draft of its integrated national energy and climate plan by 31 December 2018 and its final integrated plan until 31.12.2019 Bulgaria, as a member state of the European Union, promptly prepared and presented to the European Commission its Integrated National Environmental and Climate Plan (INECP) (Council of Ministers of the Republic of Bulgaria, 2020).

LITERATURE REVIEW

The state of energy efficiency is addressed in a number of documents adopted by forums with the participation of most member countries of the United Nations (UN). The most important sources are the normative documents of world, international and European organizations and forums. Sources from Bulgarian authors were used (Dolchinkov, 2016; Haralampiev, 2020; Manchev, 2010; Nabatov, 2015; Padarev, 2018 and others, whose works used the decisions of various national and international organizations, agencies, governments, etc.

The United Nations Framework Convention on Climate Change (UNFCCC) is one of three conventions adopted at the Earth Summit in Rio in 1992, where the international community recognized the need for collective action to protect people and the environment and to limit greenhouse gas emissions and thereby improve the energy efficiency of the world's energy resources used. The Convention has been ratified by almost all countries of the world (United Nations, 1992).

The Kyoto Protocol is an international document adopted in Kyoto, Japan on 11 December 1997 to supplement the United Nations Framework Convention on Climate Change (UNFCCC). This document is an international agreement to control global warming, committing signatory countries to reduce their greenhouse gas emissions to protect the climate. It entered into force in 2005, when it was ratified by 55 countries, as required by its signature. The US has not ratified the protocol, and Canada withdrew from it in 2011. It has been adopted by 191 countries, not all of which have ratified it (United Nations, 1997).

In 2015, a conference was held in Paris and as a result of this meeting, the Paris Agreement was signed, which prepares an action plan to limit global climate change and increase the temperature of the earth's surface. The United Nations Framework Convention on Climate Change (UNFCCC), which is the main international agreement on climate action. The Paris Agreement was adopted at the UNFCCC Meeting of the Parties in 2015. EU countries strongly support the Paris Agreement and its goal of keeping global warming at safe levels. By 2050, the EU will be climate neutral (United Nations, 2015).

In October 2022, the Council approved conclusions that will serve as the EU's main negotiating position for the 27th United Nations Climate Change Conference (COP27) in Sharm el-Sheikh (Egypt), which took place from 6 to 18 November 2022 and did not achieve the expected results.

The European Union has been one of the leading institutions in the field of efficient use of energy resources in recent decades. The current Integrated National Ecological and Climate Plan (INECP) of the European Union has been prepared in accordance with the requirements of Regulation 2018/1999 and reflects all recommendations of the EC on the draft Integrated Plan. INEKP defines the main goals and measures for implementing national policies in the field of energy and climate, in the context of European legislation, principles and priorities for energy development (Council of Ministers of the Republic of Bulgaria, 2019).

The main goals set in the Bulgarian INPEK are:

- Stimulation of low-carbon development of the economy;
- Development of competitive and secure energy;
- Reducing dependence on fuel and energy imports;
- Guaranteeing energy at affordable prices for all consumers.

National energy priorities can be summarized as follows:

- Increasing energy security and diversification of energy resource supplies;
- Development of an integrated and competitive energy market;
- Use and development of energy from renewable sources, according to the available resource, network capacity and national specifics;
- Increasing energy efficiency by developing and applying new technologies to achieve modern and sustainable energy;
- Consumer protection by guaranteeing fair, transparent and non-discriminatory conditions for using energy services.

The overall plan is fully compliant with the legislation and the main strategic documents at the European and national level (Council of Ministers of the Republic of Bulgaria, 2020).

Bulgarian legislation is fully synchronized with current international and European legislation. There is a Development Plan for Bulgaria, but due to the frequent change of governments in Bulgaria, each successive government changes the indicators of the plan, according to its own views. This leads to constant changes and the European Commission is having difficulty with our amendments to the plan and its subsections.

A good picture of the development of the Bulgarian energy market is presented by Nabokov and others in his book Electric power of Bulgaria (Nabatov N. et al, 2015).

DATA AND METHODOLOGY

Two years have passed since the adoption of the plan, but in the last six months there have been significant changes in Europe and the world. From the short-sighted policy of many of the political leaders and the transition from long-term contracts for the supply of energy carriers to fully exchange-based supplies, where the important role is played not by producers and consumers, but very often by exchange players, intermediaries and proxies of politicians and large wholesalers. This led to a complete divergence between the accepted forecast prices and the prevailing market prices and caused instability in the energy market and a significant increase in prices. In Bulgaria, there are many actions that remain hidden from the public and bypass generally accepted rules, leaving great doubts about dirty deals. When concluding deals, the main parameters are not always clarified and only learned about them after the fact. For example, the long-term contracts with Gazprom were criticized, but it turned out that other long-term gas supply contracts were concluded in their place, but not with better parameters. Such are the examples of the Turkish company "Botaş", which forces Bulgaria from January 2023 to pay 178 million dollars each month for natural gas supplies, and the fines in it are over 2 billion dollars. This is for delivery only and it is not clear who will deliver the gas to the LNG terminals, at what price, etc. Separately, the Bulgarian state has a 20% share of the terminal in the Greek port city of Alexandroupolis, and no analysis was made before signing the contracts of Bulgaria's consumption, taking into account the supplies from Azerbaijan and the Turkish Stream transit pipe to Serbia, Hungary and Europe (Ministry of Energy of the Republic of Bulgaria, 2023).

The electricity market in the Republic of Bulgaria is characterized as national and is played by producers, energy companies, power transmission companies, consumers and customers of different caliber. The device and its organization are regulated by the Rules for Trading in Electric Energy in the Republic of Bulgaria. The electricity market consists of an electricity market through bilateral contracts concluded on the platform of the exchange operator, an exchange market, a market for balancing energy, a market for reserve and additional services, a market for the provision of intersystem transmission capacity (Dolchinkov, 2016).

The Bulgarian electricity transmission network is part of the unified transmission network of the countries of continental Europe and its development is closely related to the development of the networks of the neighboring countries. From the reports of the Bulgarian National Energy Exchange, we can note that the total physical quantity traded in Bulgaria in the last 5 years is equal to 2.2 million MWh per year, with 94% of the quantity being of Romanian origin. Total physical exports for the same period amounted to 10 million MWh, distributed: Serbia (23%), Republic of North Macedonia (23%), Greece (21%), Turkey (21%) and Romania (12%). This shows that Bulgaria is primarily an exporter of electricity to all neighboring Balkan countries (NRA, 2023). During the different days of the exchange, the distribution is not uniform, with the main influence being the weather conditions, the consumers and producers included in the energy system, the load on the energy system and requests for the supply of electrical energy from neighboring countries. Bulgaria still meets the region's electricity needs, but for example, when one of the units of the Kozloduy Nuclear Power Plant (NPP) is shut down for recharging, its absence is immediately felt, and with increased electricity consumption, energy systems are seriously threatened. The energy capacities needed for the country at the current stage of the country's development are sufficient, but with the projected development of Bulgaria's economy, it is necessary to build new capacities for the production of electrical energy in the next 10 years (Kozloduy NPP, 2023). The structure of Bulgaria's electricity industry is such that Kozloduy NPP and thermal power plants (CHP) from own energy sources provide the balance of consumption (90% of consumption), CHP plants with imported energy sources work for the additional load, and hydroelectric power plants (HPP) with 2.7 MWh provides the peak load. In the last decade, many hydroelectric plants were built in the wrong place, and others necessary for our energy and time-proven were stopped, such as the Chaira PAVEC, the Belmeken - Sestrimo cascade, or were unprofessionally managed and made impossible to use.

RESULTS

Most of the transactions take place in the segment of the Centralized Bilateral Contracts Market, which has grown significantly, with their growth starting from 2018 and increasing in volume every year. Day-ahead segment volumes were also up 43% year-on-year. Also, trading in intraday segments started in April 2018 according to the requirements of the European Union and has been continuously developed in the last 5 years. Not all neighboring countries have yet built such segments, and this limits the exchange between countries, because the rules must be uniform in the countries that trade with each other. In my opinion, it is a mistake to remove medium-term and long-term contracts, which does not allow planning the operation of energy capacities and their load and achieving predictable prices, rather than a spontaneous change in prices determined by stock market speculators. Likewise, electricity producers cannot make their medium and long-term plans in advance in terms of personnel, purchase of consumables, planned repairs and other activities.

The price of electricity has also changed significantly in the last 2-3 years and instead of the set values in the integral plan, they already significantly exceed even those that were set for 2030. The set values were up to 95 €/MWh by 2030 and 106 € /MWh until 2040, but as early as October 2022, exchange prices exceeded €300/MWh. After the end of the winter season at the beginning of 2023, prices have fallen, but they are still well above what was predicted 3 years ago and are at a level that is predicted for 5-8 years and is above 100 €/MWh. This has necessitated a complete overhaul of the short-term and long-term programs and has already led to chaos in consumption and major cost overruns for producers. These high priccs, in my opinion, are also the result of the short-sighted policy led by the European Union and the leaders of many of the major economic and political countries and unions. This is based on the fact that the market and prices in Europe are the same and the burden on households is different and their economic situation is not the same in different parts of the European continent. Rich countries, which also have higher incomes, have lower energy prices than Eastern European countries, which have lower incomes for their residents. This leads to the impoverishment of the population and difficulties in servicing the payments for the used electricity by both household subscribers and industrial enterprises (Kozloduy NPP, 2023).

This is a problem not only for Bulgaria, but also for many countries in Europe and the world. Even a China in early 2023 experienced power shortages and some industrial plants were operating on a significantly reduced production schedule. This has led to delays in the supply of essential components to companies in all industries around the world.

The electricity produced in Bulgaria can be grouped into several main groups: from hydropower plants, thermal power plants, nuclear energy, wind generators and photovoltaics. Bulgaria has been and still is a gross exporter of electricity, but the conditions imposed on us by the European Commission and the actions of our politicians may soon turn Bulgaria into an importer, and thus the country's national and energy security will depend on other countries.

Bulgaria uses the existing potential of local resources to the maximum extent while complying with environmental requirements. The main energy carriers for energy production are solid fuels in the Mariska basin and the nuclear power plant.

Local coal-fired power plants currently provide about 48% of electricity production and are a guarantor of Bulgaria's energy and national security and the competitiveness of the Bulgarian economy. Bulgaria will use to the maximum extent the existing potential of the local coal in the country while complying with the environmental requirements, as they can provide a resource for the production of electrical energy for the next 60 years. Here, a reduction of the relative share by 2040 to the order of 3-4% of the total electricity production is foreseen (Bulatom, 2022).

Nuclear energy is an important energy carrier that guarantees base electricity production with predictable and competitive prices. Kozloduy NPP EAD provides over 33% of electricity production in the country and is the guarantor of Bulgaria's energy security. According to the plan, the increase in energy from nuclear capacity to almost 60% by 2040, with a net doubling from 15 GWh to almost 31 GWh (Dolchinkov & Karaivanova-Dolchinkova, 2020).

The use of energy from renewable sources is the third most important domestic energy resource, which has been increasing in recent years. A major contributor to this is the increased consumption of biomass, as well as the use of solar and wind energy for electricity generation. The comprehensive plan envisages an increase in the share of electricity production from wind generators, biomass and solar panels. In the last 4-5 years, numerous scandals have arisen in Bulgaria, specifically related to the unregulated import, storage and incineration of waste from Western European countries and especially from Italy. Among the waste there were also very dangerous and toxic wastes that significantly pollute the environment.

With Bulgaria's entry into the European Union, we were forced to close the first 4 units of the Kozloduy NPP, each with a capacity of 440 MWh. At this stage, these power blocks are irretrievably destroyed and cannot be recovered. Over the years, Bulgaria has purchased and subsequently sold 2 VVER 1000 units for the Belene NPP. After arbitration in Geneva, our country purchased under current contracts 2 more similar units of the third generation, which have been packed for more than 4 years instead of being used. 4-6 years ago, Serbia, Greece and private companies were interested in acquiring a stake in the planned Belene NPP, but the project has stalled and its termination seems preordained (Dolchinkov, 2016). There is talk of building new capacities at the Kozloduy NPP, diversification of fuels and others, but this is in the realm of fairy tales and political pressure and lobbying for certain companies that do not have the necessary experience and are compromised in the Czech Republic, Ukraine, the Philippines. and other countries. The Nuclear Regulatory Agency (NRA) of Bulgaria has already sent back several times for revision the documents for licensing new nuclear fuel for our operating reactors. The fuel being lobbied for has not received a license from the regulatory authorities of the European Union, but it will for Bulgaria, as an expert commission has been appointed with representatives of the Czech Republic and Ukraine, but without representatives of the reactor manufacturer. On 31.07.2023, the first AP 1000 a Westinghouse reactor was launched in the USA. This is the first reactor of this type to be introduced in parallel with the US power system and in general in the world. It is planned to build 12 such by 2030. There's no word yet on how the reactor will work, and the company itself admits that this is the first reactor to go live in 30 years, so I think a thorough analysis should be done before committing to something that doesn't know how it works. And our operating reactors are one of the most reliable and checked by international agencies and hold the world record for continuous trouble-free operation – more than 11 years.

When entering the EU, Slovakia, for example, was also forced to close some of its blocs, but after 2-3 months it reopened them and did not agree to the terms of closure. In this way, the state protected its national interests.

In the last 2 years, the European Commission has changed its position regarding nuclear energy, and personally its chairman, Jan Timmerman, said that if we want, we can develop our nuclear energy with new units in Kozloduy, and why not the construction of the plant in Belene. 10 EU countries, including France, Bulgaria and others, submitted a document for the continuation of the development of nuclear energy in the European Community. Nuclear energy does not produce greenhouse gases and does not pollute the environment, and with the development of technology, it is much safer and does not generate waste, unlike some of the green energies.

The US has appetites to supply small and medium mobile NPPs to Eastern European countries, but this is not a good solution, because firstly, these plants are not yet built, secondly, it is not a good solution to have many small NPPs that are a potential risk and a target of the many terrorist attacks that are taking place around the world and thirdly they will eventually get a license in 10 years. The US Secretary of Energy's visit to Central and Eastern Europe in early October 2022 was to lobby for such plants (IAEA, 2023).

Bulgaria failed in the years of transition to protect its energy and national security well enough by closing units 1-4 of the Kozloduy NPP, agreeing to premature closure of the TPP in the following years, instead of the terms reached by Poland and Germany, for example, to operate and subsidize these central government. After numerous failed negotiations and lack of negotiations, the Belene project also did not move forward, despite the presence of 2 modern 3+ generation power units at the plant. At the same time, Romania and Turkey are building new nuclear power plants and thus will fill the niche in the energy market in the region. Mistakes have been made and it is time for politicians to stop serving foreign interests and protect Bulgarian interests for the development of Bulgarian society.

Bulgaria and its politicians are under pressure to abandon nuclear power, build new capacity and switch to another fuel supplier under the pretext of "diversification". Contracts for the supply of fuel from certain companies are hastily concluded, without even an application for fuel licensing being submitted by the Nuclear Fuel Agency in Bulgaria. The fuel is also not approved by European regulators. The manufacturing company has a political umbrella, but no expert evaluation and practically working reactor and fuel. This is not a good decision for the safe operation of nuclear energy and the safety of the population, and the motto of the Kozloduy NPP is production safety.

Hastily and under pressure, a decision was made to sell the blocks for the Belene NPP to Ukraine on the day of the visit of the Ukrainian president to our country in the spring of 2023, without consulting experts in the field and protecting the interests of Bulgaria as a net exporter of electricity in the region . With these short-sighted decisions, taken under pressure, the energy and national security of Bulgaria is at risk.

If we add the increasingly high requirements to thermal power plants and the release of gases into the atmosphere, the prospects for Bulgaria are not good at all. Nuclear energy serves to produce about 35% of the country's electricity, adding 35-40% of thermal power plants, the loss of 2/3 of our energy capacity is looming over the next decade. This will inevitably lead to the fact that we will have to import electricity from other countries. And if adequate measures are not taken by the Bulgarian rulers, there will soon be talk of energy dependence. Because Turkey and Romania are developing their nuclear energy and will soon displace us from our market niche in energy (IAEA, 2018).

In order to overcome the energy crisis at the local level, it is necessary for politicians to consult with a wider range of specialists and to protect national interests, not to serve foreign interests. Because Bulgaria has always suffered from its politicians, not from the specialists. Because we have many specialists in the field of energy who can lead the country out of the current situation.

The development of green energy is good, but powering serious industries requires serious energy, while green energy can power smaller power plants and homes.

CONCLUSION

1. Bulgaria must actively work to increase the operational life of thermal power plants and to develop nuclear energy with new capacities in Kozloduy and construction of the existing reactors in Belene;
2. The EC officially names the Belene NPP as one of the three examples of a third generation nuclear project and recommends that future new nuclear facilities only have a level of safety and economic efficiency similar to that of third generation reactors;
3. The delay in the implementation of the energy projects, the numerous commissions, expertises, etc. procedures made all energy projects in Bulgaria more expensive, which further burdens the Bulgarian taxpayer and we pay colossal commissions to foreign analyst companies;
4. It is necessary to find a strategic investor for the development of our nuclear energy, since Bulgarian national and energy interests must be protected, not foreign and lobbyist interests.

REFERENCES

Bulatom. (2022). Nuclear Energy - The Basis for Sustainable Development. https://www.bulatom-bg.org/

Council of Ministers of the Republic of Bulgaria. (2020). Integrated Plan in the Field of Energy and Climate of the Republic of Bulgaria 2021 – 2030. Author.

Council of Ministers of the Republic of Bulgaria. (2019). *Resolutions and decisions of the Council of Ministers of the Republic of Bulgaria, Sofia*. Author.

Dolchinkov, N. (2016). History, development and prospects of the Belene NPP project. Scientific conference "Radiation safety in the modern world", NSU "V. Levski", 81-90.

Dolchinkov, N., & Karaivanova-Dolchinkova, B. (2020). The role of nuclear energy in the world economy. *Scientific conference "Radiation safety in the modern world", NSU "V. Levski"*, 250-260.

Dolchinkov, N., & Karaivanova-Dolchinkova, B. (2021). Modern plans for development of production of electricity worldwide and energy independence of *Bulgaria, Scientific conference "Radiation safety in the modern world", NSU "V. Levski"*, 392-399.

Haralampiev, M. (2020). The development of atomic energy and nuclear arsenals. *Collection of reports from the Scientific Conference "Current Security Issues", 6*, 123-133.

IAEA. (2023, May 1). International Atomic Energy Agency. https://www.iaea.org/

Kozloduy NPP. (2023, May 10). Kozloduy Nuclear Power Plant. https://kznpp.org/

Manchev, B. (2010). Belene. NPP - Lectures Before the "Energetik" Club.

Ministry of Energy of the Republic of Bulgaria. (2023, May 18). https://www.me.government.bg/

Mitev, M. (2021). Aspects of radiation protection in licensing of nuclear facility. *Scientific conference "Radiation safety in the modern world", NSU "V. Levski",* 88-93.

Nabatov, N. (2015). Electric power of Bulgaria. TANGRA TanNakRa IC.

NRA. (2023, may 15). Nuclear Regulatory Agency. https://bnra.bg/bg/

Padarev, N. I. (2018). Analysis of the Relationship Between Climate Changes and Security Area. *International Conference Knowledge-Based Organization, Vol. XXIV. Conference proceedings 3, Applied technical Sciences and Military Technologies,* 169-173. https://www.iaea.org/sites/default/files/publications/reports/2018/gc63-5_rus.pdf

United Nations. (1992). *United Nations Framework Convention on Climate Change, 4 June 1992.*

United Nations. (1997). *Kyoto Protocol to the United Nations Framework Convention on Climate Change.*

United Nations. (2015). *Paris Agreement.*

Chapter 2
The Multidimensional Spillover Effects of Energy Transformations on Economic and Political Development

Elizabeth Dimitrova Yoneva
University of National and World Economy, Sofia, Bulgaria

ABSTRACT

The chapter explores the principal dimensions of energy transformations and their repercussions for specific shifts in the economic and political realms. The research showcases the main vectors in the development of the energy sector with emphasis on contemporary metamorphoses in the context of the impact of the 2020 pandemic crisis, the 2021 energy crisis, and the continuing war in Ukraine, resulting in a redrawing of the world energy map. The author discusses explicit aspects of energy policy from the perspective of the evolutions in the last years, outlining the conceptual frame of the diversification efforts of different players in the energy chain, and their attempts to resolve energy dilemmas. Special attention is paid to the significant focus on global plans, launched with the goal of achieving "sustainable recovery," so as to take advantage of the opportunities generated by the current crises to switch to a new energy model.

INTRODUCTION

Presently, the global energy landscape is undergoing substantial shifts with regard to the recent challenges for this crucial sector, induced by various complications in its development with respect to the endogenous and exogenous dynamics. The disturbed operation of the energy industry exhibits the appearance of a unique synthesis of the composite internal defects and malformations, and the dissonant spill-over effects from the stormful external environment. Overall, the different crises and paralyses of energy markets unsettled almost all regions and countries, and disarranged their structural adjustment

DOI: 10.4018/979-8-3693-0400-6.ch002

to the new realities. Against the backdrop of the transformations in the world energy map over the past years, it seems only natural that issues of securing supplies and minimizing political and economic risks in capturing precious commodities should come to the fore. Undoubtedly, the pertinent topic of energy security is attracting increasing attention at international level and generating new impulses for a more widespread debate, especially within the areas with higher import dependency. The pressing energy issues are now at the top of not only the European but also the global political agenda, mainly because of the imperative of taking decisive action to address the long-ignored problems.

Energy security has set, and will continue to set, a number of parameters for diverse processes across the globe, and this is precisely the reason for the orientation of the current research work towards this topic. There is not a single state or zone, which are not facing the test to adapt to the novel texture of the energy field and the measures undertaken and planned to improve their energy situation reconstruct the geopolitical and geoeconomic patterns. In the light of recent developments, the paper explores the principal dimensions of energy transformations and their repercussions for specific shifts in the economic and political realms. Especially interesting are not only the ecological but also the other motivational factors for the energy revolution, especially as the green reforms can mitigate international tensions by making several countries less reliant on unstable regions or transit choke points in energy transportation routes. The research showcases the main vectors in the development of the energy sector with emphasis on contemporary metamorphoses in the context of the impact of the 2020 pandemic, the 2021 energy crisis and the continuing war in Ukraine, resulting in a redrawing of the world energy map. The author discusses explicit aspects of energy policy from the perspective of the evolutions in the last years, outlining the conceptual frame of the diversification efforts of different players in the energy chain, and their attempts to resolve energy dilemmas. Special attention is paid to the significant focus on global plans, launched with the goal of achieving "sustainable recovery", so as to take advantage of the opportunities generated by the current crises to switch to a new energy model. In view of these trends, the aim of the study is to discuss the main dimensions of the green energy transformations and the potential to embark on an energy transition in line with worldwide ambitions in this area.

1. The Energy Controversies: Between the Theory and the Practice

At the end of the 20th century, the attempts to find a new factor for economic development and growth in the context of globalization processes succeeded in getting on the track of the concept of the "knowledge economy". It was rapidly adopted as the appropriate model to reflect the new realities, as the dynamic development of information and communication technologies, combined with the progressive increase in the resources devoted to innovation and training, provided the basis for the emergence of the "Third Industrial Revolution" - after the agrarian and industrial era, the time of the "new economy" in human history has already come. This vision offered new and more precise tool for measuring and analyzing economic advancement. This redefinition of the forces that influence and contribute to the well-being and prosperity of individuals, companies and countries brings up the knowledge as a fundamental source of progress that could replace in importance the traditional factors of industrial production - land, labor and capital. Material and energy resources no longer play a leading role, as the center of gravity shifts from physical to intellectual activity (Cĕric, 2001). It is evident that through this approach is sought a means to describe a significant transition and the changing nature of the economy (Barkham, 2008), but it is slightly misleading, when it comes to the importance of energy resources.

In the light of today's global challenges, it is a duty to recognize the unabated importance of energy and raw materials, even in the context of the knowledge economy. The energy issues could be ignored to some extent or often remain outside the focus of economic and political theory. However, the real world is always far more complicated and the immediate entanglements demand extra determined and intensive attempts to integrate energy factors into miscellaneous analyses with a view to their role in production and growth, in terms of ecology, in the field of international relations, etc. At the same time, it would be far from an exaggeration to argue that energy in general (and energy innovation in particular) is still a driving force in global economic development. They also have an enormous impact on societies, whereas energy utilization is a relevant indicator of living standards. This is due to the fact that energy consumption "has defined, is defining and will continue to define the level of material civilization" (Beaudreau, 1998, p. 5.).

In the early 1880s, the exhaustion of the technological paradigm of the First Industrial Revolution created incentives to carry out radical transformations in the productive sphere. The time of coal, iron and steam engines was passing, and the world was entering the age of steel, oil, internal combustion engines and electricity (Stearns, 2021). The automobile molded not only a leading industry but also became a kind of symbol of the Second Industrial Revolution, and electricity entered all economic sectors as well as people's everyday lives thanks to the construction of the first power stations and innovations such as the light bulb and the electric tram. Gradually, energy resources were taken for granted, and for this reason, economic theory did not pay close attention to energy for most of the 20th century. However, there have also been periods of increased study, with the ups and downs in interest in energy issues triggered by a number of modifications in the world economy directly related to energy factors. The oil crises of 1973 and 1979 demonstrated in a strong way that economists have not properly considered the importance of the energy dimensions of production (Venn, 2002). The explosion in oil prices (from \$3 to \$12 per barrel during the first crisis and from \$13 to \$32 per barrel during the second oil shock) generated a flurry of serious research on the risks to economic growth and welfare evoked by eventual shortages of energy and other resources (Jacobs, 2017).

With the price normalization in the energy sector in the 1980s, the interest in this matter began to decline. At the same time, nuclear power was discredited in the wake of the 1979 Three Mile Island and 1986 Chernobyl accidents, raising the topic about atomic safety standards (Mahaffey, 2015). Increased public attention to the ecological degradation caused by environmental pollution, in particular with regard to global warming and climate change, stimulated the next major wave in energy research in the early 1990s. The favored solution to the existing difficulties was concentrated in the formula "renewable energy", but its unhurried evolution was not able to produce expeditious results leading to its push to the forefront of energy production. At the same time, there was an intensifying talk on the "resurrection" of nuclear power and the options for using coal as a "clean" energy source.

The first decade of the 21st century was marked by the peak oil concepts (Deffeyes, 2006). A growing corpus of studies began to present pessimistic scenarios towards the imminent depletion of the finite hydrocarbon resources and the approaching end of the fossil fuels era (Heinberg, 2005). Undoubtedly, the process of globalization has led to an increasing number of countries across the globe (especially in the group of the developing ones) moving towards an industrial stage in their development, which is inducing expanding energy needs. There are multiplying indications that the scale of extraction of several energy resources is nearing its possible maximum, after which their production will begin to decline. In this connection, peak theories have even given rise to ideas about the need for a new economic model (Heinberg, 2011).

Even if we disregard such visions as too extreme in the hope that some appropriate solutions will be found to solve the existing complications, it is obvious that energy resources can no longer be taken for granted. In view of the above, the vision of a dematerialized modern economy seems to be more of a popular myth than an empirical phenomenon born of statistical facts (Buenstorf, 2004, p. 2.). Apparently, the relationship between the "knowledge economy" and energy resources is symbiotic, as they are a critical component of it. Energy may not be the most important factor driving technological and structural change, but the "new economy" is far from replacing the traditional one - it can only build, but remains dependent on the long-established models.

One of the cardinal attributes of the Third Industrial Revolution was the addition of intelligent technologies and the expectations for their maturation provoked the conceptualization of the Fourth Revolution with the underlying idea of a flowering use of artificial intelligence. Subsequently, the second decade of the 21st century was stamped with the concerns for energy cybersecurity. The adaptation of the energy industry to the opportunities and risks arising from the entry into the digital age produced new type of discourse, embracing the cyber threats as an integral part of the broader orbit of energy security. Cyberattacks on critical infrastructure are considered extremely dangerous, as they could discompose the normal functioning of the societies. The integral role of the energy sector in the debate on the new menace is irrefutable in view of the colossal effects that can be generated by affecting electricity grids, oil and gas pipelines, and other infrastructure components such as power plants, refineries, etc. As most paralyzing is acknowledged a potential attack on electricity systems, because it could plunge us into a dark age (King, 2012). In connection to the growing cybersecurity threats, many analysts recommended to maneuver from a reactive to a more strategic position on the topic (Baker Institute, 2012). This implies moving beyond the perception of the matter as a trouble of information and communication technologies, because for the energy industry, cybersecurity is not simply a technological problem, but rather one that encompasses the broader dynamics of information and operations (Falk, 2012). The increasing number of cyberattacks against critical infrastructure demonstrates in a clear way the crucial need to improve security in this area and implement adequate measures to protect vital components and facilities. The changeover, inflamed by innovative devices is beyond avoidance, as it is part of the history of technological progress. However, in the present context, it creates opportunities to wreak catastrophic devastation, even without firing a single bullet, but through the sole use of a computer keyboard.

Perhaps it is too early at this point to draw the proper conclusions about the energy challenges of the current decade, but the turn of events up-to date indicates that the present focus of concernment is on the crisis processes in this crucial sector. The heavy blows of the COVID-19 pandemics served as a catalyst for the energy crisis in 2021 and recently the war in Ukraine gave rise to new turmoil in the energy domain. Looking at the historical context, this is obviously not the first energy crisis, but now the energy markets are extremely interconnected and every disruption has large spill-over effects. The latest energy disturbances intensified the calls for "sustainable recovery" that will help to attack the complications caused by the amalgam between the approaching depletion of fossil fuels and the ecological imperatives to reduce their use. Nevertheless, the ambitions to hasten the energy transition were blocked by the continuing eruption of new forms of energy unrest, vitalizing the urgency to find innovative approaches and alternative paths. The energy crises in last years eliminated abounding chances to unlock probable solutions for the energy hardships. The 2022 re-drawing of the world energy map resulting from the war in Ukraine cemented the trend towards polarization of energy issues, which goes hand in hand with the more dangerous inclination towards militarization of energy security (Moran, 2010). Both of them are providing additional incentives for many countries to expand their palette of instruments and approaches to obtain the needed energy resources. The praised antidote prescribing diversification with regard to the energy mix, the transport routes and the suppliers verified its meaningfulness but has not turned into a panacea for the energy sector. Yet, the crises brought up the question of search for models for consistent and unfluctuating energy performance that will be enabled by a kind of solid and stable energy setting with deep-routed apparatus for balancing in situations of disturbances.

The transformations of the energy markets in the early 21st century led to the expansion of the research efforts in this field, which helped to establish and grow the thematic area of "energy geopolitics". Along with more general studies (Wright & Conca, 2007), special attempts were focused on identifying the factors that will dictate future energy consumption trends and resource choices in the context of a changing geopolitical landscape (Verrastro et al., 2010). In this regard, economic, foreign policy and environmental considerations and priorities were taken into account to forecast developments. Additionally, scientific products offered analyses with a narrower regional or thematic scope. With regard to the problematic energy dependency of Europe, some experts devoted their attention to the challenges in front of the continent (Bressand, 2012). Encompassing the metamorphoses in many emerging economies, especially intriguing was the topic of energy geopolitics in the Asia-Pacific region (Pardesi et al., 2006). With regard to specific energy resources, engaging outputs presented different unrolled scenarios – for example concerning the problems with natural gas (The Geopolitics of Natural Gas, 2012).

Beyond the larger studies on energy geopolitics, notable was also the contribution to this topic of specialized periodicals and prestigious scientific institutions. Several journals offered interviews with experts in the field (Rothkopf, 2011) or formed special sections and rubrics for articles on energy geopolitics - for example such was promoted on the website of the American Foreign Policy Association (offering materials such as Sweet, 2012). Consequently, energy resources were accepted as an important factor in formulating national strategies, exerting external influence and shaping the contours of the international system. The analysts draw on the idea that, in view of the new challenges, the countries are trying to situate their energy concepts within the broader context of their foreign policy. As a result, there was a need for energy geopolitics to study the interrelationship between security, international relations and energy issues (Pascual, 2008). By taking energy security as a starting point, it became possible to analyze not only how different states build own strategies to secure their resource needs, but also how their actions affect other players and the international system. Particular attention was paid to the topic of how states exploit their more conventional military, political and economic power to protect their energy resources or secure the supplies they need.

Not surprisingly, the emphasis of this kind of reserach was laid on the ways in which energy sources can possibly be used to project power. Given that energy is treated as an important geopolitical factor, awareness of its importance is identified as crucial to our understanding of the international system. An interesting approach to the subject was elaborated in line with the scholarly efforts, distinguished by the ambition to develop indicators that can be monitored in order to predict changes in energy geopolitics. For example, Steve LeVine outlined 10 such indicators:

1) Oil prices with regard to their impact on producing and importing countries;
2) Transportation of energy resources with reference to "the ability to move and choke off energy";
3) Big personality, in order to accentuate on the role of national leaders in the energy field (e.g. Vladimir Putin, Muammar Qaddafi, Hugo Chávez);
4) Technological shift - innovations and technical breakthroughs in the energy realm;
5) Supply - taking into account the behavior of exporters;

6) Public opinion - with a view to its sensitivity on energy issues;
7) War - seen as a threat to energy supply and as a factor influencing the outcome of a military conflict;
8) Domestic or local politics - with a view, for example, to the spill-over effects of internal turbulences;
9) Corruption - the gains of certain circles through energy dividends could induce internal conflicts;
10) "The mountains" such as Russia, China, Saudi Arabia, as their actions create or disrupt geopolitical trends (LeVine, 2012).

Although the establishing of such indicators is an important topic, the comprehensiveness and adequacy of this list could certainly be questioned. Nevertheless, these aspects should not be neglected in the implementation of the monitoring of the energy geopolitical situation.

The application of geo-economic approaches to energy analysis is also a common exploration instrument. The aim of this type of research is to link the geo-economic perspective with international energy policy, focusing on the interrelationship between certain factors (such as reserves, production, transportation and trade opportunities for commodities) and international relations (Bilgin, 2010.). Blending between geopolitical and geo-economic approaches is also often implemented in energy research. Furthermore, it is not uncommon to encounter studies that aim to analyze and contextualize energy security, synchronizing geopolitical, geo-economic and geo-strategic perspectives (Makube, 2012).

The high-priority tackling of energy deadlocks demonstrates that nowadays energy theory has not to be simply a virtual product that remains far away from reality. To become more pragmatic, therefore, it will have to make its way to material nucleus and people's everyday lives, otherwise it would remain based on empty of content concepts. In this context, the presently identified energy challenges pose several cardinal tasks for the "new economy": to shape better educated and responsible consumers, to stimulate innovation potential and to provide a basis for informed decision-making on strategic energy issues. To avoid apocalyptic predictions about future unfolding of energy wars, additional resources have to be mobilized in the search for a new vision that will help to find cures for the current disorders and to translate calculations into political action.

2. The Energy Sector in the Grasp of the Politico-Economic Duality

Considering that every step in modern production and lifestyle is tied in an immediate or indirect way to energy, its role is of colossal importance in terms of supporting industrial and commercial processes, transport, communications, etc. Access to energy resources is crucial for the socio-economic development of any country and for the standard of living of its population. Furthermore, the recent trends in the development of world energy business are bringing preferences to accept foreign policy and the fundamental national security requirements as key determinants in the energy sphere, with a complementary role given to the economic dimensions of energy, industrial needs and market patterns in the sector. Thus, the exploration of energy issues entered immensely into the domain of international relations.

The reasons why energy is less and less seen as an economic matter are mainly to be found in the emerging global competition for resources, as securing supplies from definite importers or gaining access to undeveloped or hard-to-reach resources is associated with corresponding geopolitical influence. It is no coincidence that energy is referred to as a kind of "currency of power" in the international system (Heinberg, 2021). Delving into the intersections between the foreign relations of different countries and their energy policies has turned into catalyst for cultivation of the theme of energy diplomacy (Bovan at al., 2020). The criss-cross between these brands of problematics serves as an indicator for the complexity of the multidimensional energy integrality. Lately, the high priority for an effective regulation of energy affairs determines the unbroken unanimity with regard to the importance of energy security, but the conceptual debate is also distinguished by the lack of consensus on its nature and content. Commonly, it emerges as a strategic issue especially for large consumers, whose interest is naturally focused on securing supplies in terms of imports. It is associated with the existence of a combination of conditions necessary for a country to ensure its energy supply in a way that allows a stable and harmonious socio-economic and political development of the society, as well as meeting current and future needs for affordable and high-quality energy. Furthermore, it corresponds to the capacity of the energy sector to operate in critical situations, as well as the ability of the state to deal with existing or potential threats for the energy system arising from the negative impact of internal and external factors.

Major importers of energy resources such as the US, EU, China and India view energy security from a consumption perspective and define it in terms of households and business access to affordable energy for the foreseeable future and without significant risks of major disruption. On the other hand, large-scale producers and exporters of energy commodities have unrolled an apprehension from a different perspective - in the direction of capturing guaranteed markets for their products, which they can sell at prices that allow them to continue to invest in the chrysalis of their energy industry. As a mixture of these two visions, the reserach spotlight was on the interdependence between producers and consumers. At the same time, the role of transit countries in the energy chain was not sufficiently well understood, but after the first Russian-Ukrainian gas crisis, such a segment was added to the concept of energy security as well.

The perceptions about the anatomy of energy security has also undergone a series of transfigurations, initially emerging from concerns about the physical risks to supply associated with transport and infrastructure considerations. Subsequently, the focal point drifted predominantly towards the economic conditions that could affect the supply. Lastly, the political factors have also been calculated in energy analysis involving the use of energy resources as a tool to put pressure on importers on the one hand, and the threats posed by the unstable political climate in exporting countries on the other. Thus, the factors that can breed threats to energy security now cover a wide spectrum, including such as political interventions, sanctions, invasions, terrorist attacks, sabotage, technical breakdowns, lack of investment (in terms of exploration, extraction and refining), infrastructure failures, economic problems, natural disasters, etc.

With respect to energy security conceptualization, it is crucial to emphasize that reliance on energy imports should not necessarily be seen as a strategic weakness. Increasing security of supply does not mean definitely seeking to maximize energy self-sufficiency, nor to minimize dependence, but to limit the risks associated with that dependence. A World Energy Council's study on the effects of potential energy crises on Europe (World Energy Council, 2008) is also oriented in this angle, highlighting the distinction between energy vulnerability and energy dependence, as the latter does not always automatically lead to the former. For example, a country that imports most of its energy at stable prices and ensures its security of supply through well-diversified sources will be dependent but not vulnerable. At the same time, a country that produces the bulk of its energy itself, but at too high price or using outdated technologies, will be vulnerable even if it is not dependent on external suppliers.

Another embodiment of the politico-economic dualism of energy affairs could be found in the facet of resource conflicts. Globally, the accelerating economic development is driving a boost in energy consumption. In a situation of limited spare capacity of production over demand, logical becomes a price increase. It has a negative impact on the budgets of large importers, but at the same time supports the economic advancement of exporting countries. Having in mind the growing scarcity of energy resources, the behavior of market entities has to be adjusted. Until recently, exporters were eager to attract a larger market share and were afraid of losing consumers because of the available competition, but in the last years the current has changed radically. The center of the rivalry is shifting from sellers to buyers, who, competing with each other for finite supply, are ready to offer higher prices, which benefits export-oriented countries. The expanding activity on the international energy scene of players such as China and India makes them serious competitors of Europe in terms of securing the needed resources. On the other hand, the uneven geographical distribution of oil and gas provokes a struggle for them that is imprinted with different strategies. For example, the US turned to military and political safeguarding of strategically important regions like the Middle East. China embarked on an intense campaign to acquire stakes in energy projects and companies in different zones, while the EU is pursuing an approach of building a diversified energy supply network.

With regard to the growing competition, it will be also difficult to find an adequate approach along the lines of the producers. As resources gradually deplete, their prices will rise, increasing the revenues of export-oriented countries and stimulating their economic growth. This in turn will lead to a hike in domestic energy demand. As long as national production expands, these trends will naturally not be troublesome. However, when production begins to decline after its peak, the volumes of energy available for export will become progressively scarce. Thus, the generated problems can be solved in two ways. Those countries that choose to continue with exports for the sake of the earnings face the threat of rising internal discontent. Others who decide to keep the relevant reserves for themselves will face a wave of nationalization of the energy sector. The importers are then left with the choice of either reducing their consumption or securing their supply by force (Vanderbruck, 2010).

With reference to theory, the term "resource wars" became popular in the US in the early 1980s in relation to perceptions of the Soviet threat to American access to oil in the Middle East and mineral resources in Africa. The promotion of this concept led to the foregrounding of the idea that resource flows, rather than ideological and political segmentation, drew the dividing lines on the world map. Alongside this, the competition for control over scarce and unevenly distributed resources will be marked over time by an increasing intensity. For a long period of time, cheap and affordable energy has stood at the center of a pattern of enlarging global wealth. For this reason, a reduction in energy supplies, even if it does not provoke the unfolding of a scenario in the spirit of energy wars, will generate extremely painful economic and social effects. The expectation of imminent difficulties in the sector is conclusively leading to a rethinking of the nature of energy security. In the light of the latest developments, it could be interpreted as manifesting itself as a peculiar combination of cooperation and competition between states. Although its absolute achievement is considered an illusory ambition, the mechanisms through which it can be fulfilled at a certain level offer a spacious terrain for experimentation.

The conflicting dimensions of the energy rivalry are not the only ones that can have a serious influence on the countries. The very impact of the use of energy resources on the respective producing economy is generally laden with controversy. In this regard, analysts look particularly into the economic and political nuances of the "resource curse" (Auty, 1993). As well as examining the economic benefits of energy exports, research on this topic also draws attention to the negative effects of the reliance on oil and gas revenues. However, the extent to which the funds acquired from such activities become a "curse" or a "blessing" for a country depends on the ability of the governing structures to deal with the challenges arising from the production and export of commodities. The search for the consequences associated with the unfolding phenomenon known as the "Dutch disease" shows that oil and gas revenues have a detrimental effect on other sectors of the economy (Frankel, 2012). The boom in the natural resources sector is transformed into a decline, notably pronounced in the area of agriculture and labor-intensive industries, generating further unemployment. The term "Dutch disease" itself came into use in studies of the impact of energy revenues on the country's economy after the discovery of oil and gas deposits in the North Sea in the 1960s. The additional amount of foreign currency entering the Netherlands due to the sale of oil and natural gas has led to an increase in the exchange rate, which in turn makes its exports more expensive and less competitive. Under the influence of these shifts, factors of production are withdrawing from non-oil industries to flow into the resource sector, thus deepening the economy's dependence on these revenues.

The availability and increased exploitation of hydrocarbon resources is not bound to ruin an economy. If appropriate management practices are applied, they can also help the advancement of the state concerned. The policies of countries such as Norway, Malaysia and Botswana are cited as successful examples in this regard. Clearly, the role of the executive is key here, as its actions determine the positive or negative impact of energy resources on national political and economic development. Taking into account both short-term and long-term considerations, and finding the balance between them, governments have to take the most appropriate decisions for the moment - for example, whether to invest the available funds from energy exports in the production of public goods (infrastructure projects, etc.) or to deposit them outside the country to avoid increasing inflation. If invested adequately, energy revenues can serve as a means to achieve sustainable development and long-term prosperity. Looking at the strategies adopted by various states to circumvent the resource curse, specific research products suggest to use the term "peril" instead of "curse" to refer to the consequences of energy export because the dangers from oil and gas export might not materialize, if appropriate policies enable to avert or minimize them (Ziyadov, 2012).

The main problems faced by countries that are heavily dependent on the sale of energy resources are related to the volatility of revenues in view of fluctuations in commodity prices, as well as the threat of depletion of non-renewable reserves before the national economic reorientation processes start. The major challenge for such cases is therefore to stimulate the non-oil sectors of the economy before this point is reached. They need to build up such an economic base that will serve as a solid foundation for development once the country's natural capital is spent. In the case of non-renewable resources, there is also the logical issue of sharing the benefits between generations. Often its long-term dimensions are neglected at the expense of short-term security for the ruling structures through the use of energy export revenues for investment in economically unviable projects with high political returns - the so-called "white elephants" (Robinson & Torvik, 2005). These have a negative impact on the future economic development of the country concerned, as their inefficiency leads to the loss of its scarce resources and especially of their long-term potential, even though such projects generate momentary political support.

Along with studying the economic aspects, research has subsequently begun to pay attention to the political dimensions of the "resource curse". Observations in a number of cases show that the government is under considerable temptation to misuse these funds, which could be employed not to improve the living standards of the population, but to crush rival parties and eliminate opposition. Energy revenues can thus not only contribute to increased corruption, but also influence the political system, undermining democracy and fostering authoritarian tendencies or reinforcing the resilience of established regimes of this nature. The manifestation of the negative impact of energy export funds on the political system could be sought in the following directions: 1) making governments less dependent on tax revenues, as they no longer rely predominantly on them; 2) extending the elite's ability to "buy" political support; 3) providing capital to suppress democratization processes. Consequently, there is an increasing likelihood of an overall reduction in transparency, a restriction of media freedom, manipulation of election results, and interference in the work of the judiciary. Therefore, alongside the consideration of other factors influencing the rise of authoritarian phenomena, the energy export revenues should not be overlooked in view of their potential to consolidate power and strengthen the chances of political survival. On the other hand, in the absence of strong institutions, resource revenues will mainly serve the dominant elites, who will have an interest in ever closer ties with the oil and gas business.

Conceptualizing the links between commodity profits and democratization, Thomas Freedman formulated the now popular "first law of petro-politics": the price of oil and the progress of democratic freedom are inversely related (Friedman, 2006). This assumption implies that lower resource prices, and therefore more limited revenues, encourage the development of more open and transparent political systems. Undoubtedly, the study of the relationship between export-obtained funds and features of domestic political life has resulted in some conclusions, which, however, are by no means universally valid. The abundance of resources does not necessarily condemn every state to autocratic rule, civil wars and internal conflicts. The role of a numerous factors should also be taken into account, such as the nature of political institutions, governance and national traditions, social forces, the external political and economic environment, etc. For example, Michael Ross finds that the "resource curse" appears more significant as a basis for the continued existence of authoritarianism that has already unfolded than as a cause of its establishment (Ross, 2015). When there are not only serious energy gains, but also specific local factors, then combining the two can already lead to their feeding off each other.

A notable case study within this perspective represents the analysis of the experience of the three Caspian countries Azerbaijan, Kazakhstan and Turkmenistan. As important energy actors not only in the Caucasus region and Central Asia, but also with regard to the broader context of energy security, they share a number of common characteristics, both internally and externally, as well as identical problems. In view of the energy potential of these states, serious attention has been paid to analyzing specific aspects of their political and economic functioning. At the beginning of the first decade of the 21st century, the export revenues from energy resources provided significant opportunities for the three countries not only to boost their economic development, but also to increase their role on the international stage. However, the global financial and economic crisis of 2008-2009 and the resulting collapse in the oil prices led to a sudden drop in the profits. At the same time, this Caspian group showed symptoms of the "Dutch disease" in the form of a weakening agricultural sector. With regard to the impact of energy revenues on the political system, analysts point out that, without ignoring the other factors driving the manifestation of the authoritarian characteristics of these countries, they are undoubtedly heavily dependent on oil and natural gas exports, and not only in economic terms. Azerbaijan, Kazakhstan and Turkmenistan qualify as "hybrid regimes" in view of the combination of democratic and authoritarian elements in the system of governance (Overland et al. 2010).

Other relevant examples for the spill-over effects of the "resource curse" could be found in the events in the Middle East and North Africa in the framework of the so-called "Arab Spring". Since December 2010, the region witnessed a series of revolutions and protests in countries such as Tunisia, Egypt, Libya, Bahrain, Syria, Yemen, Algeria, Iraq, Jordan, Morocco, Oman, etc. In the context of the rising tide of discontent in the zone, research was focused on the implications of these events for global energy security, while also looking at the role of energy resources as a factor in stimulating unrest. The negative consequences for the economies of exporters because of their decades-long reliance on easy oil revenues are highlighted as a cause of the problems of these countries. Consequently, the strong emphasis on the resource sector has led to a collapse in the agricultural area and so most of them have become food importers. As a number of Middle Eastern states have passed or are close to their peak oil production, declining revenues will have an increasingly detrimental impact on their economies. The situation in

Egypt was seen as a typical proof of these trends. The country's 2011 revolution, which led to the ouster of President Hosni Mubarak, was due to, among other factors, existing economic complications. While in the 1960s Egypt almost entirely met its demand for food through domestic production, it turned gradually to import of such products, relying on oil sales revenues to subsidize domestic prices. In 1996, however, the African country reached its peak oil production of 922,000 barrels per day, and by 2011 production had already fallen by 26% (Vanderbruck, 2011). As is the case with most Middle Eastern energy exporting countries, revenues were of critical importance to Cairo, and their decline served as a catalyst for a number of economic problems. At the same time, rising global food prices have a multiplier effect on importers like Egypt, especially if they have a weak currency.

Generally, along with the impact of energy resources on the internal political development, their influence on external relations is also sought. In a situation when valuable commodities and especially their sales have a negative effect on democratic processes, the respective regime would orient its foreign policy towards cooperation with countries with similar characteristics, which would not be inclined to interfere in the internal affairs of the country. Thus, the patterns of domestic political life, and especially the type of regime, also in turn influence foreign affairs, including energy relations. Considering the economic and political aspects of the "resource curse", as well as the amalgam between its internal and external dimensions, it appears striking that maintaining a balance between the short- and long-term objectives of the governing structures and the state emerges as a cardinal task. As the experience of countries such as Norway, Canada and Australia shows, by finding an adequate trade-off between these and taking appropriate measures to eliminate the negative effects of the "resource curse", export revenues can become a catalyst for successful national development.

In recent years, the scientific debate has also focused on resource nationalism, especially when it comes to energy protectionism, because their unfolding is widely noticeable in times of crises. While reaching full energy independence or isolationism for individual countries is considered a difficult, if not almost impossible, task to achieve, the discussions on the subject of energy protectionism in its various manifestations are still very dynamic. Determining the degree of national/state participation in the development and exploitation of available energy resources, as well as ownership in the sector, is undoubtedly a sovereign right of each country. Incentives to increase control over valuable raw materials naturally correspond to the desire for greater profits generated by their extraction and export, so to provide more finance, in order to invest in the country's development (Kendall-Taylor, 2010). Another positive effect of concentrating energy resources in the hands of the state could be to strengthen the competitive advantages of national companies. In order to achieve these objectives, legislative and regulatory measures have to be taken, as well as the introduction of specific conditions and requirements for energy-related contracts and projects. Often these actions are accompanied by patriotic rhetoric, which shows that such policies can also serve as a propaganda tool.

The upward trend in energy prices in the first decade of the 21st century has created a reasonable desire in exporting countries to make the most of the situation. The steps taken to realize this objective were aimed at imposing measures to strengthen domestic energy companies and limit access to strategic resources for external firms. The pursuit of such policies was based on increasing state control over natural resources, associated with the terms "resource nationalism" or "resource protectionism". In most cases, however, its implementation leads to a weakening of those sectors of the economy that are not commodity-oriented. Extractive industries attract most of the investment, while the spill-over effects to generate growth outside this sector are relatively weak. The downsides of this phenomenon are often reflected in the lack of capital for reinvestment and R&D, as well as insufficient expertise and technology in purely domestic energy companies compared to those of large international corporations. Recent bouts of resource nationalism have, not coincidentally, raised concerns that the problem in the short and medium term is not the threat of running out of non-renewable energy resources, but the likelihood of not developing the necessary extractive capacity. These fears do not appear to be unfounded, as the expansion of control over reserves by national companies has not been accompanied by the planned increase in their output.

Despite the significant steps taken on EU level with regard to overcome energy protectionism, there are still various complications. In the context of the building of the common market, logical conflicts have arisen over attempts by foreign companies to acquire national energy giants. A key example in this respect was the effort by the German colossus E.ON to gain control of the largest Spanish electricity company, Endesa, in 2006. The Spanish authorities underlined that in a strategic sector such as energy, it is in their interest to have a company run by national business actor (Crawford, 2006). The resistance was eliminated by the European Commission, but it was symptomatic for other acts of opposition to the creation of a free market in the energy field. Notwithstanding the sensitivities regarding national "energy champions", the current trend is towards increasing concentration in the electricity and gas sectors in the EU. The transactions became predominantly cross-border in nature, as energy companies are inclined to expand internationally (Leveque & Monturus, 2008).

While the consolidation of the European energy sector and the removal of national barriers to competition have undoubtedly progressed, European companies used every opportunity to denounce the manifestations of energy protectionism outside the EU borders. Criticism towards China was a case in point, concentrated in particular in the area of renewables. European energy companies (along with a number of American ones) complained that they were gradually squeezed out of the wind energy sector (Johnson, 2009). Certainly, PRC used these kind of protectionist measures to build its national capacity in the sector and to eliminate strong external competition from solid and experienced companies. The application of a "negative list" helped to prevent foreign investment in a number of strategic sectors and ignited various trade disputes.

The picture of the current dimensions of energy protectionism on a global scale certainly shows that it is seen as a potential tool for economic development and for eradicating competition. Regardless of the arguments for and against the orientation towards resource nationalism, it has established itself as a real global phenomenon that is characterized by cyclical manifestations. Its application can take different forms, from extreme types of state domination to more moderate types of balanced public participation. Along with domestic reasons for choosing such protectionist apparatus, intentions to achieve foreign policy goals may also lie behind the preference. Apparently, the impulses towards protectionism in the energy sector, whatever their appearance, have proved to be a common occurrence in recent years. Their even greater deployment in the context of different crises is also understandable in view of the perceived impact of such measures on the national economy. At the same time, in a situation that many experts have described as a harbinger of imminent "energy chaos", in view of the increasing competition for energy resources and the indications of an end to the fossil fuel era, "energy nationalism" is undoubtedly being given a major boost.

3. Pandemic, Energy Crisis, War: The Devastating Sequence for the Energy Sector

In recent years, the energy sector has suffered a severe series of blows induced by various factors. The pandemic triggered by the spread of COVID-19 has produced shocks of various kinds in the energy industry, which had not yet fully recovered from the negative repercussions of the global financial and economic crisis of 2007-2008. Earlier predictions, that the recovery would kindle energy disturbance did not materialize simply because the full rehabilitation from the economic difficulties was blocked in 2020 by a new collapse, this time caused by the pandemic. The concept from a decade ago that we would henceforth be living in a cycle of mutually reinforcing crises, which at the time was seen as portending an extremely misanthropic vision of the future, is now gaining ground in present circumstances.

The negative impact of the pandemic in economic, political and social terms have provoked the experts to label 2020 "the lost year". For the energy markets this line could not be far from the truth, as they were damaged because of the limited transport, commercial and industrial activities. The spillover effects of this paralysis vitalized shrinkages in the consumption of various energy resources, blocking of certain ventures and operations in the sector, deterioration of the investment climate, job cuts, rise in energy poverty, etc. Notwithstanding the recognition of the massive destruction in large-scale economies, particular attention has been paid to the claim that the damage from the crisis is not being distributed on a proportional basis, so that developing countries actually end up as the big losers from the situation. Undoubtedly, for less developed areas the effects of reduced investment activity will be more severe, as limited funding opportunities for new projects will on the one hand block their ability to achieve diversification and on the other hand will increase their energy vulnerability. For 2020, energy-related investment declined by 20% globally (International Energy Agency, 2020a), with the most serious outflow in the oil industry.

The first year of the pandemic was marked by a 4.5% reduction in global primary energy consumption, a "record" for the period since the end of the Second World War. Within Europe, the decline was 7.8%, the same as that in Central and South America, and slightly lower than that in North America (8.0%). The highly industrialized countries logically suffered more economically from the shock waves, which is also evident against the backdrop of a smaller drop in primary energy consumption in areas such as Africa (by 6.7%) and the Middle East (3.1%). Impressive was the modest negative growth for the Asia-Pacific region of 1.6%, to which China made a major contribution, even posting a 2.1% increase in its energy consumption (BP, 2021a). However, the collapse in energy use as a result of the pandemic had a beneficial environmental impact in terms of reducing carbon dioxide emissions (International Energy Agency, 2020b) – again a record post-1945 cut of 6.3%. In the case of the EU, the fall was 13.4%, which was more significant than the levels in the case of the US (11.5%). In contrast, China was again in contrast with a 0.6% increase.

The hydrocarbons proved to be the biggest victim of the pandemic crisis. The oil shock was the largest, accounting for about ¾ of the decline in overall energy demand. Its consumption fell by 9.3% or 9.1 million barrels per day, mainly on account of the downturns in the US (11.8%), the EU (13.5%) and India (9.3%). Compared to the oil situation, natural gas use was less affected, declining globally by only 2.3% or about 81 bcm. This reduction is comparable to the effects experienced in 2009 as a result of the then financial and economic crisis. The demonstrated better resilience of the "blue fuel" relies on its promotion as the bridge over which the world will move from oil-centric to green energy. Such an insignia has helped to expand its position in the global energy mix and undoubtedly led to an increase in investment interest in infrastructure operating on natural gas. A different change is 2020 was observed with regard to LNG, where there was a modest increase of 0.6% or 4 bcm. However, this is a far lower than the rate at which it was progressing before the crisis. The growing interest in LNG appears logical in view of the options for diversification in terms of suppliers. With the onset of the pandemic, coal consumption was also curtailed by 4.2%, mainly due to collapses in North America (by 21.2%) and the EU (19.4%). Only in rare cases such as China and Malaysia was detected an increase in their use.

Despite being classified as a type of "clean energy", nuclear power has lost one position in the global energy mix, going in 2020 to sixth place with a consumption fall by 4.1% - the biggest reduction since the 2011 and 2012 crunch generated by the Fukushima accident. In contrast to the trends for hydrocarbons, renewables stood out as the most resilient in the face of the pandemic. Their consumption increased in 2020 by 9.7%. Thanks to being the least affected by the crisis, they reached the fifth place in world primary energy use, ahead of nuclear power. Within the EU, the 6.7% increase in renewables consumption was more modest compared to the overall picture, but by achieving it, they took the third position in the European energy mix behind oil and natural gas, climbing a full two positions in the rankings, and leaving both nuclear and coal behind. In global production, record growth of 20.5% was seen in solar energy, 11.9% in wind energy and 5.3% in other types of renewables (geothermal, biomass, etc.). 2020 was a successful year especially for the wind industry, as the new installed capacity piled up 93 GW (75% of them in China and the US). This brings the total global capacity to 743 GW, which contributes to saving 1.1 billion tons of carbon dioxide per year, equivalent to South America's annual emissions (GWEC, 2021).

Hydropower was relatively little disturbed in 2020, but its growth was also extremely minimal - only 1%. A major contributor to this is again China, which continues with the implementation of its large-scale hydropower deployment plans. The pandemic crisis has by no means prevented it from putting into operation the first two generators of the world's second largest hydropower plant, the Baihetan Dam (Stanway, 2021), launched in the summer of 2021. The Asian giant also has on its territory the world's largest hydropower plant - the Three Gorges on the Yangtze River.

Compared to the sketched landscape for primary energy consumption, the situation for electricity in 2020 has proved to be considerably more stable. This is not surprising, however, as reduced mobility in the early months of the pandemic led to increasing household's' use during lockdowns, but this far outweighed the overall negative effect of losses in industrial and commercial activities. The International Energy Agency reports that the first stages of the crisis resulted in a 15-20% drop in electricity demand, depending on the measures imposed in different countries, with economies with a larger share of services being the hardest hit (International Energy Agency, 2021). Electricity generation was shrinking more severely than in the aftermath of the 2008 financial and economic crisis, although in 2020 it dropped only by 0.9%. However, its structure is undergoing a significant transformation, where the share of coal has decreased at the expense of a rise in that of renewables. Especially remarkable was the achievement of the EU, where the renewables became the most significant component in electricity generation (BP, 2021b).

The second year of the pandemic brought with itself another kind of challenges. The winter of 2020-2021 was marked by cold temperatures and longer duration, which devoured the resource stocks of several countries. Attempts to compensate for these effects and accumulate new supplies in the summer of 2021 were not successful, as high temperatures increased electricity demand for cooling purposes, but the lack of precipitation prevented large-scale mobilization of hydroelectric power plants. At the same time, weak winds in Europe limited renewables generation, so these shortfalls could not help but immediately push prices upwards. These events stimulated the emanation of a novel understanding about the particular importance of "energy meteorology", in order to support forecast-based projections of energy consumption and generation. The eye-catching trends towards a worsening of the "wind drought" have raised further concerns about the future of this type of renewable energy, as analyses have provided pointers in the direction of an 8-10% reduction in wind speeds in Europe (Ranasinghe et al., 2021). The phenomenon of the so-called "global stilling" is associated with modifications in the thermal wind balance, as the heating of the Arctic zones as a result of climate change curtails the temperature differences between warmer and colder zones, which in turn reflects in wind reduction (Bloomfield, 2021).

Alongside this, plans to move away from coal have led to an increase in demand for natural gas. The rise in its prices to record levels in European countries such as the UK, France, Spain, Germany and Italy have spurred measures to limit the social impact so that vulnerable households are protected (Pescatori et al., 2021). The unfolding processes have shown that in going through a fundamental transformation, the global energy system becomes more vulnerable to shocks, and the emerging energy crisis demonstrates how complex the energy transition actually is to implement. Consequently, the public debate was dominated by the question of whether the blame for the worsening situation lies precisely in the shift towards renewables (Dewan, 2021). According to the observations of the experts, the reason for the complications could be found in the lack of funds for developing conventional energy sources, that is leading to a situation where the old energy industry is starving while the new one is being overfed with investment" (Baker et al., 2021). In this connection, there are arguments, that this is a case of a poorly managed energy transition, which means that the crisis is actually provoked by insufficient political foresight (Nuttall, 2021).

While such debates have been on the agenda, trying to figuring out what is happening in the energy sector, the start of the war in Ukraine has further deepened the swirling energy crisis. Logically, the 2022 worldwide discussions on energy dilemmas centralized on the repercussions from the hostilities with regard to the disruptions in supplies and markets. The deterioration of the political situation and the imposed sanctions on Russia forced the EU to search for alternatives to obtain the necessary energy. Rising resource and electricity prices in Europe began to fuel accelerating inflation, and as the energy crisis worsened, mechanisms to protect consumers from rising bills had to be implemented. With crude prices hitting new highs, several countries and regions had to reconstruct their energy affairs and forge new bonds with prospective exporters. In these turbulent times, China obtained the chance to shine and was even described as a winner in the turmoil – it used wisely the options for buying or increasing stakes in Russian energy companies, purchasing vacant resources and reselling them to the nations in need.

The redrawing of the world energy map induced various transformations in different dimensions. Looking at the energy statistics for 2022 (BP, 2023), it is notable that the Asian giant it still capturing the position as a world's largest consumer of energy with a share of 26.4%, followed by the US with 15.9% and EU with 9.6%. PRC has not overthrown its status as a biggest polluter despite the drop in the carbon dioxide emissions of 0.1% - it's share in world's total emissions (30.7%) is extensive compared to that of the US (14.0%) or EU (7.9%). Different models are observed in the hydrocarbons department – as concerns oil consumption the leader is the US with a share of 19.7% of the global use, followed by China with 14.7%, and the EU with 11.1%; for natural gas the US (with a share of 22.4%) is ahead of Russia (10.4%) and China (9.5%). Thanks to its gas savings in 2022, the EU switched its position with the Asian country and moved to the fourth place (with a share of 8.7%). PRC has pushed up its imports with regard to pipeline volumes by 9.7%, but scaled down its LNG lure by 15.2%. Its imports from the US fell to 2.6 bcm (compared to 12.4 bcm in 2021) – a confirmation for the new major destination of American LNG tankers in the figure of the EU. Europe drew to itself 31.4% of global LNG supplies, while the Asia Pacific region obtained 64.1%, with Japan on the top of the rankings as world's largest LNG importer. With regard to coal, China is not only the largest producer and consumer (with a share of 50.6% and 54.8% respectively), but also increased its production by 10.5% in 2022 as a result of its 2021 crisis measures.

Outside the fossil fuels department, relevant changeover is registered with reference to nuclear energy. Behind the runner US (with a share of 30.3% of global consumption), the second position is for China with 15.6%, but it continues to enlarge its distance from France, after the two countries switched their positions at the beginning of the pandemic. However, the Asian colossus is on the guiding position with respect to hydroelectricity consumption (with a share of 30.1% of world's total). Impressive are also its advances in renewable energy – in 2022, China was responsible for the largest portion of solar (37%) and wind (41%) growth with respect to global capacity addictions. Its renewable energy generation expanded by 18.3%, resulting in a hike in its share in world's total to 32.3% (compared to 19.3% for the EU and 16.8% for the US).

The reopening of the Chinese economy since the beginning of 2023 is watched closely by the experts, because its status of biggest consumer of commodities provokes polar expectations – not only for fresh funds for investments, but also for driving a rise in global fuel prices. The International Energy Agency highlights in a report, that the global demand for oil could reach an all-time high of 101.7 million barrels per day in 2023, with PRC contributing to almost half of the increase (International Energy Agency, 2023). Especially in the second half of the year, analysts predict that oil prices could hit $95 a barrel (Cooban, 2023a) due to more dynamic travel and consumption, in combination with the more active restocking activities ahead of the winter season. In the opinion of Christine Lagarde, president of the European Central Bank, the LNG amount that the Asian leader "will be buying from the rest of the world will be higher than we have seen". She argues, the extra demand in energy and in commodities in general will produce added inflationary pressure (Cooban, 2023b). Evidently, the energy crisis is far from its end, so new waves of instability could hit the markets. Eventually, an adequate redirection of energy flows could ease the current tensions, as major Asian importers such as China and India would be able to buy Russian resources at a discount, leaving free volumes from other suppliers to be directed towards the EU.

Apparently, Europe's competition with the Asian countries will also take place along the lines of important regions from which the necessary resources can be extracted. Currently, the focus is turning to the Mediterranean as a source of natural gas, with the search for alternative suppliers focusing, for example, on countries such as Egypt, Israel and Nigeria alongside traditional EU partners such as Algeria and Libya. However, this opens the door to new risks in tying up with areas characterized by political and economic instability. Until recently, the rhetoric regarding hydrocarbon-rich countries such as Algeria, Nigeria, Angola, etc., was based on the claims that they were threatened by internal disruptions in view of their unwillingness to abandon fossil fuels, but now they are seen as significant instruments for European distancing from the Russian supplies. On the other hand, regional political turbulence in various areas in Africa is testing the EU to find a new basis for developing relations with a number of countries, accentuating on the dilemma whether these will be dominated by pragmatism or carry the moral color of EU's role as a transformational force. The Union needs to find the right modus operandi for regaining its position in Africa, as the continent is not only an important part of China's expanding operational field for provision of energy commodities, but Beijing has also pursued a highly effective approach to capturing resources, relying on the conclusion of long-term agreements for exploitation rights, the acquisition of stakes in energy companies and projects, and investment in various types of energy infrastructure.

At the same time, the issue of the EU finding new energy partners cannot be taken out of the context of the debate on European strategic autonomy (Baudson, 2022). Achieving isolation and self-sufficiency is clearly not possible in a globalized world where the answer to the question of how to achieve a reduction in external dependence is contained in the realization of diversification. Europe must undoubtedly show that it has learnt the necessary lessons from the current crisis, that dependencies should not only not be underestimated, but also not substituted for one another.

4. The Energy Sector: On the Course Towards Sustainable Recovery?

Beyond shadow of a doubt, the present emphasis on energy issues is driven by their bond to the ecological footprint considering that energy resources are a crucial segment of the natural capital and their consumption represents an important part of the human impact on the environment. The alarming necessity to safeguard the biosphere transforms gradually our perceptions about the attitudes and the ways in which we should manage the use of resources throughout the economy and in our daily lives. As a result, the issue of the environmental protection in general, and in particular, the efficient use of energy resources and the quest for finding alternatives to traditional fossil fuels entered both the worldwide public awareness and the international political scene.

Nowadays, the subject of energy transformations provokes special attention on a global level in view of the climate change concerns and the call for sustainable development. Slowly the world is overcoming the perceptions that renewables are only suitable for local applications and are not an effective tool for powering large economies. Crushing the labels of "fashion trend" and "costly experiment" is increasingly becoming a tendency, especially as renewables have long been a brand for Western powers, but in view of the ongoing developments in the Asia-Pacific region, this kind of impression is now completely inaccurate. The previous economic crisis of 2008 brought to the fore comments that the introduction of the low-carbon model was oriented towards securing growth for the economies of the developed countries. They were indeed used by the EU and the US to revive their economy after the sharp downturn. Nonetheless, this kind of energy is no longer perceived as an expensive luxury only confined to developed nations. Presently, it is recognized as likewise affordable for countries in the developing world.

With respect to the forerunners in renewables, there are several states, which have proved in the last decades their ability to adapt the basis for the development of green energy, implementing a consistent optimizing process on their energy policies. However, behind their current prosperity of this sector lies a specific chain of motives, driving its expansion. The mix of domestic reasons is seriously intertwisted with impulses, coming from the international realm. Including diversification as an integral part of the plans for energy progress, the leaders aim not only at dealing with ecological complications, but also with several economic and political hardships. A drop in energy dependence would create various advantages and lessen the burden of militarization of energy security. In consequence, energy transformations should be encouraged in the international context. Exploring the most interesting examples of modern energy layout and searching for parallels should assist in answering the question, if successful mechanisms could be replicated in other countries.

For Europe, boosting renewable energy supported its ambition to become a world leader in climate change actions. However, it has paid a heavy price for this, as the burden imposed on industry has led to a loss of competitiveness. On the other hand, these ambitions of the EU have given it a reason to claim that, by having a successful environmental policy, it is in fact pursuing a 'new type of foreign policy' that will help in regaining the lost prestige of the continent.

Notwithstanding, the European efforts were overshadowed by the achievement of the new leader in green energy in the face of China. The Asian giant has leaned on the experience gained from the EU and the US, but has also managed to establish its own unique model of renewable energy advancement (ESCAP, 2012), which has propelled it to the forefront of wind and solar power generation, and secured its status as the world's largest producer and exporter of green energy technologies. Activating initially the import of components and equipment, by constantly refining energy policies in this segment, the country has been able to apply successful tools to build its own industry. Starting with protectionist measures in the initial phases of its development, China shielded itself from strong external competition, and after assembling sufficient capacity, the imposed ones were lifted so that the sector became open again (Chiu, 2017). This inclination towards energy protectionism has been strongly criticized by the EU, but its aptness has been proven by the success of the Asian colossus, which has not only managed to shorten its distance to Western countries, but also to overtake them. China's assumption of the position of world leader in renewable energy is indicative enough of the transformations that have taken place in this field. Beijing's targets of peaking carbon dioxide emissions before 2030 and reaching carbon neutrality before 2060 are extremely impressive, especially in terms of the time gap between them of just 30 years, which stands out when compared with the fixed 71 years for the EU and 43 years for the US. The Asian giant has not only become involved as a factor in the development of green technologies, but has also managed to lead the race, which raises the question of whether it will be a partner or competitor to the West in this realm.

In the context of the pandemic crisis, the emphasis on renewable energy was again noticeable with respect to the ideas to use the momentum for accomplish advanced arrangement of the energy domain with amended foundation and structure. In the search for remedial tools for the affected economies, the vision of achieving "green growth" to bring about a "sustainable recovery" has been floated. The calls to use the turmoil as a chance to make an energy transition have produced various designs for a complete overhaul of the energy sector. A "Sustainable Recovery Plan" (International Energy Agency, 2020c), was presented by the International Energy Agency in collaboration with the International Monetary Fund to support the conversion to a new energy model. Additionally, the EU has reaffirmed its commitment to the Green Deal adopted before the pandemic, so that despite the difficulties encountered, it can reach its goals of making Europe climate neutral by 2050 on the basis of building a circular economy (European Commission, 2019).

With the start of the war in Ukraine, a number of questions are being raised as to whether the turmoil will eliminate the green targets set, both under the Paris Agreement and within the EU. The expectations pointed towards an increased interest in short-term investments in oil, gas and coal, but it remains to be seen whether these will also provoke a wider return to fossil fuels. Military action has definitely pushed ecological issues off the top of the agenda. However, the EU has demonstrated that it is far from abandoning its environmental policies. On 18 May 2022, the European Commission presented proposals to accelerate the energy transition, focusing on increasing wind and solar energy capacity, as well as improving energy efficiency. The RePowerEU plan (European Commission, 2022) is geared towards increasing European energy independence by 2027, and under the new fixed targets the share of renewable energy is to rise to 45% by 2030, and with the same time horizon energy efficiency should have reached 13%. There is also an obligation to install solar panels on all public and commercial buildings by 2025 and on all residential buildings by 2029. The plan is worth €300 billion, as around €10 billion will be directed towards building new natural gas and green hydrogen infrastructure, while €2 billion will be allocated to laying oil pipelines.

Whether the war in Ukraine will really become an engine for accelerating the green transition, however, remains a problematic question. The EU is so mired in its own dilemmas that it is struggling to find adequate responses to the new situation. On the one hand, the prevailing view is that new investment in renewables is needed, as everything else is "energy of the past" that should not distract from the chosen course. However, according to the European Commission, for the purposes of distancing from coal, natural gas and nuclear energy could be qualified as sustainable. However, the war provokes quite naturally negative perceptions regarding dependence on natural gas. On the other hand, the member states are divided in their positions on nuclear energy. In the current complicated situation, the concrete decisions at national level rather point to the conclusion that we will witness a reversal of energy policies and a rethinking of the solutions launched so far to implement a green transition.

With regard to the crisis, special emphasis is placed on energy efficiency. In 2022, the International Energy Agency prepared a report (IEA, 2022a) on the topic, highlighting that its prioritizing is reasonable because of "its ability to simultaneously meet affordability, supply security and climate goals". The global pandemic recovery proved the urgency of implementing energy conservation measures and their application helped IEA member countries to curtail their energy bills by $680 billion in 2022 (around 15% of the total energy bill of USD 4.5 trillion). Since 2020, around $1 trillion were invested in various initiatives for improving energy efficiency, making up two-thirds of all clean energy and recovery spending. The energy efficiency-related investment amount of governments, industry and households reached the record $560 billion in 2022, marking a 16% growth compared to the data for 2021.

A crucial component in this expansion formed the sales of electric vehicles. Their worldwide purchases reached 11 million units in 2022, compared to just 1 million in 2017. Currently, they occupy a share of 13% of the sales of new vehicles, meaning that one of eight cars sold around the globe is now electric. Electric vehicle purchases contributed to a growth of almost 50% in transport efficiency-related investment. Several governments created the needed incentives and offered subsidies for them, in order to spark the progress in this sector. Nearly 42% of total efficiency-related transport investment is based on spending for the electrification of transport. China appears as a forerunner in all dimensions, marking almost 9.5 million or 95% of electric two- and three-wheeler registrations worldwide and 90% of e-bus and e-truck registrations in 2021.

Certainly, other instruments were deployed as well in the wake of the energy crisis for mitigating its negative effects for households and businesses, especially dealing with the extremely rising energy bills. With a range of government interventions encompassing miscellaneous apparatus from new or increased broad-based fuel subsidies to direct cash payments, the value of this kind of public emergency spending climbed over $550 billion. International bodies such as the IMF and the OECD expressed their reservation about broad-based energy subsidies. According to the recommendations of the OECD, the governments should aim better because the offered support "so far has been largely untargeted and often fiscally costly", so it might "reduce incentives to save energy and transition away from fossil fuels" (OECD, 2023). Trying to draw lessons from the current complications for enhancing the preparedness to future energy shocks, it suggests that reducing vulnerability to forthcoming crises is possible via diversifying energy sources and accelerating the green transition. The report is focused on guiding countries to design and implement more properly addressed policy responses. It shows that economies with larger energy import dependencies were tied to costlier support measures, especially in the case of Europe. Consequently, such countries are "more vulnerable to the impacts of energy geopolitics".

The recommendations of the IMF also point in the same direction. They suggest that broad-based support and the resolution to suppress the rising energy prices could cause additional damage. Experts highlight that "in some countries the fiscal cost of the energy crisis response is set to exceed 1.5 percent of GDP in the first year alone—with more than half of that in costly non-targeted measures" (Celasun & Iakova, 2022). Therefore, they advocate for a shift from price-suppressing instruments to income relief targeted to the vulnerable, combined with "strong incentives to save energy and switch out of fossil fuels". Added argumentation supporting this viewpoint could be found in an analysis of the policy responses to high energy and food prices. It confirms that the measures that have been taken to dampen the price pass-through are suboptimal, so "more targeted support to vulnerable households is preferred, especially in countries with strong social safety nets. Countries with weaker social safety nets can consider alternative targeting approaches relying, for example, on digital solutions and big data to provide targeted support" (Amaglobeli et al., 2023).

Especially relevant is the international collaboration with regard to solving energy problems. When it comes to designing energy policies, the countries could benefit from the others' experience, exchange best practices and even harmonize approaches and standards. A noteworthy event was the 7th Annual Global Conference on Energy Efficiency, organized by IEA in June 2022 in Sønderborg, Denmark. An important product of the forum was the joint statement (Danish Ministry of Climate, Energy and Utilities, 2022), issued by 26 countries, calling on governments, industry, and stakeholders to bolster their action on energy efficiency under the motto: "The cleanest energy is the energy we don't use". In order to support the implementation of upgraded apparatus, IEA offered the Sønderborg Action Plan on Energy Efficiency, outlining a set of strategic principles and policy toolkits (IEA, 2022b). The specific report of IEA for the conference highlights that scaling up investment could result in an extra 10 million jobs by 2030 in efficiency-related fields such as in new construction and building retrofits, manufacturing and transport infrastructure (IEA, 2022c).

As concerns the broader context of energy cooperation, the topic of diplomacy becomes once again crucial for consideration. In times of crisis, it is quite normal every country to strive for a better positioning in the current and future energy landscape. Furthermore, the opposition between multilateral and bilateral diplomacy becomes more easily detectable, as multilateral formats will help in aligning the interests of multiple stakeholders, but the bilateral mode enables a more direct and speedy pursuit of national aims and ambitions. However, analysts highlight that the "bounded notion of energy governance creates a "paradox of sovereignty" whereby countries fail to act collectively despite the fact that globalization of energy markets increasingly diminishes their control over their individual energy interests" (Griffiths, 2019). However, energy diplomacy is identified as a valuable instrument with regard to energy transition and the shift toward renewables (Kresnawan & Wijaya, 2021).

Another relevant aspect within the perspective of cooperation represents the model of regional communities building. The EU endeavor serves as an example that provides inspiration for the evolution of this mold for achieving energy security. In a regional framework, on the grounds of closer partnership and collaboration, the actors will be able to channel their mutual interests and, through the intertwining of the energy and the overall economic sectors, to use the generated interdependencies as a basis for long-term and lasting engagement. Within such communities, it will be far easier to balance the triangle of interests of producers, transit actors and consumers. However, these developments are becoming the fundament for predictions that a focus on long-term goals towards liberalization and internal consolidation on a broader regional footing, in parallel with the erection of external protectionist walls, will take center stage in the process of building a new global energy order. This may serve as a source of concerns for the future, as the realization of scenarios for the formation of a fragmented world would be unwelcomed. Definitely, the attempts to find common solutions to the energy problems via cooperation and solidarity could be overshadowed by a rush towards deglobalization and energy nationalism, induced by the instinct for self-preservation, which is normally intensified in times of crisis.

CONCLUSION

In the last decades, different events demonstrate the interdependence and interconnectedness of energy networks, where any single disturbance in a particular segment reflects rapidly through a chain propagation to other parts. An extremely thorny question now is whether disruptions in the energy sector will cloud efforts to achieve a green transition. Any return to ideas of expanding hydrocarbon use to minimize the effects of the energy crisis will have a devastating environmental impact. On the other hand, intensifying the use of renewables requires investments that will be difficult to secure in a deteriorating economic climate. Beyond the political element of taking measures and seeking solutions, the public response will also be essential, as changing attitudes and perceptions of businesses and households about energy production and consumption will be key to implementing a shift in the energy model.

The recent energy crises clearly offers more questions than answers. In the last years, the turmoil in the global energy system even calls into question the benefits of globalization. For several countries, reaching energy self-sufficiency is unachievable - they can not become energy islands, which increasingly drives them to seek novel solutions to common problems, pushing even the development of regional approaches. However, the extent to which ideas of solidarity and consolidation in the face of crisis will prove sustainable, is going to become apparent as energy complications continue to escalate. At the same time, a stance should be taken on which energy sources we will turn our backs on and which we will priorities in a complicated situation. If natural gas will no longer be the bridge to the new energy, then a supporting factor for renewables must be aired - will it be identified in the face of nuclear power or will the faster option of coal mining be preferred? The prescriptions that will be favored will also determine the results, which will show whether the world has actually hit a bad moment for the implementation of energy transition or whether, on the contrary, this is the most appropriate one.

In the current circumstances, the term “diversification” sounds more relevant than ever. However, securing new partners for the supply of energy resources implies that politics is back on the agenda. The war in Ukraine has stimulated a redrawing not only of the European but also of the global energy map. The transformations generated cannot be without geopolitical dimensions. In the words of German Chancellor Olaf Scholz: “we are in a new era and the world today is not the same as it was before” (Crawford et al., 2022). Today’s energy imperatives can also be interpreted as a source of chance for an energy paradigm shift. Only its metamorphosis can eliminate the possibilities for energy resources to be used as weapons in modern conflicts.

REFERENCES

Amaglobeli, D. (2023). *Policy Responses to High Energy and Food Prices.* IMF Working Paper, WP/23/74, March 2023. Available at: https://www.imf.org/-/media/Files/Publications/WP/2023/English/wpiea2023074-print-pdf.ashx

Andrea, P. (2021). *Energy prices: When will costs go down?* World Economic Forum, 27 October 2021. Available at: https://www.weforum.org/agenda/2021/10/surging-energy-prices-may-not-ease-next-year-2022/

Auty, R. (1993). *Sustaining Development in Mineral Economies: The Resource Curse Thesis*. Oxford University Press.

Baker, D. (2021). *Today's global energy crisis is just the first in the "clean power" era*. World Oil. Available at: https://www.worldoil.com/news/2021/10/5/today-s-global-energy-crisis-is-just-the-first-in-the-clean-power-era

Baker Institute. (2012). *Cybersecurity Issues and Policy Options for the U.S. Energy Industry, 2012.* Baker Institute Policy Report, Rice University. Available at: https://www.bakerinstitute.org/media/files/Research/ba7df664/IT-pub-PolicyReport53.pdf

Barkham, P. (2008). What is the knowledge economy? *The Guardian*. Available at: www.guardian.co.uk

Baudson, V. (2022). EU's strategic autonomy requires new investment momentum. *Financial Times*. Available at: https://www.ft.com/content/40756ab8-7307-45d7-aaee-eb33efe16f37

Beaudreau, B. (1998). Energy and Organization: Growth and Distribution Reexamined. Westport.

Bilgin, M. (2010). Geo-Economics of European Gas Security: Trade, Geography and International Politics.. *Insight Turkey*, *12*(4), 185–209.

Bloomfield, H. (2021). *What happens when the wind doesn't blow? Building the energy systems of the future*. World Economic Forum. Available at: https://www.weforum.org/agenda/2021/10/europe-low-winds-future-energy-grid-power/

Bovan. (2020). Negotiating Energy Diplomacy and its Relationship with Foreign Policy and National Security. *International Journal of Energy Economics and Policy, 10*(2), 1-6. Available at: https://www.researchgate.net/publication/338720574_Negotiating_Energy_Diplomacy_and_its_Relationship_with_Foreign_Policy_and_National_Security

BP. (2021a). Statistical Review of World Energy – all data, 1965-2020. BO.

BP. (2021b). EU's energy market in 2020. Statistical Review of World Energy – 2021. BP.

BP. (2023). Statistical Review of World Energy – 2022. BP.

Bressand, A. (2012). *The Changed Geopolitics of Energy and Climate and the Challenge for Europe: A Geopolitical and European Perspective on the Triple Agenda of Competition, Energy Security and Sustainability*. Clingendael. Available at: www.clingendael.nl

Buenstorf, G. (2004). The Economics of Energy and the Production Process: An Evolutionary Approach. Academic Press.

Celasun, O., & Iakova, D. (2022). *Helping Europe's Households*. International Monetary Fund. Available at: https://www.imf.org/en/Publications/fandd/issues/2022/12/helping-europe-households-Celasun-Iakova

Čerić, V. (2001). Building the Knowledge Economy. *Journal of Computing and Information Technology, 9*(3), 177–183..

Chiu, D. (2017). The East Is Green: China's Global Leadership in Renewable Energy. *New Perspectives in Foreign Policy, 13*. Available at: https://www.csis.org/east-green-chinas-global-leadership-renewable-energy

Cooban, A. (2023a). *China's reopening isn't all good news. Inflation could get a second wind*. CNN. Available at: https://edition.cnn.com/2023/01/27/business/china-commodities-energy-inflation/index.html

Cooban, A. (2023b). *Global interest rate hikes are 'yet to bite,' says IMF head*. CNN. Available at: https://edition.cnn.com/2023/01/20/economy/imf-economy-davos/index.html

Crawford, A. (2022). *A New World Energy Order Is Emerging From Putin's War on Ukraine*. Bloomberg. Available at: https://www.bloomberg.com/news/articles/2022-03-11/a-new-world-energy-order-is-emerging-from-putin-s-war-on-ukraine#xj4y7vzkg

Crawford, L. (2006). Spain vows to prevent foreign takeover. *Financial Times*. Available at: www.ft.com

Danish Ministry of Climate, Energy and Utilities. (n.d.). *Joint Statement: Urgent Action on Energy Efficiency, No. 2022 – 85, 10 June 2022*. Available at: https://en.kefm.dk/Media/637904431073034736/joint%20statement.pdf

Deffeyes, K. (2006). *Beyond Oil: The View from Hubbert's Peak*. Hill and Wang.

Dewan, A. (2021). *Europe's gas crisis is also a renewables crisis, but there are ready solutions*. CNN. Available at: https://edition.cnn.com/2021/09/22/business/europe-energy-gas-renewables-climate-cmd-intl/index.html

ESCAP. (2012). *Finding a Green Engine for Economic Growth: China's Renewable Energy Policies, Low Carbon Green Growth Roadmap for Asia and the Pacific*. Economic and Social Commission for Asia and the Pacific. Available at: https://www.unescap.org/sites/default/files/14.%20CS-China-Renewable-Energy-Policies.pdf

European Commission. (2019). *The European Green Deal, Brussels, 11.12.2019, COM(2019) 640 final*. Author.

European Commission. (2022). *REPowerEU: Joint European Action for more affordable, secure and sustainable energy, Strasbourg, 8.3.2022, COM(2022) 108 final*. Author.

Falk, J. (2012). *Energy firms must acknowledge cybersecurity as more than an IT problem, according to new Rice University paper*. Rice University. Available at: http://news.rice.edu

Frankel, J. (2012). *The Natural Resource Curse: A Survey of Diagnoses and Some Prescriptions*. Harvard Kennedy School, HKS Faculty Research Working Paper Series, RWP12-014.

Friedman, T. (2006). The First Law of Petro-politics. *Foreign Policy, 154*(3), 28-36.

Griffiths, S. (2019). Energy Diplomacy in a Time of Energy Transition. *Energy Strategy Reviews, 26*. Available at: https://www.sciencedirect.com/science/article/pii/S2211467X19300793

GWEC. (2021). *Global wind power growth must triple over next decade to achieve Net Zero*. Global Wind Energy Council. Available at: https://gwec.net/global-wind-power-growth-must-triple-over-next-decade-to-achieve-net-zero/

Heinberg, R. (2005). *The Party's Over: Oil, War and the Fate of Industrial Societies*. New Society Publishers.

Heinberg, R. (2011). *The End of Growth: Adapting to Our New Economic Reality*. New Society Publishers.

Heinberg, R. (2021). *Understanding Power*. Post Carbon Institute. Available at: https://www.postcarbon.org/understanding-power/

International Energy Agency. (2020a). *World Energy Investment 2020*. IEA. Available at: https://www.iea.org/reports/world-energy-investment-2020

International Energy Agency. (2020b). *Global Energy Review 2020. The Impacts of the Covid-19 Crisis on Global Energy Demand and CO2 Emissions*. Flagship Report. Available at: https://www.iea.org/reports/global-energy-review-2020/

International Energy Agency. (2020c). *Sustainable Recovery*. Available at: https://www.iea.org/reports/sustainable-recovery

International Energy Agency. (2021). *Covid-19 impact on electricity*. Available at: https://www.iea.org/reports/covid-19-impact-on-electricity

International Energy Agency. (2022a). *Energy Efficiency*. https://iea.blob.core.windows.net/assets/7741739e-8e7f-4afa-a77f-49dadd51cb52/EnergyEfficiency2022.pdf

International Energy Agency. (2022b). *7th Annual Global Conference on Energy Efficiency Policy Toolkit*. Available at: https://iea.blob.core.windows.net/assets/ef170f7d-606a-4adc-ac32-565f9b6c0579/7thAnnualGlobalConferenceonEnergyEfficiency-PolicyToolkit.pdf

International Energy Agency. (2022c). *7th Annual Global Conference on Energy Efficiency - The Value of Urgent Action on Energy Efficiency*. Available at: https://www.iea.org/reports/the-value-of-urgent-action-on-energy-efficiency

International Energy Agency. (2023). *Oil Market Report, 18 January 2023*. Available at: https://iea.blob.core.windows.net/assets/6b994ae3-17fe-4a44-8bb8-eb1217cc4604/-18JAN2023_OilMarketReport.pdf

Jacobs, M. (2017). *Panic at the Pump - The Energy Crisis and the Transformation of American Politics in the 1970s*. Macmillan.

Johnson, K. (2009). Protectionist Breezes: Wind-Power Companies Cry Foul on China. *Wall Street Journal*. Available at: http://europe.wsj.com

Kendall-Taylor, A. (2010). *Domestic balancing acts in the Caspian petro-states. - Caspian Energy Politics. Azerbaijan, Kazakhstan and Turkmenistan*. Routledge.

King, L. (2012). *The Devastating Effects of a Cyber-Attack Against a Country's Energy Grid*. http://oilprice.com

Kresnawan, M., & Wijaya, T. (2021). *Energy Diplomacy: A Vital Piece to Boost Renewable Energy Investment.* ASEAN Centre for Energy. Available at: https://aseanenergy.org/energy-diplomacy-a-vital-piece-to-boost-renewable-energy-investment/

Leveque, F., & Monturus, R. (2008). *Mergers & Acquisitions within the European Power and Gas Sectors. Cases and Patterns.* Report of the CERNA - Mines ParisTech. Available at: www.microeconomix.com

LeVine, S. (2012). *Ten Indicators You Should Watch to Predict the Geopolitics of Energy*. Quartz. Available at: https://qz.com/17335/ten-indicators-you-should-watch-to-predict-the-geopolitics-of-energy

Mahaffey, J. (2015). *Atomic Accidents: A History of Nuclear Meltdowns and Disasters; From the Ozark Mountains to Fukushima*. Pegasus Books.

Makube, S. (2012). *South African Oil Dependency: Geo-political, Geo-economic and Geo-strategic Considerations*. University of Johannesburg. ujdigispace.uj.ac.za

Moran, D., & Russell, J. (2010). *Energy Security and Global Politics - The Militarization of Resource Management*. Routledge.

Nuttall, P. (2021, September). The power trap: Why the energy crisis is a crisis of politics. –. *New Statesman (London, England), 28*. https://www.newstatesman.com/international-politics/climate-international-politics/2021/09/the-power-trap-why-the-energy-crisis-is-a-crisis-of-politics

OECD. (2023). *Aiming Better: Government Support for Households and Firms during the Energy Crisis.* OECD Economic Policy Paper No. 32. Available at: https://www.oecd-ilibrary.org/docserver/839e3ae1-en.pdf?expires=1692914306&id=id&accname=guest&checksum=0341DA666836280BAC460A99A84531BE

Overland, I. (2010). *The Resource Curse and Authoritarianism in the Caspian Petro-states. - Caspian Energy Politics. Azerbaijan, Kazakhstan and Turkmenistan*. Routledge. doi:10.4324/9780203865231

Pardesi, M. (2006). Energy and Security: The Geopolitics of Energy in the Asia-Pacific. Institute of Defence and Strategic Studies - Nanyang Technological University.

Pascual, C. (2008). *The Geopolitics of Energy: From Security to Survival.* Brookings Institution. http://www.brookings.edu

Ranasinghe, R. (2021). Climate Change Information for Regional Impact and for Risk Assessment. In *Climate Change 2021: The Physical Science Basis. Contribution of Working Group I to the Sixth Assessment Report of the Intergovernmental Panel on Climate Change*. Cambridge University Press.

Robinson, J., & Torvik, R. (2005, February). White Elephants. *Journal of Public Economics, 89*(2–3), 197–210. doi:10.1016/j.jpubeco.2004.05.004

Ross, M. (2015). What Have We Learned About the Resource Curse? *Annual Review of Political Science, 18*(1), 239–259. doi:10.1146/annurev-polisci-052213-040359

Rothkopf, D. (2011, October). The Geopolitics of Energy in the 21st Century. *Foreign Policy, 5*. http://www.foreignpolicy.com

Stanway, D. (2021). *China starts Baihetan hydro project, biggest since Three Gorges*. Reuters. Available at: https://www.reuters.com/business/energy/chinas-giant-baihetan-hydro-plant-begins-generating-power-cctv-2021-06-28/

Stearns, P. (2021). *The Industrial Revolution in World History*. Routledge.

Sweet, W. (2012). *Energy Geopolitics: Quandaries Intensify*. Great Decisions, Foreign Policy Association. Available at: http://www.fpa.org

The Geopolitics of Natural Gas. (2012). *Report of Scenarios Workshop of Harvard University's Belfer Center and Rice University's Baker Institute Energy Forum*. Available at: http://belfercenter.ksg.harvard.edu

Vanderbruck, T. (2010). *Can the World Survive the Impending Oil Crisis?* Available at: http://www.oil-price.net

Vanderbruck, T. (2011). *Egypt Riots and Oil*. http://www.oil-price.net

Venn, F. (2002). *The Oil Crisis*. Routledge.

Verrastro, F. (2010). *The Geopolitics of Energy: Emerging Trends, Changing Landscapes, Uncertain Times*. Center for Strategic and International Studies. Available at: https://csis.org/

World Energy Council. (2008). *Europe's Vulnerability to Energy Crises*. Author.

Wright, J., & Conca, J. (2007). *The GeoPolitics of Energy: Achieving a Just and Sustainable Energy Distribution by 2040*. BookSurge Publishing.

Ziyadov, T. (2012). *Beyond the Resource Curse*. University of Pennsylvania Press.

Chapter 3
Taking Off to Economic Growth and Uncovering the Impact of Electricity Consumption on Regional Development:
Case Study for Cities With Airports in Türkiye

Enver Erdinç Dinçsoy
https://orcid.org/0000-0002-3927-0724
Trakya University, Turkey

Muhammet Atlas Doğan
https://orcid.org/0000-0002-4943-223X
Istanbul Technical University, Turkey

ABSTRACT

In the study, a panel data analysis is used for examining the relationship between gross domestic product per capita (GPC) and airport activity index (AAI), electricity consumption per person (EPP), physicians per 1,000 people (PPT), and credit volume (CRE). Panel data analysis results suggest that AAI has a statistically significant positive effect on the lagged GPC. This suggests that increased airport activity is associated with higher economic output in the cities of Türkiye. Both EPP and PPT have positive and significant impacts on GPC, indicating that higher electricity consumption and better access to health-care contribute to economic development in these cities. In contrast, the study identifies a negative and statistically significant relationship between CRE and GPC, suggesting that higher credit volumes might be linked to lower economic output. In conclusion, this research highlights the importance of electricity consumption, airport activities, and access to healthcare in fostering economic growth in cities of Türkiye with airports.

DOI: 10.4018/979-8-3693-0400-6.ch003

1. INTRODUCTION

Globalization in the world economy has become increasingly important in recent years. In fact, the phenomenon of globalization is the name of a study that has been going on since the 19th century and shows the most important results after the 1980s. It seems that the definition of globalization cannot be made fully and effectively, but it can be expressed as the spread of socio-economic interaction between countries and the growth of political developments. In this context, we can also express globalization as the integration of the national economy with the world. With the industrial revelations, capital and commodity markets gained an international dimension and global markets became open to each other by several technological developments and improvements (Okur Dinçsoy, 2020). It is also seen that the mobility of human, capital, energy and production components has increased with globalization. In crisis periods, developments such as instability in growth, low growth rates, business bankruptcies, decrease in factor mobility, price instability and high inflation ratios are observed in many countries (Dinçsoy & Okur Dinçsoy, 2020). These problems in the world economy have caused globalization to be replaced by regionalization in some areas. Today, it is seen that the concept of "Regional Imbalance" is being mentioned more and more as the economic differences between regions (countries) begin to increase. Regional imbalances are a concept that is evaluated at the national and international level and funds are mobilized by international organizations and institutions.

The reasons for the differences are due to many different factors. The severity and impact of these factors vary according to geographical location, cultural and sociological structure, historical processes and demographic characteristics including the scope of regional development projects and plans carried out in the regions (Dincsoy & Ichiminami, 2006). In this respect, regional imbalances can be seen not only in underdeveloped countries, but also in developed countries.

In terms of regional imbalances; It can be divided into three as "natural or geographical imbalances", "economic and functional imbalances" and "social and cultural imbalances". While some regions are advantageous in the distribution of natural resources, other regions are not, or some regions have poor capacity and opportunities to use their resources. Similarly, factors of production may cause different gains in different regions due to market difference. Depending on the education level of people, there are differences in their social positions, value judgments, behavior patterns and attire. Climate conditions, wars, epidemics, inadequacy of natural resources, inadequacy of logistics and communication infrastructure, technological backwardness, energy supply security problem are also important obstacles to regional development (Dincsoy, 2016). The construction sector, which is considered as one of the important levers of economic growth and development, due to its internal dynamics and its immersive position on many different sectors; provides many services such as airport, power generation facility, dam, housing and infrastructure services (Taşdemir, 2021). In this context, airport investments can provide very favorable conditions for the development of regions, despite the disadvantages of geographical location.

Regions that are above the highway and railway connections or provide transit can become a center in terms of geographical location. The tourism potential of some regions may also cause these regions to separate from other regions. Another geographical advantage is that the regions provide the advantage of suitable establishment location for domestic and foreign investors. The fact that some regions are on very important routes such as energy and oil or have underground and surface resources with economic value can bring these regions to the forefront in their economic development. In these regions, apart from the industry, it is seen that the service sector has also developed in order to meet the needs with the development of transportation over time.

How regions are affected by climatic changes is another important issue. Due to global warming, food supply will gain more importance in the coming period due to the decreases in agricultural supply. There is also the possibility that some regions will lose their geographical advantages or that some disadvantaged regions will gain advantage (Okur Dincsoy, 2016). In some cases, geographical conditions seem to be a factor that increases the differences in development between countries as well as between regions within the country. In short, one of the most important geographical disadvantages for the regions is being in mountainous areas and having a location where transportation costs are very high. When we say geographical advantages, we think of favorable climatic conditions, underground and surface resources, natural conditions, proximity to important centers, transportation and communication opportunities.

Mostly emerging and developing economies have transformed their production structures from agriculture to mass industrialization with the use of technology in agriculture. Undoubtedly, it is not possible to progress in the industry and service sector without an efficient energy sector. These sectors contribute to economic growth in developing economies in a healthy way due to the increase in government revenues. It also benefits development by creating employment. The industry and services sector, which does not have an effective infrastructure, cannot achieve its high growth targets. Airports contribute to the development of sectors in the region on a wide scale, from the development of communication systems to the improvement of energy infrastructure. The highly skilled workforce in these sectors is also an important part of development. From this point of view, it is clear that the energy sector is the lifeblood of the economy as it contributes to all sectors and that one of the most important production factors for the proper functioning of the economy by providing new employment opportunities (Ahmad and Mehmood, 2016: 130).

On the other hand, it is important to examine the role played by FDI in investigating the relationship between electricity consumption and economic growth. Policy makers should consider foreign direct investments in the energy sector as a policy tool for economic growth, also in terms of regional development. Energy consumption is a good indicator of economic performance, and its relationship with macroeconomic developments and its impact on financial markets should be well understood by policy makers.

Although the relationship between economic growth and energy use is generally accepted, some changes in energy use cannot be explained by GDP alone. Investment has a significantly positive effect on the increase in energy use. It means that economies with higher investment rates will expect faster growth in energy use. In estimating long-term energy consumption, apart from the per capita GDP growth, the impact of investments should also be taken into account (Liao et al., 2022: 21-22).

The aviation sector is a key driver of economic development, as it provides air transport services that can boost productivity, competitiveness, trade, tourism, investment, innovation, and spillovers in the regions they serve (Button et al., 1999; Brueckner, 2003; Green, 2007; Bel and Fageda, 2008; Chi and Baek, 2013). However, the sector has faced unprecedented challenges due to the COVID-19 pandemic, which has disrupted air connectivity and demand worldwide. Türkiye, a developing country with a large and diverse aviation market, has also experienced a significant drop in passenger traffic and cargo volume in 2020 compared to 2019, which caused a significant decline of energy intensity (Senalp, 2021; DHMI, 2021). Despite these difficulties, the sector is expected to recover gradually, with revenue passenger kilometers (RPKs) projected to reach 61% of pre-pandemic levels by 2022 (IATA, 2021). This recovery will have significant implications for regional economic growth in Türkiye, where airports play a vital role in connecting local economies with domestic and international markets.

The relationship between airport activity and income growth is complex and can vary depending on regional characteristics and heterogeneity (Zhang & Graham, 2020). While previous studies have examined this relationship using different indicators of airport activity, such as passenger traffic, cargo volume, aircraft movements, or airport connectivity (Button & Yuan, 2013; Hindawi, 2022), most of these studies have focused on developed countries or regions, with limited evidence from developing countries or emerging markets. Moreover, few studies have used panel data analysis to account for unobserved heterogeneity and dependence across regions over time.

Air transportation's effect on the regional economy has been widely examined, with research indicating that enhanced air connectivity and accessibility can boost regional economic growth. Airports can spur local economies through job creation, increased spending, and providing air transport services, leading to regional economic structure changes (Button & Yuan, 2013). However, the connection between airport activity and economic growth is intricate and varies based on regional development levels. Various factors, including airport activity, influence income growth, a key measure of economic development and social welfare. Airport activity, which captures the volume and quality of air transport services, can improve income growth by increasing productivity, competitiveness, trade, tourism, investment, innovation, and spillovers (Button et al., 1999; Brueckner, 2003; Green, 2007; Bel and Fageda, 2008; Chi and Baek, 2013).

In addition to airport activity, electricity consumption is another indicator of local economic activity that can affect income growth. Electricity consumption reflects the level of production, consumption, and development in a region, as well as the availability and quality of energy supply and infrastructure (Narayan & Smyth, 2009). For example, Can (2017) examined the relationship between renewable energy production and domestic output for Turkey for the period 1960-2013 using VAR analysis, he concluded that the increase in energy consumption caused an increase in the demand for renewable energy, and the increase in renewable energy production did not have a statistically significant effect on GDP.

Electricity consumption can also be influenced by airport activity, as airports require a large amount of electricity to operate and provide services to passengers and cargo (Güngör et al., 2017). Previous studies have found a positive and causal relationship between electricity consumption and income growth in Türkiye, suggesting that energy conservation policies may hamper economic development (Acaravci & Ozturk, 2010; Bildirici & Kayikci, 2012). However, these studies have not considered the role of airport activity as a potential mediator or moderator of this relationship. Therefore, this study includes electricity consumption as a key variable in the analysis of income growth and airport activity in Türkiye.

It is seen that the studies conducted with the airport are grouped under two important directions: *the effect of airports on regional economic development* and *the relationship between airport activities and economic development*. Airports play an important role in regional and national economic growth by inviting new domestic and foreign businesses through capital flows which encourage governments to invest in expanding existing airports or building new (but more ambitious) airports (Yao and Yang, 2008: 4-7). Existing economic structure, topography, population density, energy consumption, level of human development, and cost of capital play an important role in the need to expand or build an airport. However, the relationship between income growth and airport activity is multifaceted, potentially influenced by economic development level, country size and location, airport service quality, air transport market competition and regulation, and external shocks or crises. Understanding these complexities and the specific dynamics in Türkiye is crucial for formulating effective policies and strategies to promote regional economic growth.

This study aims to explore how income growth varies with different indicators of airport activity in a panel of 33 countries over 14 years. The objectives include estimating the relationship between income growth and various indicators of airport activity, controlling for other factors that may affect income growth, accounting for unobserved heterogeneity and dependence across countries using a fixed-effects linear model with Driscoll-Kraay standard errors, and conducting robustness tests to validate the results.

The study's contributions include using a comprehensive dataset, applying a suitable econometric method, and providing policy implications and recommendations on promoting income growth through enhancing airport activity or improving efficiency or quality. The remainder of the paper is organized as follows: Section 2 reviews the relevant theoretical and empirical literature on income growth and airport activity. Section 3 describes the data sources, variables, and samples used in the study and the econometric method employed. Section 4 presents the results of the tests. Finally, Section 5 concludes the paper by summarizing the findings and implications.

2. LITERATURE REVIEW

The related literature on the relationship between airport activity and income growth is reviewed in this section. It describes how airport activity can affect income growth through various channels and mechanisms and what the existing empirical evidence shows about the magnitude and direction of this effect. It also identifies the gaps and limitations in the existing literature and explains how the current study fills these gaps and limitations.

The theoretical literature on the relationship between airport activity and income growth can be divided into two main groups: the production function approach and the spatial equilibrium approach. The production function approach views airport activity as an input or a factor of production that influences income growth through its effect on productivity, competitiveness, trade, tourism, investment, innovation, and spillovers. This approach suggests that airport activity can enhance income growth by reducing transportation costs, improving market access, facilitating knowledge diffusion, stimulating demand, attracting foreign direct investment, and generating multiplier effects (Button et al., 1999; Brueckner, 2003; Green, 2007; Bel and Fageda, 2008; Chi and Baek, 2013). The spatial equilibrium approach views airport activity as an amenity or a feature of a location that influences income growth through its effect on the population, migration, labor supply, human capital, and quality of life. This approach suggests that airport activity can enhance income growth by increasing population size, attracting skilled workers, improving labor mobility, enhancing human capital accumulation, and improving quality of life (Glaeser et al., 1995; Gyourko et al., 1999; Black et al., 2002; Moretti, 2012; Cohen and Paul, 2014).

The empirical literature on the relationship between airport activity and income growth can be categorized into three main types: cross-sectional studies, time-series studies, and panel data studies. Cross-sectional studies use data from a single point in time to estimate the effect of airport activity on income growth across different regions or countries. Time-series studies use data from a single region or country to estimate the effect of airport activity on income growth over time. Panel data studies use data from multiple regions or countries over time to estimate the effect of airport activity on income growth across regions or countries and over time. The empirical literature has used various measures of income growth and airport activity, such as gross domestic product per capita, passenger traffic, cargo traffic, aircraft movements, and airport quality. The empirical literature has also used various econometric techniques to deal with issues such as endogeneity, heterogeneity, dependence, nonlinearity, and dynamics. The empirical literature has found mixed results on the effect of airport activity on income growth. Some studies have found a positive and significant effect of airport activity on income growth (e.g., Button et al., 1999; Brueckner, 2003; Green, 2007; Bel and Fageda, 2008; Chi and Baek, 2013), while others have found a negative or insignificant effect (e.g., Glaeser et al., 1995; Gyourko et al., 1999; Black et al., 2002; Moretti, 2012; Cohen and Paul, 2014). The mixed results may reflect different factors, such as the level of economic development, the size and location of the region or country, the type and quality of airport services, the degree of competition and regulation in the air transport market, and the occurrence of external shocks or crises. The existing literature has some gaps and limitations that need to be addressed. First, most existing studies have focused on developed countries or regions with high-income growth levels and airport activity. There is a lack of studies on developing countries or regions with low-income growth levels and airport activity. Second, most existing studies have used simple indicators of income growth and airport activity that may not capture the complexity and diversity of these phenomena. There is a need for more comprehensive and reliable indicators of income growth and airport activity that can reflect different aspects of economic development and air transport services. Third, most existing studies have used inappropriate methods or data that may not account for unobserved heterogeneity and dependence across regions or countries or over time. There is a need for more suitable econometric methods that can control for unobserved country-specific factors and account for heteroskedasticity, autocorrelation, and cross-sectional dependence in the error terms.

The current study addresses these gaps and limitations by using a more comprehensive and reliable dataset on income growth and airport activity for 33 cities over 14 years, obtained from various official and reputable sources, by applying a more suitable econometric method that allows for controlling for unobserved city-specific factors and accounting for heteroskedasticity, autocorrelation, and cross-sectional dependence in the error terms; and by conducting various robustness tests to check the validity and sensitivity of the results. The current study also contributes to the literature by providing policy implications and recommendations on promoting income growth through enhancing airport activity or improving efficiency or quality.

The relationship between income growth and airport activity may not be linear or additive but somewhat nonlinear or interactive. Nonlinearity means that the relationship between income growth and airport activity may change in shape or direction depending on the level or range of income growth or airport activity. Interaction means that the relationship between income growth and airport activity may depend on or be influenced by other variables that affect income growth or airport activity (Button et al., 1999; Brueckner, 2003; Green, 2007; Bel and Fageda, 2008; Chi and Baek, 2013).

The existence of nonlinearities or interactions between income growth and airport activity variables may have significant implications for estimation and policy. Nonlinearities or interactions may mean that the effect of airport activity on income growth is not stable or uniform across regions, countries, or over time. Nonlinearities or interactions may also mean that the effect of airport activity on income growth is not simple but rather complicated or subtle. Therefore, nonlinearities or interactions may demand more advanced or flexible econometric techniques to measure or account for them. Nonlinearities or interactions may also demand more cautious or customized policy interventions to address or exploit them (Button et al., 1999; Brueckner, 2003; Green, 2007; Bel and Fageda, 2008; Chi and Baek, 2013).

3. DATA AND METHODOLOGY

Here, the data sources, variables, and samples used in the study are described and the econometric method is also explained to carry out the aim of the study.

The variables used in this study are the dependent variable, gross domestic product per capita (GDP), which measures the economic output per person in each city, and the independent variables, airport activity index (AAI), electricity consumption per person (EPP), physicians per 1,000 people (PPT), and credit volume (CRE), which capture different aspects of local economic activities in each city. The airport activity index (AAI) is a composite indicator that combines four indicators of airport activity: passenger traffic, cargo traffic, aircraft movements, and airport quality. The AAI is constructed using principal component analysis (PCA), which assigns weights to each indicator based on their contribution to the common variance. The AAI is normalized to have a mean of zero and a standard deviation of one. The natural logarithms of all variables were taken to avoid scale effects and to avoid nonlinearity.

The sample used in this study is a balanced panel of 33 cities over 15 years (2005-2019), resulting in 495 observations. The cities, which are selected based on data availability and represent different regions and levels of economic development, covered in the sample are;

Adana, Antalya, Isparta, and Kahramanmaraş in Mediterranean Region,
Ankara, Kayseri, Konya, Nevşehir, and Sivas in Central Anatolia Region,
Balıkesir, Bursa, Çanakkale, İstanbul, and Tekirdağ in Marmara Region,
Ağrı, Elazığ, Erzincan, Erzurum, Kars, Malatya, Muş, and Van in South Anatolia Region,
İzmir, Denizli, and Muğla in Aegean Region,
Adıyaman, Diyarbakır, Gaziantep, Mardin, Siirt, and Şanlıurfa in Southeastern Region,
Trabzon and Samsun in Black Sea Region

We use a fixed-effects linear model to estimate the effect of various indicators of airport activity, employment, population, and credit on income growth. A fixed-effects linear model is a kind of panel data model that enables us to control for unobserved factors specific to each country that may influence income growth and the explanatory variables. These factors are captured by the fixed effects, which are treated as parameters to be estimated along with the coefficients of the explanatory variables. The fixed-effects model assumes that the effect of the explanatory variables on income growth is constant and varies across countries. The model can be expressed as follows:

$$y_{it} = x_{it}\beta + \alpha_i + \epsilon_{it}$$

where y_{it} is the income growth of country i at time t, x_{it} is a vector of explanatory variables, β is a vector of coefficients, α_i is the fixed effect of city i, and ϵ_{it} is the error term.

This study uses the fixed effects model with Driscoll-Kraay standard errors to estimate the effect of local economic activities on GDP per capita. The fixed effects model enables us to eliminate the potential bias caused by omitted variables that are constant over time but vary across units. The Driscoll-Kraay standard errors enable us to account for heteroskedasticity, autocorrelation, and cross-sectional dependence in the error terms without imposing any parametric assumptions on the error covariance matrix. The advantage of using this method is that it provides consistent and robust estimates even when the number of periods is small and the error terms are spatially correlated (Driscoll and Kraay, 1998;

Hoechle, 2007). The disadvantage of using this method is that it may not be efficient if the error terms are not spatially correlated or if there are other sources of endogeneity in the model (Arellano and Bover, 1995; Anselin et al., 2006). Driscoll-Kraay standard errors use a nonparametric method to estimate the covariance matrix of the error terms without imposing any specific structure or assumption on the nature or form of dependence. The Driscoll-Kraay standard errors can be written as:

$$\widehat{V_{DK}}\left(\hat{\beta}\right)=\left(\sum_{i=1}^{N} x_i' x_i\right)^{-1}\left(\sum_{i=1}^{N}\sum_{j=1}^{N} x_i' \widehat{\Omega_{ij}} x_j\right)\left(\sum_{i=1}^{N} x_i' x_i\right)^{-1}$$

where $\widehat{\Omega_{ij}}$ is a nonparametric estimator of the long-run covariance matrix between city i and city j, which can be computed using a kernel function and a bandwidth parameter.

The econometric method used in this study is the panel least squares estimation method with robust standard errors. The panel least squares estimation method allows for estimating the relationship between GDP per capita and local economic activities using pooled or fixed effects models. The robust standard errors allow for accounting for heteroskedasticity or autocorrelation in the error terms. The model specification is as follows:

$$\ln\left(GPC_{it}\right)=\alpha_i+\lambda_t+\beta_1\ln\left(AAI_{it}\right)+\beta_2\ln\left(EPP_{it}\right)+\beta_3\ln\left(PPT_{it}\right)+\beta_4\ln\left(CRE_{it}\right)+u_{it}$$

Where i indexes cities and t indexes years. α_i and λ_t are city-specific and time-specific fixed effects, respectively. β_j are the coefficients of interest, and u_{it} is the error term. $\ln(GPC_{it})$ is the natural logarithm of gross domestic product per capita for city i in year t; $\ln(AAI_{it})$ is the natural logarithm of airport activity index for city i in year t; $\ln(EPP_{it})$ is the natural logarithm of electricity consumption per person for city i in year t; $\ln(PPT_{it})$ is the natural logarithm of physicians per 1,000 people for city i in year t; $\ln(CRE_{it})$ is the natural logarithm of credit volume for city i in year t. The model is estimated using Stata with the *xtscc* command with the fe option for fixed effects, and lag(#) is the option for specifying the maximum lag for the Driscoll-Kraay standard errors.

The panel data analysis has some advantages and disadvantages compared to other methods for data analysis. One advantage is that it can exploit the variation across and within units over time, increasing efficiency and reducing the estimates' bias. Another advantage is that it can control unobserved heterogeneity or individual-specific effects that may confound the relationship between the dependent and independent variables. A third advantage is that it can capture the dynamics and complexity of human behavior that may change over time or depend on past experiences. One disadvantage is that it may face some challenges in dealing with endogeneity, measurement errors, missing data, attrition, or sample selection issues that may arise in panel data. Another disadvantage is that it may require some assumptions or specifications about the structure or distribution of the error terms, such as homoskedasticity, independence, stationarity, or normality. A third disadvantage is that it may need some tests or criteria to choose among different models or methods for panel data analysis, such as pooled, fixed effects, random effects, dynamic, spatial, or nonlinear models (Hsiao, 2007; Baltagi, 2008; Wooldridge, 2010).

4. RESULTS AND DISCUSSION

The results of the unit root tests for all variables in the study, namely Gross Domestic Product per Capita (GPC), Airport Activity Index (AAI), Electricity Consumption per Person (EPP), Physicians per 1,000 people (PPT), and Credit Volume (CRE), are presented in the table. Both the Levin-Lin-Chu and Im-Pesaran-Shin tests were employed to examine the stationarity of the panel data.

Table 1. Unit root results

Variable	Test	Adjusted t-Statistic	Z-t-Tilde-Bar	P-Values
GPC	Levin-Lin-Chu	-8.0823		0.0000
	Im-Pesaran-Shin		-9.1179	0.0000
AAI	Levin-Lin-Chu	-3.2168		0.0006
	Im-Pesaran-Shin		-8.1477	0.0000
EPP	Levin-Lin-Chu	-9.2237		0.0000
	Im-Pesaran-Shin		-10.0532	0.0000
PPT	Levin-Lin-Chu	-11.9121		0.0000
	Im-Pesaran-Shin		-11.6356	0.0000
CRE	Levin-Lin-Chu	-7.6661		0.0000
	Im-Pesaran-Shin		-9.869	0.0000

The Levin-Lin-Chu test assumes a common unit root process, or in other words, that each individual series in the panel shares the same autoregressive parameter (Levin, Lin, & Chu, 2002). On the other hand, the Im-Pesaran-Shin test allows for individual unit root processes, meaning that each series in the panel can have its unique autoregressive parameter (Im, Pesaran, & Shin, 2003).

The null hypothesis for the Levin-Lin-Chu test is that the panels contain unit roots (i.e., the series are non-stationary), while for the Im-Pesaran-Shin test, the null hypothesis is that all panels contain unit roots. A lower (more negative) Adjusted t-statistic in both tests leads to the rejection of the null hypothesis.

For all variables (GPC, AAI, EPP, PPT, and CRE), the null hypotheses of both tests were rejected at the 1% significance level, as indicated by the asterisks next to the Adjusted t-statistics. This suggests that the series are stationary and do not contain unit roots. Stationarity is a crucial assumption in time series and panel data analysis, as non-stationary data can lead to spurious regression results (Hsiao, 2007). Therefore, the findings of stationarity for all variables provide a solid foundation for the subsequent econometric analysis.

Table 2 reports the results of a fixed-effects regression with Driscoll-Kraay standard errors for the dependent variable GPC, using a panel of 33 groups and a maximum lag of 2, and the independent variables are the natural logarithms of airport activity index, electricity consumption per person, physicians per 1,000 people, and credit volume also the first difference of the credit volumes as a control for the term difference.

Table 2. Fixed effects model with Driscoll-Kraay standard errors

Variable	Coefficient	Standard Error	t-Statistic	p-Value
AAI	0.001	0.0002	4.67	0.000
EPP	1.2428	0.1438	8.64	0.000
PPT	0.4224	0.1084	3.9	0.002
CRE	-0.0665	0.0209	-3.19	0.007
CRE D1	0.0498	0.0143	3.47	0.004
Constant term	0.2789	1.3329	0.21	0.837

The study's main findings, all the independent variables had positive and significant effects on GDP per capita, except for ln CRE, which had a negative and significant effect. This means that higher levels of airport activity, electricity consumption, health care, and credit growth were associated with higher levels of economic output per person in the cities of Türkiye with airports, while higher levels of credit volume were associated with lower levels of economic output per person.

The R-squared value of 0.857 suggested that the model explained a large proportion of the variation in GDP per capita across and within cities over time. The standard errors were adjusted for heteroskedasticity, autocorrelation, and cross-sectional dependence using the Driscoll-Kraay method, which made the estimates more robust and reliable.

The positive and significant effect of the airport activity index on GDP per capita confirmed the hypothesis that airport activity was a key driver of local economic growth, as it reflected the demand and supply of air transport services, which were connected to trade, tourism, investment, and innovation (Green, 2007; Bel and Fageda, 2008; Chi and Baek, 2013). This result was also in line with previous studies that had found positive and significant effects of airport activity on income growth using cross-sectional or panel data (Button et al., 1999; Brueckner, 2003; Appold and Kasarda, 2011). This result suggested that enhancing airport activity could positively spillover effects on local economic growth, especially in cities well connected to domestic and international markets. Therefore, policymakers and airport managers should invest in improving airports' infrastructure, quality, and efficiency and promoting the demand and supply of air transport services.

The positive and significant effect of electricity consumption per person on GDP per capita confirmed the hypothesis that electricity consumption was an indicator of energy use and industrial development, which were vital for economic growth (Stern, 1993; Wolde-Rufael, 2006; Apergis and Payne, 2011). This result was also in line with previous studies that had found positive and significant effects of electricity consumption on income growth using cross-sectional or panel data (Lee and Chang, 2008; Narayan and Prasad, 2008; Ozturk et al., 2010). This result suggested that increasing electricity consumption could foster industrial development and economic growth, especially in cities with abundant and reliable energy sources. Therefore, policymakers and energy providers should invest in expanding the capacity, quality, and accessibility of electricity supply and encouraging efficient and sustainable use of energy.

The positive and significant effect of physicians per 1, 000 people on GDP per capita confirmed the hypothesis that health care was an indicator of human capital and social welfare, which were vital for economic growth (Barro, 1991; Bloom et al., 2004; Acemoglu et al., 2009). This result was also in line with previous studies that had found positive and significant effects of health care on income growth using cross-sectional or panel data (Bhargava et al., 2001; Baldacci et al., 2008; Gyimah-Brempong et al., 2011). This result suggested that improving health care could enhance human capital and social welfare, which were vital for economic growth, especially in cities with low health indicators. Therefore, policymakers and health providers should invest in increasing the availability, quality, and affordability of health services and promoting disease prevention and treatment.

The analysis of the data showed a complex relationship between credit volume, credit growth, and GDP per capita. Initially, the negative and significant effect of credit volume on GDP per capita opposed the hypothesis that credit availability was an indicator of financial development and intermediation conducive to economic growth (Levine, 1997; King & Levine, 1993; Beck et al., 2000). This finding was inconsistent with previous studies that had found positive and significant effects of credit availability on income growth using cross-sectional or panel data (Levine et al., 2000; Aghion et al., 2005; Law & Singh, 2014). It indicated that credit volume may have had a negative effect on economic growth by creating financial instability, crowding out productive investment, or increasing inequality.

A different picture emerged when controlling for the lagged data of the credit volume. The positive and significant effect of credit growth on GDP per capita supported the hypothesis that credit availability was an indicator of financial development and intermediation conducive to economic growth. This finding was consistent with previous studies that had found positive and significant effects of credit growth on income growth using cross-sectional or panel data. It implied that credit growth could facilitate financial development and intermediation, especially in cities that had limited access to formal financial institutions.

The results underscore the need for policymakers and financial regulators to monitor and control the level and quality of credit supply while investing in developing the financial sector's legal, institutional, and informational framework. This would promote the inclusion and diversification of financial services, thereby fostering economic growth.

5. CONCLUSION

This study examined the effect of various factors, including airport activity, electricity consumption, healthcare provision, and credit volume and growth, on the GDP per capita across the cities with airports in Türkiye. The findings showed that all independent variables had a positive and significant effect on GDP per capita, except for credit volume, which showed a negative and significant effect. This suggests that higher levels of airport activity, electricity consumption, healthcare provision, and credit growth are associated with higher levels of economic output per person, while higher levels of credit volume are associated with lower levels of economic output per person.

The model used in this study, which adjusted for heteroskedasticity, autocorrelation, and cross-sectional dependence using the Driscoll-Kraay method, explained a large proportion of the variation in GDP per capita across and within cities over time, as indicated by the R-squared value of 0.857. The findings aligned with previous research in the field (Green, 2007; Bel & Fageda, 2008; Chi & Baek, 2013; Levine, 1997; King & Levine, 1993; Beck et al., 2000; Stern, 1993; Wolde-Rufael, 2006; Apergis & Payne, 2011; Barro, 1991; Bloom et al., 2004; Levine et al., 2000; Aghion et al., 2005; Law & Singh, 2014), and provide valuable insights for policymakers, airport managers, energy providers, health providers, and financial regulators.

Future research could explore the area by using instrumental variables, panel vector autoregression, dynamic panel data models, or natural experiments to tackle endogeneity issues; spatial econometric models, factor models, or cluster-robust standard errors to account for cross-sectional dependence; and threshold models, spline models, or interaction terms to capture nonlinearities or interactions.

In conclusion, this study contributes to understanding the factors influencing economic output per person in the cities of Türkiye with airports. The findings underscore the importance of enhancing airport activity, increasing electricity consumption, improving healthcare provision, and controlling credit volume while promoting credit growth for economic development. Future research addressing the limitations of this study could provide further insights into these relationships and inform policy decisions.

REFERENCES

Acaravci, A., & Ozturk, I. (2010). Electricity consumption-growth nexus: Evidence from panel data for transition countries. *Energy Economics*, *32*(3), 604–608. doi:10.1016/j.eneco.2009.10.016

Aghion, P., Howitt, P., & Mayer-Foulkes, D. (2005). The effect of financial development on convergence: Theory and evidence. *The Quarterly Journal of Economics*, *120*(1), 173–222.

Ahmad, M. I. S., & Mehmood, B. (2016). Energy-Headed-Growth Hypothesis: Evidence from Emerging Economies. *Bulletin of Energy Economics*, *4*(2), 126–132.

Anselin, L., Le Gallo, J., & Jayet, H. (2006). Spatial panel econometrics. In L. Mátyás & P. Sevestre (Eds.), *The econometrics of panel data: Fundamentals and recent developments in theory* (3rd ed., pp. 625–660). Kluwer Academic.

Appold, S. J., & Kasarda, J. D. (2011). Seeding growth at airports and airport cities: Insights from the two-sided market literature. *Research in Transportation Business & Management*, *1*(1), 91–100. doi:10.1016/j.rtbm.2011.06.011

Arellano, M., & Bover, O. (1995). Another look at the instrumental variable estimation of error-components models. *Journal of Econometrics*, *68*(1), 29–51. doi:10.1016/0304-4076(94)01642-D

Baltagi, B. H. (2008). *Econometric analysis of panel data* (4th ed.). John Wiley & Sons.

Beck, T., Levine, R., & Loayza, N. (2000). Finance and the sources of growth. *Journal of Financial Economics*, *58*(1-2), 261–300. doi:10.1016/S0304-405X(00)00072-6

Bel, G., & Fageda, X. (2008). Getting there fast: Globalization, intercontinental flights and location of headquarters. *Journal of Economic Geography*, *8*(4), 471–495. doi:10.1093/jeg/lbn017

Bildirici, M., & Kayikci, F. (2012). Economic growth and electricity consumption in former Soviet Republics. *Energy Economics*, *34*(3), 747–753. doi:10.1016/j.eneco.2012.02.010

Brueckner, J. K. (2003). Airline traffic and urban economic development. *Urban Studies (Edinburgh, Scotland)*, *40*(8), 1455–1469. doi:10.1080/0042098032000094388

Button, K., Drexler, J., & Pels, E. (1999). Economic efficiency in the provision of airport services: A summary report. *Journal of Air Transport Management*, *5*(4), 177–184. doi:10.1016/S0969-6997(99)00013-2

Button, K., Lall, S., Stough, R., & Trice, M. (1999). High-technology employment and hub airports. *Journal of Air Transport Management, 5*(1), 53–59. doi:10.1016/S0969-6997(98)00038-6

Button, K., & Yuan, J. (2013). Airfreight transport and economic development: An examination of causality. *Urban Studies (Edinburgh, Scotland), 50*(2), 329–340. doi:10.1177/0042098012446999

Can, H. (2017). *Yenilebilir enerjinin makroekonomik etkileri: Türkiye örneği.* Namık Kemal Üniversitesi, Sosyal Bilimler Enstitüsü, Yayımlanmamış Yüksek Lisans Tezi.

Chi, J., & Baek, J. (2013). Dynamic relationship between air transport demand and economic growth in the United States: A new look. *Transport Policy, 29*, 257–260. doi:10.1016/j.tranpol.2013.03.005 PMID:32288380

Chi, J., & Baek, J. (2013). Dynamic relationship between air transport demand and economic growth in the United States: A new look. *Transport Policy, 29*, 257–260. doi:10.1016/j.tranpol.2013.03.005 PMID:32288380

DHMI. (2021). *Statistics report 2020. General Directorate of State Airports Authority of Turkey.* https://web.shgm.gov.tr/documents/sivilhavacilik/files/Istatistikler/2020_istatistik_raporu.pdf

Dinçsoy, E. E. (2016). Environmental, Social and Economic Factors of Development Axes in terms of Spatial Planning: An Analysis of Thrace Region in Turkey. *International Journal of Statistics & Economics, 17*(2), 85–96.

Dincsoy, E. E., & Ichiminami, F. (2006). An Assessment of the Southeastern Anatolia Region in Turkey in Terms of the Sustainable Development Targets. *Journal of the Faculty of Environmental Science and Technology. Okayama University, 11*(1), 75–81.

Dinçsoy, E. E., & Okur Dinçsoy, M. (2020). Ekonomik büyümenin enflasyon üzerine etkisinin Türkiye ekonomisi açısından analizi. *Balkan ve Yakın Doğu Sosyal Bilimler Dergisi*, (6), 118–124.

Driscoll, J., & Kraay, A. C. (1998). Consistent covariance matrix estimation with spatially dependent panel data. *The Review of Economics and Statistics, 80*(4), 549–560. doi:10.1162/003465398557825

Gillen, D. (2011). The evolution of airport ownership and governance. *Journal of Air Transport Management, 17*(1), 3–13. doi:10.1016/j.jairtraman.2010.10.003

Green, R. K. (2007). Airports and economic development. *Real Estate Economics, 35*(1), 91–112. doi:10.1111/j.1540-6229.2007.00183.x

Güngör, A., Güngör, G., & Ünal, E. (2017). Electricity consumption of airports: A case study for Turkey. *Energy and Building, 139*, 1–9. doi:10.1016/j.enbuild.2016.12.052

(2022). Hindawi. (2022). Research on development strategy of Henan aviation economy based on SWOT analysis. *Wireless Communications and Mobile Computing*. Advance online publication. doi:10.1155/2022/4212090

Hoechle, D. (2007). Robust standard errors for panel regressions with cross-sectional dependence. *The Stata Journal, 7*(3), 281–312. doi:10.1177/1536867X0700700301

Hsiao, C. (2007). Panel data analysis—Advantages and challenges. *Test*, *16*(1), 1–22. doi:10.100711749-007-0046-x

IATA. (2021). *COVID-19 outlook for air travel in the next 5 years*. International Air Transport Association. https://www.iata.org/en/iata-repository/publications/economic-reports/covid—19-outlook-for-air-travel-in-the-next-5-years/

Im, K. S., Pesaran, M. H., & Shin, Y. (2003). Testing for unit roots in heterogeneous panels. *Journal of Econometrics*, *115*(1), 53–74. doi:10.1016/S0304-4076(03)00092-7

IMF. (2011). *Global shocks and their impact on low-income countries: Lessons from the 2007–09 crisis* (Working Paper No WP/11/27). https://www.imf.org/external/pubs/ft/wp/2011/wp1127.pdf

King, R. G., & Levine, R. (1993). Finance and growth: Schumpeter might be right. *The Quarterly Journal of Economics*, *108*(3), 717–737. doi:10.2307/2118406

Law, S. H., & Singh, N. (2014). Does too much finance harm economic growth? *Journal of Banking & Finance*, *41*, 36–44. doi:10.1016/j.jbankfin.2013.12.020

Levin, A., Lin, C. F., & Chu, C. S. J. (2002). Unit root tests in panel data: Asymptotic and finite-sample properties. *Journal of Econometrics*, *108*(1), 1–24. doi:10.1016/S0304-4076(01)00098-7

Levine, R. (1997). Financial development and economic growth: Views and agenda. *Journal of Economic Literature*, *35*(2), 688–726.

Levine, R., Loayza, N., & Beck, T. (2000). Financial intermediation and growth: Causality and causes. *Journal of Monetary Economics*, *46*(1), 31–77. doi:10.1016/S0304-3932(00)00017-9

Liao, H., Peng, Y., Wang, F. Z., & Zhang, T. (2022). Understanding energy use growth: The role of investment-GDP ratio. *Structural Change and Economic Dynamics*, *63*, 15–24. doi:10.1016/j.strueco.2022.08.007

McKinsey. (2020). *COVID-19's impact on the global aviation sector*. https://www.mckinsey.com/industries/travel-logistics-and-infrastructure/our-insights/taking-stock-of-the-pandemics-impact-on-global-aviation

Narayan, P., & Smyth, R. (2009). Multivariate granger causality between electricity consumption, exports and GDP: Evidence from a panel of Middle Eastern countries. *Energy Policy*, *37*(1), 229–236. doi:10.1016/j.enpol.2008.08.020

OECD. (2020). *COVID-19 and the aviation industry: Impact and policy responses*. https://www.oecd.org/coronavirus/policy-responses/covid-19-and-the-aviation-industry-impact-and-policy-responses-26d521c1/

Okur Dincsoy, M. (2016). A Comparative Study on Population and Employment Risks in Vulnerable Countries to Climate Change. *International Journal of Ecological Economics and Statistics*, *37*(2), 103–120.

Okur Dinçsoy, M. (2020). Sustainable Development and Industry Revolutions. In New Approaches to CSR, Sustainability and Accountability, Volume I. Accounting, Finance, Sustainability, Governance & Fraud: Theory and Application (pp. 61-79). Singapore: Springer. doi:10.1007/978-981-32-9588-9

Senalp, U. E. (2021). Covid-19 Küresel Salgınının Sanayi ve Hizmet Sektörlerinde Enerji Yoğunluğuna Etkisi. In H. Ö. Sarıdoğan & F. Çelebi (Eds.), İktisadi ve İdari Bilimlerde Özgün Çalışmalar (pp. 143–161). Academic Press.

Stern, D. I. (1993). Energy use and economic growth in the USA: A multivariate approach. *Energy Economics*, *15*(2), 137–150. doi:10.1016/0140-9883(93)90033-N

Taşdemir, F. D. (2021). Relationship Between Economic Growth and Construction Sector in Turkey. In Academic Research and Reviews in Social Sciences. Platanus Publishing House.

Wooldridge, J. M. (2010). *Econometric analysis of cross section and panel data* (2nd ed.). MIT Press.

YaoS.YangX. (2008). *Airport Development and Regional Economic Growth in China.* Reseach Paper, The University of Nottingham. https://ssrn.com/abstract=1101574 doi:10.2139/ssrn.1101574

Zhang, F., & Graham, D. J. (2020). Air transport and economic growth: A review of the impact mechanism and causal relationships. *Transport Reviews*, *40*(4), 506–528. doi:10.1080/01441647.2020.1738587

Chapter 4
China's Economic Development:
Digital Transformation, Energy Efficiency, and Climate Change

Mohamad Zreik
https://orcid.org/0000-0002-6812-6529
Independent Researcher, Lebanon

ABSTRACT

This chapter examines China's economic development in detail, focusing on the role that digital transformation, energy efficiency, and climate change have played. How digital technologies are driving China's economy and the difficulties local governments have in adapting to these changes are explored. China's response to the global energy crisis is analyzed, and the implications of energy transitions on the country's development are laid out in depth. The effects of climate change on the Chinese economy and the country's efforts to adapt to these changes are examined empirically. Nutrition is examined for its impact on a country's economy, namely its productivity and literacy rates. This chapter adds to the literature on economic growth and policy by providing fresh perspectives on China's complex economic rise.

1. INTRODUCTION

The story of China's economic progress over the past few decades is one of unprecedented change and expansion. China's economy has transformed from its rural roots in the middle of the twentieth century to become the world's second largest (Schoppa, 2019). China's economic transformation may be traced back to a number of implemented changes and transformations. These changes helped hasten the economy's shift from central planning to market forces, leading to tremendous industrial growth since their implementation, and Special Economic Zones (SEZs) were set up to attract international investment (Chaisse & Ji, 2020).

DOI: 10.4018/979-8-3693-0400-6.ch004

China's rapid economic growth continued through the 1990s and into the early 2000s, when the country finally joined the World Trade Organization (Jenkins, 2022). During this time, China underwent rapid urbanization and industrialization, turning it into the "world's factory" (Du et al., 2020). China has sustained strong economic growth despite various difficulties. These include socioeconomic inequality, environmental damage, and an aging population. This shift from an export- and investment-led paradigm to a consumer-led one exemplifies the nation's developing economic might.

In addition, the Chinese government has recently placed an emphasis on technology development and digital transformation as the primary drivers of the country's future growth (Awan, Sroufe, & Shahbaz, 2021). These efforts are expanding the country's economic story and altering the country's industrial landscape.

Developing economies like China's are feeling the effects of digital revolution, energy efficiency, and climate change more acutely than most. To revolutionize corporate processes and increase consumer value, digital transformation is a must. It would be impossible to exaggerate the importance of this shift for China. By encouraging innovation, raising productivity, and giving rise to entirely new economic sectors, digital technology has been crucial to China's rapid economic development in recent decades. These advancements in technology have been crucial in helping China tackle problems like its growing urban-rural divide and its aging population.

China's economic growth also depends on improvements in energy efficiency. China, as the largest energy consumer, plays a crucial role in reducing energy waste in the midst of a worldwide energy crisis (Aktar, Alam, & Al-Amin, 2021). Increasing energy efficiency helps in three ways: it lowers energy costs, makes industries more competitive, and encourages long-term growth. The results of China's efforts in this field will have far-reaching effects on energy markets and international initiatives to combat climate change, as well as on the country's own economic and political stability.

The urgency of the problem of climate change cannot be denied. It presents a major challenge and potential opportunity for China, the largest producer of greenhouse gases in the world (Nukusheva et al., 2021). A number of areas of China's economy are vulnerable to the effects of climate change, including agriculture, water resources, and public health. On the other hand, it gives China a push in the direction of a more environmentally friendly and sustainable economic model. To combat climate change and adapt to its effects, new technologies, businesses, and economic opportunities can be developed.

Therefore, digital transformation, energy efficiency, and climate change are not just important to China's current economic development but also crucial to the country's future economic trajectory. To fully appreciate the nuances of China's dynamic economy, an appreciation of these forces is essential.

In this work, the analytical method was employed as a foundational approach to decipher the complex interplay of factors affecting China's economic growth. This methodological choice allowed for a rigorous examination of the data and its patterns, facilitating a deeper understanding of the intricate relationships and variables at play. By leveraging the analytical method, it was possible to sift through vast amounts of information, distilling it down to the essential elements that offer a holistic perspective on the subjects discussed, ensuring both accuracy and comprehensiveness in the findings.

The chosen topic, focusing on the interplay of digital transformation, energy efficiency, climate change, and nutrition in influencing China's economic growth, holds immense importance in the contemporary global landscape. As nations grapple with the challenges and opportunities of the 21st century, understanding how these multifaceted elements converge and impact a nation's economic trajectory is critical. In the context of China, a major global player, such insights not only reflect its domestic policy dynamics but also have broader implications for global economic, environmental, and health strategies.

2. THE ROLE OF DIGITAL TRANSFORMATION

2.1. Understanding Digital Transformation in a Global Context

The term "digital transformation" is used to describe the wholesale adoption of digital technology across an organization or country, which radically alters the way in which business is conducted and value is produced (Ziółkowska, 2021). Traditional company models are being revised all around the world as a result of digital transformation, which is also opening up new markets and disrupting entire sectors. Artificial intelligence (AI), big data, the internet of things (IoT), blockchain, and cloud computing are all driving forces (Zreik, 2023).

Many governments and corporations throughout the world have made digital transformation a top goal. Benefits including higher efficiency and productivity, better customer experiences, and the flexibility to innovate and compete in a dynamic digital market have contributed significantly to this transition. Digital technologies are being used by a wide variety of sectors, from manufacturing and retail to healthcare and education, to improve efficiency, accuracy, and the quality of decision-making and service delivery (Rabah, 2018).

But the digital shift is not without its difficulties. The necessity for substantial investment, difficulties in integrating new technologies, and the demand for a digitally skilled labor force are all factors in this equation. Despite these difficulties, the benefits of digital transformation are enormous, prompting countries and enterprises to speed up their digital transformation efforts.

When it comes to growth, competitiveness, and resilience in today's linked world, digital transformation is no longer a nice-to-have. For national economies like China's, where digital transformation is playing a critical role in altering the economic landscape, an appreciation of this global context is essential.

One area that merits further exploration is China's strategic planning and its implementation in the realms discussed. A noteworthy example is the 'Made in China 2025' initiative, which is a state-led industrial policy aimed at making China dominant in global high-tech manufacturing. This ambitious plan seeks to transform China from being merely the world's factory for basic goods into a global tech leader, emphasizing innovation, quality, and advanced production techniques. Particularly in the context of digital transformation, this initiative illustrates China's foresight in harnessing digitalization, automation, and advanced technologies to supercharge its economy and increase its global competitiveness.

2.2. Impact of Digital Transformation on China's Economy

The advent of digital technologies has been instrumental in China's recent economic growth. China's economy has entered a new phase of growth thanks to the adoption of digital technologies, which have contributed to greater productivity, innovation, and international competitiveness.

The rise of China's economy and the country's technological sophistication are both direct results of China's use of digital technologies. For example, e-commerce platforms like Alibaba and JD.com have transformed the retail industry by fostering the growth of a thriving online market and ushering in novel shopping habits among consumers (Zi, 2019; Marzuki et al., 2023). Meanwhile, digital payment systems like Alipay and WeChat Pay have revolutionized the financial sector by making digital financial services available to millions of people previously excluded from such services (Kapron, 2018).

Industry 4.0 technologies have helped China's manufacturing sector become more efficient and productive, allowing the country to make the transition from low-cost to high-value production. These technologies include artificial intelligence (AI), the internet of things (IoT), and robotics. China's digital transformation has helped the country take the lead in several fast-growing sectors, including electric vehicles, digital health, and renewable energy (Yang et al., 2021).

Even more importantly, digital technology has been crucial in helping China tackle some of its social and economic problems. The digital divide between urban and rural areas has been narrowed, more people have had access to healthcare and education, and problems associated with an aging population have been tackled.

2.3. Challenges Faced by Subnational Governments During Transition and Adaptation

Subnational governments in China, including provinces, cities, and regions, confront a number of issues throughout the transition and adaptation period as the country continues to integrate digital technology into its economy. Those who have easy access to digital technologies have an advantage over others who do not, creating a digital divide that is a serious obstacle. In contrast to forward-thinking metropolises like Beijing and Shanghai, rural and underdeveloped regions are often years behind the digital innovation curve due to lack of investment in infrastructure and access to digital services (Dou & Gao, 2022). This discrepancy has the potential to deepen preexisting economic and social divides.

Protecting the privacy and security of sensitive information is difficult. The likelihood of data breaches and assaults grows as more services are brought online. Local governments need to strike a balance between encouraging technological progress and safeguarding individuals' personal information.

Investments of significant size are also needed to put digital transformation into action. Investing in things like broadband networks and data centers can get pricey quickly. In addition, keeping up with the most recent digital innovations requires constant investment due to the rapid pace at which technology is evolving.

Data privacy and security concerns, the digital gap, and the need for a qualified workforce to drive and manage this transition are just some of the new problems brought about by the digital transformation. Despite these obstacles, digital transformation continues to play a significant role in China's economic development strategy, which bodes well for the country's future economic growth and development.

The problem of finding and nurturing top talent is a major one. The digital transition necessitates a skilled labor force. A lack of such skills, however, can hamper the spread and success of digital initiatives in many areas (Hai, Van, & Thi Tuyet, 2021).

Despite these difficulties, local governments must embrace digital transformation to take advantage of its many benefits, including increased economic growth, better public services, and increased competitiveness. They need to invest in digital infrastructure and education, as well as create robust legislative frameworks for data protection, in order to meet these difficulties.

3. ENERGY EFFICIENCY IN THE MIDST OF GLOBAL ENERGY CRISIS

3.1. Examination of China's Current Energy Situation

The sheer size and speed of China's economic development have created an energy landscape that is both unprecedented and intricate. China has a pivotal role in the global energy market as both the largest user and producer (An, Dorofeev, & Zhu, 2020).

Coal, which is both abundant in China and inexpensive to produce, accounts for a disproportionate share of the country's energy use (Zhang et al., 2023). Significant environmental and health problems, including as air pollution and greenhouse gas emissions, have emerged from this reliance on coal (Ahmad et al., 2018).

China, on the other hand, has come a long way in diversifying its energy supply. The government has made significant progress toward its goal of increasing the share of renewables in its energy consumption, and it is now the world's largest investor in renewable energy sources like solar, wind, and hydropower (Li et al., 2022). China is also making significant investments in nuclear energy, with multiple reactors either now under construction or in the planning stages (Xu et al., 2022).

The energy sector in China is likewise facing serious difficulties. Rapid urbanization, industrialization, and an increasingly affluent population have all contributed to an ever-increasing demand for energy. Meanwhile, environmental concerns and the scarcity of fossil fuels are putting a damper on the country's ability to produce its own energy.

In light of these difficulties and the ongoing global energy crisis, energy efficiency has assumed central importance in China. Reducing energy use, lowering emissions, and maintaining long-term economic growth all depend on boosting energy efficiency. This move in energy policy is going to have a major impact on China's energy future, and the emphasis on energy efficiency is a big part of it.

3.2. Analysis of China's Approach to Enhancing Energy Efficiency

China's strategy for improving energy efficiency is comprehensive, incorporating a variety of legislative initiatives, technological advances, and financial incentives. The Chinese government has released multiple policies and guidelines to increase energy efficiency. Consistent with the goals of the country's Five-Year Plans, energy efficiency and reduction have been prioritized (Zreik, 2020). They establish lofty goals for lowering energy intensity, which is the amount of energy used per dollar of GDP, and assign specific responsibilities to certain sectors (Paramati, Shahzad, & Doğan, 2022).

China's policy also heavily emphasizes the development of cutting-edge technology. The government has poured resources into R&D to improve energy-efficient technology. The industrial, building, and transportation industries are just few of the many that have adopted these technologies. High-efficiency motors and energy-efficient furnaces, for instance, see extensive use in the manufacturing industry (Zheng et al., 2018). Energy-saving components and layouts in construction are actively encouraged. Electric automobiles and high-speed rail systems also contribute to the transportation sector's lower energy needs (Wang, Zhou, & Ou, 2021).

When it comes to encouraging people to be more energy efficient, financial incentives are also crucial. To encourage commercial and residential adoption of energy-efficient technologies, the government offers subsidies, tax advantages, and low-interest loans. China has also established a nationwide carbon trading market and energy-saving quotas to incentivize businesses to reduce energy consumption (Karplus & Zhang, 2017).

However, there are still obstacles for China to overcome in order to improve energy efficiency, such as the need for additional technological innovation and the poor implementation of energy efficiency regulations. China recognizes the importance of enhancing energy efficiency in the face of rising demand and growing environmental concerns, and despite these obstacles, it remains dedicated to this goal.

3.3. Discussion on the Impacts of Energy Transformations on China's Development

Improvements in energy efficiency and the shift to renewable energy sources are two examples of China's energy transitions that will have far-reaching effects on the country's economic growth. Energy efficiency initiatives may increase economic productivity and competitiveness by lowering expenses for businesses and consumers. Industries can become more competitive on the domestic and international markets by reducing their operational costs through increased energy efficiency. Additionally, the renewable energy sector benefits greatly from the shift to greener energy sources because it opens up new sectors and job prospects.

China, as the world's largest energy consumer, has launched various policies and practical measures to curb its energy intensity. The 13th Five-Year Plan for Energy Development clearly states its intent to lower energy consumption per unit of GDP by 15% from 2015 levels (Rycroft, 2017). According to the National Bureau of Statistics, by the end of 2020, the country successfully reduced its energy consumption per unit of GDP by 13.5% (Liu et al., 2022). Additionally, programs such as the 'Top 10,000 Enterprises Energy-Saving Program' target the country's largest energy-consuming firms, pushing for an aggregate reduction in energy use of 250 million tons of coal equivalent by 2020 (Tan et al., 2020). These facts not only showcase China's commitment to energy efficiency but also underscore the tangible steps the nation has taken in this direction.

China's energy modernization has the potential to improve the country's political status abroad (Zreik, 2022). China can boost its worldwide standing and clout if it takes the lead in the transition to a low-carbon economy. China can gain a strategic advantage from its leadership in this area by helping to shape international energy standards.

Energy innovations have the potential to enhance people's quality of life. Air pollution is a major threat to public health in many Chinese cities, although it can be mitigated by more efficient energy use (Perera, 2018). Making the switch to renewable energy sources can also reduce the negative effects of climate change on people and their way of life.

However, these changes also bring about new difficulties. Without careful planning, the transition to a low-carbon economy might cause a loss of jobs and societal unrest as traditional industries are phased out. There must also be major shifts in public policy and individual conduct in order for a society to fully embrace and benefit from new technology and practices.

The effects of energy changes on China's development are mostly beneficial, despite these obstacles. They offer China a chance to solve pressing environmental and social problems without slowing its economic expansion.

3.4. Implications of China's Response to the Energy Crisis at National, Regional, and Global Levels

There will be major effects on a national, regional, and global scale from China's response to the energy crisis. China's national goals of sustainable economic development and environmental improvement are consistent with the country's push for energy efficiency and a more sustainable energy mix. It allows China to satisfy its rising energy needs without increasing its dependency on fossil fuels, thereby mitigating pollution's negative effects on the environment and people's health. In addition to bolstering ongoing economic growth, these developments pave the way for more innovation and the creation of new jobs in the renewable energy sector.

The energy choices China makes have far-reaching effects across the Asia-Pacific. China's transition to greener energy has the potential to stimulate regional markets for renewables, helping to promote sustainable development throughout the region (Wang et al., 2020). Efforts made by China to improve energy efficiency may also inspire those in the region to do the same when confronted with comparable problems.

The Chinese energy policy will have far-reaching effects around the world. China is the greatest contributor to global greenhouse gas emissions, making its efforts to boost energy efficiency and expand the use of renewables essential to international efforts to slow climate change (Dong, Miao, & Wen, 2021). It can drive worldwide progress toward global climate targets with its dedication to a more sustainable energy future. And if China continues to invest in renewable energy, that may mean lower prices and better technology for everyone.

The shift toward a more sustainable energy future presents opportunities and problems alike. The transition's speed and scope necessitate substantial expenditures and legislative changes. Energy choices made in China will have far-reaching effects around the world, thus international cooperation and understanding will be essential.

4. CLIMATE CHANGE AND ITS EFFECT ON ECONOMIC GROWTH

4.1. Empirical Exploration of the Correlation Between Climate Change and China's Economic Development

There are several facets to consider when examining the link between climate change and China's economic growth and development. There is empirical data to imply that climate change affects China's economy in both direct and indirect ways. Particularly vulnerable to shifts in average temperatures and precipitation amounts are industries like agriculture, water resources, and coastal infrastructure (Instanes et al., 2016).

The agricultural and industrial sectors are also negatively impacted by climate change, as higher temperatures diminish crop yields and more frequent and severe droughts strain water supplies. Coastal infrastructure can be damaged by harsh weather and increasing sea levels, which can disrupt economic activity and lead to high expenditures for adaptation and repair (Malhi, Kaur, & Kaushik, 2021).

Health and labor productivity are two areas where climate change is having unintended consequences. Heat-related illnesses and other disorders may become more common as temperatures rise, cutting into worker output and driving up healthcare expenditures (Moda, Filho, & Minhas, 2019). These results can potentially cause fatalities, which has enormous monetary and societal repercussions.

New business opportunities may also arise as a result of climate change. Examples include renewable energy, energy efficiency, and climate resilience, all of which can benefit from increased investment as a result of the need to combat and adapt to climate change.

4.2. Examination of Climate Change Impacts on Various Sectors of China's Economy

The effects of climate change on China's economy are far-reaching, touching on agriculture, manufacturing, and the service sector. Crop yields and animal productivity are both impacted by climate change in the agriculture industry. Reduced crop yields and livestock loss are possible results of climate change's increased temperatures, changing rainfall patterns, and frequency of extreme weather events like floods and droughts (Kumar et al., 2018). Food security and the livelihoods of individuals who rely on agriculture might be jeopardized by these changes, which can disrupt food supply chains.

The effects of climate change extend to the manufacturing sector as well. Water-intensive industries like power generating and manufacturing may feel the effects of shifts in precipitation patterns and evaporation rates on water supply. Energy production efficiency, especially at thermal power plants, can be negatively impacted by rising temperatures. Sea level rise and stronger storms also pose a threat to coastal economies (Yildiz, 2019).

Tourism and insurance are two service industries that may feel the effects. Examples of tourist places that may be negatively impacted by climate change include ski resorts and beach vacations. However, claims made by policyholders as a result of damage to property, human health, and agricultural output from extreme weather occurrences may rise.

While these industries certainly have their share of problems, they also have chances for growth and change. Adapting agricultural operations to changing climate conditions, implementing more water- and energy-efficient industrial processes, and expanding service offerings are all examples. These changes can help lessen the blow of climate change while simultaneously bolstering the economy's long-term health and stability.

4.3. Adaptive Strategies Deployed by China to Counteract the Impacts of Climate Change

China has implemented numerous sector-wide adaptive techniques to counteract the effects of climate change. China is encouraging climate-smart farming methods, such as precision farming, crop diversity, and the adoption of drought- and heat-tolerant crop types (Mwangi, 2023), to improve agricultural productivity while reducing adverse effects on the environment. This overarching goal guides these strategies.

China is working to make its manufacturing sector less susceptible to climate change by funding the development of cleaner, more efficient technologies. For instance, it encourages the use of water- and energy-saving technologies in industrial production and electricity generation. In addition, China is strengthening its ability to identify climate risk in order to effectively manage climate hazards in sectors like the building and infrastructure sectors (Coenen et al., 2021).

China is taking many steps to adapt to climate change in its metropolitan regions. These include building green infrastructure, creating climate-resilient city plans, and enhancing emergency response capabilities. These actions are meant to make cities more resistant to the effects of climate change, such as extreme weather and rising sea levels.

The Chinese government is also investing in climate monitoring and early warning systems to better anticipate and deal with catastrophic weather. This involves spending money on things like satellites, weather prediction, and data analysis.

China is also working to strengthen its society as part of its climate adaptation initiatives. Policies to aid vulnerable communities and industries in adapting to climate change are a part of this effort. So are public awareness efforts about climate hazards and adaptation methods (Stange et al., 2023).

5. THE ROLE OF NUTRITION IN SOCIO-ECONOMIC DEVELOPMENT

5.1. Understanding the Link Between Nutrition and Economic Development

There is a strong and complex relationship between adequate nutrition and a nation's economic growth, with far-reaching consequences for both social and economic development.

Human capital development, which is aided by proper nutrition, is a major force in economic expansion. Mind and body both benefit greatly from proper nutrition, especially in the formative years. Stunted growth, reduced cognitive function, and lower educational attainment are among potential outcomes of malnutrition, especially in the first 1,000 days after conception (Mayneris-Perxachs & Swann, 2019). These consequences can have long-lasting repercussions on a person's ability to work productively and make a living as an adult, ultimately impacting a nation's GDP.

On the other hand, economic growth can also affect people's diets. The nutritional condition of a population can be improved by raising incomes so that more people have access to healthy food, medical care, and education. Obesity and other non-communicable diseases can be exacerbated by the shifts in eating habits that accompany economic growth, such as the increased consumption of processed and unhealthy foods (Cuevas García-Dorado et al., 2019).

Furthermore, healthy eating habits might strengthen resistance to calamities like epidemics and economic downturns. The immune systems of healthy people are stronger, making them more resistant to illness and helping them to make quicker recoveries when they do get sick. This can help lower healthcare expenses and lost productivity, which is a boon to the economy.

5.2. Analysis of How Improved Nutrition Contributes to Increased Productivity and Better Education Outcomes

Increased productivity and better learning outcomes are two ways in which better nutrition helps a country's economy grow and thrive. The ability to work physically is directly impacted by one's diet. Diets high in key nutrients and energy boost performance on the job by providing the building blocks the body needs to thrive. Malnutrition, on the other hand, can lower one's resistance to illness and make it harder to do one's job. Long-term, a healthier, more productive workforce is a key factor in economic expansion, and better nutrition can help make that happen (Fanzo, 2019).

Proper nutrition is a cornerstone of academic success since it promotes brain growth and enhances academic performance. Proper nourishment is especially important for young children because their brains are still developing at this age. Memory and attention problems are just two of the cognitive impairments that malnourished youngsters frequently face (Kabatas, 2021). Therefore, improved diet can increase children's cognitive abilities, leading to more successful academic outcomes. Over time, a well-educated populace can make major contributions to the economy through improved proficiency and fresh ideas.

Additionally, better nutrition can help kids pay attention in class and cut down on absences. The increased susceptibility to illnesses brought on by nutrient deficits can result in more frequent school absences. Similarly, youngsters who are undernourished may have trouble focusing on their schoolwork. Therefore, making sure kids have access to healthy, well-rounded meals helps their brains and their bottom lines.

Investment in better nutrition can be a potent instrument for boosting productivity and educational achievements in China's environment, where the economic and nutritional landscape is changing quickly. This, in turn, can power long-term improvements in society and the economy.

6. CONCLUSION

Factors such as digital transformation, energy efficiency, climate change, and nutrition were examined in depth in this chapter as they relate to China's economic growth. It looked into how these factors affect China's political and economic climate and demonstrated their links to the success of the country and its people.

This analysis of digital transformation shows that the widespread use of digital technology in China has contributed significantly to the country's rapid economic development. It also highlighted the challenges faced by local governments throughout the transition and the necessity for efficient strategies and policies to facilitate the transfer.

The issue on energy efficiency shed light on China's response to the global energy crisis. It went into greater into on China's commitment to energy efficiency and its effects on the country's economic and political development. China's outsized impact on the energy business was also shown through depicting the global, regional, and national implications of China's energy strategy.

The revolutionary consequences of climate change on many sectors of China's economy are explored in this chapter, which goes deeply into the topic of climate change by drawing connections between empirical facts and China's economic development. The research highlighted China's adaptive strategies for dealing with these repercussions, serving as an example for other countries experiencing the same or similar issues. Studies on the role of nutrition in China's economic development have demonstrated the topic's importance to China's development. The study's conclusions offer a simple path to societal progress by highlighting the benefits of improved nutrition on worker output, student achievement, and the economy as a whole.

The research presented in this chapter makes a substantial contribution to the literature on economic growth and policy. By connecting previously unrelated variables, our analysis paints a more complete picture of the complex forces shaping China's economic growth. It completes our understanding and provides a nuanced perspective on the many factors contributing to economic expansion.

Experts in economics, finance, and development strategy will gain much insight from this chapter's findings. They provide fresh insight into how changes in technology, energy efficiency, global warming, and people's eating patterns have impacted China's economic growth. Policymakers, investors, and planners may be able to make better decisions for long-term growth as a result of having this information at their disposal.

REFERENCES

Ahmad, M., Ur Rahman, Z., Hong, L., Khan, S., Khan, Z., & Naeem Khan, M. (2018). Impact of environmental quality variables and socio-economic factors on human health: Empirical evidence from China. *Pollution*, *4*(4), 571–579.

Aktar, M. A., Alam, M. M., & Al-Amin, A. Q. (2021). Global economic crisis, energy use, CO2 emissions, and policy roadmap amid COVID-19. *Sustainable Production and Consumption*, *26*, 770–781. doi:10.1016/j.spc.2020.12.029 PMID:33786357

An, J., Dorofeev, M., & Zhu, S. (2020). Development of energy cooperation between Russia and China. *International Journal of Energy Economics and Policy*, *10*(1), 134–139. doi:10.32479/ijeep.8509

Awan, U., Sroufe, R., & Shahbaz, M. (2021). Industry 4.0 and the circular economy: A literature review and recommendations for future research. *Business Strategy and the Environment*, *30*(4), 2038–2060. doi:10.1002/bse.2731

Chaisse, J., & Ji, X. (2020). The pervasive problem of special economic zones for international economic law: Tax, investment, and trade issues. *World Trade Review*, *19*(4), 567–588. doi:10.1017/S1474745620000129

Coenen, J., Bager, S., Meyfroidt, P., Newig, J., & Challies, E. (2021). Environmental governance of China's belt and road initiative. *Environmental Policy and Governance*, *31*(1), 3–17. doi:10.1002/eet.1901

Cuevas García-Dorado, S., Cornselsen, L., Smith, R., & Walls, H. (2019). Economic globalization, nutrition and health: A review of quantitative evidence. *Globalization and Health*, *15*(1), 1–19. doi:10.118612992-019-0456-z PMID:30786909

Dong, L., Miao, G., & Wen, W. (2021). China's carbon neutrality policy: Objectives, impacts and paths. *East Asian Policy*, *13*(1), 5–18. doi:10.1142/S1793930521000015

Dou, Q., & Gao, X. (2022). The double-edged role of the digital economy in firm green innovation: Micro-evidence from Chinese manufacturing industry. *Environmental Science and Pollution Research International*, *29*(45), 67856–67874. doi:10.100711356-022-20435-3 PMID:35524847

Du, Z., Jin, L., Ye, Y., & Zhang, H. (2020). Characteristics and influences of urban shrinkage in the exo-urbanization area of the Pearl River Delta, China. *Cities (London, England)*, *103*, 102767. doi:10.1016/j.cities.2020.102767

Fanzo, J. (2019). Healthy and sustainable diets and food systems: The key to achieving Sustainable Development Goal 2? *Food Ethics*, *4*(2), 159–174. doi:10.100741055-019-00052-6

Hai, T. N., Van, Q. N., & Thi Tuyet, M. N. (2021). Digital transformation: Opportunities and challenges for leaders in the emerging countries in response to COVID-19 pandemic. *Emerging Science Journal*, *5*(1), 21–36. doi:10.28991/esj-2021-SPER-03

Instanes, A., Kokorev, V., Janowicz, R., Bruland, O., Sand, K., & Prowse, T. (2016). Changes to freshwater systems affecting Arctic infrastructure and natural resources. *Journal of Geophysical Research. Biogeosciences*, *121*(3), 567–585. doi:10.1002/2015JG003125

Jenkins, R. (2022). *How China is reshaping the global economy: Development impacts in Africa and Latin America*. Oxford University Press. doi:10.1093/oso/9780192866356.001.0001

Kabatas, M. (2021). A Study on Healthy Eating Children's Music Lessons and School Performance. *American Educational Research Journal*, *9*(1), 112–120.

Kapron, Z. (2018). From digital payments to digital finance: How China's tech companies are redefining banking in Asia and soon Europe. *Journal of Payments Strategy & Systems*, *12*(1), 68–73.

Karplus, V. J., & Zhang, X. (2017). Incentivizing firm compliance with China's national emissions trading system. *Economics of Energy & Environmental Policy*, *6*(2), 73–86. doi:10.5547/2160-5890.6.1.vkar

Kumar, P., Tokas, J., Kumar, N., Lal, M., & Singal, H. R. (2018). Climate change consequences and its impact on agriculture and food security. *International Journal of Chemical Studies*, *6*(6), 124–133.

Li, Z., Kuo, T. H., Siao-Yun, W., & Vinh, L. T. (2022). Role of green finance, volatility and risk in promoting the investments in Renewable Energy Resources in the post-covid-19. *Resources Policy*, *76*, 102563. doi:10.1016/j.resourpol.2022.102563

Liu, Z., Deng, Z., He, G., Wang, H., Zhang, X., Lin, J., Qi, Y., & Liang, X. (2022). Challenges and opportunities for carbon neutrality in China. *Nature Reviews. Earth & Environment*, *3*(2), 141–155. doi:10.103843017-021-00244-x

Malhi, G. S., Kaur, M., & Kaushik, P. (2021). Impact of climate change on agriculture and its mitigation strategies: A review. *Sustainability (Basel)*, *13*(3), 1318. doi:10.3390u13031318

Marzuki, S. Z., Zreik, M., Buyong, S. Z., Goyipnazarov, S., Mirzaliev, S., & Bakhramovna, I. A. (2023). An Importance Satisfaction Analysis of Hosting Events in Hangzhou, China: A Pilot Study. *Advances in Social Sciences Research Journal*, *10*(6.2), 107–117. doi:10.14738/assrj.106.2.14996

Mayneris-Perxachs, J., & Swann, J. R. (2019). Metabolic phenotyping of malnutrition during the first 1000 days of life. *European Journal of Nutrition*, *58*(3), 909–930. doi:10.100700394-018-1679-0 PMID:29644395

Moda, H. M., Filho, W. L., & Minhas, A. (2019). Impacts of climate change on outdoor workers and their safety: Some research priorities. *International Journal of Environmental Research and Public Health*, *16*(18), 3458. doi:10.3390/ijerph16183458 PMID:31533360

Mwangi, L. (2023). Impact of Climate Change on Agricultural Food Production. *International Journal of Agriculture*, *8*(2), 1–10. doi:10.47604/ija.1994

Nukusheva, A., Ilyassova, G., Rustembekova, D., Zhamiyeva, R., & Arenova, L. (2021). Global warming problem faced by the international community: International legal aspect. *International Environmental Agreement: Politics, Law and Economics, 21*(2), 219–233. doi:10.100710784-020-09500-9

Paramati, S. R., Shahzad, U., & Doğan, B. (2022). The role of environmental technology for energy demand and energy efficiency: Evidence from OECD countries. *Renewable & Sustainable Energy Reviews, 153*, 111735. doi:10.1016/j.rser.2021.111735

Perera, F. (2018). Pollution from fossil-fuel combustion is the leading environmental threat to global pediatric health and equity: Solutions exist. *International Journal of Environmental Research and Public Health, 15*(1), 16. doi:10.3390/ijerph15010016 PMID:29295510

Rabah, K. (2018). Convergence of AI, IoT, big data and blockchain: a review. *The Lake Institute Journal, 1*(1), 1-18.

Rycroft, R. (2017). *The economics of inequality, discrimination, poverty, and mobility*. Routledge. doi:10.4324/9781315638867

Schoppa, R. K. (2019). *Revolution and its past: Identities and change in modern Chinese history*. Routledge. doi:10.4324/9781315182025

Stange, G., Pagogna, R., Sterly, H., Sakdapolrak, P., Borderon, M., Schraven, B., & Serraglio, D. A. (2023). Impeded migration as adaptation: COVID-19 and its implications for translocal strategies of environmental risk management. *Advances in Southeast Asian Studies, 16*(1), 157–169.

Tan, X., Choi, Y., Wang, B., & Huang, X. (2020). Does China's carbon regulatory policy improve total factor carbon efficiency? A fixed-effect panel stochastic frontier analysis. *Technological Forecasting and Social Change, 160*, 120222. doi:10.1016/j.techfore.2020.120222

Wang, Y., Zhang, D., Ji, Q., & Shi, X. (2020). Regional renewable energy development in China: A multidimensional assessment. *Renewable & Sustainable Energy Reviews, 124*, 109797. doi:10.1016/j.rser.2020.109797

Wang, Y. Z., Zhou, S., & Ou, X. M. (2021). Development and application of a life cycle energy consumption and CO2 emissions analysis model for high-speed railway transport in China. *Advances in Climate Change Research, 12*(2), 270–280. doi:10.1016/j.accre.2021.02.001

Xu, S., Lu, Y. H. M., Mutailipu, M., Yan, K., Zhang, Y., & Qvist, S. (2022). Repowering Coal Power in China by Nuclear Energy—Implementation Strategy and Potential. *Energies, 15*(3), 1072. doi:10.3390/en15031072

Yang, J., Yu, Y., Ma, T., Zhang, C., & Wang, Q. (2021). Evolution of energy and metal demand driven by industrial revolutions and its trend analysis. *Zhongguo Renkou Ziyuan Yu Huanjing, 19*(3), 256–264. doi:10.1016/j.cjpre.2021.12.028

Yildiz, I. (2019). Review of climate change issues: A forcing function perspective in agricultural and energy innovation. *International Journal of Energy Research, 43*(6), 2200–2215. doi:10.1002/er.4435

Zhang, H., Xiong, P., Yang, S., & Yu, J. (2023). Renewable energy utilization, green finance and agricultural land expansion in China. *Resources Policy, 80*, 103163. doi:10.1016/j.resourpol.2022.103163

Zheng, S., Lam, C. M., Hsu, S. C., & Ren, J. (2018). Evaluating efficiency of energy conservation measures in energy service companies in China. *Energy Policy*, *122*, 580–591. doi:10.1016/j.enpol.2018.08.011

Zi, L. (2019). *Online urbanization: Online services in China's rural transformation*. Springer. doi:10.1007/978-981-13-3603-4

Ziółkowska, M. J. (2021). Digital transformation and marketing activities in small and medium-sized enterprises. *Sustainability (Basel)*, *13*(5), 2512. doi:10.3390u13052512

Zreik, M. (2020). The Dimensions of the US-China trade war. *Open Political Science*, *3*(1), 47–55. doi:10.1515/openps-2020-0004

Zreik, M. (2022). Contemporary geopolitics of Eurasia and the Belt and Road Initiative. *Eurasian Research Journal*, *4*(1), 7–26. doi:10.53277/2519-2442-2022.1-01

Zreik, M. (2023). The Integration of China's Belt and Road Initiative Into Global Supply Chains: New Pathways for Social and Environmental Responsibility. In *Government Impact on Sustainable and Responsible Supply Chain Management* (pp. 74–94). IGI Global. doi:10.4018/978-1-6684-9062-4.ch005

Chapter 5
The Relationship of Renewable Energy Generation, Renewable Energy Consumption, and Economic Growth:
The Case of Türkiye

Meltem Okur Dinçsoy
Trakya University, Turkey

Hamit Can
https://orcid.org/0000-0002-6918-3234
Trakya University, Turkey

ABSTRACT

Renewable energy production and consumption has a triggering effect on the components associated with the energy sector. This study aims to analyze the effects of renewable energy generation and consumption on economic growth in Türkiye for the period 1990-2020 based on annual data. For the analyses in the study, the vector autoregression model (VAR) and Johansen cointegration test, vector error correction, and Granger causality are used for the data of renewable energy consumption (REC, percentage of total final energy consumption), renewable electricity generation (REG, per capita electricity generation from renewables), and economic growth (GDP constant 2010 US$). According to the findings from the study, no causality was found from production to gross domestic product from renewable energy consumption in the short run, but causality from renewable energy consumption to gross domestic product was found. In the long run, it can be said that renewable energy consumption is not the cause of gross domestic product, but gross product is the cause of renewable energy consumption.

DOI: 10.4018/979-8-3693-0400-6.ch005

INTRODUCTION

Energy, which is an indispensable element in production activities, also forms the basis of development. The possible increase in growth also triggers the demand for energy, goods and services. The fact that manufacturers produce goods with new industries at the point of meeting the demand explains the connection between energy and economic growth (Saidi et al., 2017). Energy is also an important element for science, economy, and modern society. The level of development of countries can be measured by the amount of energy they consume per capita. As the degree of economic development increases, the need and demand for energy increases. Although the energy demand differs in terms of countries, the studies that have been/will be done show that it will come to an important place in meeting the energy need in the coming years.

Energy is also a necessary element for economic growth and development. Although the countries of the world have different levels of natural resources and economic development, the need for energy on a global scale is constantly increasing. Therefore, there is a differentiation in the energy supply and demand of countries (Wang, Zhang, & Li, 2014). With this differentiation, the high demand for goods has diversified energy into renewable energy and non-renewable energy. In this diversity, renewable energy sources have started to take their place in the first place. On the other hand, the fact that most of the global energy systems are dependent on fossil fuels and together with the strong economic development, the depletion problems of fossil fuels, as well as the environmental damage caused by greenhouse gas emissions, have been effective (Afsharzade, Papzan, & Ashjaee, 2016).

The rapid industrialization process has had an impressive effect on the process inputs. With this effect, the rate of energy demand increased somewhat. Along with this demand, fossil resources are used in energy supply in many countries. The depletion of fossil resources has revealed supply security problems. Considering the cost and environmental impact for the sustainability of energy demand, it has been seen that the most suitable solution is renewable energy sources.

While struggling with the current climate change, it has been the basic vision all over the world not to experience any loss in economic output and to prevent a decrease in the welfare level. Oil, natural gas, and coal, which are the primary energy sources in the world, mostly in the Middle East, where political instability is experienced, are rapidly depleted. Harmful emissions that occur during energy production and consumption cause climate change. This disrupts the ecological balance and has negative effects on public health in the long run. The high dependence on exhaustible resources indicates that energy supply security will be faced in the near future. Turning to alternative energies and increasing savings and efficiency in energy use are the most effective and environmentally friendly policies to be implemented against energy supply problems. Along with the growth stages and development of the countries, consumption and demand show an increasing trend. Considering that this increasing trend will continue, it is very important to switch to up-to-date technological energy solutions in meeting the demands. The uncertainty of fossil resources, the shaping of the import and export future of countries by energy-based political crises, the long-term spread of renewable energy resources have increased the concerns of countries about their energy strategies. In order to eliminate these concerns, new energy supply searches have arisen, taking into account the cost, sustainability, security of supply, environmental impact, and maintenance-repair costs.

Studies examining the effects of renewable energy use on the economy and environment are increasing day by day. In addition, according to the policies implemented after the oil crisis, the insecurity in accessing fossil fuels brought the problem of energy diversity to the agenda and efforts were made to prevent dependence on fossil resources. Many of the search for solutions for energy supply are combined with renewable and cheap energy sources. In order to ensure sustainability in the field of energy, other countries such as Türkiye need to switch to renewable energies quickly and effectively. In addition, considering the environmental and health dimensions, this transition is very important in order to minimize its negative effects on the environment and other living organisms.

Türkiye is an energy importer country as its domestic fossil fuel reserves are limited and insufficient. In order to reduce its dependence on other countries, Türkiye needs to use its sustainable resources. Türkiye has the problem of not using the energy it buys from abroad effectively in the production process. The fact that the energy used is predominantly fossil fuel also increases carbon emissions. The use of renewable energy is an important policy in reducing harmful emissions. In addition to reducing the negative effects and dependence on fossil fuels, it has been predicted that the transition to the use of renewable energy will affect the country's economy.

The current account deficit increased significantly during the periods when the Türkiye economy developed and grew, and decreased during the periods when it contracted. Despite the developments in the economy and the increase in exports, Türkiye allocates a huge resource to imported energy. Although Türkiye has invested heavily in renewable energy sources in recent years, it is still a developing country in terms of energy dependency. The increase in energy imports imposes a cost on the country and causes the current account balance to deteriorate in the country. It is known that the measures to be taken to reduce Türkiye's dependence on foreign energy are also necessary to reduce the current account deficit. It is predicted that the current account deficit will decrease and economic growth will gain momentum if foreign dependency on energy is reduced.

Energy economics plays a vital role in developing strategies for finding alternative solutions to dependence on fossil resources, transition methods to renewable energies and their economic analysis, and minimizing economic crises. As a result of the econometric analyses conducted in this study, we aimed to raise awareness about Türkiye's renewable energy strategies and emphasize the importance of renewable energy sources compared to other energy sources both in Türkiye and in other countries. We aimed to draw a conclusion that will guide the investments to be made.

LITERATURE REVIEW

Fahrani's (2013) study, which states that economic growth and CO2 emissions have an impact on renewable energy consumption in the long run, and that there is no causality between the variables in the short run, covers the period 1975-2008 for 12 MENA countries. Granger causality, Panel FMOLS and DOLS methods were used in the study.

Apergis and Danuletiu (2014) concluded that there is a causal relationship from renewable energy to GDP in the long run, covering the period 1990-2012 for 80 countries. Granger, Canning and Perdoni tests were used in the study.

Doğan (2015) reached results that support the growth hypothesis between economic growth (GR) and electricity consumption from renewable energy sources (RELC) for Türkiye in the long run, and that support the feedback theory between electricity consumption from non-renewable energy sources (NRELC) and economic growth (GR), and (ARDL), Granger Causality, Gregory Hansen Cointegration Test used vector error correction models.

Bhattacharya et al. (2016) used panel estimation techniques for the period 1991-2012 across 38 countries in his study, where he found that renewable energy consumption has a positive effect on economic output.

Can (2017) stated that the increase in energy consumption will trigger an increase in renewable energy demand, but that renewable energy production has no effect on GDP covers the period of 1960-2013 for Türkiye. In the study, ADF, Zivot Andrews, CUSUM and Var Analysis were used.

Ntanos et al. (2018) concluded that there is a higher correlation between renewable energy resources (RES) consumption and the economic growth of countries with high GDP, covers the period of 2007-2016 for 25 European Countries. Cluster analysis and autoregressive distributed lag (ARDL) were used in the study.

Can and Korkmaz (2019) examined the period of 1990-2016 for Bulgaria in their study, which found that renewable energy consumption and renewable energy output have an effect on economic growth. In the study, Toda–Yamamoto analysis and Autogressive Distributed Latency (ARDL) bounds test were used.

Khobai et al. (2020) found that renewable energy consumption has a negative and significant effect on unemployment in the long run, covering the period 1990-2014 for South Africa. Autoregressive distributed lag model was used in the study.

Balsalobre-Lorente and Leitão (2020) concluded that trade openness and the use of renewable energy stimulate economic growth in the country, covering the period 1995-2014 for 28 European Union countries. FMOLS and DOLS econometric techniques were used in the study.

Yikun et al. (2021) state that renewable energy sources have significant effects on economic development among SAARC countries, covers the period 1995-2018 FOR South Asian Association for Regional Cooperation (SAARC) countries. The fixed-effect test and panel vector error correction model (PVECM) model was used in the study.

Li et al. (2021) examined the positive and significant impact of renewable energy consumption sources on economic growth in SAARC economies over the period 1995-2018.

Zhao et al. (2022) used MCDA method, Fuzzy-AHP, followed by data development analysis (DEA) in their study, which concluded that the development of wind energy projects for Pakistan can meet local energy needs and minimize fossil energy use.

Usman et al. (2023) examined the relationships between renewable energy, GDP, and trade openness on CO2 emission in G-7 nations. Using the Panel ARDL approach, the results show that, in the long run, there is a positive and significant correlation between GDP and trade openness on nitrous oxide emission in G-7 countries. Additionally, there is an insignificant but positive link between renewable energy and N2O emissions. Our proposal to political leaders and government officials is that they should strongly encourage foreign investors to participate in the production of clean and renewable energy, such as green energy, rather than conventional energy, in order to both support the activities of our economy and promote environmental stability. The government has to impose rigorous environmental laws and regulations, as well as come up with incentives for people to follow those policies, in order to enhance the overall quality of the environment.

METHODOLOGY AND DATA

This study examines the existence and direction of the possible causal relationship between total energy consumption, renewable energy production and economic growth for the period 1990-2020 in Türkiye. Annual data from 1990 to 2020 were obtained from the website World Bank and BP Statistical Review of World Energy. REC percentage of total final energy consumption, REG, per capita electricity generation from renewables, and economic growth (GDP constant 2015 US$) were used.

$$GDP_{it} = \beta_0 + \beta_1 REC_{it} + \beta_2 REG_{it} + \phi_{it} \; (i=1, \ldots, N \, ; \, t=1, \ldots\ldots, T) \qquad (1)$$

First of all, descriptive statistics about the variables used in the study are given. Relevant findings are given in Table 1:

Table 1. Descriptive stats

	GDP	REC	REG
Mean	57.63677	16.84194	724.1613
Median	56.55000	15.34000	640.0000
Maximum	84.72000	24.37000	1584.000
Minimum	36.00000	11.40000	374.0000
Std. Dev.	15.53995	4.417619	305.9287
Skewness	0.212528	0.493154	1.408329
Kurtosis	1.773083	1.750453	4.338228
Jarque-Berra	2.177746	3.273305	12.56070
Probability	0.336596	0.194630	0.001873
Observation	31	31	31

Table 2. Unit root tests

Unit Root Test	ADF		PP		KPSS
Test for Unit Root In	**Level**		**Level**		**Level**
	p-Value	t-Statistics	p-Value	t-Statistics	LM-Stat.
GDP	0.1711	-2.918647	0.1637	-2.944561	0.173434
REC	0.8324	-1.425053	0.8704	-1.292916	0.180175
REG	0.8588	-1.336402	0.8588	-1.336402	0.173724
	1st difference		1st difference		1st difference
	p-value	t-Statistics	p-value	t-Statistics	LM-Stat.
GDP	0.2624	-2.651115	0.8149	-1.475537	0.137980
REC	0.0001	-6.161128	0.0000	-7.777770	0.139150
REG	0.0783	-3.370550	0.0000	-7.010300	0.157815
	2nd difference		2nd difference		2nd difference
	p-value	t-Statistics	p-value	t-Statistics	LM-Stat.
GDP	0.0042	-4.698698	0.0125	-4.225400	0.123752
REC	0.0000	-8.467730	0.0000	-21.92832	0.067009
REG	0.0322	-3.876641	0.0000	-24.95710	0.482759

According to the results in Table 1, all variables are normally distributed. ADF, PP and KPSS tests were used to examine the levels and differences of the variables. The unit root results obtained as a result of the tests are as shown in Table 2.

Causality Relationship Between Variables in the Short Term

According to the Vector Autoregression and causality results, the causality relationship between the variables in the short term was examined. Short-term causality results are presented in Table 3, Table 4, and Table 5:

Table 3. Economic growth and renewable energy consumption causality results

Dependent Variable: D(GDP)			
Excluded	**Chi-sq**	**df**	**Prob.**
D(REC)	3.437703	2	0.1793
All	3.437703	2	0.1793
Dependent variable: D(REC)			
Excluded	**Chi-sq**	**df**	**Prob.**
D(GDP)	8.136086	2	0.0171
All	8.136086	2	0.0171

According to the results in Table 3, it can be said that there is no causality from REC to GDP, but causality from GDP to REC. According to these results, it can be said that possible income increase and inputs for development may have an impact on renewable energy consumption.

Table 4. Economic growth and renewable energy generation causality results

Dependent Variable: D(GDP)			
Excluded	**Chi-sq**	**df**	**Prob.**
D(REG)	4.079732	2	0.1300
All	4.079732	2	0.1300
Dependent Variable: D(REG)			
Excluded	**Chi-sq**	**df**	**Prob.**
D(GDP)	3.614847	2	0.1641
All	3.614847	2	0.1641

According to the results in Table 4, it can be said that there is no causality from REG to GDP or from GDP to REG. Thus, it can be said that the steps to be taken towards the production of renewable energy in the short term do not have a significant effect on the gross domestic product as well as on the renewable energy production of the gross domestic product.

Table 5. Renewable energy consumption and renewable energy generation causality results

Dependent Variable: D(REC)			
Excluded	**Chi-sq**	**df**	**Prob.**
D(REG)	0.099740	2	0.9514
All	0.099740	2	0.9514
Dependent Variable: D(REG)			
Excluded	**Chi-sq**	**df**	**Prob.**
D(REC)	0.109233	2	0.9468
All	0.109233	2	0.9468

According to the results in Table 5, no causality from REG to REC and no causality from REC to REG was found. Thus, it can be said that there is no relationship between renewable energy production and renewable energy consumption in the short term.

Causality Relationship Between Variables in the Long Run

According to the results of Vector Autoregression and causality, the long-term causality relationship between the variables was examined. Short-term causality results are presented in Table 6, Table 7, and Table 8:

Table 6. Economic growth and renewable energy consumption causality results

Error Correction	D(GDP)	D(REC)
CointEq1	0.032435	0.087091
	(0.02832)	(0.02574)
	[1.14545]	[3.38321]

According to Table 6, it is concluded that renewable energy consumption is not the cause of gross domestic product (|1.14545| < 1.96). On the contrary, it has been concluded that the gross domestic product is caused by renewable energy consumption (3.38321 > 1.96).

According to Table 7, it is concluded that renewable energy generation is not the cause of gross domestic product (|1.19875| < 1.96). On the contrary, it has been concluded that the gross domestic product is caused by renewable energy generation (2.59585 > 1.96).

Table 7. Economic growth and renewable energy generation causality resultsr

Error Correction	D(GDP)	D(REG)
CointEq1	0.027547	7.175325
	(0.02298)	(2.76415)
	[1.19875]	[2.59585]

Table 8. Renewable energy consumption and renewable energy generation causality results

Error Correction	D(REC)	D(REG)
CointEq1	-0.082036	-7.220658
	(0.04007)	(4.88528)
	[-2.04732]	[-1.47804]

According to Table 8, it is concluded that renewable energy generation is caused by renewable energy consumption (-2.04732 > 1.96). On the contrary, it is concluded that renewable energy consumption is not the cause of renewable energy generation (1.47804 < 1.96).

CONCLUSION

Today, the fact that energy inputs are mostly based on fossil fuels, their limitedness and the damage they cause to the environment reveal the importance of renewable energy sources. The fact that these resources have various advantages due to their clean, reliable and inexhaustible features has increased the demand and popularity for them. The continuous increase in energy on a global scale, which is a necessary element of economic growth and development, has made it necessary to increase investments in order to meet the demand. Türkiye's rapid economic growth and population growth rate have increased the need for energy rapidly and has become a country dependent on foreign sources in terms of energy resources. It is observed that Türkiye has grown in the production of these resources with the investments made to increase renewable energy production in order to reduce foreign dependency on energy resources. Expectations that Türkiye's current situation in total energy consumption will increase in the future, however, may also be an indication that it should attach more importance to renewable energy investments.

According to the findings from the study, no causality was found from production to gross domestic product from renewable energy consumption in the short run, but causality was found from renewable energy consumption to gross domestic product. According to this result, the determination of energy investments according to the size of the impact of the changes in energy consumption on development, shaping the strategic goals in this direction and conducting R&D studies on the size and diversification of energy consumption, the studies on the direction and form of energy supply security will be very important. can be said to be important. In addition, there is no causality from renewable energy production to gross domestic product, from gross domestic product to renewable energy production, from renewable energy production to renewable energy consumption, and from renewable energy consumption to renewable energy production in the determined periods for the short term.

In line with the results obtained from the study, it has been determined that renewable energy consumption in the long term is not the cause of gross domestic product, but gross product is the cause of renewable energy consumption. In addition, renewable energy production is not the cause of gross domestic product in the long run, but gross domestic product is the cause of renewable energy production. In the same period, it was concluded that renewable energy production was the reason for renewable energy consumption, but renewable energy consumption was not the reason for renewable energy production.

REFERENCES

Afsharzade, N., Papzan, A., Ashjaee, M., Delangizan, S., Passel, S., & Azad, H. (2016). Renewable energy development in rural areas of Iran. *Renewable & Sustainable Energy Reviews*, *65*, 743–755. doi:10.1016/j.rser.2016.07.042

Apergis, N., & Danuletiu, D. C. (2014). Renewable energy and economic growth: Evidence from the sign of panel long-run causality. *International Journal of Energy Economics and Policy*, *4*(4), 578–587. https://www.econjournals.com/index.php/ijeep/article/view/879

Balsalobre-Lorente, D., & Leitão, N. C. (2020). The role of tourism, trade, renewable energyuse and carbon dioxide emissions on economic growth: Evidence of tourism-led growthhypothesis in EU-28. *Environmental Science and Pollution Research International*, *27*(36), 45883–45896. doi:10.100711356-020-10375-1 PMID:32803615

Bhattacharya, M., Paramati, S. R., Ozturk, I., & Bhattacharya, S. (2016). The effect of renewable energy consumption on economic growth: Evidence from top 38 countries. *Applied Energy*, *162*, 733–741. doi:10.1016/j.apenergy.2015.10.104

Can, H. (2017). *Yenilebilir enerjinin makroekonomik etkileri: Türkiye örneği* [Master's thesis]. Namık Kemal Üniversitesi.

Can, H., & Korkmaz, Ö. (2020). The relationship between renewable energy consumption and economic growth: The case of Bulgaria. *International Journal of Energy Sector Management*, *13*(3), 573–589. doi:10.1108/IJESM-11-2017-0005

Dickey, D. A., & Fuller, W. A. (1979). Distribution of the estimators for autoregressive time series with a unit root. *Journal of the American Statistical Association*, *74*(366a), 427–431. doi:10.1080/01621459.1979.10482531

Dogan, E. (2015). The relationship between economic growth and electricity consumption from renewable and non-renewable sources: A study of Turkey. *Renewable & Sustainable Energy Reviews*, *52*, 534–546. doi:10.1016/j.rser.2015.07.130

Farhani, S. (2013). Renewable energy consumption, economic growth and CO2 emissions: Evidence from selected MENA countries. *Energy Economics Letters, 1*(2), 24-41. Retrieved from https://archive.aessweb.com/index.php/5049/article/view/149

Khobai, H., Kolisi, N., Moyo, C., Anyikwa, I., & Dingela, S. (2020). Renewable Energy Consumption and Unemployment in South Africa. *International Journal of Energy Economics and Policy, 10*(2), 170–178. doi:10.32479/ijeep.6374

Kwiatkowski, D., Phillips, P. C., Schmidt, P., & Shin, Y. (1992). Testing the null hypothesis of stationarity against the alternative of a unit root: How sure are we that economic time series have a unit root? *Journal of Econometrics, 54*(1-3), 159–178. doi:10.1016/0304-4076(92)90104-Y

Li, Q., Cherian, J., Shabbir, M. S., Sial, M. S., Li, J., Mester, I., & Badulescu, A. (2021). Exploring the relationship between renewable energy sources and economic growth. The case of SAARC countries. *Energies, 14*(3), 520. doi:10.3390/en14030520

Ntanos, S., Skordoulis, M., Kyriakopoulos, G., Arabatzis, G., Chalikias, M., Galatsidas, S., Batzios, A., & Katsarou, A. (2018). Renewable energy and economic growth: Evidence from European countries. *Sustainability (Basel), 10*(8), 2626. doi:10.3390u10082626

Phillips, P. C. B., & Perron, P. (1988). Testing for a unit root in time series regression. *Biometrika, 75*(2), 335–346. doi:10.1093/biomet/75.2.335

Saidi, K., Rahman, M. M., & Amamri, M. (2017). The causal nexus between economic growth and energy consumption: New evidence from global panel of 53 countries. *Sustainable Cities and Society, 33*, 45–56. doi:10.1016/j.scs.2017.05.013

Usman, M., Rahman, S. U., Shafique, M. R., Sadiq, A., & Idrees, S. (2023). Renewable Energy, Trade and Economic Growth on Nitrous Oxide Emission in G-7 Countries Using Panel ARDL Approach. *Journal of Social Sciences Review, 3*(2), 131–143. doi:10.54183/jssr.v3i2.219

Wang, W., Zhang, M., & Li, P. (2014). Exploring Temporal And Spatial Evolution Of Global Energy Production And Consumption. *Renewable & Sustainable Energy Reviews, 30*, 943–949. doi:10.1016/j.rser.2013.11.027

Yikun, Z., Gul, A., Saleem, S., Shabbir, M. S., Bilal, K., & Abbasi, H. M. (2021). The relationship between renewable energy sources and sustainable economic growth: Evidence from SAARC countries. *Environmental Science and Pollution Research International, 28*(25), 33390–33399. doi:10.100711356-021-12795-z PMID:33641094

Zhao, Patwary, Qayyum, Alharthi, Bashir, Mohsin, Hanif, & Abbas. (2022). The determinants of renewable energy sources for the fueling of green and sustainable economy. *Energy, 238*(PC). doi:10.1016/j.energy.2021.122029

Chapter 6
The Effect of Industrial Growth on Carbon Dioxide Emissions in Africa:
Can Mobile Technology Adoption and Renewable Energy Moderate the Impact?

Paul Adjei Kwakwa
University of Energy and Natural Resources, Ghana

Solomon Aboagye
https://orcid.org/0000-0001-6801-6234
University of Cape Town, South Africa & Lancaster University Ghana, Ghana

ABSTRACT

The rising levels of carbon dioxide (CO_2) emissions on the African continent has been an issue of concern. Consequently, this study analyses the mitigating role of renewable energy and mobile technology in the effect of industrial sector growth on carbon dioxide emissions. Using data from 32 African countries for the period 2002-2021, the study finds that expansion in industrial sector increases CO_2 emissions for the region, while renewable energy consumption and mobile technology reduce carbon emissions. Also, renewable energy and mobile phone technology are found to moderate the effect of industrial growth on CO_2 emissions. Other findings are that trade openness, urbanization, and income increase carbon dioxide emissions. The study recommends the removal of financial impediments in the way of industrial firms to enhance their acquisition of efficient technologies for operations to reduce carbon dioxide emissions. Also, governments in the region should increase financial support for the development and adoption of renewable energy.

DOI: 10.4018/979-8-3693-0400-6.ch006

1. INTRODUCTION

The 21st century has been marked by a continuous surge in the pace of global industrialization. There is a plethora of associated socio-economic gains that are frequently observed, including but not limited to job creation, poverty reduction, economic expansion, gender equality, improvement in labour standards, and greater access to quality education and healthcare. As a result, it is considered an important catalyst towards achieving aspects of the Sustainable Development Goals (SDGs). Indeed, over the past few decades, most African economies are seeking to make industrial expansion a key component of their drive towards sustainable growth and development. However, it must be noted at the same time that, industrial processes can have substantial negative environmental impacts – climate change, loss of natural resources, air and water pollution and extinction of species (Kwakwa et al., 2020; Aboagye et al., 2020; Kleemann and Abdulai, 2013).

Following the material balance principle, it is widely known that environment and industrial activities are linked inextricably. A key implication is the mass of anthropogenic carbon dioxide (CO_2) emissions flowing into the atmospheric environment which is regarded as a lead drive behind the growing trends in global warming and climate change. Today, the devastating effects of human-induced CO_2 emissions, such as those emitted through the industrial sector, are now more obvious. These devastating effects have long been envisaged culminating into several environmental treaties. It is among these dangers that the 2015 United Nations Framework Convention on Climate Change (UNFCCC) Paris Agreement, for instance, set the goal to limit global warming to well below 2°C above pre-industrial levels and aim for 1.5°C (Keramidas et al. 2018). Annual emissions need to be about half (25-30 GtCO2e/year on average) by 2030 to limit warming to 1.5˚C. However, a year after the agreement, total global greenhouse gas emissions rose by about 0.5% and have been projected to be 52-58 GtCO2e by 2030 (Keramidas et al. 2018).

Even though, Africa's share of global CO_2 emissions of about 7.1% is still relatively low (World Bank 2023), total CO_2 emissions in the continent could rise if current trends persist unabated or unregulated. Over the past few decades, Africa's natural resources have depleted remarkably resulting from accelerated pace of economic and social transformation. The observation is that activities such as manufacturing, construction, mining which fall within the industrial sector, do not only contribute to the depletion of the stock of natural resources but also add stress to the environmental system by increasing the stock of wastes. In addition, industry, is a highly energy-intensive sector, responsible for more than 37% of energy use which could be another major source of environmental degradation given the significant share of fossil energy in Africa's energy mix (IEA 2022). Inasmuch as industrial expansion remains key to the economic prosperity of the continent, understanding the mechanisms by which the adverse environmental effects of industry could be mitigated is imperative as the concerns of environmental sustainability intensify. Moreover, the extent that the environment serves as both the resource base and waste sink for industrial activities implies that the sustainability of industry itself partly depends on the supply and quality of natural and environmental resources.

In the modern economy, technological improvement and renewable energy are two notable avenues or mechanisms frequently debated to exert downward pressure on environmental effects of human socio-economic activities including industrial expansion. The global economy is now in a digital age with digital technology leading a global technological revolution and industrial change (Schwab, 2017; Altinoz et al., 2021). In an era characterized by rapid globalization process and diffusion of information and communication in recent years, there is a growing body of debate on the role of the digital, information-driven, globalized economy in driving or mitigating greenhouse gas emissions (Shahbaz et al. 2017; Shahnazi and Shabani 2019; Usman et al. 2021). One of the technological advances in the digital economy is in the aspect of communication and information with mobile technology being a notable component. Yet, the extent to which the adoption of mobile technology is influencing the level of atmospheric CO_2 emissions especially in African has not been subjected to rigorous quantitative evaluation by many studies (Kwakwa et al., 2023).

A fundamental driver of the overall carbon footprint of mobile communications is the number of mobile subscriptions or the level of adoption (Fehske and Fettweis, 2011). The observation is that the adoption of mobile technology facilitates the use of information communication technology (ICT). This is because mobile phones are a core device for the digital and ICT economy. Mobile technologies contribute to reduction in CO_2 emission via ICT when they facilitate the research and development of energy-efficient technology, cheaper movement, and cheaper access to clean energy[1] (Raheem et al. 2020). Similarly, they reduce CO_2 emissions through dematerialization and digitization, online delivery, intelligent transport systems, transport and travel substitution, smart buildings, and smart grids (Zhang and Liu, 2015; Asongu et al., 2018; Amri, 2018; Park et al., 2018; Danish et al., 2018; Cheng et al., 2021). Nonetheless, mobile technology adoption could have some adverse environmental effects that could invariably contribute to CO_2 emission either directly, indirectly or both. For instance, most of the direct effects are mainly caused by energy consumption in production, distribution and use of mobile technology and devices. The manufacturing process entails resource and material consumption that may drive CO_2 emission (Chatti, 2020). This is worsened further if the manufacturing process relies on fossil energy. There is also evidence that improper disposal of mobile devices threatens the quality of the environment (Chatti, 2020). Indirectly, mobile technology adoption affects CO_2 emissions through its impact on other sectors of the economy (Danish, 2019) and the behavioural changes it induces in economic agents (Asongu et al., 2018). Indeed, there are several studies that argue that mobile communication could accelerate the level of economic expansion and industrial activities, increase energy consumption, primarily fossil energy and ultimately exert upward pressure on CO_2 emission (Raheem et al. 2020; Ulucak et al. 2020; Haftu 2019; Danish, 2019; Asongu et al., 2018; Malmodin and Lundén, 2018). Meanwhile the adoption of mobile technology continues to rise in Africa. It is projected that there will be 87% smartphone adoption by *2030* in sub Saharan African region alone (Business Insider Africa 2023). How could such mobile adoption affect environmental degradation is worthy of investigation.

Renewable energy is not only available in abundance and replenished by nature but more importantly clean and emit no or little greenhouse gases or pollutants into the air. Given energy-intensive orientation of industrial activities, it is intuitively plausible to expect considerable reductions in energy-related emissions when the sector increases its utilization of renewable energy away from fossils (Kwakwa, 2020). The use of renewable energy also promotes energy efficiency relative to conventional (fossil) energy and thus, it can be used to achieve more production/output than conventional energy (Gyamfi et al., 2022); this is another important avenue to reducing emissions even in the era of heightened industrial drive. With this, it is possible for the continent to continue with its pursuit of industrial expansion without escalating the current levels of CO_2 emissions and thereby, contributing to the global fight against environment degradation, global warming and climate change. In other words, beyond industrialization, renewable energy consumption remains an important avenue to achieve sustained declines in GHG emissions particularly CO_2 emissions (Aboagye, 2017).

Globally, the prevalent of energy crises have also necessitated the need for the development of renewable energy. For instance, in the early 2000s the proportion of households using polluting fuels stood at the following: Central and Southern Asia – 37%; Eastern Asia – 38% Sub-Saharan Africa (SSA)–19%;

Rest of the World – 6%. As of 2010, these proportions have changed moderately: Central and Southern Asia – 37%; Eastern Asia – 33% Sub-Saharan Africa – 25%; Rest of the World – 5% (Stoner et al., 2021). By the turn of 2015, SSA has taken a remarkable lead to over 70% of households cooking with polluting fuels (Stoner et al., 2021). The International Energy Agency (IEA) estimates show that compared to the less than 60% in Asia (Central and Southern Asia – 22%; Eastern Asia – 26%), there are more than 900 million (80%) people in Africa who use biomass as primary cooking fuel (IEA, 2022; World Economic Forum 2022; Stoner et al., 2021) which is a principal cause of CO_2 emissions and thus, a shift towards the use of renewable energy for house holds' cooking is an expressway to exert downward pressure on CO_2 emissions. Efforts to address the above issue has resulted in significant investment in the renewable energy sector. At the global level, of the total investment made into the power sector in 2020, the International Energy Agency (IEA) reveals that 45% was for renewable energy and its network infrastructure (IEA, 2021). There has been about 300% growth in investment for renewable energy between 2001-2009 and 2010-2019 (UNEP, 2019). Also, from 2007 to 2015, the share of global renewable energy in total final energy consumption has increased from 16.6% to 17.54% (World Bank 2023).

Despite the abundance of renewable energy resources in Africa the continent is noted for its remarkably high level of energy poverty as access to affordable, reliable and sufficient modern energy that is regarded as a precondition to attaining several human development goals (World Bank, 2019; United Nations, 2012). There are however, some notable renewable energy projects in some countries on the continent. For instance, in East and Central Africa, Congo and Cameroon are constructing a $700 million hydroelectric station on the Dja River with an estimated production capacity of 600MW and project completion expected in 2025 (Energy Capital Power, 2021a). In southern Africa, Namibia has commissioned a $9.4 billion project that will help position Namibia as a green hydrogen economy while a 100MW solar photovoltaic plant at the Mogalakwena mine and another estimated 2,600MW of renewable energy of which 1,600MW comprises onshore wind and 1,000MW solar in South Africa is under construction (Energy Capital Power, 2021a). In West Africa, Ghana is constructing eight solar plants with capacities ranging from 10MW to 100MW each. Cabo Verde is investing towards a goal of transitioning to 50% renewable energy by 2030 (Energy Capital Power, 2021b). In Nigeria, through the Nigerian Electrification Project (NEP) with support from the African Development Bank (AfDB) and other partners, the country seeks to extend clean, safe, reliable and affordable electricity through renewable power sources (AfDB 2018). Similar renewable energy projects are ongoing in North Africa which, over the last decade, has managed to increase its renewable energy production by 40%, by adding 4.5 GW of wind, solar PV and solar thermal capacity to its renewable energy power fleet. Renewables generation capacity grew by 80% over the past ten years, and almost by 560%, excluding hydropower (Energy Capital Power, 2021a).

From the foregoing it can be argued that renewable energy and mobile technology can moderate the effect of industrial growth on carbon emissions. Thus, the cleanliness nature of renewable energy can abate the carbon emissions associated with industrial growth. Regarding mobile technology it can abate carbon emission effect of industrialization if it promotes industrial efficiency. However, if it increases production without efficiency then mobile technology will increase the carbon emission effect of industrial growth. While moderation analysis is becoming common in energy and environmental economics literature (Ehigiamusoe and Dogan 2022; Kwakwa et al., 2023; Ehigiamusoe et al., 2023) there is little evidence on how renewable energy and mobile technology moderate the carbon emissions effect of industrial growth.

Consequently, the study aims at assessing the effect of industrial growth, renewable energy and mobile technology on carbon emission. Specifically, the study seeks to address two broad objective a) the direct effect of industrial growth, renewable energy and mobile technology on carbon emissions in Africa; b) the moderating effect of renewable energy and mobile technology on the carbon emissions effect of industrial growth in Africa. The study utilizes the Stochastic Impacts by Regression on Population, Affluence, & Technology (STIRPAT) model with secondary data on 32 African countries (see Table 1) over the 2002-2021 period from the WDI database of the World Bank.

The study makes two important empirical contributions. Foremost, even though mobile technology is a major foundation for ICT, most studies assessing the environmental effect of communication technology have focused disproportionately on the superstructure (i.e., ICT) rather than the foundation (i.e., mobile technology). Thus, this study improves upon the extant literature by shifting emphasis to mobile technology. Secondly, given the theoretical expectation of technology and renewable energy in reducing CO2 emission, the study further examines the extent to which they could serve as potential mitigations mechanisms for upward pressure exerted on CO_2 emissions by the industrial sector.

2. LITERATURE REVIEW

2.1 Mobile Technology and Carbon Emission Nexus

Ecological modernization theory, ICT-energy consumption effect and e-waste argument are among the reasons to explain the relationship between mobile technology and carbon emissions. From the ecological modernization perspectives mobile technology like other ICTs facilitates economic growth, improves technology and supports the development of environmental framework to reduce environmental pollution including carbon emission (Simpson et al. 2019; Sadorsky 2014). The ICT-energy usage argument suggests the production of ICT gadgets including mobile phones requires energy and resources extraction that can pollute the environment (Raghutla and Chittedi 2020). Mobile phones and other gadgets functions well on electricity. They energy requirement may be high which can increase carbon emissions (Kwakwa et al., 2023). However, mobile technology can reduce energy consumption by supporting innovation or research and development (Musah et al., 2023) and promoting efficient production methods (Kouton 2019). Thirdly, Baris-uzemen et al. (2020) and Shabani and Shahnazi (2019) mention that improper disposal of mobile technology equipment is a source of e-waste which pollutes the environment.

Empirical studies have revealed a conflicting effect of mobile technology on carbon emission. Raghutla and Chittedi (2020) found technology increases carbon emission for BRICS countries. Raihan et al., (2022) obtained a negative effect of technological innovation on carbon emission for Bangladesh. Chatti and Majeed (2022) in their analysis for developed and developing countries found that telephone usage reduces carbon emission thereby increasing environmental quality although it is very weak. Fang (2023) found green technological innovation reduces carbon emissions in China. Balsalobre-Lorente et al., (2019) assessment revealed that mobile technology reduces carbon emisisons among BRICS countries. Anochiwa (2022) found a negative effect of mobile usage on carbon emissions in Sub-Saharan African countries. However, Kwakwa et al., (2023) found for the South African economy that mobile technology increases carbon dioxide emission. A comparative study by Gyamfi et al., (2023) focusing on MINT, BRICS and G7 countries found that telephone subscription reduces carbon emission in BRICS and G7 economies but increases emissions in MINT economies. However, they found export of ICT services increases carbon emissions for all blocks. Hussain et al., (2023) found mobile phone usage increases carbon emissions in India. A study on 9 thermonuclear energy-producing countries (the USA, France, China, Japan, Russia, South Korea, Canada, the United Kingdom, and Spain) by Jahanger et al., (2023) found mobile phone usage and other ICT gadgets are helpful in reducing carbon emissions. Raheem et al. (2020) reported a positive effect of mobile usage on carbon emissions in G7 countries.

2.2 Renewable Energy and Carbon Emission Nexus

The channel through which renewable energy affects carbon emission is that it is efficient and therefore enhances productivity. Through this less energy is consumed and eventually lower carbon emission is realized. Moreover, it is cleaner than conventional fossil fuel as a result it enhances cleaner environment through lower carbon emissions. It can also propel economic growth to enable economies to invest in efficient energy technologies (Bekun et al., 2022). Empirically, evidence of carbon emission reducing effect associated with renewable energy has been reported in many studies. In an analysis for China's economy Zheng et al., (2021) reported that renewable energy inhibit carbon dioxide emission. It was found that across all quantiles renewable energy helps reduce carbon emissions. Yu et al., (2020) also found for Chinese provinces that renewable energy reduces carbon emission. For countries of the Belt and Road Initiative (BRI), Sherez et al., (2022) that used method of moments (GMM) for 2003-2018 found the usefulness of renewable energy in reducing carbon emissions. Li et al., (2022) in their analysis of renewable energy and carbon emission nexus for South Eastern Asian countries found that renewable energy reduces carbon dioxide emissions. Usman and Radulescu (2022) found renewable energy reduces carbon emission to improve environmental quality. Sheraz et al., (2022) focusing on Belt and Road (BRI) countries found renewable energy reduces carbon emission. Kirikkaleli et al., (2022) noted for the Chilean economy that renewable energy reduces carbon emissions. Sarkodie and Adams (2018) reported of a carbon decreasing effect of renewable energy usage for South Africa. Acheampong et al., (2019) found renewable energy usage triggers lower carbon emissions in Africa. Similar finding was reported by Adams and Acheampong (2019) in another study on African countries. Njoh (2021) found renewable energy usage is helpful in reducing carbon emission in Africa. However, the works of Long et al. (2015) as well as Hasnisah et al. (2019) for China and group of Asian countries respectively found renewable energy increases carbon emissions.

2.3 Industrial Growth and Carbon Emission Nexus

The contribution to industrialization to economic growth and development cannot be ignored. However, because it thrives on energy it tends to increase carbon emission. Industrial growth is accompanied by increased manufacturing which is energy intended. It requires transportation of raw materials as well as finished goods for distribution. It may be associated with the construction of more building facilities. The combination of these may cause higher carbon emissions (Kwakwa 2020). Adom (2014) argues that an efficient industrial sector may lead to lower carbon emissions. Thus, as industrialization expands firms may be able to acquire modern and efficient technologies which can lower energy usage and eventually reduce carbon emissions. Idowu et al., (2023) analysis for eight Organization of the Petroleum Exporting Countries (OPEC) and nine High Industrialized Countries over the period 1985 to 2020 found industrial growth increases carbon emission through energy consumption. Fang (2023) industrial structure decreases carbon emissions for the Chinese economy. China's carbon emission was reported by Tang et al (2022) to be reduced by higher levels of deindustrialization. Raihan et al., (2022) found industrial growth increases carbon emission for Bangladesh. Kwakwa (2022) found industrialization in Ghana is associated with higher carbon emissions. Mentel et al., (2022) found that industrialization does not affect carbon emissions in sub Saharan Africa. Majeed and Tauqir (2020) found for a panel of 156 countries that industrial growth harms the environment through higher levels of carbon emissions. Assessment by Zhang and Chen (2021) for Yangtze River Economic Belt reported of a U-shaped relationship between industrialization and carbon emission. Khan and Majeed (2023) found the level of carbon emission in Pakistan is positively affected by industrialization. However, Afriyie et al., (2023) obtained a negative effect of industrial growth on carbon emission in Sub Saharan Africa. Raihan (2023) obtained a positive effect of industrialization on carbon emission in Philippine.

2.4 Trade and Carbon Emission Nexus

While trade openness can lead to transfer of efficient technology to promote sustainable development via low carbon emission it can also increase energy consumption when there is influx of inefficient or energy intensive goods (Aboagye 2017). Li et al., (2022) found trade increases carbon emission among South Eastern Asian countries. Acheampong et al (2019) found trade openness triggers higher carbon emissions in Africa. Similar finding was reported by Adams and Acheampong (2019). Mehmood (2021) found trade openness increases carbon emission for South Asian Association for Regional Cooperation (SAARC) countries. Also, Mentel et al., (2022) found that trade openness decreases carbon emissions in Sub-Saharan Africa. In their study Balsalobre-Lorente et al., (2020) found trade openness surges carbon emissions in BRICS economies. Raheem et al., (2020) also found trade openness triggers carbon emissions in G7 countries.

2.5 Income and Carbon Emission Nexus

Expansion in economic activities often puts stress on environment which may cause destruction in the environment including carbon emissions. Consequently, as income increases consumption increases which would require more resources are pushed to produce goods. More energy is thus consumed during the process which may increase carbon emissions (Aboagye 2017). On the other hand, increase in income may enable firms and households secure energy-efficient goods which will lead to lower carbon emissions (Adom et al., 2018). For SAARC countries Mehmood (2021) found economic growth reduces carbon emissions. Also, Emir et al., (2022) found income increases carbon emission in Turkey. Lv et al., (2019) obtained increased emission effect of income. Sarwar and Alsaggaf (2019) obtained a positive effect of income on carbon emission in China. Tang et al., (2022) found for the Chinese economy that increase in income increases carbon emissions. Hussain et al., (2022) found income eventually reduces carbon emissions in Africa. Raihan et al., (2022) found income growth increases carbon emission for Bangladesh. Majeed and Tauqir (2020) found that income reduces levels of carbon emissions of a group of 156 countries. Khan and Majeed (2023) found economic growth increases the level of carbon emission in Pakistan. Afriyie et al., (2023) obtained a negative effect of economic growth on carbon emission in Sub Saharan Africa. Philippine economic growth was found to be positively affected by Raihan (2023). Anochiwa et al., (2022) found income growth also increases carbon emission in SSA.

2.6 Urbanization and Carbon Emission Nexus

Urbanization effect on environmental is argued from various perspective. A school of thought suggests that urbanization leads to traffic congestion and more energy consumption will lead to higher emissions (Kwakwa et al., 2018). However, the conglomeration of industrialization in urban towns can lead to economies of scale which will promote energy efficiency and lower carbon emissions (Adom et al., 2018). This is often referred to as the compact city theory. Ecological modernization theory posits countries need to urbanize to promote industrialization in order to grow out of environmental degradation (York and Rosa 2003). Thus, it suggests that urban development which eventually becomes associated with modern efficient production is the order of the day for environmental degradation to decrease (*Gwynne 2009*). Urban transition theory presents the argument that as towns get urbanized they transition from low income or agricultural based economy to high income or service based economy . It is at a higher income level that is when urbanization can propel low environmental degradation (Moore et al., 2018).

Empirically, Kwakwa (2023) observed that urbanization pressure increases carbon dioxide emissions in Africa. Emir et al., (2022) in their study for Turkey found urbanization positively affects carbon emissions. Zhang et al., (2017) used a panel data of 141 countries to assess the effect of urbanization on carbon emissions. They found there is an inverted U-shaped relationship between urbanization and carbon emissions and the turn point is around 73.80%. This suggests that initial level of urbanization may increase carbon emissions until urbanization rate gets to 73.8% of the population where carbon emission will decrease. Sun et al., (2022) examined the carbon emission effect of urbanization for Middle East and North African (MENA) countries. They reported a positive effect of urbanization on carbon emissions. For USA, Elliot (2014) analysis using both cross sectional and panel data found various indicators of urbanization to increase carbon emissions. Lv et al., (2022) assessment also confirmed that urbanization increases carbon emission for China. Tan et al., (2022) carbon emission is positively enhanced by urbanization in China. Lv et al., (2019) obtained a negative effect of urbanization on carbon emission in China. Khan et al., (2021) analyzed optimal level of urbanization on carbon emisisons for newly industrialized countries (NIC) and found an inverted U shape relationahip between the two. Mehmood (2021) analysis for carbon emission in South Asian Association for Regional Cooperation (SAARC) countries for urbanization reduces carbon emission. Tang et al., (2022) found for the Chinese economy that higher urbanization reduces carbon emissions. Sarwar and Alsaggaf (2019) obtained a positive effect of urbanization on China's carbon emission. Hussain et al., (2022) found urbanization increases carbon emission in Africa. Raghutla and Chittedi (2020) urbanization reduces carbon emission for BRICS countries. Chatti and Majeed (2022) found urbanization reduces Carbon emission for developed and developing countries.

2.7 Moderation Analysis

Researchers in recent times have argued that innovations such as renewable energy and mobile technology may have direct effect on the environment and indirect effect. The latter effect is argued to mean that they may exert their influence through a particular sector (Kwakwa 2023b; Li et al., 2022). Some studies for example Li et al., (2022) reported that renewable energy moderates the effect of trade openness on carbon emission. Mentel et al., (2022) found that renewable energy moderates the effect of industrialization on carbon emissions in Sub-Saharan Africa. Kwakwa (2023b) found renewable energy moderates the effect that sectoral growth has on carbon emission in Africa. However, studies to assess the moderation effect of mobile technology on the carbon emission-industrial growth nexus is limited. In summary while studies on carbon emission in Africa is gaining attention more needs to be done. The conflicting results, the scarce evidence of the effect of mobile adoption and the moderation role of mobile technology and renewable energy in the industrial growth-carbon emission nexus make it essential for studies like this to be done for the African continent.

3. METHODOLOGY

3.1 Theoretical Framework and Empirical Modelling

The Stochastic Impacts by Regression on Population, Affluence, & Technology (STIRPAT) model due Dietz and Rosa (1997) has been the basis for many studies that explore the drivers of environmental degradation. Built upon the conventional IPAT model, the STIRPAT model specifies that the level of impact on the environment (I) is determined by population pressure (P), affluence or economic growth (A) and technology (T). Growth in human population requires more production to cater for human needs. This puts stress on the environment as more resources are extracted which can lead to higher environmental degradation. Expansion of economic activities also has the capacity to negatively affect the quality of the environment through extraction of natural resources and increase energy consumption (Aboagye 2017). However, with right policies in place higher economic growth promote environmental quality. Technology which signifies the method of transforming input into output will affect the environment depending on the state of technology. An advanced technology that promotes efficiency will improve environmental quality while the opposite reduces environmental quality (Adom et al., 2018; Musah et al., 2023). Considering the growth performance of African economies in recent times; the share of Africans in global population and the lower technological development it is justified to relate the work to the STIRPAT model.

The relationship between economic growth, population pressure and technology is stated in mathematical form as:

$$I = a.P^{\beta}.A^{\lambda}.T^{\sigma}.v \tag{1}$$

where *a, β, λ, σ, δ, e and v* stand for parameters to be estimated. It is undeniable fact that CO_2 emissions posses the most greatest threat to environmental quality. It would make sense to have that as the level of environmental Impact (I). The pressure posed by urban population (UP) has gained global attention thereby making it appropriate to represent population pressure. Economic growth Affluence is represented by income (YPC). According to Dietz and Rosa (1997) technology includes both machines for transforming input to output as well as the prevailing socio-economic conditions of a country. In this light, technology is denoted by industrialization (IND), mobile technology (MOT) and renewable energy (RE). Moreover, trade openness (TO) has been identified to be significant in modeling carbon dioxide emissions. By incorporating the above variables based on the objectives of the study and reflection of what prevails in Africa equation 1 is modified as:

$$CO_2 = a(UP)^{\lambda}(YPC)^{\gamma}(TO)^{\sigma}(REN)^{\delta}(IND)^{\beta}(MOP)(v) \tag{2}$$

where $a, \gamma, \lambda, \sigma, \delta, \beta$ *and* v are parameters to be estimated in addition to those already explained. Transforming equation 2 into natural logarithm for panel data gives:

$$LCO_{2it} = \upsilon + \gamma_1 LUB_{it} + \gamma_2 LYPC_{it} + \gamma_3 LTO_{it} + \gamma_4 LREN_{it} + \gamma_5 LIND_{it} + \gamma_6 LMOP_{it} + \vartheta_{it} + \varepsilon_{it} \quad (3)$$

where i and t denote the individual countries and time(year) dimension correspondingly; ϑ and ε represent the county effect and error term respectively, L is the symbol for natural logarithm; and the rest remains the same. As argued already, there is enough reasons to believe that renewable energy and mobile technology can moderate the effect of industrialization. To assess this claim, interactive terms between renewable energy and industrialization (*LREN x LIND*) as well one between mobile technology and industrialization (*LMOP x LIND*) are derived and included in the models separately to get:

$$LCO_{2it} = \upsilon + \gamma_1 LUB_{it} + \gamma_2 LYPC_{it} + \gamma_3 LTO_{it} + \gamma_4 LREN_{it} + \gamma_5 LIND_{it} + \gamma_6 LMOP_{it} + \theta_1 LREN_{it} \, x \, LIND_{it} + \vartheta_{it} + \varepsilon_{it}$$

$$LCO_{2it} = \upsilon + \gamma_1 LUB_{it} + \gamma_2 LYPC_{it} + \gamma_3 LTO_{it} + \gamma_4 LREN_{it} + \gamma_5 LIND_{it} + \gamma_6 LMOP_{it} + \theta_2 LMOP_{it} \, x \, LIND_{it} + \vartheta_{it} + \varepsilon_{it}$$

To assess the role of renewable and mobile technology in the nexus between industrialiazation and carbon dioxide emission the following interpretations are key:

If $\gamma_5 > 0$ *and* $\theta_1 > 0$ it implies industrial sectoral growth increases CO_2 emissions and it is reinforced by renewable energy.

If $\gamma_5 > 0$ *and* $\theta_1 < 0$ it implies industrial growth increases CO_2 emissions but the effect is reduced by renewable energy.

If $\gamma_5 < 0$ *and* $\theta_1 > 0$ it denotes industrial growth decreases CO_2 emissions and it is reversed by renewable energy.

If $\gamma_5 < 0$ *and* $\theta < \theta_1$ it denotes industrial growth decreases CO_2 emissions and it is reinforced by renewable energy.

If $\gamma_5 > 0$ *and* $\theta_2 > 0$ it implies industrial sectoral growth increases CO_2 emissions and it is reinforced by mobile technology.

If $\gamma_5 > 0$ *and* $\theta_2 < 0$ it implies industrial growth increases CO_2 emissions but the effect is reduced by mobile technology

If $\gamma_5 < 0$ *and* $\theta_2 > 0$ it denotes industrial growth decreases CO_2 emissions and it is reversed by mobile technology

If $\gamma_5 < 0$ *and* $\theta < \theta_2$ it denotes industrial growth decreases CO_2 emissions and it is reinforced by mobile technology.

3.2 Data Source and Description

This research falls on data from 32 African countries (see Table 1a) with enough data for the key variables over the 2002-2021 period. The World Bank's (2023) World Development Indicators is where the data were taken from. The measurement of each variable is reported in Table 1b. Table 2 shows the descriptive statistics and correlation of the variables to get an initial picture of the data used for the analysis.

Table 1a. List of countries used for the study

Countries		
Algeria Ghana Namibia Guinea Congo Rep Liberia Sierra-Leone Comoros Madagascar South Africa Tanzania	Angola Nigeria Benin Guinea. Bissau Senegal Cameroon Kenya Uganda Rwanda Botswana	Congo. DR Mauritania Tunisia Cote D'voire Mozambique Togo Egypt Mauritius Gambia Morocco Burkina Faso

Table 1b. Measurement of variables

Variable	Measurement
Carbon dioxide emissions	CO_2 metric tons per capita
renewable energy	Renewable energy consumption (% of total final energy consumption)
Industrialization	Industry (including construction), value added (% of GDP)
Urbanization	was measured as urban population (% total population)
Trade openness	Total Trade (% of GDP).
Mobile technology	Mobile cellular subscriptions
Income	GDP per capita

Table 2. Descriptive statistics and correlation analysis

Statistic							
	LCO_2	LYPC	LUB	LTO	LMOB	LIND	LREN
Mean	-0.758096	7.262415	3.681154	4.126803	15.35086	3.162797	3.695966
Median	-0.956484	7.158737	3.740321	4.089974	15.55347	3.191504	4.170300
Maximum	2.148572	9.301947	4.293045	5.055365	19.03366	4.192366	4.587719
Minimum	-3.483007	5.811188	2.748936	3.031221	7.150701	1.516429	-2.813411
Correlation							
	LCO_2	LYPC	LUB	LTO	LMOB	LIND	LREN
LCO_2	1.000000						
LYPC	0.929037	1.000000					
LUB	0.546538	0.403866	1.000000				
LTO	0.409139	0.364280	0.339248	1.000000			
LMOB	0.266107	0.254928	0.300054	-0.038724	1.000000		
LIND	0.416812	0.431994	0.265642	0.412625	0.271507	1.000000	
LREN	-0.716069	-0.630353	-0.445520	-0.193921	-0.272825	-0.287562	1.000000

3.3 Estimation Procedures

Panel data often exhibit cross dependency tendencies which affects the results generated when the appropriate techniques are not used. It is essential to examine the cross-sectional dependence of the variables before further analysis are done. The study relied on the Breusch-Pagan LM, Pesaran scaled LM and Pesaran CD tests to ascertain the cross sectional dependency of the variables. More so, the data may contain unit root (that is they may not be stationary) which can impair the results. As a result, the unit root condition of the series is examined. Unit root tests as proposed by Im, Pesaran, and Shin (2003), and Maddala and Wu (1999) are employed when there is no cross sectional dependency among the series while the Pesaran (2007) Panel Unit Root test (cross-sectionally augmented IPS, CIPS) is employed in the presence of cross sectional dependency among the variables. Next, the study assesses the long run relationship between carbon emission and the selected explanatory variables by employing the Pedroni and Westerlund cointgeration tests.

These cointegration tests hypothesizes that cointegration does not exist among the variables. A rejection of no cointegration implies there is long run relationship. To determine the impact of industrialization, renewable energy, mobile technology, urbanization and income on carbon emission the study relied on the fully modified ordinary least squares (FMOLS) approach panel data as proposed by Pedroni (2000). Reasons for using the FMOLS include the fact that it addresses the problem of endogeneity and serial correlation often associated with panel data which can generate inappropriate results (Pedroni 2000).

The panel FMOLS estimator is generally given by:

$$\hat{\beta}_{fmol} = \left[\sum_{i=1}^{N} \sum_{t=1}^{T} (x_{it} - \overline{x}_i)' \right]^{-1} \left[\sum_{i=1}^{N} (\sum_{t=1}^{T} (x_{it} - \overline{x}_i) \hat{y}_{it}^{+} + T \hat{\Delta}_{\varepsilon\mu}^{+} \right] \quad (5)$$

where $\hat{\Delta}_{\mu\varepsilon}^{+}$ is the serial correlation correction term and $\hat{y}_{it}^{+}$ is the transformed variable of y_{it} to achieve the endogeneity correction.

4. RESULTS

4.1 Cross-Sectional Dependence, Unit Root, and Cointegration

Results reported in Table 3a and Table 3b confirms the presence of cross sectional dependence among the variables for the series. This is not strange due to the fact that economic variables for countries have been closely interrelated due globalization and information technology. This evidence implies the study should should the CIPS test for the examination of the unit root property of the variables. The results shown in Table 4 indicates that at levels no single variable is found to be stationary. At first difference however, they are all found to be stationary meaning they are free from unit root. The implication is they can be used for analysis and the results generated can be reliable. Prior to embarking on regression analysis, cointegration test is performed. This is meant to examine the long run relationship among the variables. The study employed the Pedroni and Kao test. Per evidence from Table 5 all the test provide evidence of a long run relationship between carbon emissions on one side and the remaining variables on the other side. It suggests that in the long run, carbon emissions in Africa can be influenced by the level of industrialization, trade openness, urbanization, renewable energy, mobile technology and income.

Table 3a. Cross-sectional dependence of residuals results

Test	Statistic	Prob.
Breusch-Pagan LM	1829.825	0.0000
Pesaran scaled LM	44.75437	0.0000
Pesaran CD	4.943770	0.0000

Ho: No cross-section dependence

Table 3b. Cross sectional dependence of series results

Series	Breusch-Pagan LM	Pesaran Scaled LM	Bias-Corrected Scaled LM	Pesaran CD
LCO_2	3559.125***	97.2543***	96.3365***	43.700***
LUB	8817.741***	264.2156***	263.3734***	72.4653***
LYPC	55547.827***	160.3957***	159.5535***	61.044***
LMOP	8754.026***	262.1926***	261.355***	93.4883***
LREN	3866.250***	107.005***	106.115***	52.029***
LIND	2635.99***	67.9450***	67.1029***	67.1029***
LTO	1916.064***	47.5827***	46.7664***	12.8505***

*** denote 1% level of significance

Table 4. CIPS unit root test results

Series	At Levels	First Difference	Conclusion
LCO_2	-2.56	-4.02***	I(1)
LUB	-1.06	-2.61*	I(1)
LYPC	-2.09	-3.49***	I(1)
LMOP	-0.717	-3.47***	I(1)
LREN	-2.77	-3.88***	I(1)
LIND	-2.70	-3.42***	I(1)
LTO	-2.54	-4.05***	I(1)

*** and * denote 1% and 10% level of significance respectively

Table 5. Pedroni cointegration test for model

Pedroni Test Statistic Prob Weighted Statistic Prob.				
Alternative hypothesis: common AR coefs. (within-dimension)				
Panel v-Statistic	-2.544668	0.9945	-5.003972	1.0000
Panel rho-Statistic	4.901967	1.0000	5.007539	1.0000
Panel PP-Statistic	-6.326553	0.0000	-8.966865	0.0000
Panel ADF-Statistic	-2.059544	0.0197	-3.958278	0.0000
Alternative hypothesis: individual AR coefs. (between-dimension)				
	Statistic	**Prob.**		
Group rho-Statistic	6.772740	1.0000		
Group PP-Statistic	-18.00926	0.0000		
Group ADF-Statistic	-1.781310	0.0024		
Kao test	Statistic	Prob.		
ADF	-4.702020	0.0000		

4.2 Regression Analysis

Table 6 reports results for the direct effect of renewable energy and mobile technology together with other variables while in Table 7 the results focuses on the moderation effect of renewable energy and mobile technology on the industrial growth-carbon emission nexus. From both tables the results show that income, urbanization, trade openness and industrialization have positive effect on carbon emissions in Africa. On the other hand mobile technology and renewable reduces carbon emission directly. Indirectly, renewable energy helps to reduce the effect of industrial growth on carbon emissions while mobile adoption increases the carbon emission effect of industrial growth. The results reported in both tables render support to the assertion that the activities of the industry sector of the continent is detrimental to the environment in the form of increased CO_2 emissions. Explicitly, given the elasticity coefficients on the industry variable in both tables, a 1% expansion in African's industry sector is accompanied by a direct proportionate increase in CO_2 emissions by approximately 0.03-0.33% and the converse also holds.

It is also observed that 1% growth renewable energy usage is associated with about 0.23-34% direct reduction in carbon emissions while a 1% growth in mobile technology adoption lowers carbon emissions directly by 0.006-0.06%. The estimates also show that greater openness of the continent's economy to international trade exerts upward pressure on CO_2 emissions. Since trade openness comprise exports and imports, then greater trade openness contributing to increases in the level CO_2 emissions could be emanating from a rise in either one of these components or both. In particular, efforts that yield a 1% upsurge in trade openness also tend to contribute to a 0.23-0.43% increase in CO_2 emissions. The results further suggest that a rise in income translates into an increase in CO_2 emissions to the extent the latter rises by about 0.15-0.5% following 1% increase in the former. Urbanization is also found to contribute to increases in CO_2 emissions as 1% rise in the percentage of urban population relative to the total population is accompanied by about 1.04-1.08% surge in CO_2 emissions.

Regarding the moderation effect it is seen that renewable energy negatively moderates the effect of industrial growth on carbon emission. The adoption on renewable energy for industrial activities reduces emission from industrialization by 0.038%. On the other hand adoption of mobile technology for industrialization process increase emission effect of industrial growth by 0.01%

Table 6. FMOLS results with no interaction terms

Variable	Coefficient	Std. Error	t-Statistic	Prob.
LYPC	0.504896	0.022733	22.21019	0.0000
LUB	1.018488	0.034950	29.14165	0.0000
LTO	0.227047	0.009669	23.48313	0.0000
LMOP	-0.006539	0.002857	-2.288619	0.0225
LIND	0.034135	0.012273	2.781311	0.0056
LREN	-0.237294	0.012051	-19.69076	0.0000
Adj-R^2	**0.99**			

Table 7. FMOLS results of moderation analysis

	Model 1			Model 2		
Variable	Coefficient	Std. Error	t-Statistic	Coefficient	Std. Error	t-Statistic
LYPC	0.3927***	0.007449	52.72180	0.500***	0.007518	66.56728
LUB	1.0203***	0.000407	2507.733	1.0306***	0.000428	2408.989
LTO	0.5022***	0.001671	300.5406	0.4637***	0.001678	276.4269
LMOP	-0.0479***	0.000562	-84.92299	-0.0607***	0.000558	-108.8458
LIND	0.3395***	0.001352	251.1187	0.2649***	0.001276	207.7387
LREN	-0.4172***	0.001159	-360.6801	-0.3859***	0.001116	-345.9463
LMOP x LIND	0.0105***	0.000339	31.11309			
LREN x LIND				-0.0368***	0.000467	-78.93000
Adj-R^2	0.98			0.98		

***, means 1% level of significance

5. DISCUSSIONS

The overarching objective of the study is to evaluate the extent to which renewable energy consumption on the one hand and technology, in the form of mobile communication technology, on the other hand act to mitigate or moderate the theoretical adverse effects of industrial activities on CO_2 emission. The results of the study confirm that industrial activities, indeed, contribute to higher levels of CO_2 emission. This finding is not far from plausibility especially given that industrial activities in these countries, and even in the rest of Africa, rely heavily on fossil energy which is a notable contributor to CO_2 emission. Moreover, the manufacturing of pharmaceuticals, cement, plastics and other construction activities in most African economies also entail substantial consumption of diverse and several material and resources which can also contribute to CO_2 emission. Mining is also an active component of the industrial sector of these countries as some of them are quite endowed with notable mineral resources. Furthermore, in both direct and indirect ways, the activities of the mining subsector could also contribute to various emissions including CO_2. These findings are broadly consistent with Aboagye et al., (2020), Kwakwa et al. (2014), Wang et al (2013) and Zhang (2012).

In respect of renewable energy consumption, we find evidence that is theoretically unsurprising as it tends to reduce CO_2 emission. Renewable energy emanates from the sun, wind, water, waste, and heat from the Earth. Both the production and consumption of renewable are associated with no or little CO_2 emissions. Thus, when countries tend to increase the consumption of renewable energy CO_2 emissions consequently declines. This could be achieved when households shift towards the use of LPG, electricity, biogas and other clean/modern energy sources in meeting domestic fuel energy. Similar gains would be made when all other sectors of the economy increase their consumption of renewable energy relative to fossils. This suggests that even with the relatively less development state of renewable energy development in the continent, countries that consume more renewable energy stand to experience declines in CO_2 emissions (Kwakwa 2023; Gyamfi et al 2022). In line with the SDGs which was agreed upon by world leaders in 2015 many African countries have designed their own strategies and policies to promote renewable energy development. The finding suggests that should these strategies become successful it can cause a reduction in carbon emissions.

Mobile technology adoption also reduces CO_2 emissions as shown in the results. It has been espoused earlier that mobile technology facilitates ICT which in turn contributes to declines in CO_2 emission through research and development of energy-efficient technology, cheaper access to clean energy, dematerialization and digitization, online delivery, intelligent transport systems, transport and travel substitution, smart buildings, and smart grids (Musah et al., 2023; Simpson et al. 2019; Sadorsky 2014). In recent years, mobile technology adoption has increased in the continent with some countries making significant strides in ICT and its related components particularly digitization, online delivery, innovation among others. While crucial aspects of ICT such as research and development of energy-efficient technology, dematerialization intelligent transport systems, transport and travel substitution, smart buildings, and smart grids remain less developed in most African countries, adoption of mobile technology in particular has remained on the ascendancy (World Bank 2023). Besides, most countries on the continent are not directly involved in the manufacturing of mobile technology devices and thus are less likely to experience the underlying harsh environmentally adverse effects. Even though, we acknowledge the adverse effect of improper device disposal could be pervasive, putting everything together it appears the continent stands to gain environmentally with increased adoption of mobile technology in ways consistent with the results of the study and other studies (Raihan et al., 2022; Chatti and Majeed 2022; Fang 2023; Anochiwa 2022).

The results suggests that renewable energy consumption, in addition to reducing CO_2 emissions on its own, could also be deployed effectively to mitigate against the extent to which industry sector contributes to the upsurge in CO_2 emissions in the continent. The industrial sector, by its very nature, is highly energy intensive and given that renewable energy sources emit little to no greenhouse gas emissions, then it is not unreasonable that it is contributing to declines in CO_2 emissions in the era of mass industrial activities in the continent. This is very much consistent with many authors (Kwakwa 2021; Musah et al., 2023; Gyamfi et al., 2023) who argue that renewable energy have environmentally-friendly components and that a rise in their adoption/consumption can actually be expected to drive down the levels of CO_2 emissions. The negative moderation effect of renewable energy is also in line with Kwakwa (2023). However, mobile technology increases carbon emission effect of industrialization. Although innovation, efficiency and dematerialization can be achieved through ICT which is driven by mobile technology (Musah et al., 2023; Simpson et al. 2019; Sadorsky 2014) their adoption for industrial activities exacerbate the carbon emission generated from industrialization process. The outcome could be attributed to the fact that mobile technology helps to increase industrial output or industrial growth. However, because the industrial sector in Africa is energy intensive and efficient it will trigger carbon emissions to increase.

In the process, we also found evidence that that greater openness to trade in the selected African countries exerts upward pressure on CO_2 emissions. Most of these countries selected for the study, like the rest of Africa, have chunk of exports emanating largely from the extractive and agricultural sectors such as crude oil, mineral resources, timber, cocoa etc. Imports, on the other, are widely diversified including daily consumables, durables, automobiles, technology etc. The very nature of the export composition has the potential to contribute to an increase in CO_2 emission because agricultural, lumber activities as well as land preparation for the mining of mineral resources entail substantial forest loss which directly reduce the forest's carbon sequestration capacity. Beyond forest loss, there are supplementary activities associated with agriculture, lumbering and mining that could indirectly as well put upward pressure on CO_2 emissions in other indirect ways. Thus, the eventual detrimental effect of trade openness on CO_2 emission observed in the study suggests that the destructive effects of exports have outweighed the potential gains that may be accrued through its import composition. The results could also indicate that trade openness has created space for pollution haven hypothesis, a situation where lax trade regulation has allowed the location/relocation of environmentally-unfriendly production plants in these countries. This is particularly true as many of these countries and the larger continent do not enforce stringent trade regulations. Hence, with greater openness to trade coupled with weakly enforced trade-related environmental laws, a rise in CO_2 emissions could be a natural consequence. This finding suggests that Africa cannot remain on its current trade openness trajectory if it desires to contribute meaningfully to the global fight against CO_2 emissions, global warming and climate change otherwise. These findings are consistent with Mentel et al., (2022) for Sub-Saharan Africa economies; Balsalobre-Lorente et al., (2020) for BRICS economies; and Raheem et al., (2020) for G7 countries.

Similarly, in other results, the estimates also suggest CO_2 emission increases with income. This is quite plausible especially in the context of developing economies where higher income induces behavioural lifestyle at the household level towards consumption of modern gadgets such as air-conditioners, refrigerators, microwave ovens, vehicles etc. almost all of which rely extensively on energy. Thus, they result in higher energy consumption and since fossil energy dominates the energy basket of most of these countries, a rise in CO_2 emission is not unexpected. Kwakwa and Alhassan (2018) for instance observed that the higher income level enables households to afford high energy intensive gadgets which leads to higher carbon dioxide emissions. Gyamfi et al., 2018) also demonstrated how a single refrigerator could generate up to about 0.7 tons of CO2 emissions annually in Ghana. At the state level, an increase in income also affords economies to undertake more projects that require substantial capital outlays. Some of these projects are in response to the behavioural and lifestyle changes of citizens. For instance, more roads and extensive electrification projects are necessary to ensure use of automobiles and electrical equipment respectively. Information communication technology (ICT) infrastructure, factories, schools, hospitals are also imminent in the face of higher income. These do not only contribute to considerable forest loss but also increase material and energy use which could cause CO_2 emission levels to rise. It must be acknowledged that the literature highlights instances where increase in income could reduce CO_2 emission through household's behavioural changes (Aboagye 2017). In such instances, households with higher income begin to see environmental quality as a superior good and consequently demand for cleaner environment. They do not only shift consumption towards environmentally goods and energy-efficient gadgets but also exert pressure on authorities to enforce and promote environmental regulations capable of stimulating environmental quality. However, the evidence observed in this study suggests that this does not hold in the selected African countries. Perhaps, this environmental-friendly behavioural changes associated with increase in income is typical among developed countries than less developed countries. This is because in developing economies higher income may not even be enough to finance basic needs of life. Thus, it is not unreasonable not to expect significant consumption shifts towards energy-efficient technologies which are relatively expensive or citizens/households contributing financial resources, in the form of taxes, to enable government have enough revenue to enforce and promote environmental quality.

The harmful effect of urbanization on the level of CO_2 emission in the selected countries of the continent could be driven mainly by the structure and process of urbanization in these countries which also typifies most African countries. Undoubtedly, the process of urbanization in the continent is almost always a result of industrial expansion/booms and rural-urban migration. This often translates into rapid increase in demand for land for building factories, housing and other residential as well as constructing supporting socio-economic infrastructure (World Bank 2022) which frequently outweigh the usable land capacity of the urban centres. Consequently, non-negligible portions of forest have to be sacrificed to pave for these residential and socio-economic infrastructure. The activities of construction and industry imply substantial material and energy use which could contribute to CO2 emission. Moreover, urbanization in most of these countries is such that the underlying mass industrial activities are usually clustered in the same few urban cities. This is because these cities/towns, being manufacturing hubs, tend to have reliable power supply and ready market. This culminates into heavy traffic congestion creating situations where more fuel is burned which contributes indirectly to CO2 emissions. Sometimes, these urban centres struggle further with slum conditions and waste management problems. Again, this could lead indirectly to higher carbon dioxide emissions. Clearly, the combined effects of all these channels are a rise in carbon dioxide emissions. This is consistent with the evidence that cities are responsible for close to 70% of global CO2 emissions associated with energy consumption. The findings corroborate Musah et al., (2021) for West Africa and Aboagye (2017) for Sub-Saharan Africa. In particular, Aboagye (2017) found urbanization, alongside industrial expansion, to worsen several environmental quality indicators including CO2 emission.

The results further show that renewable energy negatively moderates the effect of industrialization on carbon emissions in Africa while mobile technology positively moderates the effect of industrialization on carbon emissions. This means that by adopting renewable energy industrialization can progress with a reduced impact on the environment. The outcome is reasonable given the fact that without energy (Aboagye 2017) industries will come to a halt. Relying on energy source that is environmentally unfriendly such as those from fossil fuel for industrial operations will lead to higher carbon emissions (Gyamfi et al., 2023). However, per their nature energy from environmentally friendly sources such as renewable energy can be utilized for economic activities with little or no emission effect. This therefore implies that industrial firms that have adopted renewable energy in Africa are polluting less than those relying on non-renewable source of energy. The evidence in this study is in line with the works of Kwakwa (2023) and Mentel et al., (2022). Tied to the SDG 7, in 2022, African leaders adopted the African Common Position on Energy Access and Just Energy Transition which aims at meeting the energy needs on the continent by relying on the renewable resources available. The reported results suggest that a successful implementation of this programme can help decarbonize activities of the industrial sector on the continent.

On the other hand, observing mobile technology exerting positive effect on the industrial-carbon emission nexus suggests that mobile technology may overall promote clean environment through means such as efficiency enhancement as well the promotion of research and development in an economy (Raheem et al. 2020). That notwithstanding mobile technology may harm the environment through the industrial sector. This does not mean that mobile technology is bad per se but rather its adoption is causing industries to contribute to carbon emission the more. The results can be explained that mobile technology might have enhanced the efficiency of industrial firms enabling them to produce more goods and expand. However, as industries grow through adoption of mobile technology they would have to rely on more energy for production. Since most industries in Africa rely on non-renewable source of energy it suggests that eventually, the mobile technology-induced-industrial growth will lead to the consumption of environmentally unfriendly energy. Consequently, carbon emissions will increase.

6. CONCLUSIONS AND POLICY RECOMMENDATIONS

Promoting development that meets the needs of the present generation without compromising the ability of future generations to meet their needs remains central to the global community. However, the continuous rise in the amount of environmental degradation, particularly CO_2 emissions, in recent decades raises important developmental concerns. These emissions have been attributed mainly to human activities that are directly linked with industrial activities. Yet, industrial expansion is at the core of the development agenda of many countries in Africa. Increasing activity in this sector without any simultaneous mitigating mechanisms would only lead to further resource depletion, fossil fuel overutilization and a rise in CO2 emissions. It is against these concerns that this study sets out to evaluate the extent to which mobile technology adoption and renewable energy consumption – two important aspects of the modern and digital – could serve as partial mitigation avenues.

Therefore, we employed a panel of 32 countries carefully and purposely selected from different economic and geographical blocs of the continent with data from 2002-2021. The study finds activities of industry sector in Africa to contribute to increases in CO_2 emissions. However, both mobile technology adoption and renewable energy consumption have beneficial individual effects on CO_2 emissions. Moreover, while renewable energy moderates the industrial growth to reduce CO_2 emissions, the opposite is observed for mobile technology. Given that renewable energy sources emit little to no greenhouse gas emissions, then it is not unreasonable that it contributes to declines in CO_2 emissions even in the era of environmentally-unfriendly industrial activities in the continent. In other results, the study further observed that greater openness to international trade, rising urbanization and increased income/economic growth in these countries are additional ways by which atmospheric CO2 emissions are generated in the continent.

The results of this study reveal that one of the most direct ways for African economies to achieve their nationally determined contributions (NDC) in respect of CO_2 emission is to reduce industrial activities. This suggestion is however economically unrealistic and inconsistent with the continent's growth and development agenda as industrial expansion remains pivotal. Thus, policies capable of moderating the environmentally destructive aspects of industrial activities could enable the continent achieve a twin objective of sustainable development and sustainable environment. In this regard, policies that promote the use of renewable energy in industrial activities is key. We suggest that, for maximum impact, renewable energy consumption should be promoted beyond the industry sector. Perhaps, a broader economy-wide renewable energy consumption should be the ultimate of policy. The household sector should be included in such framework because a switch from its heavy reliance on biomass consumption to renewable energy consumption to add to the continent's overall renewable energy basket and invariably contribute to CO_2 emission reductions. This is certainly incumbent on policy to create the enabling environment that supports substantial private sector investment in renewable energy development. Some of the possible pathways to incentivize private sector participation in such electrification projects include independent power production schemes. Again, the private sector could be involved in the setting up of off-grid solutions provided that these are profitable, and they can charge market-based prices. The model prescribed by the African Development Bank for Nigeria could also be adapted by other countries in the continent. Specifically, with support from the African Development Bank (AfDB) and other partners, the Nigerian Electrification Project (NEP) is extending clean, safe, reliable and affordable electricity through renewable power sources to unserved and underserved communities in the country including but not limited to households and industries. This could be bolstered further with carbon-neutral industrial policy and enforcement of energy efficiency standards and promotion of saving technology standards. South Africa has adopted a carbon tax regime as a pragmatic way of promoting carbon-neutral industrial activities. The official carbon tax rate was set at R120 (or about \$7) per ton of CO_2e initially and increased to R134 (or about \$8) by the end of 2022 (IMF 2023). Ghana and Nigeria among others are also targeting about 20-30% energy efficiency improvement in industrial facilities (IEA 2022; EPA and MESTI 2021). These are commendable policy initiatives that ought to be implemented by other African countries in ways compatible with their unique sustainable development agenda to avert rising CO_2 emission emanating from industrial expansion.

The fact that mobile technology reduces carbon emission directly but positively moderates the effect on industrial suggests that there is the tendency for economies to benefit from mobile technology for environmental gains if well deployed. It is suggested that promoting energy efficiency in the industrial sector can cause the industrial sector in Africa to benefit from mobile technology for its growth while promoting a cleaner environment. Just as Ghana (EPA and MESTI 2021) and Nigeria (IEA 2022) following COP 26 have resolved to increase energy efficiency within the industrial sector, other countries in Africa should follow suit. Also, environmental policies for the industrial sector related to mobile technology adoption should be developed to ensure that mobile adoption by industries does not generate negative environmental outcomes in Africa. Consequently, it is highly recommended that countries in Africa reduce taxes on mobile technology devices, accessories and services to incentivize mass adoption and consumption. Although in 2018 Uganda, for instance, imposed a daily levy of UGX 200 (USD 0.05) in respect of using some ICT services, public outcry led to its abandonment. However, a new digital services tax of 12% tax on internet data for non-resident companies in Uganda has been proposed effective the financial year 2023 – 2024 (Gillwald et al., 2019). While these may be an innovative domestic revenue mobilization scheme it is likely to reduce the intensity of mobile technology adoption/use and thus must be reconsidered by the country and should be discouraged elsewhere.

The paper was limited by data availability for which reason the paper used the period 2002-2021 for the analysis for 32 African countries. Unavailability of data on different types of renewable energy and components of industrial sector did not allow for analysis of disaggregated effect. To unearth more insight, it is suggested that future studies in the instance where data is available should look at the effect of the various forms of renewable energy on carbon emissions. The moderation effect of mobile technology and renewable energy for the various sub sectors of the industrial sector can also be considered in the future.

REFERENCES

Aboagye, S. (2017). Economic Expansion and Environmental Sustainability Nexus in Ghana. *African Development Review*, *29*(2), 155–168. doi:10.1111/1467-8268.12247

Acheampong, A. O., Adams, S., & Boateng, E. (2019). Do globalization and renewable energy contribute to carbon emissions mitigation in Sub-Saharan Africa? *The Science of the Total Environment*, *677*, 436–446. doi:10.1016/j.scitotenv.2019.04.353 PMID:31059886

Adams, S., & Acheampong, A. O. (2019). Reducing carbon emissions: The role of renewable energy and democracy. *Journal of Cleaner Production*, *240*, 118245. doi:10.1016/j.jclepro.2019.118245

Adom, P. K., Kwakwa, P. A., & Amankwaa, A. (2018). The long-run effects of economic, demographic, and political indices on actual and potential CO2 emissions. *Journal of Environmental Management*, *218*, 516–526. doi:10.1016/j.jenvman.2018.04.090 PMID:29709820

African Development Bank. (2018). Nigeria Electrification Project: Appraisal Report, PESR/ PERN/ RDNG November 2018. Abidjan: Cote d'Ivoire.

Afriyie, D., Wang, Z., Hu, S., Ampofo, G. K. M., & Asante, D. A. (2023). Exploring the dynamic nexus between urbanization and industrialization with carbon emissions in sub-Saharan Africa: Evidence from panel PMG-ARDL estimation. *Environmental Science and Pollution Research International*, *30*(3), 6373–6389. doi:10.100711356-022-22597-6 PMID:35997879

Altinoz, B., & Dogan, E. (2021). How renewable energy consumption and natural resource abundance impact environmental degradation? New findings and policy implications from quantile approach. *Energy Sources B Energy Econ. Plann.*, *1–12*, 301–302. https://doi.org/. doi:10.1080/15567249.2021.1885527

Altinoz, B., Vasbieva, D., & Kalugina, O. (2021). The effect of information and communication technologies and total factor productivity on CO2 emissions in top 10 emerging market economies. *Environmental Science and Pollution Research International*, *28*(45), 63784–63793. doi:10.100711356-020-11630-1 PMID:33201509

Amri, F. (2018). Carbon dioxide emissions, total factor productivity, ICT, trade, financial development, and energy consumption: Testing environmental Kuznets curve hypothesis for Tunisia. *Environmental Science and Pollution Research International*, *25*(33), 33691–33701. doi:10.100711356-018-3331-1 PMID:30276690

Anochiwa, L. I., Agbanike, T. F., Chukwu, A. B., Ikpe, M., & Otta, N. N. (2022). Urbanization and carbon emissions: Looking at the role of mobile phone adoption in Sub-Saharan African countries. *Environmental Science and Pollution Research International*, *29*(52), 78526–78541. doi:10.100711356-022-20994-5 PMID:35697981

Appiah, K., Du, J., Yeboah, M., & Appiah, R. (2019). Causal relationship between industrialization, energy intensity, economic growth and carbon dioxide emissions: Recent evidence from Uganda. *International Journal of Energy Economics and Policy*, *9*(2), 237.

Asongu, S. A., Le Roux, S., & Biekpe, N. (2018). Enhancing ICT for environmental sustainability in sub-Saharan Africa. *Technological Forecasting and Social Change, 127*, 209–216. doi:10.1016/j.techfore.2017.09.022

Balsalobre-Lorente, D., Driha, O. M., Bekun, F. V., & Osundina, O. A. (2019). Do agricultural activities induce carbon emissions? The BRICS experience. *Environmental Science and Pollution Research International, 26*(24), 25218–25234. doi:10.100711356-019-05737-3 PMID:31256399

Chatti, W. (2020). Information and communication technologies, road freight transport, and environmental sustainability. *Environment and Ecology, 11*(1), 124.

Chatti, W., & Majeed, M. T. (2022). Information communication technology (ICT), smart urbanization, and environmental quality: Evidence from a panel of developing and developed economies. *Journal of Cleaner Production, 366*, 132925. doi:10.1016/j.jclepro.2022.132925

Cheng, C., Ren, X., Dong, K., Dong, X., & Wang, Z. (2021). How does technological innovation mitigate CO2 emissions in OECD countries? Heterogeneous analysis using panel quantile regression. *Journal of Environmental Management, 280*, 111818. doi:10.1016/j.jenvman.2020.111818 PMID:33360390

Danish, K., Khan, N., Baloch, M. A., Saud, S., & Fatima, T. (2018). The effect of ICT on CO2 emissions in emerging economies: Does the level of income matters? *Environmental Science and Pollution Research International, 25*(23), 22850–22860. doi:10.100711356-018-2379-2 PMID:29855885

Dietz, T., & Rosa, E. A. (1997). Effects of population and affluence on CO2 emissions. *Proceedings of the National Academy of Sciences of the United States of America, 94*(1), 175–179. doi:10.1073/pnas.94.1.175 PMID:8990181

Ehigiamusoe, K. U., & Dogan, E. (2022). The role of interaction effect between renewable energy consumption and real income in carbon emissions: Evidence from low-income countries. *Renewable & Sustainable Energy Reviews, 154*, 111883. doi:10.1016/j.rser.2021.111883

Ehigiamusoe, K. U., Shahbaz, M., & Vo, X. V. (2023). How does globalization influence the impact of tourism on carbon emissions and ecological footprint? Evidence from African countries. *Journal of Travel Research, 62*(5), 1010–1032. doi:10.1177/00472875221113886

Elliott, J. R., & Clement, M. T. (2014). Urbanization and carbon emissions: A nationwide study of local countervailing effects in the United States. *Social Science Quarterly, 95*(3), 795–816. doi:10.1111squ.12079

Emir, F., Philip, L. D., & Sertoglu, K. (2022). Assessing the influence of urbanization and energy on carbon emissions of Turkey: Evidence using the new RALS analysis. *Environmental Science and Pollution Research International, 29*(38), 57905–57917. doi:10.100711356-022-19953-x PMID:35355189

Energy Capital Power. (2021a). *Renewable energy projects in West Africa*. Retrieved from https://energycapitalpower.com/top-5-innovative-renewable-energy-projects-in-west-africa/

Fang, Z. (2023). Assessing the impact of renewable energy investment, green technology innovation, and industrialization on sustainable development: A case study of China. *Renewable Energy, 205*, 772–782. doi:10.1016/j.renene.2023.01.014

Gillwald, A., Mothobi, A., Ndiwalana, A., & Tusubira, T. (2019). *The state of ICT in Uganda. Policy Paper Series No. 5 After Access: Paper No. 8*. International Development Research Centre.

Gwynne, R. N. (2009). *Modernization theory*. Elsevier.

Gyamfi, B. A., Onifade, S. T., & Ofori, E. K. (2023). Synthesizing the impacts of information and communication technology advancement and educational developments on environmental sustainability: A comparative analyses of three economic blocs—BRICS, MINT, and G7 economies. *Sustainable Development (Bradford)*, *31*(2), 744–759. doi:10.1002d.2416

Gyamfi, S., Diawuo, F. A., Kumi, E. N., Sika, F., & Modjinou, M. (2018). The energy efficiency situation in Ghana. *Renewable & Sustainable Energy Reviews*, *82*, 1415–1423. doi:10.1016/j.rser.2017.05.007

Haftu, G. G. (2019). Information communications technology and economic growth in Sub-Saharan Africa: A panel data approach. *Telecommunications Policy*, *43*(1), 88–99. doi:10.1016/j.telpol.2018.03.010

Hussain, M. M., Pal, S., & Villanthenkodath, M. A. (2023). Towards sustainable development: The impact of transport infrastructure expenditure on the ecological footprint in India. *Innovation and Green Development*, *2*(2), 100037. doi:10.1016/j.igd.2023.100037

Hussain, M. N., Li, Z., & Sattar, A. (2022). Effects of urbanization and nonrenewable energy on carbon emission in Africa. *Environmental Science and Pollution Research International*, *29*(17), 1–15. doi:10.100711356-021-17738-2 PMID:34837625

Idowu, A., Ohikhuare, O. M., & Chowdhury, M. A. (2023). Does industrialization trigger carbon emissions through energy consumption? Evidence from OPEC countries and high industrialised countries. *Quantitative Finance and Economics*, *7*(1), 165–186. doi:10.3934/QFE.2023009

IEA. (2021). *Key world Energy Statistics*. https://www.iea.org/reports/key-world-energy-statistics-2021/final-consumption

International Energy Agency. (2018). *World Energy Outlook 2018*. International Energy Agency.

Jahanger, A., Zaman, U., Hossain, M. R., & Awan, A. (2023). Articulating CO2 emissions limiting roles of nuclear energy and ICT under the EKC hypothesis: An application of non-parametric MMQR approach. *Geoscience Frontiers*, *14*(5), 101589. doi:10.1016/j.gsf.2023.101589

Keramidas, K., Tchung-Ming, S., Diaz-Vazquez, A. R., Weitzel, M., Vandyck, T., Després, J., Schmitz, A., Rey Los Santos, L., Wojtowicz, K., Schade, B., Saveyn, B., Soria-Ramirez, A. (2018). *Global energy and climate outlook 2018: Sectoral mitigation options towards a low-emissions economy*. JRC Science for Policy Report (No. JRC113446)

Khan, K., & Su, C. W. (2021). Urbanization and carbon emissions: A panel threshold analysis. *Environmental Science and Pollution Research International*, *28*(20), 26073–26081. doi:10.100711356-021-12443-6 PMID:33481196

Khan, S., & Majeed, M. T. (2023). Toward economic growth without emissions growth: The role of urbanization & industrialization in Pakistan. *Journal of Environmental Studies and Sciences*, *13*(1), 43–58. doi:10.100713412-022-00797-3 PMID:36118988

Kirikkaleli, D., Güngör, H., & Adebayo, T. S. (2022). Consumption-based carbon emissions, renewable energy consumption, financial development and economic growth in Chile. *Business Strategy and the Environment*, *31*(3), 1123–1137. doi:10.1002/bse.2945

Kleemann, L., & Abdulai, A. (2013). The impact of Trade and Economic Growth on the Environment: Revisiting the Cross-Country Evidence. *Journal of International Development*, *25*(2), 180–205. doi:10.1002/jid.1789

Kwakwa, P. A. (2020). The long-run effects of energy use, urbanization and financial development on carbon dioxide emissions. *International Journal of Energy Sector Management*, *14*(6), 1405–1424. doi:10.1108/IJESM-01-2020-0013

Kwakwa, P. A. (2022). The effect of industrialization, militarization, and government expenditure on carbon dioxide emissions in Ghana. *Environmental Science and Pollution Research International*, *29*(56), 85229–85242. doi:10.100711356-022-21187-w PMID:35794324

Kwakwa, P. A. (2023). Sectoral growth and carbon dioxide emission in Africa: Can renewable energy mitigate the effect? *Research in Globalization*, *6*, 100130. doi:10.1016/j.resglo.2023.100130

Kwakwa, P. A. (2023b). Climate change mitigation role of renewable energy consumption: Does institutional quality matter in the case of reducing Africa's carbon dioxide emissions? *Journal of Environmental Management*, *342*, 118234. doi:10.1016/j.jenvman.2023.118234 PMID:37327731

Li, Y., Alharthi, M., Ahmad, I., Hanif, I., & Hassan, M. U. (2022). Nexus between renewable energy, natural resources and carbon emissions under the shadow of transboundary trade relationship from South East Asian economies. *Energy Strategy Reviews*, *41*, 100855. doi:10.1016/j.esr.2022.100855

Lv, Q., Liu, H., Yang, D., & Liu, H. (2019). Effects of urbanization on freight transport carbon emissions in China: Common characteristics and regional disparity. *Journal of Cleaner Production*, *211*, 481–489. doi:10.1016/j.jclepro.2018.11.182

Lv, T., Hu, H., Zhang, X., Wang, L., & Fu, S. (2022). Impact of multidimensional urbanization on carbon emissions in an ecological civilization experimental area of China. *Physics and Chemistry of the Earth Parts A/B/C*, *126*, 103120. doi:10.1016/j.pce.2022.103120

Majeed, M. T., & Tauqir, A. (2020). Effects of urbanization, industrialization, economic growth, energy consumption, financial development on carbon emissions: An extended STIRPAT model for heterogeneous income groups. *Pakistan Journal of Commerce and Social Sciences*, *14*(3), 652–681.

Malmodin, J., & Lundén, D. (2018). The Energy and Carbon Footprint of the Global ICT and E&M Sectors 2010–2015. *Sustainability (Basel)*, *10*(9), 3027. doi:10.3390u10093027

Mehmood, U. (2021). Transport energy consumption and carbon emissions: The role of urbanization towards environment in SAARC region. *Integrated Environmental Assessment and Management*, *17*(6), 1286–1292. doi:10.1002/ieam.4463 PMID:34009742

Mentel, U., Wolanin, E., Eshov, M., & Salahodjaev, R. (2022). Industrialization and CO2 emissions in Sub-Saharan Africa: The mitigating role of renewable electricity. *Energies*, *15*(3), 946. doi:10.3390/en15030946

Moore, T., Horne, R., Gleeson, B. J., & de Haan, F. (2018). *Urban sustainability transitions*. Springer Nature Singapore. doi:10.1007/978-981-10-4792-3

Njoh, A. J. (2021). Renewable energy as a determinant of inter-country differentials in CO2 emissions in Africa. *Renewable Energy*, *172*, 1225–1232. doi:10.1016/j.renene.2021.03.096

Oliver Stoner, O., Lewis, J., Martínez, I. L., Gumy, S., Economou, T., & Adair-Rohani, H. (2021). Household cooking fuel estimates at global and country level for 1990 to 2030. *Nature Communications*, *12*(1), 5793. doi:10.103841467-021-26036-x PMID:34608147

Park, Y., Meng, F., & Baloch, M. A. (2018). The effect of ICT, financial development, growth, and trade openness on CO2 emissions: An empirical analysis. *Environmental Science and Pollution Research International*, *25*(30), 30708–30719. doi:10.100711356-018-3108-6 PMID:30178410

Raghutla, C., & Chittedi, K. R. (2020). Financial development, energy consumption, technology, urbanization, economic output and carbon emissions nexus in BRICS countries: An empirical analysis. *Management of Environmental Quality*, *32*(2), 290–307. doi:10.1108/MEQ-02-2020-0035

Raheem, I., Tiwari, A., & Balsalobre-Lorente, D. (2020). *The role of ICT and financial development in CO2 emissions and economic growth* (No. 105605). https:// mpra. ub. uni- muenc hen. de/ 105605/1/ MPRA_ paper_ 105605. Pdf

Raheem, I. D., Tiwari, A. K., & Balsalobre-Lorente, D. (2020). The role of ICT and financial development in CO2 emissions and economic growth. *Environmental Science and Pollution Research International*, *27*(2), 1912–1922. doi:10.100711356-019-06590-0 PMID:31760620

Raihan, A. (2023). The dynamic nexus between economic growth, renewable energy use, urbanization, industrialization, tourism, agricultural productivity, forest area, and carbon dioxide emissions in the Philippines. *Energy Nexus*, *9*, 100180. doi:10.1016/j.nexus.2023.100180

Raihan, A., Muhtasim, D. A., Farhana, S., Pavel, M. I., Faruk, O., Rahman, M., & Mahmood, A. (2022). Nexus between carbon emissions, economic growth, renewable energy use, urbanization, industrialization, technological innovation, and forest area towards achieving environmental sustainability in Bangladesh. *Energy and Climate Change*, *3*, 100080. doi:10.1016/j.egycc.2022.100080

Sarkodie, S. A., & Adams, S. (2018). Renewable energy, nuclear energy, and environmental pollution: Accounting for political institutional quality in South Africa. *The Science of the Total Environment*, *643*, 1590–1601. doi:10.1016/j.scitotenv.2018.06.320 PMID:30189575

Sarwar, S., & Alsaggaf, M. I. (2019). Role of urbanization and urban income in carbon emissions: Regional analysis of China. *Applied Ecology and Environmental Research*, *17*(10), 303–310. doi:10.15666/aeer/1705_1030310311

Schwab, K. (2017). *The Fourth Industrial Revolution*. Currency.

Shabani, D. Z., & Shahnazi, R. (2019). Energy consumption, carbon dioxide emissions, information and communications technology, and gross domestic product in Iranian economic sectors: A panel causality analysis. *Energy*, *169*, 1064–1078. doi:10.1016/j.energy.2018.11.062

Shahbaz, M., Raghutla, C., Song, M., Zameer, H., & Jiao, Z. (2020). Public-private partnerships investment in energy as new determinant of CO2 emissions: The role of technological innovations in China. *Energy Economics*, *86*, 104664. doi:10.1016/j.eneco.2020.104664

Sheraz, M., Deyi, X., Mumtaz, M. Z., & Ullah, A. (2022). Exploring the dynamic relationship between financial development, renewable energy, and carbon emissions: A new evidence from belt and road countries. *Environmental Science and Pollution Research International*, *29*(10), 14930–14947. doi:10.100711356-021-16641-0 PMID:34623587

Sheraz, M., Deyi, X., Sinha, A., Mumtaz, M. Z., & Fatima, N. (2022). The dynamic nexus among financial development, renewable energy and carbon emissions: Moderating roles of globalization and institutional quality across BRI countries. *Journal of Cleaner Production*, *343*, 130995. doi:10.1016/j.jclepro.2022.130995

Sun, Y., Li, H., Andlib, Z., & Genie, M. G. (2022). How do renewable energy and urbanization cause carbon emissions? Evidence from advanced panel estimation techniques. *Renewable Energy*, *185*, 996–1005. doi:10.1016/j.renene.2021.12.112

Tan, F., Yang, S., & Niu, Z. (2022). The impact of urbanization on carbon emissions: Both from heterogeneity and mechanism test. *Environment, Development and Sustainability*, 1–17.

Tang, Y., Zhu, H., & Yang, J. (2022). The asymmetric effects of economic growth, urbanization and deindustrialization on carbon emissions: Evidence from China. *Energy Reports*, *8*, 513–521. doi:10.1016/j.egyr.2022.05.076

Ulucak, R., Danish, K., & Khan, S. (2020). Does information and communication technology affect CO2 mitigation under the pathway of sustainable development during the mode of globalization? *Sustainable Development (Bradford)*, *28*(4), 857–867. doi:10.1002d.2041

United Nations. (2012). *Secretary-General to Global Development Center: 'Energy is the Golden Thread' Connecting Economic Growth, Social Equity, Environmental Sustainability*. Retrieved from https://www.un.org/press/en/2012/sgsm14242.doc.htm

Usman, A., Ozturk, I., Hassan, A., Zafar, S. M., & Ullah, S. (2021). The effect of ICT on energy consumption and economic growth in South Asian economies: An empirical analysis. *Telematics and Informatics*, *58*, 101537. doi:10.1016/j.tele.2020.101537

Usman, M., & Radulescu, M. (2022). Examining the role of nuclear and renewable energy in reducing carbon footprint: Does the role of technological innovation really create some difference? *The Science of the Total Environment*, *841*, 156662. doi:10.1016/j.scitotenv.2022.156662 PMID:35718170

World Bank. (2019). *Nigeria - North-West Geo-Political Zone: Energy Access Diagnostic Report Based on the Multi-Tier Framework*. World Bank.

York, R., & Rosa, E. A. (2003). Key challenges to ecological modernization theory: Institutional efficacy, case study evidence, units of analysis, and the pace of eco-efficiency. *Organization & Environment*, *16*(3), 273–288. doi:10.1177/1086026603256299

Yu, S., Hu, X., Li, L., & Chen, H. (2020). Does the development of renewable energy promote carbon reduction? Evidence from Chinese provinces. *Journal of Environmental Management*, *268*, 110634. doi:10.1016/j.jenvman.2020.110634 PMID:32389898

Zhang, C., & Chen, P. (2021). Industrialization, urbanization, and carbon emission efficiency of Yangtze River Economic Belt—Empirical analysis based on stochastic frontier model. *Environmental Science and Pollution Research International*, *28*(47), 66914–66929. doi:10.100711356-021-15309-z PMID:34236609

Zhang, C., & Liu, C. (2015). The impact of ICT industry on CO2 emissions: A regional analysis in China. *Renewable & Sustainable Energy Reviews*, *44*, 12–19. doi:10.1016/j.rser.2014.12.011

Zhang, N., Yu, K., & Chen, Z. (2017). How does urbanization affect carbon dioxide emissions? A cross-country panel data analysis. *Energy Policy*, *107*, 678–687. doi:10.1016/j.enpol.2017.03.072

Zheng, H., Song, M., & Shen, Z. (2021). The evolution of renewable energy and its impact on carbon reduction in China. *Energy*, *237*, 121639. doi:10.1016/j.energy.2021.121639

ENDNOTE

1 Even though not all clean energy sources are necessarily renewable and hence green, the study uses clean energy, green energy, and renewable energy interchangeably to convey a similar notion of renewable energy.

Chapter 7
A Causality Analysis of Economic Growth and Primary Energy Supply in Türkiye's Economy

Fatma Dila Taşdemir
https://orcid.org/0000-0001-8440-7200
Independent Researcher, Turkey

ABSTRACT

Energy is an important input for economic growth and development of countries. The concepts of energy and economic growth have been prominent topics for economics literature and policy makers for many years. In this note, the existence and the direction of causality between primary energy supply (PES) and gross domestic products (GDP) for Türkiye's economy is examined using data for the period 1970-2021. The variables are subjected to augmented Dickey-Fuller and Phillips-Perron unit root tests, and then the Toda-Yamamoto causality test is performed to determine the direction of causality. Based on the causality test, bidirectional causality is observed between the primary energy supply variable and the GDP variable.

INTRODUCTION

Energy has been an indispensable part of human life by using it in different ways for different purposes from the primitive ages to the present day. Technological developments that make life easier for people inevitably increase energy consumption (briefly EC). With the events such as the industrial revolutions, the second world war and oil shocks, the effect of energy on society and economy has gradually increased and clean energy technologies additionally gained importance during the third and the fourth industrial revolutions (Okur Dinçsoy, 2020). The use of energy, which is one of the important needs of life and humanity, as an input in production increases the importance of energy in terms of economic growth. Countries make great efforts to avoid events that will hinder their economic development. In

DOI: 10.4018/979-8-3693-0400-6.ch007

order for countries to grow and develop economically, they must increase their production levels in a way that does not disrupt their foreign trade balance (Kazaz & Dinçsoy, 2019). With the increase in production, EC will also increase and it will be an essential input to the energy production process (Yanar & Kerimoğlu, 2011).

Although macroeconomic stability is an indispensable part of a sustainable economic growth, it is directly or indirectly affected by several internal and external progresses (Dinçsoy & Okur Dinçsoy, 2020). Energy is also an important civilization tool and is a critical factor that provides information about the development levels of countries around the world. The fact that the production costs of countries with energy resources decreases significantly makes energy a strategic product. Therefore, countries aim to increase energy production regionally and globally and to become a regional trade center in energy. Factors such as reducing foreign dependency in energy, increasing the use of national resources, increasing the rate of renewable energy sources (briefly RES) in the local energy mix are among the strategies developed by countries in order to contribute to their economies (MFA, 2023).

The unequal distribution of energy in the world, scarcity of energy, environmental pollution and the need for new energy sources have necessitated some developments in the system of economic thought. In addition to these, increasing environmental problems have increased the importance of RES, which are a sustainable energy source in the world. RES are important in terms of preventing environmental pollution caused by carbon emissions and meeting the increasing energy need (Karamıklı & Şaşmaz, 2021). Renewable energy source is defined as "the energy source that can be available the next day in the evolution of nature itself" (Republic of Türkiye Ministry of Foreign Affairs, 2023). The most important feature of RES is that they are environmentally friendly by reducing carbon dioxide emissions. In addition, the fact that it reduces foreign dependency in energy due to its domestic nature increases the importance that should be given to RES. Wind energy, wood, geothermal energy, hydrogen energy, biomass energy, hydroelectric energy, wave energy and solar are among the RES. Being clean and sustainable means that RES have low carbon emissions, and that they are produced in harmony with the environment without harming the natural balance of the world, leaving a clean world for future generations (Republic of Türkiye Ministry of Foreign Affairs, 2023).

It is needed to ascend the importance given to RES in order to use energy resources effectively, to descent of energy costs in the economy and to protect the environment. Increasing the allocation of RES in EC and reducing energy import dependency constitute an important part of energy policies. Some of the policies that countries should implement in order to minimize sustainable growth and environmental problems are as follows: Supporting RES, increasing domestic production, diversification of energy sources, increasing and promoting production facilities based on RES, subsidies to investments made by the private sector in this area and/or introduction of applications such as low-interest loans (Republic of Türkiye Ministry of Foreign Affairs, 2023).

Energy, along with many different economic indicators, has been studied by many authors. In this study, it is aimed to provide a broader perspective on the concept of energy by using the concept of energy export, energy import, energy production, international bunkers and stock changes, which are all evaluated together and defined as primary energy supply by the OECD.

LITERATURE

Some important studies in the literature on energy are mentioned below. Kraft and Kraft (1978), who first explored the relationship between energy and GDP variables, found that a causal relationship from GDP to EC by analyzing data from the US economy for the period 1947-1974. Lise and Montfort (2007) analyzed the existence of causality between EC and GDP in Türkiye by analyzing data from 1970 to 2003. Based on applied tests, it has been seen that the GDP and EC data are cointegrated. In Türkiye's economy, a unidirectional causality running from GDP to EC has been identified and it has been argued that energy expenditures will increase as the economy grows. In addition, it has been claimed that the restriction in energy expenditures will not negatively affect economic growth. Mucuk and Uysal (2009), who investigated the existence of causality between EC and GDP by analyzing data from 1960 to 2006, used cointegration and Granger causality test in their studies. Based on the applied tests, it was concluded that the variables discussed were cointegrated. In addition, by determining the causality from EC to GDP, it has been stated that EC positively impacts GDP.

Tsani (2010) examined the relationship between aggregated and disaggregated EC levels and GDP variables using the Toda-Yamamoto causality analysis in his study using the Greek economy data for the period 1960-2006. Based on the tests, a causal relationship from total EC to real GDP was seen.

Yanar and Kerimoğlu (2011) examined the relationship between the variables of GDP, current account deficit and EC for the Türkiye economy using the 1975-2009 period data. According to the tests results, they found a strong causality from EC to GDP. As a result of the applied Johansen cointegration test, a long-term relationship was found between the variables considered. In addition to these, it has been argued that the ascent in EC will ascend GDP. Akpolat and Altıntaş (2013) examined the relationship between energy expenditures and real GDP by using cointegration test and causality analysis in their study for the Türkiye economy using the 1961-2010 period data. According to the applied tests, a long-term relationship was found between the variables discussed and bidirectional causality was determined between the two variables. Romano and Scandurra (2013) examined the relationship between real GDP and EC for the Italian economy using yearly data for the period 1980-2007. According to the applied tests, bidirectional causality was detected between the variables discussed in both the short term and the long term. Another study examining the existence of causality between EC and GDP for Türkiye's economy was carried out by Topallı and Alagöz (2014). In the study, the period of 1970-2009 was discussed and one-way causality was determined from real gross domestic product to electricity consumption. It has been argued that with the growth of economy in the country, EC, especially electricity consumption, will increase and it has been argued that consumers will consume more energy with a higher income level.

Usta (2016) examined the effects of regional EC on GDP in Türkiye's economy using the panel regression analysis method based on the 2004-2011 period data and the level two regions of the Statistical Regional Units Classification. A positive relationship was found between total electricity consumption and added value in all Level 2 regions covering 26 regions. It has been obtained that a 1% increase in total electricity consumption will increase the added value by approximately 0.38%. According to the applied tests, it has been determined that regional EC will positively affect economic growth. Fizaine and Court (2016) examined the relationship between energy expenditure, unemployment rate, capital formation and population rate variables for the US economy for the period 1850-2012. It has been stated that more than 11% of the GDP in the US economy is allocated to energy expenditures and the sudden increase in energy expenditures affects economic growth negatively. Demirgil and Birol (2020) examined the existence of causality between renewable energy consumption (briefly REC) and GDP for Türkiye's economy between 1980 and 2018 years. ARDL bounds test and Toda-Yamamoto causality analyzes were applied in the study. According to the tests results, it has been determined that a 1% growth in REC will increase GDP by 0.91%. Moreover, a unidirectional causal relationship was observed from REC to GDP.

Zhao and his co-authors (2021) used a multivariate linear regression model in their study for the Chinese economy, using the 1987-2015 period. According to the tests results, it has been obtained that the rate of energy expenditures in economic growth should not exceed 45.44% in order to achieve an average economic growth of over 5% in the 2030s. Magazzino et al. (2022) aimed to present a more environmentally friendly approach to energy by addressing the variables of CO2 emissions, GDP and renewable energy use. In this study, which examines the Scandinavian countries using the 1990-2018 period data, it is claimed that reducing CO2 emissions by increasing the use of renewable energy will support GDP and energy efficiency. It has been argued that the way to achieve sustainable economic growth is to make renewable energy investments by reducing greenhouse gas emissions. In addition, no causality running from REC to GDP has been found. It has been determined that the ascent in REC descend carbon dioxide emissions and there is a bidirectional causality relationship between these variables. Tran et al. (2022) used the threshold regression model to examine the relationship between GDP and EC by using the data of 26 OECD member countries for the period 1971-2014. When real GDP per capita is below $48170, a unidirectional causality running from electricity consumption to GDP is detected in the short and long term, when it exceeds this figure; It has been determined that causality relationship cannot be determined in the short run, but GDP is the cause of electricity consumption in the long run. According to the applied tests, it has been claimed that energy saving policies should be used in order to maintain sustainable growth when economic development exceeds a certain level. Bello and Ch'ng (2022) analyzed the energy intensity convergence of economic growth for the West African economy using the 1988-2019 period data and found that economic growth converged for most of the West African countries. Claiming that coping with the climate crisis and producing a clean environment is through REC, Su et al. (2022) investigated the effects of social, economic and demographic variables on per capita REC. The threshold panel regression model was used in this study, in which the data of 116 countries were used for the period 2000-2014. It has been determined that the change in the level of urbanization significantly encourages REC when it exceeds the threshold value. It has been observed that the increase in the level of industrialization negatively affects the per capita REC, but this effect decreases when the threshold value is exceeded. Examining the dependence of economic growth on the level of EC, Komarova et al. (2022) used the data of the last 30 years for 77 countries. In the study, which argued that there is a relationship between EC and gdp, it was determined that economic growth in non-OECD countries was dependent on EC. It has been determined that energy efficiency is higher in OECD member countries compared to developing countries. It has been determined that 44.8% of the world's EC is realized by Asia Pacific countries, 21.1% by North America, 14.7% by Europe, 6.5% by the Middle East and 2.3% by African countries. On the other hand, when the per capita EC is analyzed, it was seen that Singapore, South Korea and Australia have the highest consumption amount. When the regions are ranked in terms of energy efficiency, it is seen that Europe is the leading region, followed by Central and South America, North America and the Asia Pacific region. Dealing with the 1971-2014 period of the Thai economy, Bunnag (2023) used VECM and ARDL models in his study where he used CO2 emissions, foreign direct investments, EC and economic growth variables. As a result of the analyzes, no cointegration relationship was detected between the variables discussed. In addition, as a result of the Granger causality tests applied, bidirectional causality was found between EC and economic growth in the short run. In addition, unidirectional causality has been determined from CO_2 emissions to EC and from foreign direct investments to EC. Claiming that there is a feedback effect between economic growth and EC, Sadiq et al. (2023) used data from South Asian countries for the period 1972-2019. As a result of the Granger causality test, they determined that economic growth is the cause of CO_2 emissions. When the literature review is evaluated, it is seen that; While energy is the cause of economic growth in some studies, economic growth has been the cause of energy in some studies. In some studies, bidirectional causality was found. Although there is no clear consensus on the direction of causality, it is an undeniable fact that energy is an input of production and has a structural link with other sectors. When all this information is evaluated together; The issue of energy is of great importance for economists and policy makers.

DATA AND METHODOLOGY

In this study, the relationship between economic growth and energy in Türkiye was investigated. The relationship between the variables in question was examined using annual data for the period 1970-2021. The variables used in the analysis were obtained from the OECD database. Gross Domestic Product data from the OECD (2023) official website has been used for economic growth. Primary Energy Supply data from the OECD (2023) official website was used for energy. Table 1 contains the notations of the variables used in the paper, the definitions of the variables, and the source of the datasets of the variables.

Table 1. Variables used in analyzes

Notations	Variables	Period	Information About Variables	Sources
gdp	Gross Domestic Producs (Total, Million US dollars)	1970-2021	*"Gross domestic product (GDP) is the standard measure of the value added created through the production of goods and services in a country during a certain period."*	(OECD, 2023)
pes	Primary Energy Supply (Total, Million US dollars)	1970-2021	*"Primary energy supply is defined as energy production plus energy imports, minus energy exports, minus international bunkers, then plus or minus stock changes."*	(OECD, 2023)

In this study, first of all, the stationarities of the series are examined by using the time series method. To achieve this objective, series undergoes ADF and PP unit root tests. Then, the direction of causality is determined by performing the Toda-Yamamoto causality test to our series.

Unit Root Test

The stationarity of the time series is of great importance in econometric analysis. Non-stationary series do not have a long-term mean, their variance and covariance do not remain constant over time (Gujarati & Porter, 2018). Working with non-stationary series may cause a spurious regression problem (Granger & Newbold, 1974). For this reason, in the study, firstly, the stationarity of the series will be analyzed.

Extended Dickey-Fuller (1979) and Phillips Perron (1988) analysis are performed to investigate the stationarity of the series under consideration. The hypotheses of these tests are as follows:

H_0: Series contain unit root. (that is, the series are not stationary.)
H_1: Series do not contain unit root. (that is, the series are stationary.)

While applying the unit root test, intercept, trend and intercept and none models are compared for the series and the most suitable one is preferred for the series. The results obtained as a result of the tests applied are shown in the tables below:

Table 2. Unit root test results for GDP

Augmented Dickey-Fuller Test I(0)				**Phillips–Perron Test I(0)**		
		t-statistic	**Prob.***		**Adj. t-statistic**	**Prob.***
ADF Test statistics		0.854012	0.9997	PP Test statistics	-0.622469	0.4428
Test critical values	1% level	-4.180911		1% level	-2.611094	
	5% level	-3.515523		5% level	-1.947381	
	10% level	-3.188259		10% level	-1.612725	
Augmented Dickey-Fuller Test I(1)				Phillips–Perron Test I(1)		
		t-statistic	Prob.*		Adj. t-statistic	Prob.*
ADF Test statistics		-5.859830	0.0001	PP Test statistics	-17.15083	0.0000
Test critical values	1% level	-4.180911		1% level	-3.568308	
	5% level	-3.515523		5% level	-2.921175	
	10% level	-3.188259		10% level	-2.598551	
*MacKinnon (1996) one-sided p-values						

Table 3. Unit root test results for PES

Augmented Dickey-Fuller Test I(0)				**Phillips–Perron Test I(0)**		
		t-Statistic	**Prob.***		**Adj. t-Statistic**	**Prob.***
ADF Test statistics		-0.752418	0.3854	PP Test statistics	-1.250006	0.1916
Test critical values	1% level	-2.612033		1% level	-2.611094	
	5% level	-1.947520		5% level	-1.947381	
	10% level	-1.612650		10% level	-1.612725	
Augmented Dickey-Fuller Test I(1)				Phillips–Perron Test I(1)		
		t-statistic	Prob.*		Adj. t-statistic	Prob.*
ADF Test statistics		-12.54337	0.0000	PP Test statistics	-15.25347	0.0000
Test critical values	1% level	-2.612033		1% level	-2.612033	
	5% level	-1.947520		5% level	-1.947520	
	10% level	-1.612650		10% level	-1.612650	
*MacKinnon (1996) one-sided p-values						

When Tables 2 and 3 are examined, it is seen that the series in question are not stationary at the level, but become stationary at the first difference. We will denote appropriate lag lenghth by k and maximum degree of integration by d_{max}. It is seen that $d_{max}=1$, and then we look at selection criterias to determine k. Obtained results are given in Table 4.

Table 4. Determination of the optimal lag length

Lag	LogL	Likelihood Ratio	Final Prediction Error	Akaike Information Criterion	Schwarz Information Criterion	Hannan-Quinn Information Criterion
0	-924.5000	NA	2.00e+14	38.60417	38.68213	38.63363
1	-911.1773	24.98003	1.36e+14	38.21572	38.44962	38.30411
2	-905.6654	9.875495	1.27e+14	38.15272	38.54256	38.30004
3	-892.0469	23.26495*	8.56e+13	37.75195	38.29772*	37.95820*
4	-886.9130	8.342537	8.20e+13*	37.70471*	38.40641	37.96988

* demonstrates lag order selected by the criterion

By the Table 4, it is evident that the optimal lag length for the model is k=4 considering the Akaike information criterion.

Although the causality test developed by Toda and Yamamoto (1995) is based on the Granger causality test, even if the series are not stationary, the test can be applied without taking the differences of the series. Toda-Yamamoto causality test, which is based on the Vector Autoregressive (VAR) model, neglects the cointegrated state of the series, allowing causality to be determined even if the series under consideration are not integrated at the same degree (even if one is I(0) and the other is I(1)). In other words, with the Toda-Yamamoto causality test, the VAR model is constructed by using the level values of the series, regardless of the degree of integration of the series. The created VAR model is modified by considering $k+d_{max}$. Seemingly Unrelated Regression method is applied to the model formed after modify, as suggested in Toda-Yamamoto (1995). Obtained Wald test results are given in Table 5.

Table 5. Toda-Yamamoto causality (modified Wald) test results

Direction of Causality	Test Statistics	Value	$k+d_{max}$	Prob.
gdp ⇒ pes	Chi-square	11.16592	5	0.0482
pes ⇒ gdp	Chi-square	11.82890	5	0.0372

As can be seen from Table 5, there is a causal relationship from primary energy supply to GDP and from GDP to primary energy supply. In other words, a change in the primary energy supply will cause a change in gdp, and vice versa.

CONCLUSION

With the development of technology, energy has become the main factor of economic and social life. The gradual growth of the mechanization and industrial sector has increased the energy needs of countries. For a country to grow and develop economically, it needs to produce more. In order to produce more, the energy used as input in production must be consumed more.

There are many papers in the literature investigating the relationship between energy and GDP. In this paper, it is aimed to present a wider perspective to the concept of energy by evaluating all the variables of energy export, energy import, energy production, international bunkers under the name of energy.

In this article, the relationship between energy and economic growth is examined by analyzing data from 1970 to 2021 yearly data for the Türkiye economy. For the energy concept, the concept of primary energy supply, which we obtained from the OECD database, is used for the economic growth, and the concept of GDP is used. As a result of the analyzes, it is seen that the level values in the two series are not stationary, but they become stationary when the first difference is taken. After the unit root tests, the VAR model is established, the optimal lag length is determined, and Toda-Yamamoto causality test is performed.

Based on the performed tests, it is seen that there was bidirectional causality between the variables discussed. It has been seen that the increase in the energy item will increase the growth, and similarly, the increase in the growth will increase the energy. In this direction, it is clear that policy makers need to produce effective policies on energy in order to achieve their economic growth and development goals in a sustainable way.

REFERENCES

Akpolat, A. G., & Altıntaş, N. (2013). Enerji tüketimi ile reel GSYH arasındaki eşbütünleşme ve nedensellik ilişkisi: 1961-2010 dönemi [Cointegration and casuality relation between energy consumption and real GDP: 1961-2010 period]. *Bilgi Ekonomisi ve Yönetimi Dergisi, 8*(2), 115-127.

Bello, M. O., & Ch'ng, K. S. (2022). Convergence in energy intensity of GDP: Evidence from West African countries. *Energy*, *254*, 1–10. doi:10.1016/j.energy.2022.124217

Bunnag, T. (2023). Analyzing Short-run and Long-run Causality Relationship among CO2 Emission, Energy Consumption, GDP, Square of GDP, and Foreign Direct Investment in Environmental Kuznets Curve for Thailand. *International Journal of Energy Economics and Policy*, *13*(2), 341–348. doi:10.32479/ijeep.14088

Demirgil, B., & Birol, Y. E. (2020). Yenilenebilir enerji tüketimi ve ekonomik büyüme ilişkisi: Türkiye için bir Toda-Yamamoto nedensellik analizi [The relationship of energy consumption and economic growth: A TodaYamamoto causality analysis for Turkey]. *Cumhuriyet Üniversitesi İktisadi ve İdari Bilimler Fakültesi Dergisi, 21*(1), 68-83.

Dickey, D. A., & Fuller, W. A. (1979). Distribution of the estimators for autoregressive time series with a unit root. *Journal of the American Statistical Association*, *74*(366), 427–431. doi:10.2307/2286348

Dinçsoy, E. E., & Okur Dinçsoy, M. (2020). Ekonomik Büyümenin Enflasyon Üzerine Etkisinin Türkiye Ekonomisi Açısından Analizi. *Balkan ve Yakın Doğu Sosyal Bilimler Dergisi*, *6*, 118–124.

Fizaine, F., & Court, V. (2016). Energy expenditure,economic growth,and the minimum EROI of society. *Energy Policy*, *95*, 172–186. doi:10.1016/j.enpol.2016.04.039

Granger, C. W., & Newbold, P. (1974). Spurious Regressions in Econometrics. *Journal of Econometrics*, *2*(2), 111–120. doi:10.1016/0304-4076(74)90034-7

Gujarati, D. N., & Porter, D. C. (2018). Temel Ekonometri [Basic Econometrics]. İstanbul: Literatür Yayıncılık.

Karamıklı, A., & Şaşmaz, M. Ü. (2021). Türkiye'de Yenilenebilir Enerji Tüketiminin Ekonomik Büyüme ve Sağlık Harcamaları Üzerindeki Etkisi. *Pamukkale Üniversitesi Sosyal Bilimler Enstitüsü Dergisi*, (46), 293–304.

Kazaz, İ., & Dinçsoy, E. E. (2019). Sermaye Yatırımları, İthalat ve İhracat Değişkenleri Arasındaki İlişkinin Ekonometrik Analizi: Kosova Ekonomisi Üzerine Örnek Çalışma. *Sosyal Bilimler Araştırma Dergisi*, *8*(3), 179–190.

Komarova, A., Filimonova, I., & Kartashevich, A. (2022). *Energy consumption of the countries in the context of economic development and energy transition. TMREES22-Fr.* Energy Reports.

Kraft, J., & Kraft, A. (1978). On the relationship between energy and GNP. *Journal of the Energy Division*, *3*, 401–403.

Lise, W., & Montfort, K. V. (2007). Energy consumption and GDP in Turkey: Is there a co-integration relationship? *Energy Economics*, *29*(6), 1166–1178. doi:10.1016/j.eneco.2006.08.010

Magazzino, C., Toma, P., Fusco, G., Valente, D., & Petrosillo, I. (2022). Renewable energy consumption, environmental degradation and economic growth: The greener the richer? *Ecological Indicators*, *139*, 1–12. doi:10.1016/j.ecolind.2022.108912

Ministry of Foreign Affairs of the Republic of Türkiye. (2023). *Türkiye's International Energy Strategy*. https://www.mfa.gov.tr/turkiye_nin-enerji-stratejisi.tr.mfa

Mucuk, M., & Uysal, D. (2009). Türkiye ekonomisinde enerji tüketimi ve ekonomik büyüme [Energy consumption and economic growth in Turkish economy]. *Maliye Dergisi*, (157), 105-114.

OECD. (2023a). *Gross domestic product (GDP) (indicator)*. doi:10.1787/dc2f7aec-en

OECD. (2023b). *Primary energy supply (indicator)*. doi:10.1787/1b33c15a-en

Okur Dinçsoy, M. (2020). *Accounting, Finance, Sustainability, Governance & Fraud: Theory and Application* (Vol. I). Springer., doi:10.1007/978-981-32-9588-9

Phillips, P. C., & Perron, P. (1988). Testing for a unit root in time series regression. *Biometrika*, *75*(2), 335–346. doi:10.1093/biomet/75.2.335

Republic of Türkiye Ministry of Foreign Affairs. (2023). https://www.mfa.gov.tr/yenilenebilir-enerji-kaynaklari.tr.mfa#:~:text=Yenilenebilir%20enerji%20kaynaklar%C4%B1n%C4%B1n%20en%20b%C3%BCy%C3%BCk,yayg%C4%B1n%20ve%20g%C3%BC%C3%A7l%C3%BC%20destek%20almalar%C4%B1d%C4%B1r

Romano, A. A., & Scandurra, G. (2013). *Energy consumption–gross domestic product causal relationship in the Italian regions. In Classification and Data Mining*. Springer Berlin Heidelberg.

Sadiq, M., Kannaiah, D., Khan, G. Y., Shabbir, M. S., Bilal, K., & Zamir, A. (2023). Does sustainable environmental agenda matter? The role of globalization toward energy consumption, economic growth, and carbon dioxide emissions in South Asian countries. *Environment, Development and Sustainability, 25*(1), 76–95. doi:10.100710668-021-02043-2

Su, M., Wang, Q., Li, R., & Wang, L. (2022). Per capita renewable energy consumption in 116 countries: The effects of urbanization, industrialization, GDP, aging, and trade openness. *Energy, 254*, 1–18. doi:10.1016/j.energy.2022.124289

Toda, H. Y., & Yamamoto, T. (1995). Statistical inference in vector autoregressions with possibly integrated processes. *Journal of Econometrics, 66*(1-2), 225–250. doi:10.1016/0304-4076(94)01616-8

Topallı, N., & Alagöz, M. (2014). Energy consumption and economic growth In Turkey: An empirical analysis. Selçuk Üniversitesi Sosyal Bilimler Enstitüsü Dergisi, (32), 151-159.

Tran, B.-L., Chen, C.-C., & Tseng, W.-C. (2022). Causality between energy consumption and economic growth in the presence of GDP threshold effect: Evidence from OECD countries. *Energy, 251*, 1–12. doi:10.1016/j.energy.2022.123902

Tsani, S. Z. (2010). Energy consumption and economic growth: A causality analysis for Greece. *Energy Economics, 32*(3), 582–590. doi:10.1016/j.eneco.2009.09.007

Usta, C. (2016). Türkiye'de enerji tüketimi ekonomik büyüme ilişkisinin bölgesel analizi [Regional analysis of relationship between energy consumption and economic growth in Turkey]. *Uluslararası Ekonomi ve Yenilik Dergisi, 2*(2), 181-201.

Yanar, R., & Kerimoğlu, G. (2011). Türkiye'de enerji tüketimi, ekonomik büyüme ve cari açık ilişkisi [Energy consumption, economic growth and current account deficit relations in Turkey]. *Ekonomi Bilimleri Dergisi, 3*(2), 191-201.

Zhao, K., Feng, J., & Feng, L. (2021). Analysis of the long-term impact of energy expenditure on economic growth: A case study of China. *Biophysical Economics and Sustainability, 6*(11), 2–16. doi:10.100741247-021-00094-7

Chapter 8
The Relationship Between CO_2 Emissions, Renewable Energy, GDP, and Oil Prices in Türkiye

Adjera Alitoska Kazaz
https://orcid.org/0009-0005-8544-4368
Trakya University, Turkey

Davut Kazaz
Trakya University, Turkey

ABSTRACT

This study aims to examine the long-run causal relationship between CO_2 emissions, renewable energy consumption, GDP growth, and oil prices in Türkiye. The study covers the period 1990-2020. Toda-Yamamoto's causality test is used to avoid some of the problems faced by Granger's causality test. Furthermore, the study also utilizes variance decomposition and impulse-response function methods. The Toda-Yamamoto causality test indicates a two-way causal relationship between renewable energy and economic growth and between renewable energy and oil prices. The study revealed an undeniable and evident causality relationship in only one direction, from economic growth towards CO_2 emissions and oil prices. Also, a unidirectional causal relationship between CO_2 emissions and both oil prices and renewable energy was found. In order to achieve sustainable development and protect the environment, Türkiye requires renewable energy. Solar, wind, and hydropower can lessen the dependency on fossil fuels, generate employment opportunities and stimulate economic progress.

1. INTRODUCTION

As a fundamental component in the evolution of humanity, energy is an essential component. The energy demand is constantly increasing as society progresses and the population grows. However, energy resources are limited, at risk of depletion shortly, and growing environmental problems have led economies to continuously reduce energy consumption and save energy (Özbek & Naimoğlu, 2021).

DOI: 10.4018/979-8-3693-0400-6.ch008

Energy plays a crucial role in manufacturing, and its sustainability is paramount. The literature widely discusses the relationship between energy resources, production, and the environment. Therefore, it is necessary to efficiently use energy, considering the risks of depletion and environmental impacts, as energy resources are limited despite the ever-increasing population and needs (Ağır et al., 2020).

Renewable energy provides excellent potential for increasing energy efficiency. Particularly in developing countries and also at the global level, renewable energy sources have an essential role to play in ensuring energy independence, reducing environmental impacts, and generating economic opportunities. Increased use of renewable energy, combined with energy conservation and efficiency measures, contributes to the effective management of energy systems and steps towards a sustainable energy future. In this way, renewable energy can help achieve targets such as reducing energy bills, lowering CO_2 emissions, and improving the environment's quality (Ağır et al., 2020).

As energy-intensive activities have increased over the past century, both developed, and developing countries have faced two major challenges. First, we are in danger of running out of easily accessible energy resources (oil, natural gas, coal, etc.). Second, the environmental impacts of these activities lead to problems such as greenhouse gas emissions and climate change (Okur Dincsoy, 2016). The future sustainability of energy supplies is, therefore of concern. Secondly, there is the problem of the emission of gases (CO_2, methane, etc.) that are the cause of global warming. By creating a greenhouse effect and adversely affecting the world's climate, these gases cause environmental problems. These problems increase the search for sustainable and environmentally friendly innovations in the energy sector (Apergis & Danuletiu, 2014).

Although the limited energy resources based on fossil fuels do not cause an energy crisis for the time being, there is a risk that these resources will be depleted in the future. It is crucial to further research and develop alternative energy sources due to the accumulation of greenhouse gases, such as carbon dioxide, in the atmosphere causing global warming and climate change. This situation has emerged as a problem that needs to be addressed along with factors such as economic growth, increasing energy demand, and environmental pollution (Keleş & Hamamcı, 2002; Evrendilek & Ertekin, 2003; IEA, 2009).

Volatile oil prices, rising energy costs, climate change due to excessive use of fossil fuels, and unchecked GHG emissions have all contributed to rising environmental awareness in communities. This situation highlights the need for more efficient and sustainable management of energy systems. With increasing environmental sensitivity, the shift towards energy efficiency and renewable energy sources is seen as an important step towards a cleaner and healthier environment in the future. In addition, the goal of leaving a cleaner environment for future generations is brought to the forefront through the efficient use of energy. It is well known that non-renewable energy sources (fossil fuels) are more responsible for environmental pollution than renewable energy sources. Therefore, the choice of the type of energy is of great importance. This situation emerges as a factor that both increases the cost and decreases the quality of life in the economy of many countries (Özbek & Naimoğlu, 2021b; Emodi et al., 2015; Rexhäuser & Löschel, 2015).

Renewable energy sources refer to energy derived from sources such as solar, wind, geothermal, and biomass. These sources are clean, reliable, and inexhaustible, which is why they are rapidly expanding on a global scale. Renewable energy sources reduce CO_2 emissions, increase employment, and provide energy security. They also decrease dependence on foreign energy sources and improve trade balance, making renewable energy increasingly important (Korkmaz & Develi, 2012; Lund, 2009).

Renewable energy is crucial for countries heavily reliant on foreign energy. It promotes domestic energy production, decreases import, and reduces balance of payments deficits. Additionally, it lowers energy costs and encourages eco-friendly production processes.

Türkiye has undergone significant changes since 1980, particularly in terms of its connection to the modern World focusing on hydroelectric power plants by the development projects (Dinçsoy & Ichiminami, 2006). However, this has come at a cost, as the country has become increasingly reliant on fossil fuels such as oil, natural gas, and coal. This dependence on imported energy is a serious concern, as it undermines the balance of payments and reduces the competitiveness of goods and services. To address this issue, Türkiye must take proactive steps to harness renewable energy resources, such as solar, wind, and geothermal power. By doing so, the country can increase its energy security and reduce its external dependence while also achieving significant savings in energy consumption and costs. Additionally, a focus on improving energy efficiency will be crucial in achieving these goals and ensuring a sustainable future for Türkiye (Ayman et al., 2007). Policy makers recently introduced the National Energy Efficiency Action Plan, which successfully improved energy efficiency except for the COVID-19 period (Senalp, 2021).

Current oil production of Türkiye is insufficient to meet the country's increasing energy demand. Although the oil demand is soaring, the limited production capacity makes it difficult for the country to keep up. Therefore, it is essential for Türkiye to shift its focus towards renewable energy sources like solar, wind, and geothermal power. These resources are not only easy to produce but also have a lower carbon footprint, provide sustainable energy, and do not deplete over time. Türkiye has a variety of renewable energy sources at its disposal, including hydropower, wind, solar, geothermal, biomass, and wave energy. By actively utilizing these resources, Türkiye can reduce its energy dependency and play a significant role in creating an environmentally friendly energy sector. By doing so, Türkiye can ensure energy security and contribute to global efforts towards climate change mitigation (Pamir, 2003).

In this context, our study investigates the interplay between CO_2 emissions, renewable energy consumption, GDP growth, and oil prices in Türkiye from 1990 to 2020. To achieve this goal, we employ the Toda-Yamamoto approach to analyze the causal relationship among these variables. In addition to discussing the methodology, our paper provides an overview of the relevant literature and presents the data set used for our analysis. Lastly, we report the findings of our study, which shed light on the complex relationship between these critical factors in the Turkish economy.

2. LITERATURE REVIEW

Nowadays, the study of environmental factors and energy production has become a complex and high-priority issue in the international arena. Analyzing the factors of energy production in-depth is crucial for establishing sustainable energy systems and devising environmental protection strategies for the future. Therefore, numerous studies in academic literature aim to comprehend the varied variables that affect energy production and the dynamic relationships among them. These studies aim to analyze the complex interactions among energy production, environmental impact, and economic growth using various methodologies and analytical approaches. In this context, the relevant studies are given below.

Bamati & Raoofi (2020), in their study of energy production determinants, cover the period 1990-2015 using Least Squares (LSS). The findings show that economic, financial, environmental, and technological factors affect renewable energy production. In contrast, per capita income and oil prices positively affect renewable energy production, while CO_2 emissions decrease the effect in developed nations. Similarly, Şimşek & Yiğit (2017) investigated the relationship among carbon dioxide emissions, renewable energy consumption, oil price, urbanization, and GDP per capita in real terms in the BRIC (Brazil, Russia, India, and China) countries. Using panel VAR analysis methods, the study covers the period 1990-2015. The findings reveal a one-way causal relation between the GDP - carbon dioxide emissions, oil prices, renewable energy, and urbanization.

Öcal and Aslan (2013) investigated the causal relationship between renewable energy consumption and economic growth in Türkiye from 1990 to 2010. The results indicated a unidirectional causality from economic growth to renewable energy consumption, suggesting that renewable energy consumption negatively affects economic growth. Can (2017) examined the relationship between renewable energy production and output for Türkiye for the period 1960-2013 using VAR analysis, he concluded that the increase in energy consumption caused an increase in the demand for renewable energy, and the increase in renewable energy production did not have a statistically significant effect on GDP. Durğun & Durğun (2018) examined the relationship between energy consumption and GDP per capita. In the study, which covered the period 1980-2015, ARDL bounds test and the Toda-Yamamoto causality test were used. In contrast to Ocal and Aslan (2013), the results indicate unidirectional causality from renewable energy consumption to growth. On the other hand, Karaaslan and Çamkaya (2022), who obtained results similar to those of Öcal and Aslan (2013), examined the impact of economic growth, health expenditures, and renewable/nonrenewable energy consumption on Turkish CO_2 emissions from 1980-2016. To analyze the long-run and short-run effects, the ARDL method was used, and to analyze the relationships between the variables, the Toda-Yamamoto causality test was used. The study found that CO_2 emissions increase with GDP and non-renewable energy consumption, while they decrease with healthcare expenditure and renewable energy consumption in the long term. For the short term, only the GDP and renewable energy consumption are related to increased carbon dioxide emissions. According to the findings of the Toda-Yamamoto test, there is a one-way causality between GDP, health expenditure, renewable and non-renewable energy use, and emissions of CO_2.

Emir and Bekun (2018) analyzed the relationship between energy intensity, CO_2 emissions, renewable energy consumption, and economic growth in Romania from 1990 to 2014. The study applied the ARDL model for cointegration analysis and the Toda-Yamamoto model for causality analysis. The findings suggest a two-way relationship between energy intensity and economic growth, while renewable energy consumption has a one-way impact on economic growth. Similar to Emir & Bekun (2018) research, Khan (2013) analyzed the relationship between economic growth, CO_2 emissions, and energy consumption in Bangladesh from 1965-2007. Results show that energy consumption and economic growth have a bi-directional causality, while CO_2 emissions only have a unidirectional relationship with economic growth. In another study, Sulaiman et al. (2014) investigated the relationship among energy consumption, CO_2 emissions, and economic growth in Nigeria from 1970 to 2010. The research revealed a unidirectional causality from energy consumption to carbon dioxide emissions and from carbon dioxide emissions to growth, also a two-way causality among GDP growth and energy consumption. Morelli and Mele (2020) conducted a study on Vietnam's GDP per capita, CO_2 emissions, and energy consumption from 1970 to 2014. In contrast to Sulaiman et al. (2014), their findings suggest a one-way causal relationship to energy consumption from economic growth.

Magazzino (2014) analyzed Italy's energy consumption, CO_2 emissions, and economic growth from 1970-2006. The study found no cointegrating relationship between the three variables. However, bi-directional causality exists from CO_2 emissions to both economic growth and energy consumption, as indicated by the Toda and Yamamoto Granger causality test. Jebli and Kahia (2020) analyzed data from 65 countries between 1980 and 2014 to investigate the relationship between CO_2 emissions, growth, energy production, and value-added services. Similar to Magazzino (2014), the study highlighted the importance of renewable energy as CO_2 emissions have a two-way causal relationship with energy consumption, growth, and value-added services in both the short and long term. Also, the results support the existence of an environmental Kuznets curve. The study concludes that an effective policy for reducing greenhouse gas emissions would promote renewable energy and reduce the use of fossil fuels.

Sahoo & Sahoo (2020) analyzed the relationship between CO_2 emissions, non-renewable and renewable energy consumption in India using disaggregated data from 1985-2018. The study utilized the Toda-Yamamoto Granger causality test to determine the causality directions of the variables. The long-term findings show that hydropower consumption has a positive but insignificant impact on CO_2 emissions. Meanwhile, nuclear energy consumption has a negative impact on CO_2 emissions. Additionally, non-renewable energy consumption has a positive and significant effect on CO_2 emissions. Similar to Sahoo & Sahoo (2020) research, Udemba et al. (2021) investigated the relationship among CO_2 emissions, energy intensity, and economic growth in India from 1975 to 2017. The study employed Toda-Yamamoto and ARDL analyses and included variables like energy consumption and trade openness. Findings indicate a long-run equilibrium relationship and a significant negative correlation among economic growth and CO_2 emissions. Furthermore, there is a one-way causal relationship between energy consumption and income growth.

Bozkurt and Okumuş (2015) analyzed the relationship between CO_2 emissions, economic growth, energy consumption, trade openness, and population density variables in Türkiye from 1966 to 2011 to test the Environmental Kuznets Curve (EKC) hypothesis. Their findings indicate a positive correlation between economic growth and CO_2 emissions. Similar to Bozkurt and Okumuş (2015), Gokmenoglu & Taspinar (2015) analyzed the EKC hypothesis in Türkiye during the 1974-2010 period. They used variables such as CO_2 emissions, energy consumption, economic growth, and FDI. The Toda-Yamamoto causality test results suggest two-way causality between CO_2 emissions and FDI, energy consumption, and CO_2 emissions. Furthermore, economic growth and energy consumption are one-way causally related. The findings support the existence of the scale effect and the validity of the EKC for Türkiye. Furthermore, Adebayo & Akinsola (2021) examined the link between CO_2 emissions, economic growth, and energy consumption in Thailand from 1971 to 2018. They discovered that economic growth has an impact on Thailand's CO_2 emissions at varying frequencies. Furthermore, they found that CO_2 emissions and energy consumption have a mutual causal relationship, which is positive in both the short and long term. Using ARDL bounds test and Toda-Yamamoto analysis, Can & Korkmaz (2019) examined the relationship between renewable energy and economic growth in Bulgaria from 1990 to 2016. The findings indicate that economic growth is driven by renewable energy consumption and renewable electricity generation, with no long-term relationships between the variables.

3. DATA AND METHODOLOGY

This study analyzes the causal relationship between Tükiye's CO_2 emissions, renewable energy consumption, Gross Domestic Product (GDP) growth, and oil prices. Most of the current energy production is based on fossil fuels. As a result, fluctuations in oil prices can have a significant impact on the cost of energy. To explain energy prices, our model includes the price of oil, the main source of fossil fuels. The study covers the period 1990-2020, utilizing data sourced from the Organization for Economic Cooperation and Development (OECD) and World Development Indicators (WDI) databases.

To contend with complex multivariate interactions, the study implements the Toda-Yamamoto approach. This approach represents a favorable option, particularly for analyses utilizing time series data. It is also utilized to test for Granger causality and determine the direction of the causal relationship between variables.

Additionally, the Toda-Yamamoto approach is well-suited for discerning the dynamic interactions between variables. The primary aim of this study is to comprehend the fluctuations of factors, including energy consumption, economic growth, and environmental factors, over time. Using this approach, the goal is to gain a comprehensive understanding by further analyzing the dynamic connections among variables.

3.1. Unit Root Tests

Stationary time series has a consistent mean and variance over time, where the mean does not shift, and the variance remains constant. In addition, the covariance between two periods is determined solely by the time lag between them, indicating that the relationship between observations does not change over time (Gujarati, 1999). Non-stationary series are called unit root series. In the standard regression model, spurious regressions can occur against non-stationary variables (Dinçsoy & Okur Dinçsoy, 2020).

The Augmented Dickey-Fuller (ADF) unit root test and the Phillips-Perron (PP) unit root test are two common unit root tests used to analyze the stationarity properties of time series data.

The ADF unit root test is a statistical test used to determine the stationarity of a time series. This test tests the unit root hypothesis and evaluates whether the time series has a unit root. The unit root hypothesis states that the time series is non-stationary and exhibits random fluctuations over time. The ADF test also considers the trend and autoregressive (AR) terms when testing the unit root hypothesis (Dickey & Fuller, 1979).

The PP unit root test is another unit root test used to assess the stationarity of a time series. This test tests the unit root hypothesis and assesses whether the time series is stationary (Pillips & Perron, 1988). The PP test, like the ADF test, considers the trend and autoregressive terms and generally produces similar results to the ADF test.

Two-unit root tests commonly used in analyzing time series stationarity are the ADF and PP tests. These tests are crucial in statistical analysis of time series, econometric studies, and financial data analysis. The results have implications for understanding changes in time and stationarity in time series. If variables have the same trend, we can conclude a strong correlation. However, in the case of spurious regression, R2, and t statistics can be misleading. Parameter estimates may be insignificant (Sevüktekin & Nargeleçekenler, 2010). A long-term relationship between the variables should be examined to detect spurious regression.

$$Yt = \alpha 0 + \alpha 1\ Zt + \varepsilon\ t \quad (1)$$

$$\Delta Yt = \alpha 0 + \alpha 1\ \Delta\ Zt + \Delta\varepsilon\ t \quad (2)$$

Suppose variables with unit roots become stationary when their first differences are taken. In that case, a stationary structure may emerge with respect to the residuals of these variables when their non-stationary states are combined. Equation 2 is the first-difference version of equation 1. It examines whether the time series is stationary or not. If it is found that the series is not stationary at the level, they are re-specified as stationary.

3.2. Toda-Yamamoto Causality

While the Granger test (1969) states that the series must be stationary, there is no such condition for the Toda-Yamamoto test (1995). Therefore, the Toda-Yamamoto test can be included in the analysis without being sensitive to the degree of stationarity of the series. Successful results can be obtained by providing more information. In applying the causality test, the variables must satisfy the stationarity condition. Non-stationary series should be made stationary by taking the difference. The Granger causality test analyzes the causal relationship between non-stationary series, and it is crucial to determine the appropriate number of lags. It was developed by Granger in 1988.

The Toda-Yamamoto test method is an effective means of conducting a time-series analysis, as it does not necessitate that the series under examination possess the same degree of integration or a cointegrated relationship (Çalışkan et al., 2017). Before delving into the analysis process, unit root tests are typically conducted to ensure the data is stationary and determine the ideal number of lags that should be incorporated into the model. This preliminary step is integral to establishing a solid foundation for the following analysis.

4. FINDINGS

Data obtained from the Organization for Economic Co-Operation and Development (OECD) and World Development Indicators (WDI) databases covering the period 1990-2020 were used in the empirical analysis. Renewable energy consumption (RWC) and gross domestic product (GDP) data are obtained from the WDI database, while carbon emissions per capita (CO2PC) and oil prices (OP) data are obtained from the OECD database.

Table 1. Description of the variables

Symbol	Description	Sources
CO2PC	Carbon emissions per capita	OECD
RWC	Renewable energy consumption	World Bank
OP	Oil prices	OECD
GDP	Gross domestic product	World Bank

Note: In the models, the abbreviations of the series included in the model are preceded by the letter L by taking the logarithm.

For our analysis, we utilized the Eviews 10 package and employed the time series analysis method. Since the series considered for the analyses to be performed must be stationary, to ascertain the stationarity properties of the variables, we conducted unit root tests (Lutkepohl, 2005). Our analysis involved three models: 'with constant,' 'with constant and trend,' and 'without constant and trend.' The results obtained from the models mentioned above are presented in Tables 2 and 3.

Table 2. Unit root test (ADF)

	ADF		
	With Constant	**With Constant and Trend**	**Without Constant and Trend**
LRWC	-1,6556 (-0,4380)	-2,7360 (-0,2335)	-1,9339 (0,0520)*
LOP	-1,8070 (0,3670)	-1,6373 (0,7425)	0,5258 (0,8211)
LCO2TPC	-1,8743 (0,3357)	-2,6212 (0,2755)	1,7339 (0,9758)
LGDP	-1,1743 (0,6721)	-1,0613 (0,9191)	1,7549 (0,9782)
D(LRWC)	-5,5945 (0,0002)***	-5,3926 (0,0017)***	-5,5440 (0,0000)***
D(LOP)	-3,8374 (0,0094)***	-3,9221 (0,0306)**	-3,8371 (0,0006)***
D(LCO2TPC)	-4,5052 (0,0023)***	-3,4982 (0,0700)*	-3,5705 (0,0012)***
D(LGDP)	-5,6190 (0,0001)***	-5,7213 (0,0003)***	-5,1175 (0,0000)***

Note: 1%, 5% and 10% significance levels are denoted by ***, **, * respectively.

Table 3. Unit root test (Phillips-Perron (PP))

	PP		
	With Constant	**With Constant and Trend**	**Without Constant and Trend**
LRWC	-1,6556 (-0,4380)	-2,736 (-0,2335)	-2,6195 (0,0106)**
LOP	-1,753 (-0,3918)	-1,6209 (-0,7494)	0,5916 (-0,8361)
LCO2TPC	-0,5262 (-0,8672)	-2,1137 (-0,5093)	1,9733 (-0,9850)
LGDP	-1,1743 (0,6721)	-1,1664 (0,8995)	1,8315 (0,9814)
D(LRWC)	-5,8049 (0,0001)***	-5,5985 (0,0011)***	-5,5758 (0,0000)***
D(LOP)	-3,7627 (0,0110)**	-3,8322 (0,0362)**	-3,7761 (0,0007)***
D(LCO2TPC)	-4,6638 (0,0016)***	-6,8173 (0,0001)***	-3,5705 (0,0012)***
D(LGDP)	-5,6181 (0,0001)***	-5,7213 (0,0003)***	-5,1817 (0,0000)***

Note: 1%, 5% and 10% significance levels are denoted by ***, **, * respectively.

According to the results of both tests in Table 2 and Table 3, the RW (renewable energy) variable is stationary at the first difference in the fixed, fixed-trend, and fixed-trend models and stationary at level in the fixed and trendless models, while the OP (oil prices) variable is stationary at the first difference in the fixed, fixed-trend, and fixed and trendless models, CO2PC (carbon dioxide per capita) variable is stationary at the first difference in the fixed, fixed-trend, and constant and trendless models, and GDP (gross domestic product) variable is stationary at the first difference in the fixed, fixed-trend, and constant and trendless models. Some variables are stationary at I(1), and some at I(0). The Toda-Yamamoto causality test was applied. In order to examine the long-term relationship, it is necessary to estimate the VAR model and determine the appropriate lag length beforehand. This step is crucial to ensure accurate and reliable results in the analysis.

Table 4. Lag length of VAR model

Lag	LogL	LR	FPE	AIC	SC	HQ
0	31.24757	NA	1.79e-06	-1.879143	-1.690550	-1.820078
1	115.7935	139.9382*	1.61e-08*	-6.606451*	-5.663489*	-6.311127*
2	126.5155	14.78885	2.49e-08	-6.242446	-4.545113	-5.710862

As shown in Table 4, the VAR model order is 1 for all information criteria. In this regard, diagnostic tests were performed for the one-lag model.

Table 5. Diagnostic test

Diagnostic Test		
Serial Correlation LM Tests	F= 0.799262	p= 0.6801
Normality Tests (Jarque-Berra)	JB= 1.125149	p= 0.5697
Heteroskedasticity Tests	Chi-sq = 75.71946 df = 80	p= 0.6147

Note: Probability values are denoted by "p".

In Table 5, we have presented diagnostic tests for our model. These tests have shown that the data follows a normal distribution, which is a positive sign. Furthermore, no serial correlation is present between the error term and independent variables, as indicated by the LM test. This result is also reassuring as it suggests that our model is not biased. The results of the heteroskedasticity test indicate that there is a constant variance in the VAR model. This is an important finding as it suggests that our model is stable and reliable. Overall, these diagnostic tests provide us with valuable information about the quality and accuracy of our model.

Figure 1. Inverse roots of AR characteristic polynomial

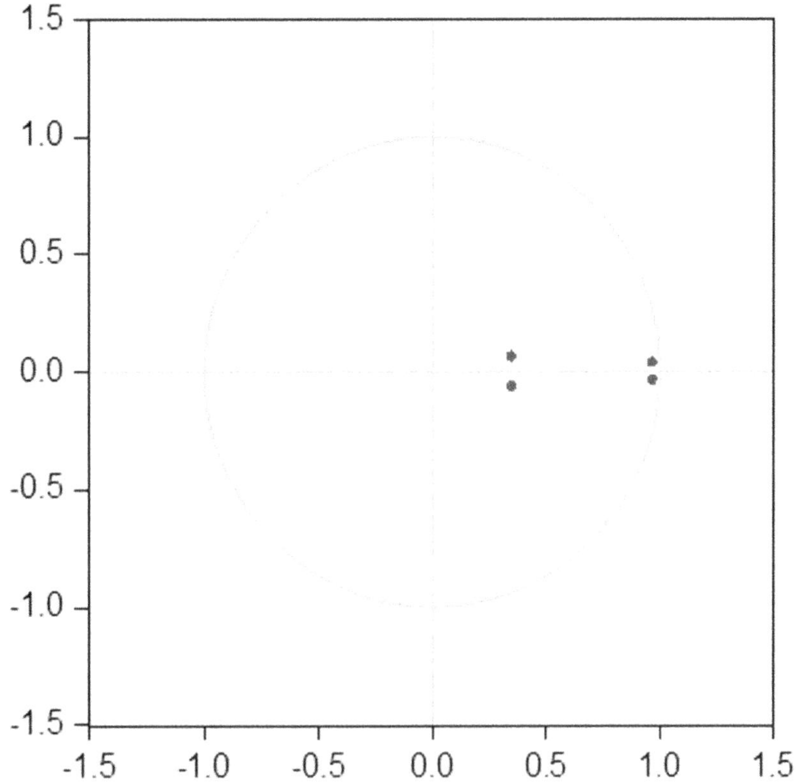

In order to fulfill the conditions of stationarity and stability of the VAR model, the model and all autoregressive (AR) roots should lie within the unit circle (+/-1 interval) (Lütkepohl, 2005). These conditions are necessary and essential for the VAR model to provide statistically accurate results and to make long-term forecasts. Once the lag length was established, we proceeded with autoregressive unit root analysis to examine the stationarity of the VAR model. As depicted in Figure 1 and Table 6, our results show that all inverse characteristic roots were well within the unit circle and all less than 1. This discovery indicates that our VAR model is stationary and appropriate for use. Subsequently, the Toda-Yamamoto Granger causality test was applied to determine the causal relationships between the variables, and the results are presented in Table 7.

Table 6. Stability test of the VAR model

Root	Modulus
0.967396 - 0.037637i	0.968128
0.967396 + 0.037637i	0.968128
0.348014 - 0.063868i	0.353826
0.348014 + 0.063868i	0.353826

Table 7. Toda-Yamamoto summary

Hypothesis			$k+d_{max}$	X^2 Statistics	Prob.	Casuality
LGDP	≠>	LCO2TPC	1+1	5,293**	0,0214	Yes
LOP	≠>	LCO2TPC	1+1	1,991	0,1582	No
LRWC	≠>	LCO2TPC	1+1	0,392	0,5312	No
LCO2TPC	≠>	LGDP	1+1	0,702	0,4020	No
LOP	≠>	LGDP	1+1	0,107	0,7440	No
LRWC	≠>	LGDP	1+1	4,323**	0,0376	Yes
LCO2TPC	≠>	LOP	1+1	8,343***	0,0038	Yes
LGDP	≠>	LOP	1+1	9,963***	0,0015	Yes
LRWC	≠>	LOP	1+1	3,931**	0,0474	Yes
LCO2TPC	≠>	LRWC	1+1	3,251*	0,0713	Yes
LGDP	≠>	LRWC	1+1	12,564***	0,0003	Yes
LOP	≠>	LRWC	1+1	6,641***	0,0009	Yes

Note: The Seeminghly Unrelated Regression method was used in the causality analysis. Lag length k was selected as 1 according to SC and AIC. 1%, 5% and 10% significance levels are denoted by ***, **, * respectively.

Renewable energy and economic growth have a bidirectional causality relationship according to the Toda-Yamamoto Causality test, which aligns with Toster et al. (2018), Apergis and Payne (2010), Büyükyılmaz and Mert (2015), Sadorsky (2009). However, this is different from Alper (2018), Durğun and Durğun (2018), and Öcal and Aslan (2013). Furthermore, unlike Brini et al. (2017), Abumunshar et al. (2020), a bidirectional causality relationship was found between renewable energy and oil prices.

On the other hand, in line with Joo et al. (2015), Bastola and Sapkota (2015), Wang et al. (2016), and Abumunshar et al. (2020), unlike Yang and Zhao (2014), a unidirectional causality relationship was found from economic growth to CO_2. In contrast to Sarwar et al. (2017) and Shahbaz et al. (2017), we find a unidirectional causality from economic growth to oil prices, which is in line with Bouzid (2012) and Kamacı and Göktaş (2020). Moreover, different from Zaghdoudi (2017) and consistent with Şimşek and Yiğit (2017), we find a unidirectional causality from CO_2 to oil prices. Unlike Dogan and Seker (2016), Paramati et al. (2017), Apergis and Payne (2014), unidirectional causality from CO_2 to renewable energy is found, which is in line with Menyah et al. (2010) and Sebri and Ben-Salha (2014).

Impulse response functions are used to determine how other variables will react and how long that reaction will last to a shock in one variable.

Figures 2, 3, and 4 show generalized impulse response functions with 5% confidence bands that reflect +/- two SEs of the response of carbon emissions following one SEs shock in GDP, oil prices, and renewable energy consumption in 10 years.

Figure 2 shows that a shock to GDP has a Positive and highly statistically significant impact on CO_2 emissions. Figure 3 and Figure 4 shows that a shock to oil prices and renewable energy has no statistically significant effect on carbon emissions over ten years.

Figure 2. Response of LCO2TPC to LGDP innovation using Cholesky (d.f. adjusted) factors

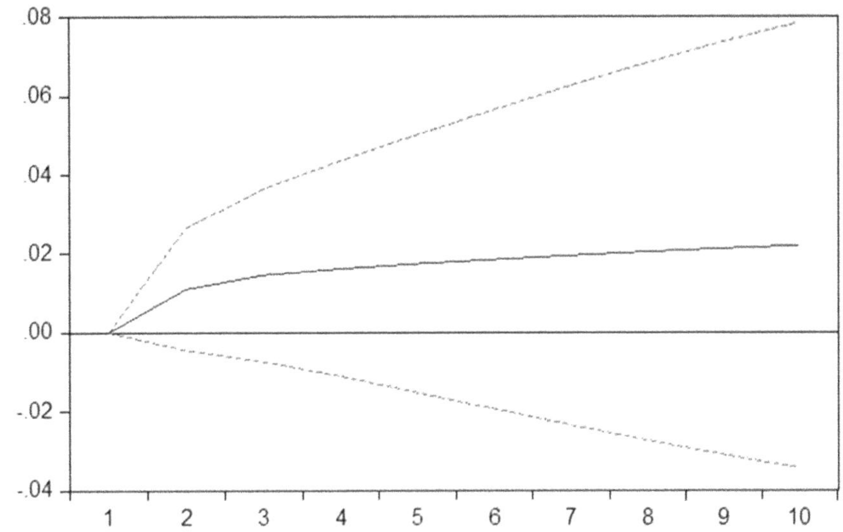

Figure 3. Response of LCO2TPC to LOP innovation using Cholesky (d.f. adjusted) factors

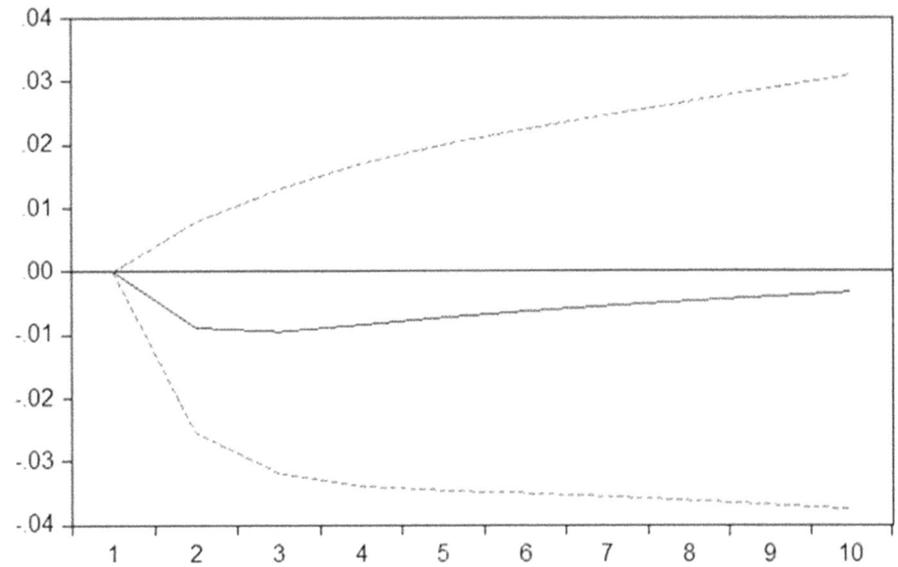

According to the variance decomposition results given in Table 8, it is seen that the change in carbon emission is explained 100% by itself in the first period. However, this situation changes in the following periods, and by the tenth period, it is determined that 84.85% of the change in carbon emission is explained by itself, 13.11% by economic growth, 1.81% by oil prices and 0.23% by renewable energy consumption.

Figure 4. Response of LCO2TPC to LRWC innovation using Cholesky (d.f. adjusted) factors

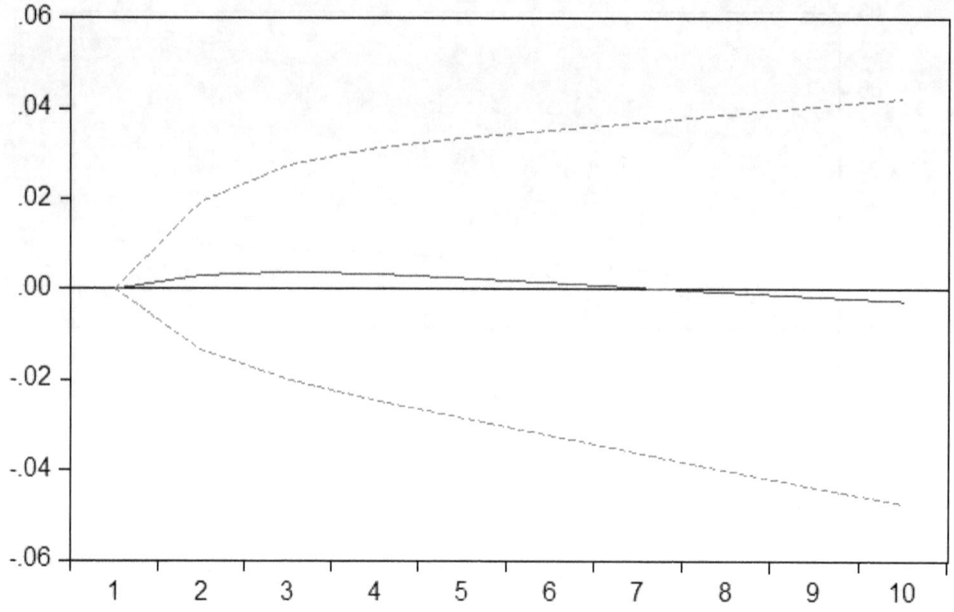

Table 8. Variance decomposition of carbon dioxide emissions per capita

Period	S.E.	LCO2TPC	LGDP	LOP	LRWC
1	0.051893	100.0000	0.000000	0.000000	0.000000
2	0.072513	96.03917	2.295935	1.493897	0.171002
3	0.087987	93.22503	4.297507	2.178440	0.299021
4	0.100615	91.39857	5.887323	2.372752	0.341355
5	0.111411	90.05215	7.252654	2.366308	0.328884
6	0.120915	88.91784	8.506329	2.281980	0.293855
7	0.129439	87.87238	9.701592	2.168654	0.257369
8	0.137184	86.86053	10.86152	2.046681	0.231268
9	0.144284	85.85795	11.99523	1.925252	0.221559
10	0.150834	84.85469	13.10557	1.808876	0.230863

5. CONCLUSION AND DISCUSSION

Energy has been the most crucial resource since the existence of humanity. When we look at the historical process of energy, we see that it is in an extensive framework from the use of animal power to nuclear resources today. However, as our world develops, our population is growing, and so are our needs. To meet growing energy needs, more energy is being used, which consumes scarce energy resources and causes incredible environmental damage. Fossil fuels are the most widely used energy source today. Fossil fuels are both polluting and have become one of the major concerns of governments in terms of cost, as they are becoming increasingly scarce. Therefore, energy has become a very costly input, especially for countries dependent on foreign energy. However, due to the relationship between production and energy, countries aiming for economic growth want to increase their production, but energy costs increase simultaneously. On the other hand, using more energy means more environmental damage and a significant sacrifice in terms of sustainability. In this regard, renewable energy has become a very important issue.

This study analyses the long-term causal relationships between carbon emissions, economic growth, renewable energy consumption, and oil prices in Türkiye. The variables used in the study are CO_2 emissions, renewable energy consumption, economic growth, and oil prices, and annual data are used for the period 1990-2020. Causal relationships between variables were investigated using a VAR model developed by Toda and Yamamoto (1995). Unit root tests were carried out on the stationarity of the series used in the model, and their maximum integration was determined. MWALD test was performed by adding extra lags to the VAR model up to the maximum integration degree of the series. According to the results of MWALD test at 5% significance level and Toda-Yamamoto causality test, we find a bidirectional causality between renewable energy and economic growth, which is consistent with Toster et al. (2018), Apergis and Payne (2010), Büyükyılmaz and Mert (2015) and Sadorsky (2009) and different from Alper (2018), Durğun and Durğun (2018) and Öcal and Aslan (2013). Furthermore, unlike Brini et al. (2017), Abumunshar et al. (2020), a bidirectional causality relationship was found between renewable energy and oil prices. On the other hand, in line with Joo et al. (2015), Bastola and Sapkota (2015), Wang et al. (2016), Abumunshar et al. (2020), and unlike Yang and Zhao (2014), a unidirectional causality relationship was found from economic growth to CO_2. In contrast to Sarwar et al. (2017) and Shahbaz et al. (2017), we find a unidirectional causality from economic growth to oil prices, which is in line with Bouzid (2012) and Kamacı and Göktaş (2020). Moreover, different from Zaghdoudi (2017) and in line with Şimşek and Yiğit (2017), there is a unidirectional causality from CO_2 to oil prices. Unlike Dogan and Seker (2016), Paramati et al. (2017), Apergis and Payne (2014), unidirectional causality from CO_2 to renewable energy is found, which is in line with Sebri and Ben-Salha (2014) and Menyah et al. (2010). The variance decomposition results show that in the first period, carbon emission change is 100% explained by itself. However, this situation changes in the following periods, and by the tenth period it is found that 84.85% of the change in carbon emissions is explained by itself, 13.11% by economic growth, 1.81% by oil prices, and 0.23% by the consumption of renewable energy.

There is a reciprocal relationship between renewable energy and economic growth. Investment in renewable energy supports economic growth, while economic growth supports the growth of the renewable energy sector. Renewable energy projects contribute to economic growth through benefits such as job creation, technological advances, and reduced energy costs. Oil prices can affect interest in renewable energy. High oil prices can increase demand for alternative energy sources and encourage investment in renewable energy. Similarly, increased production of renewable energy can reduce the oil demand, which in turn can reduce oil prices. While economic growth increases energy demand, renewable energy sources provide a sustainable energy transition by reducing environmental impacts. This helps to reduce CO_2 emissions. Therefore, the transition to renewable energy is essential for the harmonized progress of environmental sustainability and economic growth.

Consequently, a complex relationship exists between renewable energy, economic growth, and oil prices. Encouraging investment in renewable energy is crucial for sustainable economic growth and supports environmental sustainability.

REFERENCES

Abumunshar, M., Aga, M., & Samour, A. (2020). Oil price, energy consumption, and CO2 emissions in Turkey: New evidence from a bootstrap ARDL test. *Energie, 13*(21), 1-15. Retrieved from https://econpapers.repec.org/article/gamjeners/v_3a13_3ay_3a2020_3ai_3a21_3ap_3a5588-_3ad_3a434882.htm

Adebayo, T. S., & Akinsola, G. D. (2021). *Investigating the causal linkage among economic growth, energy consumption and CO2 emissions in Thailand: An application of the wavelet coherence approach.* Retrieved from https://www.proquest.com/openview/1de1167ce15f07271182482f7232d5c3/1?pq-origsite=gscholar&cbl=1416335

Ağır, H., Özbek, S., & Türkmen, S. (2020). Türkiye'de yenilenebilir enerji kaynaklarının belirleyicileri: Ampirik bir tahmin. *International Journal of Economic Studies*, *6*(4), 39–48. https://dergipark.org.tr/en/download/article-file/1280974

Alper, F. Ö. (2018). Yenilenebilir enerji ve ekonomik büyüme arasındaki ilişki: 1990-2017 Türkiye örneği. *Journal of the Faculty of Economics and Administrative Sciences*, *8*(2), 223–242. https://dergipark.org.tr/en/pub/ckuiibfd/issue/41863/466782

Amaira, B. (2012). The relationship of oil prices and economic growth in Tunisia: A vector error correction model analysis. *The Romanian Economic Journal, 43*, 3-22. https://d1wqtxts1xzle7.cloudfront.net/54262849/The_Relationship_of_Oil_Prices_and_Econo20170827-16260-1wfgtap-libre.pdf?1503903071=&response-content-disposition=inline%3B+filename%3DThe_Relationship_of_O

Apergis, N., & Danuletiu, D. C. (2014). Renewable energy and economic growth: Evidence from the sign of panel long-run causality. *International Journal of Energy Economics and Policy*, *4*(4), 578–587. https://dergipark.org.tr/en/pub/ijeeep/issue/31911/350841?publisher=http-www-cag-edu-tr-ilhan-ozturk

Apergis, N., Payne, J. E., Menyah, K., & Wolde-Rufael, Y. (2010). On the causal dynamics between emissions, nuclear energy, renewable energy, and economic growth. *Ecological Economics*, *69*(11), 2255–2260. doi:10.1016/j.ecolecon.2010.06.014

Appiah, M. O. (2018). Investigating the multivariate Granger causality between energy consumption, economic growth and CO2 emissions in Ghana. *Energy Policy*, *112*, 198–208. doi:10.1016/j.enpol.2017.10.017

Ayman, G., Kılıçdağı, T. A., & Sezer, A. (2007). Avrupa Birliği'ne katılım sürecinde Türkiye'nin komşu ve çevre ülkeler politikası: Stratejik yaklaşımlar. *TÜSİAD Basın Bülteni*. Retrieved from https://tusiad.org/tr/yayinlar/raporlar/item/3633-avrupa-birligine-katilim-surecinde-turkiyenin-komsu-ve-cevre-ulkeler-politikasi--stratejik-yaklasimlar

Bamati, N., & Raoofi, A. (2020). Development level and the impact of technological factor on renewable energy production. *Renewable Energy*, *151*, 946–955. doi:10.1016/j.renene.2019.11.098

Bastola, U., & Sapkota, P. (2015). Relationships among energy consumption, pollution emission, and economic growth in Nepal. *Energy*, *80*, 254–262. doi:10.1016/j.energy.2014.11.068

Bozkurt, C., & Okumuş, İ. (2015). Türkiye'de ekonomik büyüme, enerji tüketimi, ticari serbestleşme ve nüfus yoğunluğunun CO2 emisyonu üzerindeki etkileri: Yapısal kırılmalı eşbütünleşme analizi. *Mustafa Kemal Üniversitesi Sosyal Bilimler Enstitüsü Dergisi, 12*(32), 23-35. Retrieved from https://dergipark.org.tr/tr/pub/mkusbed/issue/19578/208976

Brini, R., Amara, M., & Jemmali, H. (2017). Renewable energy consumption, International trade, oil price and economic growth inter-linkages: The case of Tunisia. *Renewable & Sustainable Energy Reviews, 76*, 620–627. doi:10.1016/j.rser.2017.03.067

Büyükyılmaz, A., & Mert, M. (2015). CO2 emisyonu, yenilenebilir enerji tüketimi ve ekonomik büyüme arasındaki ilişkinin MS-VAR yaklaşımı ile modellenmesi: Türkiye örneği. *Journal of World of Turks, 7*(3), 103–117. https://atif.sobiad.com/index.jsp?modul=makale-detay&Alan=sosyal&Id=AWANUin4oDuH9Br_drwT

Çalışkan, Ş., Karabacak, M., & Meçik, O. (2017). Türkiye ekonomisinde eğitim harcamaları ve ekonomik büyüme ilişkisi: Bootstrap Toda-Yamamoto nedensellik testi yaklaşımı. *Kocaeli University Journal of Social Sciences*, (33), 45-56. Retrieved from https://dergipark.org.tr/en/pub/kosbed/issue/43231/524915

Can, H. (2017). *Yenilebilir enerjinin makroekonomik etkileri: Türkiye örneği*. Namık Kemal Üniversitesi, Sosyal Bilimler Enstitüsü, Yayımlanmamış Yüksek Lisans Tezi.

Can, H., & Korkmaz, Ö. (2019). The relationship between renewable energy consumption and economic growth: The case of Bulgaria. *International Journal of Energy Sector Management, 13*(3), 573–589. doi:10.1108/IJESM-11-2017-0005

Chindo, S., Abdulrahim, A., Waziri, S. I., Huong, W. M., & Ahmad, A. A. (2015). Energy consumption, CO2 emissions and GDP in Nigeria. *GeoJournal, 80*(3), 315–322. doi:10.100710708-014-9558-6

Dickey, D. A., & Fuller, W. A. (1979). Distribution of the estimators for autoregressive time series with a unit root. *Journal of the American Statistical Association, 74*(366a), 427–431. https://www.tandfonline.com/doi/abs/10.1080/01621459.1979.10482531

Dinçsoy, E. E., & Ichiminami, F. (2006). An Assessment of the Southeastern Anatolia Region in Turkey in Terms of the Sustainable Development Targets. *Journal of the Faculty of Environmental Science and Technology. Okayama University, 11*(1), 75–81.

Dinçsoy, E. E., & Okur Dinçsoy, M. (2020). Ekonomik büyümenin enflasyon üzerine etkisinin Türkiye ekonomisi açısından analizi. *Balkan ve Yakın Doğu Sosyal Bilimler Dergisi*, (6), 118–124.

Dogan, E., & Seker, F. (2016). Determinants of CO2 emissions in the European Union: The role of renewable and non-renewable energy. *Renewable Energy, 94*, 429–439. doi:10.1016/j.renene.2016.03.078

Durğun, B., & Durğun, F. (2018). Yenilenebilir enerji tüketimi ile ekonomik büyüme arasında nedensellik ilişkisi: Türkiye örneği. *International Review of Economics and Management, 6*(1), 1–27. https://dergipark.org.tr/tr/pub/iremjournal/issue/36427/347200

Emir, F., & Bekun, F. V. (2019). Energy intensity, carbon emissions, renewable energy, and economic growth nexus: New insights from Romania. *Energy & Environment, 30*(3), 427–443. doi:10.1177/0958305X18793108

Emodi, N. V., Shagdarsuren, G., & Tiky, A. Y. (2015). Influencing factors promoting technological innovation in renewable energy. *International Journal of Energy Economics and Policy*, *5*(3), 889–900. https://dergipark.org.tr/en/download/article-file/361553

Evrendilek, F., & Ertekin, C. (2003). Assessing the potential of renewable energy sources in Turkey. *Renewable Energy*, *28*(15), 2303–2315. doi:10.1016/S0960-1481(03)00138-1

Gökmenoğlu, K., & Taşpınar, N. (2016). The relationship between Co2 emissions, energy consumption, economic growth and FDI: The case of Turkey. *The Journal of International Trade & Economic Development*, *25*(5), 706–723. doi:10.1080/09638199.2015.1119876

Granger, C. (1988). Causality, cointegration, and control. *Journal of Economic Dynamics & Control*, *12*(2-3), 551–559. doi:10.1016/0165-1889(88)90055-3

Gujarati, D. (1999). *Essentials of econometrics*. Irwin/McGraw-Hill.

Jebli, M. B., & Kahia, M. (2020). The interdependence between CO2 emissions, economic growth, renewable and non-renewable energies, and service development: Evidence from 65 countries. *Climatic Change*, *162*(2), 193–212. doi:10.100710584-020-02773-8

Joo, Y.-J., Kim, C. S., & Yoo, S.-H. (2015). Energy consumption, Co2 emission, and economic growth: Evidence from Chile. *International Journal of Green Energy*, *12*(5), 543–550. doi:10.1080/15435075.2013.834822

Kamacı, A., & Göktaş, S. (2020). Petrol fiyatları ile ekonomik büyüme ilişkisi: Türkiye örneği. *Bartın Üniversitesi İktisadi ve İdari Bilimler Fakültesi Dergisi*, *11*(22), 547-556. Retrieved from https://dergipark.org.tr/en/pub/bartiniibf/article/797897

Karaaslan, A., & Çamkaya, S. (2022). The relationship between CO2 emissions, economic growth, health expenditure, and renewable and non-renewable energy consumption: Empirical evidence from Turkey. *Renewable Energy*, *190*, 457–466. doi:10.1016/j.renene.2022.03.139

Keleş, R., & Hamamcı, C. (2002). *Çevrebilim*. İmge Kitabevi Yayınları.

Khan, Z. S. (2013). Causality between economic growth, energy consumption and green house gas emissions in Bangladesh: A Toda-Yamamoto approach. *Journal of Academic Research in Economics*, (2), 245-257. Retrieved from https://www.ceeol.com/search/article-detail?id=70322

Korkmaz, Ö., & Develi, A. (2012). Türkiye'de birincil enerji kullanımı, üretimi ve gayri safi yurt içi hasıla (GSYİH) arasındaki ilişki. *Dokuz Eylül Üniversitesi İktisadi ve İdari Bilimler Fakültesi Dergisi*, *27*(2), 1-25. Retrieved from https://dergipark.org.tr/tr/pub/deuiibfd/issue/22727/242544

Lund, P. (2009). Effects of energy policies on industry expansion in renewable energy. *Renewable Energy*, *34*(1), 53–64. doi:10.1016/j.renene.2008.03.018

Lütkepohl, H. (2005). *New introduction to multiple time series analysis*. Springer Science & Business Media. doi:10.1007/978-3-540-27752-1

Magazzino, C. (2014). The relationship between CO2 emissions, energy consumption and economic growth in Italy. *International Journal of Sustainable Energy*, *35*(9), 844–857. doi:10.1080/14786451.2014.953160

Menyah, K., & Wolde-Rufael, Y. (2010). CO2 emissions, nuclear energy, renewable energy and economic growth in the US. *Energy Policy*, *38*(6), 2911–2915. doi:10.1016/j.enpol.2010.01.024

Morelli, G., & Mele, M. (2020). Energy consumption, CO2 and economic growth nexus in Vietnam. *International Journal of Energy Economics and Policy*, *10*(2), 443–449. doi:10.32479/ijeep.8248

Nain, M. Z., Ahmad, W., & Kamaiah, B. (2015). Economic growth, energy consumption and CO2 emissions in India: A disaggregated causal analysis. *International Journal of Sustainable Energy*, *36*(8), 807–824. doi:10.1080/14786451.2015.1109512

Ocal, O., & Aslan, A. (2013). Renewable energy consumption–economic growth nexus in Turkey. *Renewable & Sustainable Energy Reviews*, *28*, 494–499. doi:10.1016/j.rser.2013.08.036

Okur Dincsoy, M. (2016). A Comparative Study on Population and Employment Risks in Vulnerable Countries to Climate Change. *International Journal of Ecological Economics and Statistics*, *37*(2), 103–120.

Organisation for Economic Co-Operation and Development (OECD). (2023). *OECD Data*. Retrieved from https://data.oecd.org/

Özbek, S., & Naimoğlu, M. (2021b). Enerji verimliliğinin dinamikleri: VAR analizi ile Türkiye üzerine ampirik bir tahmin. *19 Mayıs. Journal of Social Sciences*, *2*(2), 314–326. https://dergipark.org.tr/en/download/article-file/1569393

Pamir, A. N. (2003). Dünyada ve Türkiye'de enerji, Türkiye'nin enerji kaynakları ve enerji politikaları. *Metalurji Dergisi*, 1-39. Retrieved from https://metalurji.org.tr/dergi/dergi134/d134_73100.pdf

Paramati, S. R., Mo, D., & Gupta, R. (2017). The effects of stock market growth and renewable energy use on CO2 emissions: Evidence from G20 countries. *Energy Economics*, *66*, 360–371. doi:10.1016/j.eneco.2017.06.025

Phillips, P. C., & Perron, P. (1988). Testing for a unit root in time series regression. *Biometrika*, *75*(2), 335–346. doi:10.1093/biomet/75.2.335

Rexhäuser, S., & Löschel, A. (2015). Invention in energy technologies: Comparing energy efficiency and renewable energy inventions at the firm level. *Energy Policy*, *83*, 206–217. doi:10.1016/j.enpol.2015.02.003

Sadorsky, P. (2009). Renewable energy consumption and income in emerging economies. *Energy Policy*, *37*(10), 4021–4028. doi:10.1016/j.enpol.2009.05.003

Sahoo, M., & Sahoo, J. (2020). Effects of renewable and non-renewable energy consumption on CO2 emissions in India: Empirical evidence from disaggregated data analysis. *Journal of Public Affairs*, *22*(1), 1–12. https://onlinelibrary.wiley.com/doi/abs/10.1002/pa.2307

Sarwar, S., Chen, W., & Waheed, R. (2017). Electricity consumption, oil price and economic growth: Global perspective. *Renewable & Sustainable Energy Reviews*, *76*, 9–18. doi:10.1016/j.rser.2017.03.063

Sebri, M., & Ben-Salha, O. (2014). On the causal dynamics between economic growth, renewable energy consumption, CO2 emissions and trade openness: Fresh evidence from BRICS countries. *Renewable & Sustainable Energy Reviews*, *39*, 14–23. doi:10.1016/j.rser.2014.07.033

Şenalp, U. E. (2021). In Ö. Sarıdoğan & D. Çelebi (Eds.), *Covid-19 Küresel Salgınının Sanayi ve Hizmet Sektörlerinde Enerji Yoğunluğuna Etkisi* (pp. 143–161). İktisadi ve İdari Bilimlerde Özgün Çalışmalar.

Sevüktekin, M., & Nargeleçekenler, M. (2010). *Ekonometrik Zaman Serileri Analizi*. Nobel Akademik Yayıncılık.

Shahbaz, M., Sarwar, S., Chen, W., & Malik, M. N. (2017). Dynamics of electricity consumption, oil price and economic growth: Global perspective. *Energy Policy*, *108*, 256–270. doi:10.1016/j.enpol.2017.06.006

Şimşek, T., & Yiğit, E. (2017). BRICT ülkelerinde yenilenebilir enerji tüketimi, petrol fiyatları, co2 emisyonu, kentleşme ve ekonomik büyüme üzerine nedensellik analizi. *Eskişehir Osmangazi Üniversitesi İktisadi ve İdari Bilimler Dergisi, 12*(3), 117-136. Retrieved from https://dergipark.org.tr/tr/pub/oguiibf/issue/30939/335630

The World Bank Data. (2023). *Worldbank Indicator*. Retrieved from https://data.worldbank.org/

Toda, H. Y., & Yamamoto, T. (1995). Statistical inference in vector autoregressions with possibly integrated processes. *Journal of Econometrics*, *66*(1-2), 225–250. doi:10.1016/0304-4076(94)01616-8

Udemba, E. N., Güngör, H., Bekun, F. V., & Kirikkaleli, D. (2021). Economic performance of India amidst high CO2 emissions. *Sustainable Production and Consumption*, *27*, 52–60. doi:10.1016/j.spc.2020.10.024

Wang, S., Li, Q., Fang, C., & Zhou, C. (2016). The relationship between economic growth, energy consumption, and CO2 emissions: Empirical evidence from China. *The Science of the Total Environment*, *542*, 360–371. doi:10.1016/j.scitotenv.2015.10.027 PMID:26520261

Yang, Z., & Zhao, Y. (2014). Energy consumption, carbon emissions, and economic growth in India: Evidence from directed acyclic graphs. *Economic Modelling*, *38*, 533–540. doi:10.1016/j.econmod.2014.01.030

Zaghdoudi, T. (2017). Oil prices, renewable energy, CO2 emissions and economic growth in OECD countries. *Economic Bulletin*, *37*(3), 1844–1850. http://accessecon.com/Pubs/EB/2017/Volume37/EB-17-V37-I3-P167.pdf

Chapter 9
China's Alternative Approach to Global Development:
Implications for World Order

Antonina Habova
https://orcid.org/0000-0002-0406-6360
University of National and World Economy, Sofia, Bulgaria

ABSTRACT

The Global Development Initiative, announced by China's President Xi Jinping in 2021, demonstrates China's ambition not only to strongly contribute to global development but also to have its voice in designing the dominant narrative when it comes to global development as well as to international order. This further enhances the strategic competition between China and the United States. Hence, the aim of the chapter is to study China's alternative approach to global development as an integral element of the transformation of the international order. It will analyze in comparative perspective the specific Chinese approach, key ideas, underlying values, and understanding of global development. The study will also examine China's economic, political, and geopolitical interests and motives that drive the country's approach to global development. Methodologically, the chapter will move away from the strict framework of Western theories on international development. It will rather look for better understanding of Chinese views on global development.

INTRODUCTION

A tectonic shift is taking place within the international system. The West is losing its world dominance established after the end of the Cold war and the Western liberal model of development faces significant challenges from alternative development models. It is the impressive economic growth of China in the end of the 20th and the beginning of the 21st century that has mostly challenged the very idea of the universality of the Western social and political system and the Western way of development. People's Republic of China preserved its political system that challenges the Western standards of human rights

DOI: 10.4018/979-8-3693-0400-6.ch009

and liberal democracy but still attained significant and sustainable economic growth and development. In an unprecedentedly short period of time, China made the transition from one of the poorest countries to the status of the second largest economy in the world. Thus, the "Washington Consensus" followed and imposed by the Western countries to the rest of the world was effectively contested by the "Beijing Consensus" as an alternative development model.

As China becomes stronger economically, Chinese interests become increasingly global and diverse. China's rise as a global power has been followed by increased China's ambition to play a more significant role in the international system and global governance, including by offering alternative approach when addressing development deficits of the countries.

While the war is back in Europe and it is high on the international community's agenda, serious problems and challenges facing global development are still pending. Against the background of further securitization of international relations enhanced by the war in Ukraine, Chinese President Xi Jinping calls for peace, confidence, justice, equity and win-win cooperation. After the launch of the Belt and Road Initiative (BRI) in 2013, President Xi offers to the world its Global Development Initiative (GDI), Global Security Initiative (GSI) and Global Civilization Initiative (GCI). It is considered that the development of the three initiatives will make possible the achievement of "a community of shared future for mankind", which is China's concept of global governance. Hence, the aim of the paper is to analyse China's alternative approach to global development as an integral element of the transformation of the international order.

Global Development from Western Theoretical Perspective

In 1982, UNESCO published the book entitled "Different Theories and Practices of Development". Discussing the emergence of new theoretical concepts on national and international development, the authors of the book appealed for a "scientifically based theory of development" (Alechina, 1982, p. 9). More than 30 years later it is difficult to detect a consensus on a single theoretical concept.

"Global development" is a broad concept and western scientific knowledge includes several theories and approaches in global development that form the framework of the Western debate about "development". In the middle of the 20th century, the debate was dominated by the modernization theory based on the historical experience of North America and Western Europe. Then, "development" was associated with economic growth and prosperity. It focused on internal factors (religious, cultural traditions) and shortcomings as the major reasons for the underdevelopment of third world's countries and societies. As to global development, modernization theory postulates that underdeveloped societies could develop and experience progress if they strictly follow Western values and adopt the Western model of development that includes industrialization, urbanization, rationalization, education and democratic institutions. Modernization theory is based on W.W. Rostow's five stages of economic growth and development – the traditional society; the preconditions for take-off; the take-off; the drive to maturity; the age of high mass consumption (Rostow, 1959).

In the domain of international politics modernization theory serves as an explanatory framework for the imposition of one and the same (Western) standards and models of development – considered as universal and the best - to the underdeveloped countries. In this sense, in the view of proponents of the modernization theory, development is equal to Westernisation. Hence, as Willis (2011) points out, the concept of 'Eurocentrism' also becomes quite relevant and important (p. 18) as Eurocentric discourse dominate the global development debate for a long time.

Neoliberalism, like modernization theory, focuses on internal hindrances to development. However, it put aside cultural traditions and emphasizes the importance of economic policies (free market, free trade, reduced role of the state, privatization, deregulation, etc.) as well as political and economic institutions. That's how provision of international aid was bound to the fulfilment of certain political and economic conditions based on Western practices and experience.

Dependency theory (a structuralist one) is another theory that is also conceptualized by Western scholars but it is a critical response to modernization theory. It focuses on the interaction between internal and external factors (colonialism, among others) and thus explains the divide between developed and underdeveloped countries. According to dependency theorists, "the relationship between the Northern core and the Southern periphery, far from being a relationship of mutual-interest cooperation, connotes both the subordination of the latter to the former and the exploitation of the latter by the former" (Dougherty and Pfaltzgraff, 2001, p. 455). Hence, in this theoretical model the world system is marked by global inequality where core (developed, Global North) countries still exploit periphery (underdeveloped, Global South) countries for their natural resources and cheap labour which significantly impedes their further development.

World system theory, associated with Immanuel Wallerstein, is another theory of international development. It is closely related to dependency theory and also regards global development primarily in economic terms. However, it tries to understand "the uneven development of the world capitalist system as a whole, in its various political, economic, and social aspects, and to fit the historical evolution of each country or region into a global spatiotemporal perspective encompassing the capitalist world economy since the sixteenth century transition from feudalism" (Dougherty and Pfaltzgraff, 2001, p. 458). The world system is divided into three areas i.e. core (developed, powerful states), periphery (technologically underdeveloped, weak states) and semiperiphery. However, it is the rise of China that poses a serious challenge to this theory. The country does not belong to the periphery nor to the semiperiphery anymore. China's impressive development in the last four decades helped it move to the core zone of the world system though it still regards itself as a developing country.

This brief review of the Western theoretical thought on global development could not miss to pay attention to the postdevelopment theory that challenges theoretical debate on development and contests the very meaning of "development". Part of the postdevelopment theorists do not belong to the Western world by origin but they are closely integrated in the Western academic community.

Postdevelopment theory accuses all development theories for being too ethnocentric, Western and technocratic (Escobar, 1995). Post-development theorists contest the universality of the model of development of the Western countries and argue that the aim of development – as seen by the West - is further extension of the control of the West over the developing world (Rapley, 2004). As Björklund (2020) summarizes it, "Critical theory on Western civilization, development, and modernity came to be categorized under post-development to act as a counterbalance to the hegemonic discourse of modern science which spearheads development and sees Western modernization as the only alternative towards the future" (p. 2).

Postdevelopment theory prepares also the ground for the concept of "people-centered development" that rejects the absolutization of economic growth's contribution to human development. China, under the leadership of Xi Jinping, adheres to a people-centered development philosophy postulating that people's well-being is a goal of the country's economic development. "The happiness and well-being of the people are the ultimate goals of promoting high-quality development", declares President Xi (2023, para. 2).

As the chapter analyses the implications of China's alternative approach to global development for the transformation of the world order, the theoretical framework of the analysis takes into consideration also the soft power concept introduced by J. Nye as well as institutionalism as an approach in social sciences that emphasizes the role of institutions.

China's Approach to Global Development

This paper aims to move away from the strict framework of Western theories on international development that are dominated by the Western culture, philosophies and historical experiences and practices. It rather looks for better understanding of Chinese views on global development. Based on specific Chinese principles, values, cultural and political traditions, Chinese approach to global development differs from the Western one.

Certain parallels could be drawn between contemporary Chinese foreign policy and China's approach to global development, on the one hand, and Mao Zedong's Three Worlds Theory, on the other hand. Launched in 1974, Three Worlds Theory divides geopolitically the world into three zone – the two superpowers (The United States and the Soviet Union); developing, formerly colonized, countries in Asia, Africa, Latin America and other regions (the third world); and the developed countries in between the two zones (the second world). The focus in the theory is put on the third world (the periphery countries). The theory postulates that China has to develop its relations with these countries and support their efforts to achieve independence. So, in Mao's period China's aid to the countries from the third world was politically motivated in the context of the Sino-Soviet split and Mao's ambition to get recognition in the United Nations. Vieira (2019) notes that "by selecting strategic partners in Africa and Asia, China was able to meet its political goals, solidifying itself as a leader between countries in the Third World, supporting revolutionary struggles, exporting its development model based on the countryside, especially in Africa, and redefining co-operation between periphery states" (p. 535).

China's current foreign policy keeps this focus on the relations with the developing countries from the Global South, which means countries from Africa, Latin America and the Caribbean as well as Asian countries without Israel, Japan, and the Republic of Korea, and Oceania without Australia and New Zealand, according to the United Nations Conference on Trade and Development (UNCTAD). Since the beginning of the reforms under Deng Xiaoping's leadership, however, international aid followed not political but domestic modernisation and economic growth objectives (Vieira, 2019, p. 543). This is the period when one of the major goals of China's foreign policy is to support the economic development of the country.

Xi Jinping's rise to power has also brought about changes both in China's foreign policy and in China's approach to foreign aid. Though economic interests remain of key importance, as Yuan, Su and Ouyang (2022) point out, "China is paying increasing attention to the importance of top-level design in its foreign aid programme to pursue both political and economic interests" (p. 9).

Mao's theory argues that the real power in the world system belongs to the third world and assigns China the task of uniting the second and the third world (against the two superpowers). At the same time, China – under the leadership of Xi Jinping – though insisting that it is still a developing country, demonstrates readiness to help former colonies and developing countries achieve the progress China itself achieved in the last 40 years of reforms (Bermingham, 2021).

Here, we come to the issue of the specific Chinese model of development, which is also a key to understanding China's approach to global development. As Cao Fangjun (2009) points out, China has development its own ideas on social and economic development "drawing on the useful and discarting the unfit elements found in modernization theory' (p. 7).

The People's Republic of China has developed and followed the concept of "socialism with Chinese characteristics". The country embarked on a new economic development strategy in the late 1970s, while preserving the existing political system with the leading role of the Chinese Communist Party and maintaining political stability. The goal of the declared "policy of reforms and openness" was to achieve a qualitative change of the existing model of economic development by implementing a gradual transition from a highly centralized planned economy to a "socialist market economy" (planned economy but with elements of market regulation and competition). Public ownership remained dominant and the economy remained strongly regulated by the central government. Article 6 of the Constitution of the People's Republic of China, adopted in 1982, states that "the foundation of the socialist economic system of the People's Republic of China is socialist public ownership of the means of production". The Constitution stipulates that "socialist public property is sacred and inviolable" (Article 12) but it also guarantees that citizens' lawful private property is inviolable (Article 13).

Specific focus of the new policy, initiated by Deng Xiaoping, was the gradual opening of the country to the world as an instrument to give impetus to the Chinese economy and to improve social relations. The main task was to carry out the "four modernizations" which include renovation of industry, agriculture, defence, and science and technology (Stefanov and Koleva, 2015). Adhering to the philosophy of "crossing the river by touching the stones", the Chinese government rejected "shock therapy" policies and stick to the gradual reform policies - trialed development policies (market policies, ownership reforms, trade reforms, liberalizing capital flows, financial exchanges, etc.) first in Special Economic Zones and if successful, introduced them nationwide.

That specific development model proved successful and, in an unprecedentedly short period of time, China made the transition from one of the poorest countries to the status of the second largest economy in the world. China GDP annual growth rate in the 1970s was 6.3%, it was 11.2% in 1990-97 (Tselishchev, 2012, p. 6) and it averaged 7.7% in the 2010s (World bank, 2023). China became the world's largest holder of foreign exchange reserves in 2006. In 1980, country's foreign exchange reserves were measured at 2 billion USD. In 1993, they rose to 20 billion USD and in 2014, to a record 4 trillion USD. As of July 2023, China's foreign exchange reserves totaled more than 3 trillion USD (CEIC, 2023). China is the largest exporter of goods in the world since 2009 and the world's largest trading power since 2013. The implementation of the Going Out Strategy, initiated by the Chinese government in 1999 to encourage Chinese companies to invest abroad, contributed to the improvement of their competitiveness.

The country's leadership, however, had to address some side effects of China's impressive economic growth such as rising inequality and environmental concerns. Both the widening gap in prosperity and environmental degradation are seen as a danger for social stability. Hence, the government put an emphasis on environment policy and inclusive growth that care about the shape and distribution of growth across the population.

The extraordinary accomplishments achieved by China since 1978 allowed experts to start talking about China's alternative model of development. Joshua Cooper Ramo introduced the phrase "Beijing Consensus" in 2004 as an alternative to the "Washington Consensus", followed and imposed by the Western countries to the rest of the world after the end of the Cold war. Back in 2004, noting that "China's rise is already reshaping the international order by introducing a new physics of development and power"

(2004, p. 2), J.C. Ramo (2004, p. 3) comes to the conclusion that "what is happening in China at the moment is not only a model for China, but has begun to remake the whole landscape of international development, economics, society, and, by extension, politics". This assumption is even more convincing since the beginning of the structural transformation of the Chinese economy being implemented under the leadership of President Xi Jinping.

Moving away from the export-led growth strategy, China focused on a consumer-led growth, innovation and services. This rebalancing away from the external market to the internal market was in response to the global financial crisis. It was further upgraded to a "dual circulation model" (internal circulation and external circulation), introduced in 2020 as a reaction to the U.S.-China trade war started by U.S. President Trump in 2018 as well as to the Covid-19 pandemic. The new model does not only move further away from the investment-stimulated Western liberal model and relies on increasing the contribution of domestic demand to China's growth. The dual circulation strategy is much more focused on self-reliance (especially in terms of resources and technology) i.e. the increased domestic demand to be met by domestic production rather than by imports (Herrero, 2021).

In 2013, Chinese President Xi Jinping (2014), during a visit to Africa, declared: "There is no one-size-fits-all development model in the world. The diversity of civilizations and development models should be respected by all" (p. 337). On the one hand, using cultural diversity narrative (further developed through the Global Civilization Initiative), Beijing challenges Western dominance and the universality of the Western model of development. On the other hand, its starts to more actively emphasize the advantages of its own specific model of development.

China, however, does not actively seek to impose its model of development to countries from the Global South. It rather increasingly relies on the success and attractiveness of its own development model (Kissinger, 2012, pp. 5-22). Xi Jinping (2014), in a speech at the opening ceremony of the Sixth Ministerial Conference of China-Arab States Cooperation Forum, declares China's will to share its development knowledge with other countries: "We are willing to share our experience of governance with our Arab friends, so that each can draw on the wisdom of the other's time-honored civilization and development mode" (p. 346).

China's model has attracted a great deal of attention in the context of 2008-2009 global financial and economic crisis. While Western countries were hit hard by the crisis, China registered only a slight slowdown in its economic growth and further increased its share of global GDP. In 2021, the country achieved the first centenary goal – a "moderately prosperous society in all respects" was built, lifting millions of people out of extreme poverty and eradicating absolutely poverty (The State Council Information Office, 2021). More than 700 million Chinese were lifted out of extreme poverty in 40 years (Goldin, 2019, p. 002). This Chinese success further increases the attractiveness of China model as it is of great interests to developing countries and their efforts for poverty alleviation.

Emphasizing on its role as a "responsible major power", China declares also that it aims to provide "global development with public goods" (The State Council, 2021). In order to achieve global common development, Beijing has increased its aid to other developing countries, which has been enabled by China's own economic development. For China, however, global development is not primarily about international aid. It is also about domestic development, internal economic growth and improving living standards. Achieving sustainable economic and social development is one of the three core national interests of China along with upholding the political system and national security as well as maintaining national sovereignty and territorial integrity, as defined by State Councilor Dai Bingguo back in 2009 (U.S. Department of State, 2009).

In this sense, China openly brings out the correlation between its own development and the development of the other countries. Chinese leaders, especially after the launch of the Belt and Road Imitative, talk about "common development", which is perceived as "the very foundation of sustainable development" and which "meets the long-term and fundamental interests of all the people in the world" (Xi, 2014, p. 362). Chinese President also maintains that in the era of deepening economic globalization China "should vigorously promote a global development partnership and work for the common prosperity of all countries" (p. 356). "A single tree does not make a forest", Xi Jinping (Xi, 2014, p. 356) notes endorsing the key idea of Beijing's global development narrative i.e. that China's own development and stability depends on global development. That understanding is illustrated through the very characteristics of the Chinese aid model, which includes not only aid but also trade and investment projects. The White Paper on China's International Development Cooperation, adopted in 2021, gives a broad definition to "international development cooperation" – it refers to "China's bilateral and multilateral efforts, within the framework of South-South cooperation, to promote economic and social development through foreign aid, humanitarian assistance, and other means" (The State Council, 2021).

This approach is explained by Rudyak (2019) through the idea that China defines itself as a developing state. Hence, its aid spending should serve both China's and recipients' interests. Justin Yifu Lin and Yan Wang (2017) explain the alternative Chinese model of development cooperation with the alternative Chinese model of economic development. In the context of the new challenges related to the implementation of the Sustainable Development Goals (SDGs), the two experts insist on the idea of economic development through structural transformation that was the case of China's economic reform itself. However, according to Lin and Wang, traditional development aid is not enough for developing countries to achieve structural transformation. Therefore, different types of foreign aid are needed.

Chinese White Paper on international development cooperation defines the three main categories of foreign aid - grants, interests-free loans and concessional loans. Grants aim at helping other developing countries "build small and medium-sized social welfare projects and to fund projects for cooperation in human resources development, technical cooperation, material assistance, amid emergency humanitarian assistance". Grants provision is in line with an old Chinese saying "It is more helpful to teach people how to fish than to just give them fish". Interest-free loans are used to support developing countries in constructing public facilities and improving local people's live. Concessional loans aim at helping developing countries "undertake industrial projects and large and medium-sized infrastructure projects that yield economic and social benefits" (The State Council, 2021).

China's specific concept of global development cooperation and of international assistance, in particular, contrasts with the Western patterns of international assistance. Abiding by the principle of non-interference in internal affairs of other countries (one of the Five Principles of Peaceful Co-existence), Beijing does not openly apply the Western principle of conditionality, fostering economic and political changes in recipient countries. Chinese White Paper on international development cooperation stipulates that: "When cooperating with other countries for development, no country should interfere in their efforts to find a development path suited to their own national conditions, interfere in their internal affairs, impose its own will on them, attach political strings, or pursue political self-interest" (State Council, 2021). This approach has made China a preferred finance provider among the developing countries.

China has also initiated the establishment of various cooperation platforms in different parts of the world – 17+1 format for cooperation between China and the countries from Central and Eastern Europe; the China-Arab States Cooperation Forum, the Forum of China and the Community of Latin American and Caribbean States; Forum on China-Africa Cooperation (FOCAC); China-Pacific Island Countries

Economic Development and Cooperation Forum, among other. These platforms and cooperation mechanisms provide framework for further coordination, economic cooperation and promotion of foreign aid. They have also facilitated further economic engagement and increasing presence of Chinese projects around the world. Growing China's economic engagement with different countries on different continents brings about further dissemination and readiness for replication of China's model of development, as well. It also provides access to new markets for Chinese goods as well as access to natural resources that are important for China's economy (especially in the area of new technologies). South America, for example, is such important sources of natural resources (petroleum, oil, copper, lithium, among others) for China.

China's Global Initiatives

One phrase has been dominating China's foreign policy discourse since 2017. It says that the world is experiencing "great changes unseen in a century". These words are often repeated by President Xi (Ministry of Foreign Affairs of the People's Republic of China, 2023). R. Dashi (2021) interprets them as a paraphrase of the phrase pronounced in 1872 by the general Li Hongzhang saying that the world was experiencing "great changes unseen in 3000 years". Though these two phrases mark two totally different periods in China's history, as Doshi (2021) argue, "both capture something essential: the idea that world order is once again at stake because of unprecedented geopolitical and technological shifts, and that this requires strategic adjustments" (para. 2).

The impressive economic growth of China in the last four decades as well as Xi Jinping's sense of history and vision allows China to seize this strategic opportunity, to expand its global influence and power and to challenge global hegemony of the United States. China has become one of the key factors of change in the international system with an expanding role in global governance. Beijing demonstrates growing ambition to actively participate in the formulation of international system's norms and rules that better suit China's core national interests. In terms of global development, as a survey of 93 representatives of organizations working in the sector proves (Ingram and Lord, 2019, p. 6), the rise of China is already one of the long-term trends that will transform global development.

Moreover, China's alternative approach to global development becomes an integral part of the transformation of the liberal international order. In the context of world order transition, the postdevelopment theorists' assertion that development discourse is part of the articulation of power sounds quite relevant. Foreign aid is quite frequently used as a foreign policy instrument.

In the case of China, the correlation between foreign aid and foreign policy interests is also visible. Rudyak (2019) shares the results of a project disclosing the correlation between the foreign aid provided by China and the UN voting behaviour of recipient countries. Growing economic engagement provides stronger economic but also political leverage over host countries. The case with the EU debate on an international court ruling on China's claims to maritime rights and resources in the South China Sea in 2016 is often given as an example. Then, Greece and Hungary, which relied on Chinese investments, blocked the adoption of a common EU position condemning China.

Institutional reforms in China's development policy are indicator of the growing importance China attaches to foreign aid and global development issues, in general. In 2018, China International Development Cooperation Agency (CIDCA) was established and most of China's responsibilities in this field are transferred from the Ministry of commerce to the newly established agency. The agency coordinates, monitors and evaluates the implementation of development projects. According to Rudyak (2019), the very name of the agency (international development and cooperation agency and not a foreign aid agency) illustrates China's changing self-perception of its international development role.

China launched also several initiatives in the last ten years that constitute important elements of Chinese evaluation and challenge to the existing international order – the Belt and Road Initiative, the establishment of the Asian Infrastructure Investment Bank, Global Development Initiative, Global Security Initiative, Global Civilization Initiative, among others. On the one hand, these new initiatives provide a new framework for China's international cooperation and development. On the other hand, however, they are policies projections of Beijing's ambitions for expanded role at both regional and global level.

The Belt and Road Initiative

The Belt and Road Initiative (BRI), officially announced by President Xi Jinping in 2013, appears as one of the main factors influencing global development. The initiative (with its land and maritime dimension) is a key element in China's foreign policy strategy for 21st century. Though the major focus is put on the infrastructure connectivity between Asia, Europe and Africa, BRI's underlying motives are much more diverse. They are related to China's economic but also political, geopolitical and security interests.

Chinese leadership identifies the Belt and Road Initiative as a "major platform for international development cooperation" (The State Council, 2021) and claims that the win-win approach is applied within the initiative. Through the BRI, as argued by Ferchen (2020), China is billing itself as a leader of international development.

According to a report prepared by researchers from the World Bank, Harvard Kennedy School, Aid Data and the Kiel Institute for the World Economy and cited by Savage (2023), China spent $240 billion bailing out of 22 developing countries between 2008 and 2021. Recipients are mainly middle-income countries (Argentina, Mongolia, Pakistan). Data from China Africa Research Initiative (CARI, 2023) of John Hopkins School of Advanced International Studies also shows that China's global foreign aid expenditure increased steadily in the last twenty years, growing from USD 631 million in 2003 to USD 3.18 billion in 2021.

At the same time, the development of the BRI allows China to gradually establish a global network of political and economic relations (with the leading role of Beijing) that challenges the interests of the other major powers but also the influence and global dominance of the West/the United States established after the end of the Cold war. And in the context of the dual circulation strategy, the BRI could be an important guarantee that keeps the markets of the BRI countries open for Chinese goods in case of further U.S. and EU decoupling from China.

Within the framework of the Belt and Road Initiative China has already succeeded in strengthening its positions and in projecting influence in different parts of the world. It has increased its economic presence in Southeast Asia, Central and Eastern Europe, Africa, and even in Latin America, considered to be a "US backyard". In 2021, for example, there was a strong shift of China's engagement to countries from the Global South. Analysing data released by the Chinese Minister of Commerce, Nedopil (2022, p. 9) points out that "African and Middle Eastern countries received an increasingly large share of Chinese engagement, up from 8% in 2020 to about 38% of BRI engagement in 2021" and construction engagement in South America increased by 643%.

Growing economic engagement allows China to more self-confidently challenge the dominant positions of the Western countries at regional and global level. The COVID pandemic and the rising confrontation among states, however, has significantly shrunk the opportunities for China to proceed to advance its interest worldwide.

The West has, on the other hand, become increasingly critical towards China's foreign policy and the Belt and Road Initiative, in particular. Beijing's policy is criticized for being too assertive and realist, for imposing China's economic interests around the world and for not offering moral values to third countries. Hence, "The China threat" narrative gains momentum. It has been further enforced by cases of overdependence on China (Myanmar), China's "debt trap" cases (Montenegro), etc. - all of them associated with the BRI.

Global Development Initiative

In response to the accusations of the Western world but also in the context of the relative decline in BRI implementation in terms of lending and investments as well as of the concerns regarding the idea of China's "debt trap diplomacy" among developing countries, China has tried to recalibrate and upgrade its development policy and has launched three new initiatives – Global Development Initiative (GDI), Global Security Initiative (GSI), and Global Civilization Initiative (GCI), in 2021, 2022 and 2023, respectively.

The Global Development Initiative, which was announced by China's President Xi Jinping in a video address to the UN General Assembly in 2021, is linked with the United Nations 2030 Agenda for Sustainable Development. It addresses a significant number of challenges the world faces in the post-COVID pandemic period – from poverty alleviation, food security, and development financing to climate change, green development, digital economy and industrialization. Thus, it addresses the changing needs of the global development sector where "ending extreme poverty is no longer the defining lens through which development is viewed" (Ingram and Lord, 2019, p. 4). The initiative is also in accordance with the new China's development philosophy based on the idea of innovative, coordinated, green, open, and shared development (Xi, 2021). This idea was proposed by President Xi at the Fifth Plenary Session of the 18th CPC Central Committee in 2015.

As the BRI, the GDI is based on the principle of openness and inclusiveness and does not set any pre-conditions. As in the case of the BRI, China declares its commitment to allocate resources in order to achieve tangible results in global development cooperation. Initially, China allocated USD 3 billion for developing countries for the next three years. One year later, South-South Cooperation Assistance Fund was upgraded to a Global Development and South-South Cooperation Fund and USD 1 billion were added to the fund. Xi Jinping announced also that China would increase its support for the UN Peace and Development Trust Fund (Xinhua, 2022).

Unlike the BRI, which is more realistic and pragmatic, the Global Development initiative as well as the other two new Chinese initiatives pretend to be more value-oriented ones. Besides, as Hoang Thi Ha (2023) points out, while the BRI is growth-oriented and focused on large infrastructure projects, the GDI is development-oriented and relies on small-sized projects in areas as public health, poverty reductions, green economy, digital industry and innovation. This transformation on China's development policy is explained by Carmody, Zajontz and Reboredo (2022) as "a substantial reorganization towards soft power initiatives in response to (geo)political backlashes arising from previous implementation of the BRI" (p. 198).

Launching its own global initiatives, China demonstrates ambition not only to strongly contribute to global development but also to have its voice in designing the dominant narrative when it comes to global development as well as to international order. The GDI further endorses China's specific approach to international relations that focuses on development as a prerequisite for peace and stability. In contrast to Western concept of development, China's state-centric approach to development prioritizes economic development over human rights. This is related to the conceptual gap between China and the West that is underlied by different traditional values, cultures, historical experience, political values (Pan, 2012). Both sides have different interpretations of such major political concepts as sovereignty, global governance, human rights, multilateralism, soft power. For example, economic rights and economic prosperity are given priority over civil and political rights in China's human rights discourse. This principle is strictly applied both at domestic (Xinjiang, Tibet) and international level. It is acknowledged by the countries from the Global South and makes them more supportive to China's economic engagement endeavours.

It is also acknowledged by the developing countries that China sticks to different development discourse when providing them aid. Unlike the Western countries, Beijing keeps on insisting on its role as a partner rather than as a donor. As it is stipulated in the 2021 White Paper on China's International Cooperation in the New Era, "China's development cooperation is a form of mutual assistance between developing countries. It falls into the category of South-South cooperation and therefore is essentially different from North-South cooperation" (The State Council, 2021). Moreover, drawing lessons from the BRI implementation and insisting on the existence of shared interests of both developed and developing countries in peace, development and prosperity, China has even declared willingness to pay attention to the existing trade imbalances in China's relations with third countries. It has been declared by Chinese leaders that China will adopt some trade facilitation measures and will increase imports (primarily agricultural) from ASEAN countries (Global Times, 2021) and Africa (Thomas, 2021). The fact that more than 60 countries have already joined the Group of Friends of the GDI is indicative of the success of the Chinese efforts.

The launch of the GDI further challenges the reputation of the United States in the Global South, as well. The new Chinese initiative sharply contrasts with the US security-centric policy. While Chinese President Xi Jinping calls for peace, equity, win-win cooperation and common development, Washington and its allies are focused on providing resources and support to Ukraine in its war with Russia. Definitely, developing countries are much more attracted to China's approach as their concerns are related to post-pandemic challenges to their economies as well as problems ensuing from the war in Ukraine. In this context, Hoang Thi Ha (2023) quotes the words of Indian foreign minister S. Jaishankar that best illustrate this divide: "One is the East-West divide centering around Ukraine and the other is a North-South divide centering around development" (para. 21). The expert also draws attention to the significant differences between the US development assistance pledged at ASEAN-US summit in 2022 (in the amount of USD 150 million) and the US support for Ukraine in the amount of USD 40 billion (Hoang Thi Ha, 2023, para. 21).

Community of Shared Future for Mankind

The development of the three new China's initiatives (GDI, GSI and GCI) are perceived as key steps to promoting a new type of international relations through building a "community of shared future" at global level. Prof. Wang Yiwei (2022) describes GDI and GSI as two wings of the "community of shared future for mankind". The first initiative strives for achieving global development goals, while the second one will work for secure international environment as an important precondition for development. Shuman, Fulton and Gering (2023, para. 4) argue that the GDI and GSI are "interconnected through the Chinese Marxist belief that 'security is a prerequisite for development, and development is a guarantee for security', otherwise known as "peaceful development".

The concept of a "community of shared future" is central to Xi Jinping's foreign policy. It was announced by the Chinese president in his speech at the Moscow State Institute for International Studies in March 2013. Xi Jinping (2014, p. 298) declared: "Mankind, by living in the same global village in the same era and on the same earth where history and reality meet, has increasingly emerged as a community of common destiny in which everyone has in himself a little bit of other". The concept was then presented at the World Economic Forum in Davos in 2017. Strongly defending economic globalization in a period when the then US President Donald Trump followed his "America first" strategy, the Chinese leader sets out the goal to build a "community of shared future for mankind" that will make possible the creation of a "better world" and "better lives for our peoples" (The State Council Information Office, 2017). China's White Paper on International Development Cooperation stipulates also that "promoting a global community of shared future is the mission of China's international development cooperation" (The State Council, 2021).

This all-encompassing concept is perceived by China's leadership as the bases for a new model of regional and global development. Moreover, it hints at country's strategic intentions and aspirations for restructuring global governance. It hints also at the alternative (to the Western one) tactic China will apply in realizing its intentions. China will stay away from the image of an expansionist power and it will not seek to impose aggressively its values and model of development. It would rather seek to gradually gain centrality in global governance system expanding its influence and gaining further support across the world.

CONCLUSION

After a long period of time when China was accused for abstaining from active participation in international efforts to respond to global challenges, the country - under the leadership of Xi Jinping - demonstrates a strong ambition for a leading role in global governance and in global development, in particular. The realm of global development appears as a new dimension of geopolitical competition between China (contesting the post-Cold war international order) and the Western countries (maintaining the global status quo).

Beijing has launched several initiatives that, on the one hand, offer a new framework for global development, and on the other hand, provide a framework for a soft restructuring of the existing Western-oriented international order. The Belt and Road Initiative as well as the recently announced GDI, GSI and GCI – are made possible thanks to China's own economic success and development, achieved through the application of its own development model, which is alternative to the Western liberal model. China, rebalancing its inclusive, state-centered model of sustainable development further challenges the Western approach focused on the stability of free market institutions and liberal democracy. Moreover, China's specific development experience underlies China's alternative approach to global development, which pretends to be more inclusive and more responsive to the development deficits of the Global South.

While the United States still follows a security-centric policy, Beijing further strengthens its cooperation and expands influence in different parts of the world. China is gradually consolidating its position in global governance and reshaping the international order in line with its values, principles and interests.

REFERENCES

Alechina, I., Furtado, C., Galtung, J., Preiswerk, R., Wemegah, M., Loubser, J., Lapin, N., Richta, R., & Gombo-Yn-Miyegombo, G. (1982). *Different theories and practices of development*. UNESCO.

Bermingham, F. (2021). Xi Jinping tells G20 'developed countries' should lead on global emissions. *South China Morning Post*. https://www.scmp.com/news/china/article/3154308/chinas-xi-tells-g20-developed-countries-should-lead-global-emissions

Björklund, R. (2020). *A Post-development Critique of Chinese Development Discourse*. Lund University. https://lup.lub.lu.se/luur/download?func=downloadFile&recordOId=9026103&fileOId=9026104

Cao, F. (2009). Modernization Theory and China's Road to Modernization. *Chinese Studies in History*, *43*(1), 7–16. doi:10.2753/CSH0009-4633430101

CARI. (2023). *Data: Chinese Global Foreign Aid*. John Hopkins School of Advanced International Studies. http://www.sais-cari.org/data-chinese-global-foreign-aid

Carmody, P., Zajontz, T., & Reboredo, R. (2022). From 'debt diplomacy' to donorship? China's changing role in global development. *Global Political Economy.*, *1*(2), 198–217. doi:10.1332/UZHW7185

CEIC. (2023). *China Foreign Exchange Reserves*. https://www.ceicdata.com/en/indicator/china/foreign-exchange-reserves

Constitution of the People's Republic of China. 1982. http://www.npc.gov.cn/englishnpc/constitution2019/201911/1f65146fb6104dd3a2793875d19b5b29.shtml

Degterev, D. (2021). Незападные теории развития в эпоху глобального капитализма [Non-Western Theories of Development In The Global Capitalism Era]. *World Economy and International Relations*, *65*(4), 113–122. doi:10.20542/0131-2227-2021-65-4-113-122

Doshi, R. (2021). "Great Changes Unseen in a Century": The Elusive Phrase Driving China's Grands Strategy. *China Leadership Monitor*. https://www.prcleader.org/dashi

Dougherty, J., & Pfaltzgraff, R. (2001). *Contending Theories of International Relations. A Comprehensive Survey*. Longman.

Escobar, A. (1995). *Encountering Development. The Making and Unmaking of the Third World*. Princeton University Press.

Ferchen, M. (2020). *How China is Reshaping International Development*. Carnegie Endowment for International Peace. https://carnegieendowment.org/2020/01/08/how-china-is-reshaping-international-development-pub-80703

Global Times. (2021). *China to buy $150b in farm goods from ASEAN, almost double current level.* https://www.globaltimes.cn/page/202111/1239626.shtml

Goldin, I. (2019). Chinese Lessons in Poverty Eradication. In *China Watch.* The Sleeping Giant Awakes.

Herrero, A.G. (2021). What is Behind China's Dual Circulation Strategy. *China Leadership Monitor, 69.*

Hoang Thi Ha. (2023). Why is China's Global Development Initiative Well Received in Southeast Asia? *FULCRUM.* ISEAS – Yusof Isak Institute. https://fulcrum.sg/why-is-chinas-global-development-initiative-well-received-in-southeast-asia/

Ingram, G., & Lord, K. (2019). *Global Development Disrupted: Findings from a Survey of 93 leaders.* Global Economy and Development at Brookings.

Kissinger, H. (2012). *On China.* Penguin Press HC.

Lin, J. Y., & Wang, Y. (2017). *Going Beyond Aid: Development Cooperation for Structural Transformation.* Cambridge University Press. doi:10.1017/9781316597354

Ministry of Foreign Affairs of the People's Republic of China. (2023). *Xi Jinping Attends and Addressed the Opening Ceremony of the Plenary Session of the Second Eurasian Economic Forum of the Eurasian Economic Union.* https://www.fmprc.gov.cn/mfa_eng/zxxx_662805/202305/t20230528_11084920.html

Nedopil, Ch. (2022). *China Belt and Road Initiative (BRI) Investment Report 2021.* Green Finance & Development Center. FISF Fudan University. https://greenfdc.org/brief-china-belt-and-road-initiative-bri-investment-report-2021/?cookie-state-change=1689081894767

Pan, Zh. (2012). *Conceptual Gaps in China-EU Relations: Global Governance, Human Rights and Strategic Partnerships.* Palgrave Macmillan. doi:10.1057/9781137027443

Ramo, J. C. (2004). *The Beijing Consensus.* The Foreign Policy Center.

Rapley, J. (2004). Development studies and the post-development critique. *Progress in Development Studies, 4*(4), 350–354. doi:10.1191/1464993404ps095pr

Rostow, W. W. (1959). The Stages of Economic Growth. *The Economic History Review, 12*(1), 1-16. https://www.ufjf.br/oliveira_junior/files/2009/06/rostow.pdf

Rudyak, M. (2019). *The Ins and Outs of China's International Development Agency.* Carnegie Endowment for International Peace. https://carnegieendowment.org/2019/09/02/ins-and-outs-of-china-s-international-development-agency-pub-79739

Savage, R. (2023). China spent $240 billion bailing out 'Belt and Road' countries – study. *Reuters.* https://www.reuters.com/markets/china-spent-240-bln-bailing-out-belt-road-countries-study-2023-03-27/

Shuman, M., Fulton, J., & Gering, T. (2023). *How Beijing's newest global initiatives seek to remake the world order.* Atlantic Council. https://www.atlanticcouncil.org/in-depth-research-reports/issue-brief/how-beijings-newest-global-initiatives-seek-to-remake-the-world-order/

Stefanov, N., & Koleva, A. (2015). *Китай. Социално-икономическо развитие от древността до наши дни* [China. Social and Economic Development from Ancient Times to the Present Day]. East-West Publishing House.

The State Council. (2021). *China's International Development Cooperation in the New Era*. The State Council Information Office of the People's Republic of China. https://english.www.gov.cn/archive/whitepaper/202101/10/content_WS5ffa6bbbc6d0f72576943922.html

The State Council Information Office. (2017). *Jointly Shoulder Responsibility of Our Times, Promote Global Growth.* Keynote Speech by H.E. Xi Jinping, President of the People's Republic of China at the Opening Session of the World Economic Forum Annual Meeting. Davos. http://www.china.org.cn/node_7247529/content_40569136.htm

The State Council Information Office. (2021). *Xi declares China a moderately prosperous society in all respects*. http://english.scio.gov.cn/topnews/2021-07/01/content_77599525.htm

Thomas, D. (2021). What did FOCAC 2021 deliver for Africa? *African Business*. https://african.business/2021/11/trade-investment/what-can-africa-expect-from-focac-2021

Tselishchev, I. S. (2012). *Восточная Азия: новая волна роста и структурная трансформация* [East Asia: A New Wave of Growth and Structural Transformation]. IMEMO RAS.

UNCTAD. (n.d.). https://unctadstat.unctad.org/EN/Classifications.html

U.S. Department of State. (2009). *Closing Remarks for U.S.-China Strategic and Economic Dialogue.* https://2009-2017.state.gov/secretary/20092013clinton/rm/2009a/july/126599.htm

Vieira, V. C. (2019). From Third World Theory to Belt and Road Initiative. *Contexto Internacional, 41*(3), 529–551. doi:10.15900102-8529.2019410300003

Wang, Y. (2022). *Global Security Initiative and Global Development Initiative: Two Wings for Building a Community with a Shared Future for Mankind.* Boym Institute. https://instytutboyma.org/en/global-security-initiative-and-global-development-initiative-two-wings-for-building-a-community-with-a-shared-future-for-mankind/

Willis, K. (2011). *Theories and Practices of Development*. Taylor & Francis. doi:10.4324/9780203844182

World Bank. (2023). *GDP growth (annual %) – China*. https://data.worldbank.org/indicator/NY.GDP.MKTP.KD.ZG?end=2019&locations=CN&start=2010&view=chart

Xi, J. (2014). *The Governance of China*. Foreign Languages Press.

Xi, J. (2021). Understanding the new development stage, applying the new development philosophy, and creating a new development dynamic. *China Daily*. https://www.chinadaily.com.cn/a/202107/12/WS60ec3e56a310efa1bd6614fb.html

Xinhua. (2022). *Xi hosts High-level Dialogue on Global Development*. https://english.news.cn/20220624/b373551325e8468c976463eb9e33b9e7/c.html

Xinhua. (2023). *Xi Focus: China pursues development for people's well-being*. https://english.news.cn/20230309/dbf2e73bf1724030ad7f4b435237a86b/c.html

Yuan, J., Su, F., & Ouyang, X. (2022). *China's Evolving Approach to Foreign Aid*. Stockholm International Peace Research Institute. doi:10.55163/WTNJ4163

Chapter 10
The Interplay Between Energy Factors and Economic Growth in OECD Countries:
Insights From a Panel ARDL Model

Muhammet Atlas Doğan
https://orcid.org/0000-0002-4943-223X
Istanbul Technical University, Turkey

ABSTRACT

This study examines the interplay between energy consumption, environmental impact, and economic development by analyzing the relationship between GDP per capita and electric power consumption, energy use, renewable energy consumption, and research and development expenditure. The study uses panel ARDL methodology, analyzing data from OECD countries covering the period from 1996 to 2020. The results suggest that electric power consumption and energy use have a positive long-run relationship with GDP per capita, while renewable energy consumption and research and development expenditure have a negative relationship. The findings of this study provide valuable insights for policymakers seeking to promote sustainable economic growth while mitigating environmental degradation. The chapter concludes by highlighting the need for a holistic approach that takes into account the complex interplay between these variables and promotes policies that foster sustainable economic growth and environmental sustainability.

1. INTRODUCTION

In the era of rapid globalization and technological advancements, sustainable economic growth has become a central focus for policymakers and researchers alike (Dincsoy & Icihiminami, 2006). The intricate relationship between energy consumption, environmental impact, and economic development has generated significant research in recent years (Burakov & Freidin, 2017). A growing concern for climate change resulting in vulnerability on agriculture, production, natural sources, biodiversity, envi-

DOI: 10.4018/979-8-3693-0400-6.ch010

ronmental hazards and human life increases the need for a transition towards cleaner, renewable energy sources (Okur Dincsoy, 2016). This book chapter delves into the complex interplay between electric power consumption, GDP per capita, energy use, research and development expenditure, and renewable energy consumption to shed light on the underlying mechanisms that drive economic growth and environmental sustainability.

The 21st century has witnessed a paradigm shift in the global economy, with knowledge and innovation becoming pivotal factors for economic development. Grounded in the theories of endogenous growth and the Environmental Kuznets Curve (EKC), our analysis aims to provide a comprehensive understanding of how renewable research and development expenditure and energy consumption influence economic growth while mitigating the environmental impact. Furthermore, the chapter examines the role of energy use and electric power consumption in shaping the trajectory of GDP per capita across countries with different income levels.

One of the important topics that economists, policymakers, and academics are interested in is how energy consumption affects economic growth. This chapter explores this topic by examining how GDP per capita, electric power consumption, energy use, renewable energy consumption, and research and development expenditure are related. These variables are selected because they reflect economic development and environmental sustainability.

Electric power consumption (EPC) and energy use (EUSE) are two closely related variables that represent the demand for energy in a country. While EPC measures the amount of electric power consumed per capita, EUSE represents the amount of energy used in various forms, including fossil fuels, nuclear, and renewable energy sources. GDP per capita (GDP) is an essential indicator of economic development, while renewable energy consumption (RENEW) represents clean and sustainable energy sources. Research and development expenditure (RND) indicates a country's investment in innovation and technological progress, which are crucial for sustainable economic growth.

Many studies have explored how these variables are related. For instance, empirical research in the field of economics and sustainability provides evidence to substantiate the assertion that there is a positive correlation between energy consumption and economic growth, meaning that more energy use and consumption may result in more economic growth (Burakov & Freidin, 2017; Sari & Soytas, 2007). Others claim that economic growth can cause a transition to cleaner and more sustainable energy sources, such as renewable energy (Chen & Lei, 2018; Jin & Kim, 2018; Lee & Jung, 2018). In addition, the research and development expenditure relationship with economic growth has been shown to be positive (Gumus & Çelikay, 2015; Thombs, 2017), indicating that investment in innovation and technology can support sustainable economic development.

Nonetheless, the interaction between these variables is not always linear and may hinge on several factors, including economic development level, institutional factors, and policy structures. Furthermore, the interplay between these elements could vary from one country to another, underscoring the importance of a comprehensive cross-country study.

Using the panel ARDL approach, this chapter investigates the long-term and short-term interactions among electric power consumption, energy usage, per capita GDP, renewable energy consumption, and research and development spending. This study will provide valuable knowledge for academics and policymakers who are interested in the mitigation of environmental deterioration and advocating for economic development that supports long-term prosperity without depleting natural resources or causing harm to the environment.

The structure of this chapter is outlined in the following manner: The second section presents a review of existing literature pertaining to the relationships between electric power usage, energy consumption, GDP per capita, utilization of renewable energy, and expenditure on research and development. The third section illustrates the utilized data and the underlying methodologies. Subsequently, in the fourth section, results obtained from the empirical investigation are showcased and subjected to thorough analysis. Finally, the fifth section concludes the study by providing a summary of the research findings, alongside the proposition of potential policy recommendations based on the insights gained from the study.

2. REVIEW OF RELEVANT LITERATURE

As the multifarious nexus of energy consumption, economic growth, and environmental factors is delved into, it is pivotal for exploring the insights gathered from numerous geographical and economic contexts. This literature review is centered on the application of the Autoregressive Distributed Lag (ARDL) model in various studies, with the aim of unraveling the complexities of these relationships. Through the lens of different economies and countries, patterns and commonalities are sought to be discerned, along with an understanding of the distinctive variations that arise from unique economic conditions and policies.

In the realm of renewable energy, economic growth, and emissions, several seminal works ought to be brought into focus. The literature demonstrates that renewable energy consumption is pivotal to economic growth. Focusing on Türkiye, Ocal & Aslan (2013) found a significant positive correlation between renewable energy consumption and economic growth, highlighting the role of renewable energy in diversifying the energy mix and potentially reducing reliance on fossil fuels. This is consistent with the findings of Hung-Pin (2014), who, while analyzing nine OECD countries, discovered a long-run relationship between economic growth and renewable energy consumption, suggesting renewable energy is an enabler of sustainable economic growth.

Transitioning to the broader Middle Eastern and North African context, it is essential to understand how different countries with diverse economic conditions interact with renewable energy. In Tunisia, Cherni & Jouini (2017) examined the complex relationship between CO2 emissions, economic growth, and renewable energy consumption. They observed a long-term equilibrium between these variables, indicating that renewable energy consumption has a role in influencing CO2 emission trends. However, they found no significant relationship between renewable energy consumption and CO2 emissions, which they attributed to high investment costs in renewable technologies. This differs from the Turkish context, where renewable energy was more evidently linked with economic growth.

Moving further east to the Indian subcontinent, the role of trade liberalization and foreign direct investment in environmental sustainability becomes more prominent. Akalpler & Hove (2019) investigated the Indian context and observed that economic growth was positively linked with energy use and carbon emissions. However, they emphasized the significance of trade liberalization and foreign direct investments as mitigating factors for carbon emissions.

Expanding the scope to a global context, several studies demonstrate the interplay between energy consumption, economic growth, and environmental factors. Sari et al. (2008) examined the United States and found energy consumption to drive industrial production. Similarly, in the ASEAN-5 countries, Kisswani (2017) revealed a nonlinear, positive long-term relationship between energy consumption and GDP. Conversely, Tong et al. (2020) observed a positive correlation between economic growth and energy consumption within the E7 nations but a negligible influence of CO2 emissions on economic expansion. In examining Malaysia, Khan et al. (2021) identified a reciprocal causal relationship between energy consumption and economic growth. Finally, Pachiyappan et al. (2021) demonstrated that while GDP had a long-term negative effect on CO2 emissions, energy consumption and population growth were positively correlated with CO2 emissions.

Synthesis of literature demonstrates the multifaceted relationships between renewable energy consumption, economic growth, and environmental sustainability. The geographical contexts reveal varied outcomes influenced by regional economic conditions, policy frameworks, and investment in renewable technologies. This highlights the need for geographically tailored energy policy approaches and sustainable economic development approaches.

3. DATA AND THE METHODOLOGY

This study explores the interrelationship among electricity consumption, energy use, GDP per capita, consumption of renewable energy, and R&D spending. In order to achieve this, the panel Autoregressive Distributed Lag (ARDL) method is utilized. This methodology enables the estimation of the short-term and long-term correlations among variables while considering the inherent heterogeneity at the country level (Farhani & Rejeb, 2012).

3.1. Data

The relationship between electric power consumption (EPC), energy use (EUSE), GDP per capita (GDP), consumption of renewable energy (RENEW), and research and development expenditure (RND) is examined from 1996 to 2020 in 25 OECD countries that included in the dataset. The countries have been selected according to the data availability.

Table 1. Descriptive statistics

	lngdp	lnepc	lneuse	lnrenew	lnrnd
Mean	10.13645	8.786216	8.188099	2.756591	1.536897
Number of Obs.	800	800	800	800	800
Standard Deviation	0.798975	0.591069	0.458318	0.696748	0.186432
Min.	7.75381	7.17944	6.93229	1.28333	1.178861
Max.	11.72547	10.1501	9.151843	4.204543	2.055981

The World Development Indicators (WDI) database is the source of information on GDP per capita, electric power consumption, energy usage, and renewable energy consumption. For the research and development expenditure information, the Research and Development subsection within the WDI database of the World Bank is used.

In this analysis, the per capita electricity consumption is quantified in kilowatt-hours (kWh/capita), while energy utilization is measured in terms of kilograms of oil equivalent per person (kg/capita). The share of renewable energy consumption is evaluated by assessing its proportion in relation to total final energy consumption. Gross Domestic Product (GDP) per capita is expressed in constant U.S. dollars of the year 2010. Furthermore, the expenditure on research and development is gauged as a fraction of the GDP, denoted in percentage terms.

Table 2. Correlation matrix

	lngdp	lnepc	lneuse	lnrenew	lnrnd
lngdp	1				
lnepc	0.2896	1			
lneuse	0.1936	0.5357	1		
lnrenew	-0.1069	-0.1971	-0.2947	1	
lnrnd	-0.1039	-0.0252	-0.0416	0.041	1

Estimations of the long-term and short-term impacts of the variables on each other are conducted employing a panel Autoregressive Distributed Lag (ARDL) model. The Akaike Information Criterion (AIC) is utilized as the model selection method for estimations, with the number of lags for the dependent variable set at a maximum of three. A constant term is also incorporated into the model to account for potential fixed effects. The following section will discuss the methodology used to estimate the panel ARDL model and the results obtained from the analysis.

3.2. Methodology

The objective is to explore the enduring relationship between factors such as electric power consumption, energy usage, GDP per capita, renewable energy intake, and research and development expenditure, utilizing the panel ARDL model. For analyzing the connection among variables within a panel data context, especially when the data display cross-sectional dependency, as seen in our research, the panel ARDL approach is a fitting method (Harris & Tzavalis, 1999).

The Pooled Mean Group ARDL (PMG ARDL) estimator has various advantages compared to other methods for estimating dynamic heterogeneous panels. First, it does not require pre-testing for unit roots or co-integration, which can be problematic in finite samples. Second, it allows for the flexible specification of the lag structure and the short-run dynamics. Third, it is consistent and asymptotically normal under weak assumptions on the error terms and the explanatory variables.

The Pooled Mean Group ARDL (PMG ARDL) method serves as a tool for determining the lasting connection between variables in dynamic heterogeneous panels. These panels are datasets that incorporate multiple groups (like nations, regions, businesses, etc.) which exhibit different short-term dynamics but share a common long-term equilibrium. PMG ARDL accommodates distinct intercepts, short-term coefficients, and error variances for various groups while maintaining the long-term coefficients as constant. This estimator finds its foundation in the autoregressive distributed lag (ARDL) model that manages variables that are integrated of distinct orders and cointegrated (Humpe & McMillan, 2020). PMG ARDL can be used in panels where the number of groups and time periods are both substantial and of a similar scale (Chudik et al., 2021).

The model can be shown as follows:

$$y_{it} = \alpha_i + \sum_{j=1}^{p} \lambda_{ij} y_{it-j} + \sum_{j=0}^{q} \beta_{ij}^{'} x_{it-j} + \epsilon_{it}$$

where y_{it} is the dependent variable for group i at time t, α_i is the group-specific intercept, x_{it} is a vector of explanatory variables for group i at time t, λ_{ij} and β_{ij} are the short-run coefficients for group i, and ϵ_{it} is the error term for group i at time t. The long-run relationship between y_{it} and x_{it} can be obtained by imposing the restriction that the sum of the coefficients on the lagged dependent variable is equal to one:

$$\sum_{j=1}^{p} \lambda_{ij} = 1$$

This implies that:

$$y_{it} = \alpha_i + \theta_i^{'} x_{it} + \sum_{j=0}^{q} \left(\beta_{ij}^{'} - \theta_i^{'} \right) x_{it-j} + \epsilon_{it}$$

where $\theta'_i = -\frac{\beta'_{i0}}{1 - \sum_{j=1}^{p} \lambda_{ij}}$ is the vector of long-run coefficients for group i. The PMG ARDL estimator imposes that $\theta'_i = \theta'$ for all i, meaning that all groups have the same long-run coefficients. This estimator can be obtained by applying maximum likelihood or nonlinear least squares methods to the ARDL model.

The variables that are to be included in the model need to be specified to apply the PMG ARDL method. GDP per capita is chosen as the dependent variable, as the level of economic development and welfare of the countries is reflected by it. Four explanatory variables that are expected to have positive effects on GDP per capita, in the long run, are also chosen: electric power consumption per capita, energy use per capita, renewable energy consumption, and research and development expenditure. The aspects of energy consumption, productivity, and innovation that are relevant for economic growth are captured by these variables. The following equation shows our PMG ARDL model with these variables:

$$gdp_{it} = \alpha_i + \sum_{j=1}^{p} \lambda_{ij} gdp_{it-j} + \sum_{j=0}^{q} \beta_{ij1}^{'} epc_{it-j} + \sum_{j=0}^{q} \beta_{ij2}^{'} euse_{it-j} + \sum_{j=0}^{q} \beta_{ij3}^{'} renew_{it-j} + \sum_{j=0}^{q} \beta_{ij4}^{'} rnd_{it-j} + \epsilon_{it}$$

where gdp_{it} is the natural logarithm of GDP per capita for group i at time t, epc_{it} is the natural logarithm of electric power consumption per capita for group i at time t, $euse_{it}$ is the natural logarithm of energy use per capita for group i at time t, $renew_{it}$ represents the portion of renewable energy consumption within the total final energy consumption for the group i during the time period t, and rnd_{it} is the percentage of research and development expenditure in GDP for group i at time t. The other terms are as defined before.

The model considers GDP per capita as the variable to be explained and the other variables as the variables that explain it. It also considers that there is a long-run link between GDP per capita and the other variables, which can be found by imposing the condition that the sum of the coefficients on the lagged GDP per capita is equal to one:

$$\sum_{j=1}^{p} \lambda_{ij} = 1$$

This implies that:

$$gdp_{it} = \alpha_i + \theta_i' x_{it} + \sum_{j=0}^{q} \left(\beta_{ij}' - \theta_i' \right) x_{it-j} + \epsilon_{it}$$

where $\theta_i' = -\frac{\beta_{i0}'}{1-\sum_{j=1}^{p} \lambda_{ij}}$ is the vector of long-run coefficients for group i and x_{it} is a vector of explanatory variables for group i at time t. The PMG ARDL estimator imposes that $\theta_i' = \theta'$ for all i, meaning that all groups have the same long-run coefficients.

The optimal lag structure for the dependent and independent variables is selected using the Akaike information criterion (AIC). The maximum lag length for each variable is set to three, providing sufficient flexibility while avoiding the risk of overfitting the model. Dynamic regressors are also incorporated into the model, including the independent variables' lagged values to capture any short-run dynamics. Including dynamic regressors is a critical aspect of the panel ARDL approach, as it enables more accurate estimates of the long-run coefficients by controlling for short-run dynamics that may affect the relationship between the variables.

The stationarity of the data is tested by performing the Levin-Lin-Chu (LLC) unit root test, which is suitable for panel data with a small sample size (Levin et al., 2002). The Pesaran CD test is also used to check for cross-sectional dependence (M.H Pesaran, 2004). Pedroni (1999, 2004) and Kao (1999) panel co-integration tests are used to test for co-integration. The Pedroni test is based on the residual-based method, while the Kao test is based on the eigenvalue approach.

The panel ARDL model is estimated using the PMG estimator proposed by Pesaran et al. (1999) once the existence of a long-run relationship between the variables is established. The PMG estimator is a robust method that accounts for heterogeneity and cross-sectional dependence in the data. Diagnostic tests are also performed, including the Breusch-Pagan Lagrange Multiplier (L.M.) test for heteroscedasticity and the Ramsey test for omitted variable bias.

A Granger causality test is conducted to explore the short-run dynamics among the variables. This test facilitates the investigation of any significant causal impact of the independent variables on the dependent variable in the short run (Tsaurai & Ngcobo, 2020; Dinçsoy & Okur Dinçsoy, 2020). Dumitrescu & Hurlin's (2012) test, which is designed for panel data and allows for cross-sectional dependence, is used in this process.

4. RESULTS

Before embarking on an assessment of the interrelationships among variables within our panel data model, it is vital to confirm their stationarity. In cases where the regression models incorporate non-stationary variables, the accuracy of the derived estimations can be compromised. To verify the stationarity of the panel variables, a series of tests, including the Levin-Lin-Chu (LLC), Im-Pesaran-Shin (IPS), Fisher-

Augmented Dickey-Fuller (Fisher-ADF), and Fisher-Phillips-Perron (Fisher-PP), are carried out. The LLC test assumes that there is a common unit root process for all cross-sections, while the IPS test and the two Fisher-type tests allow for individual unit root processes for each cross-section.

Table 3. Results of panel unit root tests

Variables	Levin, Lin & Chu t Value		Im, Pesaran and Shin W-Stat		ADF- Fisher Chi-Square		P.P. - Fisher Chi-Square	
LNGDP	-4.4900**	(0.0000)	0.6400	(-0.738)	46.0100	(-0.9562)	44.6000	(-0.9690)
D(LNGDP)	-14.9800***	(0.0000)	-12.5600***	(0.0000)	268.2400***	(0.0000)	273.1700***	(0.0000)
LNEPC	3.0989	(-0.999)	6.9056	(-1.0000)	53.6060	(-0.8196)	102.2430**	(-0.0017)
D(LNEPC)	-12.8598***	(0.0000)	-12.4388***	(0.0000)	311.1060***	(0.0000)	363.3610***	(0.0000)
LNEUSE	3.1125	(-0.9991)	3.3771	(-0.9996)	62.8898	(-0.5158)	36.5283	(-0.9977)
D(LNEUSE)	-19.5426***	(0.0000)	-18.3579***	(0.0000)	431.3140***	(0.0000)	509.7690***	(0.0000)
LNRENEW	-1.2673*	-0.1025	4.4774	(-1.0000)	35.9589	(-0.9982)	37.3273	(-0.9969)
D(LNRENEW)	-20.0761***	(0.0000)	-19.4442***	(0.0000)	432.5920***	(0.0000)	488.5850***	(0.0000)
LNRND	-0.0188	-0.4925	4.2787	(-1.0000)	48.5443	(-0.9243)	42.5602	(-0.9821)
D(LNRND)	-13.9047***	(0.0000)	-15.4616***	(0.0000)	344.0680***	(0.0000)	335.1170***	(0.0000)

The determination of optimal lag lengths is determined by the modified Akaike information criterion, denoted by the *p* values enclosed in parentheses.

The statistical significance levels employed in this study are 10%, 5%, and 1% significance levels shown by *, **, and ***, respectively.

The null hypothesis for all tests is that a unit root is present. Table 3 depicts the outcomes of the panel unit root tests both at the level and the first difference for each variable (LNEPC, LNEUSE, LNRENEW, and LNRND). The general non-significance at the level (LNEPC, LNEUSE, LNRENEW, LNRND) corroborates that a unit root is found within all the panels. Nevertheless, the first difference (D(LNEPC), D(LNEUSE), D(LNRENEW), and D(LNRND) displays significance, demonstrating that the variables become stationary at the first difference stage.

In conclusion, the findings from unit root tests broadly substantiate that all variables became stationary at their first differenced version, which means variables are integrated of order one, I(1), implying that some variables are non-stationary at their level, yet their first difference resulted as stationary. As such, panel co-integration tests and analysis can be deployed to investigate the correlation between these variables further.

4.1. Panel Co-integration Test

Investigating potential long-run relationships between the study variables (LNGDP, LNEPC, LNEUSE, LNRENEW, LNRND) forms a crucial part of our research; two sophisticated panel co-integration tests, designed by Pedroni (1999, 2004) and Kao (1999) used for this purpose. These particular tests are a progression of the original two-step residual-based co-integration analysis, a concept introduced by Engle & Granger (1987). By using these advanced methods, our research deepens the exploration into the persisting interactions that might be present among the variables under consideration.

Table 4. Results of Pedroni residual co-integration test

		Within-Dimension (Panel Statistics)		Between-Dimension (Individual Statistics)		
	Test	**Statistic**	**Probability**		**Statistic**	**Probability**
Pedroni (1999)	Panel v-Statistic	-0.1009	0.5402	Group rho-Statistic	5.4445	1.0000
	Panel rho-Statistic	3.7667	0.9999	Group PP-Statistic	-0.9658	0.1671
	Panel PP-Statistic	-0.0858	0.4658	Group ADF-Statistic	-2.9572	0.0016
	Panel ADF-Statistic	-1.5858	0.0564			
Pedroni (2004) weighted	Panel v-Statistic	-0.1874	0.5743			
	Panel rho-Statistic	3.6189	0.9999			
	Panel PP-Statistic	-0.9938	0.1601			
	Panel ADF-Statistic	-2.9863	0.0014			
	Kao Residual Co-integration Test					
	ADF	-6.5821	0.0000			
	Residual variance (Kao)	0.0101				
	HAC variance (Kao)	0.0142				

The determination of optimal lag lengths is accomplished by employing the Schwarz information criterion (SIC).
The significance levels used in this study are set at 10%, 5%, and 1%, shown by *, **, and ***, respectively

Pedroni's tests are used to address heterogeneity in trends and intercepts across sections and to evaluate the stationarity of the residuals. When residuals exhibit stationarity, it signifies the potential rejection of the null hypothesis that rules out co-integration. Pedroni's co-integration analysis consists of seven statistical tests that examine two different hypotheses. The first is the homogenous alternative hypothesis, usually called the within-dimension test, while the second is the heterogeneous alternative hypothesis, referred to as the between-dimension test. This second test allows heterogeneous ρ coefficients across sections under the alternative hypothesis.

The results from our Pedroni tests are not entirely conclusive in rejecting the null hypothesis of non-cointegration across all statistical tests. The panel ADF-statistic from the within-dimension weighted test and the group ADF-statistic from the between-dimension test are able to discard the null hypothesis with a 1% level of significance. However, the remaining statistical tests do not decisively reject the null hypothesis at conventional levels of significance, suggesting inconclusive evidence of co-integration.

For robustness, the Kao Residual Co-integration Test has been used, which is a method that places intercepts that is specific to cross-sectional and homogenous coefficients on independent variables. At the 1% level of significance, the ADF t-statistic from the Kao test rejects the null hypothesis of non-cointegration, indicating the presence of co-integration—or a long-term relationship—between the variables LNGDP, LNEPC, LNEUSE, LNRENEW, and LNRND.

In conclusion, the Pedroni Residual Co-integration Test yields more inconsistent results than the Kao Residual Co-integration Test, which supports the existence of co-integration among the variables. The Pedroni test's panel ADF-statistic (within-dimension) and group ADF-statistic (between-dimension) were able to reject the null hypothesis of non-cointegration, but the remaining statistical tests could not, leading to a less clear-cut interpretation.

Moreover, given the dynamic nature of the study variables—such as economic growth, energy production and consumption, renewable energy usage, and research and development—there may be structural shifts over time that could influence the co-integration relationship among the variables. Future research efforts might consider dividing the data into smaller periods or exploring time-varying co-integration methodologies to account for this.

4.2. Examination of Long-Term Associations and Short-Term Variations

Upon completing all requisite preliminary examinations, this section concentrates on exploring enduring associations and transient fluctuations between GDP per capita, per-person energy use, per-person renewable energy consumption, and per-person R&D spending. Additionally, their individual short-term adjustment procedures are covered. Owing to the possible association between the mean-differenced independent variables and the error term, conventional Auto Regressive Distributed Lag (ARDL) models with fixed effects, along with ordinary least squares (OLS) estimation, may yield asymptotically biased estimators (Hotak et al., 2020). This study uses the Panel Pooled Mean Group ARDL (PMG-ARDL) model to address these potential problems, following the same methodology as Bekun et al. (2019) and Sarkodie & Strezov (2019). This model, which Pesaran et al. (1999) built on integrating ARDL (p, q) models and PMG estimators, offers flexibility by allowing different coefficients for each unique cross-section. Additionally, it exhibits its efficacy in a variety of situations, such as when variables display various orders of integration or a combination of them.

4.2.1. Long-Run Relationships

The results of our study delineate important relationships in the context of per capita GDP growth.

Starting with the influence of per capita electric power consumption (LNEPC(-1)), we observe a compelling positive correlation in the long run. To quantify, an elevation of 1% in electric power consumption per capita corresponds to an approximate growth of 1.19% in GDP per capita. This relationship underscores the role of electricity consumption in fostering economic output, reinforced by a statistically significant coefficient.

Turning to the role of per capita energy usage (LNEUSE(-1)), our analysis points to a significant long-term positive relationship with GDP per capita. Specifically, a 1% surge in energy use per capita is tied to an enhancement of 1.66% in GDP per capita. The strength of this correlation signifies that escalating per capita energy consumption can be a robust propellant of economic expansion.

In contrast, the analysis reveals a contrasting trend for renewable energy consumption (LNRENEW(-1)). In the long run, a 1% rise in the proportion of consumption of renewable energy from total final energy consumption correlates with a 0.56% contraction in GDP per capita. This inverse relationship might stem from existing inefficiencies or elevated costs tied to renewable energy adoption. However, with the rapid progression of renewable technologies, this dynamic might undergo a transition.

Table 5. PMG-ARDL results

Variable	Coefficient	Std. Error
	Long-Run Equation	
LNEPC(-1)	1.188599***	0.258755
LNEUSE(-1)	1.662852***	0.268439
LNRENEW(-1)	-0.560784***	0.100841
LNRND(-1)	1.725502***	0.245754
	Short-Run Equation	
COINTEQ01	-0.20442***	0.066846
D(LNGDP(-1))	0.222425***	0.066988
D(LNGDP(-2))	-0.334068***	0.056015
D(LNEPC(-1))	-0.423931	0.359605
D(LNEPC(-2))	-0.647139	0.47471
D(LNEPC(-3))	-0.103898	0.531952
D(LNEUSE(-1))	-0.342486	0.337862
D(LNEUSE(-2))	-0.288609	0.456017
D(LNEUSE(-3))	0.343516	0.300631
D(LNRENEW(-1))	0.291113	0.36734
D(LNRENEW(-2))	-0.207067	0.234769
D(LNRENEW(-3))	-0.044051	0.168582
D(LNRND(-1))	-0.118093	0.489309
D(LNRND(-2))	-1.147118**	0.512517
D(LNRND(-3))	-0.150885	0.63384
C	-3.062924**	0.980808

Note: Significance levels: ***: 1%, **: 5%, *: 10%.
Akaike information criterion is used for the lag selection.

Lastly, the impact of research and development expenditure (LNRND (-1)) is evaluated. The analysis verifies a robust positive correlation, where a 1% rise in expenditure, in terms of GDP, is associated with a projected 1.73% long-term growth in GDP per capita. The criticality of investments in research and development as an impetus for economic growth is amplified by this correlation.

4.2.2. Short-Run Dynamics

Our research findings present a rich narrative about the interplay between GDP per capita growth and key determinants and how these relationships evolve in the short and long run.

The error correction term (COINTEQ01), indicating the speed of adjustment towards long-term equilibrium, stands at -0.20, suggesting that approximately 20.4% of the disequilibrium in the GDP per capita rectifies each period, implying a moderate pace of adjustment.

In the short-term horizon, the interdependencies between GDP per capita growth and the examined variables exhibit less clarity regarding statistical significance. However, a few key findings can be observed:

The first lag of GDP per capita growth (D(LNGDP(-1))) displays a 1% increase associated with a 0.22% growth in GDP per capita. This positive relation denotes that historical GDP growth benefits current GDP growth, reinforced by a statistically significant coefficient. Interestingly, a 1% rise in the second lag of GDP per capita growth (D(LNGDP(-2))) aligns with a 0.33% reduction in GDP per capita growth. This inverse relation could reflect business cycles or macroeconomic factors.

The second lag of research and development expenditure growth (D(LNRND(-2))) also shares an inverse relation with GDP per capita growth in the short term. A 1% boost in the second lag corresponds to a 1.15% drop in GDP per capita growth, possibly due to the lag between R&D investments and their tangible economic outcomes.

Although the remaining coefficients in the short-term dynamics equation lack statistical significance, the significant long-term correlations spotlight the significance of electric power consumption, energy use, renewable energy consumption, and research and development expenditure in economic growth.

The panel ARDL model underscores significant long-run associations between GDP per capita and the scrutinized variables, where electric power consumption, energy use, and research and development expenditure contribute positively, while renewable energy consumption impacts negatively. The short-run adjustment process toward long-run equilibrium is measured at 20.4%.

Aligning with existing literature, our study confirms a positive long-run relationship between electric power consumption and GDP per capita growth (Ozturk & Acaravcı, 2010; Shahbaz, 2015) between energy use and GDP per capita growth (Apergis & Payne, 2009) and between research and development expenditure and GDP per capita growth (Akinwale, 2018; Grossman & Helpman, 1991; Romer, 1990). The observed negative long-run relationship between renewable energy consumption and GDP per capita growth aligns with Apergis & Payne (2010).

This study highlights the importance of targeted policies in areas such as electricity consumption, energy use, renewable energy, and research investment for achieving long-term economic growth. Panel ARDL model results are consistent with previous literature and provide valuable insights for sustainable economic growth policy design. The long-term effects of these factors on economic development and environmental sustainability should be taken into account by policymakers.

4.3. Panel Granger Causality

Dumitrescu & Hurlin's (2012) heterogeneous panel causality test was employed in our study to discern the directionality of relations among variables. This methodology is aptly chosen for our research as it acknowledges the heterogeneity within both the regression model and the causal relationships across diverse countries, given their varied trade structures and energy utilization patterns. Our investigation primarily concentrates on the short-term correlations between variables, as all of them are stationary at the first difference.

The Pairwise Dumitrescu Hurlin Panel Causality Test outcomes illustrate a range of causal correlations among the variables. Firstly, there is a noticeable bidirectional causality between LNEPC and LNGDP. This implies that energy production and GDP exert mutual influence over each other. Additionally, bi-directional causality was identified between LNEUSE and LNGDP and between LNEUSE and LNEPC. This suggests that energy utilization and production are intertwined and influence GDP in the short-term.

Table 6. Pairwise Dumitrescu Hurlin panel causality tests results

Null Hypothesis:	W-Stat.	Zbar-Stat.	Prob.
LNEPC(-1) does not homogeneously cause LNGDP(-1)	4.25855***	4.34709	0.0000
LNGDP(-1) does not homogeneously cause LNEPC(-1)	7.52486***	11.4755	0.0000
LNEUSE(-1) does not homogeneously cause LNGDP(-1)	3.92347***	3.61582	0.0003
LNGDP(-1) does not homogeneously cause LNEUSE(-1)	5.02882***	6.02812	0.0000
LNRENEW(-1) does not homogeneously cause LNGDP(-1)	2.66260	0.86409	0.3875
LNGDP(-1) does not homogeneously cause LNRENEW(-1)	8.16636***	12.8755	0.0000
LNRND(-1) does not homogeneously cause LNGDP(-1)	2.31224	0.09946	0.9208
LNGDP(-1) does not homogeneously cause LNRND(-1)	5.44638***	6.93940	0.0000
LNEUSE(-1) does not homogeneously cause LNEPC(-1)	6.49201***	9.22139	0.0000
LNEPC(-1) does not homogeneously cause LNEUSE(-1)	4.09415***	3.98830	0.0001
LNRENEW(-1) does not homogeneously cause LNEPC(-1)	8.96871***	14.6265	0.0000
LNEPC(-1) does not homogeneously cause LNRENEW(-1)	4.76930***	5.46175	0.0000
LNRND(-1) does not homogeneously cause LNEPC(-1)	7.25479***	10.8861	0.0000
LNEPC(-1) does not homogeneously cause LNRND(-1)	5.37524***	6.78416	0.0000
LNRENEW(-1) does not homogeneously cause LNEUSE(-1)	5.24717***	6.50464	0.0000
LNEUSE(-1) does not homogeneously cause LNRENEW(-1)	3.63118***	2.97791	0.0029
LNRND(-1) does not homogeneously cause LNEUSE(-1)	2.73292	1.01754	0.3089
LNEUSE(-1) does not homogeneously cause LNRND(-1)	5.70729***	7.50882	0.0000
LNRND(-1) does not homogeneously cause LNRENEW(-1)	4.78494***	5.49588	0.0000
LNRENEW(-1) does not homogeneously cause LNRND(-1)	4.97230***	5.90478	0.0000

Variables are transformed into their first difference.
*10% significance level(W-statistics)
**5% significance level (W-statistics)
***1% significance level (W-statistics)

Furthermore, we detected a unidirectional causality originating from LNGDP leading to LNRENEW and from LNGDP to LNRND. This suggests that economic growth propels the incorporation of renewable energy technologies and fuels research and development endeavors in the near term. The causality results also display a unidirectional relationship from LNEPC leading to LNRENEW and from LNEPC to LNRND, indicating that energy production triggers the adoption of renewable energy technologies and prompts research and development activities.

Moreover, the test results signal a bidirectional causality between LNEUSE and LNRENEW and between LNEUSE and LNRND. This intimates that energy usage is tightly intertwined with the deployment of renewable energy technologies and research and development operations. Finally, we observe a unidirectional causality emerging from LNRENEW leading to LNRND, underscoring the influence of renewable energy technologies on research and development initiatives.

Table 7. Summary of the pairwise Dumitrescu Hurlin panel causality tests

Direction of Relationship			
LNGDP		↔	LNEPC (Electric Power Consumption)
LNGDP		↔	LNEUSE (Energy Use)
LNGDP		↔	LNRENEW (Renewable Energy Consumption)
LNGDP		↔	LNRND (R&D Expenditure)

In summary, the Dumitrescu-Hurlin Panel Causality Test results provide valuable insights into the complex web of causal relationships among energy production, GDP, energy use, renewable energy technologies, and research and development efforts in the short run. Understanding these relationships is crucial for policymakers seeking to promote sustainable economic growth, reduce energy consumption, and encourage the development and adoption of cleaner energy technologies (Indriani, 2022).

5. CONCLUSION

This research has delved into the long-term associations and short-term fluctuations between GDP per capita growth, per capita electric power consumption, per capita energy usage, renewable energy consumption, and research and development expenditure utilizing panel pooled mean group ARDL (PMG-ARDL) models. Our findings offer significant insights, particularly for policymakers striving to foster sustainable economic growth while considering the significance of energy consumption and technological progression.

The findings derived from the panel ARDL model illuminate that, in the long-term, GDP per capita growth is positively impacted by electric power consumption, energy use, and research and development expenditure, whereas renewable energy consumption exerts a negative influence. This infers that enhancing economic output necessitates an increase in electric power consumption and energy use, and capital allocated for research and development is vital for spurring technological advancement and innovation. The existing inverse relationship between renewable energy use and GDP per capita growth could originate from inefficiencies or high costs associated with renewable energy sources. As advancements in renewable energy technologies continue, the characteristics of this relationship could evolve, highlighting the need for continual policy adjustments.

Within the short-term scope, the progression towards the long-term equilibrium is rather measured, with an adjustment pace of approximately 20.4%. The interconnections between GDP per capita growth and the independent determinants become somewhat ambiguous, albeit a handful of statistically significant associations are observable, particularly the lagged aspects of GDP per capita growth and the expansion of research and development expenditure. These relationships underscore the intricate dynamics of the short-term interplay between these elements and economic growth, a complexity that must be integrated into policy design by decision-makers.

The discoveries from this investigation add a valuable perspective to the continuing discourse around sustainable development and energy-oriented policies. The affirmative linkage between GDP per capita and both electric power consumption and energy utilization underscores the challenge of equating economic expansion with environmental conservation. The inverse relationship observed between GDP per capita and both renewable energy consumption and research and development expenditure calls for increased commitments toward technological innovation to foster sustainable growth.

The outcomes derived from our panel ARDL model correlate well with numerous preceding studies found in the literature, thus re-emphasizing the importance of incorporating energy consumption, renewable energy application, and research and development expenditure in formulating policies to promote sustainable economic advancement. To tackle the hurdles presented by climate change and environmental preservation, a focus on transitioning towards cleaner and more efficient energy sources is imperative, paralleled by encouraging research and development endeavors that catalyze innovation and productivity enhancements.

Future explorations could explore the factors influencing the short-term relationships between GDP per capita growth and the independent determinants and the potential ramifications of other energy-centric factors on economic expansion. For the promotion of sustainable economic growth, it is vital for policymakers to understand and react to the sway of a plethora of elements like national strategies, global energy cost fluctuations, and advancements in energy sector technology. Moreover, international collaborations, public-private synergies, and initiatives aimed at raising awareness and education have pivotal roles in advancing the adoption of cleaner energy alternatives and spurring innovation in research and development. Considering the complex interaction between these variables and endorsing policies that encourage sustainable economic growth alongside environmental preservation, a comprehensive approach can enable nations to attain long-term economic stability while minimizing the negative impacts of climate change and resource scarcity.

REFERENCES

Akalpler, E., & Hove, S. (2019). Carbon emissions, energy use, real GDP per capita and trade matrix in the Indian economy-an ARDL approach. *Energy*, *168*, 1081–1093. doi:10.1016/j.energy.2018.12.012

Akinwale, Y. O. (2018). An empirical analysis of short run and long run relationships between energy consumption, technology innovation and economic growth in Saudi Arabia. *International Journal of Energy Economics and Policy*, *8*(4), 139–146.

Apergis, N., & Payne, J. (2009). Energy consumption and economic growth in Central America: Evidence from a panel co-integration and error correction model. *Energy Economics*, *31*(2), 211–216. doi:10.1016/j.eneco.2008.09.002

Apergis, N., & Payne, J. (2010). Renewable energy consumption and economic growth: Evidence from a panel of OECD countries. *Energy Policy*, *38*(1), 656–660. doi:10.1016/j.enpol.2009.09.002

Bekun, F. V., Alola, A. A., & Sarkodie, S. A. (2019). Toward a sustainable environment: Nexus between CO2 emissions, resource rent, renewable and nonrenewable energy in 16-EU countries. *The Science of the Total Environment*, *657*, 1023–1029. doi:10.1016/j.scitotenv.2018.12.104 PMID:30677870

Burakov, D., & Freidin, M. (2017). Financial development, economic growth and renewable energy consumption in Russia: A vector error correction approach. *International Journal of Energy Economics and Policy*, *7*(6), 39–47.

Chen, W., & Lei, Y. (2018). The impacts of renewable energy and technological innovation on environment-energy-growth nexus: New evidence from a panel quantile regression. *Renewable Energy, 123*, 1–14. doi:10.1016/j.renene.2018.02.026

Cherni, A., & Jouini, S. E. (2017). An ARDL approach to the CO2 emissions, renewable energy and economic growth nexus: Tunisian evidence. *International Journal of Hydrogen Energy, 42*(48), 29056–29066. doi:10.1016/j.ijhydene.2017.08.072

Chudik, A., Mohaddes, K., & Raissi, M. (2021). Covid-19 fiscal support and its effectiveness. *Economics Letters, 205*, 109939. doi:10.1016/j.econlet.2021.109939 PMID:36540861

Dincsoy, E. E., & Ichiminami, F. (2006). An Assessment of the Southeastern Anatolia Region in Turkey in Terms of the Sustainable Development Targets. *Journal of the Faculty of Environmental Science and Technology, 11*(1), 75–81.

Dinçsoy, E. E., & Okur Dinçsoy, M. (2020). Ekonomik büyümenin enflasyon üzerine etkisinin Türkiye ekonomisi açısından analizi. *Balkan ve Yakın Doğu Sosyal Bilimler Dergisi, 6*, 118–124.

Dumitrescu, E. I., & Hurlin, C. (2012). Testing for Granger non-causality in heterogeneous panels. *Economic Modelling, 29*(4), 1450–1460. doi:10.1016/j.econmod.2012.02.014

Engle, R. F., & Granger, C. W. J. (1987). Co-Integration and Error Correction: Representation, Estimation, and Testing. *Econometrica, 55*(2), 251–276. doi:10.2307/1913236

Farhani, S., & Ben Rejeb, J. (2012). Energy consumption, economic growth and CO2 emissions: Evidence from panel data for MENA region. *International Journal of Energy Economics and Policy, 2*(2), 71–81.

Grossman, G. M., & Helpman, E. (1991). Trade, knowledge spillovers, and growth. *European Economic Review, 35*(2), 517–526. doi:10.1016/0014-2921(91)90153-A

Gumus, E., & Çelikay, F. (2015). R\&D Expenditure and Economic Growth: New Empirical Evidence. *Margin - the Journal of Applied Economic Research, 9*(3), 205–217. doi:10.1177/0973801015579753

Harris, R., & Tzavalis, E. (1999). Inference for unit roots in dynamic panels where the time dimension is fixed. *Journal of Econometrics, 91*(2), 201–226. doi:10.1016/S0304-4076(98)00076-1

Hotak, S., Islam, M., Kakinaka, M., & Kotani, K. (2020). Carbon emissions and carbon trade balances: International evidence from panel ARDL analysis. *Environmental Science and Pollution Research International, 27*(19), 24115–24128. doi:10.100711356-020-08478-w PMID:32304055

Humpe, A., & McMillan, D. G. (2020). Macroeconomic variables and long-term stock market performance. A panel ARDL co-integration approach for G7 countries. *Cogent Economics & Finance, 8*(1), 1816257. doi:10.1080/23322039.2020.1816257

Hung-Pin, L. (2014). Renewable Energy Consumption and Economic Growth in Nine OECD Countries: Bounds Test Approach and Causality Analysis. *TheScientificWorldJournal, 919167*, 1–6. Advance online publication. doi:10.1155/2014/919167 PMID:24558343

Indriani, D. (2022). Tourism and Economic Growth: Evidence from ASEAN countries. *Journal of Indonesian Applied Economics, 10*(2), 100–131. doi:10.21776/ub.jiae.2022.010.02.4

Jin, T., & Kim, J. (2018). What is better for mitigating carbon emissions – Renewable energy or nuclear energy? A panel data analysis. *Renewable & Sustainable Energy Reviews*, *91*, 464–471. doi:10.1016/j.rser.2018.04.022

Kao, C. (1999). Spurious regression and residual-based tests for co-integration in panel data. *Journal of Econometrics*, *90*(1), 1–44. doi:10.1016/S0304-4076(98)00023-2

Kisswani, K. M. (2017). Evaluating the GDP–energy consumption nexus for the ASEAN-5 countries using nonlinear ARDL model. *OPEC Energy Review*, *41*(4), 318–343. doi:10.1111/opec.12113

Lee, S.-H., & Jung, Y. (2018). Causal dynamics between renewable energy consumption and economic growth in South Korea: Empirical analysis and policy implications. *Energy & Environment*, *29*, 1298–1315.

Levin, A., Lin, C.-F., & James Chu, C.-S. (2002). Unit root tests in panel data: Asymptotic and finite-sample properties. *Journal of Econometrics*, *108*(1), 1–24. doi:10.1016/S0304-4076(01)00098-7

Ocal, O., & Aslan, A. (2013). Renewable energy consumption–economic growth nexus in Turkey. *Renewable & Sustainable Energy Reviews*, *28*, 494–499. doi:10.1016/j.rser.2013.08.036

Okur Dincsoy, M. (2016). A Comparative Study on Population and Employment Risks in Vulnerable Countries to Climate Change. *International Journal of Ecological Economics and Statistics*, *37*(2), 103–120.

Ozturk, I., & Acaravcı, A. (2010). CO2 emissions, energy consumption and economic growth in Turkey. *Renewable & Sustainable Energy Reviews*, *14*(9), 3220–3225. doi:10.1016/j.rser.2010.07.005

Pachiyappan, D., Ansari, Y., Alam, M. S., Thoudam, P., Alagirisamy, K., & Manigandan, P. (2021). Short and Long-Run Causal Effects of CO2 Emissions, Energy Use, GDP and Population Growth: Evidence from India Using the ARDL and VECM Approaches. In Energies (Vol. 14, Issue 24). doi:10.3390/en14248333

Pedroni, P. (1999). Critical Values for Co-integration Tests in Heterogeneous Panels with Multiple Regressors. *Oxford Bulletin of Economics and Statistics*, *61*(s1, S1), 653–670. doi:10.1111/1468-0084.61.s1.14

Pedroni, P. (2004). *Panel Co-integration: Asymptotic and Finite Sample Properties of Pooled Time Series Tests with an Application to the PPP Hypothesis* (Department of Economics Working Papers, Issues 2004–15). Department of Economics, Williams College. https://econpapers.repec.org/RePEc:wil:wileco:2004-15

Pesaran, M., Shin, Y., & Smith, R. P. (1999). Pooled Mean Group Estimation of Dynamic Heterogeneous Panels. *Journal of the American Statistical Association*, *94*(446), 621–634. doi:10.1080/01621459.1999.10474156

Pesaran, M. H. (2004). General Diagnostic tests for Cross Section dependence in Panels:Cambridge working Paper in Economics. *IZA Discussion Paper, 1240.*

Romer, P. M. (1990). Endogenous Technological Change. *Journal of Political Economy*, *98*(5), S71–S102. doi:10.1086/261725

Sari, R., Ewing, B. T., & Soytas, U. (2008). The relationship between disaggregate energy consumption and industrial production in the United States: An ARDL approach. *Energy Economics*, *30*(5), 2302–2313. doi:10.1016/j.eneco.2007.10.002

Sari, R., & Soytas, U. (2007). The growth of income and energy consumption in six developing countries. *Energy Policy*, *35*(2), 889–898. doi:10.1016/j.enpol.2006.01.021

Sarkodie, S. A., & Strezov, V. (2019). Effect of foreign direct investments, economic development and energy consumption on greenhouse gas emissions in developing countries. *The Science of the Total Environment*, *646*, 862–871. doi:10.1016/j.scitotenv.2018.07.365 PMID:30064112

Shahbaz, M. (2015). Electricity Consumption, Financial Development and Economic Growth Nexus in Pakistan: A Visit. *Bulletin of Energy Economics*, *3*(2), 48–65. https://EconPapers.repec.org/RePEc:ijr:beejor:v:3:y:2015:i:2:p:48-65

Thombs, R. P. (2017). The Paradoxical Relationship between Renewable Energy and Economic Growth: A Cross-National Panel Study, 1990-2013. *Journal of World-systems Research*, *23*(2), 540–564. doi:10.5195/jwsr.2017.711

Tong, T., Ortiz, J., Xu, C., & Li, F. (2020). Economic growth, energy consumption, and carbon dioxide emissions in the E7 countries: A bootstrap ARDL bound test. *Energy, Sustainability and Society*, *10*(1), 20. doi:10.118613705-020-00253-6

Tsaurai, K., & Ngcobo, L. (2020). Renewable Energy Consumption, Education and Economic Growth in Brazil, Russia, India, China, South Africa. *International Journal of Energy Economics and Policy*, *10*(2), 26–34. doi:10.32479/ijeep.8497

Chapter 11
The Effect of the COVID-19 Pandemic on the Health Insurance Market in Bulgaria:
Empirical Analysis of Market Concentration

Valentina Nikolaeva Ninova
https://orcid.org/0000-0002-6147-2293
Tsenov Academy of Economics, Bulgaria

Nikolay Blagoev Ninov
https://orcid.org/0000-0003-1029-1318
Tsenov Academy of Economics, Bulgaria

ABSTRACT

The chapter is focused on the study of the effect of the processes caused by the global COVID-19 pandemic on the health insurance market in Bulgaria – a field of business with a high return on investment and an exceptional public benefit, while at the same time suffering from a deficit of research, which necessitates the need for more in-depth and up-to-date scientific analysis and studies. In this regard, referring to the official statistical data of the Financial Supervision Commission, an analysis is made of the key indicators for the development of the insurance market in Bulgaria during the period 2017-2022, indicating the factors that influence the main processes taking place in it. The main result is expressed in confirmation of the thesis, that there is high market concentration in the current health insurance market, in favor of a few insurance companies performing a key role in it, and on the market, there is growth in terms of gross written premium income, also provoked by COVID-19.

DOI: 10.4018/979-8-3693-0400-6.ch011

1. INTRODUCTION

The health insurance market as we see it today is the result of several processes, but three of them are particularly important: the process of relicensing social health insurance companies; the attempt to involve insurance companies as an active party within the social health insurance model operating in Bulgaria and the COVID-19 pandemic. These processes can be defined as key "catalysts" for health insurance market development.

The first of them is the process of relicensing social health insurance companies as insurance companies (formed public relations in this sphere by the legislative power and as a new stage of the ongoing health reform in Bulgaria, assigning their role to the second pillar of the current social health insurance model), which started in 2012. This major change, which occurred by the requirements of Council Directive 73/239/EEC15 and Council Directive 92/49/EEC16 and amending Directives 73/239/EEC and 88/357/EEC17, aimed at (Ministry of Health (Bulgaria); Ninova, 2021; Ninova, 2016):

- unification of Bulgarian and European legislation expressed in actions to eliminate inconsistencies in the regulatory framework of the activity on supplementary social health insurance;
- strengthening financial supervision over social health insurance companies; elimination of the insufficiency and limitation of the information included in the program of their activity, as a result of which it is impossible to assess its reliability, its adequacy, and feasibility; increased companies' capital and solvency requirements, caused by the specifics of the activity related to the health of individuals;
- increasing the quality and security of the offered services. According to the provisions of the Insurance Code, the criteria for insurance companies are higher, which automatically guarantees the users of insurance services that the companies admitted to the market are financially stable, responsible, and apply good business practices;
- strengthening competition in the sector, through a more diverse portfolio of innovative health insurance products and services, and hence the provision of greater options for choosing the same on the part of the users – corporate clients and citizens.

After calming down the relationships that arose among the various entities brought about by this reform, the activity of insurance companies offering health insurance policies in the form of additional health protection (voluntary health insurance) was channelized, and their efforts were directed towards capturing a larger market share. The offered aid, materialized in an insurance product offering a package of medical care, supplementing the basic package of medical assistance provided under the public compulsory social health insurance in Bulgaria, administered by the National Health Insurance Fund (NHIF), has provoked great interest between the business environment and citizens. The logical explanation for the stated interest lies, on the one hand, in the emerging trends of ever greater demand and attention to this type of need, subject to the prioritization and increased demands of individuals for their health, and from the business point of view – for the health of employed associates (employees and workers). On the other hand, the constant interest of the citizens is dictated by the desire to reduce to the maximum extent the existing systemic obstacles to accessing receiving timely, quality, and effective health care, which is also considered one of the serious shortcomings of the current Bulgarian healthcare system. On the third hand, it is an attempt to find an alternative option for getting quality health services outside the public healthcare system, financed through the compulsory social health insurance system in Bulgaria, due to its chronic state of underfunding, shortage of specialists, unsatisfactory infrastructure and equipment and so on, which largely has a deterrent and socially demotivating effect.

In 2018, two fundamentally different models for reforming the current social health insurance model were presented to Bulgarian society. In both models, an important role was given to insurance companies offering health insurance policies. In the first proposed reform option, the demonopolisation of the National Health Insurance Fund was foreseen, and the provision of an opportunity for private insurance companies to compete with it on an equal footing (performing a substitute role), for "customers" and, accordingly, for their social health insurance contributions. The second option for health reform envisaged a modification of the current model in the manner of the three-pillar pension insurance model applied in Bulgaria, with the introduction of the first pillar – the previous compulsory social health insurance, the second pillar – compulsory health insurance and the third pillar – voluntary health insurance. The concept of this variant further develops the operating model in the direction of further upgrading the basic package of healthcare services guaranteed by the NHIF with the involvement of insurance companies as participants in this process, on the principle of obligation for citizens regarding their participation and the principle of voluntariness, regarding the choice of the insurance company, in which to pay a fixed amount (insurance premium), providing them with an additional package of health services. The third pillar – "voluntary insurance" aims to satisfy the personal needs of individuals and enable them to receive health services that remain outside the scope of the packages offered by the first and the second pillars (such as related to covering costs for corrections of aesthetic imperfections in patients in a state of clinical health, with no existing personal health problem in the area of the change being performed). This ultimately failed reform of the social health insurance model had the effect of increasing interest and attention to the products of the insurance companies competing in the health insurance market and confirmed their ever-increasing role in the healthcare sector.

The COVID-19 pandemic, which has become a real threat to the entire Bulgarian population, not only to public health but also to the socio-economic situation, has created an opportunity for insurers in Bulgaria to demonstrate their inherent flexibility and business acumen. Apart from several negative consequences, they also saw new opportunities in the created situation. These opportunities are related to the desire and especially the demand formed by people and business structures to obtain additional protection through the purchase of an insurance product with coverage for a disease caused by COVID-19. It is important to clarify that the insurances related to the Coronavirus are outside the scope of the publicly built and functioning social security systems, which at times have shown slowness and hesitation regarding their effectiveness and efficiency. Only two months after 13 March 2020, when a state of emergency was declared due to a pandemic crisis in Bulgaria, insurance companies offered flexible conditions, which responded to the emerging interest in insurance protection in case of infection and subsequent treatment of COVID-19. For potential policyholders, the protection offered is rather financial (in the form of financial compensation), since the Coronavirus could also lead to the occurrence of extraordinary costs related mostly to treatment. Insurance companies in Bulgaria offered coverage against the Coronavirus risk, and this was done in the following two ways:

- Inclusion of the Coronavirus risk as part of already existing insurance policies. Practice shows that this risk can be covered under "Sickness", "Accident" or "Travel assistance abroad" insurance;
- The Coronavirus risk can also be a stand-alone insurance, but it has some inherent characteristics in any of the insurances listed above.

The specifics of the insurance policy related to the Coronavirus (whether it exists as a stand-alone insurance policy or is part of the coverage of another) were related to the duration of the insurance policy; the risks covered and the number of insured persons.

With the described three main processes, which reflected mainly on the behavior of the participants in the health insurance market in particular, and the market in general, the set of factors that influence its development is exhausted. We believe that emphasizing them to a large extent contributes to clarifying the economic and social logic of what is happening there, which is of particular importance for the correct interpretation of the results of the present study.

2. LITERATURE REVIEW

After clarifying the main processes that provoked the development of the health insurance market in Bulgaria, we should indicate the authors and, accordingly, the papers in which the subject and object of the present study have common points.

A detailed study and corresponding derivation of the specifics, state, development, and trends of the health insurance market in Bulgaria can be found in the works of Valentina Blinded for Review "Health Insurance Market in Bulgaria – State, Development and Trends" (2021) (Ninova, 2021); Valentina Blinded for Review, Nikolay Ninov "Specifics and Features of Insurance Products with Coverage for COVID-19 Offered on the Bulgarian Insurance Market" (2021) (Ninov & Ninova, 2021); Valentina Blinded for Review "Socio-Economic Characteristics of Health Insurance as the Second Pillar of the Social Health Insurance Model in Bulgaria" (2016) (Ninova, 2016); Valentina Blinded for Review, "Health Insurance – A Tool for Achieving the Goals of the National Health Strategy (2014-2020)" (2015) (Ninova, 2015). Here is the place to point out that at the present moment in Bulgaria, there is still no research specifically on the market concentration of the health insurance market, but only one on the non-life insurance market – Stoyan Prodanov, "Competition and Concentration of the Bulgarian Non-Life Insurance Market (2011-2020). Structural Analysis and Empirical Observations" (2021) (Prodanov, 2021).

Regarding current other research related to measuring market concentration in the field of insurance activity, we can note the following: Milan Kostić, Ljiljana Maksimović & Boban Stojanović, "The limitations of Competition in the Insurance Markets of Slovenia, Croatia and Serbia" (2016) (Kostic et al., 2016) and Banerjee, S., Savitha, B. "Competition Reduces Profitability: the Case of the Indian Life Microinsurance Industry" (2021) (Banerjee & Savitha, 2021). Other research papers representing studies of individual health insurance markets that deserve attention are Rodríguez Sandra Acosta – "Effects of Health Insurance Concentration Market on Insurance Coverage in Colombia" (2014) (Rodríguez, 2014), Erin E. Trisha, Bradley J. Herring –"How Do Health Insurer Market Concentration and Bargaining Power with Hospitals Affect Health Insurance Premiums?" (2015) (Trish & Herring, 2015), Mitchell K. Ng, Kenneth K. Ng, Simon Song, Ahmed K. Emara, Jason Ngo, Anooj Patel, Nihar Shah, Elias Mossialos, Sebastian Salas-Vega, Michael Mont, Nicolas Piuzzi – "U.S. Healthcare Insurance Market Concentration from 2001 to 2016: Increased Growth in Direct Written Premiums and Overall Decreased Market Consolidation" (2020) (Ng et al., 2020), Caroline Hanson, Bradley Herring, Erin Trish – "Do Health Insurance and Hospital Market Concentration Influence Hospital Patients' Experience of Care?" (2019) (Hanson et al., 2019), Erfan Kharazmi, Shima Bordbar, Hanie Gholampoor – "The pattern of Health Insurance Economic Resilience in the Covid-19 Pandemic Shock" (2021) (Kharazmi et al., 2021).

3. DATA COLLECTION AND METHODOLOGY

The type of market structure is determined by measuring market concentration, which is considered a key indicator. Its results could demonstrate high market concentration, the interpretation of which could be in the direction of consistent behavior among larger business units in a given market that can co-ordinately establish and maintain prices higher than marginal costs (so-called "cartel agreement"). The results of the measurement of high market concentration, however, could be taken for the same larger business units, and as a sign of higher efficiency, which gives them leading market positions, apropos – a higher market share. It is that which prioritizes the studies of the effects of changes in the levels of market concentration, and scientific research in this direction is significant both for theory and for practice, and above all for the conducted policy in the field of competition.

3.1. Concentration Ratio

The concentration ratio (the concentration ratio of n – insurance companies) is among the most applied indicators in the field of insurance scientific research, and it is based on the relative shares of the first n largest insurance companies. First of all, it is necessary to calculate the relative shares of the insurance companies – in percentages (Todorov, 2015):

$$S_i = \frac{x_i}{\sum_{i=1}^{N} x_i} \qquad (1)$$

where:

x_i – the gross written premium income from health insurance policies;
N – total number of insurance companies.

Summing up the relative shares of the leading insurance companies will serve to determine the concentration ratio (Kostic et al., 2016):

$$CR_n = \sum_{i=1}^{n} S_i \qquad (2)$$

where: n – the number of the largest insurance companies

For this research and given the market situation, a study and subsequent calculation of the first 2, 3, 4, and 5 insurance companies offering health insurance products in the life insurance market and the non-life insurance market is made.

In the present research, the levels of market concentration for the obtained values at CR3 and CR4 for the health insurance market in Bulgaria can be determined as follows (Communications regulation commission, 2012):

- Normal competitive market with a low level of concentration – with CR3 less than 40 and CR4 less than 50;

- Relatively competitive market with an average level of concentration – at values of CR3 from 40 to 70 and of CR4 from 50 to 85;
- Weakly competitive market with a high level of concentration – with values of CR3 over 70 and of CP4 over 85.

3.2 Herfindahl-Hirschman Index

Herfindahl-Hirschman Index is a coefficient used to determine market concentration. It is also applicable in determining the competitive environment of the health insurance market in Bulgaria. In insurance theory, its determination is based on the number of insurance companies in the market (in the case of the health insurance market in Bulgaria) and it reflects the inequality in the distribution of their market shares. The significance of the individual insurance companies corresponds to the value of their market (wi=si). Herfindahl-Hirschman Index presents the ratio of gross written insurance premiums for each insurance company offering health insurance and operating in the case of the Bulgarian insurance market, divided by the total amount of gross written insurance premiums generated by all insurers, respectively: 1) insurance companies working in the non-life insurance market and offering health insurance; 2) insurance companies working in the field of life insurance in Bulgaria and offering health insurance, and 3) summing up gross written premium income generated in non-life and life insurance (Kostic et al., 2016; Cummins & Nini, 2002; Liebenberg & Sommer, 2008; Cole & Karl, 2016; Krivokapic et al., 2017; Herfindahl, 1950). Determining the value of the Herfindahl-Hirschman Index is the result of the calculation of 1) the gross written insurance premiums for individual health insurance (representing a percentage of the sum of the premium income of all insurance companies for health insurance, and 2) the squares of the resulting percentages are summed up to calculate the Herfindahl-Hirschman Index (Cummins & Nini, 2002; Liebenberg & Sommer, 2008).

$$HHI = \sum_{i=1}^{N} \left(S_i^2 \right) \tag{3}$$

where: S_i – market share of i-insurance company.

The use of the Herfindahl-Hirschman Index guarantees a more accurate idea of the level of market concentration compared to the results obtained after calculations using the concentration ratio. The squares of the market shares of the insurance companies offering health insurance in Bulgaria are used here. This, in turn, affects the significance of insurance companies, i.e. companies with a larger market share will be more significant, and those with a smaller one will be less significant. High values of the Herfindahl-Hirschman Index indicate the concentration of the health insurance market, which allows the charging of increased insurance premiums for health insurance, and this would lead to a greater potential for insurance companies to generate supernormal profits. In the present study, the values of the Herfindahl-Hirschman Index are presented in the interval between 0 and 10 000. It is also possible for the value to be in the range between 0 and 1. This depends on the method of calculating market share. Reference values of the Index are shown in Table 1 (Kostic et al., 2016).

Table 1. Reference values of the HH index

HH Index Value	Supply Concentration Level
1 < HHI > 1 500	Highly competitive environment
1 500 < HHI >5 000	High concentration and low competition
HHI =5 000	Duopoly
HHI =10 000	Full monopoly.

Source: (Prodanov, 2021)

3.3 Entropy Index

Another measure of concentration used for the study is the Entropy Index (Spuretling, 1970):

$$E = -\sum_{i=1}^{n} S_i \ln S_i \tag{4}$$

where:

E is entropy index,

S_i – market share of *i*-insurance company,

$\ln S_i$ – the natural logarithm of the market share of *i*-insurance company.

Entropy Index is based on the market share held by insurance companies and its natural logarithm. In this way, a different approach is applied to determine the market concentration of the health insurance market in Bulgaria, compared to the approach used, for instance, in calculating the Herfindahl-Hirschman Index.

The mutual relation between the level of competition and the Entropy Index is presented in the economic literature. Seen through the prism of health insurance, we can note that a growing number of insurance companies offering health insurance on the health insurance market (in Bulgaria), by its very nature, results in more intensively increasing competition. The Entropy Index can be seen as a measure of market competition, which is affected by the concentration of the health insurance market (Horowitz & Horowitz, 1968).

4. EMPIRICAL RESEARCH

The study presents data from the Financial Supervision Commission on the gross written premium income for health insurance policies offered on the insurance market in Bulgaria and the number of insurance companies that offer them. A specific feature of the health insurance market in Bulgaria is that insurance products aimed at individuals' health are offered by companies that work in non-life and life insurance. After the relicensing of social health insurance companies as insurance companies in the period 2012-2013, health insurance acquired a new role – that of the second pillar in the funding model in Bulgaria. This is also the reason for presenting summarised data for the health insurance market in Bulgaria (non-life health insurance and life health insurance). Data by individual segments and summarised are presented in the following table:

Table 2. Gross written premium income on the health insurance market in Bulgaria by sectors for the period 2017-2021

Year	Health Insurance (Non-Life Insurance Market)		Health Insurance (Life Insurance Market)		Health Insurance (Non-Life + Life Insurance Market)	
	(BGN)	Number of Insurance Companies	(BGN)	Number of Insurance Companies	(BGN)	Number of Insurance Companies
2017	51 751 005	14	45 720 197	7	97 471 202	21
2018	53 036 642	13	70 788 518	7	123 825 160	20
2019	65 731 968	11	109 232 699	7	174 964 667	18
2020	69 898 663	13	68 223 737	7	138 122 400	20
2021	78 905 815	14	77 560 542	7	156 466 357	21

Source: FSC (Financial Supervision Commission, 2021).
* *Note:* Data for 2021 are as of the end of the fourth quarter.

For the period 2017-2019, the number of insurance companies operating in the field of non-life insurance decreased by 3 companies, from 14 in 2017 to 11 in 2019 (Ninova, 2021). In 2020, the number of insurers operating on the insurance market in Bulgaria increases to 13, and in 2021, their number again is 14 (corresponding to the number of insurance companies at the beginning of the period considered in the present study – 2017). After the declaration of the COVID-19 pandemic (in 2020) (Ninov & Ninova, 2021; Ninova, 2021), some of the active insurance companies operating in the non-life insurance market in the country are oriented toward the offer of health insurance products. In the field of life insurance (Ninov & Ninova, 2018), the number of participants in the market does not change and remains constant – 7 insurance companies. Considering the health insurance market in Bulgaria as a separate segment, the number of companies offering health insurance products decreased from 2017 to 2019, and increased in the following two years, reaching 21 market participants again.

In the case of "Sickness" insurance offered by companies working in the field of non-life insurance (Ninova, 2018), dynamics are observed for the considered period from 2017 to 2021 (Ninova, 2021). Growth of the indicator – gross written premium income is established during the entire period. Insurance companies working in the field of non-life insurance and offering health insurance do not report a decline in gross written premium income, even in 2020 and 2021.

There is an increase in the gross written premium income of about 54-55% in 2018 and 2019 for health insurance offered in the life insurance sector. Factors for the increase can be found in the following directions: 1) towards the reporting of zero gross written premium income under "Permanent Health Insurance" and the subsequent reorientation of insurance candidates (clients of life insurance companies) to short-term "Sickness" insurance; 2) enhancing the market positions of the insurers and the products offered by them regarding health insurance (Ninova, 2021). A decrease in interest in this insurance – by -37.54% is observed in 2020, as a result of the COVID-19 pandemic declared in the country in March of the same year – a trend that changes in the next year 2021.

So far, we have considered the gross written premium income generated by insurance companies offering health insurance in Bulgaria. Next, we present the results of a study on the market concentration of the health insurance market in Bulgaria. The specific data are presented in the following tables.

Table 3. CR2, CR3, CR4, and CR5 concentration ratios of the health insurance market separately for the non-life and life sectors for the period 2017-2021

Year	CR2		CR3		CR4		CR5	
	Non-Life Insurance	Life Insurance	Non-Life Insurance	Life Insurance	Non-Life Insurance	Life Insurance	Non-Life Insurance	Life Insurance
2017	51.27	71.37	70.87	87.93	78.05	94.87	85.05	98.99
2018	43.52	77.83	64.77	91.86	75.09	97.35	83.41	99.22
2019	46.04	82.94	64.74	93.91	75.70	97.93	84.72	99.64
2020	48.48	67.92	65.43	90.27	77.91	96.66	85.92	99.45
2021	50.34	68.69	64.98	91.63	73.98	96.83	82.44	99.41

Source: FSC (Financial Supervision Commission, 2021) & Research results

Table 3 presents the concentration ratios (CR) in percentages for the first 2, 3, 4, and 5 insurance companies in Bulgaria for the period from 2017 to 2022. Referring to the presented results for CR2, CR3, CR,4 and CR5, we find the following: 1) no values are observed to reflect the presence of a normal competitive market, with low levels of market concentration for the health insurance market, both in the non-life and life insurance sectors; 2) there is a relatively competitive market, with an average level of market concentration for insurance companies offering health insurance on the insurance market in the "Non-life" sector – for the entire period of 5 years, CR values are above 50%; 3) it is found a weakly competitive market with a high market concentration of life insurance companies offering health insurance – CR5 values reach 99%, even above 99% for 2018, 2019, 2020 and 2021, and 4) insurance companies working in the field of non-life insurance are more competitive than companies working in the life insurance market – at CR5, the values for the considered period are about 99%.

After describing the role of health insurance in Bulgaria (the second pillar in the social health insurance model), in the present research a generalized study of the concentration of non-life insurance and life insurance companies offering health insurance products in the country is done. The following table presents the summary data on the concentration ratio by determining the leading 2, 3, 4, and 5 insurance companies.

At CR2, Bulgaria's health insurance market values are below 50%. An exception to the outlined trend was found in 2019. At CR3 – for the period 2017-2021, the market concentration ratio occupies values ranging from 46.60-61.64% – we can define the health insurance market as relatively competitive and with average levels of market concentration. For the values of the same ratio, but when considering the 4 and 5 leading insurance companies in the health insurance market in Bulgaria, the results of the study demonstrate a stronger concentration – above 60% and 70% and, accordingly, lower competition on the market, but the market remains within the limits of average levels of market concentration. Based on the data presented, lower levels of market concentration for 2020 and 2021 can be found. The COVID-19 pandemic has urged more insurance companies to focus on offering insurance products aimed at the health of individuals.

Table 4. CR2, CR3, CR4, and CR5 concentration ratios of the health insurance market combined for the non-life and life sectors for the period 2017-2021

Year	CR2	CR3	CR4	CR5
2017	39.43	51.22	61.63	71.10
2018	45.37	54.48	63.59	72.24
2019	52.99	61.14	69.08	76.10
2020	34.71	46.60	58.08	69.12
2021	34.52	47.40	59.43	70.80

Source: FSC (Financial Supervision Commission, 2021) & Research results

Table 5. Herfindahl-Hirschman Index & Entropy Index of the health insurance market separately for the non-life and life sectors and combined for the period 2017-2021

Year	Health Insurance (Non-Life Insurance Market)		Health Insurance (Life Insurance Market)		Health Insurance (Non-Life + Life Insurance Market)	
	HHI	E	HHI	E	HHI	E
2017	1861.84	1.9465	3366.82	1.3335	1265.61	2.3502
2018	1659.18	1.9690	4391.33	1.1306	1739.56	2.1726
2019	1676.13	1.9654	5233.27	0.9742	2276.32	2.0085
2020	1732.79	1.9595	3084.36	1.3419	1196.27	2.3475
2021	1701.59	2.0112	3059.08	1.3338	1184.42	2.7429

Source: FSC (Financial Supervision Commission, 2021) & Research results

From the results presented in Table 5 – values for the Herfindahl-Hirschman Index & Entropy index of the health insurance market separately for the non-life and life sectors and combined for the period 2017-2021, we can sum up: 1) high market concentration and low competition are characteristic of insurance companies operating in the non-life insurance sector – the values vary in the interval 1659.18÷1861.84 (for a period of 5 years); 2) low market competition and high market concentration are also inherent to companies working in the life insurance sector, an exception to this trend is 2019, during which the HHI value is 5233.27 – a duopoly; 3) presented as a separate sector of insurance activity in Bulgaria (Non-life & Life health insurance), the health insurance market for the individual years of the study shows either a strong competitive environment or low competition with high concentration.

5. CONCLUSION

Based on the presented results of the indicators for measuring the market concentration of the health insurance market in Bulgaria, for a period of 5 years (2017-2021), the following conclusions can be drawn:

- The market participants are insurance companies working on the health insurance market in Bulgaria from non-life insurance and life insurance sectors, which is a specific feature of this market – the result of successive stages of health reform in the country (which is still not finished). During the considered period, the number of insurance companies in this market from the life insurance sector is constant – 7, while the number of those from the non-life insurance sector varies between 11 and 14. These companies have been established over the years as reliable partners and market players trying to gain a larger market share and defend their market positions;
- Referring to the presented results for the concentration ratios (CR) in percentages for the first 2, 3, 4, and 5 insurance companies in Bulgaria for the period from 2017 to 2022, we find that in the health insurance market, as in the sector "Non-life Insurance" and in the sector "Life Insurance", a normal competitive market is not observed, with low levels of market concentration. There is a relatively competitive market, with an average level of market concentration for insurance companies offering health insurance in the insurance market in the non-life insurance sector and a weakly competitive market with high levels of market concentration of insurance companies in the life insurance sector. Insurance companies working in the field of non-life insurance are more competitive than companies working in the life insurance market;
- When measuring the concentration ratio of the health insurance market (including companies offering health insurance from the non-life insurance and life insurance sectors), we find that the results obtained for CR2 are below 50% (an exception to the outlined trend established in 2019). The results obtained for CR3 varied in the interval 46.60-61.64%, i.e. the market is relatively competitive and has average market concentration levels. At CR4 and CR5, the obtained values demonstrate a stronger concentration – above 60% and 70% and, respectively, lower competition in the market (the market is within the limits of the average levels of market concentration). The lower levels of market concentration for 2020 and 2021 are results of the COVID-19 pandemic, which has urged more insurance companies to focus on offering health insurance policies (insurance products that include coverage against COVID-19);
- The values obtained when measuring the Herfindahl-Hirschman Index & Entropy Index of the health insurance market separately for the non-life and life sectors and combined for the period 2017-2021 clearly outline a trend of high levels of market concentration combined with low competition for the insurance companies working in the non-life insurance sector. As for the companies operating in the life insurance sector, their values demonstrate a tendency for low market competition and high market concentration (except for 2019). With the conditional representation of health insurance as a separate sector of insurance activity in Bulgaria (Non-life & Life health insurance) for the same period, the health insurance market is developing in a highly competitive environment or low competition with high concentration.

REFERENCES

Banerjee, S., & Savitha, B. (2021). Competition Reduces Profitability: The Case of the Indian Life Microinsurance Industry. *The Geneva Papers on Risk and Insurance. Issues and Practice*, *46*(3), 383–398. doi:10.105741288-020-00203-5

Cole, C., & Karl, J. (2016). The Effect of Product Diversification Strategies on the Performance of Health Insurance Conglomerates. *Applied Economics*, *48*(3), 190–202. doi:10.1080/00036846.2015.1076149

Communications Regulation Commission. (2012). https://crc.bg/: https://crc.bg/files/_bg/Metodika_2012_DV.pdf

Cummins, J., & Nini, G. (2002). Optimal Capital Utilization by Fnancial Firms: Evidence from the Property-liability Insurance Industry. *Journal of Financial Services Research*, *21*(1), 15–53. doi:10.1023/A:1014369617192

Financial Supervision Commission. (2021). https://www.fsc.bg/bg/

Hanson, C., Herring, B., & Trish, E. (2019). Do Health Insurance and Hospital Market Concentration Influence Hospital Patients' Experience of Care? *Health Services Research*, *54*(4), 1475-6773.13168. Advance online publication. doi:10.1111/1475-6773.13168 PMID:31095743

Herfindahl, O. C. (1950). *Concentration in the Steel Industry*. University Microfilms.

Horowitz, A. R., & Horowitz, J. (1968). Entropy, Markov Processes and Competition in the Brewing Industry. *The Journal of Industrial Economics, 16*(3), 196–211. doi:10.2307/2097560

Kharazmi, E., Bordbar, S., & Gholampoor, H. (2021). The Pattern of Health Insurance Economic Resilience in the Covid 19 Pandemic Shock. *BMC Research Notes*, *14*(1), 371. Advance online publication. doi:10.118613104-021-05779-2 PMID:34556156

Kostic, M., Maksimovic, L., & Stojanovic, B. (2016). The Limitations of Competition in the Insurance Markets of Slovenia, Croatia and Serbia. *Ekonomska Istrazivanja*, *29*(1), 395–418. doi:10.1080/1331677X.2016.1169703

Krivokapic, R., Njegomir, V., & Stojic, D. (2017). Effects of Corporate Diversification on Firm Performance: Evidence from the Serbian Insurance Industry. *Ekonomska Istrazivanja*, *30*(1), 1224–1236. doi:10.1080/1331677X.2017.1340175

Liebenberg, A., & Sommer, D. (2008). Effects of Corporate Diversification: Evidence from the Property-liability Insurance Industry. *The Journal of Risk and Insurance*, *75*(4), 893–919. doi:10.1111/j.1539-6975.2008.00290.x

Ministry of Health (Bulgaria). (n.d.). http://www.mh.government.bg

Ng, M., Ng, K., Song, S., Emara, A., Ngo, J., Patel, A., & Piuzzi, N. (2020). U.S. Healthcare Insurance Market Concentration from 2001 to 2016: Increased Growth in Direct Written Premiums and Overall Decreased Market Consolidation. *Cureus*. Advance online publication. doi:10.7759/cureus.7491 PMID:32368423

Ninov, N., & Ninova, V. (2018). The Need for Insurance during Maternity in Bulgaria. *International E-Journal of Advances in Social Sciences*, 392-405. doi:10.18769/ijasos.455664

Ninov, N., & Ninova, V. (2021). Specifics and Features of Insurance Products with Coverage for COVID-19 Offered on the Bulgarian Insurance Market. In *Annual university scientific conference "Scientific management. Social, economic and legal sciences"* (pp. 322-328). Veliko Tarnovo.

Ninova, V. (2015). Health Insurance – a Tool for Achieving the Goals of the National Health Strategy (2014-2020). In *Jubilee International scientific conference on "European practices and national planning Reflections", Collection of reports - Svishtov 24-25 April 2015* (pp. 363-368). Svishtov: Tsenov Academic Publishing House.

Ninova, V. (2016). *Socio-Economic Characteristics of Health Insurance as the Second Pillar of the Social Health Insurance Model in Bulgaria*. Academic Press.

Ninova, V. (2018). Bancassurance – Application and Advantages for the Insurance Market in Bulgaria. *Journal of Innovations and Sustainability*, *4*(2), 9–21. doi:10.51599/is.2018.04.02.09

Ninova, V. (2021). Health Insurance Market in Bulgaria – State, Development and Trends. In Dedicated to the 85th anniversary since the establishment of D. A. Tsenov Academy of Economics (pp. 281-288). Svishtov: Tsenov Academic Publishing House.

Prodanov, S. (2021). Competition and Concentration of the Bulgarian Non-life Insurance Market (2011-2020). Structural Analysis and Empirical Observations. In Dedicated to the 85th anniversary since the establishment of D. A. Tsenov Academy of Economics (pp. 116-125). Svishtov: Tsenov Academic Publishing House.

Rodríguez, S. (2014). Effects of Health Insurance Concentration Market on Insurance Coverage in Colombia. *Journal of Competitiveness*, *6*(3), 13–19. doi:10.7441/joc.2014.03.01

Spuretling, D. (1970). *Zur Messung der wirtschafi chen Konzentration*. Academic Press.

Todorov, A. (2015). Empirical Analysis of the Economic Concentration within the Largest Bulgarian Companies for the Period 2006-2013. *Dialogue*, 44–57.

Trish, E., & Herring, B. (2015). How Do Health Insurer Market Concentration and Bargaining Power with Hospitals Affect Health Insurance Premiums? *Journal of Health Economics*, *42*, 104–114. doi:10.1016/j.jhealeco.2015.03.009 PMID:25910690

Chapter 12
Renewable Energy Policies and the Future of Energy Storage in Türkiye

Umut Erksan Senalp
https://orcid.org/0000-0003-0261-3700
Trakya University, Turkey

Erisa Shehi
Trakya University, Turkey

ABSTRACT

Global renewable power capacity is growing. The intermittent nature of wind and solar, in particular, and the difficulty in forecasting generation lead to fluctuations and sometimes sudden increases in electricity prices. This leads to the need for more energy to balance the grid power. Through energy storage, the effect of these uncertainties can be partially eliminated, and potential price fluctuations can be prevented. Electricity generation from renewable sources has been increasing in Türkiye in recent years. In addition, recent legal regulations have paved the way for the installation of large-scale energy storage facilities. This chapter highlights the recent global and domestic developments in renewable energy policies and their potential reflections. The future of energy storage in Türkiye is also discussed.

1. INTRODUCTION

Fatih Birol, the head of the International Energy Agency (IEA), stated that the Russian invasion of Ukraine and the following political turmoil had triggered the First Global Energy Crisis (IEA, 2022a). Furthermore, due to the recent developments in the global energy market, energy supply security has become much more critical for countries.

The increasing world population and growing industrial production cause an increase in global energy demand. However, resources such as coal, oil, and natural gas, currently the primary energy sources, are limited. As a result, the increase in energy demand and supply-side instability led to an imbalance in the energy market and increased fossil fuel prices (IEA, 2022a).

DOI: 10.4018/979-8-3693-0400-6.ch012

Besides, global temperature has increased by 0.8 °C in the past century and is expected to increase further. Under this scenario, climate change and resulting environmental disasters will be inevitable and countries (or nations) will be more vulnerable (Blanco and Faaij, 2018; Okur Dincsoy, 2016). To keep the temperature rise at a maximum of 1.5°C, more than 70 countries, including China, the USA, and the European Union, signed the Paris Agreement, committed to reducing their carbon emissions by 45% by 2030 and set the target of zero carbon emissions by 2050.

Eventually, due to soaring energy prices, raising concerns about energy security, and decarbonization policies, renewable energy investments have experienced a severe upward trend. Moreover, another development that triggered renewable energy investments is the cost reduction observed in renewable energy technologies on a global scale. In particular, solar photovoltaic installation costs have become almost seven times cheaper in the last two decades (MIT, 2022).

Over the last ten years, global solar energy production has grown by an average of 22% annually, while wind energy increased by 46% (Schill, 2020). As a result, global renewable energy share in electricity production jumped to 28% in 2021 and is predicted to reach 38.1% in 2027. The expected global renewable energy capacity expansion between 2022 and 2027 will be equivalent to the gain achieved between 2001 and 2021, that is, in 20 years (IEA, 2022a).

However, the use of renewable energy also brings some problems. For example, wind and solar energy can create an energy supply in an intermittent form. The hours when wind energy is most intense may not coincide with the hours when electrical energy is most demanded. Similarly, when the energy demand is highest in the evenings, it is impossible to obtain solar energy (Greve and Pollitt, 2016). The intermittent nature of renewables puts pressure on the electricity distribution system in several ways. Energy storage technologies are the strongest candidates for solving this problem by allowing for storing surplus renewable electricity when electricity demand is low and returning this stored energy to the grid during peak hours (Waterson et al., 2022).

In this chapter, we will discuss recent renewable energy policies and the future of energy storage in Türkiye. First, the structure of electricity market and pricing mechanism in Türkiye will be explained. Second, we will highlight the recent renewable energy policies and their effect on electricity prices. Finally, the future of energy storage in Türkiye will be discussed.

2. ELECTRICITY MARKET IN TÜRKİYE

The Turkish electricity market has significantly transformed over the last two decades. Between 1994 and 2001, the Türkiye Electricity Authority was divided two state-owned companlies: Türkiye Electricity Generation-Transmission Corporation and Türkiye Electricity Distribution Company. During this time, the power market underwent liberalization, which was accompanied by the establishment of an energy regulatory authority.

Figure 1 depicts the structure of the Turkish Electricity Market consisting of the Energy Market Regulatory Authority (EMRA), the Turkish Electricity Transmission Corporation (TETC) and the Energy Exchange Istanbul (EXIST). EMRA is tasked with autonomous regulation, licensing, and supervision of the electricity, natural gas, and downstream petroleum and LPG markets. EXIST is serving as the country's electrical spot market, with 854 market participants trading 40% of the country's electricity (ITA, 2022). Turkish electricity market is a semi-liberalized and relatively regulated market. Following privatization, numerous reforms were made in the Turkish energy market, resulting in a functional electricity market with significant private sector involvement (Law No.: 6446, Article 7). TETC regulates the Real-Time Market, responsible for electricity providers' system operation in the Balancing Power Market and Ancillary Services Market, ensuring the network's real-time balancing and safe operation.

Figure 1. Electricity market overview

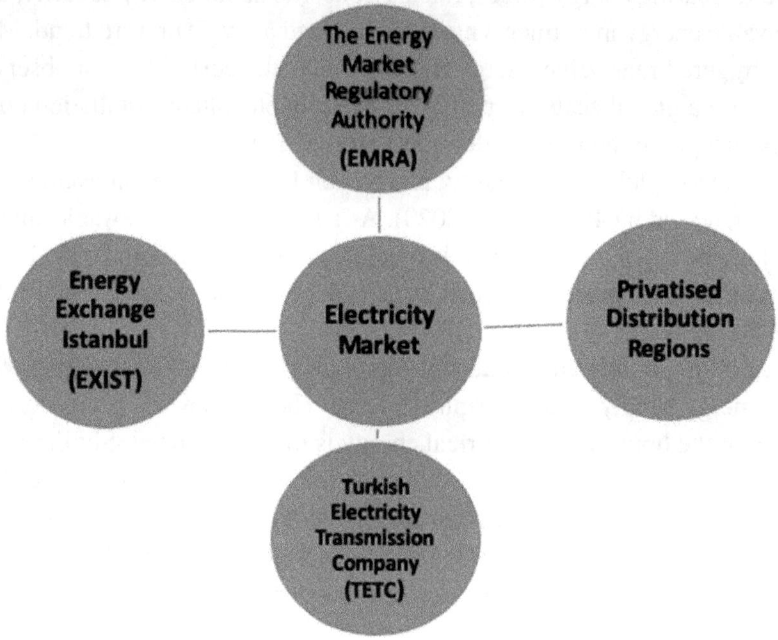

Electricity in Türkiye is traded in a variety of markets, both physical and financial. The financial markets include derivatives trading on the Istanbul Stock Exchange (BIST), while the physical markets comprise The Real-Time Market, the Organized Market, and Bilateral Agreements. The Organized Market is regulated by EMRA, which oversees three sub-markets: the Day-Ahead Market, the Intra-Day Market, and the Futures Trading Market with Physical Delivery. The primary purpose of the Organized Market is to facilitate electricity trade and protection from imbalances, ranging from price based on supply and demand (Day-Ahead Market) and imbalance management (Intra-Day Market), to risk protection and increased predictability of electricity prices.

These markets are divided into two categories based on their primary functions: Electricity Trade and Protection from Imbalances and System Operation. Bilateral Agreements, Day-Ahead Market and the Intra-Day Market help to the former function, while the Power Balancing Power Market is related to the System Operation.

Figure 2 shows that more than a half of the total electricity trade occurs via Bilateral Trade. The Day Ahead Market also has a big share of %37,9. Intra Day and Balancing Power Markets have relatively small shares of %3,7 and %2,6 respectively. These figures show that the System Operator knows around %94 of total electricity demand and supply at least one day before it actually occurs.

Figure 2. Electricity market overview

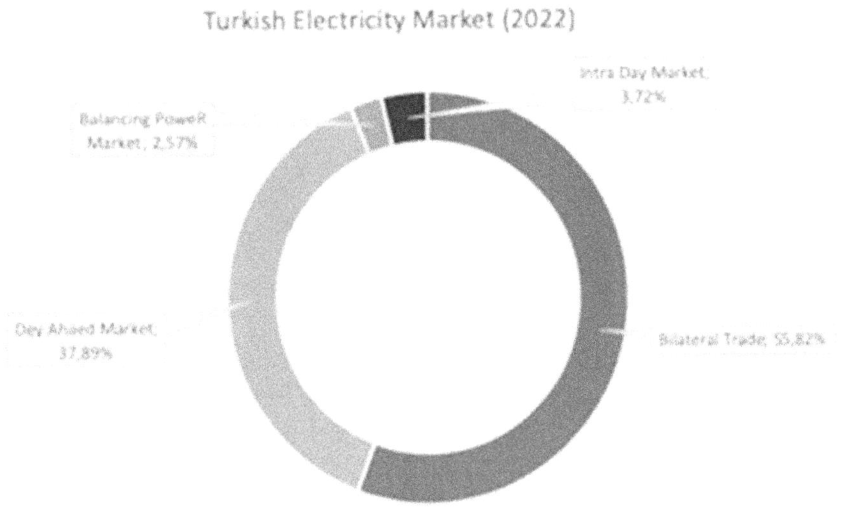

2.1 Electricity Market Pricing Mechanism

Electricity prices are a consequence of the equilibrium between supply and demand, which is affected by micro and macro factors such as temperature and economic growth. Consequently, the electricity demand has an extremely volatile structure (Şahin et al, 2021). Electricity markets are created to establish equilibrium, which entails making sure that supply and demand are as close as possible to being equal at all times. For this purpose, consumers forecast the energy demand for the following day on an hourly basis, while producers work to correctly predict the amount of energy needed hourly (EMRA, 2019). Electricity is sold in a competitive market where producers and customers offer rates to a market operator. After that, the market operator uses an algorithm to calculate the market-clearing price (MCP), which is the price of supplying an extra megawatt of electricity above the point at which supply and demand are balanced for each market period (Georgilakis, 2007). On the other hand, System Marginal Price (SMP) is the real-time cost of electricity in a specific location, which is the marginal cost of the most expensive generator meeting the demand (Lin et al., 2006). SMP is essential for electricity market participants to make informed decisions about energy production, consumption, and trading.

Figure 3 illustrates the MCP-SMP electricity prices based on monthly data provided by EMRA from December 2009 to May 2023. When the MCP is greater than the SMP, there is an excess of energy, meaning that the estimated amount of energy is higher than the actual required amount. Conversely, when the SMP is greater than the MCP, there is an energy deficit, implying that the estimated amount of energy is lower than the actual required amount. The MCP-SMP price line is anticipated to remain stable until the midpoint of 2021, followed by an increasing trend that will peak in the middle of 2022.

This can be attributed to the increased electricity demand and consumption during 2021-2022, which aligns with the recovery phase following the COVID-19 pandemic and energy crisis. Strategies aimed at reducing demand and increasing the proportion of renewable energy sources are expected to result in an energy supply imbalance in the later months (MCP>SMP). In the following chapter, we will examine the development of renewable energy policies in Türkiye.

Figure 3. MCP-SMP weighted average graph
Source: Data gained from EMRA Market& Financial Settlement Center

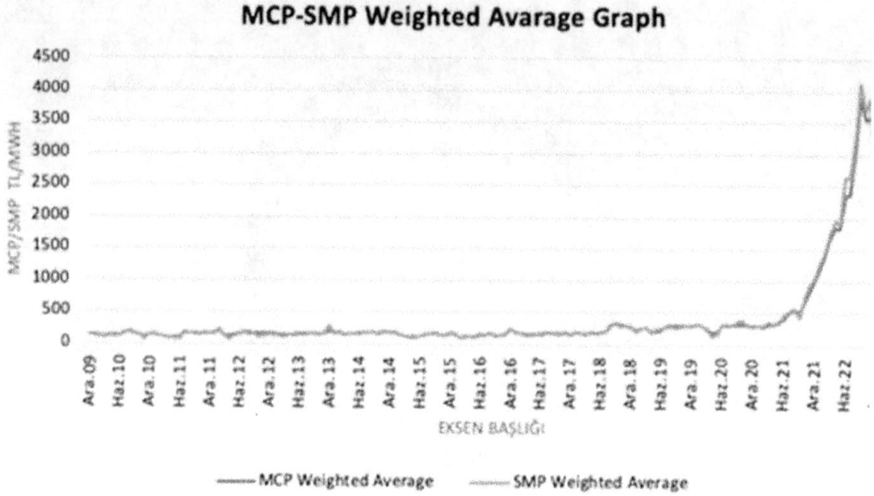

3. RENEWABLE ENERGY SUPPORT MECHANISMS IN THE EU AND TÜRKİYE

Several countries stand out with their successful renewable energy policies. For instance, the green energy transformation that Germany has been carrying out for the last twenty years has accelerated, especially after the Fukushima Nuclear accident in Japan in 2011. Following this, Germany decided to gradually close 17 nuclear power plants, having a 20% share in the total electricity production. Germany aims to reduce its dependency on fossil fuel-burning power plants and nuclear energy by increasing investments in solar and wind energy (Sinn, 2017). Following Germany, Japan has started implementing Green Transformation policies with a similar understanding, and many EU member countries have also begun preparing regulations within this framework in order to encourage the development of a renewable energy market. Table 1. displays some of the incentives and support schemes implemented by EU countries, leading to a substantial rise in the share of energy generated from renewables.

Feed-in-tariffs (FiT), tax incentives, and tradable green certificates are the three most prevalent support mechanisms (Abolhosseini and Heshmati, 2014). According to the European Environment Agency, FiT is the cost per unit of electricity that a utility or supplier must pay for renewable electricity produced by independent generators under government regulation. FiTs are advanced renewable tariffs, which are regulatory tools designed to stimulate investment in renewable energy systems and technology (ClarkII, 2018).

The feed-in tariff scheme has been the most extensively used way to fund renewable energy projects in most European countries. The fundamental goal of FiT is to give renewable energy producers with cost-based compensation while also providing price certainty and long-term contracts to help fund renewable energy development (Gipe, 2011). Its main advantages are its high efficacy and cost efficiency levels, low-risk premiums and guaranteed returns for renewable energy investors (Abdmouleh et al., 2015). Despite its success in lowering investor risks, improperly structured tariffs that are out of pace with the actual and gradually declining costs of renewable energy investment may produce inefficiencies in the energy market (Papaefthymiou et al., 2014).

Table 1. Promotion of renewable electricity production

Country	Support Schemes
Germany	Market Premium (tendering scheme), and EEG-2023 scheme, for small-scale installation are applied Feed-in-Tariff, Fixed Price, Subsidies, tax incentives
Belgium	Quota system based on certificate trade, Premium over Market Price, Quantity target, Net metering, Green Energy Ccrtificate
France	Feed-in-Tariff, tax benefits, Subsidies, Premium over Market Price
Italy	VAT (Value Added Tax) and real estate tax deduction- net metering, Green Energy Certificate, Fixed Price, Subsidy, Tender
Norway	Quota system based on certificate trade, Green Energy Certificate, Tender, Subsidy
Sweden	The quota system, tax regulation mechanism, Green Energy Certificate, and Tender.
United Kingdom	Feed-in-Tariff, Green Energy Certificate, Tender, Tax incentives
Romania	The quota system, Green Energy Certificate, Subsidy
Spain	Auctions, PPAs (Power Purchase Agreements), Fixed-Price, Green Energy Certificate, Tax incentives, Subsidy, Tender Net metering
Türkiye	Feed-in-Tariff mechanism based on "active energy costs", Green Energy Certificate, Subsidy, Tender, Rooftop Legislation

Source: Adapted from RES Legal Europe website

In order to promote investments in renewable energy, a law on the utilization of renewable energy resources was introduced in 2005. This law put into place a number of incentives, such as a waiver of license fees, eased land appropriation, and guaranteed fixed feed-in tariffs through 2011. Some financial incentives were introduced, and the Renewable Energy Resources Support Mechanism (YEKDEM) was created, in order to encourage more investments in the sector of renewable energy and prevent investors from staying away from the market due to high investment costs. In accordance with Law No. 5346, YEKDEM ensures the purchase of electricity produced by renewable energy sources at predetermined price levels. The Turkish Presidency published Decree No. 3453 on the new YEKDEM renewable energy resources support mechanism, introducing the feed-in tariff scheme that will be available to electricity generation facilities based on renewable energy sources holding YEK certificates and shifting the currency of feed-in tariff and domestic components incentive premia payments from US Dollar (USD) to Turkish Lira (TRY).

Figure 4 illustrates a comparison between the Market Clearing Price (MCP) and the YEKDEM unit costs for hydro, wind and solar, demonstrating that the spread between the YEKDEM unit cots and the spot day-ahead prices increased over the course of 2022. This spread signifies the additional income generated by participating in the YEKDEM portfolio. Power plants operating under the scope of YEKDEM sell the energy they generate on the energy exchange. These power plants produce an income over Day-Ahead prices as a result of this transaction. However, EMRA pays the difference between the amount of money obtained by the YEKDEM participant through Day-Ahead and the amount guaranteed by Law No.5346.

Figure 4. YEKDEM unit cost and day-ahead prices (quarterly)
Source: EMRA 2022 Electricity Report, graph prepared

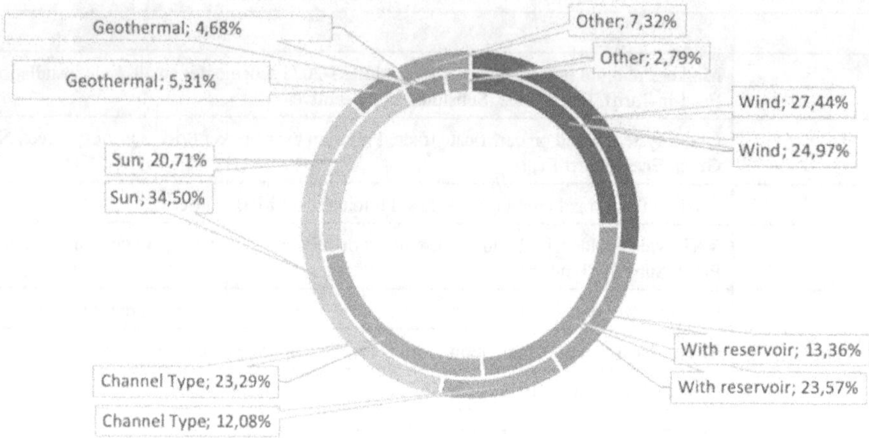

3.1 Renewable Energy in Türkiye

Türkiye has significant renewable energy potential mainly due to its geographic location, especially hydroelectric power plants in the Southeastern part of Türkiye (Dinçsoy & Icihiminami, 2006). It is reported that the annual total sunshine duration is 2,737 hours, which corresponds to an average of 7.5 hours per day (Türkiye's Solar Energy Potential Atlas, 2020). Besides, Tagliapietraet al. (2019) mention that Türkiye's wind power potential is over 100GW. All these indicators signal that renewable energy production and investments will gain importance in Türkiye.

As we discussed in the previous chapter, renewable energy investments have been increasing globally due to support mechanisms. Renewable energy trends in Türkiye are in parallel with global developments. According to the Turkish National Energy Plan (TNEP) published in 2022, the share of solar and wind in total electricity production will increase gradually to 17.5% in 2025 and 34.3% in 2035 (it was 11.7% in 2020). Considering other renewable energy sources such as hydro, geothermal, and biomass, it is estimated that the share of production from all renewable sources in total electricity production will increase to 54.8% in 2035 (TUEP, 2022). The potential for renewable energy is being utilized as fully and quickly as possible, especially for wind and solar power.

As illustrated in Figure 5, there have been considerable shifts in wind and solar energy between December 2019 and May 2023, with the installed capacity of wind energy increasing from 24.97% to 27.44% and that of solar energy from 20.71% to 34.5%.

3.2 Price Effect of Renewables: Merit Order Effect

In this subsection, we aim to explain the channel between renewable energy production and electricity prices in the market. The term "Merit Order" refers to the positioning of power plants according to their marginal costs, which are frequently influenced by the kind of fuel used, efficiency, and operating expenses. According to Tveten et al. (2013), Merit Order Effects (MOE) are typically caused by intermittent Renewable Energy Sources (RES) with grid priority and low Short-Run Marginal Costs (SRMC). As the generation of renewable energy increases, plants with higher marginal costs are being pushed out of the spot market, resulting in a shift of the supply curve to the right and a subsequent decrease in the market price of electricity (Acar and Selcuk, 2019).

Figure 5. Renewables, installed capacity
Note: Inner Circle represents the period Dec-2019 and the External circle represents data as of 31 May 2023
Source: EMRA

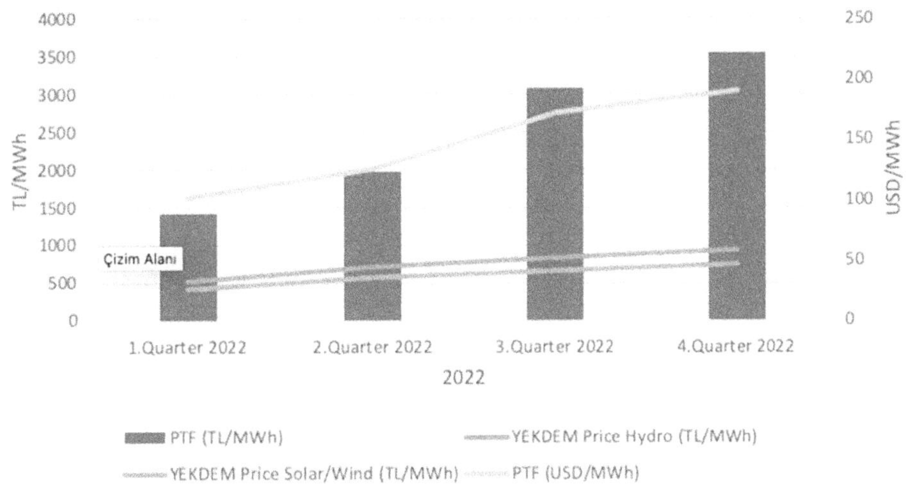

The Merit Order Curve arranges power plants according to their marginal costs, with peak demand generators situated on the right with greater fixed costs and lower variable costs (Aščerić, 2022). If the increase in renewable energy production is greater than the increase in electricity consumption, the marginal power plants in the merit order will be replaced first, resulting in a decrease in the wholesale cost of electricity (Rathmann 2007). The merit-order effect moves profits from generation corporations to consumers, but whether the savings are passed on depends on how competitive the power supply system is (Sensfuß et al., 2008).

Marginal costs determine pricing in wholesale markets. Adding more VRES (Variable Renewable Energy Systems) presents new challenges because wind and PV have low, nearly zero marginal costs. This is because they eliminate energy facilities with high variable costs from the market, which lowers the average price of electricity and lessens the incentive for all generators to increase their capacity. Furthermore, due to the loss in long-term market price incentives to invest in capital-intensive base-load power plants, the current generation of power plants is expected to include an increasing proportion of moderately flexible peak load technology (Papaefthymiou et al., 2014).

Table 2 provides an overview of various studies conducted in different countries which have utilized different methods to analyze the influence of renewable energy sources on electricity prices, ultimately demonstrating the merit order effect. The table shows that several studies confirmed price reducing effect of renewable intervention. There are few studies examining the price effect of renewable energy. For instance, Berk and Tosun (2019) conducted a nonparametric Granger causality test to analyze the efficacy of renewable subsidies in reducing electricity prices, particularly in the case of wind generation. They suggest that further research is necessary to ascertain the causal relationship between other renewable sources, such as solar and geothermal, and electricity prices. Another study, Acar and Selcuk (2019), examines Türkiye's renewable energy incentive mechanism, and conclude that it has been successful in reducing electricity prices.

Table 2. Studies on the price effects of renewables

Paper	Methodology	Country	Price Effect	Additional Information
Würzburg et al. (2013)	Time series	Germany, Austria	P↓	The price impact of solar and wind energy was roughly equal. In sizable European marketplaces, merit-order effects are weakest.
Ballester & Furió (2015)	Time series	Spain	P↓	Increases in other generation technologies such as thermal, hydropower, nuclear, and combined cycle can increase price volatility
Ketterer (2014)	Time series	Germany	P↓	Focused on wind power, the electricity price decreased, while the price volatility increased.
Gullì & Balbo (2015)	Simulation, Time series	Italy	P unchanged or P↑	In imperfectly competitive power markets, PV generation may not decrease spot prices directly.
Mulder & Scholtens (2013)	Time series	Netherland	Hardly influenced	The merit order effect of RE has no impact on where the demand and supply curves intersect in the Dutch market.
Sensfuß et al. (2008)	Time series	Germany	P↓	The reduction of the unweighted average price reaches 7.8 h/MWh in 2006.
Peña & Rodríguez (2019)	Panel, Simulation	10 EU countries	P↓	Decreases in wholesale prices, do not necessarily translate into lower household retail prices.
Csereklyei et al. (2019)	Time series	Australia (NSW, VIC, QLD, SA)	P↓	Due to increased wind and solar power, lower electricity prices were the result, according to the wind and solar merit-order effect.

Source: Data gathered from the specified authors.

3.3 Behavior of Day-Ahead Prices in Türkiye

The price fluctuations within electricity markets have become increasingly intricate in the wake of deregulation, market integration, and alterations in the input mix in various regions globally. The supply curve for electricity is convex and highly non-linear, whereas the demand curve is practically inelastic. As a result, the characteristics of electricity markets include mean reversion, seasonality, time-varying volatility, leaps, positive skewness, high kurtosis, and a complicated link to fundamentals.

The electrical power business has long placed a premium on the efficient and best economic operation and planning of electrical power generation systems. The knowledge of future electricity demand is necessary for unit commitment and is projected with adequate acuity on a weekly, daily, and hourly basis.

The electrical network's forecasted conditions and demand forecasting make it possible to plan the necessary power generation to satisfy the expected load demand. Energy load is a stochastic data series whose values depend on a wide range of variables, including the kind of receivers used, the atmosphere, the time of day, the month, and the year, sporting and cultural events, and several other uncontrollable occurrences that have an impact on receiver performance.

This paper obtained an hourly load time series from the EMRA Transparency Platform between 1 January 2019 and 31 December 2022.

Table 3. Descriptive statistics

Variable	Obs.	Mean	St. Dev	Min	Max	Skewness	Kurtosis
Price	35,064	66.27404	54.33204	0	271.63	1.871783	5.932886
Load	35,064	31327.28	4700.158	16085.56	44038.55	-.0565103	2.359946
Wind	35,064	3125.155	1842.694	107.65	9284.18	.6184072	2.707923
Solar	35,064	140.4977	267.0801	-1.7	1289.82	2.301143	7.601281

Authors calculation

Table 3 presents the descriptive statistics for electricity prices, forecasted renewables, and loads. The per-hour distribution of prices is leptokurtic (Kurtosis 5.93, which is greater than 3), indicating an asymmetric effect of extreme prices on their distribution. The mean value of Day Ahead prices is €66.27 per MWh over the sample period, with a standard deviation of 54.33. Examining the period variation, for instance, it can be seen that prices range from a minimum of €0 per MWh on 17 February 2019 at 09:00 AM to a maximum of €271.3 per MWh on 30 September 2022. For the level and volatility of day-ahead electricity prices, the sample kurtosis is noticeably higher than 3, which shows that distributions have fat tails.

On the other hand, positive skewness suggests that substantial price and volatility rises are more likely than large declines. Prices were highly volatile in the past, yet they have become more stable in recent years. This trend leads one to question whether the increasing proportion of renewable energy sources in the electricity supply has had a noteworthy influence on electricity prices. Furthermore, the mean value of the total load over the sample period was recorded to be 31327.28 MWh, with a standard deviation of 4700.158 MWh.

The minimum load was 16085.56MWh on 26 May 2020 at 05:00 AM and the maximum was 44038.55MWh on 12 August 2021 at 15:00. The sample kurtosis was slightly above 2, indicating that the distribution is not too peaked for total load generation. Additionally, the negative skewness (-0.056) implies that there is a slightly left-skewed distribution, tending towards a normal distribution, as illustrated by the graphs below for each variable.

It was observed that the mean value of wind generation over the sample period was 3125.155 MWh, with a standard deviation of 1842.694 MWh. The minimum load was recorded to be 107.65MWh and the maximum was 9284.18 MWh. The sample kurtosis was slightly above 2 (2.707), indicating that the distribution is not too peaked for total wind generation in Türkiye. Moreover, the positive skewness (0.618) implies that there is a right-skewed distribution, with a long tail on the right. Consequently, most of the values end up being left off the mean, meaning that the most extreme values are on the right side. Electricity generated from solar has the most extreme distributions, due to its nature of radiation as we cannot continuously have sun.

Figure 6. Distribution of day-ahead price (Euro)

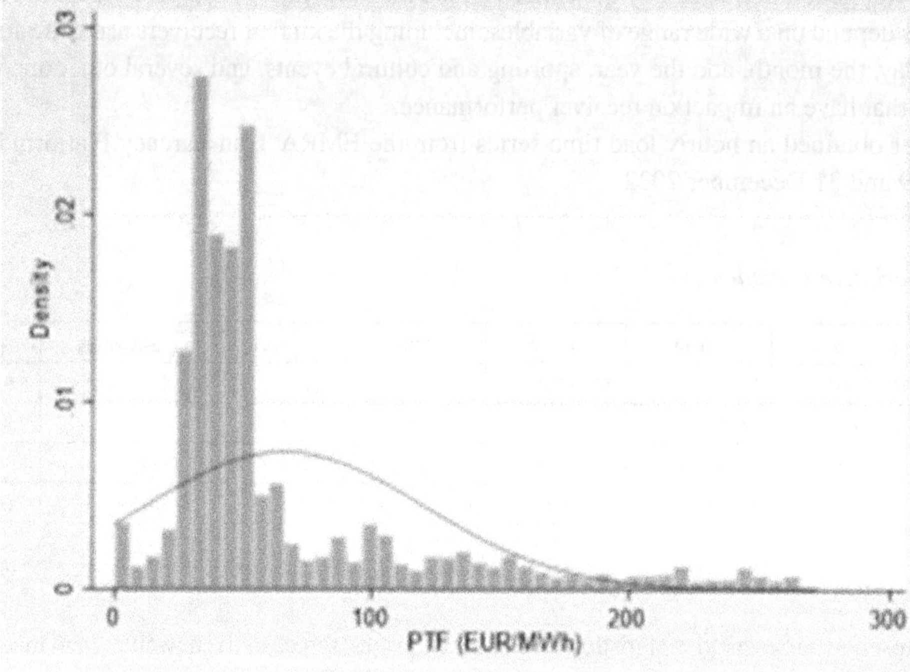

Figure 7. Distribution of total load MWh

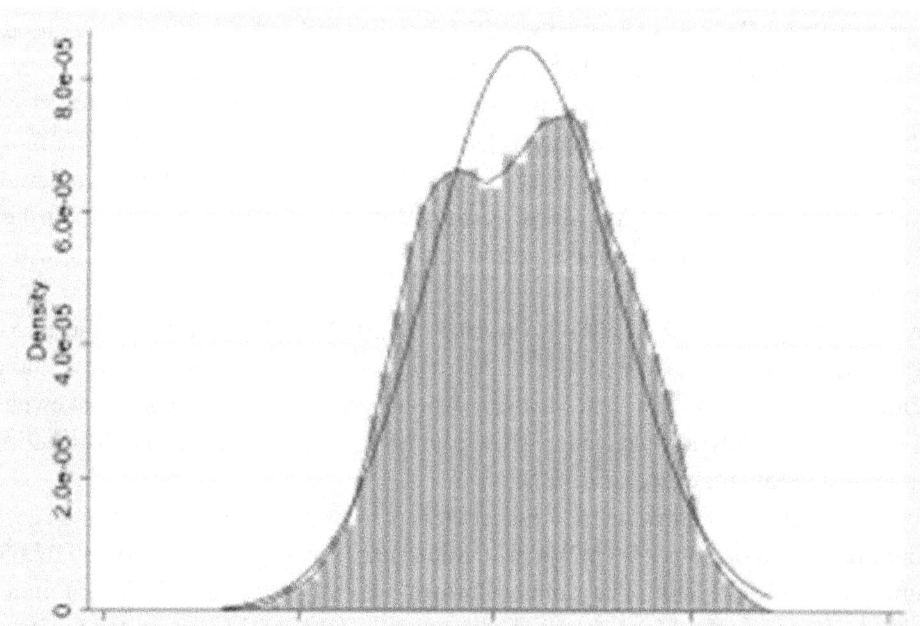

Figure 8. Distribution of wind generation

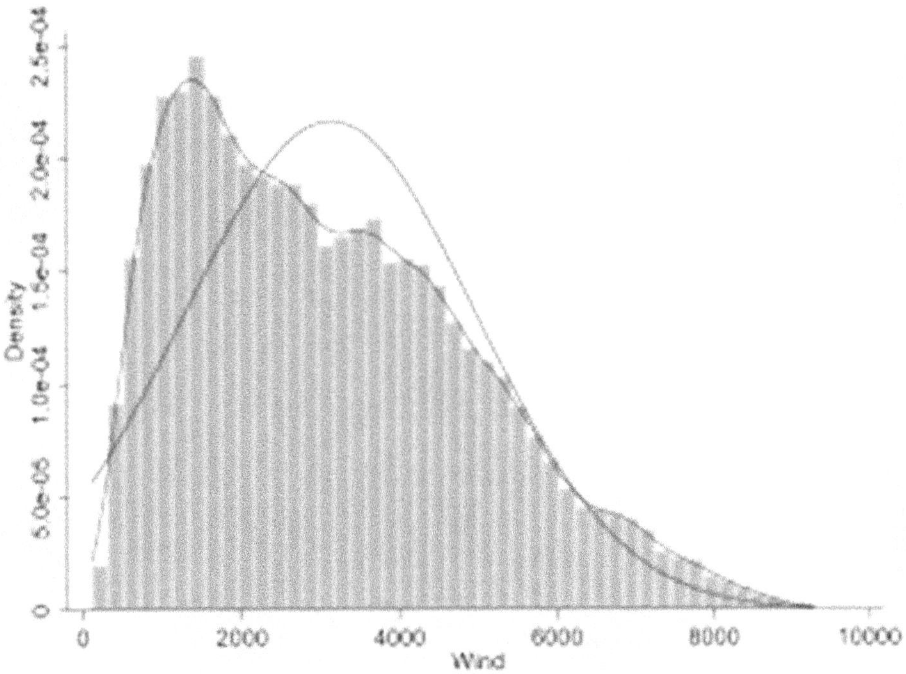

The mean value of solar generation over the sample period was 140.4977 MWh, with a standard deviation of 267.0801 MWh. The minimum solar generation was recorded to be -1.7 MWh on 11 April 2019 at 7:00 PM and the maximum was 1289.82 MWh on 26 September 2022 at 12:00 AM The sample kurtosis is high with a value of 7.6, indicating that the distribution is highly peaked for solar electricity generation, a feature observed in every country utilizing solar power. Furthermore, the positive skewness (2.3) implies that there is a right-skewed distribution, with a long tail on the right, thus, extreme values are more likely to be on the right side. This is illustrated even through Figure 6, where the distribution graph is highly skewed to the right, in comparison to wind.

The four graphs below illustrate the behavior of variables in 2022 on a daily basis, which is calculated as the arithmetic average of 24 hours a day, to gain a better understanding of spikes and the pattern that renewables and prices follow.

This is possible as long as the hourly data for a period of four years captures a wide range of observations. Prices exhibit a high degree of volatility, with extreme spikes being observable during the winter months. Furthermore, total load generation displays a continuous pattern throughout the year, with smoother waves than those generated from solar and wind. Solar energy has its extreme spikes, with the highest generation occurring in the summer months when solar radiation has the highest intensity, duration and stability. Additionally, fluctuations in wind generation are quite substantial, as one can observe spikes occurring continuously throughout the year. It is in line with the established knowledge that wind and solar energy are heavily impacted by weather conditions and can experience sudden increases or decreases.

Figure 9. Distribution of solar power generation

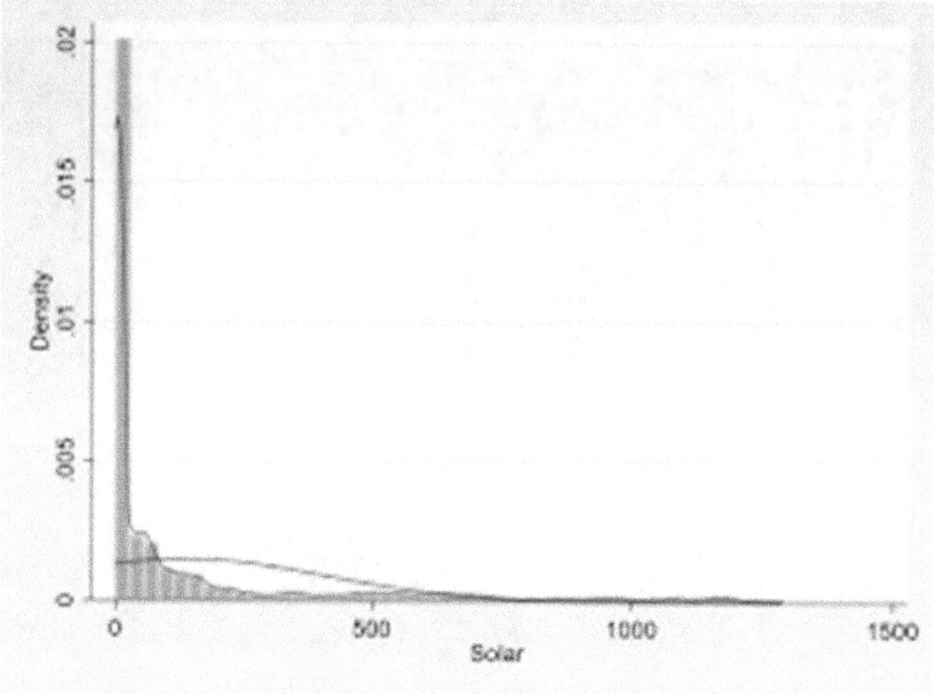

Figure 10. Daily data

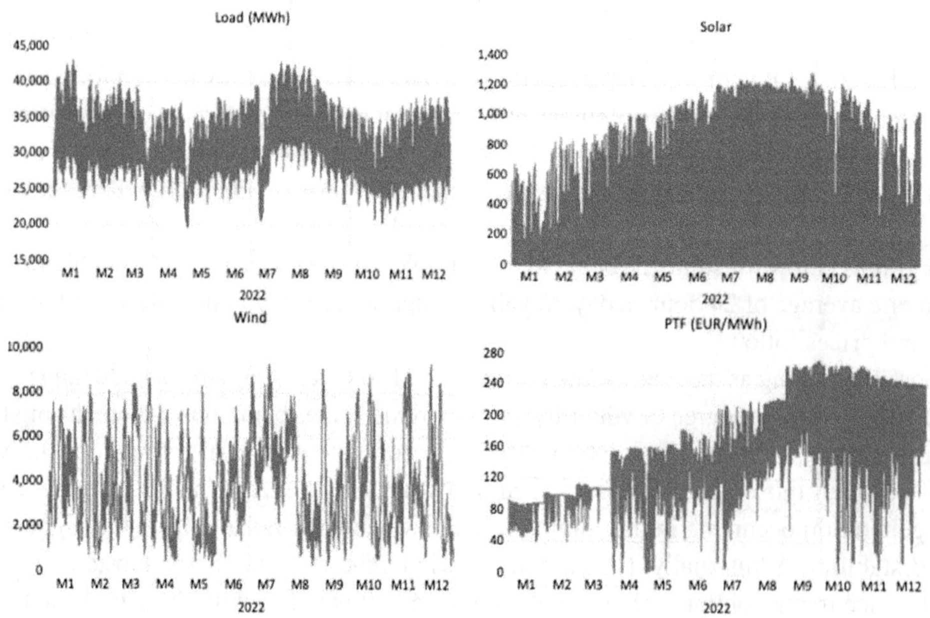

3.5 Disadvantages of Renewable Energy

The global trend is to increase the share of renewable energy and reduce fossil fuel-based production in total electricity production over time (Liu et al., 2016). However, the use of renewable energy also brings some problems. For example, wind and solar energy can create an energy supply in an intermittent form. The hours when wind energy is most intense may not coincide with the hours when electrical energy is most demanded. Similarly, when the energy demand is highest in the evenings, it is impossible to obtain solar energy (Greve and Pollitt, 2016).

In the electricity market, supply and demand must be equal at every moment of the day. However, the production from renewables may not meet the expectation due to its intermittent and unpredictable nature. For instance, Figure 10 shows the difference between predicted (blue) and actual (red) electricity production from wind in 2022 for Türkiye. In such cases, other production sources, such as gas or oil-fired plants, intervene to close the gap, which causes system inefficiency. Another problem is that the excess supply of renewable energy would be wasted and has to be paid for even though it is not used (Burlinson and Giulietti, 2017).

Figure 11. Predicted and actual wind energy

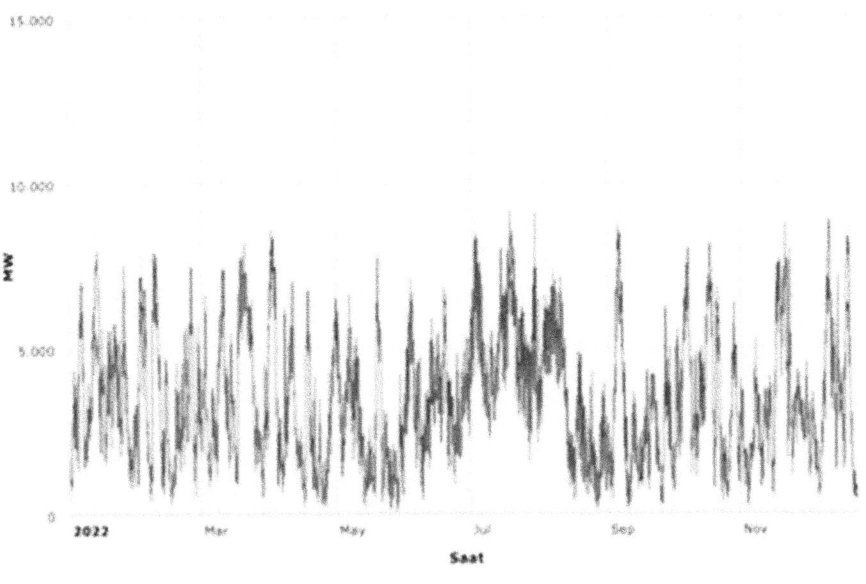

Renewable energy, especially solar and wind, can be intermittent. Holttinen (2008) focused on the negative impacts of wind power generation on the grid by considering ten different grids in European countries and the US. He concluded that more wind power generation leads to more energy needed to balance the grid power. Similarly, Miettinen and Holttinen (2019) demonstrated the unpredictable nature of wind energy causes balancing problems on the grid in the Nordic countries.

Swinand and Godel (2012) for the UK and Batalla-Bejerano and Trujillio-Baute (2016) for Spain showed that the more wind power is associated with higher grid capacity expansion and balancing cost. On the other hand, Heptonstall et al. (2017) reported that the intermittent and unpredictable nature of the renewable energy causes disruptions in the system during times of peak demand. Moreover, it is found that short-term balancing resources and additional capacity investments that can eliminate these disruptions will incur a significant cost. Finally, Hu et al. (2021) examined the effects of wind energy utilization on the intraday electricity market in Sweden between 2015 and 2018. They reported that deviations in wind forecasts negatively affected intraday market prices in regions with high wind energy generation.

4. ENERGY STORAGE

4.1 Evolution of Energy Storage Systems

One of the most challenging situations in the electricity market is the need to balance instantaneous electricity demand and supply, and to do so at all times. Besides, the intermittent nature of renewables negatively affects the electricity distribution system. Energy storage technologies are the strongest candidates for solving this problem (Waterson et al., 2022). Energy storage technologies can overcome these imbalances by converting electricity into other forms of energy (or vice versa). This technology allows for storing surplus renewable electricity when electricity demand is low and returning this stored energy to the grid during peak hours.

The increased use of energy storage is thought to increase social benefits through different mechanisms (Waterson et al., 2022);

- It can prevent electricity generation from being wasted due to electricity production exceeding demand due to disruptions in renewable energy production planning,
- It can reduce the volatility/jump in electricity prices by facilitating a balance between electricity supply and demand,
- It can be a lower-cost alternative to new grid investments in meeting growing electricity demand,
- When electricity demand exceeds supply, it has the potential to provide cheaper electricity for balancing instead of coal or gas-fired plants, which typically have a high marginal cost.

Energy is stored in three basic ways: potential energy, kinetic energy or chemical energy. Around mid 1800's, there has been developments in basic battery technologies, such as lead acid battery and nickel-cadmium battery, which are example of chemical energy. By the end of the century, flywheel energy storage system was introduced. This system stores rotational energy by utilizing the conservation of angular momentum (Hossain et al., 2020).

One of the most widely used storage methods is pumped storage hydroelectric systems, which was first used in early 1900's. This is a system of storing energy in the form of potential energy by pumping water to higher levels through a cascaded reservoir system. This type of storage offers long-term and high-capacity electricity supply and can reach the highest energy supply rate in a very short time (Bistline et al., 2020). According to a European Commission report, pumped storage hydropower plants will revolutionize smart energy management and play a key role in Europe's fight against green energy and climate change (Sinn, 2017). However, the realization of these plants requires geological characteristics. Therefore, compressed air, heat and battery storage strategies have emerged as other alternatives.

Around mid 1900's thermal energy storage and compressed energy storage has been introduced (Mitali et al., 2022). Compressed air storage technology, which is based on underground storage of compressed air or other gas, allows energy to be preserved for a long time (Mouli-Castillo et al., 2019). Heat energy storage, another energy storage method, has higher operating costs than compressed air storage. Therefore, shorter-term use of heat storage can be advantageous (Waterson, 2017).

Compared to the storage technologies mentioned above, Lithium-ion batteries are the most intensively used storage technology in recent times (Reddy et al., 2020). The installation costs of this technology, which provides flexibility of use in many ways, have been gradually decreasing over the years (Mongird et al., 2019). Next-generation battery technology has led to the emergence of powerful and fast-reacting products, but these products require frequent maintenance and replacement compared to other alternatives due to efficiency losses as a result of discharge (IEA, 2022a). Table 4 highlight the characteristics of some of the above-mentioned energy storage systems. It shows that the most efficient energy storge methods are Flow and Lithium-ion batteries, however their discharge times are relatively low compared to Pumped hydro and Compressed air. Besides, the max power of Pumped hydro is relatively high compared to other storage systems.

Table 4. Characteristics of some energy storage systems

	Max Power	Discharge Time	Lifetime	Efficiency
Pumped hydro	3000	4h-16h	30-60 years	70-85%
Compressed air	1000	2h-30h	20-40 years	40-70%
Lithium-ion batteries	100	1min-8h	1000-10000 (charge cycles)	85-95%
Lead-acid battery	100	1min-8h	6-40 years	80-90%
Flow battery	100	hours	12000-14000 (charge cycles)	70-95%

Source: The World Energy Council, 2021

4.2 Global and Local Developments in Energy Storage Policies

Countries have adopted different approaches in terms of energy storage policy. For example, grid operators cannot own storage facilities in England and Wales. However, electricity-producing companies can also operate storage facilities in Italy. On the other hand, the largest energy-producing companies in California were forced to establish electricity storage facilities by law (Burlinson and Giulietti, 2017).

The International Energy Agency predicts that the global battery storage capacity of 8GW in 2018 will reach 680 GW by 2030 (IEA, 2022b). There are two main drivers behind this recent trend. First, increasing wind and solar production require more energy storage facilities (Denholm et al., 2010; Evans et al., 2012). Second, battery storage technology is getting cheaper, mainly due to lithium-ion battery production improvements. The cost of Lithium-ion batteries, calculated in kilowatt-hours/USD units, fell to one-tenth of 2010 production prices in 2021 (MIT, 2022). Türkiye's energy storage policy is aligned with the global trend. The Turkish National Energy Plan (TUEP) aims to increase the current battery capacity of 7.5 GW (TUEP, 2022).

Türkiye has recently introduced new regulations regarding electricity storage systems. In 2021, the Regulation on Storage Activities in the Electricity Market was published. The regulation introduced the definition of electricity storage facilities and explained how a potential electricity producer could obtain licenses to set up storage facilities. In 2022, two paragraphs were added to the Electricity Market Law, which allowed potential investors to obtain renewable energy generation licenses without competition if they promised to set up an energy storage facility along with the renewable energy power plant.

The Turkish Energy Market Regulatory Authority opened the application system for this call on early December 2022. The opportunity to obtain a generation license without an auction has attracted the attention of potential investors. Within a month, 2753 applications were made (1542 applications for solar energy and 1211 for wind energy). Total investment demand has reached 91 GW in installed power and 230 billion USD in monetary terms.

4.3 Optimal Level of Energy Storage

The link between intermittent renewable energy and energy storage technology has been the subject of many studies, and one of the most important issues of interest has been the optimal energy storage capacity to be determined. In this subsection we will review some of the relevant literature to highlight the recent trends in determining the optimal level of energy storage. Rasmussen et al. (2012) analyzed the optimal amount of renewable energy generation for Europe and the amount of energy storage to accompany it through time series analysis using hourly electricity supply-demand data covering eight years. With solar and wind having a 50% share in total energy production, the study calculates that a high volume of storage will be required to avoid large energy losses and finds the ideal storage time to be 6 hours.

Similarly, Liu et al. (2016) analyzed the optimal level of combined use of renewable energy generation and accompanying energy storage technology to provide energy in addition to a fossil fuel-fired electricity generation plant. The study analyzed a scenario in which wind power generation takes place in addition to a natural gas-fired power plant and found that the scenarios in which storage-supported wind power generation has the highest share in total generation are optimal for the cities of Rugby and Aberdeen in the UK.

Sinn (2017) aimed to calculate the ideal capacity required to store electricity from wind and solar, questioning the continuity of Germany's renewable energy breakthroughs. In the scenario where all energy demand is provided by renewable energy, it was found that 61% of the energy produced would be wasted as a result of the supply-demand imbalance in the absence of any storage use. They calculated an unrealizable capacity requirement for storage that would ensure that no renewable energy is wasted. On the other hand, Zerrahn et al. (2018) criticize the corner solution strategy proposed by Sinn (2017) and argue that the optimal approach is to adopt a storage strategy in which some renewable energy can be curtailed or wasted. Their findings for the optimal storage capacity were much lower than that suggested by Sinn (2017).

Zerrahn and Schill (2017) provide a comprehensive review of the energy economics and engineering literature on renewable energy and storage. Based on the models used by the reviewed studies, they created a new model, DIETER, based on system cost minimization to examine the role of energy storage. As a follow-up study, Schill and Zerrahn (2018) use the DIETER analysis and find that for countries with a high share of renewable energy in total electricity generation, storage is efficient and the optimal storage duration is up to 12 hours. In addition, they show that long-term storage can also be profitable in a hypothetical scenario where all energy demand is met by renewable energy.

Wu and Lin (2018) analyzed the profitability and economic benefits of energy storage for China, where, unlike other examples in the literature, there is no free electricity market and the distribution, marketing and pricing mechanisms are monopolistic, and showed that the use of storage will increase profitability, but above a certain level of storage use, profitability will decrease.

Unlike previous studies that examined the short-term effects of energy storage, Mallapragada et al. (2020) conducted a long-term profit and value analysis of storage in a scenario with increased wind and solar generation. Accordingly, they find that storage generates higher value when it generates based on only one renewable energy source (only solar or wind). In addition, they emphasized that the decline in energy prices due to the increase in renewable energy production in the long run will negatively affect the profitability and value of storage projects.

The literature on the optimal level of energy storage is new and growing. Some of the review studies examined the profitability of energy storage, while others focused on the social welfare aspect. The more storage facilities used, the more data will be available to determine the optimal level of storage systems in the near future.

4.4 Future Trends in Energy Storage

The energy storage market is used to controlled by the lithium-ion battery industry. Due to their extended lifespan, low cost of maintenance, and high energy per mass, lithium-ion batteries function well in the majority of consumer gadgets. These batteries do, however, have a number of safety concerns, particularly with regard to overheating and sensitivity to high temperatures. Additionally, their performance gets worse over time. New materials are therefore being investigated for the creation of batteries and other types of energy storage. Recently, newer technologies that provide a variety of benefits started to enter the market. Each technology has advantages and limits, and the range of applications for each technology is different. Current research and development projects are taking these important distinctions into account and concentrating on solutions that are effective, affordable, and more widely accessible than lithium-based storage systems.

In the ensuing decades, the energy storage sector is anticipated to be crucial in helping a number of countries reach net zero. Despite having a promising future, the energy storage industry currently faces a number of obstacles. The initial expenditure required for exploration, research, and development of innovative energy storage technologies is substantial, which discourages some potential investors from building a healthy energy storage market. Besides, environmental issues must be considered because batteries and storage devices may have a negative influence on the environment not just during disposal but also during mining and extraction.

Other barriers to the market's expansion include the lack of long-lasting batteries, standardization and time-degradation, and the low energy density of current batteries. Energy storage technologies still lack a clearly defined market structure, and the sector is still largely dependent on government policy assistance. Future investments in the area may be expected to increase, with a focus on not only lithium but also other cutting-edge technologies including supercapacitors, redox flow batteries, and hydrogen.

5. CONCLUSION

The increase in global energy demand and supply disruptions caused a rise in energy prices. Along with the cost increases caused by high energy prices, concerns on energy supply security made it necessary to increase the share of renewable energy in total energy production over time. In addition, environmental targets such as net-zero policy leaded to a strategy for reducing fossil fuel-based energy production globally.

However, renewable energy (especially wind and solar) creates an intermittent energy supply, creating cost-increasing results in energy supply planning. The energy storage method, which is applied as a solution to this problem, enables the energy produced by wind and sun to be stored during the hours when electricity demand is low. By returning the stored energy to the grid during peak hours, the problems caused by using renewable energy are alleviated. All these developments have led to the formation of new and rapidly growing energy economy literature, analyzing the effects of renewable energy and storage activities on electricity prices.

Electricity storage getting popular around the world. According to the Regulation Amending the Regulation on Storage Activities in the Electricity Market, which entered into force in November 2022, storage units with a total capacity of 30GW will be allowed in Türkiye. Besides, it is confirmed that the level of storage will expand in the near future.

In this chapter we highlighted the recent renewable energy policy changes and the future of energy storage in Türkiye. As discussed, recent developments on renewables and electricity storage are expected to have potential effects on the electricity market, especially on pricing mechanism. We believe that future works should focus on examining such effects.

REFERENCES

Abdmouleh, Z., Alammari, R. A., & Gastli, A. (2015). Review of policies encouraging renewable energy integration & best practices. *Renewable & Sustainable Energy Reviews*, *45*, 249–262. doi:10.1016/j.rser.2015.01.035

Abolhosseini, S., & Heshmati, A. (2014). The main support mechanisms to finance renewable energy development. *Renewable & Sustainable Energy Reviews*, *40*, 876–885. doi:10.1016/j.rser.2014.08.013

Acar, B., Selcuk, O., & Dastan, S. A. (2019). The merit order effect of wind and river type hydroelectricity generation on Turkish electricity prices. *Energy Policy*, *132*, 1298–1319. doi:10.1016/j.enpol.2019.07.006

Aščerić, A., Pantoš, M., & Čepin, M. (2022). Correlation of Day-Ahead Electric Energy Market Price with Renewable Energy Sources Generation and Load Forecast. In *Advanced Technologies, Systems, and Applications VI: Proceedings of the International Symposium on Innovative and Interdisciplinary Applications of Advanced Technologies (IAT) 2021* (pp. 99-109). Springer International Publishing.

Ballester, C., & Furió, D. (2015). Effects of renewables on the stylized facts of electricity prices. *Renewable & Sustainable Energy Reviews*, *52*, 1596–1609. doi:10.1016/j.rser.2015.07.168

Batalla-Bejerano, J., & Trujillo-Baute, E. (2016). Impacts of intermittent renewable generation on electricity system costs. *Energy Policy*, *94*, 411–420. doi:10.1016/j.enpol.2015.10.024

Berk, İ., & Torun, E. (2019). Testing merit-order effect in Türkiye's electricity market: The effect of wind penetration on day-ahead electricity prices. *Akdeniz İİBF Dergisi*, *19*(1), 133–156.

Bistline, J., Cole, W., Damato, G., DeCarolis, J., Frazier, W., Linga, V., Marcy, C., Namovicz, C., Podkaminer, K., Sims, R., Sukunta, M., & Young, D. (2020). Energy storage in long-term system models: A review of considerations, best practices, and research needs. *Progress in Energy*, *2*(3), 032001. doi:10.1088/2516-1083/ab9894

Burlinson, A., & Giulietti, M. (2018). Non-traditional business models for city-scale energy storage: Evidence from UK case studies. *Economia e Politica Industriale*, *45*(2), 215–242. doi:10.100740812-017-0083-8

Clark, W. W., II. (2018). Afterword: A Sustainable Economic and Finance Proposal. In Sustainable Cities and Communities Design Handbook (pp. 573-583). Butterworth-Heinemann.

Csereklyei, Z., Qu, S., & Ancev, T. (2019). The effect of wind and solar power generation on wholesale electricity prices in Australia. *Energy Policy*, *131*, 358–369. doi:10.1016/j.enpol.2019.04.007

Dinçsoy, E. E., & Ichiminami, F. (2006). An Assessment of the Southeastern Anatolia Region in Türkiye in Terms of the Sustainable Development Targets. *Journal of the Faculty of Environmental Science and Technology, Okayama University*, *11*(1), 75–81.

Georgilakis, P. S. (2007). Artificial intelligence solution to electricity price forecasting problem. *Applied Artificial Intelligence*, *21*(8), 707–727. doi:10.1080/08839510701526533

Gipe, P. (2011). *Snapshot of Feed-in Tariffs around the World in 2011.* See also: http://www. windworks. org/FeedLaws/SnapshotofFeed-inTariffsaroundtheWorldin2011.html

Greve, T., & Pollitt, M. G. (2016). *A VCG auction for electricity storage.* EPRG working paper 1623 and Cambridge working paper in economics 1628.

Gullì, F., & Balbo, A. L. (2015). The impact of intermittently renewable energy on Italian wholesale electricity prices: Additional benefits or additional costs? *Energy Policy*, *83*, 123–137. doi:10.1016/j.enpol.2015.04.001

Holttinen, H. (2008). Estimating the impacts of wind power on power systems—Summary of IEA Wind collaboration. *Environmental Research Letters*, *3*(2), 025001. doi:10.1088/1748-9326/3/2/025001

Hossain, E., Faruque, H. M. R., Sunny, M. S. H., Mohammad, N., & Nawar, N. (2020). A comprehensive review on energy storage systems: Types, comparison, current scenario, applications, barriers, and potential solutions, policies, and future prospects. *Energies*, *13*(14), 3651. doi:10.3390/en13143651

Hu, X., Jaraite, J., & Kazukauskas, A. (2021). The effects of wind power on electricity markets: A case study of the Swedish intraday market. *Energy Economics*, *96*, 105159. doi:10.1016/j.eneco.2021.105159

IEA. (2022a), *Renewables 2022*. IEA. https://www.iea.org/reports/renewables-2022

IEA. (2022b). *International energy agency: world energy Outlook.* International Energy Agency Publications.

IEA. (2022c). *Grid-Scale Storage*. IEA. https://www.iea.org/reports/grid-scale-storage

Ketterer, J. C. (2014). The impact of wind power generation on the electricity price in Germany. *Energy Economics*, *44*, 270–280. doi:10.1016/j.eneco.2014.04.003

Lin, Z., Gao, L., & Zhang, D. (2006, June). Predictions of system marginal price of electricity using recurrent neural network. In *2006 6th World Congress on Intelligent Control and Automation* (Vol. 2, pp. 7592-7595). IEEE.

Liu, F., Giulietti, M., & Chen, B. (2016). Joint optimisation of generation and storage in the presence of wind. *IET Renewable Power Generation*, *10*(10), 1477–1487. doi:10.1049/iet-rpg.2015.0547

Mallapragada, D. S., Sepulveda, N. A., & Jenkins, J. D. (2020). Long-run system value of battery energy storage in future grids with increasing wind and solar generation. *Applied Energy*, *275*, 115390. doi:10.1016/j.apenergy.2020.115390

Miettinen, J., & Holttinen, H. (2019). Impacts of wind power forecast errors on the real-time balancing need: A Nordic case study. *IET Renewable Power Generation*, *13*(2), 227–233. doi:10.1049/iet-rpg.2018.5234

MIT. (2022). *Study on the Future of Energy Storage*. MIT.

Mitali, J., Dhinakaran, S., & Mohamad, A. A. (2022). Energy storage systems: A review. *Energy Storage and Saving*.

Mongird, K., Viswanathan, V. V., Balducci, P. J., Alam, M. J. E., Fotedar, V., Koritarov, V. S., & Hadjerioua, B. (2019). Energy storage technology and cost characterization report (No. PNNL-28866). Pacific Northwest National Lab.

Mouli-Castillo, J., Wilkinson, M., Mignard, D., McDermott, C., Haszeldine, R. S., & Shipton, Z. K. (2019). Inter-seasonal compressed-air energy storage using saline aquifers. *Nature Energy*, *4*(2), 131–139. doi:10.103841560-018-0311-0

Mulder, M., & Scholtens, B. (2013). The impact of renewable energy on electricity prices in the Netherlands. *Renewable Energy*, *57*, 94–100. doi:10.1016/j.renene.2013.01.025

Okur Dincsoy, M. (2016). A Comparative Study on Population and Employment Risks in Vulnerable Countries to Climate Change. *International Journal of Ecological Economics and Statistics*, *37*, 103–120.

Papaefthymiou, G., Grave, K., & Dragoon, K. (2014). *Flexibility options in electricity systems. Project number: POWDE14426*. Ecofys.

Peña, J. I., & Rodríguez, R. (2019). Are EU's Climate and Energy Package 20-20-20 targets achievable and compatible? Evidence from the impact of renewables on electricity prices. *Energy*, *183*, 477–486. doi:10.1016/j.energy.2019.06.138

Rasmussen, M. G., Andresen, G. B., & Greiner, M. (2012). Storage and balancing synergies in a fully or highly renewable pan-European power system. *Energy Policy*, *51*, 642–651. doi:10.1016/j.enpol.2012.09.009

Rathmann, M. (2007). Do support systems for RES-E reduce EU-ETS-driven electricity prices? *Energy Policy*, *35*(1), 342–349. doi:10.1016/j.enpol.2005.11.029

Reddy, M. V., Mauger, A., Julien, C. M., Paolella, A., & Zaghib, K. (2020). Brief history of early lithium-battery development. *Materials (Basel)*, *13*(8), 1884. doi:10.3390/ma13081884 PMID:32316390

Schill, W. P. (2020). Electricity storage and the renewable energy transition. *Joule*, *4*(10), 2059–2064. doi:10.1016/j.joule.2020.07.022

Schill, W. P., & Zerrahn, A. (2018). Long-run power storage requirements for high shares of renewables: Results and sensitivities. *Renewable & Sustainable Energy Reviews*, *83*, 156–171. doi:10.1016/j.rser.2017.05.205

Sensfuß, F. (2008). *Assessment of the impact of renewable electricity generation on the German electricity sector: An agent-based simulation approach* [Doctoral dissertation]. Karlsruhe, Univ.

Sensfuß, F., Ragwitz, M., & Genoese, M. (2008). The merit-order effect: A detailed analysis of the price effect of renewable electricity generation on spot market prices in Germany. *Energy Policy*, *36*(8), 3086–3094. doi:10.1016/j.enpol.2008.03.035

Sinn, H. W. (2017). Buffering volatility: A study on the limits of Germany's energy revolution. *European Economic Review*, *99*, 130–150. doi:10.1016/j.euroecorev.2017.05.007

Swinand, G. P., & Godel, M. (2012, May). Estimating the impact of wind generation on balancing costs in the GB electricity markets. In *2012 9th International Conference on the European Energy Market* (pp. 1-8). IEEE. 10.1109/EEM.2012.6254790

Tagliapietra, S., Zachmann, G., Edenhofer, O., Glachant, J. M., Linares, P., & Loeschel, A. (2019). The European union energy transition: Key priorities for the next five years. *Energy Policy*, *132*, 950–954. doi:10.1016/j.enpol.2019.06.060

Tveten, Å. G., Bolkesjø, T. F., Martinsen, T., & Hvarnes, H. (2013). Solar feed-in tariffs and the merit order effect: A study of the German electricity market. *Energy Policy*, *61*, 761–770. doi:10.1016/j.enpol.2013.05.060

Waterson, M. (2017). The characteristics of electricity storage, renewables and markets. *Energy Policy*, *104*, 466–473. doi:10.1016/j.enpol.2017.01.025

Waterson, M., Trujillo-Baute, E., & Giulietti, M. (2022). Intermittency and the social role of storage. *Energy Policy*, *165*, 112947. doi:10.1016/j.enpol.2022.112947

Würzburg, K., Labandeira, X., & Linares, P. (2013). Renewable generation and electricity prices: Taking stock and new evidence for Germany and Austria. *Energy Economics*, *40*, S159–S171. doi:10.1016/j.eneco.2013.09.011

Zerrahn, A., & Schill, W. P. (2017). Long-run power storage requirements for high shares of renewables: Review and a new model. *Renewable & Sustainable Energy Reviews*, *79*, 1518–1534. doi:10.1016/j.rser.2016.11.098

Zerrahn, A., Schill, W. P., & Kemfert, C. (2018). On the economics of electrical storage for variable renewable energy sources. *European Economic Review*, *108*, 259–279. doi:10.1016/j.euroecorev.2018.07.004

Chapter 13
Global Development and International Order Transition:
The Role of China

Mukesh Shankar Bharti
https://orcid.org/0000-0002-3693-7247
Jawaharlal Nehru University, India

ABSTRACT

The aim of this study is to discuss China's role in the development process in the current world order. This chapter elucidates how China's Belt and Road Initiative (BRI) connects countries from all over the world in the context of economic and trade prosperity. Thus, the revival of the China's old silk road by President Xi Jinping has initiated a global development programme on all the continents. Since 2013, China has been delivering through the successful launch of the BRI projects and dominate on their counterpart in the new world order. Now, the theory of globalisation is being pioneered by Chinese diplomacy in world politics. The concept of soft and hard power is applied to explain the main research problems of this study. The chapter relies on qualitative analysis and an empirical approach to discussion to investigate the goal of this research.

INTRODUCTION

The People's Republic of China (PRC) has emerged as the leading global economy in the last decade and is gaining world attention in the Asia-Pacific region. China has established itself as a second economic power and has been setting the agenda of globalisation in the world for trade and economic cooperation through the use of soft power politics (Pan & Lo, 2017). China had transformed its diplomacy through political debate and theoretical discourse to implement the policy that is Beijing's power strategy to establish partnerships at the global level. China's role in the new world order looms large in the age of geopolitics and geoeconomics. China is the second-largest economy in the world and has been setting the agenda for a new economic world, and its economic policy is strengthening the concept of globalisation 5.0 to create deeper geopolitical connectivity in the world. China has emerged as a major economic

DOI: 10.4018/979-8-3693-0400-6.ch013

partner for more than 170 countries in the world. China is also considered the biggest driver of the global economy. China's contribution to the world economy has been growing by around 30 percent at the annual rate of the world economy. China is seriously implementing the core agenda of the UN for sustainable development, also called "the UN 2030 Agenda for Sustainable Development" (Ministry of Foreign Affairs of the People's Republic of China, 2022). China's State Councillor and Foreign Minister of the People's Republic of China (PRC) Wang Yi addressed the United Nations General Assembly's General Debate of the 77th Session on September 24, 2022, and also made strong comments about the agenda of sustainable development and talked about China's commitment to people's happy lives through the global development program. Wang Yi also affirms that development must be at the centre of every nation in the international community.

China's Belt and Road Initiative (BRI) is connecting countries from all continents. China is promoting the BRI framework of economic cooperation to promote development as the centre of the international development agenda to provide for and uphold the legitimate human right to social development. China understands that to expedite new drivers for the development of international communities and continue to work for the partnership of global development. China understands that to accelerate new drivers for the development of international communities and continue to work for the global development partnership. China's BRI is spreading as a successful global development agenda for developing fruitful relations in a more equitable manner. China's Foreign Minister Wang Yi said that "development is the bedrock of peace. China has contributed enormously to world peace and stability through its own economic development. It is estimated that China has consistently served as one of the main drivers of the global economy in the past 30 years, becoming the largest contributor to global growth since the international financial crisis. China, a strong and dynamic locomotive, is fueling the development of many other countries, thus creating a more favourable environment and laying a more solid foundation for the noble cause of peace" (Ministry of Foreign Affairs of the People's Republic of China, 2015).

China's BRI is a comprehensive undertaking watched by world experts, commentators, and scholars who recognise Chinese diplomacy under the leadership of Xi Jinping (Zhao, 2020). The BRI framework of economic cooperation is the latest series of China's endeavours that have been getting global value with an international framework of strategic connectivity (Silvius, 2021). Since 2013, China has proven to be a rising world power and is emerging as a major player in the context of global governance. China has been using the 'western liberal internationalism' approach in its foreign affairs policy. China has proven year after year to be a confidence-builder in international politics, particularly in the field of multilateral forums and security. China's economic engagement across the world strengthens its position in international politics through cultural linkages, economic interdependence, diplomatic expansion with liberal value, interwind, and institutional development (Lampton, 1997, 2005). The rising power always gains a valuable position to pursue mutual benefits through the institutions' development. China has reduced its own embezzlement and has been trying to manipulate other states. China is aiming for absolute gains rather than relative power gains (Keohane & Joseph S. Nye Jr., 1998).

This study uses the primary and secondary resources of data collected from different private and public sector institutions' websites and published literature to answer the research problems. Further, this study also evaluates and tries to find out China's position in the "Liberal International Order" for the global development program. The qualitative nature of this study focuses on China's BRI and another worldwide connectivity programme that has had a strong presence in global politics and has strengthened its geostrategic focus on competing geoeconomics and geopolitics. Moreover, the inductive method is broadly used through the empirical approach to explain the research gap in this study.

Conceptual Framework of China's Global Development Initiatives

China started its diplomatic journey for integration into global institutions during the era of the 'Cold War' with the establishment of deeper political and economic cooperation. China had adopted strategic innovation and participation in global regimes. This changed its diplomacy after the Chinese accession to the WTO and China started the Shanghai Cooperation Organisation through a multilateral diplomatic channel to engage in deeper economic and political ties with like-minded countries (Liu, 2020). According to rationalist theorists, hegemonic stability theory is particularly associated with those countries that have been working to shape the new world order until the achievement of dominant behaviours for the establishment of hegemony in international politics (Keohane, 1980; Krasner, 1976). There are high levels of conflict of interest that have been clashing between China and the USA in global politics. In the South China Sea, both biggest economies' rivalry is ongoing for their supremacy in the maritime domain of the Asia-Pacific region. However, China's contribution to the Allied WWII effort facilitated China's recognition as an increasingly important member of the order. China has been benefiting from the economic restructuring programme initiated by the Allied member in Bretton Woods, Hampshire. From the Cold War to the era of globalisation, China has continuously pursued economic growth and connectivity around the world. (Gong, 1984; King, 2022; Mitter, 2013).

In 2021, China's President Xi Jinping put forward its international development vision, the "Global Development Initiative," at the 76th session of the "United Nations General Assembly (UNGA). Xi Jinping states that China's commitment to the agenda of development is a priority for the country to work for global development and the welfare of the common global people. The common people across the world are our focus, and we want to connect them with employment and better human facilities through innovation and skilled base development. China has been focused on and committed to harmony between nature and human beings. China's development concept is based on results-oriented steps (Yao, 2022). On August 2–5, 2022, China's Ambassador to the Seychelles Guo Wei stated that "China's latest solutions to world peace, security, and development". China's perception of development brought some basic principles of historical materialism and Marxist ideology to the formation of history through the masses. It is reflected in the way China's traditional political philosophy has been talking about "the essence of governance is livelihood, and the essence of livelihood is adequacy" (Embassy of the People's Republic of China in the Republic of Seychelles, 2022).

China's President Xi Jinping's ideas on the current world order are transforming and accelerating many changes. The coronavirus outbreak has been denting decades of development, and China is committing to fully implementing the UN 2030 Agenda for Sustainable Development to remove difficulties. Beijing is stating and understanding that there is a widening North-South gap in the world that has continued to increase, and food and energy security are key areas to work with global partners to limit future crises. At the global level, people simply want a peaceful and stable global environment, and states should be involved in economic growth and improvement, focusing on better livelihoods, job orientation, and addressing the world's major recurring challenges. In this context, China's President Xi Jinping has initiated two flagship programmes at the global level, which are the Global Development Initiative (GDI) and the Global Security Initiative (GSI). These two initiatives consider China's wisdom and solutions to the world's problems regarding security and development. In recent years, China has organised high-level conferences on the 'Global Security Initiative' to fill the gap of mutual understanding and promote dialogue at the intergovernmental level. Through this regular dialogue between states on the GSI to address multiple challenges, this kind of initiative could foster synergy in the global community (Ministry of Foreign Affairs of the People's Republic of China, 2023).

China's rise in international politics might change the dynamics of power distribution and the global order. The power pillar of the world order system has been shifting between the US and China, and both sides are in leading positions in the new world order. Despite China's emergence in global politics, there is a negligible chance that it will make a significant orderly transition. Furthermore, the US and China have a deep rivalry in the South China Sea (SCS) and in the Asia-Pacific region. However, China's economic and trade connectivity in the context of the expansion of the BRI framework of cooperation is a threat to Western economies across the world (He & Feng, 2023). There is various literature raising recurring questions about China's rising power and its power expansion towards other continents. At the international level, the main debate is here: when and how we can stop China's strong presence and its rise in the world by other major and minor global players (de Graaff et al., 2020; Krickovic, 2017; Liff, 2016). In global politics, hedging and congagment are important strategies that are significant for blending engagement and containment. On the other hand, China has been involved in the expansion of the developing agenda through the expansion of the BRI framework of cooperation. At the 2017 meeting of the World Economic Forum (WEF) and the May 2017 meeting on the New Silk Road, Chinese President Xi Jinping delivered his speech in favour of globalisation, which brought immense support to the development of people around the world. The PRC's policy is associated with a development agenda, which means that the BRI and China's infrastructure development projects have revolutionised the world (Khalilzad, 2017).

There is no doubt that China has succeeded in consolidating its reach in South, Southeast, and Central Asia. Beyond Asia, China has also made its presence in the countries of Africa, the Pacific Islands, North and South America, the countries of the European Union, and the region of the Western Balkans. In the 'Thucydides trap, at the global level, there is a complete hegemonic war ongoing between major power groups in the world. At the ideological level, despite the wearing of communist values, China is adopting a liberal approach to counter the US and other EU countries by strengthening geopolitical interests and making allies on all continents. China has also been developing institutions and mechanisms to balance the international order without using military involvement. Thus, China's diplomacy has been changed according to the global demand to accelerate the BRI projects (He, 2022). India is actively participating in the Quad, which is an Indo-Pacific' security community, but in recent years has not strongly opposed China's policy in this region. Indian Prime Minister Narendra Modi has engaged with other Western partners, including the United States, to strengthen his presence in the Indo-Pacific region (Sullivan de Estrada, 2023). Since the last decade, China has impacted the established global order and the newest international order. Chinese diplomacy and the BRI projects brought major transformations across the world. The BRI framework for economic and trade cooperation has brought great global changes and dented international authoritarianism as well (Gonzalez-Vicente, 2022).

China's diplomacy has been working deeper to earn economic benefits, and Beijing is enthusiastic about the BRI projects that are likely to bring capital to the country and cement partnerships with other countries (Henderson, 2008). China is the highest economic growth state in the Asia-Pacific region's countries. The columnists and pundits speculated a decade ago that China would be a revisionist power in the new world order. Which could aim to change the status quo in future world politics. It is the concept of the modern era of rising powers. China's Maritime Silk Route Initiative (MSRI) has been spreading from the Pacific to the Indian Ocean region and threatening the opponent side in the maritime domain.

India and France have been committed to working in the maritime domain to provide security sketches to trade and business (Bharti et al., 2022; Kim & Kim, 2022). India and France are defence partners, and both countries' navies and air forces have regular exercises in the Indian Ocean region. The EU and its Member States wish to cooperate in the Indo-Pacific region with a resident player like India. During the French Presidency, the EU started strategic partnerships with regional countries. Thus, the EU and India have been nurturing their bilateral strategic partnership. India has been supporting the EU's Asia-Europe connectivity for deeper economic and trade cooperation. The EU also supports the Indian position in the Indo-Pacific concept of multilateral partnership with major global economies, for example, the US, Japan, South Korea, Australia, and like-minded countries. India is the biggest supporter of democracy, peace and prosperity, social harmony, and secularism standards, and the EU and its member states also support what India wants to establish in the world. In this comparison, China is a totally different country with a one-man dictatorship and one-party rule, which is the negative side of this Asian giant (Bharti, 2023a).

China's Modernisation and the World

China has emerged with modernisation and development in recent decades. The Chinese economy ranks second in the world and its huge population will help spur the recovery of the global economy. China has been tackling the challenge of such a larger population in the country and answering the questions to the world community with proper development with economic prosperity. Beijing's policies also show people-oriented development programmes with the government's deeper interest in overall development. Since the beginning of the complete reform of the country, China has successfully provided all basic needs of human development to the 800 million people in the country. The nation has also worked on the alienation of poverty in many backward regions of the country. Today, China claims that more than 140 countries and some regions are trading partners across the world. Beijing also claimed that every day China makes 320 million dollars in direct investment and the country attracts more than 3,000 foreign businessmen. China has been contributing to global growth in combination with the G7 member states (Ministry of Foreign Affairs of the People's Republic of China, 2023).

China's modernisation rate is higher than any developing country and more than 1.4 billion people are on course toward full-scale modernisation which is a larger number than the combined population of developed countries from across the world. Thus, China can contribute to accelerating the global economy. China has been providing support to many African countries' peoples' welfare and many projects are under construction in the context of the implementation of BRI-oriented infrastructural development program in the Horn of Africa region (Bharti, 2022a). Modernisation brought tremendous changes in the world and China's BRI projects connect all the continents with hope of development since its inception in 2013. Globalisation 5.0 is attached to China's BRI program and the idea of Xi Jinping. China is spreading its flagship economic projects through the BRI and the GDI, China offers an economic development program to the global community. Since 2013, China started over 3,000 multiple cooperation projects which have been initiated and invested around USD 1 trillion and creating more than 420, 000 jobs in the countries which are part of these BRI projects. Many countries around the world realised that China could construct railways, big bridges and poverty alleviation as well in their countries. In the Horn of Africa region, China has been constructing railways, ports and highways under the BRI framework of economic cooperation (Bharti, 2023b; Ministry of Foreign Affairs of the People's Republic of China, 2023).

President Xi Jinping said China's role in global development has grown over the past decades and gained an important position on the international development agenda. Beijing has been operating many development programmes in Latin America, Central Asia, Central and Eastern Africa, South and Southeast Asia to Pacific countries. In the sector of peace and peacekeeping process, China has been enthusiastically participating in the establishment of universal peace and promoting stable global order through advancing international development. China is also promoting norms and ethos of pro-multilateralism and free trade and economic activities at the global level. Beijing understands that China is not supporting unilateralism and protectionism. Thus, Xi Jinping also said that China is helping to create a vibrant international economy in which cooperation is able to provide equal benefits to all countries (Embassy of the PRC in the Republic of South Africa, 2022). Climate issues and global warming are key concerns for responsible economies. China commits to work and implementation of the Paris Climate Accords to support international efforts to mitigate the upcoming environmental-related crises. Beijing has also been promoting sustainable development programmes under the BRI framework of global cooperation. Under BRI connectivity, China is cementing bilateral cooperation and mutually beneficial partnerships by using the principle of global diplomacy. China has started at the larger scale of BRI-related infrastructural work across the world. The BRI framework of trade and economic partnership boosts economic growth, improves quality of life, and creates favourable connectivity between China and the rest of the world.

China and Russia are rebuilding the mutual partnership and intensifying the common agenda for developing programmes, i.e., strategic coordination, bilateral trade and defence, technological exchange and maritime cooperation in the Pacific and Indian Oceans region. Enhancing China-Europe diplomacy and started manufacturing and infrastructural building cooperation in Central and Eastern Europe and the western Balkan region. The "17+1" projects are deeply related to infrastructural development, trade and economic cooperation under China's BRI. China-Europe started a partnership in the area of international affairs, trade liberalisation, and multilateral processes. Thus, both sides also enhance cooperation to promote conflict resolution at the international or domestic level, aware of climate emergency and common interest in tackling the crises, and unitedly work for sustainable development. China has been spreading its trade and economic partnership with regional levels such as Japan, India and South Korea. Xi Jinping explained during his many speeches that strengthening China's cooperation with the regional neighbourhood for a shared future. Through the Shanghai Cooperation Organisation (SCO) and deeper partnership with the Association of Southeast Asian Nations (ASEAN). China is also committed to working with less developed countries at a higher level. The platforms like G77 and China, FOCAC Beijing Summit, BRICS, and BRI Forum, where China has been playing an important role in supporting countries from Asia, Africa, Latin America, Pacific and Caribbean countries (Bharti, 2022b; OECD, 2018).

While new vehicles have been formed to help with the financing such a various BRI projects, such as the Silk Road Fund, most of the Chinese funding for these projects will actually come from state-directed development and commercial banks. China is also supporting a multilateral approach to investment including Multilateral development banks (MDB) and private-public partnerships. (Xi, 2017)

China's minister Kong Xiangxi concurred that China and the USA have great potential to work together for mutual benefit and set the agenda for a new global order. He also claimed that "maintaining close cooperation" with the USA would be beneficial for China in long-term partnership and as well for international economic development (King, 2022). China's President Xi Jinping said that Beijing is too much serious to work for all the communities living on the earth. Thorough promotion of green development and harmonious coexistence between nature and humanity. China has been collaborating with many countries and implementing several principles of treat on saving climate and environment, in-depth promotion of green development and harmonious coexistence between nature and mankind. President Xi Jinping also indicates an encouragement of deeper engagement with the institutional framework of economic structure facilitates green, low-carbon and promotes a transition to green economic and social development. Furthermore, China also actively participates in a different kind of governance at the international level and cooperation with prominent economies. These are as follows climate response, ocean governance, protection of global biodiversity, and other sectors as well. China has been also participating in the encouragement of a global environmental governance system of win-win cooperation. China also assures the world community at the international platforms; that we must work together to tackle the global challenges of climate change save the environment and build a clean and beautiful world.

Since 1978, China began to reform its economy and focus on deeper bilateral cooperation to run the exports and imports. Because of this reform and open-up policy, China has successfully lifted people out of poverty and about 800 million people have benefited. China's medical division also working aggressively for the welfare of mass people in the country. Thus, other prominent sectors also support the government's policy for overseas countries. China has been successfully maintaining an average GDP growth of 9 percent per year. China is now rated the upper-middle-income country in the world, which has successfully eradicated extreme poverty in the country. "China's swift reopening after the COVID-19 outbreaks in late 2022, GDP growth is expected to rebound to 5.1 percent in 2023, from 3 percent in 2022. Growth will be led by a recovery in demand, particularly for services" (World Bank, 2023).

In March 2023, China's President Xi Jinping started diplomatic relationships with Saudi Arabia and Iran. China signed an agreement with longtime antagonists Saudi Arabia and Iran. China wants to deepen partnerships with the Gulf countries to spread its flagship BRI projects in this region (Schuman et al., 2023). China's Communist Party's top official for Foreign Affairs, Wang Yi states that dialogue with Iran and Saudi Arabia is a successful diplomatic initiative of Beijing for the Global Security Initiative (GSI). It is impossible to trace by the practitioner of international relations experts on China stunned the world to restore diplomatic partnership with these two Islamic countries. He says that Chinese President Xi Jinping's charisma has been working to make partnerships with Arabian countries and launched his political intensification campaign to remake the world order (Global Times, 2023). The Global Security Initiative (GSI) and the Global Development Initiative (GDI) are interconnected through the idea of the Chinese Marxist belief that "security is a prerequisite for development, and development is a guarantee for security, it is also famous to known as "peace through development". Xi Jinping stated and outline the proposal in the United Nations General Assembly in 2021 "to help revive global efforts to achieve the ultimate of the UN's goal of Sustainable Development by 2030" (Wong, 2021).

On 26th of September 2021, China's Foreign Minister Wang Yi participated in the inaugural ceremony of the Sustainable Development Forum that emphasized the leadership of President Jinping's crucial role to bring out concrete policy on the "Global Development Initiative". These two twin initiatives of China's vision of transforming international order. It is also called Xi Jinping's "blueprint" for global connectivity to reshape the new global order. China's growing importance in world politics contains a worthy position. Today's China has been playing a significant role in changing the dynamics of developing countries through the cooperation of several BRI projects and China's 21st Century Maritime Silk Road Initiative continuously increasing the country's reach in the maritime domain (Foreign Minister of Foreign Affairs of the People's Republic of China, 2021). China introduced a new initiative in March

2023, the Global Civilisation Initiative (GCI), which promotes a state-focused and state-defined working system and accounted for this effort another landmark decision of Beijing to eliminate universal values in areas such as human rights and democracy.

The recent development of China's partnership with Saudi Arabia and Iran is a successful case of the practice of the Global Security Initiative. Through the GSI, China has incorporated trademark deals with both countries to work on issues of security and prosperity. "The Global Development Initiative (GDI) proposed by Chinese President Xi Jinping helps achieve the Sustainable Development Goals (SDGs). The holistic Global Development Initiative is a valued contribution to addressing common challenges and accelerating the transition to a more sustainable and inclusive future" (Huaxia, 2022).

From the South Asia region, Sri Lanka had signed to join the BRI-Forum and China started several infrastructural works in the country. Sri Lanka also got a loan from China, after some years Sri Lanka didn't return or repay to China. Later, China got Sri Lanka's Hambantota port on a 99-year lease instead of a loan. This is also China's 'debt trap' diplomacy. Thus, China's BRI project in Pakistan is in media and political debate, the CEPC is crossing from the disputed territory of India in Jammu & Kashmir, which has been under Pakistan's control since 1948 and is also called Pak-occupied Kashmir (PoK). The Indian government has also been protesting against this BRI project and refused to participate in the BRI Forum. The Indian authority also understands China's 'Strings of Pearls" concept in the South Asia region. China has been creating a network of commercial and military bases and ports in the Indian Ocean region to dominate opponent block.

The GSI is the concept of the Kremlin's "indivisible security" and the Russian invasion of Ukraine shows that Chinese leaders joining President Vladimir Putin. This is an unlawful invasion of Ukraine by the Russians and this is an unprovoked war against Ukraine which has been blamed by the US-Led NATO (Wenling, 2022). Western political leaders have criticized China's position in the Russian-Ukrainian war, even, though Ukraine is a partner of China's BRI projects and participated in the BRI Forum in Beijing. China is not talking to President Vladimir Putin to stop the war against Ukraine. China is a member of the UN Security Council, and the UN's prime concern is to stop the war in the world. Even though Ukrainian President Volodymyr Zelenskyy urged China to help Ukraine criticised China's act and cast a vote in the UN resolution on the Russian invasion of Ukraine against Russia but China didn't vote for Ukraine. It is a dark side of international politics where a permanent member of the Security Council is involved in the war against Ukraine and another member not voting against Russia.

China could play an active role in trying to resolve disputes in different countries around the world but China has huge border disputes with its neighbouring countries. China has border disputes with Russia, India, Mongolia, Tajikistan and Bhutan. China is unable to resolve border disputes with its friendly country Russia. China offered to mediate between Israel and Palestinians for peace and social harmony in the Gulf region. For instance, in April 2023, Chinese Foreign Minister Qin Gang offered to facilitate a peace settlement between two West Asian countries. But China should take the initiative to start to talk from both sides at the primary level. Because peace is the only solution for human beings to live without wars or crises and it must be a priority for all states. It is methods of diplomacy and concepts of global governance as superior to those of the current rules-based order. China has been deeply involving itself in global politics to mediate disputed matters for the settlement of the peace process. Beijing's diplomacy didn't achieve more success to mediate in the Russian-Ukrainian war. China's President Xi Jinping's "best friend" Russian President Vladimir Putin has exposed the inherent contradictions between the lofty principles of the GSI and Beijing's pursuit of its political and economic interests. Thus, Putin has rejected the principles of the GSI and China is not in a position to negotiate with Russia on war against Ukraine depicting the failure of an emerging international power in world politics (Reuters, 2023).

CONCLUSION

China is the fastest-growing country in the Asia-Pacific region. This book chapter explains that China has initiated deeper trade and economic cooperation across the world. China emerged strong competitor of the USA and other countries. Today, China's domestic development is praised by many philosophers and pundits in their writing. Thus, Russia, Central Asian countries, Southeast Asian and African countries are members of the BRI Forum and support China's investment. "Spanning thousands of miles, the ancient Silk Road has embodied the spirit of cooperation, mutual learning and mutual benefit. The year 2023 marks the 10th anniversary of China's proposal of the Belt and Road Initiative (BRI), another public good which has brought tangible benefits to people of participating countries and promoted people-to-people exchanges" (Xinhua, 2023). China had successfully laid the foundation of BRI projects in Pakistan. The "China-Pakistan-Economic-Corridor (CPEC) is connecting from China's Xinjiang province to the port of Gwadar in Pakistan. China has been constructing the port of Gwadar in the Baluchistan province of Pakistan, which is strategically important to reach out in the Arabian Sea to connect with the Gulf countries for the purpose of the expansion of MSI.

This study evaluates China's BRI as a success story and delivers fruitful outcomes. The study also shows that because of the BRI framework of cooperation, China has connectivity to more than 170 countries across the world. These Chinese projects brought job opportunities for partner countries' young professionals and skilled workers. The Horn of Africa (HoA) and Central Eastern European countries (CEECs) are deeply connected with BRI infrastructure works. China also uses tools of soft power politics to engage partner countries with more fruitful cooperation. China also opened the 'Confucious Study Circle or Institutes' attracting students at a larger number to enrolment in these institutions. Thus, the Chinese government made provisions to provide funds to these institutions and scholarships to students and professors to get an education in China. There are hundreds of students from CEE countries, Pakistan, Central Asia and African countries who get scholarships to pursue higher education in Chinese universities and institutions. Tourism is another sector that China is promoting for its people to visit BRI-oriented countries. There are many European airports broadcasting announcements in the Chinese language for the understanding of Chinese tourists. The airport LED display board displays the information on the flights scheduled for arrival/departure in Chinese/Mandarin language. These kinds of initiatives bond strong strategic partnerships. China is using the norms of soft power to accelerate the bilateral partnership.

This chapter reached out to the main finding points: China is getting much positive feedback from its BRI partner countries and that is why it has more than 170 partners from across the world in the cooperation of BRI. It is a much successful flagship economic project of China's President Xi Jinping's vision to connect countries from all continents. There is no doubt today's world politics that China has been setting the agenda of world politics since the success of the BRI projects in Central Asia, Pakistan, African countries, Southeast Asia and Pacific countries. China is a permanent member of the Security Council of the United Nations and has significance in international relations. There are several countries around the world that need China's help in the UN as well. There is a matter of trust building and

China is getting support from the African countries. China is an Asian giant that already has built trust through investment under the BRI framework of trade and economic cooperation in these countries and regions. Thus, China's MSRI and Silk Road Economic Belt (SREB) connect countries from across the world. Since 2013, China is celebrating 10 years of the success story of BRI projects. On the other hand, China is playing an important role in international politics through the promotion of exchanges among civilisations. China has been working on mutual accommodation, coexistence, exchanges and mutual learning among different civilizations. China is also creating social harmony and a peaceful society among different human groups in the world.

This study concludes that China's modernisation has been attracting countries from the developing world. The 2008 Olympic Games were successfully organised by China, which is an example of China's development and economic growth. Since then, China has been attracting countries from developed and developing worlds to start exporting and importing. The BRI framework of partnership is a landmark policy of China and has had a successful story since its inception in 2013. This research highlights that if China will solve border issues with neighbouring countries, then China's acceptance will be increased in the Asia Pacific. India will be one of the strongest countries in South Asia which can openly support China on the international fronts. India is now the biggest market with huge purchasing power in the countryside. It would be beneficial for all the nations that could invest in India will certainly not go to waste. China's BRI projects are working on the concept of modernising the partner countries. Many development and infrastructure works are successfully carried out by Chinese companies in BRI member states and many projects are still under construction. During the Coronavirus Outbreak, many projects were brutally affected by this worldwide pandemic. Despite COVID-19, China has been investing adequate funds to complete infrastructural work at projected times in African countries and other countries and regions. By and large, China has emerged as the biggest competitor of the US in the Indo-Pacific region and African countries. Apart from these regions, China is also a threat in the Eurasian region and CEE countries.

As a result, this study aims to find out that China is an emerging foreign investor in Africa. China had installed its first overseas military base in Djibouti in the Horn of Africa region. Which is providing strategic balance to its opponent in eastern Africa. Thus, China has been replacing the US and the EU in many African countries. China has also been involved and deeply engaged in the HoA region to resolve the domestic disputes of East African countries.

REFERENCES

Bharti, M. S. (2022a). The Development of China's Economic Cooperation in the Horn of Africa: Special Reference to the Belt and Road Initiative. *African Journal of Economics, Politics and Social Studies*, *1*(1), 17–30. doi:10.15804/ajepss.2022.1.12

Bharti, M. S. (2022b). The evolution of China's economic engagement in Central and Eastern Europe. *Economic and Regional Studies*, *15*(1), 90–106. doi:10.2478/ers-2022-0007

Bharti, M. S. (2023a). Indo–French Defence Partnership and Regional Balance in South Asia. *The Copernicus Journal of Political Studies*, *1–2*, 71–89. doi:10.12775.CJPS.2022.005

Bharti, M. S. (2023b). The Sustainable Development and Economic Impact of China's Belt and Road Initiative in Ethiopia. *East Asia (Piscataway, N.J.), 40*(2), 175–194. doi:10.100712140-023-09402-y PMID:37065271

Bharti, M. S., Kumari, S., & Bharti, S. S. (2022). Indo-French Comprehensive Bilateral Cooperation: A Roadmap to Indo-Pacific Parks Partnership and Beyond. *Economic and Regional Studies / Studia Ekonomiczne i Regionalne, 15*(3), 284–303. https://doi.org/doi:10.2478/ers-2022-0020

De Graaff, N., ten Brink, T., & Parmar, I. (2020). China's rise in a liberal world order in transition – introduction to the FORUM. *Review of International Political Economy, 27*(2), 191–207. doi:10.1080/09692290.2019.1709880

Embassy of the People's Republic China in the Republic of Seychelles. (2022, May 8). *Global Development Initiative and Global Security Initiative—China's latest solutions to world peace, security and development.* Retrieved from http://sc.china-embassy.gov.cn/eng/zxhd/202208/t20220805_10735867.htm

Embassy of the PRC in the Republic of South Africa. (2022, October 20). *The Global Development Initiative: How Useful and Prudent is Xi Jinping's Global Development Initiative for Advancing the Wellbeing of Humanity?* Retrieved from http://za.china-embassy.gov.cn/eng/sgxw/202210/t20221020_10788973.htm

Foreign Minister of Foreign Affairs of the People's Republic of China. (2021, September 26). *Wang Yi Talks about the Significance of the "Global Development Initiative."* Retrieved from https://www.fmprc.gov.cn/web/wjbzhd/202109/t20210926_9584091.shtml

Global Times. (2023, March 10). *Saudi Arabia, Iran agree to resume ties, reopen embassies after talks in Beijing.* Retrieved from https://www.globaltimes.cn/page/202303/1287076.shtml

Gong, G. W. (1984). *The Standard of 'Civilization' in International Society.* Oxford University Press.

Gonzalez-Vicente, R. (2022). In the name of the nation: Authoritarian practices, capital accumulation, and the radical simplification of development in China's global vision. *Globalizations*, 1–16. doi:10.1080/14747731.2022.2121061

He, K. (2022). China's rise, institutional balancing, and (possible) peaceful order transition in the Asia pacific. *The Pacific Review, 35*(6), 1105–1134. doi:10.1080/09512748.2022.2075439

He, K., & Feng, H. (2023). International order transition and US-China strategic competition in the indo pacific. *The Pacific Review, 36*(2), 234–260. doi:10.1080/09512748.2022.2160789

Henderson, J. (2008). China and global development: Towards a Global-Asian Era? *Contemporary Politics, 14*(4), 375–392. doi:10.1080/13569770802519284

Huaxia. (2022, September 21). *UN chief says China's Global Development Initiative helps achieve global goals.* Xinhua. Retrieved from https://english.news.cn/20220921/61b03af7cfaa45c58ea3d31a34f6f3aa/c.html

Keohane, R. O. (1980). The theory of hegemonic stability and changes in international economic regimes. In O. R. Holsti, R. M. Siverson, & A. L. George (Eds.), *Change in the International System* (pp. 131–162). Westview Press.

Keohane, R. O., & Joseph, S. Nye Jr. (1998). Power and interdependence in the information age. *Foreign Policy*, *77*(5), 81–98.

Khalilzad, Z. (2017, June 19). *The Case for Congagement with China*. The National Interest. Retrieved from https://nationalinterest.org/feature/the-case-congagement-china-21232

Kim, S., & Kim, S. (2022). China's contestation of the liberal international order. *The Pacific Review*, 1–26. doi:10.1080/09512748.2022.2063367

King, A. (2022). Power, shared ideas and order transition: China, the United States, and the creation of the Bretton Woods order. *European Journal of International Relations*, *28*(4), 910–933. doi:10.1177/13540661221118787

Krasner, S. D. (1976). State Power and the Structure of International Trade. *World Politics*, *28*(3), 317–347. https://doi.org/DOI. doi:10.2307/2009974

Krickovic, A. (2017). The Symbiotic China-Russia Partnership: Cautious Riser and Desperate Challenger. *The Chinese Journal of International Politics*, *10*(3), 299–329. doi:10.1093/cjip/pox011

Lampton, D. M. (1997). A growing China in a shrinking world: Beijing and the global order. In E. F. Vogel (Ed.), *Living with China: US/China Relations in the Twenty-first Century* (pp. 120–140). WW Norton & Company.

Lampton, D. M. (2005). China's rise in Asia need not be at America's expense. In D. L. Shambaugh (Ed.), *Power Shift: China and Asia's New Dynamics* (pp. 306–326). University of California Press.

Liff, A. P. (2016). Whither the Balancers? The Case for a Methodological Reset. *Security Studies*, *25*(3), 420–459. doi:10.1080/09636412.2016.1195624

Liu, H. (2020). Chinese perception of China's engagement in multilateralism and global governance. *The Pacific Review*, *33*(3–4), 469–496. doi:10.1080/09512748.2020.1728570

Ministry of Foreign Affair of the People's Republic of China. (2023, May 16). *Providing New Opportunities to the World Through Chinese Modernization*. Retrieved from https://www.fmprc.gov.cn/eng/wjdt_665385/zyjh_665391/202305/t20230516_11078125.html

Ministry of Foreign Affairs of the People's Republic of China. (2015, June 27). *China's Role in the Global and Regional Order: Participant, Facilitator and Contributor*. Speech at the Luncheon of the Fourth World Peace Forum By H.E. Foreign Minister Wang Yi. Retrieved from https://www.fmprc.gov.cn/eng/wjb_663304/wjbz_663308/2461_663310/201506/t20150627_468568.html

Ministry of Foreign Affairs of the People's Republic of China. (2022, September 25). *Making Every Effort for Peace and Development and Shouldering the Responsibility for Solidarity and Progress*. The United Nations General Assembly. Retrieved from https://www.fmprc.gov.cn/eng/wjdt_665385/zyjh_665391/202209/t20220925_10771160.html#:~:text=China%20is%20a%20major%20trading,2030%20Agenda%20for%20Sustainable%20Development

Ministry of Foreign Affairs of the People's Republic of China. (2023, February 21). *The Global Security Initiative Concept Paper*. Retrieved from https://www.fmprc.gov.cn/mfa_eng/wjbxw/202302/t20230221_11028348.html

Mitter, R. (2013). *China's War with Japan, 1937–1945: The Struggle for Survival*. Allen Lane.

OECD. (2018). *China's Belt and Road Initiative in the Global Trade, Investment and Finance Landscape*. Organisation for Economic Co-Operation and Development. Retrieved from https://www.oecd.org/finance/Chinas-Belt-and-Road-Initiative-in-the-global-trade-investment-and-finance-landscape.pdf

Pan, S.-Y., & Lo, J. T.-Y. (2017). Re-conceptualizing China's rise as a global power: A neo-tributary perspective. *The Pacific Review*, *30*(1), 1–25. doi:10.1080/09512748.2015.1075578

Reuters. (2023, March 16). *China Hopes Russia and Ukraine Will Hold Peace Talks, Says Senior Chinese Diplomat*. Retrieved from https://www.reuters.com/world/europe/china-hopes-ukraine-russia-will-not-close-door-political-solution-senior-chinese-2023-03-16/

Schuman, M., Fulton, J., & Gering, T. (2023, June 21). *How Beijing's newest global initiatives seek to remake the world order*. Atlantic Council. Retrieved from https://www.atlanticcouncil.org/in-depth-research-reports/issue-brief/how-beijings-newest-global-initiatives-seek-to-remake-the-world-order/

Silvius, R. (2021). China's Belt and Road Initiative as Nascent World Order Structure and Concept? Between Sino-Centering and Sino-Deflecting. *Journal of Contemporary China*, *30*(128), 314–329. doi:10.1080/10670564.2020.1790905

Sullivan de Estrada, K. (2023). India and order transition in the Indo-Pacific: Resisting the Quad as a 'security community.'. *The Pacific Review*, *36*(2), 378–405. doi:10.1080/09512748.2022.2160792

Wenling, C. (2022, April 12). *The Battlefield Is in Ukraine, but the Whole World Is a Front*. Academic Press.

Wong, K. C. (2021). The Rise of China's Developmental Peace: Can an Economic Approach to Peacebuilding Create Sustainable Peace? *Global Society*, *35*(4), 522–540. doi:10.1080/13600826.2021.1942802

World Bank. (2023, April 20). *The World Bank in China*. Retrieved from https://www.worldbank.org/en/country/china/overview

Xi, J. (2017, May). *Work Together to Build the Silk Road Economic Belt and The 21st Century Maritime Silk Road*. Opening Speech, The Belt and Road Forum for International Cooperation.

Xinhua. (2023, March 19). *Global Civilization Initiative Injects Fresh Energy into Human Development*. The State Council Information Office. Retrieved from http://english.scio.gov.cn/topnews/2023-03/19/content_85177312.htm

Yao, Y. (2022, February 25). *Global Development Initiative Provides a Blueprint for Responding to World Changes* ["全球发展倡议"为因应世界变局擘画蓝图]". Interpret: China. Retrieved from https://interpret.csis.org/translations/global-development-initiative-provides-a-blueprint-for-responding-to-world-changes/

Zhao, S. (2020). China's Belt-Road Initiative as the Signature of President Xi Jinping Diplomacy: Easier Said than Done. *Journal of Contemporary China*, *29*(123), 319–335. doi:10.1080/10670564.2019.1645483

Chapter 14
Strategic Adaptive Responses to Energy Crises From an Organizational Resilience Perspective

Korhan Arun
https://orcid.org/0000-0001-7494-9591
Tekirdağ Namık Kemal University, Turkey

Olcay Okun
https://orcid.org/0000-0002-7096-5794
NDU Turkish Military Academy, Turkey

Sercan Edinsel
Ministry of National Defence, Turkey

ABSTRACT

Energy crises have emerged as one of the most pressing and complex global challenges. As the world becomes increasingly interconnected and reliant on energy for its day-to-day operations, the repercussions of these crises are felt across societies, economies, and the natural environment. Disruptions in energy supply, fluctuating prices, and overreliance on finite and non-renewable resources demand urgent and proactive measures. In this context, strategic adaptive responses play a pivotal role in enabling organizations to navigate these challenges successfully and enhance their overall resilience. Effective crisis management constitutes a cornerstone of strategic adaptive responses to energy crises.

DOI: 10.4018/979-8-3693-0400-6.ch014

INTRODUCTION

Energy is one of the factors that create the driving force in the development of countries. Energy is one of the main production factors. In this context, countries should provide the energy they need cheaply, continuously, with high quality, safe, and "clean". Countries must diversify their energy resources within the security of energy supply. In this framework, it is necessary to plan not only to provide and produce energy but also to ensure the use of clean energy in an environmentally friendly manner (Flavin & Lenssen, 1994). In a world where energy resources are akin to treasures, the global clamor for energy amplifies its cost, reverberating across borders. Even in domains where energy prices recline, the virtuoso performance of resource efficiency remains a universal anthem, enriching individuals, nations, and the grand tapestry of humanity. Within the realm of energy corporations, the mastery of energy management crafts temporal canvases for capital infusion into nascent power plants and their allied infrastructures, an orchestration conducted for tomorrows yet to dawn (Smith & Parmenter, 2016). The main starting points of energy management can be listed as follows (Shinkawa, 1998).

- It is the optimum use of energy.
- It is an organization created to ensure the most efficient use of energy.
- All of the activities are carried out to effectively use resources in a way that does not harm nature.
- It is all the work done to use energy to provide optimum benefit at the level of money and efficiency.
- Measuring and controlling the energy used, minimizing the energy consumption per unit product or action, and assigning a responsible person for this.
- It is the work of choosing the most economical way while continuing to exist.
- Fuel + Electricity Saving = Money It is the monitoring of the energy from the beginning to the end, not wasting it, and using it adequately.
- Measures to be taken for efficient energy use are savings and development and research studies.
- It is to provide the necessary comfort and comfort for humanity for a longer period.
- It is the way and method of using money. It is the optimum use of the energy available in nature in line with human needs.
- Energy = Implementation, development, and continuity of a system to ensure the effective use of money and maximum savings.
- It is the work done to reduce energy losses and use them correctly. Briefly; It is the work done to prevent unnecessary expenditures and wasted money.
- Ensuring the efficiency of money is necessary for economic strength. It is the use of money in a business-specific manner for efficient daily life. Measures, savings, etc.
- It is to use energy in the optimum way, that is, in the most efficient way.

Energy is one of businesses' basic inputs, mainly from fossil fuels such as coal, oil, and natural gas. Energy demand is a phenomenon that is constantly increasing. The techniques used in energy management have a common structure with those required for managing any resource in a company or organization. Monitoring a performance or setting goals is important for the control of expenses and also for the motivation of employees who are related to energy use (Özbakır, 2006). Fluctuations in energy have the potential to be causes of consequences that affect the entire organization.

The term strategy entered the literature as a military term and was used in this way until the beginning of the 20th century. The purpose of strategic management is to create and consume new and different opportunities for the future. Strategic management, on the other hand, is the science and art of formulating, implementing, and evaluating cross-functional decisions that can contribute to the achievement of the purpose of the business (David, 2011). Strategic management harmonizes organizations with their environment and is based on the efficiency of adaptive responses to uncertainties rather than reflexive responses from the past. The strategic management perspective against today's energy crises can offer unique opportunities to differentiate from other organizations and create a competitive advantage.

Energy crises are turbulences that deeply affect organizations and have devastating consequences. EU countries experienced energy and inflation crises together in 2022. European countries, dependent on foreign energy, have faced rapidly increasing natural gas and electricity prices, especially since the first months of 2022. Inflation in European countries, which were helpless in the face of the rise in energy prices, also entered an upward trend, and thus, inflation in Europe exceeded the 2 percent target of the European Central Bank (ECB). Inflation in the EU and Euro Zone broke a record in the first month of the year, while the increase in inflation accelerated with the Russia-Ukraine war. The increase in energy prices has started to reflect on other products(euronews.com, 2022). It was stated that there was an energy problem in Europe after Russia cut off the natural gas supply because of the war between Russia and Ukraine. A situation that will happen has the potential to cause an energy crisis that will last for many years. While Europe has been shaken by the energy cost of approximately 1 trillion dollars in the energy shortage caused by the Ukraine war, energy crises, which have the potential to be the biggest of the last decades, appear in different forms. The President of South Africa appointed an Electricity Minister for the first time in the country in 2023 (bbc.com, 2023) to combat the electricity cuts that often negatively affect life in the country. The possibility that the crisis may be just beginning should not be ignored (bloomberg.com, 2022). It is inevitable for organizations to run every step of the strategic management from end to end to take the necessary measures against the possibility of the energy crisis continuing.

The repercussions of energy crises often manifest as a haunting specter of energy deprivation. This haunting notion encapsulates the heart-wrenching reality where individuals are robbed of their rightful access to energy sources. Think of it as a wintry chill that creeps into homes, unfazed by the feeble warmth of a heating system that remains inoperative due to energy scarcities driven by economic tumult. As a cruel twist of fate, those most susceptible, standing on the precipice of energy insecurity, are compelled into the throes of transformative change within their everyday lives. (Ortar, 2018).Similarly, crises bring about lifestyle changes related to energy consumption. During the period of staying at home during the pandemic, the energy consumption of individuals and, accordingly, their working and daily lifestyles in business life have undergone radical changes (Novianto et. al., 2022). In this context, energy crises bring many new phenomena that should be understood among organizational behavior researchers.

In today's world, where the importance of sustainable development is increasingly understood, the value of efforts toward energy efficiency is increasing at the same rate. In this context, improving energy efficiency at all stages from energy production and transmission to final consumption, preventing unconscious use and waste, and reducing energy intensity both based on sectors and at the macro level are among the priority and important components of our national energy policy. Energy efficiency is a concept that encompasses a number of national strategic goals, including ensuring the security of the energy supply, lowering the risks associated with dependence on foreign sources, stabilizing energy prices, enhancing the effectiveness of the fight against climate change, and safeguarding the environment (MERN, 2023). Strategic goals, on the other hand, will be possible with strategic management processes that focus on increasing organizational resilience.

Organizational resilience has been defined in various ways by different researchers, the common feature of the definitions is that resilience is an adaptive capacity. Organizational resilience research becomes more evident as the pandemic, global terrorist attacks, economic recession, and other important disruptions experienced after unforeseen events that deeply affect the activities of today's businesses create a climate of uncertainty and crisis. Organizational resilience refers to the ability to respond and adapt to turbulent situations, unexpected crises, and shocks (Okun, 2021). Just like humans, organizations should increase their capacity to develop positive, adaptive responses to challenges and upheavals. Organizations that have developed capacities to respond flexibly to energy crises will survive in the long run, while organizations that cannot respond appropriately will perish.

Recent energy crises can be viewed as an external shock since they have raised energy costs and put a lot of pressure on policymakers. While the energy crisis has recently hit organizations, little is known about how companies should respond to this threat. Therefore, it has become necessary to write a book chapter to fill this research gap and present ideas that can expand the scope of energy crisis management in line with the concepts of strategic management and organizational resilience. In this book chapter, energy management, energy efficiency, rational use of energy, energy saving, and strategic adaptive responses that can be applied to energy crises will be examined from the perspective of organizational resilience. This book chapter will be tried to conceptually illuminate the adaptive reactions that organizational managers can put forward at the end of strategic management processes to overcome energy-related bottlenecks in turbulent processes. It will also be explained in which areas these adaptive responses provide flexibility in the organizational resilience perspective.

ENERGY CRISES

Energy crises are emergencies that result from insufficient energy resources due to interruptions in energy supply or the continuous increase in energy demand. Energy crises are situations that negatively affect economic activities, cause energy cuts and increase energy prices. Some common examples of energy crises are (Smil, 2017; Yergin, 2008, 2012):

- Interruptions in Energy Sources: Energy crises can occur if interruptions occur in the supply of energy sources such as natural gas, oil, or coal. Source countries can cause these interruptions for geopolitical reasons or by factors such as malfunctions in production facilities or problems in transportation lines.
- Natural Disasters: Large-scale natural disasters can damage energy infrastructure and cause interruptions to electricity, natural gas, or fuel supplies. For example, hurricanes, earthquakes, or extreme weather conditions can affect power plants and lead to energy crises.
- Political Conflicts: Political conflicts at the regional or international level can affect energy supply. Factors such as blocking access to energy sources or targeting energy transmission lines can lead to energy crises.

- Demand-Supply Imbalances: Rapidly increasing energy demand can cause energy crises if there is not enough capacity to meet the supply. Such imbalances are common in developing countries where energy infrastructure is inadequate or where demand is booming in conjunction with rapid economic growth.

The ripples of energy crises extend far beyond mere power shortages; they possess the potency to disrupt economic currents, propel energy prices to new heights, cast shadows of blackouts, and even conjure the tempests of social and political unrest. Hence, the wisdom lies in channeling resources towards fortifying energy security and nurturing sustainable energy reserves – a crucial maneuver that stands as our shield against the tempests of energy turmoil.

In 2011, the Arab Spring began in Tunisia and quickly spread throughout the Middle East and North Africa. The uprisings and subsequent political instability in countries such as Egypt, Libya, and Syria disrupted oil production and exports from these regions. The turmoil led to supply disruptions and uncertainties in the oil market, causing price fluctuations and impacting energy security for both exporting and importing nations(Darbouche & Fattouh, 2011).In research covering the years 2012-2013, when oil prices peaked, it was seen that energy and economic crises changed the lifestyles in the French suburbs. Increasing consumption expenditures due to energy crises make households in the city's periphery vulnerable and necessitate a change in their lifestyles. The change affects all lifestyle areas such as home habits, consumption, and transportation(Ortar, 2014, 2018).

In 2014, the annexation of Crimea by Russia and the subsequent conflict in Eastern Ukraine created another energy crisis. The region was a crucial transit area for natural gas pipelines delivering Russian gas to Europe. The tensions between Russia and Ukraine resulted in gas supply disruptions and concerns over the reliability and stability of energy routes. This highlighted the vulnerability of countries heavily dependent on Russian gas and the need to diversify energy sources and routes (Hutter & Weber, 2022).Furthermore, conflicts in the Middle East, such as the Syrian Civil War and the rise of ISIS, have disrupted oil production and infrastructure in the region. These conflicts have caused instability and raised concerns about the safety and accessibility of energy resources. Economic sanctions imposed on countries like Iran and Venezuela have affected their oil exports, leading to supply constraints and price fluctuations in the global oil market(Karim & Islam, 2017).

The COVID-19 pandemic has had a significant impact on energy crises worldwide. The measures implemented to contain the spread of the virus, such as lockdowns, travel restrictions, and reduced economic activity, have led to a sharp decline in energy demand. This sudden drop in energy consumption has resulted in an oversupply and a surplus of energy resources, particularly in the oil and gas sectors. The decrease in energy demand has caused a significant disruption in the global energy market. Oil prices experienced a dramatic decline as demand plummeted, leading to a surplus of oil supplies. This situation created challenges for oil-producing countries heavily reliant on oil revenues, as they faced reduced income and struggled to balance their budgets (Akyildirim et.al., 2022). The pandemic also affected the renewable energy sector. While renewable energy sources continued to generate electricity, the installation of new renewable energy infrastructure faced delays due to supply chain disruptions and reduced investment(Halbrügge et. al., 2021). Additionally, the decline in economic activity impacted the financing and viability of renewable energy projects. The energy crisis resulting from the COVID-19 pandemic has also had implications for energy security and infrastructure. The surplus of energy resources, combined with reduced storage capacity, posed challenges in managing and storing excess supplies(Berahab, 2022).

It has been determined that more than 3 million UK citizens could not heat their homes in the winter of 2022 with increased energy prices. 500,000 people in the UK, struggling to pay their bills due to the rise in energy prices, spent this winter using 'public heating areas' to avoid sitting in their cold homes during the daylight hours. The idea of heated public spaces, introduced as electricity and gas bills and the cost of living became unbearable for the millions, found a response in thousands of places across England, Wales, Scotland, and Northern Ireland (Weaver, 2022). This situation indicates a change in people's daily lives with the energy crisis. Every change experienced brings with it many organizational problems that must be investigated.

Worldwide energy consumption is shown in Table-1, Table 2, Table 3, and Table 4 to make sound comments in light of the information presented above. It is seen that 3 types of energy consumption decreased between 2009 and 2020.

Table 1. Energy consumption (worldwide)

Year	Coal and Lignite (Million Tons)	Local Consumption of Petroleum Products (Million Tons)	Domestic Natural Gas Consumption (Billion Cubic Meters)	Electricity Local Consumption (Terawatt Hour)
1990	4.693	3.090	2.047	10.120
1991	4.614	3.117	2.107	10.436
1992	4.558	3.132	2.101	10.525
1993	4.538	3.130	2.136	10.724
1994	4.539	3.161	2.141	11.003
1995	4.678	3.233	2.191	11.346
1996	4.733	3.315	2.279	11.702
1997	4.719	3.424	2.315	11.975
1998	4.674	3.467	2.345	12.258
1999	4.568	3.540	2.423	12.607
2000	4.790	3.569	2.507	13.186
2001	4.869	3.598	2.533	13.393
2002	5.026	3.599	2.613	13.839
2003	5.439	3.659	2.705	14.384
2004	5.749	3.813	2.794	15.027
2005	6.103	3.853	2.863	15.681
2006	6.447	3.898	2.931	16.327
2007	6.784	3.948	3.050	17.133
2008	6.919	3.902	3.126	17.443
2009	6.953	3.800	3.048	17.353
2010	7.325	3.915	3.320	18.559
2011	7.738	3.909	3.376	19.135
2012	7.872	3.955	3.446	19.628
2013	8.001	3.999	3.491	20.246
2014	7.981	4.044	3.494	20.770
2015	7.749	4.128	3.541	21.004
2016	7.630	4.167	3.633	21.622
2017	7.772	4.245	3.742	22.367
2018	7.902	4.286	3.919	23.366
2019	7.765	4.296	3.993	23.718
2020	7.466	3.897	3.912	23.652
2021	7.964	4.137	4.100	25.024
2022	8.462	4.283	4.041	25.530
Average	**6.273**	**3.743**	**2.978**	**16.700**

Source: yearbook.enerdata.net/total-energy/world-consumption-statistics.html

The reason for this decrease can be attributed to various factors, including changes in economic conditions, advancements in energy efficiency, and the impact of global events. Notably, in the annals of 2009, the global economic stage convalesced from the repercussions of the 2008 financial crisis, an epoch characterized by tentative recovery and subdued industrial vigor. This intricate interplay yielded a discernible dip in the appetite for energy, as sectors such as manufacturing and construction retrenched operations, thereby eliciting a commensurate reduction in energy consumption (Hamilton, 2013). In parallel, the chronicle of 2020 witnessed the profound imprint of the COVID-19 pandemic on the canvas of global electricity consumption (Roidt et al., 2020). The adoption of stringent lockdown measures, imposition of travel embargoes, and the shuttering of business operations collectively engendered a seismic disruption in economic cadence. Lockdown measures, travel restrictions, and business closures disrupted economic activity, causing a significant reduction in electricity demand (Ghiani et. al., 2020).

Table 2. Electricity consumption worldwide

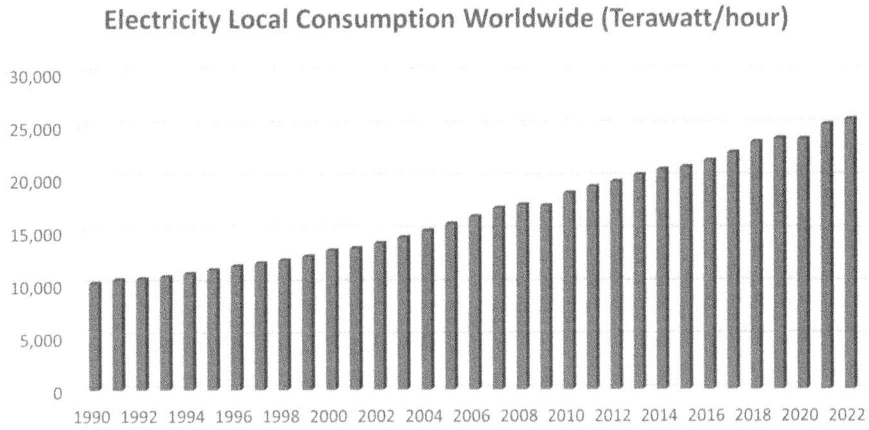

Source: yearbook.enerdata.net/total-energy/world-consumption-statistics.html

Industries, offices, and commercial establishments operated at limited capacity or temporarily shut down, leading to a substantial decrease in energy usage. Moreover, the shift to remote work and online activities during the pandemic resulted in changes in energy consumption patterns, with reduced demand for office spaces and increased reliance on home energy consumption(IEA, 2020).The increasing penetration of renewable energy sources in the electricity mix has also impacted consumption patterns. The transition towards cleaner energy sources, such as solar and wind power, has reduced reliance on fossil fuel-based energy generation. Integrating renewable energy into the grid has contributed to a more diversified and environmentally friendly energy supply, decreasing energy consumption from conventional power plants(EEA, 2023).

Table 3. Domestic natural gas consumption worldwide

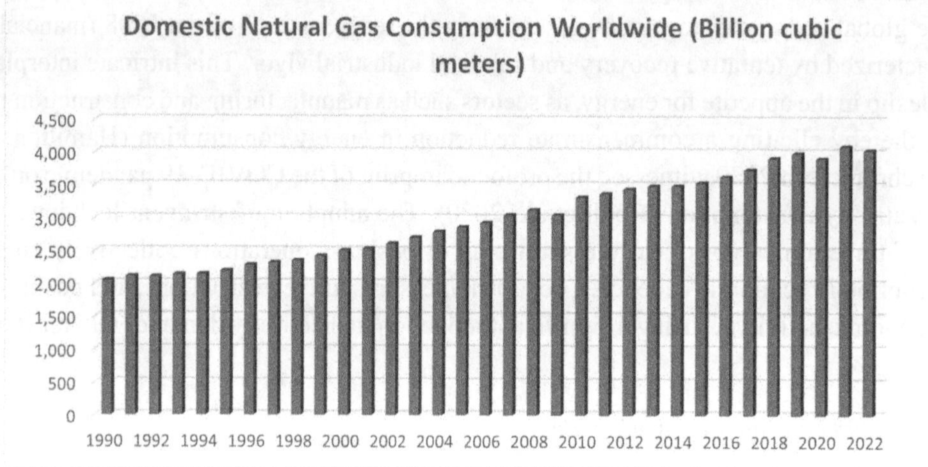

Source: yearbook.enerdata.net/total-energy/world-consumption-statistics.html

Energy efficiency measures have played a crucial role in the declining energy consumption trends. Governments, businesses, and individuals have increasingly embraced energy-saving technologies and practices to reduce environmental impact and lower energy costs (IEA,2022). Advancements in energy-efficient appliances, lighting, heating, and cooling systems have significantly reduced energy usage. The growing awareness of climate change and sustainability has also led to a greater emphasis on energy conservation and the adoption of energy-efficient practices in households, industries, and commercial buildings (Lancu et. al., 2021).

Table 4. Local consumption of petroleum products worldwide

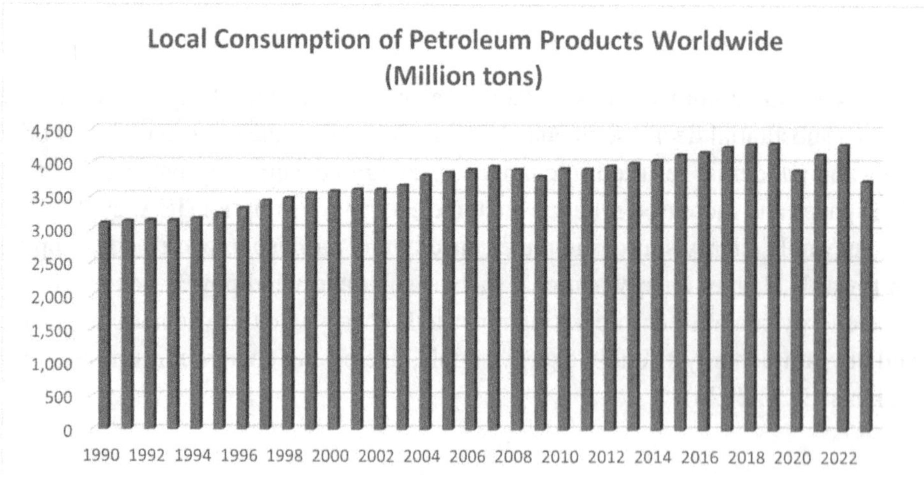

Source: yearbook.enerdata.net/total-energy/world-consumption-statistics.html

The COVID-19 pandemic had a significant impact on the consumption of petroleum in 2020. The widespread outbreak and ensuing containment measures sharply decreased global petroleum demand(Hoang et. al., 2021). Travel restrictions, lockdowns, and social distancing measures resulted in reduced travel and transportation activities, leading to a significant decline in gasoline, diesel, and jet fuel consumption. With people staying at home and businesses operating at reduced capacity or temporarily shutting down, the demand for petroleum products used in various industries also decreased. Furthermore, the unprecedented disruption in air travel due to border closures and reduced flights directly impacted the demand for aviation fuel(Global Energy Review,2020). The economic downturn caused by the pandemic further contributed to reduced industrial activities and overall petroleum consumption. These combined factors led to a significant contraction in petroleum consumption in 2020, reflecting the profound impact of the COVID-19 pandemic on the global energy landscape(OEDC,2020).

Energy crises have wide-ranging and profound effects on various aspects of daily life and socio-economic development of countries and households. At the household level, energy crises can lead to disruptions in the supply of electricity, heating, and cooking fuel, significantly affecting individuals' and families' well-being and quality of life. The lack of reliable and affordable energy sources creates challenges in maintaining adequate warmth, especially during cold seasons, posing health risks, particularly for vulnerable populations such as the elderly, children, and pre-existing medical conditions(Zukowski, 2022).Furthermore, energy crises can disrupt access to essential services within households. The lack of electricity hampers the operation of appliances, including refrigerators, lighting, and communication devices, limiting food storage, safety, and connectivity. In some cases, households may use alternative, often more expensive and less efficient energy sources, placing financial burdens on families already struggling to meet their basic needs. The increased energy cost and limited access can exacerbate poverty, inequality, and social disparities, as low-income households often bear a disproportionate burden during energy crises(Drehobl et. al., 2020).

At the national level, energy crises have significant economic implications. Industries heavily reliant on energy, such as manufacturing, transportation, and agriculture, experience disruptions, leading to decreased production, job losses (BBC, 2020), and reduced competitiveness. The lack of energy resources and infrastructure can hinder economic growth, foreign investment, and development initiatives. Additionally, energy crises can strain government budgets as subsidies and financial assistance are required to support affected households and mitigate the social and economic consequences. Countries heavily dependent on energy exports may face revenue losses and trade imbalances, impacting their overall fiscal stability(World Energy Investment, 2020).Energy crises also have environmental implications, as increased demand for alternative energy sources can lead to a surge in carbon emissions and environmental degradation. In cases where there is a reliance on fossil fuels, such as coal or oil, the increased consumption of these resources during an energy crisis can contribute to air pollution, climate change, and associated health hazards(Worlanyo & Jiangfeng, 2021).

STRATEGIC MANAGEMENT IN ENERGY CRISES

Energy is a resource of strategic importance today. Energy is a fundamental driver of economic activity, and a country's dependence on energy resources is an important factor for national security and economic stability (Kajanus et. al., 2012). Energy sustainability is of great importance in reducing environmental impacts, using energy resources efficiently, and leaving a clean energy source to future generations. Crises inevitably need to quickly adapt to new conditions, especially those arising from unexpected changes in external environmental factors. Countries and organizations should determine a plan for adapting to the situation in the face of crises. From the strategic management perspective, the scenarios to be applied in crises and the mechanisms to be used should be implemented quickly and effectively (Groh, 2014). Energy crises occur due to sudden large interruptions in energy supply or imbalances between demand and supply. Such crises can be caused by various reasons, such as interruption of energy supplies, natural disasters, political conflicts, technical failures, or economic factors (Smil, 2017; Yergin, 2008).

The function of strategic management in the face of crises is to help countries and organizations achieve their goals of exiting the crisis, by providing decision-making and action processes and the development of effective strategies (Hidayat et. al., 2022). The units responsible for the strategy production of countries and organizations should use mathematical models and simulations in the strategic management process to efficiently and effectively implement strategic planning and planning (Shtunder et. al., 2022). As stated in the previous pages, the type, intensity, and quantitative amounts of energy used by countries and organizations are tracked over the years. Optimizations to be made with modeling and simulations (for example, the transition to renewable energy sources, green energy versus a return to fossil fuels) will form the quantitative infrastructure of the scenarios to be applied in crises.

The main facts to be considered in the strategic management process in energy crises can be listed as follows.

- What are the main energy phenomena that the organization may encounter as of the country/region it is located in?
- Based on these facts, how should strategic consciousness be shaped at senior management levels?
- Determining at which levels and in what way strategists will work against possible energy crises based on energy phenomena.
- Analysis of the current internal and external environmental factors of the organization by strategists, and determination of energy vulnerabilities as a result of the analysis.
- Identifying strategies to overcome the organization's energy vulnerabilities.
- Continuous review of internal and external environmental factors. Updating the strategies to increase the adaptive capacity of the organization.

The strategic management process is a systematic and continuous process that organizations undertake to formulate, implement, and evaluate strategies. It involves environmental analysis, strategy formulation, strategy implementation, and strategy evaluation. The process is dynamic and iterative, requiring ongoing monitoring, adaptation, and learning. Effective strategic management requires the involvement and commitment of top management, effective communication, and alignment of the entire organization towards the strategic goals (David, 2011).

In the context of strategies that can be developed by the managers responsible for shaping the energy policy of countries and organizations, smart electricity savings, mandatory limitations in the hours when energy use increases, the development of wind power, hydropower, or solar power can be considered (Borowski, 2022).

Figure 1. Strategic management process in energy crises

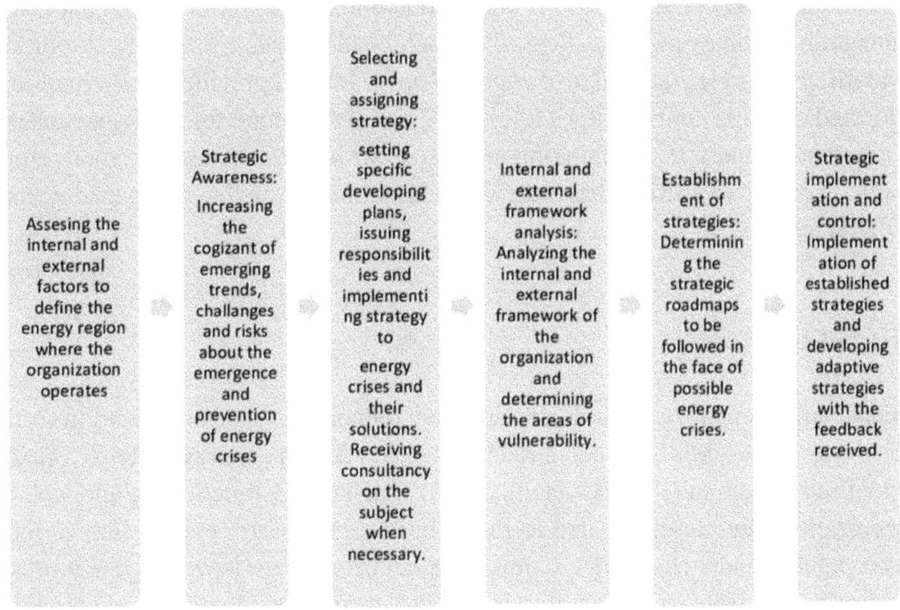

ORGANIZATIONAL RESILIENCE

Organizational resilience is a critical characteristic that enables companies to survive and thrive in the face of adversity and change. It encompasses various capabilities and strategies that allow an organization to effectively anticipate, prepare for, respond to, and recover from various disruptions and challenges(Lengnick-Hall et. al, 2011).At its core, organizational resilience involves identifying and assessing risks and vulnerabilities, both internally and externally, and proactively taking measures to mitigate and manage them(Sawik, 2013).This includes developing robust risk management processes, establishing business continuity plans, and implementing systems to monitor and address potential threats. By understanding and addressing potential risks, organizations can build a solid foundation to withstand shocks and disruptions, ensuring the continued functioning of core operations(Mcdonald, 2012). Flexibility and adaptability are also crucial elements of organizational resilience. Companies need to be agile and responsive to changing market dynamics, emerging technologies, and evolving customer demands. This requires fostering a culture that embraces change, encourages innovation, and empowers employees to think creatively and proactively. By constantly scanning the environment for emerging trends and adapting strategies and processes accordingly, organizations can seize new opportunities and stay ahead of the competition(Jaaron & Backhouse, 2014).Effective communication and collaboration play a vital role in building organizational resilience. Establishing open communication channels, both vertically and horizontally, enables the timely and effective sharing of information, coordination of actions, and collective problem-solving. This promotes a sense of unity and shared purpose within the organization, facilitating swift responses and effective decision-making during times of crisis(Seville et.al., 2008).Learning and knowledge management are key components of organizational resilience. Companies that prioritize a culture of continuous learning and knowledge sharing are better equipped to adapt and respond to changing circumstances. By capturing and analyzing lessons learned from past experiences, organizations can enhance their understanding of risks, refine their strategies, and improve their overall resilience(Godwin et.al., 2013). This iterative learning and improvement process ensures that the organization becomes more resilient with each challenge faced. Finally, strong leadership is instrumental in fostering organizational resilience. Effective leaders provide clarity, inspire confidence, and make informed decisions during times of crisis. They set the tone for resilience, championing an organization's proactive and forward-thinking approach. Strong leaders also promote employee well-being and maintain morale, ensuring that individuals remain motivated and engaged despite adversity (Stewart & O'Donnell, 2007).

ENERGY RESILIENCE

The most critical component of sustainable development for countries and organizations is the provision of uninterrupted energy. In addition to being renewable and efficient, energy systems' durability should be considered a third condition (Kharrazi et. al., 2015). The healthy functioning and wealth of nations similar to organizations are closely related to their ability to transform energy into economic output. Failure of this capability under changing circumstances and conditions leaves organizations and nations fragile. Natural disasters, wars, and economic instability encourage countries and organizations to re-examine the security vulnerabilities of their energy systems. This reinforces the importance of energy resilience (Roege et. al., 2014).

Resilience is the capacity of a system to absorb shocks and crises(Gambino, 2012). The vulnerability of countries and organizations can be determined in the context of their absorptive capacity. Today, the increase in global energy consumption and the interdependencies created by this energy consumption ecology, the necessity of providing safe and affordable energy to the people of the countries, the global uncertainties, and energy crises require countries to ensure the resilience of energy services to keep the energy system alive. In line with this assessment, resilience in the context of the energy crisis is the capacity to successfully deal with energy-related disruptions while providing affordable energy services to society. A resilient energy system can quickly recover from shock as it adapts quickly to a new situation(Erker et.al., 2017). Energy resilience is a capacity that describes how organizations can cope with or respond to tensions, disturbances, or crises. A highly resilient organization can [1] withstand an unexpected sudden critical event, [2] re-stabilize systemic functions and structures after disruptions and disruptions, [3] learn from and thrive from a crisis by adapting or transforming core characteristics of parts affected by disruption and crisis it is desirable (Erker et. al., 2017b).

Energy security is the continuous availability of sufficient and affordable energy without any adverse economic or environmental impact(UNDP, 2015). Energy security research, which began with the oil crises of the 1970s, has now expanded to cover various energy sectors and increasingly diverse topics (Cherp & Jewell, 2014). The fragility of vital energy systems is one issue addressed within the energy security scope. In this context, energy security should be included under the Energy Resilience umbrella concept.

Fuel diversification is a strategy frequently implemented by different countries in the face of unexpected crises. This strategy aims to reduce vulnerability during interruptions in energy supply processes. Alternative energies reduce over-dependence on one type of energy (Dharfizi et. al., 2020).A successful energy diversification strategy can achieve three basic goals: to supply clean, cheap, and safe energy (Aslani et. al., 2013).To meet the increasing energy demand and to reduce the effects caused by the internal and external environment of the organization, it is necessary to diversify the energy resources efficiently by applying effective energy strategies. In this context, energy diversification should be included under the umbrella of Energy Resilience.

Resilience, defined as the ability to recover from difficulty, change, and undesirable situations quickly, can be adapted to energy resilience. Energy resilience refers to the ability of an individual, community, or organization to withstand and recover from disruptions in energy supply while maintaining essential functions and minimizing negative impacts. It involves diversified and reliable energy sources and the capability to adapt and respond to changing energy needs and challenges(Gatto & Drago, 2020). Energy resilience is particularly important in natural disasters(Temby et.al., 2014), extreme weather events(Maliszewski & Perrings, 2012), or other disruptions that can cause power outages or disruptions in energy infrastructure. Measures to enhance energy resilience include investing in renewable energy sources, implementing energy-efficient technologies, and developing robust backup systems such as generators or energy storage(Ben Abdallah et.al., 2013). By prioritizing energy resilience, individuals and communities can reduce vulnerabilities, ensure access to vital services, and foster sustainable and reliable energy systems that contribute to long-term stability and well-being(Jasiūnas et.al., 2021). According to this;

Table 5. Energy resilience

Resiliency Scope	Criteria	Adopted From
A return to the baseline point in the face of sudden disruptions in the energy system.	The energy's availability decline or recovery time determines the asset's resilience to availability events.	(Hughes, 2015)
	An increase in the energy cost can be an affordable event; the flexibility of the organization is the time it takes for the Energy cost to become affordable again.	(Hughes, 2015)
	Return to a level of acceptability. It is time for the energy flow to return to an acceptable level.	(Hughes, 2015)
Energy Security	"Low probability of damage to earned values" Security for whom? Security for what values? From what threats? • Availability, • Accessibility, • Affordability, • Acceptability.	(Wolfers, 1952)
Energy Diversification	To reduce the effects caused by the internal and external environment of the organization, diversify the energy resources efficiently by applying effective energy strategies. Supply, • Clean, • Cheap, • Safe Energy.	(Aslani et. al., 2013; Dharfizi et. al., 2020; Islam et. al., 2022)
Adaptive Responses To Energy Crises	The ability to successfully manage energy-related interruptions while continuing to offer sustainable energy services to the nation or organization is resilience in the face of an energy crisis. A resilient energy system can reconfigure itself after a shock and recover swiftly.	(Erker et. al., 2017b, 2017a)
Energy Efficiency	Energy efficiency indicates how effectively a device or system can use energy as an input. Higher energy efficiency means doing the same job using less energy. As energy efficiency increases, energy savings are achieved and energy resources are used more effectively.	(Aldieri et. al., 2021; Dong et. al., 2021)

Source: Developed by the authors.

Returning to the baseline point becomes crucial in the face of sudden disruptions in the energy system. The baseline point refers to the stable and expected energy availability and flow level before the disruption occurred. It signifies a return to normalcy and restoring the energy system to its pre-disruption state. The ability of an asset or organization to return to the baseline point after an energy disruption depends on the decline or recovery time of energy availability. This period measures how quickly the energy system can recover and function normally. A shorter decline or recovery time indicates greater resilience of the asset or organization to availability events, as it can bounce back more swiftly from the disruption. During an energy disruption, the cost of energy may increase due to factors like scarcity, increased demand, or logistical challenges. However, this increase in energy cost may not be sustainable in the long run(Hughes, 2015). The affordability of energy is a critical consideration for organizations. The flexibility of an organization is measured by the time it takes for the energy cost to become affordable again. This refers to the organization's ability to adapt and adjust its operations or seek alternative energy sources until the energy cost returns to a manageable and affordable level.-(Asia Pacific Energy Research Centre, 2007). The last goal is to return the energy flow to an acceptable level. This means ensuring that the supply and availability of energy meet the organization's operational needs and are aligned with its predetermined acceptability standards. It involves managing the energy system and associated processes to restore equilibrium, reliability, and a satisfactory level of energy flow(World Energy Trilemma, 2013).

Energy Security

Energy security entails ensuring a low probability of damage to the earned values associated with energy resources. It involves providing security for specific stakeholders and the fundamental values associated with energy systems. These values include availability, accessibility, affordability, and acceptability(Sovacool, 2011). Availability refers to ensuring a consistent and reliable energy supply to meet the demands of individuals, industries, and societies. It involves maintaining adequate energy reserves, diversifying energy sources, and investing in infrastructure to mitigate the risk of disruptions and ensure a continuous flow of energy. Accessibility focuses on providing equitable access to energy resources, irrespective of geographical location or socio-economic status. It involves improving energy distribution networks, expanding electrification efforts, and promoting energy equity to ensure that all individuals and communities have access to reliable and affordable energy services(UNDP, 2015). Affordability is a key aspect of energy security, aiming to make energy services accessible and affordable for all. It involves implementing policies and mechanisms to mitigate energy poverty, promote energy efficiency, and reduce the financial burden of energy costs on individuals, businesses, and economies. Acceptability ensures that energy resources and systems align with social, environmental, and ethical considerations. It involves addressing concerns related to environmental sustainability, public health, community impacts, and ethical sourcing of energy resources. Energy systems can gain wider acceptance and support by promoting clean energy sources, minimizing environmental impacts, and involving stakeholders in decision-making processes (Asia Pacific Energy Research Centre, 2007).

Energy Diversification

Energy diversification, the strategic process of expanding and varying energy resources, plays a pivotal role in mitigating the effects caused by both internal and external factors that can impact an organization's energy supply. Organizations can reap numerous benefits by efficiently diversifying energy resources through effective energy strategies (Stirling, 2010). One key advantage is securing a reliable supply of energy that meets the organization's needs while minimizing vulnerability to disruptions. A central aspect of energy diversification is the pursuit of clean energy sources. By integrating renewable energy technologies such as solar, wind, hydro, or geothermal power into their energy mix, organizations can significantly reduce their carbon footprint and contribute to a more sustainable future. Clean energy sources not only help combat climate change but also enhance the organization's environmental stewardship, which is becoming increasingly important in today's eco-conscious world(Akrofi, 2021). However, energy diversification also takes into account the cost aspect. Finding cheap energy resources is crucial for organizations to remain competitive and financially viable. Organizations can reduce energy expenditures and enhance their bottom line by exploring cost-effective options, such as optimizing energy efficiency, leveraging energy-saving technologies, or utilizing alternative fuels. This cost-conscious approach allows organizations to allocate resources more efficiently, enabling them to invest in other areas of growth and development(Dharfizi et. al., 2020).

Furthermore, safety is a paramount consideration in energy diversification. Organizations must prioritize using energy sources and technologies that minimize risks and ensure the well-being of employees, communities, and the environment. This includes adhering to stringent safety standards, implementing robust maintenance procedures, and embracing innovative technologies to prevent accidents or hazardous incidents. By prioritizing safety, organizations can enhance their reputation, maintain regulatory compliance, and safeguard their operations against potential liabilities(Islam et. al., 2022).

Adaptive Responses

Adaptation is change and transformation to suit a changing practice or situation. It refers to the change in the behavior of an organization or group in response to a new or changed environment. The need for transformation and change arises from an organization's inability to recover from an event and return to its normal state (Hughes, 2015). Energy resilience can be classified under two definitions, engineering resilience, and adaptive resilience. In engineering resilience, the goal is to develop the capacity to withstand a stress/crisis and return to a normal state. It refers to the survival of the vital systems of the country and the organization against natural disasters such as earthquakes, storms, floods, and fires to a certain extent and returning to their normal functioning in a short time. Adaptive resilience, on the other hand, is the flexibility in the functions of the country's and organization's systems to adapt to environmental changes. At this stage, resilience involves an adaptive capacity to rearrange into alternative configurations while retaining function, going beyond the typical perceived reversion to baseline (Holling, 1973, 1996).

Adaptive strategies emerge (Mintzberg, 1972) by adapting generic scenarios developed by countries and organizations through mathematical models and simulations to real situations. The strategies that emerge with the planned strategies reveal the adaptability of countries and organizations. To avoid energy crises, the following generic strategies can be developed for initial situations (Morane, 2009; Pascual & Elkind, 2010; Smil, 2010):

- Energy Diversification: It is important to diversify the energy supply and create an energy portfolio based on different energy sources. This makes it more resilient to interruptions or price fluctuations in an energy source. For example, the production and use of energy from various sources such as coal, natural gas, nuclear energy, hydroelectricity, solar energy, and wind energy should be encouraged.
- Energy Efficiency: Energy efficiency aims to reduce energy demand by using existing energy resources more effectively. Applications such as well-insulated buildings, energy-efficient electronics, and smart grids optimize energy use and reduce the effects of energy crises.
- Renewable Energy Investments: Investments in renewable energy sources are important for a sustainable energy future. Renewable energy sources such as solar power, wind power, hydropower, and biomass provide environmentally friendly and sustainable energy. Investments in these resources contribute to the diversification of energy supply.
- Energy Storage and Resilience: Energy storage technologies can increase resilience to energy crises. Especially considering the variable nature of renewable energy sources, energy storage systems, and flexible energy consumption methods can be used to manage the imbalances between energy supply and demand.
- International Cooperation: Energy crises are a global problem and international cooperation is important. Making agreements that support access to energy resources, energy transport lines, and trade is vital for energy security.
- Energy Planning and Policies: Energy planning and policies are important for achieving energy security and sustainability goals. Energy policies should include developing energy infrastructure, managing energy resources, energy efficiency incentives, and incentives for renewable energy.

Energy Efficiency

Energy efficiency is related to the efficiency of nations and organizations in transforming energy into economic output and the extent and accessibility of energy reserves and the capacity of energy distribution infrastructure (Roege et. al., 2014). With energy efficiency, countries and organizations support energy resilience by maintaining existing local energy systems, providing stable and affordable energy for their businesses and households (Ribeiro et. al., 2015).Energy efficiency is an effective indicator for energy resilience(Aldieri et. al., 2021; Dong et. al., 2021).

FUTURE RESEARCH DIRECTIONS

Energy crises are a constant phenomenon in today's turbulent world. In this context, it is important to understand the starting points of future energy crises in the context of taking preliminary measures.

The implementation of strategic management procedures before, during and after energy crises and the determination of strategies to be created by planning each person in these procedures in detail can be suggested as another study subject.

Since identifying the determinants of energy resilience is important in the context of adaptive strategies to be developed, energy resilience criteria should be developed for countries and organizations.

CONCLUSION

One key aspect of strategic adaptive responses is crisis management. Effective crisis management involves identifying potential risks and vulnerabilities, developing contingency plans, and implementing proactive measures to mitigate the impact of crises (Mudalal, 2021). Organizations need to have robust crisis management strategies in place to respond swiftly and effectively to energy crises.

Energy crises have become a pressing global issue, posing significant challenges to societies, economies, and the environment. These crises, characterized by disruptions in energy supply, price volatility, and reliance on finite and non-renewable resources, highlight the need for proactive measures and sustainable solutions. Factors such as geopolitical conflicts, natural disasters, and economic fluctuations contribute to energy crises. The impacts are far-reaching, affecting households, industries, and countries at large.

Energy crises can have significant impacts on household life. Common effects can be grouped under the following headings (Schobert, 2014; Smil, 2010).

- Power Outages: During energy crises, the electricity supply can be limited or cause blackouts. In this case, households may have to deal with power outages. Power outages can affect the lighting, heating and cooling, electrical equipment, and communications equipment in the home.
- Heating and Cooling Issues: During an energy crisis, heating and cooling systems can be affected. In this case, households may have to find alternative heating or cooling methods to keep their home at a suitable temperature. Especially in cold climates, the problem of heating can lead to serious health problems.
- Transportation Challenges: Energy crises can cause transportation problems in the form of fuel shortages or disruptions in public transportation systems. In this case, households may have to look for alternative modes of transportation to get to work, meet their daily needs, and travel.
- Price Increases: Energy crises can lead to increases in energy prices when energy resources are limited or supply decreases. In this case, households may experience budgetary difficulties as energy bills increase. In addition, energy crises can affect the prices of basic daily necessities of food and other materials.
- Economic Impacts: Energy crises can lead to a reduction or cessation of production and activities in industries and businesses that depend on energy. This may affect households economically as unemployment rates rise and economic uncertainties arise.

These effects may vary depending on the duration and severity of energy crises. States and organizations try to minimize these effects by taking measures such as energy conservation, energy diversification, and sustainable energy sources to prevent or mitigate the effects of energy crises. Strategic management is the most important management instrument to be used at this stage. The effects of crises can be softened with flexible responses provided by strategic management. Changes in the lifestyle of households in energy crises will also affect business life. In this context, business continuity plans should be reviewed according to the energy crisis.

Another important aspect of strategic adaptive responses is the development of alternative energy sources and technologies. Energy crises often highlight the vulnerabilities of relying on a single source of energy. Diversifying the energy mix and investing in renewable energy sources can help reduce dependence on fossil fuels and enhance energy security (Gitelman & Kozhevnikov, 2023). This requires strategic planning and investment in research and development to promote the adoption of sustainable and resilient energy systems.

Furthermore, strategic adaptive responses involve collaboration and cooperation among stakeholders in the energy sector. This includes partnerships between governments, energy companies, research institutions, and international organizations to share knowledge, resources, and best practices (Kecskeméthy & Teknős, 2023). Collaborative efforts can help address common challenges, promote innovation, and build resilience in the energy sector.

In addition to crisis management, diversification of energy sources, and collaboration, strategic adaptive responses also involve the development of robust governance frameworks and policies. Governments are crucial in formulating and implementing policies that promote energy security, sustainability, and resilience (Landau et al., 2021). This includes the establishment of regulatory frameworks, incentives for renewable energy investments, and the promotion of energy efficiency measures.

The diversification and transition to different energy forms suggested throughout the department can be considered as a way out so that the household's lifestyle is least affected by energy crises. Strategic management at this stage should answer this question: To what extent do renewable energy facilities meet the energy needs of homes? What conditions favor the usage of renewable energy sources in homes? What are the barriers to the household energy transition? (Szymańska et. al., 2023). Different questions must be answered in the strategic management process for different scenarios, simulations, and modeling for each energy crisis type.

Strategic planning is a crucial component of adaptive responses to energy crises, enabling governments and organizations to navigate the challenges and uncertainties associated with disruptions in energy supply. By conducting thorough risk assessments, decision-makers can identify potential vulnerabilities and assess the likelihood and potential impact of various risks. These assessments encompass a wide range of factors, including geopolitical tensions, environmental concerns, technological dependencies, and market fluctuations. In the face of energy crises, governments and organizations must analyze the potential risks identified during the assessment process. This analysis involves evaluating the interdependencies and vulnerabilities within the energy system, such as the reliance on a single energy source or supplier, the resilience of critical energy infrastructure, and the impact of disruptions on energy supply chains. By understanding these risks, stakeholders can develop informed and targeted strategies to address energy crises effectively.

Security in the supply of energy resources affects a country's energy independence and national resilience. A country's external dependence on its energy supply can lead to problems such as exposure to geopolitical risks and fluctuating energy prices. Therefore, energy policies often include strategies such as diversifying energy supply, increasing energy efficiency, and investing in renewable energy sources.

In the face of energy crises, organizations must develop strategic adaptive responses to manage and navigate these challenges effectively. Strategic adaptiveness involves anticipating, adapting, and innovating in response to changing circumstances (Nyuur et al., 2018). Strategic adaptive responses enable organizations to enhance their resilience, maintain operations, and ensure the continuity of energy supply.

Contingency planning is a crucial outcome of strategic planning and risk assessment. This involves developing detailed plans that outline specific actions during an energy crisis. Contingency plans should consider different scenarios and outline response measures prioritizing energy security, resilience, and sustainability. These plans may include diversifying energy sources, investing in alternative technologies, enhancing energy efficiency, and promoting energy conservation measures. They should also address the potential impacts on various sectors, such as industry, transportation, and households, and propose mitigation strategies to minimize disruption. To ensure the effectiveness of these contingency plans, governments and organizations must establish robust response mechanisms. This includes creating dedicated emergency response teams, establishing clear lines of communication and coordination among relevant stakeholders, and conducting regular drills and simulations to test the efficacy of response measures. Also, close collaboration with energy suppliers, international partners, and neighboring countries is crucial for timely and coordinated responses during energy crises.

Strategic planning, risk assessment, and contingency planning are iterative processes. As the energy landscape evolves, governments and organizations must continuously monitor and reassess potential risks and update their strategies and response mechanisms accordingly. This includes staying abreast of technological advancements, market dynamics, geopolitical shifts, and emerging energy sources to adapt and optimize their approaches.

Moreover, strategic adaptive responses require organizations to invest in technological advancements and cybersecurity measures. The energy sector is increasingly vulnerable to cyber-attacks, which can disrupt critical infrastructure and compromise the security of energy systems (Cesarec, 2020). Organizations must develop robust cybersecurity strategies and invest in technologies that detect, prevent, and respond to cyber threats.

Overall, strategic adaptive responses are essential for mitigating the impact of energy crises. These responses involve crisis management, diversification of energy sources, collaboration among stakeholders, development of robust governance frameworks, and investment in technology and cybersecurity measures. By adopting strategic adaptive responses, organizations can enhance their resilience, ensure the continuity of energy supply, and contribute to a more sustainable and secure energy future.

Furthermore, strategic adaptive responses require the development of robust governance frameworks and policies. Governments play a crucial role in formulating and implementing policies that promote energy security, sustainability, and resilience. This includes the establishment of regulatory frameworks, incentives for renewable energy investments, and promoting energy efficiency measures. By implementing effective governance frameworks, nations can create an enabling environment for strategic adaptive responses and enhance their resilience to energy crises.

In conclusion, embracing sustainable energy solutions, employing robust strategic planning, and fostering cooperation among nations and industries can address the energy crisis, an urgent global problem, collectively. Through concerted efforts and proactive measures, a more resilient, secure, and sustainable energy future can be built for future generations.

ACKNOWLEDGMENT

This research received no specific grant from any funding agency in the public, commercial, or not-for-profit sectors.

REFERENCES

Accelerating energy efficiency: What governments can do now to deliver energy savings – Analysis. (n.d.). IEA. Retrieved July 13, 2023, from https://www.iea.org/commentaries/accelerating-energy-efficiency-what-governments-can-do-now-to-deliver-energy-savings

Akrofi, M. M. (2021). An analysis of energy diversification and transition trends in Africa. *International Journal of Energy and Water Resources*, *5*(1), 1–12. doi:10.100742108-020-00101-5

Akyildirim, E., Cepni, O., Molnár, P., & Uddin, G. S. (2022). Connectedness of energy markets around the world during the COVID-19 pandemic. *Energy Economics*, *109*, 105900. doi:10.1016/j.eneco.2022.105900 PMID:35529585

Aldieri, L., Gatto, A., & Vinci, C. P. (2021). Evaluation of energy resilience and adaptation policies: An energy efficiency analysis. *Energy Policy*, *157*, 112505. doi:10.1016/j.enpol.2021.112505

Asia Pacific Energy Research Centre. (Ed.). (2007). *A quest for energy security in the 21st century: Resources and constraints*. Inst. of Energy Economics.

Aslani, A., Naaranoja, M., Helo, P., Antila, E., & Hiltunen, E. (2013). Energy diversification in Finland: Achievements and potential of renewable energy development. *International Journal of Sustainable Energy*, *32*(5), 504–514. doi:10.1080/14786451.2013.766612

bbc.com. (2023). *Güney Afrika'da elektrik kesintilerini gidermek için bakanlık kuruldu.* BBC News Türkçe. https://www.bbc.com/turkce/articles/cd1d9zxeynno

Ben Abdallah, K., Belloumi, M., & De Wolf, D. (2013). Indicators for sustainable energy development: A multivariate cointegration and causality analysis from Tunisian road transport sector. *Renewable & Sustainable Energy Reviews*, *25*, 34–43. doi:10.1016/j.rser.2013.03.066

Berahab, R. (2022). *The Energy Crisis of 2021 and its Implications for Africa.* Academic Press.

bloomberg.com. (2022). *Uzmanlardan "Enerji krizi yeni başlıyor olabilir" uyarısı.* BloombergHT. https://www.bloomberght.com/uzmanlardan-enerji-krizi-yeni-basliyor-olabilir-uyarisi-2321458

Borowski, P. F. (2022). Mitigating Climate Change and the Development of Green Energy versus a Return to Fossil Fuels Due to the Energy Crisis in 2022. *Energies*, *15*(24), 9289. doi:10.3390/en15249289

Cesarec, I. (2020). Beyond Physical Threats: Cyber-Attacks on Critical Infrastructure as a Challenge of Changing Security Environment – Overview of Cyber-Security Legislation and Implementation in SEE Countries. *Annals of Disaster Risk Sciences.* doi:10.51381/adrs.v3i1.45

Cherp, A., & Jewell, J. (2014). The concept of energy security: Beyond the four As. *Energy Policy*, *75*, 415–421. doi:10.1016/j.enpol.2014.09.005

Coronavirus: "Thousands" of North Sea oil and gas jobs under threat. (2020, April 27). *BBC News.* https://www.bbc.com/news/uk-scotland-scotland-business-52446555

Darbouche, H., & Fattouh, B. (2011). *The Implications of the Arab Uprisings for Oil and Gas Markets.* Oxford Institute for Energy Studies., doi:10.26889/9781907555336

David, F. R. (2011). *Strategic management: Concepts and cases* (13th ed.). Prentice Hall.

Dharfizi, A. D. H., Ghani, A. B. A., & Islam, R. (2020). Evaluating Malaysia's fuel diversification strategies 1981–2016. *Energy Policy*, *137*, 111083. doi:10.1016/j.enpol.2019.111083

Dong, K., Dong, X., Jiang, Q., & Zhao, J. (2021). Assessing energy resilience and its greenhouse effect: A global perspective. *Energy Economics*, *104*, 105659. doi:10.1016/j.eneco.2021.105659

Drehobl, A., Ross, L., & Ayala, R. (n.d.). *An Assessment of National and Metropolitan Energy Burden across the United States*. Academic Press.

Erker, S., Stangl, R., & Stoeglehner, G. (2017a). Resilience in the light of energy crises – Part I: A framework to conceptualise regional energy resilience. *Journal of Cleaner Production*, *164*, 420–433. doi:10.1016/j.jclepro.2017.06.163

Erker, S., Stangl, R., & Stoeglehner, G. (2017b). Resilience in the light of energy crises – Part II: Application of the regional energy resilience assessment. *Journal of Cleaner Production*, *164*, 495–507. doi:10.1016/j.jclepro.2017.06.162

euronews.com. (2022). *AB, 2022'de savaş, enerji krizi ve enflasyonun etkileriyle mücadele etti | Euronews*. https://tr.euronews.com/2022/12/22/ab-2022de-savas-enerji-krizi-ve-enflasyonun-etkileriyle-mucadele-etti

Flavin, C., & Lenssen, N. (1994). *Enerjide Arayışlar*. Tema Vakfı Yayınları.

Gambino, M. (2012). Is *it too late for Sustainable Development. Dennis Meadows Thinks So. Forty Years after His Book the Limits to Growth, He Explains Why*. Available Online: Https://Www. Smithsonianmag. Com/Sciencenature/Is-It-Too-Late-for-Sustainable-Development-125411410/

Gatto, A., & Drago, C. (2020). Measuring and modeling energy resilience. *Ecological Economics*, *172*, 106527. doi:10.1016/j.ecolecon.2019.106527

Ghiani, E., Galici, M., Mureddu, M., & Pilo, F. (2020). Impact on Electricity Consumption and Market Pricing of Energy and Ancillary Services during Pandemic of COVID-19 in Italy. *Energies*, *13*(13), 13. Advance online publication. doi:10.3390/en13133357

Gitelman, L., & Kozhevnikov, M. (2023). New Business Models in the Energy Sector in the Context of Revolutionary Transformations. *Sustainability (Basel)*, *15*(4), 3604. doi:10.3390u15043604

Godwin, I., Umoh, E., & Amah, E. (2013). *Knowledge Management and Organizational Resilience in Nigerian Manufacturing Organizations*. Developing Country Studies.

Groh, M. (2014). *Strategic management in times of crisis*. Academic Press.

Halbrügge, S., Schott, P., Weibelzahl, M., Buhl, H. U., Fridgen, G., & Schöpf, M. (2021). How did the German and other European electricity systems react to the COVID-19 pandemic? *Applied Energy*, *285*, 116370. doi:10.1016/j.apenergy.2020.116370 PMID:36568698

Hamilton, J. (n.d.). Historical oil shocks. In Routledge Handbook of Major Events in Economic History. Retrieved July 13, 2023, from https://www.google.com/search?q=Hamilton%2C+J.+Historical+oil+shocks.+In+Routledge+Handbook+of+Major+Events+in+Economic+History%3B+Randall%2C+E.%2C+Whaples%2C+P.%2C+Whaples%2C+R.%2C+Eds.%3B+Routledge%3A+New+York%2C+NY%2C+USA%2C+2013%3B+pp.+239%E2%80%93265&oq=Hamilton%2C+J.+Historical+oil+shocks.+In+Routledge+Handbook+of+Major+Events+in+Economic+History%3B+Randall%2C+E.%2C+Whaples%2C+P.%2C+Whaples%2C+R.%2C+Eds.%3B+Routledge%3A+New+York%2C+NY%2C+USA%2C+2013%3B+pp.+239%E2%80%93265&gs_lcrp=EgZjaHJvbWUyBggAEEUYOdIBBzYwN2owajeoAgCwAgA&sourceid=chrome&ie=UTF-8

Hidayat, S., Yusgiantoro, P., Thamrin, S., & Widayatno, R. L. (2022). Energy Management Strategy For State Defense Toward The Energy Crisis. *Natural Volatiles & Essential Oils Journal*, 25–35.

Hoang, A. T., Sandro Nižetić, Olcer, A. I., Ong, H. C., Chen, W.-H., Chong, C. T., Thomas, S., Bandh, S. A., & Nguyen, X. P. (2021). Impacts of COVID-19 pandemic on the global energy system and the shift progress to renewable energy: Opportunities, challenges, and policy implications. *Energy Policy*, *154*, 112322. doi:10.1016/j.enpol.2021.112322 PMID:34566236

Holling, C. S. (1973). Resilience and Stability of Ecological Systems. *Annual Review of Ecology and Systematics*, *4*(1), 1–23. doi:10.1146/annurev.es.04.110173.000245

Holling, C. S. (1996). *Engineering Resilience versus Ecological Resilience*. https://www.semanticscholar.org/paper/Engineering-Resilience-versus-Ecological-Resilience-Holling/ab0dc6785ebbae3904aace0cb9e243d5379acd75

Hughes, L. (2015). The effects of event occurrence and duration on resilience and adaptation in energy systems. *Energy*, *84*, 443–454. doi:10.1016/j.energy.2015.03.010

Hutter, C., & Weber, E. (2022). *Russia-Ukraine War: Short-run Production and Labour Market Effects of the Energy Crisis*. IAB-Discussion Paper, Article 202210. https://ideas.repec.org//p/iab/iabdpa/202210.html

Iancu, I. A., Darab, C. P., & Cirstea, S. D. (2021). The Effect of the COVID-19 Pandemic on the Electricity Consumption in Romania. *Energies*, *14*(11), 11. Advance online publication. doi:10.3390/en14113146

Islam, A., Al-tabatabaie, K. F., Karmaker, A. K., Biplob Hossain, M., & Islam, K. (2022). Assessing energy diversification policy and sustainability: Bangladesh standpoints. *Energy Strategy Reviews*, *40*, 100803. doi:10.1016/j.esr.2022.100803

Jaaron, A. A. M., & Backhouse, C. J. (2014). Service organisations resilience through the application of the vanguard method of systems thinking: A case study approach. *International Journal of Production Research*, *52*(7), 2026–2041. doi:10.1080/00207543.2013.847291

Jasiūnas, J., Lund, P. D., & Mikkola, J. (2021). Energy system resilience – A review. *Renewable & Sustainable Energy Reviews*, *150*, 111476. doi:10.1016/j.rser.2021.111476

Kajanus, M., Leskinen, P., Kurttila, M., & Kangas, J. (2012). Making use of MCDS methods in SWOT analysis—Lessons learnt in strategic natural resources management. *Forest Policy and Economics*, *20*, 1–9. doi:10.1016/j.forpol.2012.03.005

Karim, S., & Islam, N. M. (2017). Syrian crisis: Geopolitics and implications. *Biiss Journal, 37*(2).

Kecskeméthy, K. S., & Teknős, L. (2023). North Atlantic Treaty Organisation's climate change risk management responsibilities. *Belügyi Szemle, 71*(1). doi:10.38146/BSZ.SPEC.2023.1.4

Kharrazi, A., Sato, M., Yarime, M., Nakayama, H., Yu, Y., & Kraines, S. (2015). Examining the resilience of national energy systems: Measurements of diversity in production-based and consumption-based electricity in the globalization of trade networks. *Energy Policy, 87*, 455–464. doi:10.1016/j.enpol.2015.09.019

Landau, L. F., Campbell, L. K., Svendsen, E. S., & Johnson, M. L. (2021). Building Adaptive Capacity Through Civic Environmental Stewardship: Responding to COVID-19 Alongside Compounding and Concurrent Crises. *Frontiers in Sustainable Cities, 3*, 705178. doi:10.3389/frsc.2021.705178

Lengnick-Hall, C. A., Beck, T. E., & Lengnick-Hall, M. L. (2011). Developing a capacity for organizational resilience through strategic human resource management. *Human Resource Management Review, 21*(3), 243–255. doi:10.1016/j.hrmr.2010.07.001

Maliszewski, P. J., & Perrings, C. (2012). Factors in the resilience of electrical power distribution infrastructures. *Applied Geography (Sevenoaks, England), 32*(2), 668–679. doi:10.1016/j.apgeog.2011.08.001

Mcdonald, N. (2012). Organisational resilience and industrial risk. Academic Press.

MERN. (2023). *Başbakanlık Mevzuatı Geliştirme ve Yayın Genel Müdürlüğü*. https://www.resmigazete.gov.tr/eskiler/2012/02/20120225-7.htm

Mintzberg, H. (1972). Research on strategy-making. *Proceedings - Academy of Management, 1972*(1), 90–94. doi:10.5465/ambpp.1972.4981316

Morane, D. (Ed.). (2009). *Energy security and global politics: The militarization of resource management* (Vol. 1). Routledge.

Mudalal, M. W. (2021). Examining the Moderating Effect of Geopolitical Environment on Crisis Management and Strategic Planning. *International Journal of Academic Research in Business & Social Sciences, 11*(9), 1025–1041. doi:10.6007/IJARBSS/v11-i9/10898

Novianto, D., Koerniawan, M. D., Munawir, M., & Sekartaji, D. (2022). Impact of lifestyle changes on home energy consumption during pandemic COVID-19 in Indonesia. *Sustainable Cities and Society, 83*, 103930. doi:10.1016/j.scs.2022.103930 PMID:35581999

Nyuur, R. B., Brecic, R., & Debrah, Y. A. (2018). SME international innovation and strategic adaptiveness: The role of domestic network density, centrality and informality. *International Marketing Review, 35*(2), 280–300. doi:10.1108/IMR-11-2015-0239

Oil – Global Energy Review 2020 – Analysis. (n.d.). IEA. Retrieved July 12, 2023, from https://www.iea.org/reports/global-energy-review-2020/oil

Okun. (2021). Örgütsel Dayanıklılık. In *Örgütsel Davranış Üzerine Literatürel Analiz ve Ölçekler* (p. 760). Nobel Kitapevi.

Ortar, N. (2014). Le quotidien peut-il être durable? Routines dans la baie de San Francisco. *Norois, 231*(231), 13–25. doi:10.4000/norois.5066

Ortar, N. (2018). Dealing with energy crises: Working and living arrangements in peri-urban France. *Transport Policy*, *65*, 72–78. doi:10.1016/j.tranpol.2016.09.008

Özbakır, P. (2006). *Enerji yönetimi*. Academic Press.

Pascual, C., & Elkind, J. (Eds.). (2010). *Energy security: Economics, politics, strategies, and implications*. Brookings Institution Press.

Ribeiro, D., Mackres, E., Baatz, B., Cluett, R., Jarrett, M., Kelly, M., & Vaidyanathan, S. (n.d.). Enhancing Community Resilience through. *Energy Efficiency*.

Roege, P. E., Collier, Z. A., Mancillas, J., McDonagh, J. A., & Linkov, I. (2014). Metrics for energy resilience. *Energy Policy*, *72*, 249–256. doi:10.1016/j.enpol.2014.04.012

Roidt, M., Chini, C. M., Stillwell, A. S., & Cominola, A. (2020). Unlocking the Impacts of COVID-19 Lockdowns: Changes in Thermal Electricity Generation Water Footprint and Virtual Water Trade in Europe. *Environmental Science & Technology Letters*, *7*(9), 683–689. doi:10.1021/acs.estlett.0c00381 PMID:37566299

Sawik, T. (2013). Selection of resilient supply portfolio under disruption risks. *Omega*, *41*(2), 259–269. doi:10.1016/j.omega.2012.05.003

Schobert, H. H. (2014). Energy and society: An introduction (2nd ed.). CRC Press, Taylor & Francis Group.

Seville, E., Brunsdon, D., Dantas, A., Le Masurier, J., Wilkinson, S., & Vargo, J. (2008). Organisational resilience: Researching the reality of New Zealand organisations. *Journal of Business Continuity & Emergency Planning*, *2*, 258–266. PMID:21339112

Share of energy consumption from renewable sources in Europe (8th EAP). (n.d.). Retrieved July 13, 2023, from https://www.eea.europa.eu/ims/share-of-energy-consumption-from

Shinkawa, N. (1998). An Outlook for Energy in Energy Conservation Point of View. Kyushu International Center, JICA & KITA,Kitakyushu, Japonya.

Shtunder, I., Kushnir, S., Perevozova, I., Kalinina, S., Savchenko, E., & Nitsenko, V. (2022). Sustainable development of the economy in the conditions of the energy crisis. *Naukovyi Visnyk Natsionalnoho Hirnychoho Universytetu*, *4*(4), 156–161. doi:10.33271/nvngu/2022-4/156

Smil, V. (2010). *Energy transitions: History, requirements, prospects*. Praeger.

Smil, V. (2017). *Energy and civilization: A history*. The MIT Press. doi:10.7551/mitpress/9780262035774.001.0001

Smith, C. B., & Parmenter, K. E. (2016). *Energy management principles: Applications, benefits, savings* (2nd ed.). Elsevier. doi:10.1016/B978-0-12-802506-2.00003-3

Sovacool, B. K. (2011). Evaluating energy security in the Asia pacific: Towards a more comprehensive approach. *Energy Policy*, *39*(11), 7472–7479. doi:10.1016/j.enpol.2010.10.008

Stewart, J., & O'Donnell, M. (2007). Implementing change in a public agency: Leadership, learning and organisational resilience. *International Journal of Public Sector Management*, *20*(3), 239–251. doi:10.1108/09513550710740634

Stirling, A. (2010). Multicriteria diversity analysis: A novel heuristic framework for appraising energy portfolios. *Energy Policy*, *38*(4), 1622–1634. doi:10.1016/j.enpol.2009.02.023

Szymańska, E. J., Kubacka, M., & Polaszczyk, J. (2023). Households' Energy Transformation in the Face of the Energy Crisis. *Energies*, *16*(1), 466. doi:10.3390/en16010466

Temby, O., Kapsis, K., Berton, H., Rosenbloom, D., Gibson, G., Athienitis, A., & Meadowcroft, J. (2014). Building-Integrated Photovoltaics: Distributed Energy Development for Urban Sustainability. *Environment*, *56*(6), 4–17. doi:10.1080/00139157.2014.964092

The impact of coronavirus (COVID-19) and the global oil price shock on the fiscal position of oil-exporting developing countries. (n.d.). OECD. Retrieved July 12, 2023, from https://www.oecd.org/coronavirus/policy-responses/the-impact-of-coronavirus-covid-19-and-the-global-oil-price-shock-on-the-fiscal-position-of-oil-exporting-developing-countries-8bafbd95/

UNDP. (2015). *World Energy Assessment Overview: 2004 Update | United Nations Development Programme*. UNDP. https://www.undp.org/publications/world-energy-assessment-overview-2004-update

Weaver, M. (2022, December 8). Millions cannot afford to heat homes as UK faces Arctic snap. *The Guardian*. https://www.theguardian.com/society/2022/dec/08/uk-weather-millions-households-cannot-afford-heat-homes

Wolfers, A. (1952). "National Security" as an Ambiguous Symbol. *Political Science Quarterly*, *67*(4), 481–502. doi:10.2307/2145138

Worlanyo, A. S., & Jiangfeng, L. (2021). Evaluating the environmental and economic impact of mining for post-mined land restoration and land-use: A review. *Journal of Environmental Management*, *279*, 111623. doi:10.1016/j.jenvman.2020.111623 PMID:33223352

World Energy Investment 2020 – Analysis. (n.d.). IEA. Retrieved July 11, 2023, from https://www.iea.org/reports/world-energy-investment-2020

World Energy Trilemma 2013: Time to get real – the case for sustainable energy investment. (n.d.). World Energy Council. Retrieved July 12, 2023, from https://www.worldenergy.org/publications/entry/world-energy-trilemma-2013-time-to-get-real-a-the-case-for-sustainable-energy-investment

Yergin, D. (2008). The prize: The epic quest for oil, money & power. Free Press.

Yergin, D. (2012). The quest: Energy, security and the remaking of the modern world. Penguin Books.

Zukowski, M. (2022). A Small Modular House as a Response to the Energy Crisis. *Energies*, *15*(21), 21. Advance online publication. doi:10.3390/en15218058

ADDITIONAL READING

Smil, V. (2010). *Energy transitions: History, requirements, prospects*. Praeger.

Smil, V. (2017). *Energy and civilization: A history*. The MIT Press. doi:10.7551/mitpress/9780262035774.001.0001

Yergin, D. (2008). The prize: The epic quest for oil, money & power. Free Press.

Yergin, D. (2012). The quest: Energy, security and the remaking of the modern world. Penguin Books.

KEY TERMS AND DEFINITIONS

Energy Crises: Energy crises are turbulences that deeply affect organizations and have devastating consequences. Energy crises are emergencies that result from insufficient energy resources due to interruptions in energy supply or the continuous increase in energy demand. Energy crises are situations that negatively affect economic activities, cause energy cuts and increase energy prices

Organizational Resilience: Organizational resilience refers to the ability to respond and adapt to turbulent situations, unexpected crises, and shocks.

Strategic Adaptive Responses: These responses include crisis management, diversification of energy sources, collaboration between stakeholders, the development of robust governance frameworks, and investment in technology and cybersecurity measures. By adopting strategic adaptive responses, organizations can increase their resilience, ensure continuity of energy supply, and contribute to a more sustainable and secure energy future.

Strategic Management: Strategic management aligns organizations with their environment and enables adaptive responses to uncertainties instead of reactive responses from the past. The strategic management perspective against today's energy crises can offer unique opportunities to differentiate from other organizations and create competitive advantage.

Chapter 15
The Labor Market Policies and Social Development in Bulgaria

Marin Petrov Georgiev
https://orcid.org/0000-0002-4530-6471
Scientific Journal Society and Health, Bulgaria

Venelin Krastev Terziev
https://orcid.org/0000-0003-1115-8877
Scientific Journal Society and Health, Bulgaria

ABSTRACT

The study comes as a result and in response to the identified priorities of the social policy in Bulgaria and logically outlines the actions for an effective management of the social processes tailored to the dynamic social environment. The essential characteristics of the social policy, its relations with the social management, and the opportunities for it to become a way of realization of important public tasks gives the chance to fit in it more delicate and important problems and the associated solutions. For this reason, the achievement of an active labor market is perceived as an objective of the social management, reachable in the conduct of relevant social policies, reflecting the registered interests of interested parties and society's need for an appropriate and irreversible change. The actually active social programs, interpreted as a system of social projects with direct feedback of social interaction, define the possibilities for adaptation of their components to the coming changes.

1. INTRODUCTION

The challenges of seeking answers to questions in terms of their usefulness, efficiency and effectiveness are related to a definite and accurate knowledge of these processes and their impact on the entire social process in which they take place, or, to be more precise, are part of it. The impact of science on our development is a process that itself does not need to be proven, because its results are obvious to all. Perceiving science as something abstract and incomprehensible would rather harm the process of its understanding and evaluating.

DOI: 10.4018/979-8-3693-0400-6.ch015

Numerous state and public institutions, Ministry of education and science of Bulgaria being one of them, are devoted to this task as part of their obligations. By developing and implementing different models and techniques in this directions there always will be support and opposition. However, in no way should this frighten, offend or discourage any of the parties. Achieving maximum justice is already a strong motivation to keep on going in the direction of objectifying the essential processes related to the scientific and research activities. Moreover, over lifelong existence it has been proven that the progress is related to scientific breakthroughs that are part of human experience (Terziev, 2020; Terziev, 2020a).

Very often people perceive things quite pragmatically and are satisfied with the explanation that their present state is acceptable enough. The changes are rather unwanted or frightening because we associate them with ourselves. The academic community is quite conservative in its pointviews and is perceived as self-sufficient. This acceptable way may be relatively good for a certain period of time, but it is by no means acceptable and progressive for the development of these processes.

The term "process" is complicated enough in the sense we use it, because on the one hand, it is continuous and has a number of characteristic features, complexity and even contradictions. It should be considered, defined and analyzed by all its participants, but mostly by those who will benefit from it, i.e. the people. Other way it will be just a pseudoscience that will bring satisfaction to a man himself without being useful to others. You will agree that the main benefit in this direction is the applicability of everything that scientists and researchers do. Historically, this has been repeated many times over the years, and in many cases scientific discoveries have been accepted and valued much later. Accepting or denying a certain scientific activity demands its understanding and approval by the society, which is not always an easy and achievable task from any point of view and sometimes impossible for a scientist (Terziev, 2020; Terziev, 2020a).

Usually, scientific discoveries, researches or scientific projects are published in specialized publications that are available to a limited number of users who are engaged in this activity or these publications have limited access which in most cases is paid. This additionally complicates the process of their approval. Due to the need of scientific research to be published in databases with reviewed content, i.e. those that contain scientific information of high value and are peer-reviewed, they have become publications with closed or limited access to this information. This is understandable, considering the effort and hard work of respective teams or specific researchers to get feedback and be assessed in an appropriate and acceptable manner (Terziev, 2020)

On the other hand, the scientists` work should reach larger number of people, since it is them who will potentially benefit from scientific achievements. For this reason, the scientists and researchers have no other choice but to constantly present their thesis statements, projects and discoveries on various forums in order to reach the consumer through different online information channels. This explanation sounds pretty simplistic, but it is relatively true. Sometimes one scientific research is presented, promoted and shown at a number of scientific conferences, round tables, symposia and exhibitions, which makes its validation rather a complicated and continuous process. This is especially true for social sciences. The resistance of the scientific community in such cases is very strong, because the search for non-traditional approaches in the validation of research violates the generally accepted slowliness of the process. This "irritates" the scientific community, which is quite introverted and even rigid in its understanding of the promotion of scientific works.

In our opinion, almost all ways of presenting scientific work are acceptable, providing that they ensure satisfactory results and reliable and true feedback and useful information. The relationship between authors (creators) and users needs to be more than just warm and sincere in order to identify omissions, drawbacks or imperfections in a sufficiently accurate and correct manner (Terziev, 2020; Terziev, 2020a).

2. ACTIVE SOCIAL PROGRAMS DEVELOPMENT IN BULGARIA: CONTEMPORARY CHALLENGES AND SOCIAL MANAGEMENT INSTRUMENTS

Under the conditions of the formation of information society new theoretical approaches are formed, a new model of active, dynamic self-improving social programs is developed (Terziev, 2015). These social programs are capable of active self-improvement and adjustment to the dynamically changing conditions of social life. In addition to the fact that under the new conditions the real need of orientation of the social programs towards solution to the problems of intellectual educational development increases, the characteristics of health and physical development do not lose their social significance (Terziev & Georgiev, 2017). Today, public health is a real indicator of a country's wealth, a reflection of the quality of life and the level of development of human resources. The state of health is directly related to the income per capita and the maintenance of the healthcare system.

In market conditions, the modern social programs have many manifestations. In turn, they have specific principles, methods, technologies for identifying and reaching social goals, ways and means of development of human resources. The general trend in the development and implementation of social programs for human resource development is the fact that their preponderant target orientation is related to solving the problem of the health and physical development of the population, the intellectual and educational development of human resources (Terziev, 2015a).

The implementation of the social programs under the conditions of the modern market system requires not only a deep knowledge and understanding of its nature and essence, but also creative skills when using the specific forms of the given method of social control. And that means to develop and implement detailed technological procedures for the creation of social programs and their implementation in accordance with the principles of systematic social management.

The objective preference for participation in active social programs, synthesizing active projects, considered as a complex of flowing projects, based on social processes directed to human development. The social processes based on active programming and projection are of unbalanced, dynamic nature and that is why they are at the forefront of the active social programs (Terziev & Arabska, 2015b). The basis of the social resources for support of the programs may be conditionally structured as a combination of at least three layers of support. Taken together, these three layers form a space of flows of social resources for support. The first layer, the first resource basis of the space of flows, consists of a chain of electronic impulses (telecommunication, computer processing systems for broadcasting and highspeed transport based information technology). The second layer of the space of flows is composed of hubs and communication centers. These are mostly large social institutions, which link the global network for support of social projects. The third important layer of the space of flows refers to the spatial organization of the dominant managerial elite, performing management functions, around which the organizational space is built.

Technocratic, financial and management elites that occupy a leading position in our society, also have their specific spatial requirements regarding the material and spatial basis of their interests and actions.

In the new conditions, the development of programs requires setting in the mechanism of their implementation of an active research and pioneering work for their self-cultivation. The adequacy of the program-targeted social management under the conditions of unstable and constantly changing way of life, is manifested in its focus to active examination of the results from the implementation of the social program (social assessment of the results from the implementation), attracting large groups of the population for its development (Terziev & Stanchev, 2015c).

The active social program is a system of social projects with direct feedback from social interaction that determines the adaptive capacity of the components of the program to the changing requirements to it (Terziev, 2015d). Moreover, in connection with the implementation of the social program, its social goals, implementation terms, partially its participants could be changed, as well as its attracted social resource to be transformed.

Under the current conditions, the active social programs in their essence reflect the transition from the traditional to the innovative model of social development. This transition namely determines the integrated use of social programs within the frames of innovative creativity, partner relations of participants within the program, the delegation of auxiliary functions to structures and collaborators, as well as widespread public participation of the population in the implementation of the programs.

In recent years, significant efforts have been made for execution of the tasks arising from the commitments of Bulgaria to the European Union strategic priorities. In many areas of labor, employment and social security relations significant steps towards the harmonization of the legislation with the European and social practice have been made (Terziev, 2015d; Terziev, 2015f). The legislation and practices in the field of employment and combating unemployment are constantly improving in view of harmonization with the directives and regulations of the EU and the successful achievement of the Europe 2020 goals. Gradually, the effects of the active measures on the labor market have been enhanced and the institutional capacity improved (Terziev & Georgiev, 2017). However, the accumulated problems in the field of employment and combating unemployment are difficult to overcome. The economic activity of the population and the employment rate of the labor force in the country are lagging behind compared to the EU average (Terziev & Arabska, 2014). The difficulties in the social policy in Bulgaria are related to several circumstances: in the first place, the relatively short period, for which the social model in the country had to be radically changed; in the second place, the low socio-economic level in Bulgaria that makes necessary the adaptation to higher goals, objectives and social standards; in the third place, the fact that the very European social policy is under continuous expansion and enrichment of adopting new principles, approaches and specific recommendations to the member states. Some of the main challenges for the social policy of Bulgaria are: the trinity "education, employment, standard of living" to be regarded as a leading practice in the socio-political practice; conditions for higher quality of life of Bulgarian citizens to be created, given the limited financial resources for health, education and security; the social policy to become a factor for productivity (Terziev & Stanchev, 2015g), which means new investments in human capital. These challenges require a qualitative change of the system for social protection. Measures to motivate and encourage citizens to be more active and autonomous should be included in it. Assuming the general principles and spirit of the European social policy, Bulgaria should comply with its national specifics and traditions.

The country is facing a serious challenge to improve the Bulgarian social model and the need to bring it into line with the EU legislation (Terziev & Georgiev, 2017). In this regard, the following priorities of the social policy and the employment policy in Bulgaria can be formulated for the next years:

- Increasing income and bringing closer the quality of life through an active social policy, consistent with the criteria, standards and achievements of the EU;
- Increasing the labor income;
- Continuation of the reforms in the pension system;
- Conducting an active social policy to overcome the negative demographic trends, targeted investment in the social development of children and young people and creation of equal opportunities for social reproduction;
- Providing equal opportunities, prevention and elimination of discrimination based on sex, age, disability, ethnicity, etc.;
- Conducting an active policy of training and promoting employment for disadvantaged people in the labor market;
- Ensuring social protection and integration of vulnerable groups of the population;
- Stimulating links between universities and the business and a life-long learning;
- Reducing regional disparities.

Moreover, now, when the country is an equal member of the euro structures and the European social policy plays an important role in building the economic strength of the EU through the development of a unique social model, the improvement of the European social model and investing in people is important to the preservation of the European social values of solidarity and justice while improving the economic achievements.

The social policy of the EU, which has begun its development as an extension and complement of the economic policy, is gradually becoming more important for the functioning of the Community and takes its place as one of the most important areas of activity of the Union.

2.1. Social Programming and Social Management

Studies, analyses, summaries and forecasts allow to derive the following cross-cutting implications accompanied by more specific suggestions.

The modern consideration of programming as a general principle of management, is associated with preliminary planned future actions and activities aimed at achieving a certain goal with certain means, in accordance with the challenges of the dynamic changes in the social environment on the basis of alternativeness of the decisions and optimal choice, contributing to the management by results (Terziev & Arabska, 2015h).

The concretization of the objectives of the social management is carried out through the social program, as a structured dynamic image and a way of action for coordinated interaction between the bodies of power, which allows the solution of important social problems according to their resource commitment, executors and deadlines for the implementation of a set of tasks and measures.

The effectiveness (economic and social) of the operating and developing social system, is always the result of the actions of all factors of the system as a whole, presented as an integrative productivity (Terziev & Arabska, 2015i). Consistency and complexity of the relationship between economic and social efficiency is determined by the methodological principle, which states that the implementation of the social program becomes in itself a catalyst for effective socio-economic development.

The validity of the objectives and tasks to assess the effectiveness of social services in Bulgaria, to provide stability and support to disadvantaged people, known as risk groups, is determined by the analytical capabilities of the social service for identification and evaluation of the "inquiries", the resource availability of the social service to meet the "inquiries"; the level of interaction between the institutions at a state (national), municipal and non-governmental level; socio-economic conditions and qualifications of the collaborators of the social service.

The theoretical and pragmatic overview of social programming allows the application of an appropriate methodology for the development of an active social program (Terziev & Georgiev, 2017), which primary goal is determined by the faster level of knowledge, prediction and achievement of socially significant consequences for the future in the forming of the general public process.

For the assessment of the effectiveness of the social program, the determination of exact criteria, specific reference points and specific indicators is necessary, which can serve as formally adopted standards for social service and as parameters of the program itself.

The people, the human resources with their actions and skills are a key factor of the social policies. The confirmation of this is the fact that the remaining components of a country's resources are synthesized and multiplied in them and thus turned into a finished product in the planning of the goals of the socioeconomic development, enabling an effective social policy.

In an environment of dynamic changes, requiring the participation of human resources in the socio-economic processes, through maintenance and development of adequate to the changes in the social environment capabilities to harmonize social relations, the need to establish an effective system of social activity is determined, which essential characteristics are the change, activities, social subject, social system, social relations.

The active role of socialization is determined by the creative activity of the human personality in the course of the gained social experience and the reproduction of a certain system of social relations (Terziev, 2015j).

Achieving an active labor market as a result, united by the overall objective of a social management as an active social policy, determines the adaptation of the model for collective qualifications on the basis of which to reveal the potential of the individual and the society, through the implementation of active social programs for social protection in the dynamically changing social environment (Terziev & Georgiev, 2017).

In the early periods of development of the labor market, its policies aim primarily at tackling the effects of the economic reforms on employment, but the policy of the labor market today has a clearly distinguished active character and is aimed at influencing processes or formation of behavior among target groups according to preliminary planned targets (Terziev, 2015k). The functioning labor market in the country is an adequate mechanism of the market environment and the conducted policy complies increasingly with the existing relationships and interactions between the periods of development of the economy and the labor market.

2.2. Methodology of Active Social Programs Development

The active social program, as a system of social projects with direct feedback from social interaction, determines the adaptive capacity of the components of the program to the changing demands to it. Their unifying social idea is a synthesis of thoughts, ideas and objectives of the participants in the program, including representatives and members of the public (Terziev, 2015d).

The methodology for the development of an active social program, shown in Figure 1 requires the focus on the following theoretical components (Terziev & Georgiev, 2017):

- the ascertainment of the social problem;
- the determination of the social objective of the program as a starting point for programming of the process for development of human resources. The external social environment provides an objective characteristic of the surrounding conditions, parameters and structure of the external objects that interact in one way or another with the given object;
- the projection of the planned trajectory for the development of human resources, which takes place within and under the reporting of the adopted for implementation comprehensive set of national and regional programs in accordance with the pre-determined social criteria.

It is noteworthy that the projection of the trajectory of development of human resources is related to the determination of eligible coordinates for changes of the social system. More specifically, it should solve the following objective tasks: first, determining the initial coordinates of the process of development of human resources; second, a description of the terms and conditions of its final states (final coordinates of the trajectory of motion); third, setting the criteria for qualitative and quantitative indicators for human resources development. That means to bind the objective with the final targeted state, which lies essentially in the basis of the management by results (Terziev & Georgiev, 2017).

Figure 1. Methodology for the development of an active social program

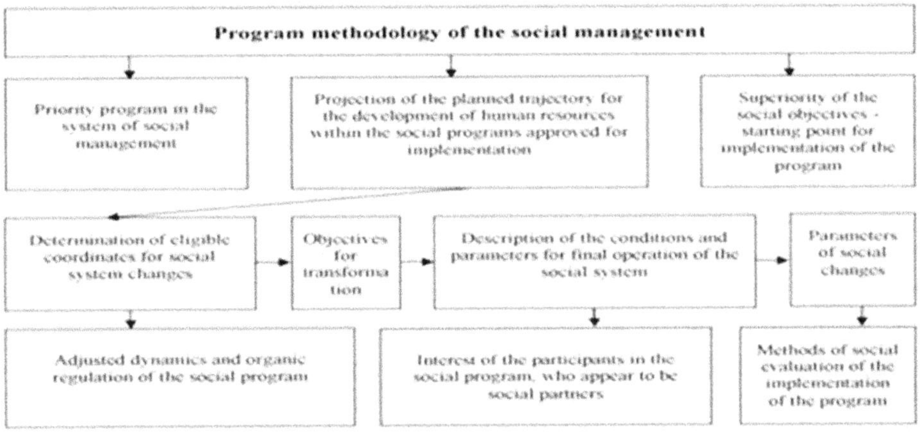

We should take into account that the most important goal of the modern social programs is determined by the faster level of knowledge, prediction and reaching of socially significant consequences for the future in shaping the overall educational process. Achieving a certain goal may serve as a criterion in the implementation of the model for a proactive education as a basis of the social construction of the faster human development. By its nature, the given social construction is a synthesis of the implementation of a complex of active social programs of society.

In the search of optimal forms of social construction, the central axis is a dynamically developing education system and the corresponding new type of dynamically developing intelligence, a new personality. This position can be argued by the fact that the education system is a social industry, which prepares specialists with one type of thinking or another. In other words, this is the spiritual targeted development of a certain type of personality, which in its essence is a system of expanded reproduction of the spiritual culture of the members of a given society. Society is transformed and developed rapidly and the system of educational institutions, educational practice is a “bottleneck” for this process. The practice shows that educational institutions of different rank demonstrate quantitative growth of graduate specialists, without taking caring about the conformity of their qualities with the growing needs of modern social development. And in order to overcome this inconsistency, the creation of conditions for competition of the structural elements of the education system is necessary. The educational development of human resources, determining the set of the acquired systematic knowledge, skills and professional habits, as well as the acquired skills for further learning and analysis of knowledge, exchange and use of information in the process of professional activity, are namely the most important factor and the social objective of the whole social policy adequate to the requirements of the labor market and the economy based on knowledge (Terziev & Georgiev, 2017).

The active social program also features the dynamic adjustment regulation by using the feedback in its implementation. The functions of the adjustment regulator are a kind of solution of the problem of optimization of its components as a result of the changes in the conditions of life activity of the population - damping down of the external disturbing social impulses, arising in the implementation of the social program.

The adjustment regulator of the program consists in turn of three interrelated parts: the systems for social studies, the organic system for planning and the organic regulatory system. The system of social studies is implemented by the methods that study the social interests of the population. As a result of the social studies, the needs and preferences of the population by certain social benefits are revealed. Among them are housing, healthcare, sport and cultural needs, retraining and rehabilitation training of the staff. Social planning is implemented with the aim of solving a social problem caused by the incompatibility of the components of the social program with the changed requirements.

The process of creating conditions for active implementation of the social program, gives an idea of social regulation. The successful implementation of the social regulation contributes to unification of the program participants, to bringing their interests and the interests of the public layers to which the program is directed, closer (Terziev & Georgiev, 2017).

The given components are completely identical in their structure and consist of the following interrelated parts:

- Predicting (anticipatory reflection of reality);
- Planning of social changes in the components of the system;

- Simulation model for the formation of the process of implementation of the program; internal immediate adapter of the system for program management, external adapter of the program management system;
- Internal adapter of the system for program management.

The principle of anticipatory reflection of reality expresses the possibility of adaptation of society to changing environmental conditions and the very possibility of existence, the ability to raise awareness of the current and future reality. The anticipatory reflection of the social reality is one of the forms to reflect future social development, which is a "historical foundation for the emergence of all higher forms of anticipating future events and above all the emergence of conditioned reflex".

The principle of anticipatory reflection of reality in the social program is expressed in the reporting of determination of the future performance of project impact: social prediction, social anticipation, social projection, social programming, social planning, social construction, social engineering. Based on the principle of anticipatory reflection of social reality, "in this dimension the principle of anticipatory reflection of social reality as a fundamental principle of social projection can be formulated" (Terziev & Georgiev, 2017).

Under the new conditions, the theoretical paradigm of social programs requires a synthesis of the theory of active systems that objectively to lead to the provision of conditions and motivational activity among the participants of the target social program. It is namely the activity of the element of the system that corresponds to a greater extent to the model for active target social program, the implementation of which is through the involvement of independent participants: the population, the government and public social institutions, as shown in Figure 2.

Figure 2. Specifics of the active social program for human development

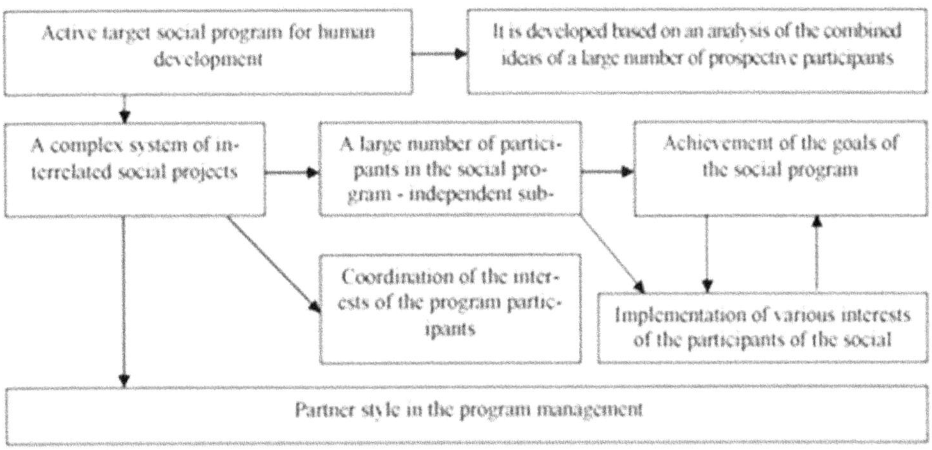

The development of an active target social program implies the presence of four components of the mechanism for its activation, which can be seen in Figure 3 (Terziev & Georgiev, 2017).

Figure 3. Components of the mechanism for activation of the social program

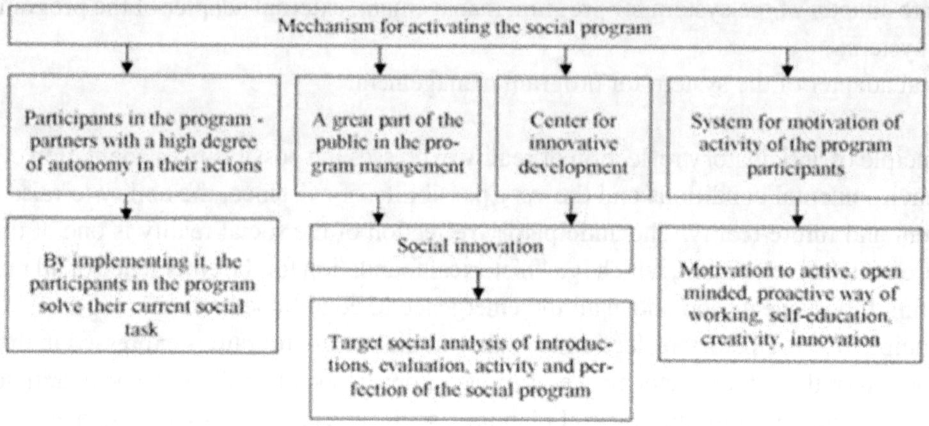

The participants in the program, who have a wide range of choice of action aiming at implementation of their interests, are the first component. This means that each participant in the social program is interested in solving a topical for them social task on the account of their participation in it.

The second component is the presence of a body with broad composition of managers of the social program and broad involvement of the public. The body shall not only examine the social results of the implementation, collect data, assess the stages of implementation of the program as a whole, but also develop guidelines for correction of the program elements.

The third component is defined by the system of motivation of a large composition of participants in the program. The development and implementation of the social program requires a special form of motivation of an open minded, active, scientific style of work that determines self-education, creativity and innovation development in any job.

The fourth component is expressed in the need for permanent operating innovation center for innovative improvement of the social program, for activation of the processes of its renewal (Terziev & Georgiev, 2017).

It is noteworthy that the highly qualified intellectual labor is combining between these four components of the mechanism for activating the social program. It is the potential of opportunity for self-improvement of the social program. The self-growing resource that has a cultural value and determines the potential for an active adaptation to the changing social environment, gives an idea of scientific innovation activity of the program participants. In other words, this is the resource of knowledge, which ranks today together with other resources (financial, material, human, information), which are subject to transformation into specific capabilities. Thus, the active social programs are aimed at solving social problems through implementation of breakthrough, innovative social technologies, attraction of investments, optimization of social resource flows, integration of social systems. The development of the social program denies the principle of ending the ongoing social measures. Each active social project is above all an innovation project, as its main objective consists in the development and use of new ideas that might be new social technologies aimed at providing social services that lead to dynamic social development and the viability of the population.

The active social program is created as a complex of social projects based on the common idea of social interaction, ensuring the coordination of the interests of the population in conditions of unstable social environment impact. The active social program is a systematic development. Each integral part of the active social program, considered separately, is interconnected and interdependent with its other parts. As a rule, in the self-realization of the individual elements of the social program, separated from one another, conditions for a sharp reduction of the effectiveness of its implementation are created (Terziev & Georgiev, 2017).

The optimal synthesis of thoughts, ideas and objectives of the program participants, the composition of which also includes representatives of the public, is the so-called common social idea of the active program. Moreover, the participants in the social program are relatively independent, act on the basis of their own interests - every participant within the framework of their participation in the social program determines their own interest. The program is developed on the basis of the creation of a common socially significant idea, in order to coordinate personal interests with the objective of the active program. The social program is developed based on the study of ideas and innovative thinking of the participants, on the basis of a comprehensive analysis in the field of implementation of the active social project through the formation of a common idea and development of schemes for the interests of the participants and the public. Based on the already obtained data, the structure of the active social program is formed, a network of organizations with the program participants is created around the representative of the common social idea, who assumes the role of coordinator and supervisor of the program implementation.

The active social programs have a number of common features. They include: a focus on achieving specific objectives; coordinated implementation of interrelated actions; limited in time action with a determined beginning and a period for development of a new program or its completion; originality and uniqueness to a certain extent (Terziev & Georgiev, 2017).

The result of the active social programming allows the implementation of the comprehensive program with a maximum efficiency under the conditions of a dynamically changing social environment. Moreover, based on the common ideas, the involvement of relatively independent functioning social institutions is ensured by coordinating their needs and interests. The active approach is primarily directed to reaching an effective development of the social object of the program by implementation of breakthrough innovation technologies, attracting to public management, optimization of the resource flows, integration of the social systems of the program participants. The term “active programming” emphasizes the continuous process of adaptation of the developed program to the conditions of the social environment of the system. Therefore, the active social program is open to self-development of the system. The success of its management implementation is largely determined by the factors of interaction of the elements of the social program with the constantly changing environment of its impact. Unlike the conventional social programs, its active form represents a creative self- developing project with a transformable final social goal, means and tasks of the process of social changes, which denies the fixed static schemes of classic social programming. The active social programs are directed to local social stabilization in unstable dynamically developing conditions of the environmental for social impact. The active projection is mainly directed towards the effective development of the social objects on the way to deployment of innovations; optimization of financial, resource and innovation flows; integration of socio- economic projects in global economic relations.

Information, as a result of the social study on the conditions for implementation of the program, is the basis for the establishment of all relevant systematically interrelated factors for social changes, reflecting the nature of the ongoing processes and phenomena. The participants in the active social program also have and implement skills for active creative conduct, related not only to the development and organization of the implementation of the social program, but with the ability to accumulate and reasonable adopt different kind of innovations as well. The implementation of the social program largely depends on the professionalism of its implementation. Nowadays, the main criterion for the quality of the program is the professionalism of its participants. These are the national and European employment services, whose coordination guarantees the effectiveness of one social program or another and the social policy of a country. This is the reason for the development of a common strategy for the future, approved by all European public employment services, subject to our further studies (Terziev & Georgiev, 2017).

3. THE ACTIVE MODEL OF A SOCIAL PROGRAMME AND ITS STRATEGIC ADVANTAGE

Classical complex targeted social programmesare traditionally used in the command-administrative (totalitarian) social system. Within that system the programmes were developed and implemented predominantly separately from each other and were bound up with the state centralised planning - namely directive, perspective and ongoing planning. These social programmes are implemented in accordance with the external social environment. They depend on state funding and budget planning. At the same time, they do not allow significant adjustments to be made by the subject and the object of management on the adjustments of the inter-programming social plan, the interaction between the participants in the social programmes and the adjustments of the relatively social assessment of the programme implementation (Terziev & Georgiev, 2017a).

The said principles of social programming are insufficiently effective in the context of democratic transformations. In situation of social instability the classical form of the social programmes needs significant adjustment. The practice of social programming should abandon the obsolete programmes, lacking flexibility, that have not been updated for a long period of time. Despite the progress in the field of labour and social development today, still, social policy is grounded to an insignifficant extent on science, on the strategy for finding human development resources, on a well-planned staff policy, on scientific and methodological principles of development of the social sphere and on scientific and practical studies of current social problems. Those factors that are inapplicable to the health of the population e.g. sustainable ecosystem development, including the quality of social education, the level of organisational culture of the institutions, the structure of the establishments in terms of professional skills and qualifications, the qualification level of the specialists working with the population, are often disregarded. The ideology of social service as a whole is gradually loosening its bonds with the old system of social protection; however, the final separation from the paternalistic position has not been achieved so far (Terziev & Georgiev, 2017a).

The democratic changes require new ideology of development and implementation of social programmes. The general public is no longer able to choose social goals as a component of targeted actions that remain unchanged over time, since the change in the conditions of the social living activity increases the necessary adjustments to be made in the implementation of the social programme. The social programmes should allow for active partnership interaction between their participants and should introduce the principle of democratic interaction with the object of social influence. The link between the contemporary social programmes and the state financial and budget planning should not be severed. The main source of resources for the said programmes should be formed on the basis of the budgets on a national and regional level.

The classical complex social programmes are focused on defining their social efficiency through the efficiency of capital investments, whilst disregarding to a certain extent other investments (including social investments, investments in educational, scientific and human capital). It is considered that under the conditions of a stable social environment it is not necessary to record the partial changes of the social programme in the accounting indicators of the latter. Consequently, the indicators of social and economic justifications, achieved with the help of the applied regulatory requirements, would be positive as a rule, while the actual social results from the human resource development would often be negative and, paradoxically, would not affect in any way the subsequent stages of the social programme implementation.

At the end of the 1980s of the last century the scientific publications put the use of the classical approach to the development of social programmes under severe criticism (Terziev & Georgiev, 2017a). It was pointed out that the social programmes underpinning the implementation of the social policy should cover the whole range of human needs and interests. The object of the social programme should be determined by the flexible impact on "the status of the classes and social groups, nations and nationalities, the social, class and national relations, the status of the individual in the society and his/her relation to it, all aspects of the national welfare pertinent to the society and its classes, social groups and ways of life". Scholars argue that it is necessary to significantly expand the area of influence of the social programmes, it is crucial to use them together with proved social technologies and new, more flexible and socially mobile, i.e. effective means of influence over social processes. "The abandonment of recognised management methods inevitably disturbed the stagnant balance of the social processes; it will reveal many latent conflicts and problems and will give surge to new ones. At the same time, the reform of the political system opens up opportunities for solving these problems by means of scientific research and democratic benchmarking of the various alternatives before the social policy"(Cherkasov, 1978; Terziev, 2003). The new conditions turn out to require an adjustment of the main approach to the development of social programmes. At a time of a reform the given basic principles require the presence of a flexible mechanism for the free formation and manifestation of the interests and wills of all classes and social groups, their flexible coordination and realisation in the process of development and implementation of social programmes, During the 1990s the social programmes were characterised not only by their rigidity and social inefficiency, but they also reflected the negative context of the corruption, which had turned into a resilient system of relations. Specific relationships were formed between entrepreneurs and officials, not as a cooperation in achieving the social goals, but rather as a means of taking away a financial resource to the benefit of a restricted group of people. The serious disruptions in the implementation of the social programmes lead to loss of their social efficiency and subsequent crisis phenomena, reflecting the ineffeciency of the social policy on a macroeconomic level, because the losses for the general public outweigh many times the social benefits it would have gained if the social programmes had been implemented (Cherkasov, 1978; Terziev, 2012).

According to people canvassed the main objective of the social programmes in Bulgaria in the last years was to ensure stability rather than development of human resources and support for disadvantaged people.

New theoretical approaches and a new model of active, dynamically self- improving social programmes capable of adapting to the changeable social life conditions have sprung up during the building of the information society. While there is a growing real need under the new conditions to orient the social programmes to solving the problems related to the intellectual educational development, the characteristics of health and physical development do not lose their social significance. Today the health of the population is a true indicator of the welfare of the country, the quality of life and the level of development of human resources. Health is directly related to per capita income and healthcare maintenance.

In summary, we can say that the contemporary social programmes unde market economy coditions can gain various forms which have their specific principles, methods, technologies for defining and achieving the social goals, paths and means of developing human resources. The general tendency in planning and implementing social programmes for human resource development is that their primary goals are oriented to solving the problems related to the health and physical development of the population and the intellectual educational development of the human resources.

The application of the social programmes under the conditions of the contemporary market production system requires not only comprehensive knowledge and understanding of its nature, but also creative skills to use the various forms of a social management method, establishing detailed technological procedures for designing and implementing social programmes in compliance with the principles of systematic social management (Terziev, 2012a; Terziev & Mladenov, 2012b; Terziev & Georgiev, 2017a).

Objectively speaking the population prefers to participate in active social programmes, consisting of active projects as a set of chain projects based on social processes directed to human development. The social processes based on active programming and project development, have an unbalanced, dynamic character and therefore they are in the foreground within the active social programmes. The foundation of the social resources used to support the programmes can be structured, so to say, of a combination of at least three support layers, which taken together, form the space of the flows of social support resources. The first layer, i.e. the first resource foundation of the space of flows, consists of a chain of electronic systems (telecommunication, computer processing, broadcasting and high-speed transport based on information technologies). The second layer of the space of flows consists of nodes and communication centres. These are mainly big social institutions which are the connection point with the world network for the support of social projects. „The third important layer of the space of flows concerns the spacial organisation of the dominant management elite which performs managerial functions and forms the center around which organisational space is built. The technocratic, financial and management elites which have a leading role in our society, have their specific spacial requirements related to the material and special foundation of their interests and actions" (Terziev, 2012c; Terziev & Georgiev, 2017a).

Under the new conditions the development of programmes requires the inclusion into the implementation mechanism of active research and innovation work aiming their self-improvement. The adequacy of the programme and targeted social management under the conditions of an unstable and constantly changing way of life is determined by its focus on the active analysis of the results from the implementation of the social programme (social assessment of the results from the implementation) and on the attraction of broad groups of people for its development. The active social programmes form a system of social projects with direct social interaction and a feedback from it which defines the possibilities for adapting the components of the programme to its changing requirements. Morover, with regard to the implementation of the social programme, its social goals, deadlines and partly its participants can be changed and the involved social resource can be transformed (Terziev, 2013; Terziev, 2013a; Terziev, 2013b; Terziev, 2013c).

Figure 4. Essential features of the active social programme

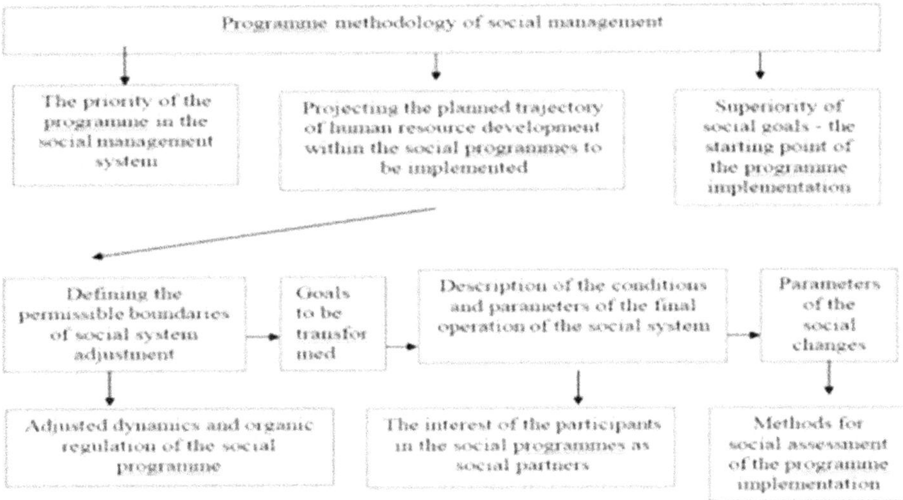

Under the present day conditions the active social programmes essentially reflect the transition from the traditional to the innovative model of social development. This transition determines the complex use of the social programmes within the framework of innovative creativity, the partnership relations between the participants in the programme, the delegation of auxiliary functions to subordinate structures, as well as the broad participation of the population in the implementation of the programmes (Figure 4) (Terziev & Georgiev, 2017a).

3.1. Material and Methods

The methodology for developing an active social programme places an emphasis on the following theoretical components:

- Identifying the social problem. "Getting a better understanding of the problem and gaining a more resonable control over certain key processes, we can turn the crisis into an opportunity, helping people not only to survive, but also to make the best of the change and to achieve a new experience of dominance over their own destiny";
- Defining the social goal of the programme is the starting point of programming the process of human resource development. The external social environment gives an objective characteristic of the surrounding conditions, parameters and structure of the external objects, which interact more or less with the given object;
- The planned trajectory of human resource development is projected within and by taking into account the set of national and regional programmes to be implemented, in accordance with the predetermined social criteria.

In order to plan the trajectory of human resource development, the following objective tasks need to be performed: First, defining the initial coordinates of the process of human resource development. Second, describing the conditions and parameters of the final state / final coordinates of the trajectory. Third, establishing criteria for qualitative and quantitative indicators of human resource development (Terziev & Georgiev, 2017a).

Many works by mathematicians have been published, related to planning and building a projected trajectory of the managed system. While examining in detail a few tests that use the results from such studies, we reached the conclusion that the mathematical approach to a problem has a limited practical significance when devising methods for influencing human resource development. The trust-worthiness of the above statement is corroborated by the fact that "each attempt to transfer the object... through management actions... from the initial state to the desired final state reveals the impossibility in principle of mathematically defining the initial conditions of the object precisely". The need for formalisation of theimpact of the external disturbance of the system on the living activity of the population faces a similar problem (Terziev & Georgiev, 2017a).

Therefore, it is relevant to maintain the conditions for material consumption and the level of the health of the population, as well as to plan the trajectory of the educational development of human resources. In the future the current system of scientific and educational institutes will become a base element of the information society as a society based on information resources, as well as on self-training educational systems. In the contemporary models of active social programmes it is necessary to provide for a trajectory of an anticipatory education of the population. The educational development should be continuous and should anticipate the targeted training, self-training, repeated training of the population and other forms of training. The anticipatory education in its abstract form looks like an ideal which the educational process could strive to achieve by shifting its development focus from the past to the present and the future. "The uncertainty of the future could be significantly reduced by setting apart the most desirable and at the same time the most realistic tendencies among the various alternatives and forecasts that stretch to the future, which is susceptible to guidance (manageable impact). Such tendencies and features of the future can turn into a normative vision of the societal development or certain spheres of its activity" (Cherkasov, 1978; Terziev, 2003).

We should mention that the most important goal of the contemporary social programmes is defined by the anticipatory level of knowledge, foreseeing and achieving socially significant consequences of the future when forming the general educational process. Reaching a certain goal can serve as a criterion during the implementation of the model of anticipatory education as a basis for the social construction of anticipatory human development. The social construction is essentially an aggregate result from the implementation of a set of active social programmes of the society. The anticipatory educational development of human resources on societal level reflects the transition of the individuals from one "social and professional stratum to another, accompanied by the development of skills and needs of the individuals through the acquisition of some or other set of cultural universalia - language, symbols, customs, traditions, societal norms, general and specific knowledge, translating into the education and self-training system of the society and presenting an opportunity for continuous objectivisation of personal skills, habits, experience in the system of the social professional activity" (Cherkasov, 1978; Terziev, 2003; Terziev, 2012; Terziev, 2012a).

The pivot in the search for optimal forms of social construction is the dynamically developing educational system and the corresponding new type of developing intellect and new kind of personality. This position can be justified with the fact that the educational system represents a social industry which trains specialists with one way of thinking or another; it is a spiritual targeted development of various types of individuals, i.e. in essence, this is a system of expanded reproduction of the spiritual culture of the members of certain society. The society transforms and develops quickly, whereas the system of educational institutions and the pedagogical practice are "a narrow space" for this process. Educational institutions of various ranking report an increase in the numbers of graduating specialists, without showing any concern about the adequacy of their qualities with regard to the increasing needs of the contemporary social development. This discrepancy can be overcome by creating conditions for competition among the structural elements of the educational system targeted at devloping the literacy of the various strata of the population". Ihe educational development of human resources, in determining the set of acquired systematic knowledge, skills and professional habits, as well as the developed abilities for further learning and analysis of the knowledge, the exchange and use of information in the professional activity, are notably the factor and the social goal of the overall social policy, which are most important.

The active social programme is characterised by a dynamic adjustable regulation through the feedback from its implementation. The functions of the adjustable regulator are some kind of a solution to the optimisation of the programme components as a result of the changed conditions of the living activity of the population - suppressing the disturbing external social impulses that occur during the implementation of the social programme (Terziev & Georgiev, 2017a).

The adjustable regulator of the programme consists of three interrelated parts: the systems for social research, the organic system for planning and the organic system for regulation. The system for social research is put into practice with the help of methods studying the social interests of the population. The social research reveals the needs and preferences of the population to certain goods: a dwelling, health improvement, sports and cultural needs, qualification improvement and retraining of the personnel. The social planning is carried out with a view to solving a social problem that has occurred as a result of the non-conformity of the components of the social programme with the modified requirements. The social regulation is a process of creating conditions for active implementation of the social programme. The successful implementation of the social regulation helps unite the participants in the programme and bring closer their interests and the interests of the population which is the target of the programme.

The components are structurally identical and consists of the following interrelated parts:

- Forecasting/anticipatory presentation of the reality;
- Planning the social changes in the system components; an imitation model of developing the programme implementation; internal direct adaptor of the programme management system, an external adaptor of the programme management system;
- An internal adaptor of the programme management system (Terziev & Georgiev, 2017a).

The principle of anticipatory reflection of reality provides for the adaptation of society to the changing conditions of the environment and the very possibility for existence - the capacity for awareness of the present and future reality. The anticipatory reflection of the social reality is one of the forms of presenting the future social development, which is "a historical foundation for the occurrence of all supreme forms of foreseeing future events and most of all for the occurrence of the conditioned reflex".

The principle of anticipatory reflection of reality within the social programme takes into account the determination of the future characteristics of the designed impact:

- Social anticipation;
- Social forecast;
- Social design;
- Social programming;
- Social planning;
- Social construction;
- Social engineering.

By using the principle of anticipatory reflection of the social reality "the principle of anticipatory reflection of the social reality can be sociologically established as a fundamental principle of social design".

Under the new conditions the theoretical paradigm of the social programmes need synthesis with the theory of active systems, which would create conditions and montivational activity among the participants in the targeted social programme. This activity of the system element corresponds most closely to the model of targeted active social programme whose implementation requires individual participants to be enlisted: the population, government and public social institutions (Figure 5) (Terziev & Georgiev, 2017a).

The theory of active systems transforms into a section of the theory of programme social management, determining the social adaptability of the social programmes, the use of more participants in the programme and their activity. This activity of the system element corresponds most closely to the active model of the social programme. The activity consists in partner independence and interest of the participants in the programme. The coordination of the efforts aimed at achieving the social goals of the programme should be combined with the deriving of social benefits by its participants (Terziev & Georgiev, 2017a).

Figure 5. Features of the targeted active social programme of human development

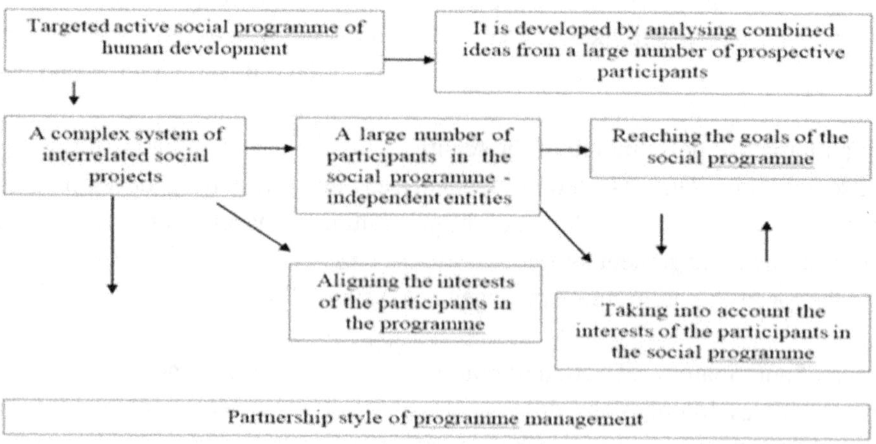

The social programmes assume an active character as a result of expanding the composition of the participants in the programme and uniting them systematically by applying the principle of partnership, as well as a result of the economic stimulation and activation of their social actions, i.e. the possibilities for making a strategic choice by the participants in the program are intentionally created within the implemented social programme. This implies that when developing the social programmes the participants undertake a social task relevant to them at the expense of their participation. The active model of the social programme provides for the creation of conditions where participants would benefit from their participation in the social programme. In the active targeted programme systems the controllable subjects are placed under certain conditions and have active increased managerial powers. Of significance here are the conditions and possibilities for a free choice of one's own state, the possibility to show one's own interests and preferences, i.e. they intentionally choose their state, but only within the priority of the implemented social programme. The active model of the social programme reflects the network structure of the social management when implementing the programme, where each participant in the targeted social programme has a high level of freedom of action and they strive to select optimal strategies in terms of the targeted results under the defined or foreseen significance of the used social potential (Terziev & Georgiev, 2017a).

3. 2. Results

The activation mechanism of the development of an active targeted social programme has four components (Figure 6).

The first component - the participants in the programme have geat freedom when selecting actions in accordance with the goals to fulfil their interests. In other words, each paticipant in the social programme has an interest in tackling a task relevant to him/her at the expense of his/her participation in it.

Figure 6. Components of the mechanism for activating social programmes

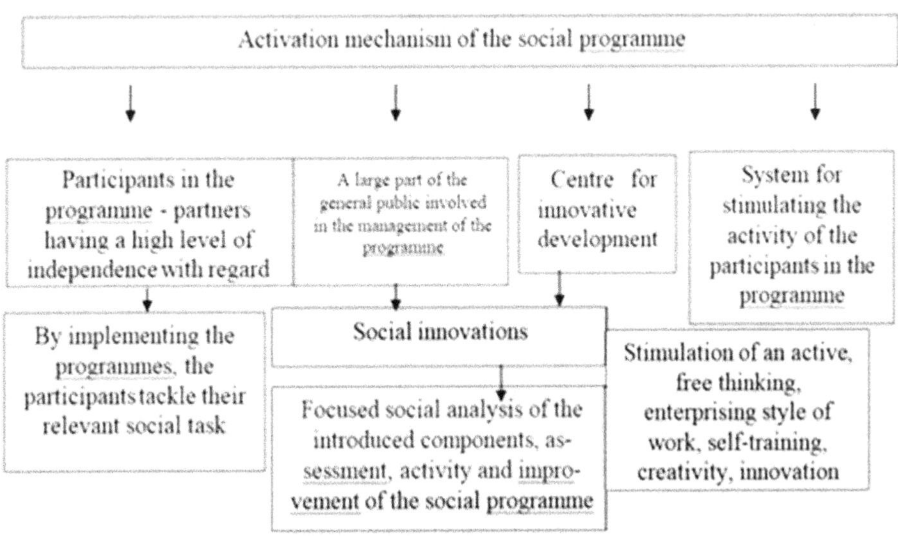

The second component - the existence of a body with a wide range of managers of the social programme and wide public participation. This body should not only examine the social results from the implementation, collect data, assess the implementation stages of the programme as a whole, but also develop guidelines for the corretion of the programme elements.

The third component is determined by the system for motivating a wide range of participants in the programme. The development and the implementation of the social programme require a specific form of stimulation the active free thinking, enterprising, scientific style of work which contributes to self-training, creativity and innovative development at the workplace.

The fourth component - the need for a permanent innovative centre which will support the innovative improvement of the social program and the activation of the processes for its renovation.

The active social programmes are thus directed to resolving social problems during the introduction of break-through, innovative social technologies, to attracting investments, to optimising the flows of social resources and to integrating the social systems. The development of the social programme renounces the principle of termination of the organised social events. Each active social project is first and foremost innovative as its main goal is to develop and use new ideas which could be new social technologies aimed at delivering social services and supporting the dynamic social development of the population (Terziev & Georgiev, 2017a).

The active social programme is created as a set of social projectsunited by the idea of social interaction which ensures the coordination of the population's interests under the conditions of an unstable social environment. The active social programme is a systematic development. Each constituent part of the active social programme, taken separately, is interrelated and dependent on the other parts. As a rule, when the individual elements of the social programmes are implemented separately and isolated from the rest, this decreases the effectiveness of the implementation of the programme as a whole (Terziev & Georgiev, 2017a).

The unifying social idea of the active programme - this is the optimal synthesis of thoughts, ideas and goals of the participants in the programme, including members of the general public. The participants in the social programme are relatively independent and they act driven by their own interests - they pursue their own interest by their participation in the social programme. The development of the programme rests on a socially significant unifying idea so that the personal interests of the participants in the active social programme could be aligned with the goal of the programme itself. The social programme is developed by studying the ideas and innovative thoughts of the participants concerning the implementation of the active social project, analysing them thoroughly to form a unifying idea and devising schemes of the interests of the participants and the population. The structure of the active social programme is shaped using the data collected, then a network of organisations is established with the participants in the programme and the representative of the unifying social idea assumes the role of a coordintor and regulator of the programme implementation.

The active social programmes share a number of common features:

- They are designed to achieve specific goals;
- They include a coordinated implementation of interrelated activities;
- They have a limited validity with a specified beginning and a deadline for designing a new programme or its implementation;
- They are unique to a certain extent (Terziev & Georgiev, 2017a).

The result from the active social programming allows the complex programme to be implemented with maximum effectiveness under the conditions of a dynamically changing social environment. Besides, based on the unifying ideas the involvement of relatively independent social institutions is ensured through the coordination of their needs and interests. The active approach is primarily focused on the effective development of the social object of the programme by introducing break-through innovative technologies, engaging the general public in the management process, optimising the flows of resources and integrating the social systems of the participants in the programme. The term "active programming" highlights the continuous process of adaptation of the developed programme to the conditions of the social environment within the system. Therefore, the active social programme allows self-development of the system. The success of its management is determined significantly by the factors behind the interaction of the elements of the social programme with the constantly changing environment that has an impact on it. Unlike the classical social programmes, the active form of the programme is a creative self-developing project with a modifiable final social aim, means and tasks of the process of social changes, which repudiates the rigid static schemes of the classical social programming. The active social programmes are oriented to local social stabilisation under the unstable, dynamically changing conditions of the environment that has a social impact. The active project development is focused mainly on the effective development of the social objects during the introduction of innovations, on the optimisation of the flows of finances, resources and innovations, on the integration of the social and economic objects in the world economic connections (Terziev & Georgiev, 2017a).

The information gained during the social study of the conditions for the programme implementation is the basis for separating all significant system interrelated factors of social changes, reflecting the nature of the processes and phenomena that are taking place. The participants in the active social programme have and apply their skills for active creative behaviour related not only to the development of the social programme and the organisation of its implementation, but also to the ability to accumulate and reasonably appreciate various types of innovations. The implementation of the social programme depends to a great extent on professionalism. Under the present day conditions professionalism is a main criterion for the qualities of the programme. To this end, specialists from abroad need to be attracted reasonably (Terziev & Georgiev, 2017a).

3.3. Discussion

The criteria for the efficiency of the social activity are dependent on the goals and tasks related to the delivery of social services to the population and the degree of their achievement. In principle, the following shall be taken into account: the goals of the social activity can be studied on the level of society, regions, towns and villages, areas, groups of population and individuals.

First, the criteria for the efficiency of the social activity need to reflect the effectiveness of all types, forms and methods of social service of the population; second, they need to demonstrate the degree of effectiveness of the activity of the administration and the social institutions under the present day conditions in Bulgaria, where sweeping and complicated reforms are in place. Third, the criteria and indicators shall reflect the degree of efficiency of the leaders and of the management of the targeted and systematic social work with the population and the individuals who need professional social support.

Several approaches for ascertaining the effectiveness of the implemented social programmes can be employed.

The first is related to the objective assessment of the ratio of achieved results (output) and the associated costs. In this case a key problem is the measurement (description) of the results (output) and the costs. As far as the costs can be estimated and planned, so can the effectiveness of the social service be presumed, planned and actually achieve (Terziev & Georgiev, 2017a).

Another approach focuses on the assessment of the effectivenss of the social activity in terms of the degree of satisfaction of the social needs and expectations of the serviced customers (users and beneficieries of the project or programme). The subjective methods of assessment e.g. opinions, judgments, views (expressed about somebody or something more or less specifically) and the specific subject who performs the assessment of the effectiveness of the social activity are of great significance here. Therefore, in this case it is important to define and select the relevant source of information for the assessment (managers, specialists, representatives of surveillance bodies, users etc.); in other words, the subject is the bearer of information that is significant for the assessment. Moreover, it shall be taken into account that the assessment-related information derived from individuals is subjective. The more subjects are engaged in the assessment, the more this assessment will seek to gain (under other equivalent conditions) an objective and reliable picture of the activity of the social services and the implementation of the specific social programme/project on employment.

The complicated nature of the assessment requires a targeted organisation of the process of obtaining opinions, judgments and conclusions, expressed through specific forms and methods. In this case, this concerns the procedural and organisational aspect of the term "assessment of the effectiveness of the social service". If we want to assess someone or something, we need to organise the process of assessment (collecting and processing the assessment information), devising and employing specific assessment procedures (including for example complex methods of assessment verification).

The whole diversity of opinions given by various subjects go through certain procedures and stages during the process of assessment and turn into the resultant (final) assessments Generally, the organisational process of assessing the final information can be used to draw practical significant conclusions, to carry out relevant events and activities and to develop programmes for enhancing the effectiveness.

Before the start of the practical measurement of the effectiveness of the social activity, the researchers inevitably have to pose a number of questions: what is the object of the assessment, what is the subject-matter of the assessment, who is the subject of the assessment, what criteria and indicators shall be used for the assessment, etc.

Effectivenss is an aggregate, integral indicator of the qualities of the system. It is determined by the external properties of the system (the meaning of the various indicators, characterising the capacity and the resources), as well as by the conditions where the specific system funcions. Therefore, it is more precise to talk about the operational effectiveness of the system when carrying out specific tasks under certain conditions, rather than about effectiveness in general. This allows all specific indicators of quality to be functionally connected in an integral indicator, i.e. effectiveness. This type of study of the quality helps to avoid many difficulties that occur during the analysis of complex systems (Terziev & Georgiev, 2017a).

Some of the factors that help define the goals and tasks of the assessment of the effectiveness of the social services are:

- The analytical capabilities of the social employment service for identification and assessment of the queries;
- The resources of the social employment service for operational response to the queries;

- The capacity of the social employment service (including its level of interaction with government, state, commercial and public organisations);
- The social and economic conditions in the administrative area where the social employment service operates;
- The qualification of the employees of the social employment service;
- Special attention shall be paid to the assessment of the quality when assessing the effectiveness.

Indeed, many issues are resolved in the light of quality and the subjects of the management of the activity of the social employment service and the objects of its activity can function as indicators of quality (experts). The most typical operation during the assessment of quality is ranking. The objects (phenomena, processes) are considered ranked if a quantitative dimension of theirs corresponds to a particular quality they possess in varying degrees. The various social employment services use ranking in different situations. For example, ordering the objects (processes, phenomena) in terms of their position in space and time according to the degree of manifestation of a quality that cannot be measured by any objective scale, according to some measurable qualities or qualities susceptible to evaluation (as a rule the degree of manifestation of a quality used as a basis of ranking can always be practically measured), according to some quality which is generally measurable, yet at a particular moment cannot be measured due to practical or theoretical reasons.

The matrix "goal: means" can serve as a typical example when using expert assessments in the management. The cells of this matrix have to be filled in with data gained from the results of the expert assessments (Terziev & Georgiev, 2017a).

Depending on the subject-matter of the assessment there are various methodologies of assessing the effectiveness of the social protection system. We can call them provisionally "first tier methodologies" Each subject-matter of the assessment can be analysed in more detail and respectively, there will be "second tier methodologies". There is a specific methodology of assessing the effectiveness of each type of social service (social domestic, legal, rehabilitation, pscychological and consulting services, material support).

A comprehensive review and analysis of the efficiency of the government social services need to be carried out when analysing the national social policy.

In the organisation and administrative management theory the efficient management is defined as the relation between the net positive results (when the desired consequences exceed the non-desired) and the admissible costs. The decision is considered efficient if the best result has been achieved in accordance with the defined time costs and with the lowest selection costs (Terziev & Georgiev, 2017a).

The modern societies experience a crisis in the efficiency of the traditional systems of state government. There are three key factors that have been conducive to the crisis situation: sociopolitical, economic and sociocultural. To overcome the crisis of modern democracies and respectively to resolve the problem associated with the administrative state government, it is necessary to construct a government paradigm corresponding as far as possible to the new cultural, social and political situation. The synergy methodology can be used as a government paradigm. It is considered that the synergy theory which distances itself from the extreme deterministic and atomistic positions with regard to the analysis of the institutional systems, lends to scholars two key categories for the conceptualisation of the term „social efficiency": „interpretative rationality" and "transaction costs". These two categories help achieve the main research objective: search for a general principle which allows the term "management decision" to be interpreted in the context of various institutional subsystems while recognising their own specific set of goals.

Apart from the "economic constituent" of the concept of efficiency (the ratio between the quantity of services delivered and the value or the quantity of resources needed for the delivery of the specified quantity of services), it necessary to mention "the technical" or the organisational constituent defined by the goals to be pursued. Technical efficiency is a term that refers to the degree of adequacy of the civil services in relation to the needs, desires and resources of their customers.

The concept of social efficiency is studied in the context of the new post- classical paradigm of state government. With regard to the concept of social efficiency the western scholars (M. Dimock, Anicet le Pors, J. Lane, etc.) study the distribution of resources using methodologies that are closer to political economy and management of organisations. Social efficiency is defined as a function of the minimization of transaction costs (exchange-related costs). Therefore, a prerequisite for socially efficient general government is the existence of an effective mechanism for the coordination of social interactions. The transaction costs that are most typical of the state government system are as follows: costs related to opportunitstic behaviour (truancy, nepotism, agent's fees, blackmail, politisation costs, etc.) (Terziev & Georgiev, 2017a).

It can be said that during a transition period there is a general system crisis that covers all spheres of society and lasts a long period of time. The success of the economic reforms is dependent on two groups of conditions: taking into account the subjects of the reforms (primarily the political elite of the country) and taking into account the need for objects of the reforms (the management teams and the personnel of enterprises with all forms of ownership, regional structures, the general public). The interests shall be taken into account on the "accounting" level and by studying more specific motivations covering the multi-layered structure of needs.

The experience of the industrial and postindustrial development of all countries in the world convincingly demonstrates the inadequacy of the purely technocratic approach to management. The new technologies, the information, taylorism and the economic and mathematical methods are very important, yet they allow true efficiency and competitiveness to be achieved only by taking into account the social motivation of the workers and by creating a well-planned system of incentives. Criteria for assessing the social efficiency of the state government are established. There two groups of such criteria: general system criteria which include equilibrium, stability, diversity, feedback, etc.; and specific social criteria the most important among which are social safety and social protection of the population.

Social efficiency is closely related to the safety of the social system. Statistically the safety of the social system can be construed as a spatial area or a state whose parameters are historically defined by a social ideal. For the contemporary Bulgarian society in particular going abroad, outside the boundary of the demarcated area implies that the society is approaching some form of a totalitarian regime (Terziev & Georgiev, 2017a).

4. IMPACT OF THE LABOR MARKET POLICIES FOR ENSURING EMPLOYMENT

Any form of human activity is related to getting ahead of any specific actions of its understanding in some way, i.e. as a particular program. This is even more important when it comes to organization and coordination of joint actions and activities, managing the whole business in social communities, starting with the smallest and ending with the national.

Compared to the existing political and governing practices, the nature of social programming is characterized by finding and justifying an algorithm for upcoming activities and actions in order to solve societal problems and to achieve the necessary and desired result. Social programming is manifested in various forms: creation of norms, normative or programming forecasting, design, planning, etc (Terziev & Georgiev, 2017b).

Justified social norms, solutions and programs containing the outcome (goal) and approach for its reach (methods and procedures for the activity) in the mselves, enable the impact on the processes in a targeted, comprehensive and systematic way.

For many years our society has created a special form of social programming, which basic forms have been the party directives and total government planning. When in the early 90's the system was exhausted, a search of new forms of social programming started, adequate to orientation to a market economy and civil society.

The use of the discovered in Western societies separate, predominantly „liberal" forms of social programming (legal ensuring of social regulation, the combination of „soft" government decisions of predictive nature and the very sound system of planning in companies, organizations, etc.), now becomes unsystematic and unprepared, without due regard for the specifics of the Bulgarian society and the specific characteristics of the regions, districts and municipalities (Terziev, 2013d; Terziev, 2013a; Terziev, 2013e, Terziev, 2013f; Terziev, 2013g).

In this first phase of reforms of all possible means the so called "Shock" method was chosen- which transfers the system from one extreme solution to another, which is also extreme.

The attempt at the national legislative level: the Constitution of the Republic of Bulgaria from 1991- to determine adequate model and reference for the development of Bulgarian society in the absence of clearly defined and legitimized programs- concepts and institutional transformations, did not and could not bring the desired result. Naturally, in these conditions the new „social" laws- the Unemployment Protection and Employment Promotion Act, the Employment Promotion Act, the Compulsory Social Insurance Code, the Social Insurance Code, the Social Assistance Act, the Integration of People with Disabilities Act etc., are bringing more methodical and technological character than are providing social and legal methods for solution in this regard. To some extent this situation is a result of the apparent insufficient general theoretical and methodological development of the problem for social programming as well as the absence of systems, assessing its effectiveness (Terziev, 2013h; Terziev, 2013i; Terziev, 2013j; Terziev, 2013k; Terziev, 2014a; Terziev, 2014b; Terziev, 2014c).

The effectiveness assessment that became apparent in the practice of the economic activity, until recently has not been used in the social field or is taken down to simple transfer of the basic principles for the assessment of economic efficiency to social processes. It is vital that today, within the given course of scientific research, the reasoning of the term „efficiency" has substantially been changed by the functioning of public systems. In particular, it is recognized that the principle of effectiveness is not limited to purely economic and market criteria.

Nowadays there are all indications that the principle of social efficiency in the nearest global perspective will not only be a means of correcting the social consequences of economic development, but also an active tool for structuring the business itself, the most important prerequisite for achieving sustainable economic effects. We can conclude that in the modern circumstances the principle of social efficiency is realized within the business activity itself. This becomes particularly evident when considering the field of employment of the population, primarily in specific administrative districts and municipalities.

This study is devoted to the problem of testing the effectiveness of social programming as a function of the state social policy (applied at the level of the administrative district and municipality) and the specific forms of its realization (regional targeted social programs) in the field of social protection and employment of the population.

The general concept implies disclosure of the nature of social programming. Moreover, we find in the classics of philosophical thought (Aristotle, Plato, Ibn Khaldun, F. Voltaire, E. Kant, Hegel, Marx and others.) a number of fundamental principles of the dialectical unity between the image and the ways of action, the outpacing nature of the mental image and the way of action in real actions, etc. Certain approaches to the study of social programming in the context of public awareness are contained in the works of modern philosophers (Terziev, 2013h; Terziev, 2013j; Terziev, 2013k; Terziev, 2014a).

The social program as the most important part of the socio-cultural process is the subject of research in a number of works of contemporary scholars and scientists. The ratio between the conscious and spontaneous inception in the programming of human activity, the relationship of social programming with scientific prediction and the use of program-target approach in science, programming of socio-economic processes are the basis for research and development. The most important forms of social programming: normative forecasting, social designing and social planning find deep and versatile reasoning in a number of works. The relation between social programming and social technologies was first discovered by K.Poper (Terziev & Georgiev, 2017b).

In recent years from the applied norms a separate research tendency aimed at summarizing the positive experience of the work of state social services and the development of a system of recommendations for improving their effectiveness has emerged. Different dimensions of the activity and social effectiveness of social services has been analyzed. Despite the private nature of many of the tested approaches and recommendations, most of the works are pushing the idea of the need to build a complete system for securing the social activity of the activities of state social services and developing an accurate system of criteria for the evaluation of its effectiveness. In this respect we can positively assess the placement of the given problem and the development of common approaches against the analysis of the effectiveness of employment and social protection authorities. However, it should be noted that many of the marked lines intersect each other and many works by different authors in most cases contain related questions.

In addition, neither of these studies aims at theoretical and methodological justification and comprehensive assessment of the social programming. As a concept that is too frequently employed and constantly used in the practice of the state government, for the present moment social programming does not imply mandatory comprehensive assessment of the effectiveness of all stages in the development of its product "social programs". In this connection the assigned objective of integrated assessment of social programming as a function of state power and its effectiveness following the example of regional social programs implemented in individual districts and municipalities is justified (Terziev & Georgiev, 2017b).

4.1. Details Experimental

The following tasks have been assigned in compliance with the objective:

- Defining the role and place of social programming within the system of sociological categories;
- Developing criteria and indicators for the effectiveness of social programs;
- Considering the effectiveness of the activity of public employment authorities;

- Analyzing the effectiveness of the national regional social protection programs (for employment) of the population in the Republic of Bulgaria, addressing specific regions and municipalities;
- Considering the social performance of the activity of employment offices as a body for the implementation of the state employment policy;
- Assessing the effectiveness of the project and the interim results of the National Program "From Social Assistance to Employment" for the period 2000 - 2015.

Subject of the study is the social protection system and ensuring employment of the population in Bulgaria.

Subject of the study is the assessment of the effectiveness of the National Program "'rom Social Assistance to Employment", its implementation at regional and local level as a means of organization of the bodies for social protection and employment of the population.

The theoretical and methodological bases of research shall be concluded in its comprehensive and systematic approach. This complex (interdisciplinary) approach, suggesting integration of sociological, theoretical and management, socio- economic and other aspects of the study is related to the system analysis.

Methodologically based on the study are the fundamental ideas of Bulgarian and foreign sociology for the specifics of social efficiency in the activity of subjects of institutional governance, including the state power bodies. Based on them, social governance is seen from the perspective of a system method, being the regulation of the relations between subject and object of management as a purposeful impact on the social system in order to bring its operation and development in accordance with socially significant goals.

Empirical basis. In addition to the theoretical methods, methods of observation and statistical analysis of sociological information have actively been used within the work (Terziev & Georgiev, 2017b).

The information sources used in the research project incorporate archival documents from the Ministry of Labor and Social Policy, the National Employment Service (later the Employment Agency), the National Social Assistance Service (later the Social Assistance Agency), the National Statistical Institute, the National Insurance Institute; documentary sources and statistical materials of the bodies of social protection and employment; programs for social support and employment of the population in the Republic of Bulgaria; information materials from the Ministry of Labor and Social Policy, the Employment Agency, the Agency for Social Assistance, the National Institute of Statistics; socio-demographic data of the population, school and university students, the professional qualification structure of employed and unemployed people in the country; materials of sociological studies of the main categories of unemployed people of working age; results of expert surveys of managers and specialists from social protection and employment offices; specific literature on the topic; materials from the media, conferences, meetings, seminars and "round tables" on the issues analyzed in the study. Local observations and impressions have a significant contribution among the information sources, which in combination with the statistical materials and expertise, allow forming an objective picture of the analyzed processes and designing optimal model for measuring the social efficiency of the activities of the Public Employment Services (the Employment Agency, "Regional Employment Services", "Labor Office" Directorates and their subsidiaries) (Terziev & Georgiev, 2017b).

The regional principle of study of the social efficiency of the activities of state social offices is selected in connection with the fact that at this level the selected methodologies for assessing the effectiveness are the most representative and specifically represent the relation between the established organization of the subject of management activities (the specific state power body in the region) and the researched subject - the national regional social programs.

Scientific novelty lies in the comprehensive evaluation of the effectiveness of the programs for social assistance and the employment programs of the population as specific products of the activity of the state social services in the region, including districts and municipalities. In this regard (Terziev & Georgiev, 2017b):

- The role and place of social programming within the system of sociological and economic categories has been defined;
- Criteria and indicators for the effectiveness of social programming in the system of social protection and employment of the population have been developed;
- The evaluation criteria for efficient operation of public employment services have been disclosed;
- Analysis of the effectiveness of the implementation of a national program at regional and local level has been performed for the first time;
- The social and structural specificity in the activities of employment offices, as an authority for implementation of the state employment policy in different districts and municipalities has been shown;
- A comprehensive evaluation of the content and the interim results of the implementation of the comprehensive program for employment assistance of the population in Bulgaria for the period 2000 - 2015 has been conducted for the first time (Terziev & Arabska, 2015l; Terziev, 2015j; Terziev, 2015a; Terziev, 2015f; Terziev, 2015m; Terziev, 2015e; Terziev, 2015k; Terziev, 2015d; Terziev, 2015n).

The basics of the study consist of the following (Terziev & Georgiev, 2017b):

- In the public institutionalization, the role of social programming is defining the norms, as it derives from the decision-making process, it sets out solution priorities and formulates the problems and the resulting tasks;
- The use of a specially developed system of metrics and indicators allows to determine the degree of efficiency of the activity of state social services in their integral significance in the evaluation of the dynamic interrelations in the changes between “internal” and “external” environment in the governance of these areas, and to set up a system of criteria and evaluations of the social efficiency in its individual functional elements;
- The analysis of the efficiency of the regional and local public employment offices and targeted social programs as products of their activity allows the adoption of the following principal points as efficiency criteria: the relevance of the program objectives with the objectives for social development and the needs of the recipients, the existence of prognosis of the socio-economic consequences from the events of the program, the use of modern methods for analysis of the organization and management of the programs accounting the resource, legal and information security of these events, achieving the goals of the program in the most optimal way, defined as the degree for solving social problems with minimum time and minimum level of material losses to society;
- The disclosed deficiencies in the programs for social protection of the population in the country and the respective regions suggest the lack of efficient program-targeted approach for solving social problems. These include insufficient funding, lack of necessary legal and information security for

their planning and implementation, lack of project management, real control in the execution of programs and evaluation of their economic efficiency;

- As a result of the analysis of the complex employment program for the population in the country for the period 2000-2015 (National Program "From Social Assistance to Employment") main drawbacks are defined as follows: At the stage of development of the draft program: the lack of legislative mechanisms for the development and implementation of targeted programs (undeveloped specific criteria and indicators for efficiency assessment of program activities). At the stage of implementation: lack of accurate control mechanisms in the use of budget funds allocated for the program implementation and for compliance of the obtained results with the program objectives. In the stage for summarizing the interim and main results: no calculations have been performed for the final evaluation of the economic efficiency of the results of the program activities and evaluation of the satisfaction of the recipients of the program;
- The functioning of a uniform mechanism for social protection and the provision of employment in the country suggests monitoring of the social sphere, development of a system of program activities, organization of the resource, legal and information security of these events.

The scientific and practical significance of the work is expressed in the fact that the concept of social programming has a direct relation to the implementation of social policies and the implementation of good governance practices in the country and the relevant administrative districts and municipalities and allows the specification of an entire line of conditions in normative legal basis for the regulation of social relations (Terziev & Georgiev, 2017b).

The results of the sociological and economic analysis allow to determine the content of the principle of social efficiency in the programming part of the activities of regional and local government social services for employment, to offer a comprehensive methodology for sociological analysis and measurement of social performance of these types of activities to identify the most important determinants in the implementation of the present principle, to evaluate and determine the main directions for improving the social performance of the work of the analyzed services.

The results of the study can be used for the compilation of training and work programs, courses related to the foundations of social development, economic sociology, economics and sociology of labor, the development of specialized courses lectured to students in higher education institutions, for additional training of managers and experts from regional and local employment offices ("Regional Employment Offices", "Labor Office" directorates and their subsidiaries) in the offices for social protection of the population ("Social assistance" directorates), in working with students and university students from professional schools, colleges and universities and others in the development of regional, district and municipal social employment programs.

Approbation of the results of the study. The study results can be implemented (Terziev & Georgiev, 2017b):

- In the practice of the public authorities for social protection, support and employment of the population a complex of sociological research has been held on "Investigation on the demanded professions and specialties on the labor market and vocational training programs for the unemployed" and „Sociological monitoring of social offices, related to the selection and recruitment in social programs". The author has participated in the development of instruments and the implementation of "Complex monitoring for compliance with the professional qualification structure of free labor force and jobs in the secondary labor market", the results of the survey were used in the practice of the Ministry of Labor and Social Policy in developing a system for programmed and targeted cost management for the implementation of social programs;

- In the program of numerous national and international conferences, scientific and practical conferences and seminars;
- The most essential implementations and results of the study are reflected in more than 100 scientific publications totaling over 500 printed sheets (Terziev & Arabska, 2016; Terziev & Arabska, 2015o; Terziev & Arabska, 2015p; Terziev & Arabska, 2016a).

The analysis of the theoretical and methodological issues of social planning allows the proposition of a comprehensive concept of the institutional and governmental foundations of social programming.

The institutional and governmental approach involves detecting the role of social programming as a function of the public institutions, power and government. Moreover, if social programming in an institutional approach brings some norms, in the government it takes the form of a solution. The interaction of social institutions and government systems depends very much on the mechanism of this transformation.

Strategic programming turns to be a major center for transformation of the program norms in the governmental decision, in which promising conceptual solutions are produced based on program- target principle (approach). Depending on the situations and the instrument that is used by the person receiving the decision, the strategic programs can take the shape of prognosis, projects, plans in various combinations. Different types apply specific range of skills. The "Firm" use of only one of them, in some cases leads to a loss of manageability, spontaneous "self-programming" of the processes and in other cases makes the governing system rigid and deprives it from the necessary flexibility and the ability for fast reconstruction of the methods for impact. This is clearly visible in the two crises of the twentieth century- the spontaneous development of market relations in the late 20s, the early 30s in the West (especially in the US) where the system for state programming was virtually absent and the stagnation in the socio-economic development of the USSR, which led to the crisis in the late 80s and the early 90s where the government system was "attached" to the total government directives (Terziev & Georgiev, 2017b).

The analysis of the interaction of institutional programming, resulting in adequate formation of norms (expressed primarily through legislation) and governmental through the program-target mechanism (through strategic, organizational and competent programming) shows that these essential parts can create efficient enough system of social programming, combining the mechanisms of the market economy with state regulation in the social sphere.

We consider necessary the clarification of the different cases in the legislation. In particular, it is necessary to define the concept of social programming (social programs) as a promising structural image and method of action, created for coordinated interaction between the bodies of power, aimed to solve important social problems using the contractors bound by resources and deadlines for the implementation of complex events.

The project approach to solving social problems, which is implicit in the given definition, allows us to assess the effectiveness of the social programs as a use of effective methods for management, concentrated with optimal use of program resources. The concept of social efficiency should not be considered as a separate type (class) but as an organic constituent component /main part/ of any social program (Terziev & Georgiev, 2017b).

It is also necessary to adopt national legislation for regional social programming, which has to ensure the unity of the legal and theoretical and methodological foundations for development and support of strategic government programs at national and local level.

In this system a particularly important role is played by the subsystem of target national and social programs, funded by the state budget (under the respective co-ordination) at all levels of the public administration. Its managing role is particularly important in the interaction at different levels (national, regional and local), as well as in the coordination of activities of the various social offices with businesses and public organizations (groups) within a single methodology, forming a unified field of social protection and ensuring effective employment of the population.

Further study of these issues and the development of progressive social technologies will enable more efficient use of the social programming in solving current problems and actions during crises.

5. IMPORTANCE OF HUMAN RESOURCES TO SOCIAL DEVELOPMENT

The key factor for socio-economic development are people. They are the foundation of social management as a separate managerial area, the goal of which is the management of the interaction between the subject and the object, (having their social character), occurring in a particular social environment. To what degree the actions of the subject and the object, as elements of social management are adequate to the changes in the environment, is determined by their activity. Moreover, the rationalization of social managerial decisions is directly dependent on the social policy carried out (Terziev & Georgiev, 2017c).

The social policy - as a set of principles, legal norms, institutions and activities, aimed at creating conditions ensuring the quality of life of the citizens of a country, is an expression of the social relations between the state and its citizens. The social policy determines the safety (social, health, economic) and security of the people in the socium. This is why it is defined as „philosophy, ideology, program for influence on the demographic situation, employment of the population, level, way and quality of living of the population, „its income level and structure of consumption of material and cultural wealth,... forms of social security, social services to the population, ... providing targeted state aid to the most unprotected, the most vulnerable and poor layers of the population,... measures aimed at creating conditions for self-defense in order to maintain and improve the level of well-being..."(Terziev, 2013l).

It is noteworthy that within the scope of social policy a wide arsenal of concepts is included (social protection, social safety, social support, social selfprotection, quality of life), defined in the quoted edition. From here, in the content of social policy are differentiated concrete actions of the state bodies, non-state institutions, public associations, related to the implementation of tactical and strategic objectives for the harmonization of public relations. Since the foundation of these relations are the people with their actions and skills, they are a crucial factor of social policy. Inside there are synthesized and multiplied the other components of a country's resources and thus they are transformed into a finished product in the planning of the goals for achieving socio-economic development, making it possible to carry out an effective social policy (Arabska, 2016b)

Moreover, researches show that 70% of the world's wealth is in the form of human capital - the skills and knowledge of the people and not in physical or financial capital. The strategy of many companies today is clearly guided by the idea of human resources, stressing on individualization, service and innovation (Terziev, 2013l).

Put another way, human resources are the people in an organization which, by their professional and personal qualities, make it possible to achieve its strategic objectives. Together with the rest of the resources, they should meet the needs of the organization, and the way they are transformed into abilities, predetermines the efficiency of their use. This means that they, human resources, together with others, become a function, a subsystem and an object of management. The reason for this is the circumstance that in terms of goal setting, they are a function of management. The application of the accumulated scientific knowledge on the general theory of systems, basing on the system approach, interacting with other management subsystems, characterizes them as a management subsystem. Through the forward and backward informational feedback, they are a subject to management, influence for the purpose of obtaining certain result. Therefore, human resource management (HRM) is defined as „a system of principles, methods, tools, legal norms, rules, criteria, requirements, standards, procedures, policies, plans and programs of formation and use of human resources in the organization, in accordance with its immediate interests and strategic objectives" (Shopov & Atanasova, 2003a; Terziev & Georgiev, 2017c)

In other words, HRM is an activity resulting from the strategic objectives of the organization, which requires the implementation of a strategic management approach in taking managerial decisions, related to this resource. In this sense, the human resources are a reflection of specific social relations in the interests of social governance, as part of a nationwide management. And in an environment of dynamic changes, requiring the participation of human resources in the socio-economic processes, by maintaining and developing adequate to the changes in the social environment abilities to harmonize social relations, there are demands on establishment of an effective system of social activity, which is also the goal of the study presented in this publication.

5.1. Details Experimental

Social activity as a factor of change in public relations The social activity is inherently associated with foresight and proactive actions. Put another way, it is directly related to the change in social relations caused by people, by the individual. From here, „...social activity is the realization of a particular new norm-measure of the activity, which norm-measure stands out as new in direct comparison with the established one, with that which is considered "normal" by common sense in life. The individual realizes this new norm-measure either in his/her own activities or in the activities of other people, their associations, public institutions activity that generates activity" (Mirchev).

What is noteworthy is that the essential characteristics of social activity are the change, the activities, the social subject, the public system, the public relations.

In all his/her actions, "the individual intentionally makes changes in the activity and its results (his/her or someone else's activity) and thus causes social change and creates conditions for change (progressive or regressive)" (Mirchev).

Social activity is objectively and subjectively conceptualized by the individual as his/her activity for the development of society from the position of the adopted by him/her specific team interests, ideals and ideas. Social activity is (1) a purposeful effort on the part of the individual (2) for a significant personal contribution to this development, (3) through the available forms and means (4) to the possible extent ((Mirchev). And this determines his/her public predestination, the expression of which is the alignment of the social system and public relations with the dynamic changes in the social environment.

Since, in the basis of these projections and activities stays the subject, the human resource, led by the private and public interest towards change, the social activity is associated with the concept of the term interest, motivation, desire for satisfaction of needs that depend on organizational changes, the intensity of these activities is directly dependent on the factors of the social environment. All this resides within the scope of social management as part of the general managerial process and in connection with the management of human resources (Zahariev & Arabska, 2014d). In order to have efficient management of social processes, it is more than ever necessary to observe certain rules, principles which in scenes are also principles of the human resources management (HRM). This concerns the following (Terziev & Georgiev, 2017c):

- Predictability, expression of which is in synchronizing social management with the longterm strategic requirements and social needs;
- Integration, the relevance of which is in the integration of social management in a unified framework, which to consolidate the planned strategic goals of social policy on the basis of fair treatment of the individual;
- Synchronization, expressed in planning, organizing, coordinating the activities in social management;
- Protection of information, consistent with the requirements for personal data protection, integrity and security of information, related to the individual and the social processes;
- Empathy, guaranteeing the identification of the needs of the individual and their satisfaction in a real social environment;
- Flexibility on the basis of which social management to adapt to changes in the social environment.

And all this is in the interest of the objectives and tasks of social policy, the achievement of which is a result of the activity of the human factor, understood as an individual, a team, the society, and the relations between the people in this team, in this society on the basis of self-awareness (Arabska, 2016b). And this activity, social in its nature, is determined by certain factors- general and specific (Kamenov & Asenow, 2000). Amongst the general factors of social activity, special attention deserve:

- The common culture, which is important for the behavior of the human factor in the team, in the society;
- The special-functional culture resulting from the behavior of the individual in the realization of professional relationships;
- The motivating factors relating to the stimulation and consideration of interests of individuals in the team and in the society.
- The specific factors of social activity include:
    - The way of taking management decisions, while leading are these two moments - one, when it is necessary to ensure the participation of the team, the society in the execution of the decision, and the second, when it is important to act immediately and in a short time to achieve the intended purpose;
    - The way of managerial communication, while extremely important is the managerial responsibility, manifested by the so called „Ruling Five" (Terziev, 2013l), illustrated by the fingers of the hand.

Through this approach the following questions receive their answers:

- Greater pressure (the thumb); who is to blame (the index finger);
- Whose is the choice (the middle finger);
- Whose are the instructions (the ring finger) and who is in control (the little finger).

The application of this approach to managerial communication is essential in the implementation of managerial decisions in the social sphere, which too often should be taken depending upon the particular situation and the implementation of which is a result of the contribution of each member of the team, of the society and their team wise interaction.

Achieving motivation in the individual sometimes determines the practice the answer to the questions of the Ruling Five to be given "face to face".

Therefore, the understanding and consideration of these factors for the social activity of the human factor is in the basis of the formation of managers at all levels in the managerial hierarchy of the social system (strategic, operational and tactical levels) with established leadership skills on the basis of collective qualification and team work (Kamenov & Asenow, 2000). This means forming ability for:

- Management of change in the social environment by bringing together experts with different backgrounds in the realization of the set objectives;
- Linking the goals with the personal interest;
- Motivating highly efficient communication between the individual experts;
- Merging the collective, the social with the personal responsibility in the tasks execution;
- Optimal use of the skills of the members of the team, corresponding to the nature and complexity of the executed tasks.

Without claiming to be exhaustive, we believe that the application of the model of collective qualification allows the disclosure of the potential of both the individual and the team, and the society as a whole, in achieving the end results, united by the global objective of social management. This, according to the theory of leadership, is the basis of focusing "on the release of human talent and realizing the potential of the people" in managing change in the social system, in public relations, in accordance with the changes in the social environment (Terziev & Georgiev, 2017c).

Adaptation of the model of collective qualification and team work allows defining the role and place of the human factor in social management by the dependency "goal-results", which is the basis of management by result and rationalization of managerial decisions (Terziev & Georgiev, 2017c).

6. IMPACTS OF ACTIVE SOCIAL PROGRAMS ON LABOR MARKET

Unfavorable negative demographic trends in Bulgaria leading to processes of decreasing and aging of labor resources, sustainably unbalanced character of labor market, characterized by high unemployment and low labor demand, the availability of vulnerable groups and significant regional discrepancies in labor market development are among the most serious challenges before the country in the XXI century (Terziev & Arabska, 2014e; Georgiev, 2017d). Among the macroeconomic policies and means a significant place is rendered to the so-called active programs and measures on the labor market which are an object of increasing attention not only because the expectations of tangible effects but also because comparatively significant financial resources necessary for their implementation (Arabska, 2016c). Furthermore, the problem of effective spending of resources gains bigger sharpness in the current situation of limited social expenses in the country and poses questions to the effectiveness of the implementation of different programs and control (Georgiev, 2017d).

Current study examines information about active programs for labor employment, makes analyses of existing good practices and determines main preferences of unemployed persons in capable of working age taking monthly social support towards transformation of social support into incomes from labor, as well as the attitude of the main institutional departments conducting the state social policy in the field of employment and unemployment and the attitude of the non-governmental organizations towards the program and their readiness for distributing the functions between state, municipalities and non-governmental organizations in implementation and financing of the program, probable problems and conflict points.

Main characteristics of active social programs and their assessment

The active programs are a means of raising the competitiveness of labor force, mobilization of labor resources and increase in economic activity of population (Terziev, 2013e). The active policy also implements a very important socially distributing function, especially in conditions of availability of vulnerable groups on the labor market (Georgiev, 2017d). For the last the participation into active programs is the only one chance of employment, avoidance of entering endmost poverty and social deprivation (isolation). Not the least, from the right determination of goals and expected results in active programs and measures and their appropriate announcement in the public space are dependent the extent, trust and support of implemented social and economic reforms (Georgiev, 2017d).

Introduced as a response to significantly increasing unemployment, active social policies incessantly expand the variety of programs and measures including the following main elements:

- Intermediary services on the labor market;
- Opening new places of work (programs of temporary employment);
- Qualification / re-qualification of unemployed and employed persons;
- Entrepreneurship encouragement;
- Subsidized employment.

The active programs could be scrutinized, in the most general plan, as an instrument of support to the effective functioning of the labor market. They contribute to the elimination of barriers and problems in the functioning of market economy. The active programs have a multidirection impact on the labor market. Emerged as a means of unemployment limitation, nowadays expected impacts of their application are too broad (Terziev, 2014a). Despite the availability of a number of modifications and concrete varieties for the implementation of the mentioned directions of active policies, the qualification is an important issue of consideration for all the countries, including conducted in the Republic of Bulgaria active policy on the labor market (Arabska, 2016c; Arabska, 2016d; Terziev, 2013i).

The building up of a capacity for executing regularly monitoring activities and assessment of the effectiveness of conducted active policies is one of the priority tasks in the strategies on the European level too. In the practical assessments of the active programs and measures, the problems most often arising are substantiated by their multigoal and multiaspect nature and they are connected to the lack of a common and consolidated methodology for assessment, as well as to mistakesin measurements and the absence of adequate statistical information, resulting in the objective impossibility to trace the persons and state "benefits" of participation in such programs (Arabska, 2016e; Georgiev, 2017d).

The starting point in the assessment of active programs and measures are the activities of clarification of goals, tasks and expected results for a concrete program (Georgiev, 2017d). Studies of different active programs in the field of labor market worldwide show ambiguity and often contradictory results regarding their effectiveness. Results are highly influenced by the examined country's peculiarities, period and way of implementation of programs. The outlined great variety of active programs gives an evidence that during the assessments of their effectiveness all probable aspects of the effectiveness should be measured, all the impacts should be considered and compared- increase in the chances of employment, increase in the level of payment, social impact, etc. Furthermore, it is important an analysis of benefits and expenditures to be made which would give an opportunity to provide a clear answer to the question to what extent spent financial resources are economically and socially justifiable (Arabska, 2016b; Arabska, 2016f).

Into the world practice four types of active measures' assessments are mainly applied (Koceva, Terziev, & Andreeva, 2003b):

- Permanent (current) monitoring and control of programs;
- Assessment of the net impact of the programs;
- Benefit- expenditure analyses;
- Assessment of institutional and organizational capacity of programs.

Full investigation means realization of the four above-mentioned assessments. In practice, this is very expensive and that's why most often the assessments of the net impact are applied. Most of the governments implement permanent monitoring and control over the implementation of programs. Very little, even into the world practice, are the comparative analyses of benefits and expenditures, although namely such a kind of assessment proves the economic effectiveness of spent financial resources under employment programs (Georgiev, 2017d).

The effectiveness of every one program is generally measured by the implementation of its goals. A program has efficiency when in its implementation a significant part of the target group is covered. On the next place, the direct impact of the active policies on employment and level of incomes is of great interest. For the evaluations of the net impact on employment it is necessary to find out what is the percentage of the program participants succeeded to find job following finishing their participation and how many would not succeed if they weren't included into the program (Terziev, 2014a). The net impact on the payment is measured as a relative share of program participants which after the end report higher incomes than before participation in the program. That way, the increase in incomes is explained by the participation into the program.

For the final measurement of the effectiveness it is necessary to compare the net impacts on employment and level of incomes with direct and indirect expenses made during the program implementation. It is also possible to assess non-monetary effects, often called just social. In order an active program to be of full effectiveness, on the macro level it is necessary the side effects to be subtracted by the net impact thus finding the real net effect or the real significance of the program as a means of decrease in unemployment and increase in new-opened places of work. The side effects could be (Georgiev, 2017d):

- Dead weight effect: the results got by the participation into the program would arise without it as well. For example, when an unemployed person is employed under a program of subsidized employment, but the same person would get the same job without the program, the effect of dead weight loss would be noticed;
- Effect of substitution: that effect emerges in the cases when an unemployed person is employed in a program of subsidized employment and gets a job which would be given to another person non-participating in the program, the net effect is null;
- Effect of shift: this side effect is noticed in regard to the production process when an organization using subsidized employment replaces on the market other organizations which do not use preferences under the program of subsidized employment.

The importance of juxtaposing of expenditures to realized incomes and benefits from every one program could be illustrated by the following example. If a program of qualification and re-qualification of unemployed persons and the intermediary services give one and the same quantitative contribution (net effect) to increase of employment, but the resources spent in qualification and re-qualification are twice higher than those of intermediary services, the first program would be twice less economically effective than the second one (Georgiev, 2017d).

Discussing the situation on the labor market in the country in connection to the overall economic conditions, the following trends should be mentioned in recent decades of transition to market economy and processes and attempts of establishment a new social system: stagnant labor demand, qualitative disbalance between labor demand and supply, high and lasting unemployment and significant levels of poverty, problems in labor integration of unemployed persons from the risky (vulnerable) groups because of their low competitiveness on the labor market and low flexibility in the changing economic environment (Georgiev, 2017d). The concentration of unemployed persons from certain risky groups in certain regions and settlements creates additional prerequisites for the high level of unemployment and as a consequence – emerging social tension.

Assessments of the impacts from the implementation of active measures on the labor market in the country, and particularly National action plan on employment, show that there are many weaknesses in both planning and implementation (Terziev, 2002; Terziev, 2005). The achievements in the last decade are accompanied by a number of problems in procedures, planning, lack of communication, etc. (Georgiev, 2017d).

The results show more pessimistic and negative than optimistic and positive attitudes and expectations. They support the conclusions that economic growth for now is not transformed into some concrete improvements in everyday life and in the material status of the people which is the case in its greatest depth for the poorest people in the community (Terziev, 2013e).

The analyses of previously existing and implemented programs of temporary employment show the relatively low effectiveness which is easily to be proved by the kept level of unemployment during and after the end of the programs. Such programs are characterized by the following more important peculiarities (Terziev, 2013i):

- Employment is provided only for a certain period of time and after that the hired unemployed persons are again without jobs and register in labor offices;

- Comparatively identical selection of activities is offered, usually unattractive and non-qualified connected to cleaning, planting, afforestation, communal infrastructure, etc. which do not contribute to acquisition of new and specific professional skills;
- Acquisition of professional qualification is not offered nor through practicing qualified activities, neither through participation in courses of professional qualification;
- Negative attitude of participating employers who isolate the most risky groups in the selection processes.

Along with negative social consequences (some of which will be commented later) the practice of "social support" instead of "labor employment" creates also economic problems as far as it leads to irrational, economically ineffective and non-perspective re-distributions of incomes from working to unemployed and socially vulnerable who could work and realized economic benefits not only for themselves but also for the state in different forms (Georgiev, 2017d).

In conjunction with the rest of the changes in economic system and social structure of the country, the transition processes lead to significant impoverishment of a big part of the population. A common conviction is that the unemployed persons from different risky groups are among the most influenced and one of the main reasons for that is the labor isolation and subsequent social marginalization (Terziev, 2014a). The motivation to get out of the poverty has many dimensions, incl. how the citizens see the trends in economic development, how they estimate their own position on the background of the overall development of the country and in comparison to the way of life of the rest. The way out of the poverty is not a problem of the society only but also a question of personal position and wish for a change. The search of some contact points between what the society wants to achieve through the National program „From social support to employment" and to what extent socially supported poor want to change their economic status and are ready for the corresponding efforts is a matter of investigation of the success of the program. Namely socially supported unemployed persons' way of assessments of their own situations, their vision for perspectives in economic development and about their personal perspectives are the initial point in determination their readiness to participate in the program (Georgiev, 2017d):

- In making assessments of the studied program there are four major moments:
- First, the program offers full employment per day and weak;
- Second, the program offers employment in certain activities;
- Third, the program offers employment in conditions of fixed payments;
- Fourth, the program envisages sanctions for those who have refused participation.

The effectiveness of the implemented programs till now is doubtful considering the level of unemployment during and after the corresponding program's end which is kept. The organized and implemented temporary employment programs are characterized by the following more important peculiarities (Georgiev, 2017d):

- Employment is provided only for a certain period of time and after that the hired unemployed persons remain again without a job and register in the labor offices;
- Relatively identical composition of unattractive and non-qualified activities is offered which are connected to cleaning, planting and afforestation, communal infrastructure, etc. Those do not contribute to the acquisition of new and specific professional skills;

- Professional qualification acquisition is not offered by practicing qualified activities neither by participation in vocational training courses giving professional qualification;
- Negative attitude of the participating employers who isolate some risky groups during the selection among the unemployed persons.

The same characteristics are relatively repeated regarding the National program "From social support to employment" having been the main program implemented on the Bulgarian labor market since the years of transition to a market economy.

The economic effect of the active policy could be sought in several directions. On the individual level, for an unemployed person the economic effect would comprise of increased level of incomes as a result of finding job after participation in an active policy. On the level of the National employment agency, the economic effect could be measured by the saved resources from compensations for unemployment in cases of ceasing payments because the unemployed person has found a job. For the government the incomes are as saved money of compensations for unemployment and increased incomes in the state budget (National insurance institute) which the unemployed person and the employer have to pay from the moment of starting the job. For society as a whole, the economic effect is in the increased level of incomes and quality of life (Georgiev, 2017d).

7. CONCLUSION

The modern application of the programming as a general principle of management, is associated with preliminary planned future actions and activities aimed at achieving a certain goal with certain means, in accordance with the challenges of the dynamic changes, resulting from the changes in the social environment based on alternativeness of the decisions and the optimal choice, contributing to the effective management. The concretization of the management objectives achieved through the social program as a structured dynamic image and a way of action for coordinated interaction between the bodies of power allows the solution of important social problems, in accordance with the specific conditions, changing circumstances and stated public interests (Terziev & Georgiev, 2017).

The development and the achieved efficiency is perceived as a multi-layered expedient process, covering identification, analysis and operational fulfillment of the established social needs on the one hand, and as an opportunity to consolidate the efforts of the institutionally stated publicly significant subjects, on the other. The established conditions and the critical analysis place the focus of attention on social programming and specifically determine the finding of a relevant methodology for the engagement of any social agenda with a concrete result perceived as a success and finding a way to effectively control and measure every success. The creation of an objective assessment of this specific efficiency challenges the science of management to turn every established social program regarded as "good practice" into a standard for efficient work.

The analysis on the nature of the social policy confirm that human resources in their purposeful activity achieve goals, influencing the other resources and other factors of the social environment transforming them into human capital. The development of this process gives the opportunity this specific mechanism of change to be interpreted as a social system with high public activity, which predetermines the improvement of public relations. Within their structure, creativity stands out, presenting the role of the individual, reproducing a certain social experience for enriching the social relations and making an application for participation in the labor process (Terziev & Georgiev, 2017).

REFERENCES

Arabska, E. (2016b). Challenges of building functioning labor market: employability and lifelong learning. *XI International scientific conference „Innovations in technology and education"*, 87-108.

Arabska, E. (2016c). Competence-based training of staff and opportunities of life-long learning. *First international scientific conference "Human resources, leadership and organizational management", 1*, 131-156.

Arabska, E. (2016c). Active Social Policies - Insights in Developing a Functioning Labor Market. *Balkan and Near Eastern Journal of Social Sciences, 2*(3), 47–63.

Arabska, E. (2016d). Bulgarian Experience in Improving Effectiveness of Activities in Public Employment Services. *Balkan and Near Eastern Journal of Social Sciences, BNEJSS, 2*(2), 76–94.

Arabska, E. (2016e). Challenges in social policies implementation and effective impact on labour market. *Proceedings of the Annual university scientific conference*, 431-448.

Arabska, E. (2016f). Problems of Employment and Unemployment in Bulgaria: Is Sustainable Development Possible? *Balkan and Near Eastern Journal of Social Sciences, BNEJSS, 2*(1), 6–19.

Georgiev, M. (2017d). Impacts of active social programs on labor market. *// International Scientific Journal Innovation Science*. http://www.assam.com/katalog115.php/

Kamenov, K., & Asenow, A. (2000). *Man, teams, leaders.* Publishing house "Luren".

Koceva, M., Terziev, V., & Andreeva, Z. (2003b). Problems in assessment of the active policies on the labor market. *Fifth National conference "Employment services and the European labor market"*.

Shopov, D., & Atanasova, M. (2003a). Human resources management. *Trakia*.

Terziev, V. (2002). National program „From social support to employment. *The Labor Lawyer, 2002*(11), 38–41.

Terziev, V. (2003). Noviyat sotsialen model, kato efektivna vazmozhnost za realizirane na aktivnata politika na pazara na truda v Balgariya. *Natsionalna nauchno-prakticheska konferentsiya „Gavkavata zaetost i problemi na neynata regulatsiya"*.

Terziev, V. (2005). A common analysis of the impact of the National program "From social support to employment" on the national labor market. *UNITECH'05*, 75-80.

Terziev, V. (2012). Social technology as a method for management of the social processes. *International Conference "Trends in economics and management for the 21st century"*, 79-80.

Terziev, V. (2012a). The active model of a social programme and its strategic advantage. *International Conference "Trends in economics and management for the 21st century"*, 77-78.

Terziev, V. (2012c). Kriterii i pokazateli za sotsialna efektivnost. *Mezhdunarodna nauchna konferentsiya*.

Terziev, V. (2013). The active model of a social programme and its strategic advantage. *The 1st AARESOC International Conference On Business and Management*.

Terziev, V. (2013a). Social technology as a method for management of the social processes. *International Conference on Business and Economy (ICBE) Interdisciplinary studies on a new economy*, 258-265. 10.2139srn.3177801

Terziev, V. (2013b). The active model of a social programme and its strategic advantage. *International Scientific Conference: Management Horizons in Changing Economic Environment & Visions and Challenges*, 917-932.

Terziev, V. (2013c). The active model of a social programme and its strategic advantage. // Spisanie za nauka "Novo znanie".

Terziev, V. (2013d). Social technology as a method for management of the social processes, VI *Mezhdunarodnaya nauchnaya konferentsiya "Innovatsii v tekhnologiyakh i obrazovanii" (KuzGTU).*

Terziev, V. (2013f). *Programni metodi za regulirane na pazara na truda.* Natsionalen voenen universitet "Vasil Levski".

Terziev, V. (2013g). *Chuzhd opit za regulirane na sotsialnoto razvitie.* Natsionalen voenen universitet "Vasil Levski".

Terziev, V. (2013h). Politika v oblastta na zaetostta i bezrabotitsata v Balgariya v perioda na prehod kam pazarno stopanstvo. *Mezhdunarodna nauchna konferentsiya UNITEH, Gabrovo.*

Terziev, V. (2013i). *Politika v oblastta na zaetostta i bezrabotitsata v Balgariya- tseli i zadachi.* Mezhdunarodna nauchna konferentsiya UNITEH.

Terziev, V. (2013j). Osobenosti na trudovite otnosheniya v Balgariya v perioda na prehod ot planovo stopanstvo kam pazarna ikonomika. Mezhdunarodna nauchna konferentsiya "Iztochnoevropeyskiyat prehod i sotsialno-ikonomicheskoto razsloyavane".

Terziev, V. (2013k). Faktori, vliyaeshti varhu ravnovesieto i efektivnostta na fuktsioniraneto na pazara na truda v usloviyata na prehod. Mezhdunarodna nauchna konferentsiya, Kolezh po ikonomika i administratsiya.

Terziev, V. (2013l). *Impact of labor market policies on employment.* Dema press.

Terziev, V. (2014a). Impact of labor market policies on employment. New Knowledge Journal of science, 3(3).

Terziev, V. (2014b). Sotsialnoto programirane v sistemata na sotsialnite kategorii. *VII Mezhdunarodnaya nauchnaya konferentsiya "Innovatsii v tehnologiyah i obrazovanii" (KuzGTU).*

Terziev, V. (2014c). Teoretichni osnovi za regulirane na pazara na truda. *VII Mezhdunarodnaya nauchnaya konferentsiya "Innovatsii v tehnologiyah i obrazovanii" (KuzGTU).*

Terziev, V. (2015). *Impact of active social policies and programs in the period of active economic transformations in Bulgaria. In East West.* Association for Advances Studies and Higher Education GmbH.

Terziev, V. (2015a). Social programming in the system of sociological categories concerning market economy and labor market development in transition economy. Proceedings of "Culture, spirituality, society", 100-123.

Terziev, V. (2015d). An active model of a social program and its strategic advantage. Proceedings of "Value system of contemporary society", 113-131.

Terziev, V. (2015e). Social policy and labor market development in Bulgarian transition period. Proceedings of "Priority scirntific directions: from theory to practice", 139-154.

Terziev, V. (2015f). Social policy development in the Republic of Bulgaria during the transition period to a market economy. Scientific works "A new look" – International scientific papers 8, 230-265.

Terziev, V. (2015j). Criteria and indicators for social efficiency. Proceedings of "State and municipal governance in XXI century: theory, methodology and practice", 46-70.

Terziev, V. (2015k). Theoretical basis of development of labor market and social policy in the Republic of Bulgaria. Proceedings of "Science and modernity 2015", 233-251.

Terziev, V. (2015m). Methodological approach to research and evaluate main states and transitions on labor market. Konferentsiya „Problemay sovremennoy ekonomiki", TSRNS.

Terziev, V. (2015n). Flows of labor force and types of labor markets in transition economy. *Konferentsiya „Sotsialyno- ekonomicheskie nauki i gumanitarnaye issledovaniya", TSRNS.*

Terziev, V. (2020). Science as a tool for social development. *Review of Socio-Economic Perspectives, 5*(3), 117-134.

Terziev, V. (2020a). Science as a tool for social development. 18th RSEP International Economics, Finance & Business Conference – Virtual/Online 26-27 August 2020.

Terziev, V., & Arabska, E. (2014). Assessment of active social policies' impacts on labor market in the Republic of Bulgaria. *Collective monograph "Socio-economic and law bases of economic development"*. UFA.

Terziev, V., & Arabska, E. (2014e). *Assessment of active social policies' impacts on labor market in the Republic of Bulgaria. Collective monograph "Socio-economic and law basis of economy development"*. UFA-Aeterna.

Terziev, V., & Arabska, E. (2015b). Social policy and social programming: key implications concerning development of active labor market policies and employment. *Proceedings of 17th International Academic Conference*, 499-513.

Terziev, V., & Arabska, E. (2015h). Theoretical and methodological basis of social programming and social activity. Collective monograph "Socio-economic and law bases of economic development", 3-183.

Terziev, V., & Arabska, E. (2015i). *Assessment of the effectiveness of social programming* (Vol. 9). Knowledge International Journal, Scientific& Applicative Papers.

Terziev, V., & Arabska, E. (2015l). Development of social policies increasing employment opportunities on labor market in periods of transition. *2nd IBESRA Conference*. 10.2139srn.3166802

Terziev, V., & Arabska, E. (2015o). Application of new instruments to increase effectiveness of implementation of social policies on labor market in Bulgaria. *Journal of Economic Development, Environment and People, 4*(3), 26-44.

Terziev, V., & Arabska, E. (2015p). Bulgarian experience in labor market development. *18th International Academic Conference*, 710-733.

Terziev, V., & Arabska, E. (2016). Social Policy Development and Implementation: Municipal level perspectives. *HASSACC 2016 - Human and Social Sciences at the Common Conference*, 19-24.

Terziev, V., & Arabska, E. (2016a). Monitoring active policies on labor market. *18th EBES Conference.*

Terziev, V., & Georgiev, M. (2017). Active social programs development in Bulgaria: Contemporary challenges and social management instruments. *International Journal of Humanities and Social Science Invention*. www.ijhssi.org

Terziev, V., & Georgiev, M. (2017). Importance of human resources to social development. *International Journal of Management and Applied Science*, *3*(4), 37-39.

Terziev, V., & Georgiev, M. (2017a). The active model of a social programme and ITS strategic advantage. *Medical Teacher, 12*(2), 1418-1437.

Terziev, V., & Georgiev, M. (2017b). Impact of the labor market policies for ensuring employment. *International Journal of Management and Applied Science*, *3*(4), 29-36.

Terziev, V., & Georgiev, M. (2017c) Importance of human resources to social development. *International Journal of Management and Applied Science*, *3*(4), 37-39.

Terziev, V., & Mladenov, Yu. (2012b). Aktivna sotsialna programa i neynoto strategichesko preimushtestvo. *Nauchni trudove. R: Rusenski universitet „Angel Kanchev".*

Terziev, V., & Stanchev, S. (2015c). Development of active social policies in Bulgaria. *First International Scientific Conference "Sustainability Challenges in Modern Organizations - Knowledge & Innovation in Management & Operation"*, 63-79.

Terziev, V., & Stanchev, S. (2015g). Challenges to labor market development in Bulgaria. *First International Scientific Conference "Sustainability Challenges in Modern Organizations - Knowledge & Innovation in Management & Operation"*, 41-62.

Zahariev, E., & Arabska, E. (2014d). Eclectic concepts for distribution and popularization of good management practices. *VII International scientific conference „Innovations in technology and education" - Belovo*, 149-153.

Chapter 16
Innovation Development of Industrial Business Organizations

Venelin Krastev Terziev
https://orcid.org/0000-0003-1115-8877
Scientific Journal Society and Health, Bulgaria

ABSTRACT

The study presents the mechanisms influencing the development of innovations in industrial business organizations in the Republic of Belarus, emphasizing the stimulation of the innovative development of organizations from the real sector of the economy, research, and education sector. The innovation policy plays an important role in the development of country`s competitiveness, creating favourable conditions for the increase of financial potential, development of intellectual resources, modernization of scientific and innovation infrastructure. Some basic economic theories, such as the cluster theory, network theory, and integration theory describe the process of increasing the efficiency of an enterprise through collaborative partnership by combining functional advantages of each partner. These theories focus on achieving synergy in the form of developed and put into practice innovative product due to shared use of resource potential of the members of such associations.

1. INTRODUCTION

In the contemporary conditions of functioning of industrial business organizations the stimulation of innovation activities is defined as the main priority for increasing competitiveness. The study proposes a model of functioning of organizations aimed at innovation development – a cooperative resource model – with functional blocks and expected results from each member of the cooperation scheme (Terziev & Klimuk, 2021).

This study analyzes the efficiency of innovative activity across countries and industries. An interpretation was offered of the concept «model of innovation development». Tools for the quantitative assessment of level of innovative development of countries and formation of the vector of economic development

DOI: 10.4018/979-8-3693-0400-6.ch016

based on indicators grouped under the following three components were developed: labor, productivity, and cost. This study also investigates the structure of domestic expenditure on innovation in the main sectors of investment (by country). Based on the testing of the developed tools, recommendations for the innovative development of the country are offered (Terziev & Klimuk, 2021a).

The study presents the mechanisms influencing the development of innovations in industrial business organizations in the Republic of Belarus, emphasizing the stimulation of the innovative development of organizations from the real sector of the economy, research and education sector The innovation policy plays an important role in the development of country`s competitiveness, creating favourable conditions for the increase of financial potential, development of intellectual resources, modernization of scientific and innovation infrastructure (Terziev & Klimuk, 2021b).

Some basic economic theories, such as the cluster theory, network theory and integration theory describe the process of increasing the efficiency of an enterprise through collaborative partnership by combining functional advantages of each partner. These theories focus on achieving synergy in the form of developed and put into practice innovative product due to shared use of resource potential of the members of such associations (Terziev & Klimuk, 2021c).

This work contains an overview of national and foreign authors working in the field of innovation ecosystems management. It presents components of the model of innovation ecosystem management, a set of compulsory elements of the model, the basic principles and functional components of the model (Terziev & Klimuk, 2021d).

This study also discusses and analyzes the financing process of innovative scientific processes that take place in parallel with innovation processes. This process is pre-emulsive as an element of the state policy under way in this area. The structure of the sources of financing of these processes in the Republic of Belarus, as well as the expenditure from the Republican budget in this direction has been analysed in details. The main place is the allocated financial resources for fundamental and applied research, as well as those related to the financing of scientific and technical programs and the development of the material and technical base (Terziev & Klimuk, 2021e; 2021f; 2021g).

2. METHODOLOGICAL CONCEPTS FOR MODERNIZATION OF INDUSTRIAL ENTERPRISES IN THE CONCEPT OF POSTINDUSTRIAL DEVELOPMENT

The modern era of rapid development of information technologies, automated systems, creative methods, and new types of products, sets tough conditions for ensuring market competitiveness. These conditions, which include originality, economy, standards, environmental friendliness, mobility and a number of others, dictate the urgent need for rapid adaptation to market metamorphoses, manifested in the activation of innovative activity on the principle of "being in the lead" (with an emphasis on the indicator of the quality of the result, and not a quantitative basis). Thus, innovations are the dominant source of socio-economic growth of a country, creating a platform that forces technical and technological excellence, economic and environmental benefits, and social security (Terziev & Klimuk, 2021a).

On the one hand, a country's total aspiration for innovation determines the potential for improving the quality of life, the diversification of economic activity, and ensures the barrier-free functioning of the state. However, on the other hand, there may be an increase in incidents of unfair competition, which can result in a significant "overflow" of capital from "underdeveloped" countries to the innovative development of "developed" countries, which will ensure an already huge economic development gap between individual countries (Figure 1) (Averina, 2006; Goldyakova, 2006a).

In Belarus, a high share of the innovative development of the country is concentrated on the acquisition of machinery and equipment (53%), which can be characterized by the consumption function (the consumption of existing innovations, rather than their independent creation) (Indicators of innovation, 2016).

Looking at the role of innovative products and technologies of any era, it is crucial to observe a country's state of development. Moreover, the comparison of the current level of development and potential opportunities, as well as the model of innovative development of the current and projected, serve as the underlying motive of this work (Lvov, Glazyev, 1986).

Modeling issues of innovative development is given the lion's share of research, which is associated with the economic effect of using their results in practice.

Figure 1. Aggregate level of innovation activity by countries, %
Source: Notation - Collection "Indicators of innovation activity – 2018".

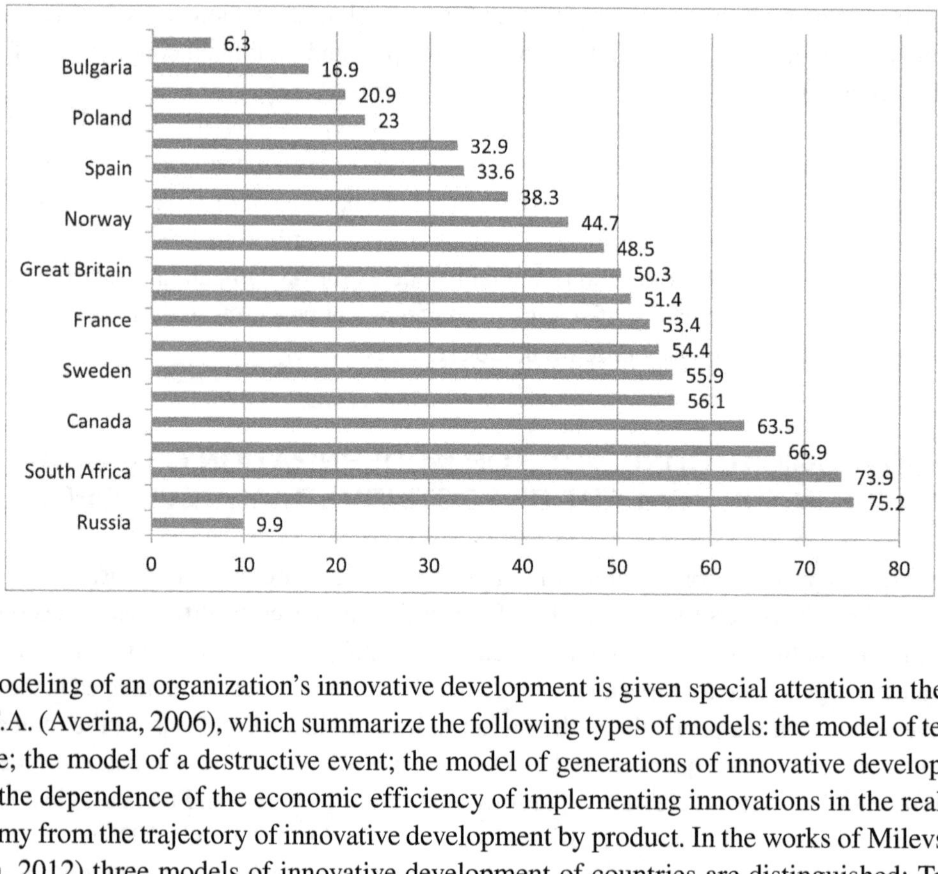

The modeling of an organization's innovative development is given special attention in the works of Averina T.A. (Averina, 2006), which summarize the following types of models: the model of technological change; the model of a destructive event; the model of generations of innovative development; the model of the dependence of the economic efficiency of implementing innovations in the real sector of the economy from the trajectory of innovative development by product. In the works of Milevskaya T.S. (Milevska, 2012) three models of innovative development of countries are distinguished: Traditional, European, Asian; all based on the life cycle of the innovation process and management structure.

The prioritization of development, the existing potential for excellence, and incentive mechanisms, explain the differentiation of the levels of innovative development of countries and possible trends in their deformation. We created a model that includes a set of tools and methods a country can use to move in a trajectory of innovation. We have proposed the following interpretation of this kind of model: "A model of innovation development is an integral vector of development based on the improvement of organizational, managerial, technical-technological, and economic processes of functioning, forming a platform of competitiveness and socio-ecological and economic security of the country" (Matveeva, Chernova & Klimuk, 2015).

Based on the methods that are used to stimulate the innovative activity of the existing technical, raw material and intellectual base of the planned positions on a global scale of economic prosperity, different types of models are singled out. The study of the works on this subject made it possible to generalize existing models on two grounds: territorial features and a set of mechanisms for the implementation of the innovation vector (Postaljuk & Gusarova, 2014).

In order to quantify the level of innovative development of countries and form the "vector of the future", the following system of relative indicators (with the aim of unifying the applicable indicators and the possibility of intercountry comparison) is proposed. The indicators are grouped according to the leading components:

- The labor component:
    - § Budget for minimum wage/wage;
    - § Proportion of population with a higher education;
    - § Proportion of those who have those who have presented their work in order to get a PhD;
    - § The proportion of researchers with a degree within the total number of researchers.
- Efficiency component:
    - § Proportion of active innovative organizations;
    - § Proportion of innovative products within total production;
    - § Proportion of exports of innovative products within the total volume of shipped products;
    - § Proportion of patents granted within the total number of applications filed;
    - § Proportion of global innovations within the country's total volume of innovative products.
- The cost component:
    - § Proportion of costs for innovation within the total volume of innovative products;
    - § Proportion of expenses for innovation activity within the total volume of investments in the country (region);
    - § Proportion of worn-out machinery and equipment.

This set of indicators will provide an opportunity to assess the level of innovation development for the current or retrospective period, and also act as a platform for the country's development strategy to improve its level of innovation (Praslov, 2007; Sampieva Tamashev, 2011; Chernov & Sadovnikov, 2015a).

One of the most important factors and conditions for the activation of innovative activity are investment funds that ensure the implementation of multi-vector functions, the development of certain tasks, as well as the approbation and implementation of innovations in practice.

The largest share in the structure of domestic costs within a country is entrepreneurship (except for Latvia, since their priority is high school), which is the lever of economic dynamics and innovative metamorphoses at the micro level. It ensures the wide-spread application of new products that have already passed the initial stage of testing (Terziev & Georgiev, 2020; Terziev, 2020a; Terziev, 2020b; Terziev, 2019b).

Mechanisms for stimulating the country's innovative development, tools for assessing its level, and prospective development trajectories all form models of innovative development, the differentiation of which can be represented in the following structure:

- Productive (each type of innovation provides high indications);
- Cloning (specialize in the development and creation of one type of innovation, not all);
- Catching up (by their own efforts, but at a slower pace, they create their own innovations).

To assess the level of innovative development, the proposed method was used to calculate and analyze, according to the algorithm described above, for the comparison of Republic of Belarus and the Russian Federation (Klimuk & Tarasova, 2019; Klimuk & Lazdins, 2019a).

As for recommendations on expanding opportunities and increasing the degree of innovative development of countries, we suggest the following:

- Strengthening of measures of material stimulation for workers in the development of the economy's innovation sector (introduction of the differentiated system of progressive awarding, expansion of programs of financing of innovative projects);
- Formation of alliance economic systems (based on vertical and horizontal integration schemes ensuring prompt delivery, quality of raw materials, real buyers);
- Development of innovative infrastructure (expansion of the number of technology parks, innovation funds, venture firms, approbation of start-up projects) (Terziev & Klimuk, 2021a).

3. MECHANISMS AFFECTING INNOVATION DEVELOPMENT OF INDUSTRIAL BUSINESS ORGANIZATIONS

Stimulation of innovation development of organizations of the real sector of the economy, research and education sector and business is determined by the need to increase country`s competitiveness in the world economy by ensuring new markets, growing demand for innovative products and additional financial flows. The successful implementation of this process, related to innovation development of organizations, is a comprehensive process of intellectual potential development, improvement of communication channels between partners (participants), search for main and alternative sources of funding for research and innovation developments (Terziev & Klimuk, 2021b).

The innovation policy plays an important role in the development of country`s competitiveness, creating favourable conditions for the increase of financial potential, development of intellectual resources, modernization of scientific and innovation infrastructure. An analysis of the level of innovation development of countries based on the main indicators of the European innovation scoreboard (2021h) indicates a high level of the Republic of Belarus compared to the average in the EU and, in particular, in the Republic of Bulgaria. These indicators include a share of employment in knowledge intensive sectors (exceeding the value of this indicator by 3,6 times and by 2,63 times compared to Bulgaria and the EU average, respectively), sale of innovations new to the market and to an enterprise (increase by 2,55 times and 1,22 times compared to Bulgaria and the EU average, respectively) (Fig. 2). Those values indicate the development of a state system for motivating organizations` innovation activity, stimulating R&D and innovation activities in the direction of intellectual potential development as the driving force of innovation development. In general, the indicators for the state funding, share of knowledge-intensive products export and share of innovative products export are at the same level in Belarus, Bulgaria and EU, which demonstrates the similar priorities for innovation policy implementation. The indicators reflecting the share of commercial funding for R&D, the share of small and medium-sized enterprises implementing internal innovation, as well as the share of participants of the joint projects are lagging behind in Belarus, which is characterised by an insufficient level of interaction between the scientific and educational organizations, the real sector of the economy, business and government authorities. To eliminate these problematic issues in the country, since 2017 an emphasis is put on the entrepreneurship development within social and economic development of Belarus, which includes the improved mechanisms for interaction between state authorities and business entities (2021i); support policies for small and medium-sized enterprises (2021j; 2021k); development of the activities of innovation infrastructure entities (2021l) and their performance.

Figure 2. Main indicators of the European innovation scoreboard in the Republic of Belarus, the Republic of Bulgaria and the European Union for 2019 (2021m)

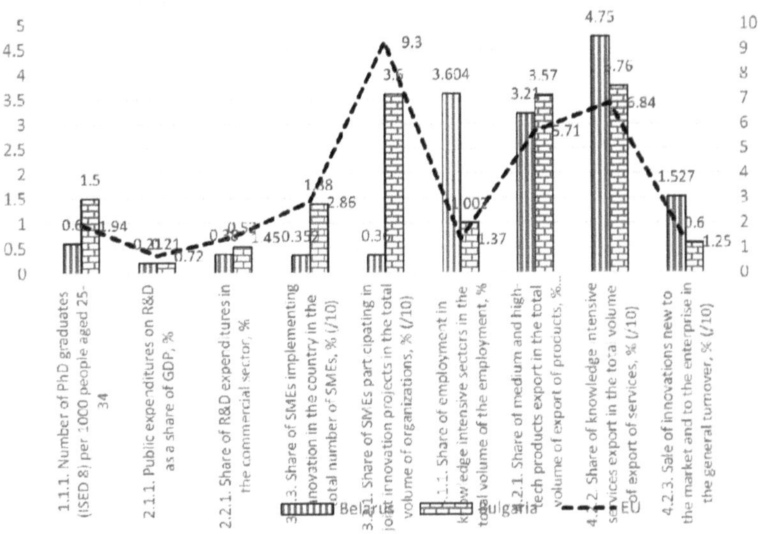

According to the Global Innovation Index reports, the Republic of Belarus ranks 64th out of 131 countries in 2020 in terms of this indicator (31,27 points, which is 1,1% more than the average), in 2019 Belarus ranked 72nd out of 129 countries (32,07 points, which is by 5,2% less than the average). For comparison, Bulgaria in 2020 ranked 37th (39,98 points, which is by 27,8% more than the average) and 2019 – 40th (40,35 points, which is by 25,8% more than the average) (Fig. 3) (2021n).

An analysis of the statistical data demonstrates a positive tendency of the global innovation index in 2020 compared to the previous years` values in the Republic of Belarus and in the Republic of Bulgaria. It should be noted that the ranking of Belarus and Bulgaria in terms of investments in innovation has deteriorated. Despite that, it is important to mention that the analyzed countries have shown a significant increase in their ranking in terms of the return of investments on innovation (the volume of produced innovative products, works and services).

Figure 3. Ranking of the global innovation index of the Republic of Belarus and the Republic of Bulgaria for 2018-2020 respectively, ranks (2021o)

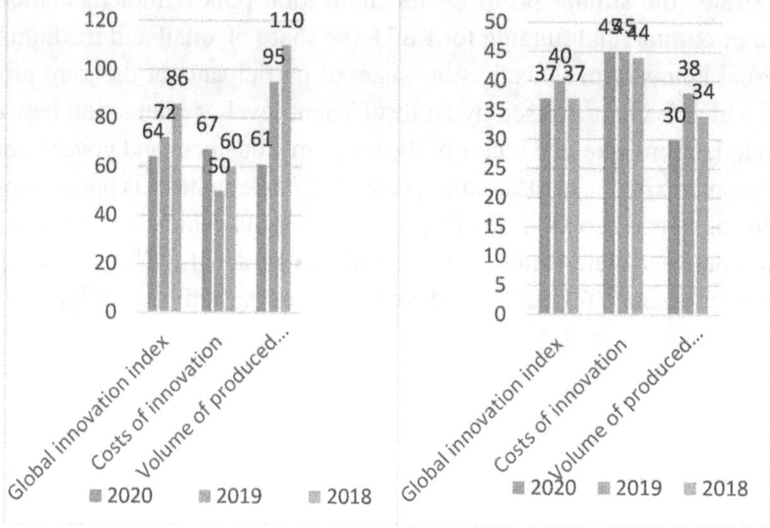

For successful implementation of innovation in organizations – creation of a finished innovative solution (product, work, service) – it is necessary to develop effective mechanisms that would make the process precise and gradual and ensure the coherence between the actions of the parties for achieving the set objectives. The mechanism of innovation development of an organization is a set of interrelated actions agreed in terms of resources (financial, intellectual, material and technological resources), deadlines of each stage, responsible contractors and partners, expected outcomes (priorities) and possible risks. Such structure of the mechanism allows considering performance (expected economic and social effect) and resource costs (needed current costs, investment resources) (Terziev & Klimuk, 2021b).

Apart from this, the mechanism acts as a universal approach to increasing innovation performance. For more specific implementation of mechanisms of innovation development in individual organizations (regions) it is necessary to develop a detailed programme of actions, i.e. a road map for innovation development.

The mentioned mechanisms affecting innovation development act as a guide to action for organizations on the basis of thorough analysis of the current development state of an organization (region, country) and the retrospective analysis of its activity. The competitive advantages and bottlenecks (drawbacks) in activities identified on the basis of these analytical procedures determine the choice and implementation of appropriate tools within the framework of mechanisms affecting innovation development.

For a clear and comprehensive implementation of innovation development mechanisms it is appropriate to use 'road maps' of innovation development created on the basis of chosen priorities (planned outcomes) and means for their achievement within financial and legal, information and knowledge-based and organizational and managerial mechanisms (Figure 4).

It would be effective to use this structure as a foundation for the development of a 'road map' for innovation development of organizations (regions, a country). It is developed on the basis of:

- A set of selected tools within each of the discussed mechanisms;

- A set of measures aimed at successfully implementing them in the activities of an organization (region, country);
- Factors and conditions necessary for a successful implementation of the planned activities;
- A schedule for each tool, activity;
- A group of contractors and interrelated partners that ensure the implementation of the activities;
- Expected results based on the success of implementation of each activity and, necessarily, a system of quantitative measures (for assessing the degree of achievement of planned results);
- Considered risks, their possible consequences and measures for their prevention (elimination, reduction);
- Means of verification (to recognize the accomplishments and compare them with the expectations);
- A set of corrective actions needed for immediate regulation of innovation processes, managerial and organizational actions in compliance with the developed plan.

Figure 4. Basic "road map" structure of innovation development of industrial business organizations

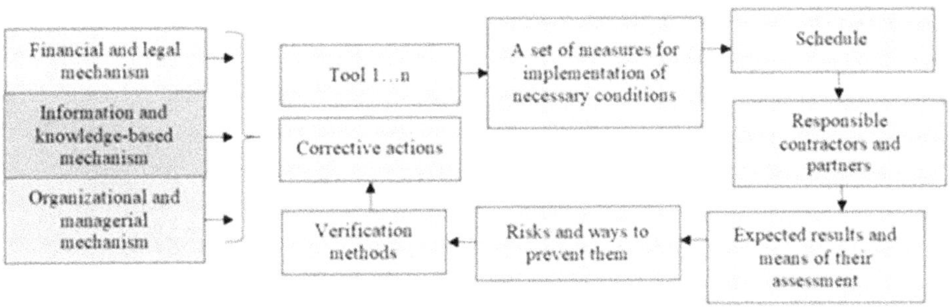

The developed mechanisms for innovation development of organizations are focused on the stimulation of innovation, improvement of its performance and the return of invested resources. The described mechanisms with the help of specific tools should ensure dynamic impact on the overall innovation development level (Figure 5).

To conclude, in the contemporary conditions an active search for organizations in the national and international markets of products (works, services) and innovations and the development of financial potential should be performed with the help of effective mechanisms of innovation development. These mechanisms would ensure a systematic, interconnected and gradual implementation of innovation policies by organizations in particular and regional and national innovation policies in general to increase competitiveness on a global level. The process of innovation development of organizations includes the following components: development of financial potential, adaptation and flexibility of legal system for stimulating innovation, research and innovation infrastructure, intellectual potential, active implementation of information and communication technologies in the main and additional activities. The mechanisms provide for tools that ensure the implementation of specific objectives, while providing the ways of their implementation, a team of contractors and partners, expected outcomes and possible risks. According to the set priorities, assessment of the current (and retrospective) state of innovation development, an organization develops a specific action plan in the form of a "road map" on the basis of tools, forms and ways of implementing each mechanism of the innovation development system. The implementation of each stage of the 'road map' for innovation development allows achieving the planned objectives by ensuring the stimulation of innovation activities of organizations within the cooperative resource model and strengthening international competitiveness (Terziev & Klimuk, 2021b).

Figure 5. Results of implementation of mechanisms for innovation development of organizations

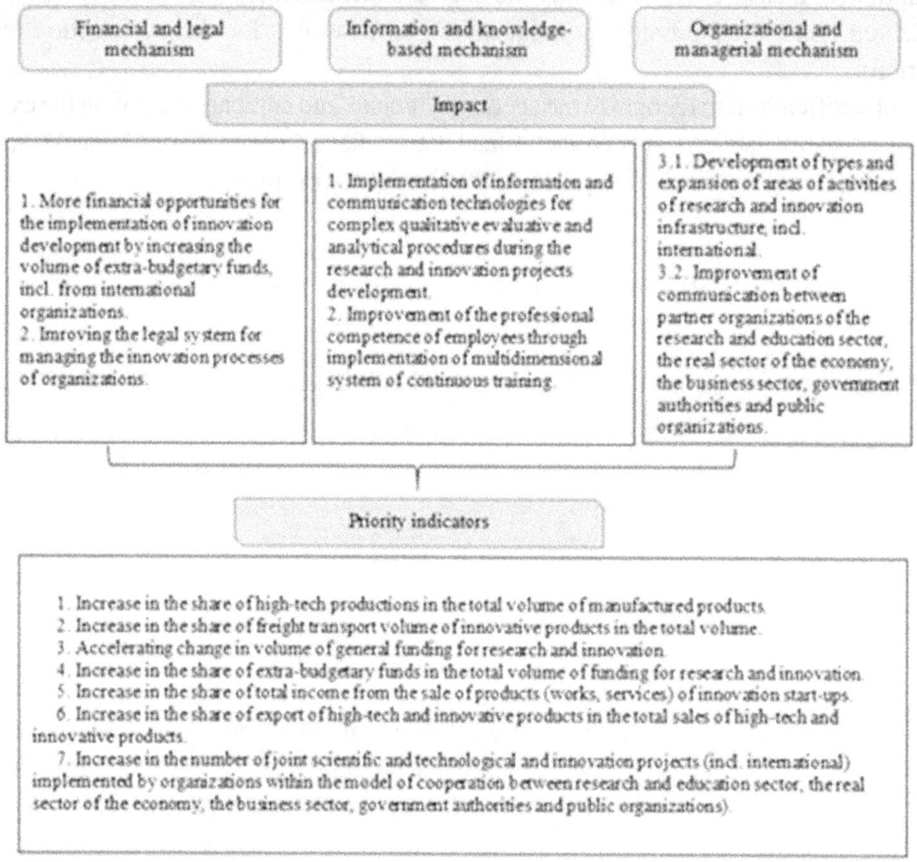

3. FACTORS AND MECHANISMS AFFECTING INNOVATION DEVELOPMENT OF INDUSTRIAL BUSINESS ORGANIZATIONS: COOPERATIVE RESOURCE MODEL

The level of competitiveness of global and national social and economic systems is determined, first of all, by the pace and level of innovation implementation by organizations of different industries. The development of information and communication technologies, the current epidemiological situation, the changed customer preferences and priorities determine the need to create new forms and implement new mechanisms of innovation development and stimulate research and development. By creating more science-based products it will be possible to develop a number of competitive advantages for the country (region, enterprise), providing an opportunity to reduce production costs, create a unique product and increase partner networks (incl. international) (Terziev & Klimuk, 2021).

A percentage of scientific activity in the GDP of the Republic of Belarus from 2015 to 2019 has increased from 0,5 to 0,59% respectively (2020c), which indicates the strengthening role of science in the state. For comparison, the percentage of scientific activity in the Republic of Bulgaria during the first 10 years after accession to the EU had been steadily decreasing (from 0,29% to 0,2% of GDP), which is 3 times less than the EU average (0,64%). The main objective of the National Development Programme of Bulgaria until 2030 is to create a high-quality research infrastructure and modernize the research ecosystem, stimulate the development and implementation of innovation in certain sectors of the economy. At the same time, cooperation between the industry and research centres, development of intellectual potential of specialists and researchers, commercialization of applied research developments should be of utmost importance (2019c).

The industrial sector is a leading contributor to the gross domestic product (25,7% in the Republic of Belarus in 2019) (2020d). A negative fact is that the freight transport volume of innovative products by industrial organizations decreased by 5,5% in 2019 compared to previous year`s value (until 2019 the average annual growth rate was 28,7%). Some of the reasons of such a transition include considerable investments in the development of material and technological infrastructure, financial incentives for labour force, changed customer preferences, etc. This is confirmed by an analysis of the industry cost structure of the Republic of Belarus (Figure 6) (2020d) that determines the development of the strategy for implementing modern high-performance equipment and new technologies, the development of intellectual potential of labour force: the share of material costs decreased to 2,3% in 2019, the share of labour costs increased to 3,8% and the share of depreciation also increased to 24,5% (2020d).

It is noteworthy that in 2019 the share of freight transport volume of innovative products in the total industrial production decreased by 10,8%. However, this indicator for small organizations increased: from 0,9% in 2018 to 1,4% in 2019, which is due to the state policy to support the development of small and medium-sized enterprises (state subsidies (to the unemployed, those willing to start their own business, incl. in the industrial sector; an annual plan for the implementation of start-up events by the country`s organizations).

The share of innovative industry organizations also increased by 1,2% (24,5% in 2019) compared to the previous year`s value, which again indicates the increased role of the state in the implementation of innovation policy. Innovation enables the growth of the competitiveness of the national economy by developing a new and unique product.

In the current conditions of development of society each country strives to stimulate the development of its innovation potential, therefore, competition in this area is growing, the process of creating an innovative product is optimized, since except for the novelty the manufacturers have to consider time and durability factors ("viability" of the product – to what extent the innovation will be useful for the industry and the country considering the duration of its impact) (Terziev & Klimuk, 2021).

Consequently, the innovation process should be complex, multifunctional, creative, time and resource efficient. Enterprises, as initiators and developers of innovation, cannot perform this task by themselves anymore, which includes the growth of competitiveness through innovation development. Enterprises, as representatives of the real sector of the economy, are one of the components of a high quality and fully-fledged process – the implementation of innovation. Cooperation of partners, that are interested in creating an innovation and receiving economic and, of course, social effect from its implementation, would be very effective in developing an innovative product. That is why, for high-quality innovations it is vital to engage as many interested parties as possible, taking into account preferences of end users – beneficiaries, the predicted level of science and technology development, the pace and vectors of the country`s social and economic development.

Figure 6. Industry cost structure in the Republic of Belarus in 2015-2019

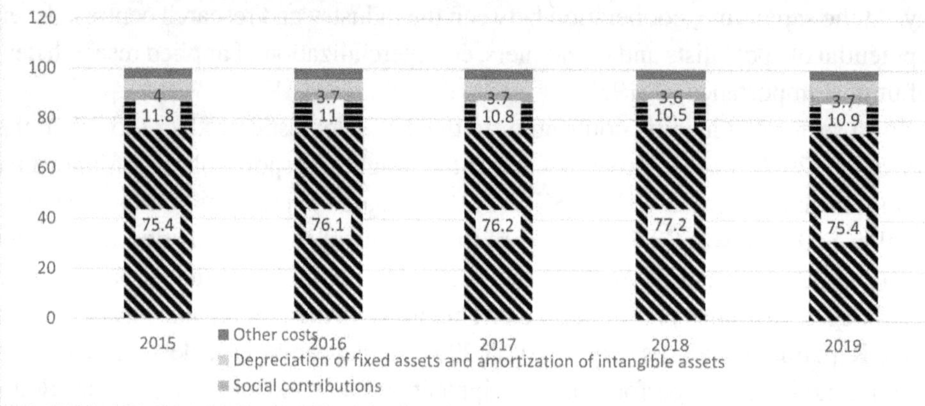

The most important resource that stimulates innovation is intellectual resource, the development of which is determined by the effective organization and functioning of the education and research sectors. Innovations are developed on the basis of new technologies, new methods, by creating new or improving the existing products (works, services), which is possible only through high-quality research (not necessarily and not always scientific). The research process itself involves a cooperative work of specialists based on the analysis of information (past, current, planned/predicted), the identification of strengths and weaknesses of the studied object (process), the search for opportunities for potential development and the efficiency of the used resources (Figure 7).

Considering the above-mentioned facts it should be noted that according to art. 19 of the Law of the Republic of Belarus "On State Innovation Policy and Innovation Activities in the Republic of Belarus" (2016a), "innovation activities" may include the following:

- Performing research and development necessary to transform a novelty into innovation;
- Developing a new or improved product, new or improved technology, creating new services and organizational and technical solutions;
- Preparing and developing the production of new or improved products, developing the production of new or improved technologies, preparing the implementation of new organizational and technical solutions;
- Producing new or improved products, producing products based on new or improved technology;
- Introducing for public or personal use new or improved products, new or improved technologies, new services and new organizational and technical solutions;
- Other activities aimed at transforming a novelty into innovation" (2016a).

Figure 7. Organizational chart of the interrelation between research and innovation

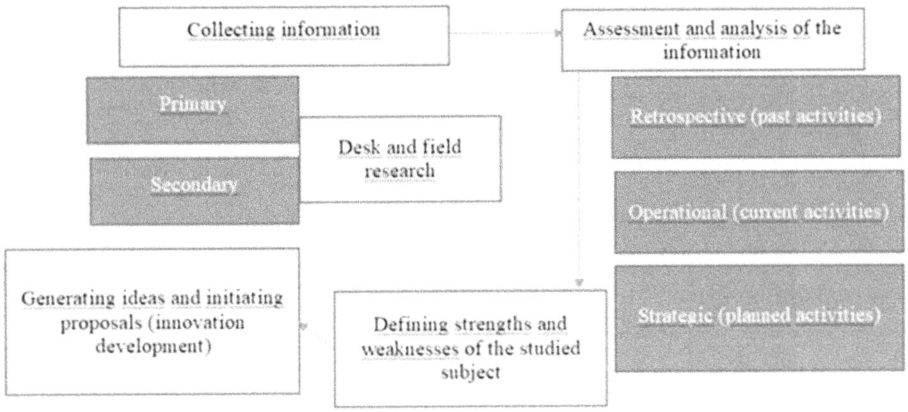

By conducting a consistent and comprehensive study it is possible to improve the process (processes), create a new product (work, service), i.e. to implement innovation. The success of this process in one enterprise, a region or country depends on a number of factors that include the development of intellectual potential, scientific and innovation infrastructure, the degree of cooperation between developers, clients, intermediaries (partners), the level of research and others. The success of the innovation is determined by the quality and effectiveness of cooperation in the process of innovation product (work, service) development between all interested parties, i.e. the real sector of the economy, the business entities, the government sector, public organization and research and education sectors. Thus, the process of innovation is determined by the usefulness of cooperation between these sectors in order to achieve a synergistic effect focused on solving social and economic issues.

We define this model of cooperation as a cooperative resource model, which is an effective mechanism of interaction between these sectors based on mutually beneficial use of the resources of partners (members of the association).

The "cooperative resource model" represents a system of interrelated and complementary partners – organizations of the real sector of the economy, research and education sector, the business entities, the government sector, public organization, working permanently or temporarily in order to achieve a synergistic social and economic effect in solving the set tasks (a complex of tasks) on the basis of mutual use of the existing and potential resources.

One of the main problematic aspects of stimulating and increasing performance (both economic and social) of innovation activity of industrial business is the degree of cooperation between economic entities of the real sector of the economy and education and scientific organizations (research and education sector), representatives of the business community (business sector), state authorities (government sector) and public organizations (consumer sector). Important –developing an innovative product (work, service) based on cooperative and purposeful work done simultaneously or sequentially by each partner-sector (Figure 8) (Terziev & Klimuk, 2021).

In order to define the main factors that have impact on the innovation activity and the increase of its effectiveness, respectively, the author has developed a survey "Factors affecting innovation development of industrial business organizations" with the help of Google Forms and which is published online (2021r) (Table 1).

Figure 8. Functional blocks and expected outcomes of organizations working within the cooperative resource model

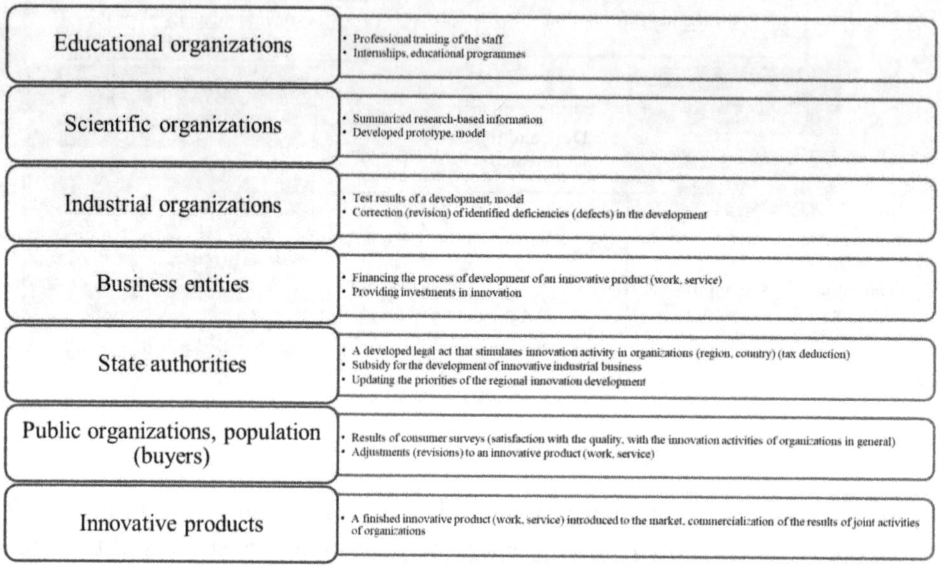

Table 1. Results of the survey "Factors affecting innovation development of industrial business organizations" (31/12/2020 – 20/01/2021)

No.	Factors	Evaluation Criteria, Points					Points, Total	Rank	Weight
		1	2	3	4	5			
1	Professional training of the staff, additional training, other forms of intellectual potential development		1	5	15	32	237	2	0,146
2	State and development of the material and technological infrastructure			1	18	34	245	1	0,151
3	Degree of cooperation between developers, users (clients, buyers), intermediaries, partners in the creation of an innovative product			6	18	29	235	3	0,145
4	Solutions to the problems with the help of scientific approach			5	22	26	233	4	0,144
5	Various government measures aimed at stimulating the innovation activity of organizations (funding, tax preferences, etc.)			7	20	26	231	5	0,142
6	Various financial incentives to stimulate innovation (funds, special programmes, credit resources, etc.)		1	7	18	27	230	6	0,142
7	Administrative procedures optimization (project approval process, reporting the results, etc.)		1	15	20	17	212	7	0,131

The greatest impact on the success of the innovation development, according to the respondents, has the state and development of material and technological infrastructure (weight coefficient = 0,151), and the least – the administrative procedures optimization (weight coefficient = 0,131) (Fig. 9).

Figure 9. Distribution of the survey results by impact on the success of industrial organization`s innovation activity within the cooperative resource model, points total

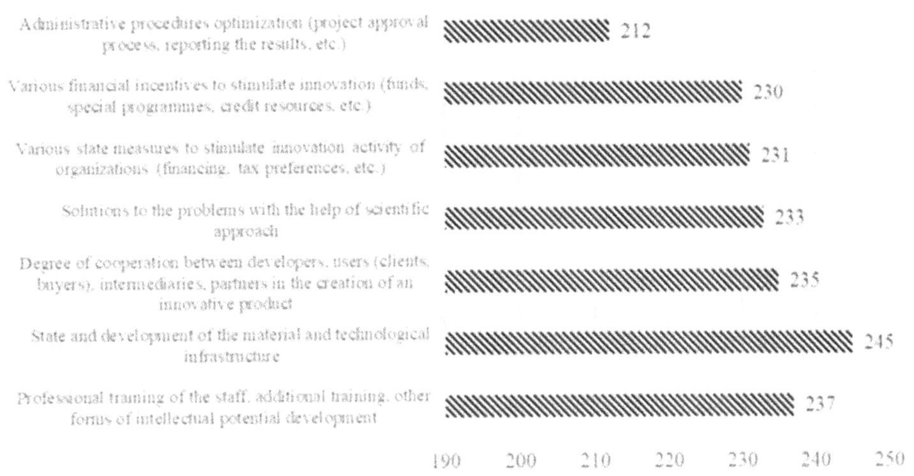

Apart from this, with the help of the survey the author obtained the respondents` opinions on defining the basic objectives for cooperation and the existing problematic aspects resulting from such cooperation between organizations within the cooperative resource model.

The analysis of the obtained survey results of representatives of industrial business organizations, representatives of the business sector, government authorities, public organizations, scientific and educational institutions, as well as from buyers of finished products (work, service) of industrial business organizations helped define the factors that have the most and least influence on the innovation success, according to the respondents, and also define the goals (motivators) of cooperation between these organizations in order to create an innovative product and define the problematic aspects. The leading motivator of cooperation between organizations is the vector of intellectual potential development (the factor "Gaining new knowledge in the process of cooperation") (Fig.10).

The results of the survey also helped define the problematic aspects that hinder the effective cooperation of the organizations in the cooperative resource model. One of the main problematic aspects include deficiency of financial resources (investments), ineffective communication between the organizations, insufficient level of national innovation infrastructure development (Figure 11).

The innovation performance of industrial business is defined as a functional relation of the performance indicator, which depends on the identified factors. As an effective indicator for assessing the performance of innovation we shall define "the share of the freight transport volume of innovative industrial products in the total volume of the production". As a factor indicator we shall define the quantitative manifestation of each factor presented in the survey with the help of Google Forms. For objectivity of the calculations and possibility of predicting the innovation development of industrial business organizations, working within cooperative resource model, each factor according to the survey results is assigned a corresponding weight coefficient (Terziev, Klimuk, 2021a; 2021f; 2021p, 2021q).

Figure 10. Distribution of the survey results by main motivators (goals) for uniting organizations of the scientific and education, real and business sectors, government sector and public organizations in the process of innovation

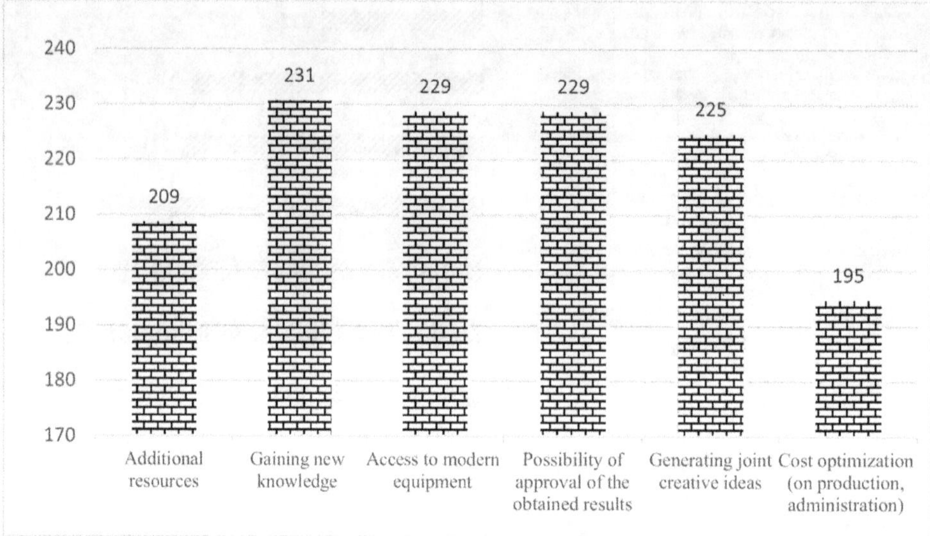

Figure 11. Distribution of the survey results by main problematic aspects that hinder the effective co-operation of the organizations

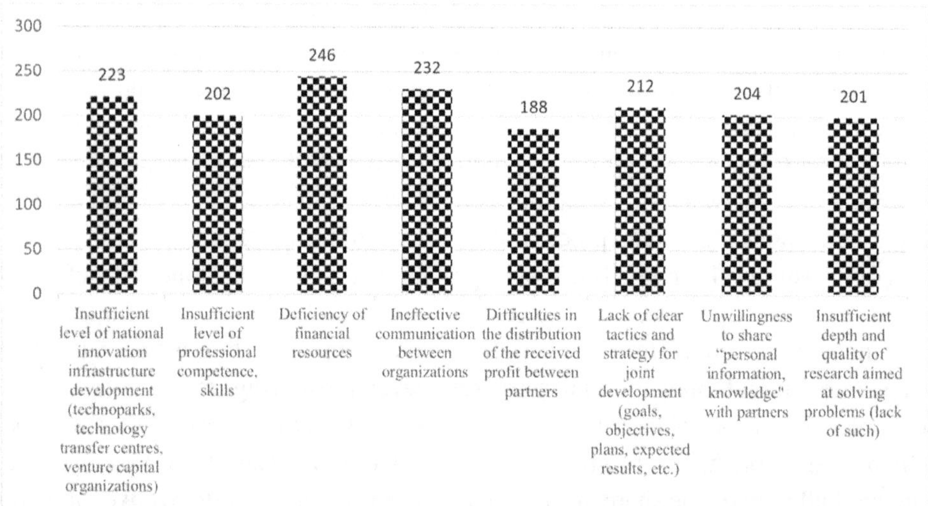

To unify the applied system of indicators and compare the cross-country results we shall present the system of these indicators on the basis of a European innovation scoreboard (Table 2) (2021s; 2021t; 2020c). This will allow applying the approach to identify weaknesses of the country`s innovation development strategy in terms of global trends and highlight priorities in international cooperation.

Table 2. System of indicators for assessing innovation development of industrial business organizations (in accordance with the European innovation scoreboard (EIS-2019))

Factor	Indicator
1. Professional training of the staff, additional training, other forms of intellectual potential development	Number of PhD graduates (ISED 8) per 1000 people aged 25-34
2. State and development of the material and technological infrastructure	Share of R&D expenditures in the commercial sector
3. Degree of cooperation between developers, users (clients, buyers), intermediaries, partners in the creation of an innovative product	Share of SMEs participating in joint innovation projects in the total volume of surveyed organizations
4. Solutions to the problems with the help of scientific approach	Share of employment in knowledge intensive sectors in the total volume of the employment
5. Various government measures aimed at stimulating the innovation activity of organizations (funding, tax preferences, etc.)	Public expenditures on R&D as a share of GDP
6. Various financial incentives to stimulate innovation (funds, special programmes, credit resources, etc.)	Share of SMEs implementing innovation in the country in the total number of SMEs
7. Administrative procedures optimization (project approval process, reporting the results, etc.)	Sale of innovations new to the market and to the enterprise in the general turnover

These indicators should be presented (listed) in a unified form based on the use of relative values (calculations of standardized coefficients) for further statistical analysis. To predict innovation development of industrial business organizations by studying the opportunities of diversification of actual and potential resources, we have analysed the statistical base in terms of the developed system of indicators for 2015-2019.

The results were obtained with the help of a powerful software programme IBM SPSS Statistics 26 (2020c), that helped write a regression equation used to develop the predictive models for innovation development of industrial business organizations in the Republic of Belarus: linear and quadratic functions. At the same time, the quadratic functions are derived from the largest correlation coefficient values (Pearson correlation coefficient) from a number of factor indicators with a statistical series of data (Table 3).

Table 3. Types of functions for predictive models for innovation development of industrial business organizations

Type of Function	Equation	R-Square	Deviation From the Actual Value of 2019
Linear	$E_{innovat} = -0{,}936 - 1{,}033*Grad_{PhD} + 7{,}5*Exp_{R\&Dpub} + 1{,}086*Sale_{innov}$	1,000	+0,002
Quadratic (correlation coefficient $Sale_{innov} = 0{,}992$)	$E_{innovat} = 27{,}638 - 2{,}342*Sale_{innov} + 0{,}105*Sale_{innov}^2$	0,986	-0,241
Quadratic (correlation coefficient $Sh_{SMEinnov} = 0{,}954$)	$E_{innovat} = -65{,}947 + 41{,}258*Sh_{SMEinnov} - 5{,}031*Sh_{SMEinnov}^2$	0,936	+0,345

Note: explanation of indicators:

$Grad_{PhD}$ – Number of PhD graduates (ISED 8) per 1000 people aged 25-34;
$Exp_{R\&Dpub}$ – Public expenditures on R&D as a share of GDP;
$Sale_{innov}$ – Sale of innovations new to the market and to the enterprise in the general turnover;
$Sh_{SMEinnov}$ – Share of SMEs implementing innovation in the country in the total number of SMEs.

Therefore, to predict the innovation development it is advisable to apply multiple linear regressions. Let us present the predicted values of the share of freight transport volume of innovative products in 2020-2022 taking into account the 5% growth rate of the factors included in the model (Figure 12).

Figure 12. Results of modelling predictive scenarios of innovation development of industrial business organizations in a cooperative resource model

Note: red line – actual values, blue line – predicted values of the share of freight transport volume of innovative products (with 5% predicted growth rate of the factors included in the model), dotted black line – predicted values of the share of freight transport volume of innovative products (considering the adjustment factors of the factors included in the model, based on the survey results)

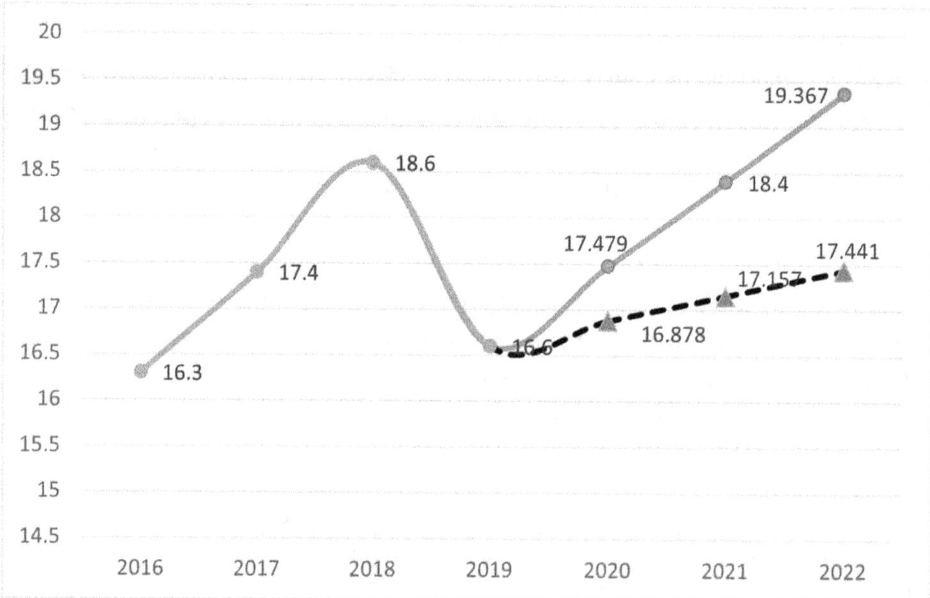

Based on the analysis of the activities of innovation infrastructure entities we believe that as an effective mechanism for stimulating innovation activity of organizations, industrial business in particular, it is necessary to create innovation alliances, based on the cooperative resource model of mutually beneficial partnerships between the science and education sector, the business sector, the real sector of the economy, the government and public organizations (Terziev & Klimuk, 2021).

4. APPROACHES TO THE APPLICATION OF THE CONCEPTS OF COOPERATIVE INTEGRATION BETWEEN ORGANIZATIONS

The term "cluster" was formulated and put forward in the 1990's by an American economist M. Porter. The author interpreted cluster as "geographically proximate group of interconnected companies" (Porter, 1998). The main criterion is the geographical proximity of partner organizations. Contemporary national science literature also contains other definitions of business cluster. For instance, a cluster is understood as "a network of complementary, territorially interconnected enterprises and organizations (incl. specialized suppliers of goods and services, as well as manufacturers and buyers) collaborating with each other, united around a research and education centre, and which is cooperating with local institutions and governing authorities with the aim of increasing the competitiveness of enterprises, regions and the national economy" (Yasheva, 2008). The aim of the cluster is to ensure effective regional development related to the growth of competitiveness, encouraging innovation in the region, eliminating of regional imbalances in the process of redistribution and reorientation of mobile capital from areas of accelerated development (cluster core) to less developed territories (Matveeva & Aguzarov, 2013; Anisova 2014a; Afonichkin 2011a; Gakashev, 2013a; Koblova, 2013b; Lavrikova, 2008a; Mingaleva, 2011a; Sergeev, 2008b; Tomashevska & Korchagina, 2010).

In general, the desire to shift the emphasis towards the territorial localization of enterprises, part of the cluster, is prevailing. These enterprises form production chains that create the final product and are concentrated around a large organization (core). This indicates the inclusion of small and medium-sized enterprises in the cluster through competitive selection (based on the selection of the most favourable, profitable conditions, quality goods and services). The main distinctive features of clusters include: concentration of production, cooperation, internal competition, and competitiveness of a cluster. The product of the cluster activity should be competitive outside the territory of the cluster itself. Its products should have a competitive advantage in the foreign market. The existence of a coordinating organization (cluster core) (Economics, 2007a; Zapariy, 2017, Prangishvili, 2000) is therefore necessary.

The performance of these enterprises is determined by the appropriateness of collaboration based on the theory of integration. Participants of such business associations strive to gain benefit due to shared resources, in other words, to obtain resources at a lower cost than in the market. This is the essence of integration.

Such forms of cooperative integration between organizations are gradually shifting the target towards the development of innovative potential, increase of the capitalization of the modernization potential of the integration structure (Chernova, 2009; Chernova & Ivanov, 2015).

It is also possible to consider the integration of enterprises as "a project, a complex of organizationally and economically separate activities", which necessitates an assessment of the effectiveness of this project both at the stage of making a decision on its implementation and at the stage of assessing the intermediate and final results obtained (Simonova, 2012a).

Analysing the existing types of networks of industrial enterprises (types of network structures according to R. Miles, Ch. Snow; network models according to R. Paturel; ways of network development according to A.L. Rvachev, E.P. Berezhkova; models of network organization of business processes according to E.P. Karlina; models of organizational networks according to A. Lamanov; models of network organizations according to O.Yu. Michurina; models of functioning of networks according to A.N. Asaul, E.G. Skumatov, G.E. Lokteva) (Mahmudova, 2010a), it should be noted that they lack the concept of innovation, which is fundamental in the modern model of society development.

Taking into account this fact, we believe it would be wise to analyse the presented classifications of network organization models with the help of such features as "process" and "resource" when creating an innovative product (manifested vertically or horizontally).

The "process" feature of the creation of a network of enterprises is based on the unification of enterprises engaged in innovation, in the process of sequentially performing each stage in the creation of innovative products: analytical stage (studying the market conditions by product groups, monitoring the dynamics of supply and demand for certain types of goods, conducting surveys, etc.), generation stage (justification of the relevance, importance of new ideas, design of innovative solutions, development of new types of products, technologies, organization of training and competitive events, etc.), production stage (design, creation of prototypes of innovative products, release of finished products, etc.), testing stage (launching a trial batch of innovative products on the market, assessing and analysing demand, attitudes of buyers to products, making the necessary adjustments, etc.), implementation stage (development of a marketing programme for bringing new products to the market, market diversification policy, release of innovative products according to the production capacities of enterprises, updating the technical and technological base, improving the resource potential of enterprises, etc.).

The "resource" feature of network organization is the pooling of resources (usually unique or scarce) from enterprises. This includes shared use of intellectual potential, unique raw materials, unique equipment, unique management technologies and other resources in order to create extraordinary, original and, consequently, competitive products that would bring economic (and social) benefit and increase competitive advantages of each member-organization (Terziev & Klimuk, 2021c).

Figure 13. Types of models of network organization of industrial enterprises by "process" and "resource" features (V.V. Klimuk)

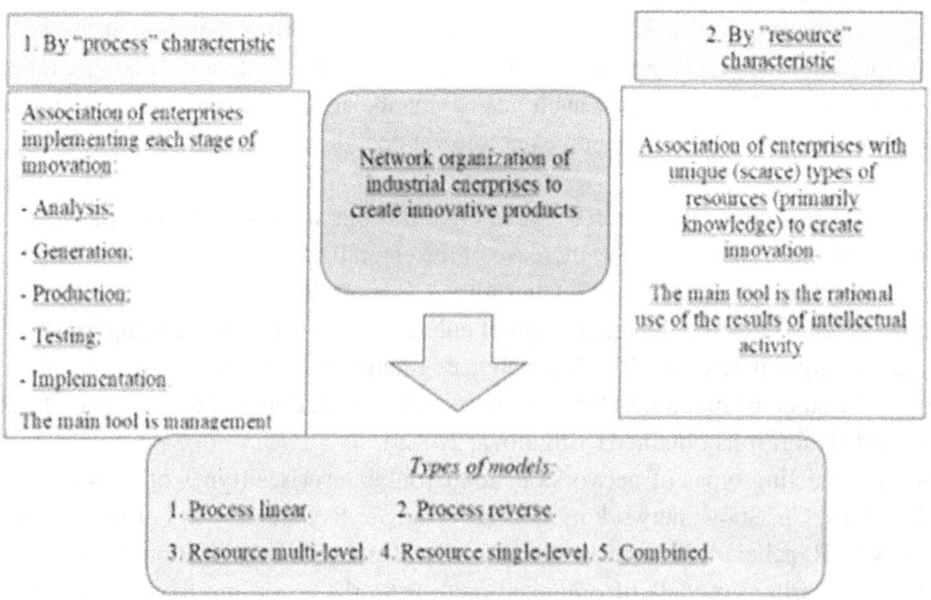

Taking into account "process" and "resource" features when forming a network organization of production by industrial enterprises, it is possible to use one of 5 alternative models:

- Process linear (the initiative of the association comes from the stage of assessing and analysing the state of the industrial goods market);
- Process reverse (the initiative of the association is generated by enterprises that implement the last stage of the process of creating innovative products - the introduction of innovative developments in the practical areas of industry);
- Resource multi-level (unique resources of enterprises of several sectors are combined to create industrial innovation);
- Resource single-level (unique resources of enterprises of the same industry are combined);
- Combined (industrial enterprises are united on the basis of a combination of two or more possible models for the creation of innovative industrial products) (Fig. 13).

The study of the main ideas of theories that determine the importance of interaction between enterprises in order to increase economic benefits, the implementation of strategic objectives, allows us to systematize these theories in relation to the main tools of influence and goals (Table 3).

Table 3. Comparative analysis of theories of interaction between partners in the sector of industrial business

Name of the Theory	Description and Goal	Distinctive Features
Cluster theory	Association of enterprises (suppliers, manufacturers, buyers) of one sector, primarily based on the principle of territorial localization. The main goal is to increase competitiveness of enterprises, regions and national economy.	The core of the association is a large industrial enterprise.
Integration theory	Based on theories of transaction costs, strategic advantages and industry life cycles. The goal is to optimize costs (primarily indirect) as a result of optimizing individual control functions.	Shared use of factors of production within the association on favourable terms. Monitoring the capacity of the industrial goods market.
Network theory	Association of enterprises according to sectoral, territorial, functional and other characteristics. The goal is to create competitive products based on the development of intellectual potential, information and communication technologies.	Association of enterprises with unique (scarce) resources to enhance innovation potential. Formation of a product and resource environment for attracting investments.
Such interaction would result in an increase in the competitiveness of enterprises due to: - access to unique (scarce) resources; - cost optimization; - development of scientific and innovative activity.		

Thus, the development of integration between organizations allows achieving synergy by optimally distributing functions between the participants of an ecosystem based on the principles of partnership, absolute advantages, flexibility of the strategy being implemented (Terziev & Klimuk, 2021c).

5. CONCLUSION

To conclude, in the contemporary conditions an active search for organizations in the national and international markets of products (works, services) and innovations and the development of financial potential should be performed with the help of effective mechanisms of innovation development. These mechanisms would ensure a systematic, interconnected and gradual implementation of innovation policies by organizations in particular and regional and national innovation policies in general to increase competitiveness on a global level. The process of innovation development of organizations includes the following components: development of financial potential, adaptation and flexibility of legal system for stimulating innovation, research and innovation infrastructure, intellectual potential, active implementation of information and communication technologies in the main and additional activities.

The mechanisms provide for tools that ensure the implementation of specific objectives, while providing the ways of their implementation, a team of contractors and partners, expected outcomes and possible risks. According to the set priorities, assessment of the current (and retrospective) state of innovation development, an organization develops a specific action plan in the form of a 'road map' on the basis of tools, forms and ways of implementing each mechanism of the innovation development system.

The implementation of each stage of the 'road map' for innovation development allows achieving the planned objectives by ensuring the stimulation of innovation activities of organizations within the cooperative resource model and strengthening international competitiveness (Terziev & Klimuk, 2022).

REFERENCES

Afonichkin, A. I. (2011a). Strategies for the coordinated development of cluster economic systems. *Journal of the V.N. Tatishchev Volzhsky University, 2011*(24), 244–252.

Anisova, N. A. (2014a). Development of cluster theory: a typical model and examples of application. BIBLIO-GLOBUS.

Annual report of the state and development of research in 2019. (2019c). Ministry of Education and Science.

Averina, T.A. (2006). Analysis of models and methods of management of the innovative development of the enterprise. *Scientific Herald of the Voronezh State Architectural and Construction University. Series: Management of construction, 1*(6), 76-83.

Chernov, O.A., & Sadovnikov, A.S. (2015a). Mechanisms of activation of innovative activity of enterprises. *Modern problems of science and education*, 759-765.

Chernova, O.A. (2009). Backbone principles of forming of innovation regional development strategy *Journal of Orenburg State University, 10*(104), 46-51.

Chernova, O.A., & Ivanov A.V. (2015/b). Models of integration cooperation of industrial enterprises: opportunities for capitalization growth. *Electronic Scientific Journal "Engineering Journal of Don"*. ivdon.ru/ru/magazine/archive/n1p2y2015/2817.

Decree of the President of the Republic of Belarus No. 7 dated 23 November 2017 "On development of entrepreneurship". (2021i), https://president.gov.by/ru/official_documents_ru/view/dekret-7-ot-23-nojabrja-2017-g-17533

Gakashev, M. M. (2013a). Methodology for the selection and formation of economic industrial clusters. *Vector of Science of Togliatti State University. Series: Economics and Management, 2013*(1), 20–23.

Goldyakova, T. V. (2006a). Concept and classification of innovations. *Russian foreign economic bulletin, 2006*(2), 20–27.

Indicators of Innovation. (2016). *Statistical compilation.* Moscow: NIU HSE.

Industry of the Republic of Belarus. (2020d). Statistical collection. Minsk: National Statistical Committee of the Republic of Belarus.

Klimuk, V., & Tarasova, A. (2019). Digital economy in Belarus and Russia: leading underpins of a new reality. *Proceedings of the 3rd International Conference on Social, Economic, and Academic Leadership (ICSEAL 2019)*, 421-427. 10.2991/icseal-19.2019.66

Klimuk, V. V., & Lazdins, V. (2019a). Interaction of education, science and business in terms of digital economy development. *Proceedings of the 2019 International Conference "Economic science for rural development". Jelgava, LLU ESAF, 9-10 May 2019*, 37-48. 10.22616/ESRD.2019.102

Koblova, Yu. A. (2013b). Virtual organizations as the latest form of network structures. *Journal of the Saratov State Social and Economic University, 2013*, 18–21.

Lavrikova, Yu. L. (2008a). Clusters: strategy of formation and development in the economics of a region. Yekaterinburg: Publishing house of the Institute of Economics of the Ural Branch of the Russian Academy of Sciences.

Law of the Republic of Belarus No. 148-3 dated 1 July 2010 (with amendmends and additions No. 91-3 dated 9 January 2018) "On the development of small and medium-sized enterprises". (2021j). https://pravo.by/document/?guid=3871&p0=H11000148

Law of the Republic of Belarus No. 425-3 dated 10 July 2012, "On State Innovation Policy and Innovation Activities in the Republic of Belarus" (as amended and supplemented on 11 May 2016), (2016a).

Lvov, D. S., & Glazyev, S. Yu. (1986).Theoretical and Applied Aspects of NTP Management. Economics and Mathematical Methods: Journal, 5, 793-804.

Mahmudova, A. I. (2010a). Varieties of network integration in industry. *Journal of Astrakhan State Technical University: Series: Economics, 2010*(1), 211–218.

Matveeva, L.G., & Aguzarov, Z.A. (2013). Institutional environment for the use of cluster strategies in the modernization of the economy of the South of Russia. *Terra Economicus, 11*(2), 67-71.

Matveeva, L.G., Chernova, OA, & Klimuk, V.V. (2015). Evaluation of the effectiveness of import substitution policies in industry: methodological tools. *News of the Far Eastern Federal University. Economics and Management, 3*(75), 3-14.

Milevska, T. S. (2012). Models of innovative development of economics. *Business Info, 2012*(7), 40–46.

Mingaleva, Zh. A. (2011a). Theoretical and methodological approaches to the analysis of the dynamics of the sectoral structure of the economy. *Journal of Economic Theory*, *2011*(4), 126–136.

Porter, M. (1998, December). Clusters and the new economics of competitiveness. *Harvard Business Review*.

Postaljuk, M. P., & Gusarova, V. U. (2014). Mechanisms for ensuring innovation in economic development structures. *Problems of modernization and transition to an innovative economy*, *2014*, 27–30.

Prangishvili, I. V. (2000). System approach and system-wide patterns / I.V. *Prangishvili. M.: SINTEG*, *2000*, 22–23.

Praslov, A. V. (2007). Classification of innovations and their essence. *News from the Russian State Pedagogical University. A.I. Herzen*, *2007*, 156–162.

Region in the new paradigm of the spatial organization of Russia. (2007a). *Economics*.

Research and innovation in the Republic of Belarus. (2020c). *Statistical collection*. Minsk: National Statistical Committee of the Republic of Belarus.

Resolution of the Council of Ministers of the Republic of Belarus No. 149 dated 23 February 2016 "State programme for the development of small and medium-sized entrprises in the Republic of Belarus for 2016-2020". (2021k). http://www.economy.gov.by/uploads/files/gos-progr-2016-2020/Postanovlenie-149-v-red.-920.pdf

Sampieva, L. D., & Tamashev, I. M. (2011). Principles and features of innovative development of enterprises of the agro-industrial complex. Terra Economicus, 9(4), 145-147.

Sergeev, A. M. (2008b). Comparative advantages of clusters. *Panorama of competition*, *2008*(3), 83–88.

Simonova, N. E. (2012a). Evaluation of the effectiveness of integration projects. *Electronic Scientific Journal "Engineering Journal of Don"*. https://cyberleninka.ru/article/n/otsenka-effektivnosti-integratsionnyh-proektov/viewer

Software programme IBM SPSS Statistics. (2021t). https://www.ibm.com/products/spss-statistics?lnk=hpmps_bupr

Terziev, V. (2019b). The role and place of social programming in public governance. *Proceedings of SOCIOINT 2019- 6th International Conference on Education, Social Sciences and Humanities 24-26 June 2019- Istanbul, Turkey*, 354-362. 10.2139srn.3411580

Terziev, V. (2020a). Social programming in the context of social economy development in Bulgaria. *51st International Scientific Conference on Economic and Social Development (Rabat, 26-27 March 2020)*, 387-396.

Terziev, V. (2020b). Programming as mechanism of managing, oriented towards results. *Economic and Social Development (Book of Proceedings), 50th International Scientific Conference on Economic and Social Development Development*, 92-98.

Terziev, V., & Georgiev, M. (2020). The place of programming in the state's social policy. *Review of Behavioral Aspect in Organizations and Society*, *2*(1), 25–30. doi:10.32770/rbaos.vol225-30

Terziev, V., & Klimuk, V. (2021). Factors and mechanisms affecting innovation development of industrial business organizations: cooperative resource model. *71st International Scientific Conference on Economic and Social Development – Online Conference*, 31-40.

Terziev, V., & Klimuk, V. (2021a). Methodological concepts for modernization of industrial enterprises in the concept of postindustrial development. *65th International Scientific Conference on Economic and Social Development – Online Conference*, 1-5.

Terziev, V., & Klimuk, V. (2021b). Mechanisms affecting innovation development of industrial business organizations. 21st RSEP International Economics, Finance & Business Conference – Virtual/Online 19-20 May 2021, HCC. St. Moritz Hotel, Barcelona, Spain, 132-141.

Terziev, V., & Klimuk, V. (2021c). Approaches to the application of the concepts of cooperative integration between organizations. *75th International Scientific Conference on Economic and Social Development – Belgrade, 02-03 December, 2021*, 383-387.

Terziev, V., & Klimuk, V. (2021d). Management of the innovation ecosystem development. *77th International Scientific Conference on Economic and Social Development – Online Conference, 27 January, 2022*, 24-28.

Terziev, V., & Klimuk, V. (2021e). Analysis of the procedures and sources of financing research and innovation. *70th International Scientific Conference on Economic and Social Development – Baku, 25-26 June, 2021*, 332-338.

Terziev, V., & Klimuk, V. (2021f). Modelling the forms of international scientific and educational cooperation. 20th RSEP International Economics, Finance & Business Conference – Virtual/Online 17-18 February 2021, Holiday Inn Vienna City, Vienna, Austria, 151-156.

Terziev, V., & Klimuk, V. (2021q). Directions for modernization of innovative youth startup design in Belarus. 20th RSEP International Economics, Finance & Business Conference – Virtual/Online 17-18 February 2021, Holiday Inn Vienna City, Vienna, Austria, 157-162.

Terziev, V., & Klimuk, V. (2022). *New incentives for development of the modern research and innovation ecosystem: a case study of Belarus.* doi:10.25313/978-611-01-2659-5

Terziev, V. & Klimuk, V. (2021g). Designing a digital education ecosystem. *68 th International Scientific Conference on Economic and Social Development – Aveiro, 24-25 May, 2021*, 218-228.

Tomashevska, Yu. N., & Korchagina, N. A. (2010). International experience in identifying clusters: Prospects for use in the Russian Federation. *Scientific works of the Institute of National Economic Forecasting of the Russian Academy of Sciences, 2010*, 727–742.

Website of the European innovation scoreboard. (2021s), https://ec.europa.eu/growth/industry/policy/innovation/scoreboards_en

Website of the European Union. (2021m), https://ec.europa.eu/growth/industry/policy/innovation/scoreboards_en

Website of the European Union. (2021h), https://ec.europa.eu/growth/industry/policy/innovation/scoreboards_en

Website of the Global Innovation Index. (2021o), https://www.globalinnovationindex.org,

Website of the World Intellectual Property Organization (WIPO). (2021n). https://www.wipo.int

Yasheva, G.A. (2008). Cluster concept of innovative development of the economy: justification and implementation mechanism. *Journal of Russian University, 4,* 64-72.

Zapariy, V. V. (2017). Formation and development of a territorial manufacturing complex for the production of heavy tanks in Chelyabinsk in 1940-1945. Economic History, 13(4), 48-58.

Chapter 17

Theory of the Firm, FDI, and Development in the Light of the Global Challenges:

Modern Firms in the Era of Digitalisation and Green Transition

Ninel Seniuk
Bratislava University of Economics and Management, Slovakia

Michal Fabus
https://orcid.org/0000-0002-3792-179X
Bratislava University of Economics and Management, Slovakia

ABSTRACT

The world economy and its energy sector are going through tough period of simultaneous imposition of the evolutionary processes of global transformation, digitalization, and green transition on the one hand, and global innovation challenges, geopolitical, and geostrategic upheavals on the other hand. Digitalization, climate mitigation programs, and the green transition contributed to the intensification of the globalization of production and services, and hence the expansion of distributed forms of multi-subject business activities—global value chains (GVC), global production networks (GPN), and global innovation networks (GIN)—and, at the same time, decentralization of green energy advancing the development of distributed generation and consumption of energy resources, as well as the widespread introduction of energy efficient technologies.

DOI: 10.4018/979-8-3693-0400-6.ch017

INTRODUCTION

Foreign Direct Investment (FDI) often plays the role of a compass, indicating the priority, innovation-oriented, directions of transformation of the World Economy, and also characterizes the intensity of these changes. That is why the analysis of the historical dynamics of the quantitative and qualitative characteristics of Global FDI flows occupies an important place in scientific research, and their results have a significant impact on economic practice. Especially, at the stages of the global post-industrial infrastructural reorganization of the economy, the leading drivers of which are the green transition and digitalization of all spheres of socio-economic life. And the results of such an analysis point to the fact that by the end of the past, the beginning of the current decade, the World found itself in a new economic reality with such significant differences from the previous stage that it causes an urgent need for a critical analysis of the institutional architecture of new business ecosystems, including renewable energy, distributed green generating, smart grid systems and cyber security, etc., as well as testing the performance in the new conditions of the old theoretical and methodological tools, starting with existing theories of the firm, FDI theoretical models in the context of global innovation challenges and UN Sustainable Development Goals (SDG).

1. A Steak of Geo-Economic Turmoil and Weak Global Recovery Amid China's Economic Expansion

The global financial and economic crisis of 2008-2009 became in fact a crisis of global overconsumption, in its depth and consequences comparable to the crisis of global overproduction of the 1930s. In fact, it pointed to the end of a whole historical post-war stage in the development of the World Economy, when controlled inflationary pumping of consumer demand acted as its main driver. That is why subsequent international efforts to restore world economic dynamics by the old neoliberal monetary methods did not lead to a sustainable result. Despite their stimulating effect on the growth of global capital flows, to reach their pre-crisis level of 2007 ($1.905T) and even slightly exceed it (up to $2.064T) only in 2015. However, further this sluggish trend was replaced by a steady, albeit fluctuating fall, breaking through in 2021, under the impact of the COVID-19 pandemic, a bottom of 1 trillion US dollars ($963B) (WIR2022), with the prospect of a further decrease in 2022 (UNCTAD2023). At the same time, the greatest volatility is observed in their very traditional form of Foreign Direct Investment (FDI) - cross-border M&A deals. Particularly FDI, as can be seen from Fig. 1, in the period 2019-2022 demonstrate the greatest volatility, and in the largest World market, the United States, this the fall exceeded 50% (more precisely - 53%) against the backdrop of a more moderate (-6%) global decline.

Undoubtedly, the pandemic and the War in Ukraine had a decisive impact on the strengthening of the negative investment dynamics and M&A volatility during this period. In contrast to the noted 6% decrease in brownfield investment with the largest (53%) drop in the American market most remote from the geopolitical tensions, 2022 simultaneously showed a global 6% increase in announced greenfield projects. It is no less significant that the European market, directly affected by the War, showed a more moderate decline of 15% (UNCTAD2023), which requires an appropriate explanation. In general, the historical and geopolitical specifics of this period sharply increased the impression of strategic uncertainty in the prospects for geo-economic dynamics, against the backdrop of the volatility of global investment flows and the mobility of their structural components.

Figure 1. Investment trends, 2019-2022 (indexed, 2019: Q1=100)
Source: Investment Ttrends Monitor, January 2023. P. 1. URL:http:// https://unctad.org/system/files/official-document/diaeiainf2023d1_en.pdf

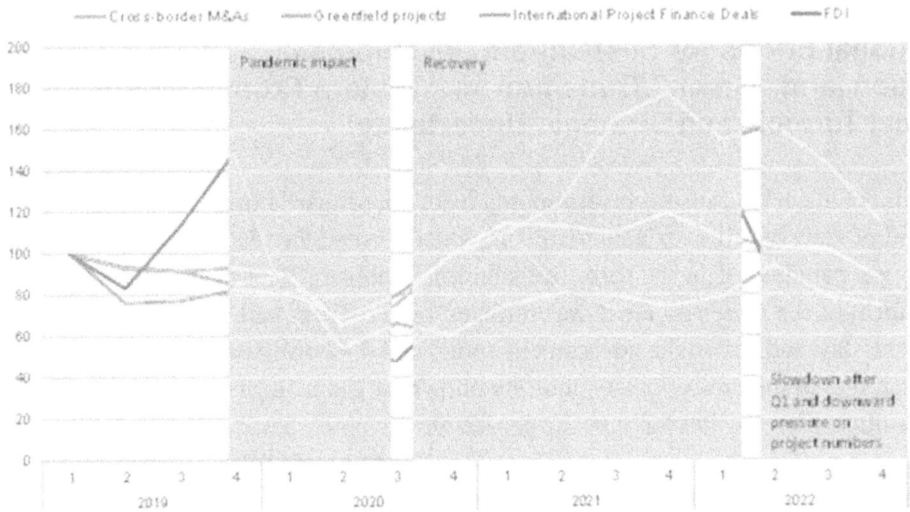

Such a strong investment volatility, on the one hand, testifies to the objective processes of the growing inconsistency of the interaction of later forms of global evolutionary dynamics generated by achievements and the industrial revolution 4.0 (IR4.0) and known as Globalization 4.0 (G 4.0 "service without borders"), with its predecessor Globalization 3.0 (G3.0 "production without borders") (Baldwin, 2018). In particular, the first half of the last decade began with a trend towards increased economic Globalization and the lengthening of Global Value Chains (GVC) under the flag of G3.0, a powerful driver of which is unilateral Chinese strategy "One Belt and One Road" (OBOR) initiated in 2013. And despite its one-sided nature, over the first 10 years, about 150 countries and more than 30 international organizations were involved in the practical implementation of OBOR, giving this initiative not only a global character, but also a global scale. Indeed, although the focus of the initial attention of the "Economic Belt" was primarily on the Eurasian continent with all the complex palette of investment interaction and opposition, however, the "Northern Sea Route" already involved the African continent, and indirectly Australia, into the area of infrastructure transformation, not to mention the well-known Second Route - the Severn of the Sea and the prospects for the economic development of Antarctica by China. Therefore, OBOR actually marked the beginning of an unprecedented historical process of global infrastructural restructuring of the entire World Economy, as its traditional industrial component and post-industrial digital, in G4.0 format. Thanks to the latter, the global networked digital economy began to develop rapidly, and with-it Global Innovation Networks (GINs) and Global Production Networks (GPNs) were formed, with the increasing participation of virtual, including in the form of smart contracts, economic actors: Non - Equity Modes (NEMs). The main Chinese manufacturer in the G3.0 format of equipment for network innovation and production infrastructure was "Huawei", while the global expansion of its 5G technologies in the sense of G4.0 became a visible reason for geopolitical opposition from the United States and one of the most striking causes of occurrence in 2017-2018 US-China trade and tariff War. All this taken together, taking into account the recent experience of China's relative strengthening during the global financial and economic crisis and the subsequent Chinese investment expansion, being perceived through the traditional prism of global competition, formed in the collective West not only geo-economic, but also geopolitical and even geostrategic (at least in the form of the Taiwan issue or the sea safety) concerns.

2. International Efforts for Sustainable Development, Digitalization, and "Green" Transition vs. Western Protectionism, Geopolitical Turmoil, and Strategic Uncertainty

Of course, this could not but cause a corresponding reaction, primarily from the United States. Moreover, from the point of view of orthodox neoliberalism, which formed the ideological basis of Globalization, the reaction was paradoxical in the form of techno-nationalism. First of all, this reaction manifested itself in the form of the trade and tariff war initiated by the Trump administration with China, which continues to this day, and also to the government-sponsored re-shoring of overseas manufacturing facilities. Moreover, due to the protectionist solidarity shown by the majority of developed economies, this created geopolitical prerequisites for opposite geo-economic processes: de-globalization, divestment and production fragmentation. In turn, this led to both the shortening of GVCs and their regionalization, and the reconfiguration of GINs and GPNs. These processes have intensified more strongly under the impact of the crushing blows of the COVID -19 pandemic, especially devastating during the global lockdown in 2020. Moreover, despite the non-economic nature of this Public Health crisis, its geo-economic consequences led not only to huge quantitative losses, but also to profound qualitative shifts, manifested both in the form of sectoral restructuring and in the form of institutional transformations. First of all, these shifts were associated with the intensification of the digitalization of many socially necessary services, as well as with the transition of a huge number of employees to remote work. At the same time, this crisis could not but affect the slowdown in the implementation of international investment programs, including climate mitigation, the development of "green energy" and the circular economy, etc. A clear example of its destructive impact on the sectoral structure of international project investments (IPI) gives Figure 2.

Figure 2. Climate change investment trend, 2022 vs. 2021, greenfield project announcements and international project finance deals (project numbers)
Source: Investment Ttrends Monitor, January 2023. P.3. URL:http://https://unctad.org/system/files/official-document/diaeiainf2023d1_en.pdf

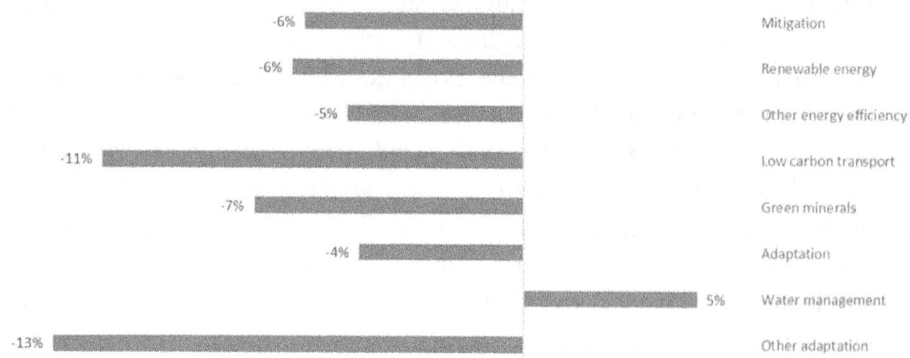

As can be seen from this figure, against the background of a 5% increase in investment in the water management sector, which is quite understandable in the context of military destruction of critical infrastructure, at the same time, there is a serious drop in IPI inflow in climate mitigation, especially in low carbon transport (-11%), green minerals (-7%), renewable energy (-6%), etc. And a 12% drop in global FDI flows in 2022, to $1.3T, and a worsening outlook for 2023 promise further strengthening of such trends. This is indicated by the trend of global FDI outflows above inflows (17% in 2021 and 15% in 2022) that has emerged over the past 2-3 years against the background of the usually shown opposite picture, and most importantly, a sharp increase in capital exports from developed economies compared to its imports. (By 2.1 times in 2021 and 2.7 times in 2022) against the background of a calmer, fluctuating at a level not exceeding 20% of their balance, observed in previous years (WIR 2023, p.197).

Realizing that international project investments are mainly focused on the implementation of the 17 sustainable development goals (SDGs) adopted by the UN in 2015, the emerging trends significantly complicate the prospect of achieving them in the time remaining until 2030. However, their role as leading drivers of the public economy and priority areas of IPI remains. At the same time, the development of the public economy contributes to the strengthening of the role of national governments as the leading macro-drivers, serving as a navigator for the micro-level of enterprises. This involuntarily puts enterprises, including MNCs, into a reactive, led position, modulating their investment motivation accordingly. In addition, this indicates a certain, and growing, gap between the idealized neoclassical conceptual representations of the market behavioral economy, which are the basis of the most popular theoretical FDI models, and that new navigated economic reality, against the backdrop of growing geo-economic volatility and geopolitical uncertainty, which is formed on our eyes. As a result, since the middle of the last decade, a number of works have appeared that have set as their goal the study of the nature of this new reality. Among them, there were also those in which the authors were convinced of the objective nature of the observed processes that did not fit into the neoclassical logic of the simple geo-economic consequences of the subjectivism of certain geopolitical decisions, starting, for example, with the US-China trade and tariff war. In their opinion, this indicates the advent of a new era in human history, which has such inherent features as Volatility, Uncertainty, Complexity and Ambiguity (VUCA) (Bennet and Lemoine, 2014, pp.311-317). In fact, the main source of this new VUCA reality is the dynamically increasing complexity of economic processes, first noted as an evolutionary phenomenon at the very end of the 20th century (Arthur, 1999). This prompted researchers to pay attention not only to its quantitative and more complicated characteristics, but also to the qualitatively different nature of their carriers as living, multi-subject Complex Adaptive Systems (CAS) (Holland, 2014). Such CAS systems are arbitrarily formed in the process of interactive interaction of business entities, called agents, who are forced to learn from each other in order to achieve common goals, accept and adapt to the jointly created rules of the collective game (Ibid, p.24). As a consequence, the individual behavior of such internationalizing firms as agents operating within the framework of these rules, in the conditions of modern network systems (Chandra & Wilkinson, 2017), becomes unpredictable and cannot be centrally controlled. At the same time, their collective interaction is very different from the traditional local behavior, becoming "quite counterintuitive" and forming large-scale patterns with their "Collective Intelligence" and "Collective Ability", formed in the "bottom-up" direction (Ibid, p.694).

As a result, a completely logical question arises about the applicability in the conditions of VUCA reality of those conceptual theoretical foundations that were once laid in the scientific foundation of the theories of International Business (IB) and FDI models. At the same time, the most radical authors (see, for example, Petrisevic and Teece, 2019, pp. 1487, 1512) consider it necessary to use other bases that are more adequate to this new era, while researchers who adhere to more conservative sentiments do not agree with this. In particular, one of the founders of the IB theory Prof. Peter Buckley believes that in order to take into account VUCA-features in the modern behavior of MNC, it is enough to modify investment models accordingly, but there is no need to change the conceptual theoretical foundation itself (Buckley, 2020). However, the growth of geopolitical turbulence at the beginning of the third decade, up to the threat of a nuclear conflict and a new World War, connected with the Russian -Ukrainian eopolitical tensions, as well as taking into account its global energy and environmental consequences, have further exacerbated the relevance of this issue. First of all, this was due to the need to take into account the impact of such geopolitical risks when making investment decisions, as a result of which many companies tried to move their business to more friendly countries, where such risks would be absent or minimized. Consequently, this led to the shortening and reconfiguration of GVC, which means it increased the processes of fragmentation and divestment of the World Economy. In addition, these processes were accompanied by qualitative changes in the global structure of the total FDI-flows and their geographical redistribution.

Based on this, it is not surprising that the processes of such de-globalization have affected China, as a result of which its fragmentation index in the beginning of 2022 has gradually increased almost twice compared to 2015, with a trend towards some stabilization. Accordingly, China's Industrial Capacity Utilization (ICU) rate began to increase, from 72.9% in March 2016 to 78% in December 2017, falling under the influence of the US-China trade tariff war to 76% in December 2018 and up to 75.9% in March 2019, demonstrating an average for the period since March 2013 to March 2019 rate of 75.5% (CEIC Data 2021) and 75.8% in Q1 2022 (Xinhua, April 23, 2023) compared to only about 60% in 2012 against almost 80% in the pre-crisis 2007 (Worldscience 2023), with an average value of 65.9% per decade 2001-2010 (Xie et al., 2023, p.6). However, after the beginning of the military conflict in Ukraine, fragmentation began to increase significantly again, in contrast to the increased economic integration demonstrated by developed countries (Ahn et al., 2023). At the same time, it seems that the possibilities of increasing domestic consumption within the framework of the "Dual Circulation model" have also been exhausted, which also affected the decrease in ICU in Q1 2023 by 1.5% compared to Q1 2022 to the level of 74.3% (Xinhua, April 23, 2023). In this dynamic picture, attention is drawn to those geopolitical events, after which the utilization of China's industrial capacities increases significantly. In particular, thanks to China's accession to the WTO at the very end of 2001, until that steadily downward trend, when in 2001 the ICU level dropped to 61.6%, but by 2010 it had already risen to 73.4%, with outpacing growth in the efficiency of using the technical capabilities of production (Ibid), then falling to almost 60% in 2012. Next year followed by the start of the Chinese global infrastructure initiative OBOR, which led to a significant increase in capacity utilization, up to the start of the US-China trade and tariff War, in place with the sanctions of Western countries, the COVID -19 pandemic and current geopolitical tensions.

Of course, the processes of increasing fragmentation, de-globalization and divestment are also changing the global distribution of political risks, the minimum level of which was demonstrated by the EU countries, and the maximum by the MENA (Middle East and North Africa) and Asia-Pacific regions. At the same time, geopolitical volatility increases, in the conditions of which, as studies have shown, the geopolitical distance becomes more important than the traditional geographic one. As a result, the processes of restoring, nearshoring and friend-shoring are intensified, which, moreover, entails additional costs on the part of MNCs for reconfiguring GVC. Estimates show that such expenditures can reach 2% of global GDP (Ahn et al., 2023), which is much higher in order of magnitude than the volumes of global

FDI flows observed in recent years. All this testifies to the obvious strengthening of the influence of geopolitical factors on geo-economic fragmentation, and so much so that this topic has not only moved to the center of political debates in recent years (IMF 2023), but also becomes an important additional factor influencing the investment behavior of MNCs.

Meanwhile, such a picture enters into a certain conceptual contradiction with the logic of classical ideas about the predictability of the rational behavior of an "economic man", as well as about the separation of the market economy from politics. This situation forces researchers to go beyond the narrow framework of neoclassical IB conceptual limits and move into the fundamental complexity of CAS, which, in turn, contributes to the tightening of the requirements imposed by practice on the quality, efficiency and predictive properties of FDI theoretical models. At the same time, it becomes obvious that making adequate investment decisions in modern VUCA conditions is hardly possible without the use of Artificial Intelligence (AI), which becomes the core of the corporate smart infrastructure, which plays role of a new attractor of outpacing (up to 40% in 2022) investment growth flows. As a result, the creation of such Creative AI becomes the main priority of innovative investment, relegating ROI goals to the background (Predictions 2022. pp.14,8). Another feature of the investment strategies of MNCs in these conditions is the desire of their top management to share the risks, as geopolitical ones, through participation in national and international programs, including the Net Zero Emissions by 2050 Scenario, as well as financial ones, in cooperation with specialized Global Investment Funds (GIF), and the Sovereign Wealth Funds (SWF). Thanks to the action of such programs and the resources attracted within their framework, net investment flows are growing at a faster pace (58% compared to 2020 and 200% in relation to 2019), having reached 2021 year $557B or 58% of the global FDI flow. Characteristic enough, that the lion's share of the growth of this kind of investment resources is concentrated in developed economies, of which 81% is concentrated in Europe, stimulating the priority increase in Green funds, which showed an increase of 26% in 2021 against 3% in the case of fossil funds. Thanks to this, the share of the EU in total investment inflows was 85%, showing a 63% increase in relation to 2020 year (WIR2022, p.164-168).

3. Existential Challenges of the Pandemic, Health-Oriented and "Green" Structural Transformations, and Inflationary Consequences of the Anti-Pandemic Strategies

At the same time, among recent sectoral shifts, special attention is drawn to health-oriented investment trends, which manifested themselves during the pandemic period not only in the sectoral structure of the economy, but also in the very conceptual basis of political and economic thinking. We are describing the emerging transition from "homo economicus" as a means of creating income and capital to some new state of human-centered consciousness and well-being, the minimum goal of which is the expanded reproduction of health, and the main material means of achieving it is some new health-oriented post-pandemic bioeconomy. This is precisely indicated by the fact that, as a result of 2021 year, the Public Health sector became the investment leader, attracting 12.7% of all global FDI flows, pushing climate change mitigation projects to the second place (7.5%), leaving only the third place for food and agriculture, despite its basic role in maintaining health population. It is curious that in the top ten of such priorities, the last three positions were telecom infrastructure (0.4%), transport infrastructure (0.2%) and education (0.1%) (ibid, p.169).

Of course, such a health-oriented structural shift, caused by fundamental existential reasons, required huge financial outlays, attracted by means of monetary and financial policy, as well as the mobilization of business resources. As for such a policy, in the end, it came down to two main areas: 1) additional spending and forgone revenue; 2) equity, guarantees and loans. It is quite expected that developed economies incurred the most large-scale expenditures, reaching an average of 17% of GDP at the end of September 2021 (most of all - $ 5.4T or about 25% for the United States, about 18% for Great Britain and 14% for Canada) against the backdrop of 6% by emerging economies and 2.5% by low-income developing countries. Moreover, the second path had less weight, on average estimated at 10% GDP in the case of developed countries (the maximum is in Italy, more than 35%, about 30% in Japan and slightly less in Germany), 3% by emerging economies and 0.2% for least developing ones (IMF 2021). Undoubtedly, all these measures had a significant negative impact on the global economy, when its real GDP in 2021 has fallen twice in comparison with 2020, and the projected cumulative impact on real GDP for the period 2020-2024 estimated at 38% in the case of the USA, of which 32% is due to domestic and 6% by external support, 32% in case of Brazil (18% for domestic and 14 for external), 30% in Germany (9% and 21%, respectively), 29% in Canada (12%/17%), 25% in Great Britain (18%/7%) and 24% in China (9%/15%) (Moody's Analytics 2022).

Meanwhile, the nominal economic dynamics does not show such a deep fall during the pandemic period. Except for the dramatic 2020, when the global GDP showed an absolute decline to the level of $85.97T, losing about 2 trillion USD compared to 2019, all subsequent years, starting from 2021 and including the predicted outlook until 2028, its dynamics will be positive (Statista 2023). Undoubtedly, such a prosperous nominal dynamic is an obvious consequence of a powerful pandemic "inflationary pump". Estimates of its quantitative impact show (Hale et al., 2023) that fiscal support at the level of 10% of GDP entails an inflationary wave, which usually reaches 40% by the end of the third month, and if it coincides with an increase in positive consumer expectations, then and all 60%. As a result of such inflationary pumping, the lion's share of which fell on developed economies, the average indicator of World inflation in 2021, it almost doubled reaching 5.4% against the background of the 5-year previous period, when its level did not exceed the range of 2.5 - 3.0% (EC2023). It is clear that this, almost twofold excess of the permissible level of inflation, also determined the above-mentioned scale of the decline in real GDP on the planet. At the same time, it sharply increased the amount of additional liquidity, creating a strong potential motivation for its concentration in the most successful companies. And unlike previous crises, when banks and other financial institutions became the main concentrators of additional government-generated liquidity, the public health crisis brought its own peculiarities. The fact is that since the demand for remote purchases of essential goods and online services at home has skyrocketed during the pandemic, the main beneficiaries of this situation have become technology companies that can provide such a service. And those of them that provided a reliable service on a global scale within the framework of G4.0 became the undisputed leaders of such a "pumping", giving rise to the so-called "Amazon effect" - when the market price of the assets of such companies soars almost an order of magnitude compared to their pre-crisis cost (ibid).

As a result of such an "inflationary pump", the number of investment mega-deals, costing at least $1B each, has sharply increased to an unprecedented 159, and their total volume almost reached $500B, i.e., almost half of the annual FDI flow. At the same time, 99 of these 159 projects (62%) were implemented by large MNEs, and their share in the total investments of all 16,000 such projects in the World in 2022 reached 54% (fDi Intelligence, May 31, 2023). Moreover, all this applies to new energy investment projects

(WIR 2023, p.145). Of course, this indicates an unprecedented concentration of investment capital, with less than 1% of all investing companies making more than half (54%) of all investments. In turn, such a superconcentration of capital also conflicts with the necessary conditions for the self-organization of free markets. This model is based on the condition of statistical insignificance of investments of each of the participants (in our case, MNEs), in comparison with the total investment flow. If this condition is violated, then oligopolistic deformations occur that change the individual behavior of participants in the World capital market, and, moreover, increase the economic, political and social polarization in society.

Such trends are also confirmed by the analysis of the country and sectoral distribution of global FDI flows. In particular, as a 2022 result Egypt took the lead in terms of the volume of their investments, raising $96.8B compared to $34.9B in 2016, outstripping the total investments in the USA (about $88B), but losing them in the total number of projects (22). Moreover, it is characteristic that in the sectoral distribution, the largest share of mega-deals (59%) fell on "green hydrogen", represented by 35% of all mega-projects (Ibid). The next year, 2023, under the influence of all the consequences of the war in Ukraine and the energy and technological sanctions imposed against Russia, marked a sharp increase in investment in 10 leading sectors of the economy, the top three of which are the production of semiconductors - an increase of 225% over the period Q2 2020 - Q1 2023 compared to Q2 2017 - Q1 2023, renewable energy - 146% and electric components - 114%, although in this group biotechnology (+98%) is in 4th place, and 9th and 10th are healthcare and medical devices (+14% each), against the backdrop of communications (+50%) and software and IT service (+22%, the 8th position), which took 5th place. At the same time, the role of global leadership in general terms of the volume and growth of attracted investments belongs to the renewable energy sector, which has attracted since April 2020 about $668B, but in terms of growth dynamics, the semiconductors sector is leading, where only for 2022 about $190B was invested this year, compared to $59B invested three years earlier through massive programs and subsidies initiated by the governments of the US, Japan, Germany and France (fDi Intelligence, June 14, 2023).

Another, very indicative trend, as a priority innovation-oriented direction of partial utilization of the consequences of global inflationary hyperpumping, has become the leadership role of large technology companies. This is noticeably different from all other crisis situations, where banks and financial companies usually acted as the main architects of anti-crisis recovery. In this case, the main recipients of inflationary bonuses were really technology companies, primarily those that are focused on the development of the digital economy. This is eloquently evidenced by the fact that the top 100 global innovation leaders in 2022 increased their R&D spending by 15.3% compared to 2021, with a total investment of around $720B, significantly more than the combined investment of 159 mega-investment deals. Among this innovative hundred, almost half (47) are technology companies, where Amazon is in the lead, concentrating 10% of the total innovation-oriented investments ($72B), and almost a quarter (24) - health-oriented, including healthcare, pharmaceutical, biotech and medical devices, and only one from the financial services sector. Among all companies, 45 are American, but their total investments exceed 58% ($420B), 28 MNCs are from the EU (28% of all investments) and 17 are from China, with a share of 12.2% of total investments. The inflation bonus made it possible for American companies to confidently hold the top five. The first among them is "Amazon", which increased its investments in science and innovation by 30% in a year, which, however, is only 10th in terms of their growth rate, followed by "Alfabet", "Google's" parent company, which invested $40B. "Meta", "Facebook's" parent company increased its investment by 43% to over $35B, followed by "Apple" ($27B) and "Microsoft"

($26.6B). Close to this "five" approached the Chinese "Huawei", investing 25% of the firm's global revenue, which amounted to $24B, but the German "Volkswagen", as the largest European MNC, with its indicator of $ 19.8B, took only seventh place (fDi Intelligence, June 19, 2023).

In general, behind these trends, demonstrating outpacing growth against the background of the general volatile and declining dynamics of investment flows in recent years, the contours of a post-pandemic future appear. In fact, these trends are responses to the most acute global existential, geopolitical and geo-economic challenges, carried out by means of predominantly public-oriented FDI, directed through national and international programs. Thus, in essence, an innovative infrastructure framework for the future post-pandemic reality is being laid in the form of Public Energy and Public Health, based on clean energy and digitalized Universal health coverage (UHC). The dominant sectoral trends today are choosing "green energy", long-term R&D investments point to a more complex technological future that requires appropriate institutional CAS, without which its successful implementation is hardly possible, while the main issue for the existential context is public health after the pandemic mobilization of all available funds and resources, is relegated to the background, requiring for its implementation a holistic approach to the creation of UHC, as follows from SDG3. In turn, this will require appropriate institutional innovations that can create local markets for technological innovations. At the same time, an important shift took place in the energy sector - 2015 was the last year when investments in fossil fuels exceeded investments in clean energy, however, starting from 2016 to 2023, the clean energy segment, including the renewable one, is steadily increasing. In particular, out of the planned volume of investments in global energy in 2023 in the amount of $2.8T, the larger half ($1.7T) will be directed to the clean energy sector, of which more than $660B will go to renewables, and a little more than $500B to oil and gas supply through compared to just over $400 in 2020 and $560B in 2019. At the same time, China invests most of all in clean energy, having invested over the period 2019-2023 about $180B into this segment compared to $150B of EU investments and slightly less than $100B against the background of the outflow (-$4B) demonstrated by Russia. As a result, in accordance with the plans for the 14th five-year plan, the PRC aims to increase the share of renewable energy up to 33% (WEI 2023, pp.9-12,14,30).

4. International Business and Global Investment Movement in the New Economic Reality

Thus, in the post-pandemic years, we are seeing a sharp increase in the share of investment mega-projects and the dominant place for their implementation by large MNEs, and at the same time, a significant increase in the orienting, guiding and supporting role of both national governments, their strategies and subsidies, and international programs and global financial institutions. As a result, it is difficult to refrain from stating that a certain convergence is actually observed, and the activities of large Western MNCs softly directed by the programs of their governments and international organizations, are increasingly reminiscent of the aggressive investment expansion of the Chinese "MNC -dragons", directed perhaps even more hard, by programs and plans of the leadership of the PRC. Moreover, the problem of involving SMEs with large companies in investment activities and business partnerships sounds very similar, the solution of which involves measures to reduce transaction costs for small and medium-sized businesses, financial, tariff and non-tariff support, assistance in establishing national and international cooperation and integration in GVC, as in the case of developed economies (Lopez-Gonzalez et al., 2019), including through the development of an entire architecture of EU institutions that support the internationalization of their small businesses (Enterprise Europe Network, Cluster Internalization, including green transition support, EU SME Center in China, EU-Japan Center for Industrial Cooperation, etc.) (European Commission, official web-site). China, worried about the slowdown in growth associated with the exhaustion of its available endogenous factors in the current conditions, at the end of 2022 developed, and at the beginning 2023 approved within the framework of the Ministry of Industry and Information Technology (MIIT) 15 measures to further stabilize growth and adjust the structure of SMEs, required financial institutions to increase their support for S&T innovation, including green transformation and expansion the consumption of green intelligent appliances at home as well as the using of new new-energy vehicles and green building materials using in rural markets. Through these measures, MIIT plans to grow over 150,000 Innovative SMEs and more than 100,000 little giant enterprises specializing in a manufacture's niches and boast cutting-edge technologies by the end of 2023 (Global Times, January 16, 2023). At the same time, to strengthen China's global dominance as "the leading producer and investor in renewable energy facilities" (WIR 2023, p.42).

This whole situation, under the influence of the complex interweaving of G3.0 and G4.0 trends implemented by IR4.0 tools, which has sharply intensified due to the intensification of digitalization and fragmentation of world production, as well as global turbulence generated by the War in Ukraine, requires critical rethinking of the entire cycle of Investment activity (IA - cycle), not only its alienated result – realized Foreign Direct Investment projects. This is especially important in the modern conditions of distributed systems of multi-subject business activity, including clusters and blockchain smart contract, as well as distributed power generation and smart grid energy systems (see, for example, (IEA 2022)). In this case, discussing FDI as an implementation of a holistic IA-cycle, we understand the need to answer a whole chain of interrelated questions WHAT? (FDI); WHO (Firm); WHY and HOW the subject-oriented activity of the firm is carried out in the new economic reality. And since world statistics allow us to have an idea of the current macro-dynamics of global FDI flows, the main focus of our attention is, first of all, the firm. Therefore, we will discuss a critical analysis of the theory of the firm and its initial conceptual foundations in the context of digitalization and global turbulence. However, since the IA-cycle under these conditions becomes a complex system of multilateral interaction, i.e. Complex Adaptive System (CAS), then it loses the meaning of the traditional (neo)classical description of the individual behavior of a firm in the market space of global capital flows. Therefore, there is a need for modeling

collective interactive behavior of all participating firms. It is clear that it is almost impossible to do this in the conditions of digitalization and smart energy systems without the involvement of AI technologies. Therefore, there is a need for such a revision and reformulation of the theory of the modern firm, so that it is accessible for perception and understanding, both from the standpoint of Human Intelligence (HI) and from the standpoint of algorithmic AI.

5. Theory of the Firm, Its Modern Problems, and Prospects for Possible Development

The firm, as a corporate system of managed transformational activity using production facilities and natural resources, was actually generated by the era of industrialization and the development of foreign trade. From the position of HI in an effort to build its general theory, the firm is usually considered in one of three aspects: Ontological; Teleological and Epistemological (OTE) (Suszynski, 2013, p.30). Although the construction of a fundamentally complete picture, it is necessary to consider it in the OTE-unity of all three components. Meanwhile, due to their constant complication occurring under the influence of evolution, if it is possible to do this, then only at the level of general philosophical reasoning. Therefore, a unified universal theory of the firm, even within the narrower framework of ontological approaches, limited to consideration of its nature, structure and components, has not yet been created (ibid, 43). It is even more difficult, within the framework of classical scientific rationality, to do this in a teleological approach, the focus of which is on the goals of the firm and the objectives of its activity, not to mention the epistemological consideration, focused on the subjective nature of the firm, its content and methods of extracting and concentration of tacit knowledge as a source of radical innovation (Suszynski, 2013, p.30). Under these circumstances, it is necessary to use differentiated within the framework of the subject specialization of the multifaced packages of the firm, primarily economic, financial, organizational and sociological, as well as technological, legal, etc. (ibid, pp. 32-36).

Naturally, in the course of evolution, such models became correspondingly more complicated and transformed. Originating at the dawn of industrialization, first in the form of small, mostly family-owned, trading companies, and then trading and manufacturing firms, by the end of the 19th and beginning of the 20th century, they acquired a more recognizable form of a manufacturing enterprise, including one that went abroad in form of MNC within the framework of Globalization 1.0 (G1.0 "Free trade"). As a consequence, the first, pre-war half of the 20th century produced a package of three basic and economic theories of the firm. Among them, the fundamental role belongs to the neoclassical approach of A. Marshall (Marshall, 1920), in which the company is considered as a "black box", which has an individualized set of factors of production (labor and capital), capable of providing a stationary reproduction process, characterized by a constant flow input in the beginning and outputs at the end. The means of production determine the capital value of the firm, while the output determines its gross income, and with it, minus costs, the firm's profit. At the same time, the main goal of the activity of such a company, within the framework of the trading logic, becomes profit maximization while minimizing costs, which is achieved by observing the equilibrium principle, in which the company provides stationary output at stable prices, when marginal cost is equal to marginal revenue. Thus, in the neoclassical approach, the attention of the company's management is focused on obtaining maximum profit through the price mechanism of balancing the volume of production (supply) according to market demand, as the basis of microeconomic equilibrium. From a methodological point of view, this neoclassical approach is based on 4 key principles: individualizm; rationality; local equilibrium and price mechanism (Walker, 2019).

Against the background of this rather static version, the more dynamic innovative approach has been developed by J. Schumpeter in its English version for the first time published in 1934 (Schumpeter, 1934, (2008)). Within the framework of his approach the company, in its desire to maximize profits, is forced to organize and timely change its own original system of innovation-oriented cyclic reproduction activities accordingly. Its factor base, in addition to the traditional external (exogenous), including natural resources, labor and technology as the basis of productive capital, also includes an internal, endogenous development factor, the source of which is innovative entrepreneurial ability. Thanks to this factor, the firm acquires the ability to respond to the imperfection of the market equilibrium through both intra-firm transformation and making appropriate changes to the environment (Schumpeter, 1939), which today we would call the business ecosystem, and the changes themselves - institutional innovations. Thanks to such institutional innovations, it is possible to build horizontally integrated cluster technological chains that can quickly implement technological innovations in a cooperative approach, and at the same time reach new, higher levels of local equilibrium. At the same time, going beyond the initiating firm in this way, the implementation cycle of such technological and institutional innovations has a devastating effect on the existing production structure and institutional architecture of the business ecosystem, simultaneously generating "innovation waves" and encouraging others to innovative development.

A more accountant approach to the theory of the firm forms the basis of Transaction Cost Theory (Coarse, 1937). Within its framework, R. Coase draws attention to the difference in the understanding of the word "firm" in the ideal economic approach in terms of costs (transaction costs) and the time required for investigating, negotiating, enforcing, coordinating contract preparations, etc., in contrast to the picture of real production. At the same time, this theory is based on the idea that due to internal organization and better use of external transactions, the company will be able to produce goods by minimizing the associated costs at a lower price than the market offers. It also contains the answer to the question - is it worth creating a company or is it better to buy what you need on the market (Make or Buy?), as well as the answer to the question of the achievable limits of the company's growth until the total external transaction and internal transaction costs do not match the market price.

This triad of theories has indeed laid a predominantly neoclassical basis for ideas about a firm, where in the simplest case its owner is at the same time a rationally acting entrepreneur in the interests of maximizing profits, who has fairly complete information both about the production, technological and organizational and economic capabilities of his own company, and about needs, requirements and conjuncture of the external market. From a theoretical point of view, we are talking about an idealistic picture of a firm seeking to find a local economic equilibrium in the external field of influence of market forces and price impulses, aimed at extracting maximum profit through the implementation of the marginalist principle. Within the framework of such a rather static picture and the simplest company, whose structure, in the first approximation, is considered as a "black box", mainly exogenous factors are taken into account, while endogenous ones, related to the internal structure of the company, are only indicated in Schumpeter's innovative approach. It is clear that in reality the picture differs, and often quite significantly, from the idealistic one. And the demand for accounting for such a reality began to grow rapidly in the post-war period of the formation of Globalization 2.0 (G2.0 - "free trade, but according to WTO rules").

The global consequences of WWII and the needs of post-war reconstruction required the ordering of the international movement of goods and capital, which, in turn, led to both the complication of the very structure of the firms participating in such movement, and the need to adapt them to the requirements of the "rules of the game" in G2.0 conditions. The complication of the internal organization of the post-war firm required a distinction between its structure and interest of various groups and motivations not only of owners, but also of managers and other stuff. Undoubtedly, all this was reflected in the market behavior of the firm, seeking to balance such interests and optimize this behavior. Therefore, the first works of this "second wave", starting with the pioneering work of H. Simon (1947), and further work begun as early as 1952 by Carnegy Mellon University ((March, 1958; Cayert and March, 1963), formed the basis of the Behavioral theories of the firm. Within its framework, the firm ceases to be a "black box", but is a system of complex interaction between groups with different interests and motives, and the management of the firm is reduced not only and not so much to maximizing profits received on the foreign market, as ensuring a balance of interests and maintaining the internal unity of the company, as a result of which the problem of profit maximization is rather replaced by the problem of optimizing the main economic parameters of the company (profits, costs and other people indicators) in conditions of information incompleteness. .

The seminal paper of E. Penrose (1958) had a significant impact on the further evolution of scientific research in this area. Despite its descriptive nature, this approach goes beyond the behavioral one and proceeds from the activity structure of the firm, where its management acts as the main driving force, and quite creative at that. Moreover, the possibility of economic growth of the company is already laid here, of course, thanks to investments in the expansion of its business activities. In this case, which is fundamentally important, it is necessary to consider already non-equilibrium processes.

The main building blocks of such a company capable of self-organized growth, in a slightly modified form by the author, are presented in Table 1.

Table 1. Explanation of the Edith Penrose's "The Theory of the Growth of the Firm"

The Concept of Firm and Its Purpose
1) Firms are institutions that are created by people to serve the purpose of people
2) Firms operate in a disequilibrium model of firm growth, and seek to maintain administrative coordination within a multistakeholder environment
The Firm as a Bundle of Resources and the Central Role of Managers
3) The firm is a collection of productive resources and the services made available from these resources are the drivers of a firm's uniqueness
4) Managers play the central role—a catalyst role—in the resource-service conversion process
5) A firm's managers provide both entrepreneurial and managerial services. Versatility of managers' entrepreneurial services matters as they shape their creative imagination and vision for the firm
6) Managers with firm-specific experience are vital in identifying the subjective growth opportunity and executing growth projects for the firm
7) Managers' experiential knowledge of the firm's resources and their entrepreneurial imagination jointly shape how the firm "sees" the demand and which opportunities it will pursue
Unused/Underutilized Resources as Drivers of Growth, Diversification, and Innovation
8) Unused and underutilized productive services of resources are a key source of firm expansion, learning, innovation, and profitable growth
9) The specialized resources and the specialize use of resources lead to a firm's
diversification of products and services, which provide a basis for firms to achieve long-run survival and profitability
growth in a changing and competitive environment
Managerial Experience as a Key Bottleneck for the Rate of Firm Growth
10) Penrose dares to be different. By going beyond the economic research literature on firm growth, she asks a new research question. Instead of the conventional question: "What is the optimal size of
the firm?" She asks: What is the optimal growth rate of the firm? (1959, p. 2).
11) Managerial capability is the binding constraint that limits the growth of the firm – the so-called Penrose effect or Penrose theorem.
12) If a firm deliberately or inadvertently grows faster than the rate at which
managers and employees in the expanding organization can obtain the experience with each other and with the firm
that is necessary for the effective operation of the group, the efficiency of the firm will suffer.
Penrose Effect on Acquisitions and International Expansion as the Mechanisms for Firm Growth
13) There is a limit to the rate of firm growth via the expansion mode of acquisitions.
14) Availability of management capability also serves as a bottleneck for the rate of international growth. However, in some cases, acquisitions of subsidiaries in foreign countries can help to reduce the need for direct administrative co-ordination, and thus, the firm can grow at a higher rate than what is possible through organic international growth (greenfield entry form).

Source: authors modifications based on Yasemin Y.Kor, Joseph T. Mahoney, Enno Siemsen, Danchi Tan " Penrose's The Theory of the Growth of the Firm: An Exemplar of Engaged Scholarship"

https://www.researchgate.net/publication/301774842_Penrose's
_The_Theory_of_the_Growth_of_the_Firm_An_Exemplar_of_Engaged
_Scholarship

Within the framework of this table, we will pay special attention to some important building blocks of Edith Penrose's firm growth theory. First of all, this would seem to be an obvious statement that a company is built from people and for people (item 1), which indirectly indicates that the potential of those who build a company and manage it should be explicitly taken into account, because it is the underused part, as well as the unused part of the company's resources and production capacities, are the source of its further growth and expansion (item 8). However, it is especially important to note the difference presented in item 5 between managerial and entrepreneurial functions, the main advantage of which is the ability to see, and therefore form the metaphysical foundations for making innovative decisions. From this part it follows that managers are responsible for the stable market functioning of the firm, while the entrepreneurial component is responsible for innovations and their implementation in the interests of its sustainable growth on an innovative basis.

Therefore, it is not surprising that the idea laid down by E. Penrose about the key role of managers was later reflected in Managerial Theories of the Firm. First of all, here we are describing the work of W. Baumol (1959), who was the first to introduce the model of a structured firm to the world, where, in the general case, the interests of managers and owners of the company do not coincide, since if the owners are interested in maximizing profits, then managers are in the stability of their position, maintaining current profitability and maximizing the self-utility function. Of course, this has to be taken into account in the company's economic growth strategy and in the choice of management tactics. Further development of this approach was carried out in the papers of R. Marris (1964; 1998) and O. Williamson (1964; 1970). All of them are characterized by a view of the firm, as a vertically integrated complex entity consisting of many productive units, managed by salaried executives. Such a vertical hierarchy forms the structural framework of the internal organization (internalization) of the firm, the features of the use of funds and resources and management decision making. Together with the comparative advantages of the location, in general, this determines the specific advantages of the firm.

Subsequently, such predominantly neoclassical theoretical approaches gave rise to a whole "family tree" that has grown rapidly since the late 70s in its quest to describe the economic development of a firm going abroad through the implementation of FDI, a certain idea of which can be obtained from Figure 3.

All of these approaches, a detailed analysis of which belongs to the field of FDI theories and is beyond the scope of this study, nevertheless indicates that until the start of the COVID-19 pandemic, attempts to build a unified universal theory of the firm that can describe the dynamics of its economic growth, and even more - development, due to the evolutionarily growing variety of factors to be taken into account, were not crowned with success. Although, in order to create theoretical and model tools for practical use, when MNCs developing their strategies for global investment expansion in the conditions of G3.0, and then G4.0, many models were developed that tried to take into account the multifaced nature of the multi-location enterprise. Perhaps the most typical and popular of them is the OLI-model of J. Dunning, where the lack of a single, organic and universal dynamic structure of the company is replaced by its Eclectic model, whose competitive advantages are constructed from three "building blocks" - the advantages of Ownership, Location and Internalization. From a methodological point of view, the totality of such models makes it possible to group objective, subjective and motivational factors, respectively, determinants, drivers and motives of an internationalizing MNC, however, mainly from the standpoint of an external observer and in the neoclassical phenomenological approach.

Figure 3. Family tree of major investment theories and models
Source: Authors

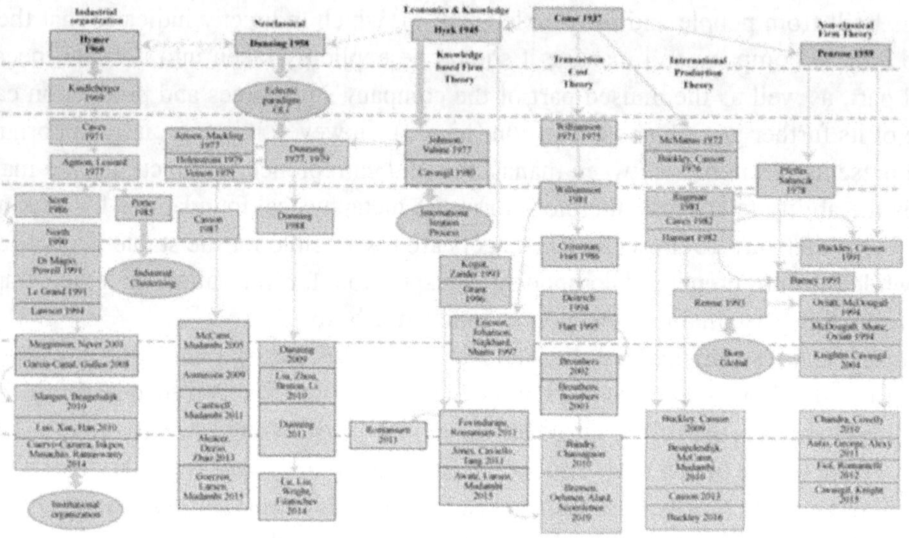

Meanwhile, there are a number of publications (see, for example, (Estola, 2014)) that pay attention to the logical inconsistency of the neoclassical theories of the firm, due to the fact that the basic idea that a firm receives a constant profit while maximizing output does not leave room for its further economic growth and does not explain how the company finds its local, and even more global economic equilibrium, and attempts to mathematically build a dynamic model of the company conflict with its static versions. But even in this dynamic case, when mathematically modeling the individual economic behavior of a firm (Ibid), it is not possible to see the content in order to assess its potential and extract them from the depths of the tacit knowledge (Nonaka & Takeuchi, 1995). Meanwhile, the modern view of the firm and the management of its global competitiveness proceeds from the fact that "the primary task of managers consists in the conversation of tacit, human capital into explicit, structural capital" (Virtanen, 2011). However, this just implies not only the ability to mathematically describe the dynamic structure and features of the functioning of the company, but also to understand the content. Only these kind of opportunity opens up a transition to the use of non-classical, quantum theoretical approaches, both to economics (see, for example: Rampling and Eddie, 2019) and management, which allowed to make "The Quantum Management Revolution", as it is for the first time, the Chinese company "Hier" demonstrated in practice (Zohar, 2022). At the same time, taking into account these deep-seated opportunities as sources of its inclusive innovative development is in itself insufficient for modeling its internationalization in the conditions of modern network-centric complex adaptive systems (Chandra and Wilkinson, 2017), where the trajectory of the firm's individual behavior is blurred, collective intelligence (CI) and norms of cooperative interactive interaction to achieve agreed goals. Moreover, in particular, in complex systems of multilocal interaction within the framework of distributed green energy generation, to control such systems, taking into account difficulties to predict weather factors that are critical for the use of solar and wind energy, it is necessary to use Neuro-Fuzzy Modeling Techniques, which are actively used recently in the economy (see, for example, Miroshnychenko et al., 2021).

CONCLUSION

Everything that has been outlined above points to a fundamentally new economic, political and cultural reality, both at the Global geo-civilizational level (states) and at the local micro-level (enterprises) and meso-level (global regions and cities). At the mega level, there is not only VUCA conditions, but also an emergent superposition of contradictory interacting forms of Globalization 2.0, 3.0 and 4.0 should be taken into account. It is also a new networked reality of the digital economy and distributed forms of non-classical business activities, starting with clusters and agglomerations, as well as GVC, GPN and GIN. Thus, the emerging new reality is rapidly evolving, trying to form adequate responses to the innovative challenges of global turbulence. The focus of these changes, primarily economic ones, is the modern firm as a new integrated innovative reality that combines both traditional corporate and virtual, non-corporate forms of activity, including distributed ones. Especially, these forms are important for modeling investment and management processes in the field of distributed green energy, where 167 GW of solar generation were put into operation in the field of distributed PV systems in just two years in 2019-2021. Of course, distributed systems of economic activity are already non-classical in nature, however, the existing theories of firms are predominantly neoclassical in nature, and, as has been shown, mostly static.

In this regard, the formulation of the problem of creating an adequate theoretical and conceptual basis and the formation of a unified language for the theory of the company and the corresponding methodology arises, which would be equally perceived at the level of both natural human and artificial intelligence. In turn, the solution of this problem, which is complex in nature, requires international cooperation of researchers, the initiation of which is one of the goals of this paper.

REFERENCES

Ahn, J., Habib, A., Malacrino, D., & Presbitero, A. F. (2023, April 5). *Fragmenting Foreign Direct Investment Hits Emerging Economies Hardest*. https://www.imf.org/en/Blogs/Articles/2023/04/05/fragmenting-foreign-direct-investment-hits-emerging-economies-hardest

AList. (2022). *PREDICTIONS 2022. Disruptive Forces Necessitate Bold Decisions*. https://www.alist-daily.com/strategy/Forrester-2022-predictions-guid

Arthur, W. B. (1999). Complexity and the economy. *Science*, *284*(5411), 107–109. doi:10.1126cience.284.5411.107 PMID:10103172

Baumol, W. J. (1959). *Business Behavior, Value and Growth*. Macmillan.

Can, H., & Paskaleva, M. (2017). Macroeconomic determinants of CDS: The case of Europe. *New knowledge. Journal of Science*, *6*(3), 1080–1096.

CEIC Data. (2021). *China Capacity Utilization Rate*. https://www.ceicdata.com/en/china/capacity-utilization-rate

Chandra, Y., & Wilkinson, I. F. (2017). Firm internationalization from a network-centric complex-systems perspective. *Journal of World Business*, *52*(5), 691–701. doi:10.1016/j.jwb.2017.06.001

Coase, R. H. (1937). The Nature of the Firm. *Economica*, *4*(16), 386–405. doi:10.1111/j.1468-0335.1937.tb00002.x

Cyert, R. M., & March, J. G. (1963). *A Behavioral Theory of the Firm.*

EC2023. Economic Commentary. (2023). *How Has the Pandemic Impacted Inflation.* https://blog.nationalwidefinancial.com/market-economy/how-has-the-pandemic-impacted-inflation

Estola, M. (2014). The Neoclassical Theory of a Firm: Correction for its errors. *Hyperion International Journal of Econophisics & New Economy*, *7*(1), 7–21.

European Commission. (2020). *Support for SME Internalization beyond the EU.* https://evening.europe.eu/growth/smes/sme-strategy/assets-to-markets/internationalization/support-tools_en

Fabuš, M., & Csabay, M. (2018). State aid and investment: Case of Slovakia. *Enterpreneurship and Sustainability Issues*, *6*(1), 369–377. doi:10.9770/jesi.2018.6.1(23)

fDi Intelligence. (2023). *Strategic Industries buck post-Covid Investment slump.* https://www.fdiintelligence.com/content/data-trends/strategic-industries-buck-postcovid-investment-slump-82621?

fDi Intelligence. (2023). *Wave of mega projects mounts in 2022.* https://www.fdiintelligence.com/content/data-trends/wave-of-mega-projects-mounts-in-2022-82551

Global Times. (2023). *China issue 15 measures to help SMEs stabilize growth, adjust structure.* https://www.globaltimes.cn/page/202301/1283861.shtml

Hale, G., Leer, J. C., & Nechio, F. (2023). Inflationary effects of fiscal support to households and firms. *National Bureau of Economic Research*, 30906. https://www.nber.org/w30906

Holland, J. H. (2014). *Complexity: A very short introduction.* Oxford University Press. doi:10.1093/actrade/9780199662548.001.0001

IEA. (2022). *Unlocking the Potential of Distributed Energy Resources.* https://www.iea.org/reports/unlocking-the-potential-of-distributed-energy-resources

IEA. (2023). *World Energy Investment 2023.* https://iea.glob.core.windows.net/assets/8834d3af-af60-4df0-9643-72e2684f7221/WorldEnergyinvestment2023.pdf

IMF. (2021). *Fiscal Monitor Database of Country Fiscal Measures in Response to the COVID-19 Pandemic.* https://www.imf.org/en/Topics/inf-and-covid19/Fiscal-Policies-Database-in-Response-to-COVID-19

IMF. (2023). *World Economic Outlook.* https://www.imf.org/en/Publications/WEO

INCTAD. (2022). *World Investment Report 2022.* https://unctad.org/publication/world-investment-report-2022

INCTAD. (2023). *World Investment Report 2023. Investing in Sustainable Energy for All.* https://unctad.org/system/files/official-document/wir2023_en.pdf

March, J. G. (1958). A Behavioral Theory of Decision Making. *The Personnel Administrator*, *21*(3), 8–10.

Marris, R. (1964). *The Economic Theory of 'Managerial' Capitalism*. Macmillan. doi:10.1007/978-1-349-81732-0

Marris, R. (1998). Managerial Theories of the Firm. In *Managerial Capitalism in Retrospect*. Palgrave Macmillan. doi:10.1057/9780230376168_5

Marshall, A. (1920). *Principal of Economics*. Macmillan.

Miroshnychenko, I., Kravchenko, T., & Drobyna, Y. (2021). Forecasting electricity generation from renewable sources in developing countries (on the case of Ukraine). *Neuro-Fuzzy Modeling Techniques in Economics*, *10*(10), 164–198. doi:10.33111/nfmte.2021.164

Moody's Analytics. (2022). *Global Fiscal Policy in the Pandemic*. https://www.moodysanalytics.com/-/media/article/2022/global-fiscal-policy-in-the-pandemic.pdf

Nonaka, I., & Takeuchi, H. (1995). *The Knowledge-Creating Company - How Japanese Companies Create the Dynamics of Innovation*. Oxford University Press.

Penrose, E. (1958). The Theory of the Growth of the Firm. Basil Blackwell.

Schumpeter, J. A. (1939). *Business Cycles. A theoretical, Historical and Statistical Analysis of the Capitalist Process*. McGraw-Hill Book Company.

Schumpeter, J. A. (2008). The Theory of Economic Development: As Inquiry into Profits, Capital, Credit, Interest and the Business Cycle. Transaction Publishers. (Original publication 1934)

Shuyan, L., & Fabuš, M. (2019). Study on the spatial distribution of China's Outward Foreign Direct Investment in EU and its influencing factors. *Entrepreneurship and Sustainability Issues*, *6*(3), 1080–1096. doi:10.9770/jesi.2019.6.3(16)

Shuyan, L., & Fabus, M. (2019). The impact of OFDI reverse technology spillover on China's technological progress: Analysis of provincial panel data. *Journal of International Students*, *12*(4), 325–336. doi:10.14254/2071-8330.2019/12-4/21

Simon, H. A. (1947). *Administrative Behavior. A study of decision-making process in administrative organizations*. Macmillan.

Simon, H. A. (1957). *Models of Man*. John Wiley & Sons.

Statista. (2023). *Global gross domestic product (GDP) at current prices from 1985 to 2028*. https://www.statista.com/statistics/268750/global-gross-domestic-product-gdp

Suszynski, C. (2013). *Business Enterprise. The Integration of Approaches*. Oficyna Wudawnicza Szkola Glowna Handlowa w Warszawie.

UNCTAD. (2023). *Investment Trends Monitor*. https://unctad.org/system/files/official-document/diaeiainf2023d1_en.pdf

Virtanen, I. (2011). Externalization of tacit knowledge implies a simplified theory of cognition. *Journal of Knowledge Management Practice*, *12*(3), 139–145.

Walker, P. (2019). *The Theory of the Firm. An overview of the economic mainstream*. Routledge.

Williamson, O. (1964). *The Economics of Discretionary Behavior: Managerial Objectives in a Theory of the Firm*. Prentice-Hall.

Williamson, O. (1970). *Corporate Control and Business Behavior*. Prentice-Hall.

Worldscience. (2023). *Industrial Overcapacity and Duplicate Construction in China: Introduction*. https://www.worldscience.com/doi/pdf/10.1142/9789813277281_0001.pdf

Xie, B., Yang, C., Song, W., Song, L., & Wang, H. (2023). The impact of environmental regulation on capacity utilization of China's manufacturing industry: An empirical research based on the sector level. *Ecological Indicators*, *148*, 110085. doi:10.1016/j.ecolind.2023.110085

Zohar, D., & Zohar, D. (2022). The Tao of Quantum Management. *Zero Distance: Management in the Quantum Age*, 71-80.

Chapter 18
Structural and Qualitative Defects in Adaptation to Digital Transformation in Local Governments

Sedat Akbiyik
Tekirdag Metropolitan Municipality, Turkey

Hamit Can
https://orcid.org/0000-0002-6918-3234
Trakya University, Turkey

ABSTRACT

Different digital transformation applications have been developed in order to provide more qualified and higher quality services to the local people by using the internet, information, and communication technologies in local governments. This study has examined which applications they have implemented by using information technology in order to respond to the needs of local people in a shorter and faster time thanks to the digital transformation applications put into practice by local governments. Suggestions have been developed in order to provide the expected benefit from digital transformation in local governments. The problems encountered in the digital transformation transition and the predictions that will be encountered if these problems are not resolved are stated. In addition, energy efficiency and the applicability of European projects with digital transformation in local governments and their effects on the economic crisis and economic development in the country are mentioned.

INTRODUCTION

Digital technologies and digitization have become a common part of daily life for both business and entertainment. It has transformed the way most people interact and communicate, as well as the way many businesses run are with the increase of competitiveness and quality of employment (Okur Dincsoy,

DOI: 10.4018/979-8-3693-0400-6.ch018

2009). Several significant developments in sectors, which are related with Information and Communication Technology (ICT), were deeply observed that it has a remarkable effect on economic and social activities as much as economic growth for countries. Many development strategies have focused on pursuing plans and policies for promoting a more attractive environment for digital transformation (Okur Dincsoy, 2008). Thanks to this digital transformation, new roles, professions, markets and services have developed. Digital technology and digitization are also expected to solve some of the great challenges of our time, such as the problems associated with an aging population and rising healthcare spending (Peine, 2015). Today, many services are offered electronically quickly, smoothly and cost-effectively. It becomes extremely important for social workers and social workers to know what services are offered on the technological ground so that they can follow current technological developments in the realization of their professional work, be a good technology literate and use their functions as a link-maker, intermediary and resource mobilizer while working with client systems. (Spensberger, 2019).

Municipalities are organizations with a complex structure with a large amount of external demand (Magnusson, 2021). Along with digitalization innovations in the field of society and industry, municipalities also make it necessary to follow these developments and integrate them into these systems (Hanna, 2016). Despite the citizen-oriented and solution-oriented services of municipalities, they need to break the general perception that they are negative and reactionary towards municipalities. One of the best ways to break this perception could be for municipalities to offer digital well-being (Magnusson, 2021). According to the studies on the subject, in order to create maximum value and ensure the transition to smart systems, the municipality should do the existing works in different ways, observe each operation and increase citizen-oriented studies as a part of digitalization. Thus, citizen-oriented satisfaction and service quality can be increased.

Digital Transformation, workflows, management, changes the rules of living in every field from start to finish. Local governments are affected by these changes. The spread of New Information (Digital) and Mobile Technologies is changing the management models and service processes of cities. For this reason, cities such as countries, non-governmental organizations, companies and universities have to find ways of digital transformation by adapting to the Digital Age. It should not be forgotten that the Digital Transformation of a city means that it becomes a Smart City (Satyam, 2017). Administrative activities are indispensable with their responsive role in eliminating the disruptions caused by technological developments in society and should be compatible with daily conditions (Janssen & van der Voort, 2016). Public institutions have been found to have a reduced skill set and limitations for upgrading their IT infrastructure (Dunleavy et al., 2006). Inappropriate managerial understanding can hinder digital transformation (Magnusson, 2021). In the transformation, it can be observed that the central administration, to which all public institutions are affiliated, cannot be organized at a sufficient level for the transformation and that the appropriateness of the infrastructures belonging to this is not determined. Therefore, it is foreseen that many main service applications that the central administration puts into use without adequate testing and work over the network structure created without infrastructure determination may not work properly, and many problems may be encountered, especially in the transport and processing of data. The inability of the personnel working in the local government to integrate into a system with an incomplete infrastructure or to try to maintain their service incompletely in areas that can be integrated may increase the workload and may create passive resistance in transformation.

While the quality, speed and efficiency of the service offered to the citizens increase with the use of digital transformation technologies by local governments in municipalities, some problems occur with digitalization. In this study, suggestions are presented about the problems that may occur in the digitalization stages and how these problems can be solved.

LITERATURE

Although there are various studies related to digital transformation in local governments, the most comprehensive study in the field of e-municipality is in the literature with the title of Seventh Global E-Governance Research: "Longitudinal Evaluation of Municipal Websites Around the World". This study was created by examining the web pages of the municipalities of the capitals of more than 120 countries and scoring them in the framework of privacy and security, usability, content, services and social participation categories. As a result of the study, the municipalities of Seoul, Tokyo, Hong Kong, Helsinki, Toronto and Barcelona were stated as the municipalities with the highest scores. According to the findings of the research, Seoul Municipality's web page includes information and services about the main organs of the city and the municipality, urban planning, international interactions, economy and investment, transportation, environment and energy, culture and tourism, welfare, health, social services, security, education. It has been reported that the services provided in the fields of crisis management, women and children were shared (Holzer & Manoharan, 2016).

According to Frennert (2021), it is very important to evaluate the purpose of digitalization. Although this development provides several benefits, the original purpose is not always taken into account. One of the biggest problems is that many municipalities aim to be modern but fail to set a goal. It is essential to have a clear goal aimed at increasing value creation. On the other hand, it is important to recognize that economic or technological goals are not always compatible with each other. It is important to reflect on whom and what value will be created from each initiative. The goal should not only be to increase efficiency, but also to consider other value creations. If the aim of initiatives is to create more value for citizens or employees, it can reduce resistance to change within the organization. In most cases, digitization is accomplished without creating value. During transformations, the organization should take the opportunity to optimize it and consider how to maximize value creation. According to some views, many initiatives against citizens may be seen as unnecessary. While the basic idea is good, many citizens have limited time to engage and often only desire the safety and smooth functioning of municipal services (Frennert, 2021). It can also be said that the modernity mentioned here is tried to be made only in visual and theoretical fields, but it cannot be filled, and this does not have a sufficient effect on the citizens, especially the employees. The result of not setting a target is the conviction that it is sufficient for the citizen to reach the most basic service or not to delay it, especially in order not to harm himself in the legal and financial field.

At the same time, public institutions have much more external responsibilities than private institutions. Combined with emerging digital technologies and the goal of staying current in the ever-increasing digital business arena, government agencies need to address challenges with citizens, including demographic changes and the evolution of life patterns. Generally, public institutions, especially municipalities, need to manage the aging population, increasing demand for municipal services and the increasing population living in cities due to urbanization (Frennert, 2018).

Soe and Drechsler (2018) argue that public value management is more applicable in a digital context than New Public Management in a public organization, as it aims to improve public and social values.

Digital transformation can offer solutions to such challenges faced by municipalities and provide more value to citizens in general. This could potentially be a municipal method of monetizing job opportunities. Digital transformations have the potential, for example, to enable municipalities to deliver better healthcare, more efficient waste management and improved sustainability efforts (Ringenson, 2021; Chang et al., 2020; Davenport & Westerman, 2018). According to Magnusson (2021), the existing administration in municipalities today opposes digital transformations. Although this perception needs to be changed during the transition to digitization, there is a risk that these phases of change will be placed on top of existing governance and thus the previous management will not change (Magnusson, 2021). Although there is a desire to make changes more adaptive, but currently adaptive management can be seen as an academic product that does not exist in practice (Frennert, 2021). There is a misconception that municipalities should be dynamic. Most of the organization is stable over time where parts can be dynamic (Magnusson, 2021). However, employees can be trained in business development by working in short intervals and soft-targeted projects (Frennert, 2021).

Most applications can be supported by digitization, but this needs to be done properly, which is not always the case. When applications fail, it's often because they haven't been thought through and planned. Sometimes the designed solutions do not take into account the individual point of view. Although the original idea was created with a good purpose, it can cause negative effects. For example, digital systems could occur that increase surveillance and can remove socially vulnerable citizens from society. Frennert (2021) agrees in emphasizing the employees' perspective on digital applications. Frennert (2021) argues that it is necessary to view digitalization as an ecosystem. Just focusing on technology and application and forgetting about adaptation and integration may seem like a simple solution. But the implementation of a new digital system is an important process that requires adapting the technology to the context, such as business processes and existing systems. Otherwise, employees will have to adapt their jobs so that the new technology works instead of supporting the job (Frennert, 2021). The increase in the number of the current works of the municipalities in line with the developing population and the demand for more comfortable service, the fact that the same increase does not occur in the income section, and therefore all the related needs and the inability to provide qualified employment create pressure on the employees. Since the current workload and forcing the service to the employees with technological development require the attention of the employees to focus on technology, it may reduce the efficiency in the timely and complete fulfillment of the service.

Municipalities can provide social services to citizens that limit their ability to use resources in experimental initiatives. Collaboration with universities can be beneficial for municipalities when the aim is to experiment as part of universities (Ringenson, 2021). In addition, scientists do not aim to make money, and it is known that public institutions can provide consultancy in a very different way than consultants. Consulting services may vary according to their dependence on consulting firms (Magnusson, 2021). However, there are difficulties in such collaborations. Research can be slow and it is possible to arrive at ambiguous, negative or unfavorable results that may conflict with the desires of municipalities wishing to invest quickly in something that pleases everyone (Ringenson, 2021). Governments should make sure they get the best use of taxpayers' money and avoid bad consequences that make public institutions afraid to take risks (Goh & Arenas, 2020). This can lead to extremely high opportunity costs (Magnusson, 2021). Therefore, public institutions need to learn to accept criticism from the media regarding their dynamic management approach and trial and error approaches (Frennert, 2021; Magnusson, 2021).

This type of management approach requires public institutions not to shy away from public value and to defend the results (Mergel et al., 2020). At the same time, there is a misconception that municipalities need to be agile and that agile methods and approaches can be inefficient in municipalities (Magnusson, 2021). Mergel et al. (2020) agree that dynamic management can be contradictory for many traditional bureaucratic organizations. Magnusson (2021) emphasizes that one part of the organization can be dynamic, but the majority of an organization should be stable over time. Versatility, which balances stability and accountability on the one hand, and adaptability and accountability on the other, is possible with adaptive governance (Janssen, 2016). As Janssen and van der Voort (2016) point out, adaptive governance can enable organizations to manage changes while keeping them stable. While emphasizing the tendency to be more adaptive to Frennert (2021), both Frennert (2021) and Magnusson (2021) agree that adaptive governance is virtually nonexistent in practice. However, technological developments are changing society and this calls for organizations to be more adaptable (Janssen & van der Voort, 2016).

DIGITAL TRANSFORMATION APPLICATIONS IN LOCAL GOVERNMENTS

Within the scope of digital transformation in local governments, it is seen that some projects have been implemented under the support of the state to facilitate cooperation and information sharing between local governments. At the same time, projects have been implemented that will ensure the participation of citizens and enable local governments to act jointly.

Smart City Automation System

These systems cover the services of storing the information of the city and the people of the city within the framework of certain standards, transferring this information to the database, establishing a relationship between the obtained data and determining this information according to the needs of the municipality and managing it correctly.

Kiosks

Thanks to the kiosks placed in certain parts of the cities, it can be ensured that the services are open to all citizens from the predetermined parts of the city. Thus, citizens who do not have internet access at their homes and workplaces will be reached. Especially in low-income neighborhoods with lower levels of internet access, it is an important regulation in eliminating the digital divide in the digital transformation process.

Cemetery Information System Application

It is a system that allows the collecting of all the information about the Cemeteries Directorate of the municipalities in a common database, collecting numerical information about the cemeteries, integrating all the information about the graves, and analyzing and querying them. MEBIS is a project prepared to carry out parcel studies of cemeteries, to determine empty burial places, and to carry out more comprehensive maintenance and repairs of cemeteries. With this project, local people can access the information of their relatives buried in the cemeteries through the kiosks located at the entrances of the cemeteries, and they can access the web pages of the municipalities. In addition, with the MEBIS application, statistical information such as the medical causes of death of individuals who died and the death rates of women and men are also obtained. With the implementation of the MEBIS project; The information about the people in the cemeteries can be accessed via the internet, the citizens outside the city can see who has passed away from the deceased menu, information about the important people and artifacts in the cemetery is obtained, the time spent by the visitors in finding the cemeteries of their relatives is reduced, and the authorized persons can obtain more accurate information about the plans to be made about the cemeteries. will be able to reach.

Video Conferencing and Webcasting

Video conferencing is a system that enables individuals in different places to communicate simultaneously with video and audio. This method is also applied in municipalities, and municipal meetings are held without coming together in a physical place. Webcasting is the broadcasting of previously prepared videos and audio recordings on the internet through a television or radio program. For example, it is possible to broadcast the municipal council meetings live or in the form of video on the web pages of the municipalities so that the citizens can watch these meetings.

Artificial Intelligence/Machine Learning

Machine learning or artificial intelligence applications, which are at the center of digital transformation, can be used in every field in local governments. Social media applications used by local governments, sharing information instantly and in real time, receiving feedback from local people, conducting surveys through social media platforms, and providing participants on the basis of streets and neighborhoods in the decision-making process may be possible. It is possible for local governments to use drones (unmanned aerial vehicles) in many areas such as crisis management and to deliver aid during natural disasters. Today, people who benefit from the services offered by local governments every day and over the internet of things, a large amount of data flow to local governments is possible. Analyzing this information in a healthy and reliable way plays an important role in ensuring institutionalization, determining the needs correctly and getting feedback from the citizens.

Big Data Analysis/Data Mining

Almost every minute, large numbers of citizens who benefit from the services of municipalities receive a large data flow to local units over the internet of people and objects. Analyzing this data in a healthy and legal way is an important practice in terms of ensuring institutional efficiency, receiving feedback from citizens and determining needs.

Virtual Reality/Augmented Reality

This technology contributes to the decision-making processes of political mechanisms, in the decision-making processes of council members or city councils, in making healthier decisions for the future. In the process of ensuring the integration of the discriminated segments, it contributes to reducing the problems they have experienced and understanding the problems.

Blockchain

This method, which was put into practice to bring solutions to cryptocurrencies, brings more transparent and reliable solutions to some issues based on cryptography. In particular, municipalities are responsible for the payment of taxes, and the distribution of social benefits.

Crowdsourcing and Mapping

In terms of local governments, it is an application used in many areas such as solidarity and volunteering activities, in times of crisis and natural disasters, in collecting information, and in delivering aid.

DISCUSSION

Transition to digital transformation and adaptation in local governments face various structural and qualitative challenges. It is very important to identify these difficulties in order not to hinder the progress and effectiveness of digital transformation initiatives. Various scientific studies have been carried out on the determination of these difficulties. The general problems identified by these studies are the lack of financial, technical, and personnel capacities. While local governments support digital transformation initiatives, legal issues can also pose challenges to digital transformation in local governments (Moon, 2002). In addition, there may be problems such as a lack of capacity, infrastructure, software, and investment allocation to qualified personnel. Local governments need to be aligned with the resolution of legal complexities and the digitization of data protection and privacy regulations. Also, the size and type of government can affect the transition to digital transformation in local governments (Moon, 2002). For example, larger cities and municipalities, as well as those with a governing council government structure, are more likely to adopt digital solutions such as municipal websites. Smaller local governments may face additional challenges in terms of limited resources and capacity. Another structural challenge in the transition to digital transformation is the slow progress toward integrated and transactional e-government (Norris and Moon, 2005). In addition, qualitative challenges in transitioning to digital transformation, resistance to change, and the lack of digital skills among employees are among the main problems that slow the transition (Gangneux and Joss, 2022). Adoption of digital technologies often requires a cultural shift in organizations. The existence of training that increases digital skills is very important for the adoption of these changes. General personnel training, especially those who lack training in the use of digital tools and technologies, is one of the issues that should be given importance. The difficult digital transformation that the state insists all institutions pass through creates serious difficulties for some local governments, while the transition of some institutions may be easy. Therefore, digital transformation conditions should be regulated by considering the structure of all institutions (Lino and Aquino, 2021). The importance of digitization also emerges in various crisis moments. The COVID-19 pandemic has highlighted the need for accelerated digitization in local governments (Gangneux and Joss, 2022). The crisis has led to the rapid adoption of digital technologies for the remote and efficient delivery of public services. But the pandemic has also exposed weaknesses and gaps in readiness and capabilities for digital transformation. Structural and qualitative difficulties encountered in the transition to digital transformation and adaptation process in local governments include lack of financial and technical capacity, legal problems, resistance to change, and lack of digital skills. These challenges can hinder the progress and effectiveness of digital transformation initiatives, and addressing them requires addressing both technical and social system-level changes within organizations. A common application of digital transformation in local governments is the adoption of open data and open government initiatives (Janssen et al., 2012). Open data refers to the practice of making government data available to the public free of charge in a readable format. This allows citizens, businesses, and other stakeholders to access and use government data for a variety of purposes such as research, innovation, and decision-making. Open government initiatives include increasing transparency, accountability, and citizen participation through the use of digital technologies. Another important application of digital transformation in local governments is the implementation of e-government services (Kuhlmann and Heuberger, 2021). The aim of e-government is to improve the efficiency, accessibility and relevance of government services. Digital transformation in local governments also includes the use of data analytics and data mining techniques to inform decision-making and policy development (Lan, 2022). By analyzing large volumes of data, local governments can gain insight into citizens' needs and preferences, identify trends and patterns, and make data-driven decisions. Data mining can also be used to evaluate the effectiveness and impact of digital transformation initiatives in local governments. In addition, digital transformation in local governments also includes the integration of digital technologies into various administrative and operational processes (Lino and Aquino, 2021). This may include automation of routine tasks, digitization of paper-based processes, and implementation of digital workflow systems. By streamlining and digitizing processes, local governments can increase efficiency, reduce costs and increase the overall effectiveness of their operations. In addition, digital transformation in local governments may also include the development and implementation of smart city initiatives (Lino and Aquino, 2021).

The fact that the e-municipality platform created for the use of municipalities is not categorically separated in terms of the characteristics, powers, and responsibilities of the municipalities, that all municipalities are evaluated in the same standard, and that this platform is theoretically difficult for municipalities to use, especially by correspondence, may complicate the process. Municipalities that do not implement this practice or fail to pass due to infrastructural problems may face the problem of being completely independent and dependent on private sector practices and may create more burden on public finances. Such practices should be prepared collectively by establishing commissions and comprehensive studies and should be put into practice after adequate tests are carried out and the results are obtained. First of all, the existing platform should be improved and made into a user-friendly form by changing the version.

Sample systems or applications established by IT personnel working in municipalities can be examined by affiliated ministries, personnel who make this contribution can be rewarded, and they can be motivated by finding different methods to contribute to digital transformation and continue their work. The personnel who produce many useful applications and systems can be included in the working groups to be held in the country, especially abroad, in a way to present their own municipal applications. The studies can be reported and the opinions that are re-evaluated by obtaining the approval of the top managers of each municipality can be matured and transformed into new practices.

Information processing units of municipalities can be established in accordance with the structures of the municipality, and the closure of these units can be prevented by the initiative of the administrator. Awareness training for senior managers can be provided by special teams to be established by the ministries. The job descriptions of the personnel to be employed in the units to be established should be clearly defined and qualified personnel should be provided.

It can be very beneficial to supervise the municipal data processing units, not by many and different institutions, but by authorized and competent public personnel through a single institution. The fact that the supervisory or regulatory bodies at the top of the institutional hierarchy take on the form of an inaccessible institution that issues, sets and publishes regulatory rules can complicate digitalization. The activities of these institutions to play an educational role open to communication and to develop encouraging projects in every field can contribute to the digitalization steps of public institutions. It is very important for the state to adopt the awareness of digital transformation from the upper level to the lower level and to identify the central coordinating authority. The main purpose of corporate audits is not to look for vulnerabilities, but to be constructive and especially by keeping the issue of cyber security in the foreground, which can facilitate digital transformation. Leaving the audit and certification processes to be carried out within the scope of information security to authorized IT companies may cause various problems. On the contrary, it is foreseen that the execution of audit and certification processes by competent public personnel appointed by the public will eliminate many problems in the digitalization of public institutions. Completion status should be followed by taking high-level measures and providing financial and technical support in order to fulfill the findings obtained in the audit results. Since the periodic inquiry of completion status will involve service units and each end user, it will play a role in triggering the transformation, mainly on basic informatics issues. While the current inspection standards and guides are being prepared, the reality of the field should not be overlooked, first of all, each municipality should be determined separately and measures that can be managed and supported from the center should be taken. It should be taken as a basis that each institution has its own unique structure, features, technical capacity, that it does not have the same standards at the same time, that the institution should be approached with this awareness and that the developments should be in this direction.

The construction of disaster recovery centers by affiliated ministries for municipalities, which are public institutions, and the integration of municipalities into these centers, not excluding even a municipality that is not included in the disaster recovery center management, will benefit the digitalization processes and will enable the system to resume from where it left off in case of emergency.

In order to ensure developments in the light of the specific evaluations listed above, first of all, studies to increase digital literacy under the roof of the central government may contribute to the developing processes. Especially in school curricula, planning education in such a way that these themes are in every classroom, other institutions and organizations, as well as planning courses for adults without schooling can facilitate these goals. In addition, fairs, conferences, project workshops, etc. that encourage digital transformation. Public personnel can be encouraged to participate in these activities by increasing the number of events. Personnel who spend energy and effort on digital transformation can be employed in appropriate positions or positions with positive distinctions and can be supported financially. Considering that the use of technology is a costly business and the technical personnel to install this system or software are very difficult to train or acquire, it is foreseen that the whole society can be included in the digital transformation process thanks to a large number of trained personnel. It should be adopted that the basic policy should be based on not losing the trained manpower in the face of economic difficulties without leaving them in a difficult situation.

The absence of a mechanism to check whether the websites of municipalities have appropriate content or the absence of a standard type of website or mobile applications that can be easily understood and used by everyone, can create reluctance in both citizens and employees to access information and services easily and can make controllability difficult. Municipalities should play a role in facilitating the processes that are likely to adopt the principles aimed at providing the ideal service by considering the comfort of the citizens in the shortest way.

The use of information technologies in local governments causes pressure on local governments by individuals, institutions, and organizations. Thanks to these pressures, important steps are being taken towards the development of participatory democracy. Despite these efforts, many problems can be encountered in the process of digital applications in local governments. These problems are; The inadequacy of the laws in legal and technical matters, the resistance of the local government units to the restructuring efforts due to insufficient information, the resistance of the employees to the use of new technology, the traditional management approach, and the conflicts among the employees consisting of different party members, bureaucratic obstacles, the e-municipality is an important area. It can be listed as the absence of a specified standard in urban information systems (Karakurt-Tosun, 2008).

The existence of problems such as the technical inadequacy of communication at the national level, the inability of the traditional government approach to the function of the e-government approach, the inadequacy of personnel, the inadequacy of budget transfer, the low administrative or institutional tendency to integration prevent the integration of all institutions in an effective digital system.

The continuation of the traditional service delivery habits, the insistence of the employees to continue their old habits due to the fear of losing their income or innovation, the thought that new systems will disrupt the workflow with the digital transformation, the pressure on the employees that will be experienced with the transition, and the problems that will occur with this pressure in the transition to the digital system. are some of the problems that occur.

Insisting on maintaining their old habits, not being able to solve the problems in the old way of transitioning to a new way of functioning, not being able to fully establish the new way of functioning, efforts to maintain the old and new system together, and incompletely, staff with high age level or lack of technology knowledge. Not being able to adapt to integration and escaping from this adaptation are among the important problems.

Another problem encountered is that e-culture has not yet been fully established in public institutions and citizens, a single form of functioning in public administrations has not been reached, digital transformation has been postponed together with the non-established culture, not being able to benefit from rapidly developing technologies and falling behind.

Not providing information security in the national area and therefore lack of trust in users, not applying sufficient sanctions to users in case of possible security violations in ensuring information security, and not being able to overcome the bureaucratic problems encountered in the implementation of these sanctions are among the important problems.

The low rate of computer literacy in public administrations and citizens, and as a result of this, the low use of the internet, and the inadequacy of training on the adaptation of employees to technology are among the problems that hinder digital transformation.

As a result of not benefiting from the brain power of the country in the production of technology, being left behind in this field, and the employment of these personnel in private sectors as a result of the financial difficulties encountered in employing competent personnel significantly hinders digital transformation.

In terms of ensuring security within the scope of the protection of personal data, the insecure attitudes of citizens towards communication technology, the failure to apply the necessary articles in case of possible violations, and the fact that this issue is put into the background alongside the daily works and projects of my institution are among the serious problems.

Lack of cooperation and coordination between the central administration and local authorities, significant problems in the integration of institutions with different bureaucratic understanding and different budgets, or the lack of integration significantly hinders digital transformation.

Another problem is the lack of sufficient inclination towards digital transformation and the inability to transfer the necessary budgets by prioritizing the resistance created by the managers of the institutions against change and the other goals and projects of the institution.

The inadequacy of qualified personnel who will adapt to innovations and follow them closely, the problems caused by the inadequacy of personnel assignment, the incompleteness or non-fulfillment of the items determined in the assignments, and the problems experienced in imposing sanctions on personnel who do not fulfill their duties are among the important obstacles.

The difficulties encountered in the transition to digital transformation, as the official web pages of most of the municipalities are useless, not updated, the web pages are used only for the purpose of informing the citizens, and there is no environment that foresees the active participation of the citizens.

One of the problems experienced in the field of digital transformation in municipalities is that each municipality implements its own application. The scarcity of projects aimed at ensuring coordination in this regard also ensures that this problem cannot be solved. At the same time, there are some problems due to not giving enough importance to information technology in municipalities. These problems cause repetition of the data used, not updating the data, lack of communication within the institution and not being able to reach the necessary information in a timely manner. For these reasons, it is possible for managers to make incomplete decisions and to experience disruptions in the service process.

Another issue experienced in the field of digital transformation in local governments is the personnel problem. It is important for municipal employees to specialize in digital applications. Otherwise, instead of holistic policies, it will be possible to present separate and independent solutions in the solution of problems. In addition, since some digital applications may exceed the scale of the city, it is necessary to perform applications on a regional or country basis in these cases. Many digital applications may require cooperation with different institutions or organizations from different sectors, in such cases care should be taken to establish horizontal and vertical collaborations.

RESULTS

In order to create smart cities, it is necessary to establish the legal infrastructure for the collection of data and to carry out administrative studies on this subject. In addition, assurance should be provided regarding the collection and sharing of data in areas such as trade secrets, state secrets, and privacy. When the developments and studies related to digitalization are examined, some changes that public institutions can make as stages of digitalization can be expressed as follows.

First of all, it requires public institutions to strengthen their efforts to inform and raise awareness regarding the law on the use of personal data. While carrying out these studies, it may be more beneficial for efficiency to develop integrated studies with the protection of personal data and information security issues.

In addition, it can be said that websites are one of the most important factors in the success of local organizations in their digitalization goals. It is very important that the news and announcements on the home pages of these organizations are up-to-date and compatible with the latest technological developments. In addition, contact and social media information of all units, working hours, introductory information about the city and districts, investments and projects made here, how other stakeholders can access the information and how they can be included in projects if needed, and their documentation information are included on the site. It is very important to receive. In addition, it may be beneficial to specify the areas of duty, authorities and responsibilities, financing sources, annual reports, and relevant legislation and workflows in a diagram on the websites. Municipalities develop e-municipal services in the provision of social services and design these services in accordance with both the service production process of social workers and the service usage process of the clients, The municipalities include the social services they offer on their web pages as separate heading and present the scope of the services in detail, It can be suggested to add search engines to the web pages in order to facilitate the use of the archive containing the works and the web page, the municipalities to update their web pages to broadcast in a foreign language, and the municipalities to add software to the web pages where the applicants can convey their wishes and complaints.

In addition to these suggestions, another important digitization stage is the efficiency of the projects to be realized in local institutions. Considering public institutions as institutions that provide services and inputs that contribute to the country's economy, it is very important that these institutions carry out efficient projects for inputs that contribute to the economy. For the realization of these projects, the employment of competent personnel and the transfer of income resources to this area play a key role. It is known that energy is one of the most important inputs in economic development. The realization of projects compatible with digitalization for energy optimization in public institutions can be seen as a trigger for economic development, firstly locally and in the following stages throughout the country. At the same time, it can be predicted that the development and economic freedom that will occur will be beneficial in the form of a circular economy when transferred to digitalization projects.

In order to create smart cities, it is necessary to establish the legal infrastructure for the collection of data and to carry out administrative studies on this subject. In addition, assurance must be provided for the collection and sharing of data in areas such as trade secrets, state secrets, and privacy.

REFERENCES

Chang, H., Mikalsen, K. S., Nesse, P. J., & Erdal, O. B. (2019). *Digitalization of municipalities through ecosystem collaboration. In Innovation, Regulation, Multi Business Model Innovation and Technology*. ICT. doi:10.13052/nbjict1902-097X.2020.006

Davenport, T. H., & Westerman, G. (2018). Why so many high-profile digital transformations fail. *Harvard Business Review*, *9*(4), 15.

Dunleavy, P., Margetts, H., Bastow, S., & Tinkler, J. (2006). New public management is dead—Long live digital-era governance. *Journal of Public Administration: Research and Theory*, *16*(3), 467–494. doi:10.1093/jopart/mui057

Frennert, S. (2018). Lost in digitalization? Municipality employment of welfare technologies. *Disability and Rehabilitation. Assistive Technology*. Advance online publication. doi:10.1080/17483107.2018.14 96362 PMID:30264649

Gangneux, J., & Joss, S. (2022). Crisis as driver of digital transformation? Scottish local governments' response to COVID-19. *Data & Policy*, *4*, e26. doi:10.1017/dap.2022.18

Goh, J. M., & Arenas, A. E. (2020). IT value creation in public sector: How IT-enabled capabilities mitigate tradeoffs in public organisations. *European Journal of Information Systems*, *29*(1), 25–43. do i:10.1080/0960085X.2019.1708821

Hanna, N. K. (2016). *Mastering digital transformation. Mastering Digital Transformation (Innovation, Technology, and Education for Growth)*. Emerald Publishing., doi:10.1108/978-1-78560-465-220151009

Holzer, M., & Manoharan, A. P. (2016). *Digital Governance in Municipalities Worldwide (2015- 16) Seventh Global E-Governance Survey: A Longitudinal Assessment of Municipal Websites Throughout the World*. National Center for Public Performance.

Janssen, M., Charalabidis, Y., & Zuiderwijk, A. (2012). Benefits, adoption barriers and myths of open data and open government. *Information Systems Management*, *29*(4), 258–268. doi:10.1080/1058053 0.2012.716740

Janssen, M., & Van Der Voort, H. (2016). Adaptive governance: Towards a stable, accountable and responsive government. *Government Information Quarterly*, *33*(1), 1–5. doi:10.1016/j.giq.2016.02.003

Karakurt Tosun, E. (2008). Türkiye de E Belediyecilik Uygulamaları Bursa Nilüfer Osmangazi Yıldırım Belediyelerinin Web Sitelerinin Analizi. *Çağdaş Yerel Yönetimler*, *2*(17), 71-94. doi:10.1111/faam.12313

Kuhlmann, S., & Heuberger, M. (2023). Digital transformation going local: Implementation, impacts and constraints from a German perspective. *Public Money & Management*, *43*(2), 147–155. doi:10.10 80/09540962.2021.1939584

Lan, P. (2022, December). Evaluation of Digital Transformation in Chinese Government from Data Mining Perspective. In *2022 3rd International Conference on Big Data and Social Sciences (ICBDSS 2022)* (pp. 134-144). Atlantis Press. 10.2991/978-94-6463-064-0_15

Lino, A. F., Aquino, A. C. B. D., & Neves, F. R. (2022). Accountants' postures under compulsory digital transformation imposed by government oversight authorities. *Financial Accountability & Management*, *38*(2), 202–222. doi:10.1111/faam.12313

Mergel, I., Ganapati, S., & Whitford, A. B. (2020). Agile: A New Way of Governing. *Public Administration Review*, *81*(1), 161–165. doi:10.1111/puar.13202

Moon, M. J. (2002). The evolution of e-government among municipalities: Rhetoric or reality? *Public Administration Review*, *62*(4), 424–433. doi:10.1111/0033-3352.00196

Norris, D. F., & Moon, M. J. (2005). Advancing e-government at the grassroots: Tortoise or hare? *Public Administration Review*, *65*(1), 64–75. doi:10.1111/j.1540-6210.2005.00431.x

Okur Dincsoy, M. (2008). A Statistical Analysis of ICT Developments and Regional GDP per capita Convergence in Major East Asian Countries. 岡山大学大学院社会文化科学研究科紀要, *26*(1), 125-143.

Okur Dincsoy, M. (2009). Can ICT Economically Catalyze a Regional GDP Per Capita Convergence? A Case Study of Major East Asian Countries. 北東アジア経済研究, *7*(1), 45-64.

Peine, A., Faulkner, A., Jæger, B., & Moors, E. (2015). Science, technology and the 'grand challenge'of ageing—Understanding the socio-material constitution of later life. *Technological Forecasting and Social Change*, *93*, 1–9. doi:10.1016/j.techfore.2014.11.010

Satyam, A. (2017). *The Smart City transformations*. Bloomsbury Publishing India Pvt. Ltd.

Soe, R. M., & Drechsler, W. (2018). Agile local governments: Experimentation before implementation. *Government Information Quarterly*, *35*(2), 323–335. doi:10.1016/j.giq.2017.11.010

Spensberger, F. (2019). The digitalization of a social work theory: Experiences of a German child welfare social worker. *International Social Work*, *62*(6), 1575–1579. doi:10.1177/0020872819865018

Chapter 19
The Role of Nutrition in Social and Economic Development

Seher Can
Trakya University, Turkey

ABSTRACT

Nutrition is the most basic need for human well-being. It also develops human capital. Foods are very important to all of us, and proper nutrition is essential for a healthy, active life. However, although the issues of access to food and healthy sustainable nutrition are very important for a healthy life, their effects on the economy cannot be ignored. There is a growing belief by many scientists that applications developed to improve the nutritional status of people, in addition to their nutritional content, have significant value in terms of economic outcomes. According to results from studies that integrate insights from nutrition and economics, many investments in nutrition are actually very good economic investments. It is thought that this study, which deals with the economic effects of nutrition in addition to a healthy lifestyle, will also have important benefits in terms of the improved design of programs and policies that aim to benefit the results related to nutrition.

INTRODUCTION

The relationship between nutrition and health economics outcomes is essential at the individual and community levels. Today, healthcare services experience high financial constraints, and policymakers and healthcare providers are under growing pressure to deliver the maximum possible health benefits with the resources available. Establishing the economic framework to evaluate the cost and benefit of nutritional interventions and medical nutrition therapy will be an essential area for future research.

Incorrect management of natural resources leads to the emergence of foods that are produced but cannot be used effectively for human consumption. Reducing food losses and recycling the resulting food waste is one of the potential measures to overcome the future danger of starvation and famine that the growing world population may face. Food waste, which can occur at all stages of the food chain from farm to fork, causes economic losses as well as an ethical issues and causes negative effects on the environment (Kilibarda et al., 2019).

DOI: 10.4018/979-8-3693-0400-6.ch019

Malnutrition is a direct indicator of poverty because food poverty is associated with poor nutrition, which increases malnutrition and therefore reduces health and future income. Malnutrition is an important global health problem, accounting for 54% of all child deaths worldwide (Teshome, 2022; Bain et al., 2013). Around the world, 70-80% of malnourished children live in underdeveloped countries. Malnutrition is responsible for 45% of child deaths under the age of 5 and causes more than three million deaths each year (Pravana et al., 2017). When the prevalence of malnutrition in children in the last 200 years is examined; while approximately 40-50% of children died before the age of 5 in the 1800s, this rate decreased to 36% in the 1900s and to 4% in 2017. In many ways, it can be thought that we are in the prime of life for children. Despite this improvement, an average of fifteen thousand children per day still die due to malnutrition (Munoz et al., 2022). Malnutrition is a pathological condition resulting from inadequate consumption of one or more essential nutrients. It also includes weight loss associated with calorie and protein deficiencies and low levels of other specific nutrients necessary for the organism to be in balance (Uribe-Quintero et al., 2022). Malnutrition may be associated with one or more adverse developmental or physiological consequences resulting from environmental starvation, or socioeconomic or behavioral factors resulting from a lack of nutrient intake. Since malnutrition is not accepted in developed countries, there is little data on long-term outcomes. Therefore, developmental and mortality data primarily come from low- and low-middle-income countries where the etiology of malnutrition is different (Corkins, 2017: 16–17). Malnutrition affects the potential life of individuals and communities. The risks of malnutrition have economic, political, and cultural implications, due to both deficiency and excess. The social and economic development of countries and the health of their populations are related to their nutritional levels. Malnutrition is caused by an unbalanced or inappropriate intake of macronutrients (proteins, carbohydrates, and lipids) or micronutrients (vitamins, minerals, and trace elements) depending on the living conditions of an individual or population (Djoumessi, 2022).

Malnutrition is a preventable source of mortality and morbidity in infants and children. The factors responsible for infant malnutrition are many and varied. These include lack of basic health services, food insecurity, inadequate access to basic survival services, and inadequate infant feeding practices (Pravana et al., 2017). Infancy is the growth period after the fetal period. Maintaining proper nutrition to ensure adequate growth and organ development is one of the vital aspects of infancy. Malnutrition in the fetal period due to placental, maternal or fetal conditions may lead to growth restriction with impaired organogenesis and decreased birth weight (Picot et al., 2012). Fetal nutrition; It is a condition that occurs in the neonatal and postnatal period due to growth restriction and inadequate nutritional intake in the postnatal period. Insufficient nutrition during infancy causes growth and development retardation and metabolic disorders in the following periods. Premature babies are especially at risk of postnatal growth retardation due to the natural difficulties encountered due to prematurity. Growth measurements are performed to define nutritional needs during infancy. It is more difficult to meet the nutritional needs of preterm premature babies (Picot et al., 2012). In low-income countries, traditional weaning foods and problems with feeding practices predispose infants to malnutrition, growth retardation, infection, and mortality. It has been observed that one of the main causes of malnutrition in the weaning age is to supplement breast milk with low energy density cereals. Therefore, protein-energy malnutrition is a common problem among infants and children in low-income countries. Insufficient growth and dwarfism in children as a result of inadequate dietary supplementation are the most important causes of malnutrition (Pemunta & Fubah, 2015). Millions of infants and young children in low- and middle-income countries are vulnerable to malnutrition and impaired neurobehavioral development. Deficiencies of micronutrients such as iron, zinc, vitamin A and B12 cause many developmental problems as a result of low micronutrient stores at birth, inadequate intake of bioavailable micronutrients and increased micronutrient requirements (Dewey et al., 2021). Most affected children have problems with their physical, mental and psychomotor development. They may suffer from biochemical and physiological disorders such as growth delays, cognitive impairments, low physical and intellectual capacity (Uribe-Quintero et al., 2022).

Severe acute malnutrition occurs as a result of a sudden shortage of food and causes a person's body fat deficiency and skeletal muscle dysfunction. Babies and toddlers need extra nourishment for growth and development and are the most vulnerable to depend on others because they have limited energy reserves. Malnutrition can have severe and far-reaching consequences for a child's development and survival. Despite efforts to treat severe acute malnutrition, it continues to have high levels of mortality and morbidity (Picot et al., 2012).

The importance of understanding the channel through which nutrition is affected by economic growth (income growth per capita) as well as its effects on income can be explained as follows. First, knowing how food intake responds to per capita income (i.e. causal relationship) is vital in designing policies to combat malnutrition in poor countries and improve nutrition in both rich and poor countries (WorldBank, 1980).

Malnutrition is a costly problem in health care. Patients with malnutrition have longer hospital stays and require more intensive care. Malnutrition is often seen as accompanying a disease, and it is difficult to differentiate from each other as each can be a cause and a result of the other. Therefore, the cost of malnutrition and related disease are considered together (Stratton et al., 2003; Elia, 2006).

LITERATURE

Globally, socioeconomic factors such as income level, occupation, education, maternal age and family size influence malnutrition. Lack of maternal and child health services, lack of adequate and safe water supply, and lack of improved environmental sanitation, which are social determinants, are also important. There are also child-related determinants such as the child's gender, age, birth weight, and nutritional diversity (Gebremaryam et al., 2022; Agedew & Shimeles, 2016).

There are two theories in the literature that describe the relationship between nutrition and income: the Engel curve framework and the productivity wage hypothesis. The Engel curve framework assumes that nutrition is determined by income growth (defined in terms of calories or protein intakes), while the activity wage hypothesis assumes that income growth is determined by improvements in nutritional status through increases in work productivity/productivity. Increasing awareness of the impact of good nutrition and income growth on well-being has led to increased interest in indicators of well-being that can be derived from the relationship between food intake and income, often referred to in the literature as nutrient-income elasticity (Ogundari et al., 2016). This is because nutrition is the basic prerequisite for human well-being and contributes to human capital development.

As Neeliah and Shankar (2008) noted, deficiency of essential nutrients such as protein, iron, calcium and vitamins is a common phenomenon in most developing countries. Earlier, Berg (1968) stated that malnutrition can hinder the economic growth of developing countries in many ways:

- by reducing the average life expectancy, which reduces the productive years expected from newborn children,
- by reducing resistance to diseases which reduces available uptime in the literature,

- by inhibiting the mental and physical development of children, which reduces their potential productivity as adults' economic growth (Correa and Cummins, 1970; Wanji and Taniguchi, 2002; Salois et al., 2012).

While Benson (2004) states that economic growth is one of the prerequisites for reducing malnutrition or nutritional poverty, per capita income is accepted as one of the main determinants of nutrition (Ogundari and Abdulai, 2013).

Salmuth et al. (2021), conducted a systematic review of mother-focused interventions to improve infant growth and nutritional status in low-middle-income countries and interventions that promote mother-focused breastfeeding to prevent or address growth arrests in infants younger than 6 years of age; education and peer support; prenatal supplementation with female empowerment; maternal mental health; conditional cash and/or agricultural support; stated that maternal support is effective during pregnancy and breastfeeding.

Prüss-Ustün et al. (2019); In an analysis of the burden of disease from inadequate water, sanitation, and hygiene for selected adverse health outcomes in low- and middle-income countries, they noted that despite recent declines in mortality rates, inadequate sanitation is an important determinant of the global burden of disease, particularly among young children. To improve the health impact of adequate sanitation, well-designed studies are needed that assess the impact of safely managed water and sanitation services, access to basic hygiene conditions, and the implementation of basic hygiene behaviors that achieve high coverage and use in communities.

Do et al. (2018) In a cohort of 371 36-month-old children from rural communities in India, Pakistan, and Zambia to evaluate nutritional practices and growth and neurodevelopmental outcomes at 36 months among children living in low- and low-middle-income countries, 47% of children received a modified minimum acceptable diet. A highly significant difference was found between children who received the minimum acceptable diet modified with mean height-weight scores and minimum meal frequency and those who did not. However, no significant correlation was found between adjusted mean height for age, weight for height scores, and weight for age, and those who received and did not receive a modified minimum acceptable diet. Similarly, no significant relationship was found between these dietary practices and the mental development index and psychomotor development index. A highly significant difference was found between children who received the minimum acceptable diet modified with mean weight-for-height scores and minimum meal frequency compared to those who did not. However, no significant correlation was found between adjusted mean height for age, weight for height scores, and weight for age, and those who received and did not receive a modified minimum acceptable diet. Similarly, no significant relationship was found between these dietary practices and the mental development index and psychomotor development index.

DISCUSSION

When the studies in the literature dealing with the relationship between nutrition and economic development are examined, it can be said that healthy and sustainable nutrition will positively affect the economy and this positive effect may also be effective on development. Various educational policies, seminars, and webinars, which start at an early age, can be very beneficial for society to adopt sustainable and healthy eating habits. Sustainable and healthy eating habits of societies can also prevent food waste.

Globally, 14 percent of an estimated US$400 billion worth of food is lost from harvest to retail (FAO, 2019). Seventeen percent or more is wasted at the retail and consumer levels (UNEP, 2021). It is known that sustainable and proper nutrition has a great effect on preventing this waste. In this context, the income to be obtained by preventing waste can be transferred to investments in many different fields such as energy, technology, scientific studies, and R&D studies in various fields. For example, considering that this gain from waste is transferred to energy investments thanks to proper nutrition, a deficit here will be closed and the budget allocated for closing this deficit can be used in different areas. Ensuring a circular economy in this way can make a great contribution to development.

RESULTS

It seems that the publications and methods related to the total cost and benefit analysis of healthy nutrition and medical nutrition therapy are limited. The benefits are mostly prevention of malnutrition of the individual and patient, improvement of quality of life, reduction of hospitalization and length of stay, reduction of medical treatment cost and high efficiency.

Health economics is a discipline used to determine the effects of intervention studies on health, to evaluate the costs and benefits of the intervention, and to make effective use of resources. The economic evaluation assesses the relationship between the measurable benefit from a nutritional intervention and the cost of the intervention. Nutrition products and intervention studies have an important place in the health care budget, and the cost of nutrition care is evaluated by research on health economics and its consequences.

It is stated that the low cost of counseling is high, and it is possible to prevent diseases such as diabetes and some types of cancer by directing the patient to a healthy diet (Lammers and Kok, 2012). Accordingly, cost-effectiveness, modelling, descriptive risk models, and budget effectiveness analyzes are examples of frequently used tools to explain the value of interventions. Nutrition economics; is a discipline based on researching and characterizing the health and economic consequences of clinical nutrition and its benefits for the individual and society. Nutrition economics investigates the effect of nutrition on health and disease by examining the disciplines of nutrition and health together, and reveals the economic dimension with a cost-effectiveness perspective in health and daily nutrition and nutritional recommendations. In summary, nutrition economics focuses on examining nutritional habits, health and public expenditures together.

Evaluation of nutritional problems and nutrition intervention studies in terms of health and nutrition economics can be the main source of information for the formation of country policies and the preparation of guidelines in clinical and community health care services.

REFERENCES

Agedew, E., & Shimeles, A. (2016). Acute undernutrition (wasting) and associated factors among children aged 6–23 months in Kemba Woreda, Southern Ethiopia: A community based crosssectional study. *Iranian Journal of Nutrition Sciences and Food Technology*, *2*(2), 59–66.

Bain, L. E., Awah, P. K., Geraldine, N., Kindong, N. P., Sigal, Y., Bernard, N., & Tanjeko, A. T. (2013). Malnutrition in Sub-Saharan Africa: Burden, causes and prospects. *The Pan African Medical Journal, 15*, 120. doi:10.11604/pamj.2013.15.120.2535 PMID:24255726

Benson, T. (2004). *Africa's food and nutrition security situation: where are we and how did we get here?* International Food Policy Research Institute.

Berg, A. D. (1968). Malnutrition and national development. *Journal of Topical Podiatry, 14*, 116. PMID:5303642

Dewey, K. G., Wessells, K. R., Arnold, C. D., Prado, E. L., Abbeddou, S., Adu-Afarwuah, S., Ali, H., Arnold, B. F., Ashorn, P., Ashorn, U., Ashraf, S., Becquey, E., Bendabenda, J., Brown, K. H., Christian, P., Colford, J. M. Jr, Dulience, S., Fernald, L., Galasso, E., ... Stewart, C. P. (2021). Characteristics that modify the effect of small-quantity lipid-based nutrient supplementation on child growth: An individual participant data meta-analysis of randomized controlled trials. *The American Journal of Clinical Nutrition, 114*(1), 15–42. doi:10.1093/ajcn/nqab278 PMID:34590672

Djoumessi, Y. F. (2022). The impact of malnutrition on infant mortality and life expectancy in Africa. *Nutrition (Burbank, Los Angeles County, Calif.), 103–104*, 111760. Advance online publication. doi:10.1016/j.nut.2022.111760 PMID:35843043

Do, B. T., Hansen, N. I., Bann, C., Lander, R. L., Goudar, S. S., Pasha, O., Chomba, E., Dhaded, S. M., Thorsten, V. R., Wallander, J. L., Biasini, F. J., Derman, R., Goldenberg, R. L., & Carlo, W. A. (2018). Associations between feeding practices and growth and neurodevelopmental outcomes at 36 months among children living in low-and low-middle income countries who participated in the BRAIN-HIT trial. *BMC Nutrition, 4*(1), 1–12. doi:10.118640795-018-0228-9 PMID:32123571

Elia, M. (2006). Nutrition and health economics. *Nutrition (Burbank, Los Angeles County, Calif.), 22*(5), 576–578. doi:10.1016/j.nut.2006.01.005 PMID:16600820

FAO. (2019). *Food Loss and Waste.* Food and Agriculture Organization of the United Nations. Retrieved: https://www.fao.org/nutrition/capacity-development/food-loss-and-waste/en/

Gebremaryam, T., Amare, D., Ayalew, T., Tigabu, A., & Menshaw, T. (2022). Determinants of severe acute malnutrition among children aged 6-23 months in bahir dar city public hospitals, Northwest Ethiopia, 2020: A case control study. *BMC Pediatrics, 22*(1), 296. doi:10.118612887-022-03327-w PMID:35596187

Kilibarda, N., Djokovic, F., & Suzic, R. (2019). Food Waste Management-Reducing and Managing Food Waste in Hospitality. *Scientific Journal Meat Technology, 60*(2), 134–142. doi:10.18485/meattech.2019.60.2.8

Lammers, M., & Kok, L. (2012). Cost-benefit analysis of dietary treatment. *Amsterdam, Países Bajos: Seo. Economic Research Journal.*

Munoz, N., Litchford, M., Cox, J., Nelson, J. L., Nie, A. M., & Delmore, B. (2022). Malnutrition and pressure ınjury risk in vulnerable populations: Application of the 2019 international clinical practice guideline. *Advances in Skin & Wound Care*, *35*(3), 156–165. doi:10.1097/01.ASW.0000816332.60024.05 PMID:35188483

Neeliah, H., & Shankar, B. (2008). Is nutritional improvement a cross or consequence of economicgrowth? Evidence from Mauritius. *Economic Bulletin*, *17*, 1–11.

Ogundari, K., & Abdulai, A. (2013). Examining the heterogeneity in calorie-income elasticities: Ameta-analysis. *Food Policy*, *40*, 119–128. doi:10.1016/j.foodpol.2013.03.001

Ogundari, K., Ito, S., & Okoruwa, V. O. (2016). Estimating nutrition-income elasticities in sub-Saharan Africa: Implications on health. *Journal of Economic Studies (Glasgow, Scotland)*, *43*(1), 59–69. doi:10.1108/JES-07-2014-0125

Pemunta, N. V., & Fubah, M. A. (2015). Socio-cultural determinants of infant malnutrition in Cameroon. *Journal of Biosocial Science*, *47*(4), 423–448. doi:10.1017/S0021932014000145 PMID:24717356

Picot, J., Hartwell, D., Harris, P., Mendes, D., Clegg, A. J., & Takeda, A. (2012). The effectiveness of interventions to treat severe acute malnutrition in young children: A systematic review. *Health Technology Assessment*, *16*(19), 1–316. doi:10.3310/hta16190 PMID:22480797

Pravana, N. K., Piryani, S., Chaurasiya, S. P., Kawan, R., Thapa, R. K., & Shrestha, S. (2017). Determinants of severe acute malnutrition among children under 5 years of age in Nepal: A community-based case-control study. *BMJ Open*, *7*(8), e017084. doi:10.1136/bmjopen-2017-017084 PMID:28851796

Prüss-Ustün, A., Wolf, J., Bartram, J., Clasen, T., Cumming, O., Freeman, M. C., Gordon, B., Hunter, P. R., Medlicott, K., & Johnston, R. (2019). Burden of disease from inadequate water, sanitation and hygiene for selected adverse health outcomes: An updated analysis with a focus on lowand middle-income countries. *International Journal of Hygiene and Environmental Health*, *222*(5), 765–777. doi:10.1016/j.ijheh.2019.05.004 PMID:31088724

Salmuth, V., Brennan, E., Kerac, M., McGrath, M., Frison, S., & Lelijveld, N. (2021). Maternal-focused interventions to improve infant growth and nutritional status in low-middle income countries, A systematic review of reviews. *PLoS One*, *16*(8), e0256188. doi:10.1371/journal.pone.0256188 PMID:34407128

Salois, M. J., Tiffin, R., & Balcombe, K. G. (2012). Impact of income on nutrient intakes: Implications for undernourishment and obesity. *The Journal of Development Studies*, *48*(12), 1716–1730. doi:10.1080/00220388.2012.658376

Stratton, R. J., Green, C. J., & Elia, M. (2003). *Disease-related malnutrition: an evidence-based approach to treatment*. Cabi. doi:10.1079/9780851996486.0000

Teshome, F., & Tadele, A. (2022). Trends and determinants of minimum acceptable diet intake among infant and young children aged 6–23 months in Ethiopia: A multilevel analysis of Ethiopian demographic and health survey. *BMC Nutrition*, *8*(1), 44. doi:10.118640795-022-00533-8 PMID:35513888

UNEP. (2021). *UN: %17 of all food available at consumer levels is wasted.* UN Enviroment Programme. Retrieved: https://www.unep.org/news-and-stories/press-release/un-17-all-food-available-consumer-levels-wasted

Uribe-Quintero, R., Álvarez-Castaño-Castaño, L. S., Caicedo-Velásquez, B., & Ruiz-Buitrago, I. C. (2022). Trends in undernutrition mortality among children under five years of age and adults over 60. *Biomédica, 42*(1), 41–53. doi:10.7705/biomedica.5937 PMID:35471169

Wanji, X., & Taniguch, K. (2002). *Does better nutrition cause economic growth? The efficiency cost ofHunger revisited.* FAO Working paper-ESA Working Paper No. 02-11.

Compilation of References

Abdmouleh, Z., Alammari, R. A., & Gastli, A. (2015). Review of policies encouraging renewable energy integration & best practices. *Renewable & Sustainable Energy Reviews*, *45*, 249–262. doi:10.1016/j.rser.2015.01.035

Aboagye, S. (2017). Economic Expansion and Environmental Sustainability Nexus in Ghana. *African Development Review*, *29*(2), 155–168. doi:10.1111/1467-8268.12247

Abolhosseini, S., & Heshmati, A. (2014). The main support mechanisms to finance renewable energy development. *Renewable & Sustainable Energy Reviews*, *40*, 876–885. doi:10.1016/j.rser.2014.08.013

Abumunshar, M., Aga, M., & Samour, A. (2020). Oil price, energy consumption, and CO2 emissions in Turkey: New evidence from a bootstrap ARDL test. *Energie, 13*(21), 1-15. Retrieved from https://econpapers.repec.org/article/gamjeners/v_3a13_3ay_3a2020_3ai_3a21_3ap_3a5588-_3ad_3a434882.htm

Acaravci, A., & Ozturk, I. (2010). Electricity consumption-growth nexus: Evidence from panel data for transition countries. *Energy Economics*, *32*(3), 604–608. doi:10.1016/j.eneco.2009.10.016

Acar, B., Selcuk, O., & Dastan, S. A. (2019). The merit order effect of wind and river type hydroelectricity generation on Turkish electricity prices. *Energy Policy*, *132*, 1298–1319. doi:10.1016/j.enpol.2019.07.006

Accelerating energy efficiency: What governments can do now to deliver energy savings – Analysis. (n.d.). IEA. Retrieved July 13, 2023, from https://www.iea.org/commentaries/accelerating-energy-efficiency-what-governments-can-do-now-to-deliver-energy-savings

Acheampong, A. O., Adams, S., & Boateng, E. (2019). Do globalization and renewable energy contribute to carbon emissions mitigation in Sub-Saharan Africa? *The Science of the Total Environment*, *677*, 436–446. doi:10.1016/j.scitotenv.2019.04.353 PMID:31059886

Adams, S., & Acheampong, A. O. (2019). Reducing carbon emissions: The role of renewable energy and democracy. *Journal of Cleaner Production*, *240*, 118245. doi:10.1016/j.jclepro.2019.118245

Adebayo, T. S., & Akinsola, G. D. (2021). *Investigating the causal linkage among economic growth, energy consumption and CO2 emissions in Thailand: An application of the wavelet coherence approach.* Retrieved from https://www.proquest.com/openview/1de1167ce15f07271182482f7232d5c3/1?pq-origsite=gscholar&cbl=1416335

Adom, P. K., Kwakwa, P. A., & Amankwaa, A. (2018). The long-run effects of economic, demographic, and political indices on actual and potential CO2 emissions. *Journal of Environmental Management*, *218*, 516–526. doi:10.1016/j.jenvman.2018.04.090 PMID:29709820

Afonichkin, A. I. (2011a). Strategies for the coordinated development of cluster economic systems. *Journal of the V.N. Tatishchev Volzhsky University*, *2011*(24), 244–252.

African Development Bank. (2018). Nigeria Electrification Project: Appraisal Report, PESR/ PERN/RDNG November 2018. Abidjan: Cote d'Ivoire.

Afriyie, D., Wang, Z., Hu, S., Ampofo, G. K. M., & Asante, D. A. (2023). Exploring the dynamic nexus between urbanization and industrialization with carbon emissions in sub-Saharan Africa: Evidence from panel PMG-ARDL estimation. *Environmental Science and Pollution Research International, 30*(3), 6373–6389. doi:10.100711356-022-22597-6 PMID:35997879

Afsharzade, N., Papzan, A., Ashjaee, M., Delangizan, S., Passel, S., & Azad, H. (2016). Renewable energy development in rural areas of Iran. *Renewable & Sustainable Energy Reviews, 65*, 743–755. doi:10.1016/j.rser.2016.07.042

Agedew, E., & Shimeles, A. (2016). Acute undernutrition (wasting) and associated factors among children aged 6–23 months in Kemba Woreda, Southern Ethiopia: A community based crosssectional study. *Iranian Journal of Nutrition Sciences and Food Technology, 2*(2), 59–66.

Aghion, P., Howitt, P., & Mayer-Foulkes, D. (2005). The effect of financial development on convergence: Theory and evidence. *The Quarterly Journal of Economics, 120*(1), 173–222.

Ağır, H., Özbek, S., & Türkmen, S. (2020). Türkiye'de yenilenebilir enerji kaynaklarının belirleyicileri: Ampirik bir tahmin. *International Journal of Economic Studies, 6*(4), 39–48. https://dergipark.org.tr/en/download/article-file/1280974

Ahmad, M. I. S., & Mehmood, B. (2016). Energy-Headed-Growth Hypothesis: Evidence from Emerging Economies. *Bulletin of Energy Economics, 4*(2), 126–132.

Ahmad, M., Ur Rahman, Z., Hong, L., Khan, S., Khan, Z., & Naeem Khan, M. (2018). Impact of environmental quality variables and socio-economic factors on human health: Empirical evidence from China. *Pollution, 4*(4), 571–579.

Ahn, J., Habib, A., Malacrino, D., & Presbitero, A. F. (2023, April 5). *Fragmenting Foreign Direct Investment Hits Emerging Economies Hardest.* https://www.imf.org/en/Blogs/Articles/2023/04/05/fragmenting-foreign-direct-investment-hits-emerging-economies-hardest

Akalpler, E., & Hove, S. (2019). Carbon emissions, energy use, real GDP per capita and trade matrix in the Indian economy-an ARDL approach. *Energy, 168*, 1081–1093. doi:10.1016/j.energy.2018.12.012

Akinwale, Y. O. (2018). An empirical analysis of short run and long run relationships between energy consumption, technology innovation and economic growth in Saudi Arabia. *International Journal of Energy Economics and Policy, 8*(4), 139–146.

Akpolat, A. G., & Altıntaş, N. (2013). Enerji tüketimi ile reel GSYH arasındaki eşbütünleşme ve nedensellik ilişkisi: 1961-2010 dönemi [Cointegration and casuality relation between energy consumption and real GDP: 1961-2010 period]. *Bilgi Ekonomisi ve Yönetimi Dergisi, 8*(2), 115-127.

Akrofi, M. M. (2021). An analysis of energy diversification and transition trends in Africa. *International Journal of Energy and Water Resources, 5*(1), 1–12. doi:10.100742108-020-00101-5

Aktar, M. A., Alam, M. M., & Al-Amin, A. Q. (2021). Global economic crisis, energy use, CO2 emissions, and policy roadmap amid COVID-19. *Sustainable Production and Consumption, 26*, 770–781. doi:10.1016/j.spc.2020.12.029 PMID:33786357

Akyildirim, E., Cepni, O., Molnár, P., & Uddin, G. S. (2022). Connectedness of energy markets around the world during the COVID-19 pandemic. *Energy Economics, 109*, 105900. doi:10.1016/j.eneco.2022.105900 PMID:35529585

Aldieri, L., Gatto, A., & Vinci, C. P. (2021). Evaluation of energy resilience and adaptation policies: An energy efficiency analysis. *Energy Policy, 157*, 112505. doi:10.1016/j.enpol.2021.112505

Alechina, I., Furtado, C., Galtung, J., Preiswerk, R., Wemegah, M., Loubser, J., Lapin, N., Richta, R., & Gombo-Yn-Miyegombo, G. (1982). *Different theories and practices of development.* UNESCO.

AList. (2022). *PREDICTIONS 2022. Disruptive Forces Necessitate Bold Decisions.* https://www.alistdaily.com/strategy/Forrester-2022-predictions-guid

Alper, F. Ö. (2018). Yenilenebilir enerji ve ekonomik büyüme arasındaki ilişki: 1990-2017 Türkiye örneği. *Journal of the Faculty of Economics and Administrative Sciences, 8*(2), 223–242. https://dergipark.org.tr/en/pub/ckuiibfd/issue/41863/466782

Altinoz, B., & Dogan, E. (2021). How renewable energy consumption and natural resource abundance impact environmental degradation? New findings and policy implications from quantile approach. *Energy Sources B Energy Econ. Plann., 1–12*, 301–302. https://doi.org/. doi:10.1080/15567249.2021.1885527

Altinoz, B., Vasbieva, D., & Kalugina, O. (2021). The effect of information and communication technologies and total factor productivity on CO2 emissions in top 10 emerging market economies. *Environmental Science and Pollution Research International, 28*(45), 63784–63793. doi:10.100711356-020-11630-1 PMID:33201509

Amaglobeli, D. (2023). *Policy Responses to High Energy and Food Prices.* IMF Working Paper, WP/23/74, March 2023. Available at: https://www.imf.org/-/media/Files/Publications/WP/2023/English/wpiea2023074-print-pdf.ashx

Amaira, B. (2012). The relationship of oil prices and economic growth in Tunisia: A vector error correction model analysis. *The Romanian Economic Journal, 43*, 3-22. https://d1wqtxts1xzle7.cloudfront.net/54262849/The_Relationship_of_Oil_Prices_and_Econo20170827-16260-1wfgtap-libre.pdf?1503903071=&response-content-disposition=inline%3B+filename%3DThe_Relationship_of_O

Amri, F. (2018). Carbon dioxide emissions, total factor productivity, ICT, trade, financial development, and energy consumption: Testing environmental Kuznets curve hypothesis for Tunisia. *Environmental Science and Pollution Research International, 25*(33), 33691–33701. doi:10.100711356-018-3331-1 PMID:30276690

Andrea, P. (2021). *Energy prices: When will costs go down?* World Economic Forum, 27 October 2021. Available at: https://www.weforum.org/agenda/2021/10/surging-energy-prices-may-not-ease-next-year-2022/

Anisova, N. A. (2014a). Development of cluster theory: a typical model and examples of application. BIBLIO-GLOBUS.

An, J., Dorofeev, M., & Zhu, S. (2020). Development of energy cooperation between Russia and China. *International Journal of Energy Economics and Policy, 10*(1), 134–139. doi:10.32479/ijeep.8509

Annual report of the state and development of research in 2019. (2019c). Ministry of Education and Science.

Anochiwa, L. I., Agbanike, T. F., Chukwu, A. B., Ikpe, M., & Otta, N. N. (2022). Urbanization and carbon emissions: Looking at the role of mobile phone adoption in Sub-Saharan African countries. *Environmental Science and Pollution Research International, 29*(52), 78526–78541. doi:10.100711356-022-20994-5 PMID:35697981

Anselin, L., Le Gallo, J., & Jayet, H. (2006). Spatial panel econometrics. In L. Mátyás & P. Sevestre (Eds.), *The econometrics of panel data: Fundamentals and recent developments in theory* (3rd ed., pp. 625–660). Kluwer Academic.

Apergis, N., & Danuletiu, D. C. (2014). Renewable energy and economic growth: Evidence from the sign of panel long-run causality. *International Journal of Energy Economics and Policy, 4*(4), 578–587. https://www.econjournals.com/index.php/ijeep/article/view/879

Apergis, N., & Payne, J. (2009). Energy consumption and economic growth in Central America: Evidence from a panel co-integration and error correction model. *Energy Economics, 31*(2), 211–216. doi:10.1016/j.eneco.2008.09.002

Apergis, N., & Payne, J. (2010). Renewable energy consumption and economic growth: Evidence from a panel of OECD countries. *Energy Policy*, *38*(1), 656–660. doi:10.1016/j.enpol.2009.09.002

Apergis, N., Payne, J. E., Menyah, K., & Wolde-Rufael, Y. (2010). On the causal dynamics between emissions, nuclear energy, renewable energy, and economic growth. *Ecological Economics*, *69*(11), 2255–2260. doi:10.1016/j.ecolecon.2010.06.014

Appiah, K., Du, J., Yeboah, M., & Appiah, R. (2019). Causal relationship between industrialization, energy intensity, economic growth and carbon dioxide emissions: Recent evidence from Uganda. *International Journal of Energy Economics and Policy*, *9*(2), 237.

Appiah, M. O. (2018). Investigating the multivariate Granger causality between energy consumption, economic growth and CO2 emissions in Ghana. *Energy Policy*, *112*, 198–208. doi:10.1016/j.enpol.2017.10.017

Appold, S. J., & Kasarda, J. D. (2011). Seeding growth at airports and airport cities: Insights from the two-sided market literature. *Research in Transportation Business & Management*, *1*(1), 91–100. doi:10.1016/j.rtbm.2011.06.011

Arabska, E. (2016b). Challenges of building functioning labor market: employability and lifelong learning. *XI International scientific conference „Innovations in technology and education"*, 87-108.

Arabska, E. (2016c). Competence-based training of staff and opportunities of life-long learning. *First international scientific conference "Human resources, leadership and organizational management"*, *1*, 131-156.

Arabska, E. (2016c). Active Social Policies - Insights in Developing a Functioning Labor Market. *Balkan and Near Eastern Journal of Social Sciences*, *2*(3), 47–63.

Arabska, E. (2016d). Bulgarian Experience in Improving Effectiveness of Activities in Public Employment Services. *Balkan and Near Eastern Journal of Social Sciences, BNEJSS*, *2*(2), 76–94.

Arabska, E. (2016e). Challenges in social policies implementation and effective impact on labour market. *Proceedings of the Annual university scientific conference*, 431-448.

Arabska, E. (2016f). Problems of Employment and Unemployment in Bulgaria: Is Sustainable Development Possible? *Balkan and Near Eastern Journal of Social Sciences, BNEJSS*, *2*(1), 6–19.

Arellano, M., & Bover, O. (1995). Another look at the instrumental variable estimation of error-components models. *Journal of Econometrics*, *68*(1), 29–51. doi:10.1016/0304-4076(94)01642-D

Arthur, W. B. (1999). Complexity and the economy. *Science*, *284*(5411), 107–109. doi:10.1126cience.284.5411.107 PMID:10103172

Aščerić, A., Pantoš, M., & Čepin, M. (2022). Correlation of Day-Ahead Electric Energy Market Price with Renewable Energy Sources Generation and Load Forecast. In *Advanced Technologies, Systems, and Applications VI: Proceedings of the International Symposium on Innovative and Interdisciplinary Applications of Advanced Technologies (IAT) 2021* (pp. 99-109). Springer International Publishing.

Asia Pacific Energy Research Centre. (Ed.). (2007). *A quest for energy security in the 21st century: Resources and constraints*. Inst. of Energy Economics.

Aslani, A., Naaranoja, M., Helo, P., Antila, E., & Hiltunen, E. (2013). Energy diversification in Finland: Achievements and potential of renewable energy development. *International Journal of Sustainable Energy*, *32*(5), 504–514. doi:10.1080/14786451.2013.766612

Asongu, S. A., Le Roux, S., & Biekpe, N. (2018). Enhancing ICT for environmental sustainability in sub-Saharan Africa. *Technological Forecasting and Social Change*, *127*, 209–216. doi:10.1016/j.techfore.2017.09.022

Auty, R. (1993). *Sustaining Development in Mineral Economies: The Resource Curse Thesis*. Oxford University Press.

Averina, T.A. (2006). Analysis of models and methods of management of the innovative development of the enterprise. *Scientific Herald of the Voronezh State Architectural and Construction University. Series: Management of construction*, *1*(6), 76-83.

Awan, U., Sroufe, R., & Shahbaz, M. (2021). Industry 4.0 and the circular economy: A literature review and recommendations for future research. *Business Strategy and the Environment*, *30*(4), 2038–2060. doi:10.1002/bse.2731

Ayman, G., Kılıçdağı, T. A., & Sezer, A. (2007). Avrupa Birliği'ne katılım sürecinde Türkiye'nin komşu ve çevre ülkeler politikası: Stratejik yaklaşımlar. *TÜSİAD Basın Bülteni*. Retrieved from https://tusiad.org/tr/yayinlar/raporlar/item/3633-avrupa-birligine-katilim-surecinde-turkiyenin-komsu-ve-cevre-ulkeler-politikasi--stratejik-yaklasimlar

Bain, L. E., Awah, P. K., Geraldine, N., Kindong, N. P., Sigal, Y., Bernard, N., & Tanjeko, A. T. (2013). Malnutrition in Sub-Saharan Africa: Burden, causes and prospects. *The Pan African Medical Journal*, *15*, 120. doi:10.11604/pamj.2013.15.120.2535 PMID:24255726

Baker Institute. (2012). *Cybersecurity Issues and Policy Options for the U.S. Energy Industry, 2012*. Baker Institute Policy Report, Rice University. Available at: https://www.bakerinstitute.org/media/files/Research/ba7df664/IT-pub-PolicyReport53.pdf

Baker, D. (2021). *Today's global energy crisis is just the first in the "clean power" era*. World Oil. Available at: https://www.worldoil.com/news/2021/10/5/today-s-global-energy-crisis-is-just-the-first-in-the-clean-power-era

Ballester, C., & Furió, D. (2015). Effects of renewables on the stylized facts of electricity prices. *Renewable & Sustainable Energy Reviews*, *52*, 1596–1609. doi:10.1016/j.rser.2015.07.168

Balsalobre-Lorente, D., Driha, O. M., Bekun, F. V., & Osundina, O. A. (2019). Do agricultural activities induce carbon emissions? The BRICS experience. *Environmental Science and Pollution Research International*, *26*(24), 25218–25234. doi:10.100711356-019-05737-3 PMID:31256399

Balsalobre-Lorente, D., & Leitão, N. C. (2020). The role of tourism, trade, renewable energyuse and carbon dioxide emissions on economic growth: Evidence of tourism-led growthhypothesis in EU-28. *Environmental Science and Pollution Research International*, *27*(36), 45883–45896. doi:10.100711356-020-10375-1 PMID:32803615

Baltagi, B. H. (2008). *Econometric analysis of panel data* (4th ed.). John Wiley & Sons.

Bamati, N., & Raoofi, A. (2020). Development level and the impact of technological factor on renewable energy production. *Renewable Energy*, *151*, 946–955. doi:10.1016/j.renene.2019.11.098

Banerjee, S., & Savitha, B. (2021). Competition Reduces Profitability: The Case of the Indian Life Microinsurance Industry. *The Geneva Papers on Risk and Insurance. Issues and Practice*, *46*(3), 383–398. doi:10.105741288-020-00203-5

Barkham, P. (2008). What is the knowledge economy? *The Guardian*. Available at: www.guardian.co.uk

Bastola, U., & Sapkota, P. (2015). Relationships among energy consumption, pollution emission, and economic growth in Nepal. *Energy*, *80*, 254–262. doi:10.1016/j.energy.2014.11.068

Batalla-Bejerano, J., & Trujillo-Baute, E. (2016). Impacts of intermittent renewable generation on electricity system costs. *Energy Policy*, *94*, 411–420. doi:10.1016/j.enpol.2015.10.024

Baudson, V. (2022). EU's strategic autonomy requires new investment momentum. *Financial Times*. Available at: https://www.ft.com/content/40756ab8-7307-45d7-aaee-eb33efe16f37

Baumol, W. J. (1959). *Business Behavior, Value and Growth*. Macmillan.

bbc.com. (2023). *Güney Afrika'da elektrik kesintilerini gidermek için bakanlık kuruldu*. BBC News Türkçe. https://www.bbc.com/turkce/articles/cd1d9zxeynno

Beaudreau, B. (1998). Energy and Organization: Growth and Distribution Reexamined. Westport.

Beck, T., Levine, R., & Loayza, N. (2000). Finance and the sources of growth. *Journal of Financial Economics*, *58*(1-2), 261–300. doi:10.1016/S0304-405X(00)00072-6

Bekun, F. V., Alola, A. A., & Sarkodie, S. A. (2019). Toward a sustainable environment: Nexus between CO2 emissions, resource rent, renewable and nonrenewable energy in 16-EU countries. *The Science of the Total Environment*, *657*, 1023–1029. doi:10.1016/j.scitotenv.2018.12.104 PMID:30677870

Bel, G., & Fageda, X. (2008). Getting there fast: Globalization, intercontinental flights and location of headquarters. *Journal of Economic Geography*, *8*(4), 471–495. doi:10.1093/jeg/lbn017

Bello, M. O., & Ch'ng, K. S. (2022). Convergence in energy intensity of GDP: Evidence from West African countries. *Energy*, *254*, 1–10. doi:10.1016/j.energy.2022.124217

Ben Abdallah, K., Belloumi, M., & De Wolf, D. (2013). Indicators for sustainable energy development: A multivariate cointegration and causality analysis from Tunisian road transport sector. *Renewable & Sustainable Energy Reviews*, *25*, 34–43. doi:10.1016/j.rser.2013.03.066

Benson, T. (2004). *Africa's food and nutrition security situation: where are we and how did we get here?* International Food Policy Research Institute.

Berahab, R. (2022). *The Energy Crisis of 2021 and its Implications for Africa*. Academic Press.

Berg, A. D. (1968). Malnutrition and national development. *Journal of Topical Podiatry*, *14*, 116. PMID:5303642

Berk, İ., & Torun, E. (2019). Testing merit-order effect in Türkiye's electricity market: The effect of wind penetration on day-ahead electricity prices. *Akdeniz İİBF Dergisi*, *19*(1), 133–156.

Bermingham, F. (2021). Xi Jinping tells G20 'developed countries' should lead on global emissions. *South China Morning Post*. https://www.scmp.com/news/china/article/3154308/chinas-xi-tells-g20-developed-countries-should-lead-global-emissions

Bharti, M. S., Kumari, S., & Bharti, S. S. (2022). Indo-French Comprehensive Bilateral Cooperation: A Roadmap to Indo-Pacific Parks Partnership and Beyond. *Economic and Regional Studies / Studia Ekonomiczne i Regionalne*, *15*(3), 284–303. https://doi.org/doi:10.2478/ers-2022-0020

Bharti, M. S. (2022a). The Development of China's Economic Cooperation in the Horn of Africa: Special Reference to the Belt and Road Initiative. *African Journal of Economics, Politics and Social Studies*, *1*(1), 17–30. doi:10.15804/ajepss.2022.1.12

Bharti, M. S. (2022b). The evolution of China's economic engagement in Central and Eastern Europe. *Economic and Regional Studies*, *15*(1), 90–106. doi:10.2478/ers-2022-0007

Bharti, M. S. (2023a). Indo–French Defence Partnership and Regional Balance in South Asia. *The Copernicus Journal of Political Studies*, *1–2*, 71–89. doi:10.12775.CJPS.2022.005

Bharti, M. S. (2023b). The Sustainable Development and Economic Impact of China's Belt and Road Initiative in Ethiopia. *East Asia (Piscataway, N.J.), 40*(2), 175–194. doi:10.100712140-023-09402-y PMID:37065271

Bhattacharya, M., Paramati, S. R., Ozturk, I., & Bhattacharya, S. (2016). The effect of renewable energy consumption on economic growth: Evidence from top 38 countries. *Applied Energy, 162*, 733–741. doi:10.1016/j.apenergy.2015.10.104

Bildirici, M., & Kayikci, F. (2012). Economic growth and electricity consumption in former Soviet Republics. *Energy Economics, 34*(3), 747–753. doi:10.1016/j.eneco.2012.02.010

Bilgin, M. (2010). Geo-Economics of European Gas Security: Trade, Geography and International Politics.. *Insight Turkey, 12*(4), 185–209.

Bistline, J., Cole, W., Damato, G., DeCarolis, J., Frazier, W., Linga, V., Marcy, C., Namovicz, C., Podkaminer, K., Sims, R., Sukunta, M., & Young, D. (2020). Energy storage in long-term system models: A review of considerations, best practices, and research needs. *Progress in Energy, 2*(3), 032001. doi:10.1088/2516-1083/ab9894

Björklund, R. (2020). *A Post-development Critique of Chinese Development Discourse*. Lund University. https://lup.lub.lu.se/luur/download?func=downloadFile&recordOId=9026103&fileOId=9026104

bloomberg.com. (2022). *Uzmanlardan "Enerji krizi yeni başlıyor olabilir" uyarısı*. BloombergHT. https://www.bloomberght.com/uzmanlardan-enerji-krizi-yeni-basliyor-olabilir-uyarisi-2321458

Bloomfield, H. (2021). *What happens when the wind doesn't blow? Building the energy systems of the future.* World Economic Forum. Available at: https://www.weforum.org/agenda/2021/10/europe-low-winds-future-energy-grid-power/

Borowski, P. F. (2022). Mitigating Climate Change and the Development of Green Energy versus a Return to Fossil Fuels Due to the Energy Crisis in 2022. *Energies, 15*(24), 9289. doi:10.3390/en15249289

Bovan. (2020). Negotiating Energy Diplomacy and its Relationship with Foreign Policy and National Security. *International Journal of Energy Economics and Policy, 10*(2), 1-6. Available at: https://www.researchgate.net/publication/338720574_Negotiating_Energy_Diplomacy_and_its_Relationship_with_Foreign_Policy_and_National_Security

Bozkurt, C., & Okumuş, İ. (2015). Türkiye'de ekonomik büyüme, enerji tüketimi, ticari serbestleşme ve nüfus yoğunluğunun CO2 emisyonu üzerindeki etkileri: Yapısal kırılmalı eşbütünleşme analizi. *Mustafa Kemal Üniversitesi Sosyal Bilimler Enstitüsü Dergisi, 12*(32), 23-35. Retrieved from https://dergipark.org.tr/tr/pub/mkusbed/issue/19578/208976

BP. (2021a). Statistical Review of World Energy – all data, 1965-2020. BO.

BP. (2021b). EU's energy market in 2020. Statistical Review of World Energy – 2021. BP.

BP. (2023). Statistical Review of World Energy – 2022. BP.

Bressand, A. (2012). *The Changed Geopolitics of Energy and Climate and the Challenge for Europe: A Geopolitical and European Perspective on the Triple Agenda of Competition, Energy Security and Sustainability.* Clingendael. Available at: www.clingendael.nl

Brini, R., Amara, M., & Jemmali, H. (2017). Renewable energy consumption, International trade, oil price and economic growth inter-linkages: The case of Tunisia. *Renewable & Sustainable Energy Reviews, 76*, 620–627. doi:10.1016/j.rser.2017.03.067

Brueckner, J. K. (2003). Airline traffic and urban economic development. *Urban Studies (Edinburgh, Scotland), 40*(8), 1455–1469. doi:10.1080/0042098032000094388

Buenstorf, G. (2004). The Economics of Energy and the Production Process: An Evolutionary Approach. Academic Press.

Bulatom. (2022). Nuclear Energy - The Basis for Sustainable Development. https://www.bulatom-bg.org/

Bunnag, T. (2023). Analyzing Short-run and Long-run Causality Relationship among CO2 Emission, Energy Consumption, GDP, Square of GDP, and Foreign Direct Investment in Environmental Kuznets Curve for Thailand. *International Journal of Energy Economics and Policy*, *13*(2), 341–348. doi:10.32479/ijeep.14088

Burakov, D., & Freidin, M. (2017). Financial development, economic growth and renewable energy consumption in Russia: A vector error correction approach. *International Journal of Energy Economics and Policy*, *7*(6), 39–47.

Burlinson, A., & Giulietti, M. (2018). Non-traditional business models for city-scale energy storage: Evidence from UK case studies. *Economia e Politica Industriale*, *45*(2), 215–242. doi:10.100740812-017-0083-8

Button, K., Drexler, J., & Pels, E. (1999). Economic efficiency in the provision of airport services: A summary report. *Journal of Air Transport Management*, *5*(4), 177–184. doi:10.1016/S0969-6997(99)00013-2

Button, K., Lall, S., Stough, R., & Trice, M. (1999). High-technology employment and hub airports. *Journal of Air Transport Management*, *5*(1), 53–59. doi:10.1016/S0969-6997(98)00038-6

Button, K., & Yuan, J. (2013). Airfreight transport and economic development: An examination of causality. *Urban Studies (Edinburgh, Scotland)*, *50*(2), 329–340. doi:10.1177/0042098012446999

Büyükyılmaz, A., & Mert, M. (2015). CO2 emisyonu, yenilenebilir enerji tüketimi ve ekonomik büyüme arasındaki ilişkinin MS-VAR yaklaşımı ile modellenmesi: Türkiye örneği. *Journal of World of Turks*, *7*(3), 103–117. https://atif.sobiad.com/index.jsp?modul=makale-detay&Alan=sosyal&Id=AWANUin4oDuH9Br_drwT

Çalışkan, Ş., Karabacak, M., & Meçik, O. (2017). Türkiye ekonomisinde eğitim harcamaları ve ekonomik büyüme ilişkisi: Bootstrap Toda-Yamamoto nedensellik testi yaklaşımı. *Kocaeli University Journal of Social Sciences,* (33), 45-56. Retrieved from https://dergipark.org.tr/en/pub/kosbed/issue/43231/524915

Can, H. (2017). *Yenilebilir enerjinin makroekonomik etkileri: Türkiye örneği* [Master's thesis]. Namık Kemal Üniversitesi.

Can, H. (2017). *Yenilebilir enerjinin makroekonomik etkileri: Türkiye örneği*. Namık Kemal Üniversitesi, Sosyal Bilimler Enstitüsü, Yayımlanmamış Yüksek Lisans Tezi.

Can, H., & Korkmaz, Ö. (2020). The relationship between renewable energy consumption and economic growth: The case of Bulgaria. *International Journal of Energy Sector Management*, *13*(3), 573–589. doi:10.1108/IJESM-11-2017-0005

Can, H., & Paskaleva, M. (2017). Macroeconomic determinants of CDS: The case of Europe. *New knowledge. Journal of Science*, *6*(3), 1080–1096.

Cao, F. (2009). Modernization Theory and China's Road to Modernization. *Chinese Studies in History*, *43*(1), 7–16. doi:10.2753/CSH0009-4633430101

CARI. (2023). *Data: Chinese Global Foreign Aid.* John Hopkins School of Advanced International Studies. http://www.sais-cari.org/data-chinese-global-foreign-aid

Carmody, P., Zajontz, T., & Reboredo, R. (2022). From 'debt diplomacy' to donorship? China's changing role in global development. *Global Political Economy.*, *1*(2), 198–217. doi:10.1332/UZHW7185

CEIC Data. (2021). *China Capacity Utilization Rate*. https://www.ceicdata.com/en/china/capacity-utilization-rate

CEIC. (2023). *China Foreign Exchange Reserves*. https://www.ceicdata.com/en/indicator/china/foreign-exchange-reserves

Celasun, O., & Iakova, D. (2022). *Helping Europe's Households*. International Monetary Fund. Available at: https://www.imf.org/en/Publications/fandd/issues/2022/12/helping-europe-households-Celasun-Iakova

Cĕric, V. (2001). Building the Knowledge Economy. *Journal of Computing and Information Technology, 9*(3), 177–183..

Cesarec, I. (2020). Beyond Physical Threats: Cyber-Attacks on Critical Infrastructure as a Challenge of Changing Security Environment – Overview of Cyber-Security Legislation and Implementation in SEE Countries. *Annals of Disaster Risk Sciences*. doi:10.51381/adrs.v3i1.45

Chaisse, J., & Ji, X. (2020). The pervasive problem of special economic zones for international economic law: Tax, investment, and trade issues. *World Trade Review, 19*(4), 567–588. doi:10.1017/S1474745620000129

Chandra, Y., & Wilkinson, I. F. (2017). Firm internationalization from a network-centric complex-systems perspective. *Journal of World Business, 52*(5), 691–701. doi:10.1016/j.jwb.2017.06.001

Chang, H., Mikalsen, K. S., Nesse, P. J., & Erdal, O. B. (2019). *Digitalization of municipalities through ecosystem collaboration. In Innovation, Regulation, Multi Business Model Innovation and Technology*. ICT. doi:10.13052/nbjict1902-097X.2020.006

Chatti, W. (2020). Information and communication technologies, road freight transport, and environmental sustainability. *Environment and Ecology, 11*(1), 124.

Chatti, W., & Majeed, M. T. (2022). Information communication technology (ICT), smart urbanization, and environmental quality: Evidence from a panel of developing and developed economies. *Journal of Cleaner Production, 366*, 132925. doi:10.1016/j.jclepro.2022.132925

Cheng, C., Ren, X., Dong, K., Dong, X., & Wang, Z. (2021). How does technological innovation mitigate CO2 emissions in OECD countries? Heterogeneous analysis using panel quantile regression. *Journal of Environmental Management, 280*, 111818. doi:10.1016/j.jenvman.2020.111818 PMID:33360390

Chen, W., & Lei, Y. (2018). The impacts of renewable energy and technological innovation on environment-energy-growth nexus: New evidence from a panel quantile regression. *Renewable Energy, 123*, 1–14. doi:10.1016/j.renene.2018.02.026

Cherni, A., & Jouini, S. E. (2017). An ARDL approach to the CO2 emissions, renewable energy and economic growth nexus: Tunisian evidence. *International Journal of Hydrogen Energy, 42*(48), 29056–29066. doi:10.1016/j.ijhydene.2017.08.072

Chernov, O.A., & Sadovnikov, A.S. (2015a). Mechanisms of activation of innovative activity of enterprises. *Modern problems of science and education*, 759-765.

Chernova, O.A. (2009). Backbone principles of forming of innovation regional development strategy *Journal of Orenburg State University, 10*(104), 46-51.

Chernova, O.A., & Ivanov A.V. (2015/b). Models of integration cooperation of industrial enterprises: opportunities for capitalization growth. *Electronic Scientific Journal "Engineering Journal of Don"*. ivdon.ru/ru/magazine/archive/n1p2y2015/2817.

Cherp, A., & Jewell, J. (2014). The concept of energy security: Beyond the four As. *Energy Policy, 75*, 415–421. doi:10.1016/j.enpol.2014.09.005

Chi, J., & Baek, J. (2013). Dynamic relationship between air transport demand and economic growth in the United States: A new look. *Transport Policy, 29*, 257–260. doi:10.1016/j.tranpol.2013.03.005 PMID:32288380

Chindo, S., Abdulrahim, A., Waziri, S. I., Huong, W. M., & Ahmad, A. A. (2015). Energy consumption, CO2 emissions and GDP in Nigeria. *GeoJournal, 80*(3), 315–322. doi:10.100710708-014-9558-6

Chiu, D. (2017). The East Is Green: China's Global Leadership in Renewable Energy. *New Perspectives in Foreign Policy, 13*. Available at: https://www.csis.org/east-green-chinas-global-leadership-renewable-energy

Chudik, A., Mohaddes, K., & Raissi, M. (2021). Covid-19 fiscal support and its effectiveness. *Economics Letters, 205*, 109939. doi:10.1016/j.econlet.2021.109939 PMID:36540861

Clark, W. W., II. (2018). Afterword: A Sustainable Economic and Finance Proposal. In Sustainable Cities and Communities Design Handbook (pp. 573-583). Butterworth-Heinemann.

Coase, R. H. (1937). The Nature of the Firm. *Economica, 4*(16), 386–405. doi:10.1111/j.1468-0335.1937.tb00002.x

Coenen, J., Bager, S., Meyfroidt, P., Newig, J., & Challies, E. (2021). Environmental governance of China's belt and road initiative. *Environmental Policy and Governance, 31*(1), 3–17. doi:10.1002/eet.1901

Cole, C., & Karl, J. (2016). The Effect of Product Diversification Strategies on the Performance of Health Insurance Conglomerates. *Applied Economics, 48*(3), 190–202. doi:10.1080/00036846.2015.1076149

Communications Regulation Commission. (2012). https://crc.bg/: https://crc.bg/files/_bg/Metodika_2012_DV.pdf

Constitution of the People's Republic of China. 1982. http://www.npc.gov.cn/englishnpc/constitution2019/201911/1f65146fb6104dd3a2793875d19b5b29.shtml

Cooban, A. (2023a). *China's reopening isn't all good news. Inflation could get a second wind.* CNN. Available at: https://edition.cnn.com/2023/01/27/business/china-commodities-energy-inflation/index.html

Cooban, A. (2023b). *Global interest rate hikes are 'yet to bite,' says IMF head.* CNN. Available at: https://edition.cnn.com/2023/01/20/economy/imf-economy-davos/index.html

Coronavirus: "Thousands" of North Sea oil and gas jobs under threat. (2020, April 27). *BBC News.* https://www.bbc.com/news/uk-scotland-scotland-business-52446555

Council of Ministers of the Republic of Bulgaria. (2019). *Resolutions and decisions of the Council of Ministers of the Republic of Bulgaria, Sofia.* Author.

Council of Ministers of the Republic of Bulgaria. (2020). Integrated Plan in the Field of Energy and Climate of the Republic of Bulgaria 2021 – 2030. Author.

Crawford, A. (2022). *A New World Energy Order Is Emerging From Putin's War on Ukraine.* Bloomberg. Available at: https://www.bloomberg.com/news/articles/2022-03-11/a-new-world-energy-order-is-emerging-from-putin-s-war-on-ukraine#xj4y7vzkg

Crawford, L. (2006). Spain vows to prevent foreign takeover. *Financial Times.* Available at: www.ft.com

Csereklyei, Z., Qu, S., & Ancev, T. (2019). The effect of wind and solar power generation on wholesale electricity prices in Australia. *Energy Policy, 131*, 358–369. doi:10.1016/j.enpol.2019.04.007

Cuevas García-Dorado, S., Cornselsen, L., Smith, R., & Walls, H. (2019). Economic globalization, nutrition and health: A review of quantitative evidence. *Globalization and Health, 15*(1), 1–19. doi:10.118612992-019-0456-z PMID:30786909

Cummins, J., & Nini, G. (2002). Optimal Capital Utilization by Fnancial Firms: Evidence from the Property-liability Insurance Industry. *Journal of Financial Services Research, 21*(1), 15–53. doi:10.1023/A:1014369617192

Cyert, R. M., & March, J. G. (1963). *A Behavioral Theory of the Firm.*

Danish Ministry of Climate, Energy and Utilities. (n.d.). *Joint Statement: Urgent Action on Energy Efficiency, No. 2022 – 85, 10 June 2022.* Available at: https://en.kefm.dk/Media/637904431073034736/joint%20statement.pdf

Danish, K., Khan, N., Baloch, M. A., Saud, S., & Fatima, T. (2018). The effect of ICT on CO2 emissions in emerging economies: Does the level of income matters? *Environmental Science and Pollution Research International, 25*(23), 22850–22860. doi:10.100711356-018-2379-2 PMID:29855885

Darbouche, H., & Fattouh, B. (2011). *The Implications of the Arab Uprisings for Oil and Gas Markets.* Oxford Institute for Energy Studies., doi:10.26889/9781907555336

Davenport, T. H., & Westerman, G. (2018). Why so many high-profile digital transformations fail. *Harvard Business Review, 9*(4), 15.

David, F. R. (2011). *Strategic management: Concepts and cases* (13th ed.). Prentice Hall.

De Graaff, N., ten Brink, T., & Parmar, I. (2020). China's rise in a liberal world order in transition – introduction to the FORUM. *Review of International Political Economy, 27*(2), 191–207. doi:10.1080/09692290.2019.1709880

Decree of the President of the Republic of Belarus No. 7 dated 23 November 2017 "On development of entrepreneurship". (2021i), https://president.gov.by/ru/official_documents_ru/view/dekret-7-ot-23-nojabrja-2017-g-17533

Deffeyes, K. (2006). *Beyond Oil: The View from Hubbert's Peak.* Hill and Wang.

Degterev, D. (2021). Незападные теории развития в эпоху глобального капитализма [Non-Western Theories of Development In The Global Capitalism Era]. *World Economy and International Relations, 65*(4), 113–122. doi:10.20542/0131-2227-2021-65-4-113-122

Demirgil, B., & Birol, Y. E. (2020). Yenilenebilir enerji tüketimi ve ekonomik büyüme ilişkisi: Türkiye için bir Toda-Yamamoto nedensellik analizi [The relationship of energy consumption and economic growth: A TodaYamamoto causality analysis for Turkey]. *Cumhuriyet Üniversitesi İktisadi ve İdari Bilimler Fakültesi Dergisi, 21*(1), 68-83.

Dewan, A. (2021). *Europe's gas crisis is also a renewables crisis, but there are ready solutions.* CNN. Available at: https://edition.cnn.com/2021/09/22/business/europe-energy-gas-renewables-climate-cmd-intl/index.html

Dewey, K. G., Wessells, K. R., Arnold, C. D., Prado, E. L., Abbeddou, S., Adu-Afarwuah, S., Ali, H., Arnold, B. F., Ashorn, P., Ashorn, U., Ashraf, S., Becquey, E., Bendabenda, J., Brown, K. H., Christian, P., Colford, J. M. Jr, Dulience, S., Fernald, L., Galasso, E., ... Stewart, C. P. (2021). Characteristics that modify the effect of small-quantity lipid-based nutrient supplementation on child growth: An individual participant data meta-analysis of randomized controlled trials. *The American Journal of Clinical Nutrition, 114*(1), 15–42. doi:10.1093/ajcn/nqab278 PMID:34590672

Dharfizi, A. D. H., Ghani, A. B. A., & Islam, R. (2020). Evaluating Malaysia's fuel diversification strategies 1981–2016. *Energy Policy, 137*, 111083. doi:10.1016/j.enpol.2019.111083

DHMI. (2021). *Statistics report 2020. General Directorate of State Airports Authority of Turkey.* https://web.shgm.gov.tr/documents/sivilhavacilik/files/Istatistikler/2020_istatistik_raporu.pdf

Dickey, D. A., & Fuller, W. A. (1979). Distribution of the estimators for autoregressive time series with a unit root. *Journal of the American Statistical Association, 74*(366a), 427–431. doi:10.1080/01621459.1979.10482531

Dietz, T., & Rosa, E. A. (1997). Effects of population and affluence on CO2 emissions. *Proceedings of the National Academy of Sciences of the United States of America, 94*(1), 175–179. doi:10.1073/pnas.94.1.175 PMID:8990181

Dinçsoy, E. E. (2016). Environmental, Social and Economic Factors of Development Axes in terms of Spatial Planning: An Analysis of Thrace Region in Turkey. *International Journal of Statistics & Economics, 17*(2), 85–96.

Dincsoy, E. E., & Ichiminami, F. (2006). An Assessment of the Southeastern Anatolia Region in Turkey in Terms of the Sustainable Development Targets. *Journal of the Faculty of Environmental Science and Technology, 11*(1), 75–81.

Dincsoy, E. E., & Ichiminami, F. (2006). An Assessment of the Southeastern Anatolia Region in Turkey in Terms of the Sustainable Development Targets. *Journal of the Faculty of Environmental Science and Technology. Okayama University*, *11*(1), 75–81.

Dinçsoy, E. E., & Ichiminami, F. (2006). An Assessment of the Southeastern Anatolia Region in Türkiye in Terms of the Sustainable Development Targets. *Journal of the Faculty of Environmental Science and Technology, Okayama University*, *11*(1), 75–81.

Dinçsoy, E. E., & Okur Dinçsoy, M. (2020). Ekonomik büyümenin enflasyon üzerine etkisinin Türkiye ekonomisi açısından analizi. *Balkan ve Yakın Doğu Sosyal Bilimler Dergisi*, (6), 118–124.

Dinçsoy, E. E., & Okur Dinçsoy, M. (2020). Ekonomik Büyümenin Enflasyon Üzerine Etkisinin Türkiye Ekonomisi Açısından Analizi. *Balkan ve Yakın Doğu Sosyal Bilimler Dergisi*, *6*, 118–124.

Djoumessi, Y. F. (2022). The impact of malnutrition on infant mortality and life expectancy in Africa. *Nutrition (Burbank, Los Angeles County, Calif.)*, *103–104*, 111760. Advance online publication. doi:10.1016/j.nut.2022.111760 PMID:35843043

Do, B. T., Hansen, N. I., Bann, C., Lander, R. L., Goudar, S. S., Pasha, O., Chomba, E., Dhaded, S. M., Thorsten, V. R., Wallander, J. L., Biasini, F. J., Derman, R., Goldenberg, R. L., & Carlo, W. A. (2018). Associations between feeding practices and growth and neurodevelopmental outcomes at 36 months among children living in low-and low-middle income countries who participated in the BRAIN-HIT trial. *BMC Nutrition*, *4*(1), 1–12. doi:10.118640795-018-0228-9 PMID:32123571

Dogan, E. (2015). The relationship between economic growth and electricity consumption from renewable and non-renewable sources: A study of Turkey. *Renewable & Sustainable Energy Reviews*, *52*, 534–546. doi:10.1016/j.rser.2015.07.130

Dogan, E., & Seker, F. (2016). Determinants of CO2 emissions in the European Union: The role of renewable and non-renewable energy. *Renewable Energy*, *94*, 429–439. doi:10.1016/j.renene.2016.03.078

Dolchinkov, N. (2016). History, development and prospects of the Belene NPP project. Scientific conference "Radiation safety in the modern world", NSU "V. Levski", 81-90.

Dolchinkov, N., & Karaivanova-Dolchinkova, B. (2020). The role of nuclear energy in the world economy. *Scientific conference "Radiation safety in the modern world", NSU "V. Levski"*, 250-260.

Dolchinkov, N., & Karaivanova-Dolchinkova, B. (2021). Modern plans for development of production of electricity worldwide and energy independence of *Bulgaria, Scientific conference "Radiation safety in the modern world", NSU "V. Levski"*, 392-399.

Dong, K., Dong, X., Jiang, Q., & Zhao, J. (2021). Assessing energy resilience and its greenhouse effect: A global perspective. *Energy Economics*, *104*, 105659. doi:10.1016/j.eneco.2021.105659

Dong, L., Miao, G., & Wen, W. (2021). China's carbon neutrality policy: Objectives, impacts and paths. *East Asian Policy*, *13*(1), 5–18. doi:10.1142/S1793930521000015

Doshi, R. (2021). "Great Changes Unseen in a Century": The Elusive Phrase Driving China's Grands Strategy. *China Leadership Monitor*. https://www.prcleader.org/dashi

Dougherty, J., & Pfaltzgraff, R. (2001). *Contending Theories of International Relations. A Comprehensive Survey*. Longman.

Dou, Q., & Gao, X. (2022). The double-edged role of the digital economy in firm green innovation: Micro-evidence from Chinese manufacturing industry. *Environmental Science and Pollution Research International*, *29*(45), 67856–67874. doi:10.100711356-022-20435-3 PMID:35524847

Drehobl, A., Ross, L., & Ayala, R. (n.d.). *An Assessment of National and Metropolitan Energy Burden across the United States*. Academic Press.

Driscoll, J., & Kraay, A. C. (1998). Consistent covariance matrix estimation with spatially dependent panel data. *The Review of Economics and Statistics*, *80*(4), 549–560. doi:10.1162/003465398557825

Dumitrescu, E. I., & Hurlin, C. (2012). Testing for Granger non-causality in heterogeneous panels. *Economic Modelling*, *29*(4), 1450–1460. doi:10.1016/j.econmod.2012.02.014

Dunleavy, P., Margetts, H., Bastow, S., & Tinkler, J. (2006). New public management is dead—Long live digital-era governance. *Journal of Public Administration: Research and Theory*, *16*(3), 467–494. doi:10.1093/jopart/mui057

Durğun, B., & Durğun, F. (2018). Yenilenebilir enerji tüketimi ile ekonomik büyüme arasında nedensellik ilişkisi: Türkiye örneği. *International Review of Economics and Management*, *6*(1), 1–27. https://dergipark.org.tr/tr/pub/iremjournal/issue/36427/347200

Du, Z., Jin, L., Ye, Y., & Zhang, H. (2020). Characteristics and influences of urban shrinkage in the exo-urbanization area of the Pearl River Delta, China. *Cities (London, England)*, *103*, 102767. doi:10.1016/j.cities.2020.102767

EC2023. Economic Commentary. (2023). *How Has the Pandemic Impacted Inflation*. https://blog.nationalwidefinancial.com/market-economy/how-has-the-pandemic-impacted-inflation

Ehigiamusoe, K. U., & Dogan, E. (2022). The role of interaction effect between renewable energy consumption and real income in carbon emissions: Evidence from low-income countries. *Renewable & Sustainable Energy Reviews*, *154*, 111883. doi:10.1016/j.rser.2021.111883

Ehigiamusoe, K. U., Shahbaz, M., & Vo, X. V. (2023). How does globalization influence the impact of tourism on carbon emissions and ecological footprint? Evidence from African countries. *Journal of Travel Research*, *62*(5), 1010–1032. doi:10.1177/00472875221113886

Elia, M. (2006). Nutrition and health economics. *Nutrition (Burbank, Los Angeles County, Calif.)*, *22*(5), 576–578. doi:10.1016/j.nut.2006.01.005 PMID:16600820

Elliott, J. R., & Clement, M. T. (2014). Urbanization and carbon emissions: A nationwide study of local countervailing effects in the United States. *Social Science Quarterly*, *95*(3), 795–816. doi:10.1111squ.12079

Embassy of the People's Republic China in the Republic of Seychelles. (2022, May 8). *Global Development Initiative and Global Security Initiative—China's latest solutions to world peace, security and development*. Retrieved from http://sc.china-embassy.gov.cn/eng/zxhd/202208/t20220805_10735867.htm

Embassy of the PRC in the Republic of South Africa. (2022, October 20). *The Global Development Initiative: How Useful and Prudent is Xi Jinping's Global Development Initiative for Advancing the Wellbeing of Humanity?* Retrieved from http://za.china-embassy.gov.cn/eng/sgxw/202210/t20221020_10788973.htm

Emir, F., & Bekun, F. V. (2019). Energy intensity, carbon emissions, renewable energy, and economic growth nexus: New insights from Romania. *Energy & Environment*, *30*(3), 427–443. doi:10.1177/0958305X18793108

Emir, F., Philip, L. D., & Sertoglu, K. (2022). Assessing the influence of urbanization and energy on carbon emissions of Turkey: Evidence using the new RALS analysis. *Environmental Science and Pollution Research International*, *29*(38), 57905–57917. doi:10.100711356-022-19953-x PMID:35355189

Emodi, N. V., Shagdarsuren, G., & Tiky, A. Y. (2015). Influencing factors promoting technological innovation in renewable energy. *International Journal of Energy Economics and Policy*, *5*(3), 889–900. https://dergipark.org.tr/en/download/article-file/361553

Energy Capital Power. (2021a). *Renewable energy projects in West Africa*. Retrieved from https://energycapitalpower.com/top-5-innovative-renewable-energy-projects-in-west-africa/

Engle, R. F., & Granger, C. W. J. (1987). Co-Integration and Error Correction: Representation, Estimation, and Testing. *Econometrica*, *55*(2), 251–276. doi:10.2307/1913236

Erker, S., Stangl, R., & Stoeglehner, G. (2017a). Resilience in the light of energy crises – Part I: A framework to conceptualise regional energy resilience. *Journal of Cleaner Production*, *164*, 420–433. doi:10.1016/j.jclepro.2017.06.163

Erker, S., Stangl, R., & Stoeglehner, G. (2017b). Resilience in the light of energy crises – Part II: Application of the regional energy resilience assessment. *Journal of Cleaner Production*, *164*, 495–507. doi:10.1016/j.jclepro.2017.06.162

ESCAP. (2012). *Finding a Green Engine for Economic Growth: China's Renewable Energy Policies, Low Carbon Green Growth Roadmap for Asia and the Pacific*. Economic and Social Commission for Asia and the Pacific. Available at: https://www.unescap.org/sites/default/files/14.%20CS-China-Renewable-Energy-Policies.pdf

Escobar, A. (1995). *Encountering Development. The Making and Unmaking of the Third World*. Princeton University Press.

Estola, M. (2014). The Neoclassical Theory of a Firm: Correction for its errors. *Hyperion International Journal of Econophisics & New Economy*, *7*(1), 7–21.

euronews.com. (2022). *AB, 2022'de savaş, enerji krizi ve enflasyonun etkileriyle mücadele etti | Euronews*. https://tr.euronews.com/2022/12/22/ab-2022de-savas-enerji-krizi-ve-enflasyonun-etkileriyle-mucadele-etti

European Commission. (2019). *The European Green Deal, Brussels, 11.12.2019, COM(2019) 640 final*. Author.

European Commission. (2020). *Support for SME Internalization beyond the EU*. https://evening.europe.eu/growth/smes/sme-strategy/assets-to-markets/internationalization/support-tools_en

European Commission. (2022). *REPowerEU: Joint European Action for more affordable, secure and sustainable energy, Strasbourg, 8.3.2022, COM(2022) 108 final*. Author.

Evrendilek, F., & Ertekin, C. (2003). Assessing the potential of renewable energy sources in Turkey. *Renewable Energy*, *28*(15), 2303–2315. doi:10.1016/S0960-1481(03)00138-1

Fabuš, M., & Csabay, M. (2018). State aid and investment: Case of Slovakia. *Enterpreneurship and Sustainability Issues*, *6*(1), 369–377. doi:10.9770/jesi.2018.6.1(23)

Falk, J. (2012). *Energy firms must acknowledge cybersecurity as more than an IT problem, according to new Rice University paper*. Rice University. Available at: http://news.rice.edu

Fang, Z. (2023). Assessing the impact of renewable energy investment, green technology innovation, and industrialization on sustainable development: A case study of China. *Renewable Energy*, *205*, 772–782. doi:10.1016/j.renene.2023.01.014

Fanzo, J. (2019). Healthy and sustainable diets and food systems: The key to achieving Sustainable Development Goal 2? *Food Ethics*, *4*(2), 159–174. doi:10.100741055-019-00052-6

FAO. (2019). *Food Loss and Waste*. Food and Agriculture Organization of the United Nations. Retrieved: https://www.fao.org/nutrition/capacity-development/food-loss-and-waste/en/

Farhani, S. (2013). Renewable energy consumption, economic growth and CO2 emissions: Evidence from selected MENA countries. *Energy Economics Letters*, *1*(2), 24-41. Retrieved from https://archive.aessweb.com/index.php/5049/article/view/149

Farhani, S., & Ben Rejeb, J. (2012). Energy consumption, economic growth and CO2 emissions: Evidence from panel data for MENA region. *International Journal of Energy Economics and Policy*, *2*(2), 71–81.

fDi Intelligence. (2023). *Strategic Industries buck post-Covid Investment slump*. https://www.fdiintelligence.com/content/data-trends/strategic-industries-buck-postcovid-investment-slump-82621?

fDi Intelligence. (2023). *Wave of mega projects mounts in 2022*. https://www.fdiintelligence.com/content/data-trends/wave-of-mega-projects-mounts-in-2022-82551

Ferchen, M. (2020). *How China is Reshaping International Development*. Carnegie Endowment for International Peace. https://carnegieendowment.org/2020/01/08/how-china-is-reshaping-international-development-pub-80703

Financial Supervision Commission. (2021). https://www.fsc.bg/bg/

Fizaine, F., & Court, V. (2016). Energy expenditure,economic growth,and the minimum EROI of society. *Energy Policy*, *95*, 172–186. doi:10.1016/j.enpol.2016.04.039

Flavin, C., & Lenssen, N. (1994). *Enerjide Arayışlar*. Tema Vakfı Yayınları.

Foreign Minister of Foreign Affairs of the People's Republic of China. (2021, September 26). *Wang Yi Talks about the Significance of the "Global Development Initiative."* Retrieved from https://www.fmprc.gov.cn/web/wjbzhd/202109/t20210926_9584091.shtml

Frankel, J. (2012). *The Natural Resource Curse: A Survey of Diagnoses and Some Prescriptions*. Harvard Kennedy School, HKS Faculty Research Working Paper Series, RWP12-014.

Frennert, S. (2018). Lost in digitalization? Municipality employment of welfare technologies. *Disability and Rehabilitation. Assistive Technology*. Advance online publication. doi:10.1080/17483107.2018.1496362 PMID:30264649

Friedman, T. (2006). The First Law of Petro-politics. *Foreign Policy, 154*(3), 28-36.

Gakashev, M. M. (2013a). Methodology for the selection and formation of economic industrial clusters. *Vector of Science of Togliatti State University. Series: Economics and Management*, *2013*(1), 20–23.

Gambino, M. (2012). Is *it too late for Sustainable Development. Dennis Meadows Thinks So. Forty Years after His Book the Limits to Growth, He Explains Why*. Available Online: Https://Www. Smithsonianmag. Com/Sciencenature/Is-It-Too-Late-for-Sustainable-Development-125411410/

Gangneux, J., & Joss, S. (2022). Crisis as driver of digital transformation? Scottish local governments' response to COVID-19. *Data & Policy*, *4*, e26. doi:10.1017/dap.2022.18

Gatto, A., & Drago, C. (2020). Measuring and modeling energy resilience. *Ecological Economics*, *172*, 106527. doi:10.1016/j.ecolecon.2019.106527

Gebremaryam, T., Amare, D., Ayalew, T., Tigabu, A., & Menshaw, T. (2022). Determinants of severe acute malnutrition among children aged 6-23 months in bahir dar city public hospitals, Northwest Ethiopia, 2020: A case control study. *BMC Pediatrics*, *22*(1), 296. doi:10.118612887-022-03327-w PMID:35596187

Georgiev, M. (2017d). Impacts of active social programs on labor market. *// International Scientific Journal Innovation Science*. http://www.assam.com/katalog115.php/

Georgilakis, P. S. (2007). Artificial intelligence solution to electricity price forecasting problem. *Applied Artificial Intelligence*, *21*(8), 707–727. doi:10.1080/08839510701526533

Ghiani, E., Galici, M., Mureddu, M., & Pilo, F. (2020). Impact on Electricity Consumption and Market Pricing of Energy and Ancillary Services during Pandemic of COVID-19 in Italy. *Energies*, *13*(13), 13. Advance online publication. doi:10.3390/en13133357

Gillen, D. (2011). The evolution of airport ownership and governance. *Journal of Air Transport Management*, *17*(1), 3–13. doi:10.1016/j.jairtraman.2010.10.003

Gillwald, A., Mothobi, A., Ndiwalana, A., & Tusubira, T. (2019). *The state of ICT in Uganda. Policy Paper Series No. 5 After Access: Paper No. 8*. International Development Research Centre.

Gipe, P. (2011). *Snapshot of Feed-in Tariffs around the World in 2011*. See also: http://www. windworks.org/FeedLaws/SnapshotofFeed-inTariffsaroundtheWorldin2011.html

Gitelman, L., & Kozhevnikov, M. (2023). New Business Models in the Energy Sector in the Context of Revolutionary Transformations. *Sustainability (Basel)*, *15*(4), 3604. doi:10.3390u15043604

Global Times. (2021). *China to buy $150b in farm goods from ASEAN, almost double current level*. https://www.globaltimes.cn/page/202111/1239626.shtml

Global Times. (2023). *China issue 15 measures to help SMEs stabilize growth, adjust structure*. https://www.globaltimes.cn/page/202301/1283861.shtml

Global Times. (2023, March 10). *Saudi Arabia, Iran agree to resume ties, reopen embassies after talks in Beijing*. Retrieved from https://www.globaltimes.cn/page/202303/1287076.shtml

Godwin, I., Umoh, E., & Amah, E. (2013). *Knowledge Management and Organizational Resilience in Nigerian Manufacturing Organizations*. Developing Country Studies.

Goh, J. M., & Arenas, A. E. (2020). IT value creation in public sector: How IT-enabled capabilities mitigate tradeoffs in public organisations. *European Journal of Information Systems*, *29*(1), 25–43. doi:10.1080/0960085X.2019.1708821

Gökmenoğlu, K., & Taşpınar, N. (2016). The relationship between Co2 emissions, energy consumption, economic growth and FDI: The case of Turkey. *The Journal of International Trade & Economic Development*, *25*(5), 706–723. doi:10.1080/09638199.2015.1119876

Goldin, I. (2019). Chinese Lessons in Poverty Eradication. In *China Watch*. The Sleeping Giant Awakes.

Goldyakova, T. V. (2006a). Concept and classification of innovations. *Russian foreign economic bulletin*, *2006*(2), 20–27.

Gong, G. W. (1984). *The Standard of 'Civilization' in International Society*. Oxford University Press.

Gonzalez-Vicente, R. (2022). In the name of the nation: Authoritarian practices, capital accumulation, and the radical simplification of development in China's global vision. *Globalizations*, 1–16. doi:10.1080/14747731.2022.2121061

Granger, C. (1988). Causality, cointegration, and control. *Journal of Economic Dynamics & Control*, *12*(2-3), 551–559. doi:10.1016/0165-1889(88)90055-3

Granger, C. W., & Newbold, P. (1974). Spurious Regressions in Econometrics. *Journal of Econometrics*, *2*(2), 111–120. doi:10.1016/0304-4076(74)90034-7

Green, R. K. (2007). Airports and economic development. *Real Estate Economics*, *35*(1), 91–112. doi:10.1111/j.1540-6229.2007.00183.x

Greve, T., & Pollitt, M. G. (2016). *A VCG auction for electricity storage*. EPRG working paper 1623 and Cambridge working paper in economics 1628.

Griffiths, S. (2019). Energy Diplomacy in a Time of Energy Transition. *Energy Strategy Reviews, 26*. Available at: https://www.sciencedirect.com/science/article/pii/S2211467X19300793

Groh, M. (2014). *Strategic management in times of crisis*. Academic Press.

Grossman, G. M., & Helpman, E. (1991). Trade, knowledge spillovers, and growth. *European Economic Review*, *35*(2), 517–526. doi:10.1016/0014-2921(91)90153-A

Gujarati, D. N., & Porter, D. C. (2018). Temel Ekonometri [Basic Econometrics]. İstanbul: Literatür Yayıncılık.

Gujarati, D. (1999). *Essentials of econometrics*. Irwin/McGraw-Hill.

Gullì, F., & Balbo, A. L. (2015). The impact of intermittently renewable energy on Italian wholesale electricity prices: Additional benefits or additional costs? *Energy Policy*, *83*, 123–137. doi:10.1016/j.enpol.2015.04.001

Gumus, E., & Çelikay, F. (2015). R\&D Expenditure and Economic Growth: New Empirical Evidence. *Margin - the Journal of Applied Economic Research*, *9*(3), 205–217. doi:10.1177/0973801015579753

Güngör, A., Güngör, G., & Ünal, E. (2017). Electricity consumption of airports: A case study for Turkey. *Energy and Building*, *139*, 1–9. doi:10.1016/j.enbuild.2016.12.052

GWEC. (2021). *Global wind power growth must triple over next decade to achieve Net Zero*. Global Wind Energy Council. Available at: https://gwec.net/global-wind-power-growth-must-triple-over-next-decade-to-achieve-net-zero/

Gwynne, R. N. (2009). *Modernization theory*. Elsevier.

Gyamfi, B. A., Onifade, S. T., & Ofori, E. K. (2023). Synthesizing the impacts of information and communication technology advancement and educational developments on environmental sustainability: A comparative analyses of three economic blocs—BRICS, MINT, and G7 economies. *Sustainable Development (Bradford)*, *31*(2), 744–759. doi:10.1002d.2416

Gyamfi, S., Diawuo, F. A., Kumi, E. N., Sika, F., & Modjinou, M. (2018). The energy efficiency situation in Ghana. *Renewable & Sustainable Energy Reviews*, *82*, 1415–1423. doi:10.1016/j.rser.2017.05.007

Haftu, G. G. (2019). Information communications technology and economic growth in Sub-Saharan Africa: A panel data approach. *Telecommunications Policy*, *43*(1), 88–99. doi:10.1016/j.telpol.2018.03.010

Hai, T. N., Van, Q. N., & Thi Tuyet, M. N. (2021). Digital transformation: Opportunities and challenges for leaders in the emerging countries in response to COVID-19 pandemic. *Emerging Science Journal*, *5*(1), 21–36. doi:10.28991/esj-2021-SPER-03

Halbrügge, S., Schott, P., Weibelzahl, M., Buhl, H. U., Fridgen, G., & Schöpf, M. (2021). How did the German and other European electricity systems react to the COVID-19 pandemic? *Applied Energy*, *285*, 116370. doi:10.1016/j.apenergy.2020.116370 PMID:36568698

Hale, G., Leer, J. C., & Nechio, F. (2023). Inflationary effects of fiscal support to households and firms. *National Bureau of Economic Research*, 30906. https://www.nber.org/w30906

Hamilton, J. (n.d.). Historical oil shocks. In Routledge Handbook of Major Events in Economic History. Retrieved July 13, 2023, from https://www.google.com/search?q=Hamilton%2C+J.+Historical+oil+shocks.+In+Routledge+Handbook+of+Major+Events+in+Economic+History%3B+Randall%2C+E.%2C+Whaples%2C+P.%2C+Whaples%2C+R.%2C+Eds.%3B+Routledge%3A+New+York%2C+NY%2C+USA%2C+2013%3B+pp.+239%E2%80%93265&oq=Hamilton%2C+J.+Historical+oil+shocks.+In+Routledge+Handbook+of+Major+Events+in+Economic+History%3B+Randall%2C+E.%2C+Whaples%2C+P.%2C+Whaples%2C+R.%2C+Eds.%3B+Routledge%3A+New+York%2C+NY%2C+USA%2C+2013%3B+pp.+239%E2%80%93265&gs_lcrp=EgZjaHJvbWUyBggAEEUYOdIBBzYwN2owajeoAgCwAgA&sourceid=chrome&ie=UTF-8

Hanna, N. K. (2016). *Mastering digital transformation. Mastering Digital Transformation (Innovation, Technology, and Education for Growth).* Emerald Publishing., doi:10.1108/978-1-78560-465-220151009

Hanson, C., Herring, B., & Trish, E. (2019). Do Health Insurance and Hospital Market Concentration Influence Hospital Patients' Experience of Care? *Health Services Research, 54*(4), 1475-6773.13168. Advance online publication. doi:10.1111/1475-6773.13168 PMID:31095743

Haralampiev, M. (2020). The development of atomic energy and nuclear arsenals. *Collection of reports from the Scientific Conference "Current Security Issues", 6,* 123-133.

Harris, R., & Tzavalis, E. (1999). Inference for unit roots in dynamic panels where the time dimension is fixed. *Journal of Econometrics, 91*(2), 201–226. doi:10.1016/S0304-4076(98)00076-1

Heinberg, R. (2021). *Understanding Power.* Post Carbon Institute. Available at: https://www.postcarbon.org/understanding-power/

Heinberg, R. (2005). *The Party's Over: Oil, War and the Fate of Industrial Societies.* New Society Publishers.

Heinberg, R. (2011). *The End of Growth: Adapting to Our New Economic Reality.* New Society Publishers.

He, K. (2022). China's rise, institutional balancing, and (possible) peaceful order transition in the Asia pacific. *The Pacific Review, 35*(6), 1105–1134. doi:10.1080/09512748.2022.2075439

He, K., & Feng, H. (2023). International order transition and US-China strategic competition in the indo pacific. *The Pacific Review, 36*(2), 234–260. doi:10.1080/09512748.2022.2160789

Henderson, J. (2008). China and global development: Towards a Global-Asian Era? *Contemporary Politics, 14*(4), 375–392. doi:10.1080/13569770802519284

Herfindahl, O. C. (1950). *Concentration in the Steel Industry.* University Microfilms.

Herrero, A.G. (2021). What is Behind China's Dual Circulation Strategy. *China Leadership Monitor, 69.*

Hidayat, S., Yusgiantoro, P., Thamrin, S., & Widayatno, R. L. (2022). Energy Management Strategy For State Defense Toward The Energy Crisis. *Natural Volatiles & Essential Oils Journal,* 25–35.

Hoang Thi Ha. (2023). Why is China's Global Development Initiative Well Received in Southeast Asia? *FULCRUM.* ISEAS – Yusof Isak Institute. https://fulcrum.sg/why-is-chinas-global-development-initiative-well-received-in-southeast-asia/

Hoang, A. T., Sandro Nižetić, Olcer, A. I., Ong, H. C., Chen, W.-H., Chong, C. T., Thomas, S., Bandh, S. A., & Nguyen, X. P. (2021). Impacts of COVID-19 pandemic on the global energy system and the shift progress to renewable energy: Opportunities, challenges, and policy implications. *Energy Policy, 154,* 112322. doi:10.1016/j.enpol.2021.112322 PMID:34566236

Hoechle, D. (2007). Robust standard errors for panel regressions with cross-sectional dependence. *The Stata Journal*, *7*(3), 281–312. doi:10.1177/1536867X0700700301

Holland, J. H. (2014). *Complexity: A very short introduction*. Oxford University Press. doi:10.1093/actrade/9780199662548.001.0001

Holling, C. S. (1996). *Engineering Resilience versus Ecological Resilience*. https://www.semanticscholar.org/paper/Engineering-Resilience-versus-Ecological-Resilience-Holling/ab0dc6785ebbae3904aace0cb9e243d5379acd75

Holling, C. S. (1973). Resilience and Stability of Ecological Systems. *Annual Review of Ecology and Systematics*, *4*(1), 1–23. doi:10.1146/annurev.es.04.110173.000245

Holttinen, H. (2008). Estimating the impacts of wind power on power systems—Summary of IEA Wind collaboration. *Environmental Research Letters*, *3*(2), 025001. doi:10.1088/1748-9326/3/2/025001

Holzer, M., & Manoharan, A. P. (2016). *Digital Governance in Municipalities Worldwide (2015- 16) Seventh Global E-Governance Survey: A Longitudinal Assessment of Municipal Websites Throughout the World*. National Center for Public Performance.

Horowitz, A. R., & Horowitz, J. (1968). Entropy, Markov Processes and Competition in the Brewing Industry. *The Journal of Industrial Economics*, *16*(3), 196–211. doi:10.2307/2097560

Hossain, E., Faruque, H. M. R., Sunny, M. S. H., Mohammad, N., & Nawar, N. (2020). A comprehensive review on energy storage systems: Types, comparison, current scenario, applications, barriers, and potential solutions, policies, and future prospects. *Energies*, *13*(14), 3651. doi:10.3390/en13143651

Hotak, S., Islam, M., Kakinaka, M., & Kotani, K. (2020). Carbon emissions and carbon trade balances: International evidence from panel ARDL analysis. *Environmental Science and Pollution Research International*, *27*(19), 24115–24128. doi:10.100711356-020-08478-w PMID:32304055

Hsiao, C. (2007). Panel data analysis—Advantages and challenges. *Test*, *16*(1), 1–22. doi:10.100711749-007-0046-x

Huaxia. (2022, September 21). *UN chief says China's Global Development Initiative helps achieve global goals*. Xinhua. Retrieved from https://english.news.cn/20220921/61b03af7cfaa45c58ea3d31a34f6f3aa/c.html

Hughes, L. (2015). The effects of event occurrence and duration on resilience and adaptation in energy systems. *Energy*, *84*, 443–454. doi:10.1016/j.energy.2015.03.010

Humpe, A., & McMillan, D. G. (2020). Macroeconomic variables and long-term stock market performance. A panel ARDL co-integration approach for G7 countries. *Cogent Economics & Finance*, *8*(1), 1816257. doi:10.1080/23322039.2020.1816257

Hung-Pin, L. (2014). Renewable Energy Consumption and Economic Growth in Nine OECD Countries: Bounds Test Approach and Causality Analysis. *TheScientificWorldJournal*, *919167*, 1–6. Advance online publication. doi:10.1155/2014/919167 PMID:24558343

Hussain, M. M., Pal, S., & Villanthenkodath, M. A. (2023). Towards sustainable development: The impact of transport infrastructure expenditure on the ecological footprint in India. *Innovation and Green Development*, *2*(2), 100037. doi:10.1016/j.igd.2023.100037

Hussain, M. N., Li, Z., & Sattar, A. (2022). Effects of urbanization and nonrenewable energy on carbon emission in Africa. *Environmental Science and Pollution Research International*, *29*(17), 1–15. doi:10.100711356-021-17738-2 PMID:34837625

Hutter, C., & Weber, E. (2022). *Russia-Ukraine War: Short-run Production and Labour Market Effects of the Energy Crisis.* IAB-Discussion Paper, Article 202210. https://ideas.repec.org//p/iab/iabdpa/202210.html

Hu, X., Jaraite, J., & Kazukauskas, A. (2021). The effects of wind power on electricity markets: A case study of the Swedish intraday market. *Energy Economics, 96*, 105159. doi:10.1016/j.eneco.2021.105159

IAEA. (2023, May 1). International Atomic Energy Agency. https://www.iaea.org/

Iancu, I. A., Darab, C. P., & Cirstea, S. D. (2021). The Effect of the COVID-19 Pandemic on the Electricity Consumption in Romania. *Energies, 14*(11), 11. Advance online publication. doi:10.3390/en14113146

IATA. (2021). *COVID-19 outlook for air travel in the next 5 years.* International Air Transport Association. https://www.iata.org/en/iata-repository/publications/economic-reports/covid—19-outlook-for-air-travel-in-the-next-5-years/

Idowu, A., Ohikhuare, O. M., & Chowdhury, M. A. (2023). Does industrialization trigger carbon emissions through energy consumption? Evidence from OPEC countries and high industrialised countries. *Quantitative Finance and Economics, 7*(1), 165–186. doi:10.3934/QFE.2023009

IEA. (2021). *Key world Energy Statistics.* https://www.iea.org/reports/key-world-energy-statistics-2021/final-consumption

IEA. (2022). *Unlocking the Potential of Distributed Energy Resources.* https://www.iea.org/reports/unlocking-the-potential-of-distributed-energy-resources

IEA. (2022a), *Renewables 2022.* IEA. https://www.iea.org/reports/renewables-2022

IEA. (2022b). *International energy agency: world energy Outlook.* International Energy Agency Publications.

IEA. (2022c). *Grid-Scale Storage.* IEA. https://www.iea.org/reports/grid-scale-storage

IEA. (2023). *World Energy Investment 2023.* https://iea.glob.core.windows.net/assets/8834d3af-af60-4df0-9643-72e2684f7221/WorldEnergyinvestment2023.pdf

IMF. (2011). *Global shocks and their impact on low-income countries: Lessons from the 2007–09 crisis* (Working Paper No WP/11/27). https://www.imf.org/external/pubs/ft/wp/2011/wp1127.pdf

IMF. (2021). *Fiscal Monitor Database of Country Fiscal Measures in Response to the COVID-19 Pandemic.* https://www.imf.org/en/Topics/inf-and-covid19/Fiscal-Policies-Database-in-Response-to-COVID-19

IMF. (2023). *World Economic Outlook.* https://www.imf.org/en/Publications/WEO

Im, K. S., Pesaran, M. H., & Shin, Y. (2003). Testing for unit roots in heterogeneous panels. *Journal of Econometrics, 115*(1), 53–74. doi:10.1016/S0304-4076(03)00092-7

INCTAD. (2022). *World Investment Report 2022.* https://unctad.org/publication/world-investment-report-2022

INCTAD. (2023). *World Investment Report 2023. Investing in Sustainable Energy for All.* https://unctad.org/system/files/official-document/wir2023_en.pdf

Indicators of Innovation. (2016). *Statistical compilation.* Moscow: NIU HSE.

Indriani, D. (2022). Tourism and Economic Growth: Evidence from ASEAN countries. *Journal of Indonesian Applied Economics, 10*(2), 100–131. doi:10.21776/ub.jiae.2022.010.02.4

Industry of the Republic of Belarus. (2020d). Statistical collection. Minsk: National Statistical Committee of the Republic of Belarus.

Ingram, G., & Lord, K. (2019). *Global Development Disrupted: Findings from a Survey of 93 leaders*. Global Economy and Development at Brookings.

Instanes, A., Kokorev, V., Janowicz, R., Bruland, O., Sand, K., & Prowse, T. (2016). Changes to freshwater systems affecting Arctic infrastructure and natural resources. *Journal of Geophysical Research. Biogeosciences*, *121*(3), 567–585. doi:10.1002/2015JG003125

International Energy Agency. (2018). *World Energy Outlook 2018*. International Energy Agency.

International Energy Agency. (2020a). *World Energy Investment 2020*. IEA. Available at: https://www.iea.org/reports/world-energy-investment-2020

International Energy Agency. (2020b). *Global Energy Review 2020. The Impacts of the Covid-19 Crisis on Global Energy Demand and CO2 Emissions*. Flagship Report. Available at: https://www.iea.org/reports/global-energy-review-2020/

International Energy Agency. (2020c). *Sustainable Recovery*. Available at: https://www.iea.org/reports/sustainable-recovery

International Energy Agency. (2021). *Covid-19 impact on electricity*. Available at: https://www.iea.org/reports/covid-19-impact-on-electricity

International Energy Agency. (2022a). *Energy Efficiency*. https://iea.blob.core.windows.net/assets/7741739e-8e7f-4afa-a77f-49dadd51cb52/EnergyEfficiency2022.pdf

International Energy Agency. (2022b). *7th Annual Global Conference on Energy Efficiency Policy Toolkit*. Available at: https://iea.blob.core.windows.net/assets/ef170f7d-606a-4adc-ac32-565f9b6c0579/7thAnnualGlobalConferenceonEnergyEfficiency-PolicyToolkit.pdf

International Energy Agency. (2022c). *7th Annual Global Conference on Energy Efficiency - The Value of Urgent Action on Energy Efficiency*. Available at: https://www.iea.org/reports/the-value-of-urgent-action-on-energy-efficiency

International Energy Agency. (2023). *Oil Market Report, 18 January 2023*. Available at: https://iea.blob.core.windows.net/assets/6b994ae3-17fe-4a44-8bb8-eb1217cc4604/-18JAN2023_OilMarketReport.pdf

Islam, A., Al-tabatabaie, K. F., Karmaker, A. K., Biplob Hossain, M., & Islam, K. (2022). Assessing energy diversification policy and sustainability: Bangladesh standpoints. *Energy Strategy Reviews*, *40*, 100803. doi:10.1016/j.esr.2022.100803

Jaaron, A. A. M., & Backhouse, C. J. (2014). Service organisations resilience through the application of the vanguard method of systems thinking: A case study approach. *International Journal of Production Research*, *52*(7), 2026–2041. doi:10.1080/00207543.2013.847291

Jacobs, M. (2017). *Panic at the Pump - The Energy Crisis and the Transformation of American Politics in the 1970s*. Macmillan.

Jahanger, A., Zaman, U., Hossain, M. R., & Awan, A. (2023). Articulating CO2 emissions limiting roles of nuclear energy and ICT under the EKC hypothesis: An application of non-parametric MMQR approach. *Geoscience Frontiers*, *14*(5), 101589. doi:10.1016/j.gsf.2023.101589

Janssen, M., Charalabidis, Y., & Zuiderwijk, A. (2012). Benefits, adoption barriers and myths of open data and open government. *Information Systems Management*, *29*(4), 258–268. doi:10.1080/10580530.2012.716740

Janssen, M., & Van Der Voort, H. (2016). Adaptive governance: Towards a stable, accountable and responsive government. *Government Information Quarterly*, *33*(1), 1–5. doi:10.1016/j.giq.2016.02.003

Jasiūnas, J., Lund, P. D., & Mikkola, J. (2021). Energy system resilience – A review. *Renewable & Sustainable Energy Reviews*, *150*, 111476. doi:10.1016/j.rser.2021.111476

Jebli, M. B., & Kahia, M. (2020). The interdependence between CO2 emissions, economic growth, renewable and non-renewable energies, and service development: Evidence from 65 countries. *Climatic Change, 162*(2), 193–212. doi:10.100710584-020-02773-8

Jenkins, R. (2022). *How China is reshaping the global economy: Development impacts in Africa and Latin America.* Oxford University Press. doi:10.1093/oso/9780192866356.001.0001

Jin, T., & Kim, J. (2018). What is better for mitigating carbon emissions – Renewable energy or nuclear energy? A panel data analysis. *Renewable & Sustainable Energy Reviews, 91*, 464–471. doi:10.1016/j.rser.2018.04.022

Johnson, K. (2009). Protectionist Breezes: Wind-Power Companies Cry Foul on China. *Wall Street Journal.* Available at: http://europe.wsj.com

Joo, Y.-J., Kim, C. S., & Yoo, S.-H. (2015). Energy consumption, Co2 emission, and economic growth: Evidence from Chile. *International Journal of Green Energy, 12*(5), 543–550. doi:10.1080/15435075.2013.834822

Kabatas, M. (2021). A Study on Healthy Eating Children's Music Lessons and School Performance. *American Educational Research Journal, 9*(1), 112–120.

Kajanus, M., Leskinen, P., Kurttila, M., & Kangas, J. (2012). Making use of MCDS methods in SWOT analysis—Lessons learnt in strategic natural resources management. *Forest Policy and Economics, 20*, 1–9. doi:10.1016/j.forpol.2012.03.005

Kamacı, A., & Göktaş, S. (2020). Petrol fiyatları ile ekonomik büyüme ilişkisi: Türkiye örneği. *Bartın Üniversitesi İktisadi ve İdari Bilimler Fakültesi Dergisi, 11*(22), 547-556. Retrieved from https://dergipark.org.tr/en/pub/bartiniibf/article/797897

Kamenov, K., & Asenow, A. (2000). *Man, teams, leaders.* Publishing house "Luren".

Kao, C. (1999). Spurious regression and residual-based tests for co-integration in panel data. *Journal of Econometrics, 90*(1), 1–44. doi:10.1016/S0304-4076(98)00023-2

Kapron, Z. (2018). From digital payments to digital finance: How China's tech companies are redefining banking in Asia and soon Europe. *Journal of Payments Strategy & Systems, 12*(1), 68–73.

Karaaslan, A., & Çamkaya, S. (2022). The relationship between CO2 emissions, economic growth, health expenditure, and renewable and non-renewable energy consumption: Empirical evidence from Turkey. *Renewable Energy, 190*, 457–466. doi:10.1016/j.renene.2022.03.139

Karakurt Tosun, E. (2008). Türkiye de E Belediyecilik Uygulamaları Bursa Nilüfer Osmangazi Yıldırım Belediyelerinin Web Sitelerinin Analizi. *Çağdaş Yerel Yönetimler, 2*(17), 71-94. doi:10.1111/faam.12313

Karamıklı, A., & Şaşmaz, M. Ü. (2021). Türkiye'de Yenilenebilir Enerji Tüketiminin Ekonomik Büyüme ve Sağlık Harcamaları Üzerindeki Etkisi. *Pamukkale Üniversitesi Sosyal Bilimler Enstitüsü Dergisi*, (46), 293–304.

Karim, S., & Islam, N. M. (2017). Syrian crisis: Geopolitics and implications. *Biiss Journal, 37*(2).

Karplus, V. J., & Zhang, X. (2017). Incentivizing firm compliance with China's national emissions trading system. *Economics of Energy & Environmental Policy, 6*(2), 73–86. doi:10.5547/2160-5890.6.1.vkar

Kazaz, İ., & Dinçsoy, E. E. (2019). Sermaye Yatırımları, İthalat ve İhracat Değişkenleri Arasındaki İlişkinin Ekonometrik Analizi: Kosova Ekonomisi Üzerine Örnek Çalışma. *Sosyal Bilimler Araştırma Dergisi, 8*(3), 179–190.

Kecskeméthy, K. S., & Teknős, L. (2023). North Atlantic Treaty Organisation's climate change risk management responsibilities. *Belügyi Szemle, 71*(1). doi:10.38146/BSZ.SPEC.2023.1.4

Keleş, R., & Hamamcı, C. (2002). *Çevrebilim.* İmge Kitabevi Yayınları.

Kendall-Taylor, A. (2010). *Domestic balancing acts in the Caspian petro-states. - Caspian Energy Politics. Azerbaijan, Kazakhstan and Turkmenistan.* Routledge.

Keohane, R. O. (1980). The theory of hegemonic stability and changes in international economic regimes. In O. R. Holsti, R. M. Siverson, & A. L. George (Eds.), *Change in the International System* (pp. 131–162). Westview Press.

Keohane, R. O., & Joseph, S. Nye Jr. (1998). Power and interdependence in the information age. *Foreign Policy, 77*(5), 81–98.

Keramidas, K., Tchung-Ming, S., Diaz-Vazquez, A. R., Weitzel, M., Vandyck, T., Després, J., Schmitz, A., Rey Los Santos, L., Wojtowicz, K., Schade, B., Saveyn, B., Soria-Ramirez, A. (2018). *Global energy and climate outlook 2018: Sectoral mitigation options towards a low-emissions economy.* JRC Science for Policy Report (No. JRC113446)

Ketterer, J. C. (2014). The impact of wind power generation on the electricity price in Germany. *Energy Economics, 44*, 270–280. doi:10.1016/j.eneco.2014.04.003

Khalilzad, Z. (2017, June 19). *The Case for Congagement with China.* The National Interest. Retrieved from https://nationalinterest.org/feature/the-case-congagement-china-21232

Khan, Z. S. (2013). Causality between economic growth, energy consumption and green house gas emissions in Bangladesh: A Toda-Yamamoto approach. *Journal of Academic Research in Economics,* (2), 245-257. Retrieved from https://www.ceeol.com/search/article-detail?id=70322

Khan, K., & Su, C. W. (2021). Urbanization and carbon emissions: A panel threshold analysis. *Environmental Science and Pollution Research International, 28*(20), 26073–26081. doi:10.100711356-021-12443-6 PMID:33481196

Khan, S., & Majeed, M. T. (2023). Toward economic growth without emissions growth: The role of urbanization & industrialization in Pakistan. *Journal of Environmental Studies and Sciences, 13*(1), 43–58. doi:10.100713412-022-00797-3 PMID:36118988

Kharazmi, E., Bordbar, S., & Gholampoor, H. (2021). The Pattern of Health Insurance Economic Resilience in the Covid 19 Pandemic Shock. *BMC Research Notes, 14*(1), 371. Advance online publication. doi:10.118613104-021-05779-2 PMID:34556156

Kharrazi, A., Sato, M., Yarime, M., Nakayama, H., Yu, Y., & Kraines, S. (2015). Examining the resilience of national energy systems: Measurements of diversity in production-based and consumption-based electricity in the globalization of trade networks. *Energy Policy, 87*, 455–464. doi:10.1016/j.enpol.2015.09.019

Khobai, H., Kolisi, N., Moyo, C., Anyikwa, I., & Dingela, S. (2020). Renewable Energy Consumption and Unemployment in South Africa. *International Journal of Energy Economics and Policy, 10*(2), 170–178. doi:10.32479/ijeep.6374

Kilibarda, N., Djokovic, F., & Suzic, R. (2019). Food Waste Management-Reducing and Managing Food Waste in Hospitality. *Scientific Journal Meat Technology, 60*(2), 134–142. doi:10.18485/meattech.2019.60.2.8

Kim, S., & Kim, S. (2022). China's contestation of the liberal international order. *The Pacific Review*, 1–26. doi:10.1080/09512748.2022.2063367

King, L. (2012). *The Devastating Effects of a Cyber-Attack Against a Country's Energy Grid.* http://oilprice.com

King, A. (2022). Power, shared ideas and order transition: China, the United States, and the creation of the Bretton Woods order. *European Journal of International Relations, 28*(4), 910–933. doi:10.1177/13540661221118787

King, R. G., & Levine, R. (1993). Finance and growth: Schumpeter might be right. *The Quarterly Journal of Economics*, *108*(3), 717–737. doi:10.2307/2118406

Kirikkaleli, D., Güngör, H., & Adebayo, T. S. (2022). Consumption-based carbon emissions, renewable energy consumption, financial development and economic growth in Chile. *Business Strategy and the Environment*, *31*(3), 1123–1137. doi:10.1002/bse.2945

Kissinger, H. (2012). *On China*. Penguin Press HC.

Kisswani, K. M. (2017). Evaluating the GDP–energy consumption nexus for the ASEAN-5 countries using nonlinear ARDL model. *OPEC Energy Review*, *41*(4), 318–343. doi:10.1111/opec.12113

Kleemann, L., & Abdulai, A. (2013). The impact of Trade and Economic Growth on the Environment: Revisiting the Cross-Country Evidence. *Journal of International Development*, *25*(2), 180–205. doi:10.1002/jid.1789

Klimuk, V. V., & Lazdins, V. (2019a). Interaction of education, science and business in terms of digital economy development. *Proceedings of the 2019 International Conference "Economic science for rural development". Jelgava, LLU ESAF, 9-10 May 2019*, 37-48. 10.22616/ESRD.2019.102

Klimuk, V., & Tarasova, A. (2019). Digital economy in Belarus and Russia: leading underpins of a new reality. *Proceedings of the 3rd International Conference on Social, Economic, and Academic Leadership (ICSEAL 2019)*, 421-427. 10.2991/icseal-19.2019.66

Koblova, Yu. A. (2013b). Virtual organizations as the latest form of network structures. *Journal of the Saratov State Social and Economic University*, *2013*, 18–21.

Koceva, M., Terziev, V., & Andreeva, Z. (2003b). Problems in assessment of the active policies on the labor market. *Fifth National conference "Employment services and the European labor market"*.

Komarova, A., Filimonova, I., & Kartashevich, A. (2022). *Energy consumption of the countries in the context of economic development and energy transition. TMREES22-Fr.* Energy Reports.

Korkmaz, Ö., & Develi, A. (2012). Türkiye'de birincil enerji kullanımı, üretimi ve gayri safi yurt içi hasıla (GSYİH) arasındaki ilişki. *Dokuz Eylül Üniversitesi İktisadi ve İdari Bilimler Fakültesi Dergisi, 27*(2), 1-25. Retrieved from https://dergipark.org.tr/tr/pub/deuiibfd/issue/22727/242544

Kostic, M., Maksimovic, L., & Stojanovic, B. (2016). The Limitations of Competition in the Insurance Markets of Slovenia, Croatia and Serbia. *Ekonomska Istrazivanja*, *29*(1), 395–418. doi:10.1080/1331677X.2016.1169703

Kozloduy NPP. (2023, May 10). Kozloduy Nuclear Power Plant. https://kznpp.org/

Kraft, J., & Kraft, A. (1978). On the relationship between energy and GNP. *Journal of the Energy Division*, *3*, 401–403.

Krasner, S. D. (1976). State Power and the Structure of International Trade. *World Politics*, *28*(3), 317–347. https://doi.org/DOI. doi:10.2307/2009974

Kresnawan, M., & Wijaya, T. (2021). *Energy Diplomacy: A Vital Piece to Boost Renewable Energy Investment.* ASEAN Centre for Energy. Available at: https://aseanenergy.org/energy-diplomacy-a-vital-piece-to-boost-renewable-energy-investment/

Krickovic, A. (2017). The Symbiotic China-Russia Partnership: Cautious Riser and Desperate Challenger. *The Chinese Journal of International Politics*, *10*(3), 299–329. doi:10.1093/cjip/pox011

Krivokapic, R., Njegomir, V., & Stojic, D. (2017). Effects of Corporate Diversification on Firm Performance: Evidence from the Serbian Insurance Industry. *Ekonomska Istrazivanja*, *30*(1), 1224–1236. doi:10.1080/1331677X.2017.1340175

Kuhlmann, S., & Heuberger, M. (2023). Digital transformation going local: Implementation, impacts and constraints from a German perspective. *Public Money & Management*, *43*(2), 147–155. doi:10.1080/09540962.2021.1939584

Kumar, P., Tokas, J., Kumar, N., Lal, M., & Singal, H. R. (2018). Climate change consequences and its impact on agriculture and food security. *International Journal of Chemical Studies*, *6*(6), 124–133.

Kwakwa, P. A. (2020). The long-run effects of energy use, urbanization and financial development on carbon dioxide emissions. *International Journal of Energy Sector Management*, *14*(6), 1405–1424. doi:10.1108/IJESM-01-2020-0013

Kwakwa, P. A. (2022). The effect of industrialization, militarization, and government expenditure on carbon dioxide emissions in Ghana. *Environmental Science and Pollution Research International*, *29*(56), 85229–85242. doi:10.100711356-022-21187-w PMID:35794324

Kwakwa, P. A. (2023). Sectoral growth and carbon dioxide emission in Africa: Can renewable energy mitigate the effect? *Research in Globalization*, *6*, 100130. doi:10.1016/j.resglo.2023.100130

Kwakwa, P. A. (2023b). Climate change mitigation role of renewable energy consumption: Does institutional quality matter in the case of reducing Africa's carbon dioxide emissions? *Journal of Environmental Management*, *342*, 118234. doi:10.1016/j.jenvman.2023.118234 PMID:37327731

Kwiatkowski, D., Phillips, P. C., Schmidt, P., & Shin, Y. (1992). Testing the null hypothesis of stationarity against the alternative of a unit root: How sure are we that economic time series have a unit root? *Journal of Econometrics*, *54*(1-3), 159–178. doi:10.1016/0304-4076(92)90104-Y

Lammers, M., & Kok, L. (2012). Cost-benefit analysis of dietary treatment. *Amsterdam, Países Bajos: Seo. Economic Research Journal.*

Lampton, D. M. (1997). A growing China in a shrinking world: Beijing and the global order. In E. F. Vogel (Ed.), *Living with China: US/China Relations in the Twenty-first Century* (pp. 120–140). WW Norton & Company.

Lampton, D. M. (2005). China's rise in Asia need not be at America's expense. In D. L. Shambaugh (Ed.), *Power Shift: China and Asia's New Dynamics* (pp. 306–326). University of California Press.

Lan, P. (2022, December). Evaluation of Digital Transformation in Chinese Government from Data Mining Perspective. In *2022 3rd International Conference on Big Data and Social Sciences (ICBDSS 2022)* (pp. 134-144). Atlantis Press. 10.2991/978-94-6463-064-0_15

Landau, L. F., Campbell, L. K., Svendsen, E. S., & Johnson, M. L. (2021). Building Adaptive Capacity Through Civic Environmental Stewardship: Responding to COVID-19 Alongside Compounding and Concurrent Crises. *Frontiers in Sustainable Cities*, *3*, 705178. doi:10.3389/frsc.2021.705178

Lavrikova, Yu. L. (2008a). Clusters: strategy of formation and development in the economics of a region. Yekaterinburg: Publishing house of the Institute of Economics of the Ural Branch of the Russian Academy of Sciences.

Law of the Republic of Belarus No. 148-3 dated 1 July 2010 (with amendmends and additions No. 91-3 dated 9 January 2018) "On the development of small and medium-sized enterprises". (2021j). https://pravo.by/document/?guid=3871&p0=H11000148

Law of the Republic of Belarus No. 425-3 dated 10 July 2012, "On State Innovation Policy and Innovation Activities in the Republic of Belarus" (as amended and supplemented on 11 May 2016), (2016a).

Law, S. H., & Singh, N. (2014). Does too much finance harm economic growth? *Journal of Banking & Finance*, *41*, 36–44. doi:10.1016/j.jbankfin.2013.12.020

Lee, S.-H., & Jung, Y. (2018). Causal dynamics between renewable energy consumption and economic growth in South Korea: Empirical analysis and policy implications. *Energy & Environment, 29*, 1298–1315.

Lengnick-Hall, C. A., Beck, T. E., & Lengnick-Hall, M. L. (2011). Developing a capacity for organizational resilience through strategic human resource management. *Human Resource Management Review*, *21*(3), 243–255. doi:10.1016/j.hrmr.2010.07.001

Leveque, F., & Monturus, R. (2008). *Mergers & Acquisitions within the European Power and Gas Sectors. Cases and Patterns.* Report of the CERNA - Mines ParisTech. Available at: www.microeconomix.com

Levin, A., Lin, C. F., & Chu, C. S. J. (2002). Unit root tests in panel data: Asymptotic and finite-sample properties. *Journal of Econometrics*, *108*(1), 1–24. doi:10.1016/S0304-4076(01)00098-7

LeVine, S. (2012). *Ten Indicators You Should Watch to Predict the Geopolitics of Energy.* Quartz. Available at: https://qz.com/17335/ten-indicators-you-should-watch-to-predict-the-geopolitics-of-energy

Levine, R. (1997). Financial development and economic growth: Views and agenda. *Journal of Economic Literature*, *35*(2), 688–726.

Levine, R., Loayza, N., & Beck, T. (2000). Financial intermediation and growth: Causality and causes. *Journal of Monetary Economics*, *46*(1), 31–77. doi:10.1016/S0304-3932(00)00017-9

Liao, H., Peng, Y., Wang, F. Z., & Zhang, T. (2022). Understanding energy use growth: The role of investment-GDP ratio. *Structural Change and Economic Dynamics*, *63*, 15–24. doi:10.1016/j.strueco.2022.08.007

Liebenberg, A., & Sommer, D. (2008). Effects of Corporate Diversification: Evidence from the Property-liability Insurance Industry. *The Journal of Risk and Insurance*, *75*(4), 893–919. doi:10.1111/j.1539-6975.2008.00290.x

Liff, A. P. (2016). Whither the Balancers? The Case for a Methodological Reset. *Security Studies*, *25*(3), 420–459. doi:10.1080/09636412.2016.1195624

Lin, Z., Gao, L., & Zhang, D. (2006, June). Predictions of system marginal price of electricity using recurrent neural network. In *2006 6th World Congress on Intelligent Control and Automation* (Vol. 2, pp. 7592-7595). IEEE.

Lin, J. Y., & Wang, Y. (2017). *Going Beyond Aid: Development Cooperation for Structural Transformation.* Cambridge University Press. doi:10.1017/9781316597354

Li, Q., Cherian, J., Shabbir, M. S., Sial, M. S., Li, J., Mester, I., & Badulescu, A. (2021). Exploring the relationship between renewable energy sources and economic growth. The case of SAARC countries. *Energies*, *14*(3), 520. doi:10.3390/en14030520

Lise, W., & Montfort, K. V. (2007). Energy consumption and GDP in Turkey: Is there a co-integration relationship? *Energy Economics*, *29*(6), 1166–1178. doi:10.1016/j.eneco.2006.08.010

Liu, F., Giulietti, M., & Chen, B. (2016). Joint optimisation of generation and storage in the presence of wind. *IET Renewable Power Generation*, *10*(10), 1477–1487. doi:10.1049/iet-rpg.2015.0547

Liu, H. (2020). Chinese perception of China's engagement in multilateralism and global governance. *The Pacific Review*, *33*(3–4), 469–496. doi:10.1080/09512748.2020.1728570

Liu, Z., Deng, Z., He, G., Wang, H., Zhang, X., Lin, J., Qi, Y., & Liang, X. (2022). Challenges and opportunities for carbon neutrality in China. *Nature Reviews. Earth & Environment*, *3*(2), 141–155. doi:10.103843017-021-00244-x

Li, Y., Alharthi, M., Ahmad, I., Hanif, I., & Hassan, M. U. (2022). Nexus between renewable energy, natural resources and carbon emissions under the shadow of transboundary trade relationship from South East Asian economies. *Energy Strategy Reviews*, *41*, 100855. doi:10.1016/j.esr.2022.100855

Li, Z., Kuo, T. H., Siao-Yun, W., & Vinh, L. T. (2022). Role of green finance, volatility and risk in promoting the investments in Renewable Energy Resources in the post-covid-19. *Resources Policy*, *76*, 102563. doi:10.1016/j.resourpol.2022.102563

Lund, P. (2009). Effects of energy policies on industry expansion in renewable energy. *Renewable Energy*, *34*(1), 53–64. doi:10.1016/j.renene.2008.03.018

Lütkepohl, H. (2005). *New introduction to multiple time series analysis*. Springer Science & Business Media. doi:10.1007/978-3-540-27752-1

Lvov, D. S., & Glazyev, S. Yu. (1986).Theoretical and Applied Aspects of NTP Management. Economics and Mathematical Methods: Journal, 5, 793-804.

Lv, Q., Liu, H., Yang, D., & Liu, H. (2019). Effects of urbanization on freight transport carbon emissions in China: Common characteristics and regional disparity. *Journal of Cleaner Production*, *211*, 481–489. doi:10.1016/j.jclepro.2018.11.182

Lv, T., Hu, H., Zhang, X., Wang, L., & Fu, S. (2022). Impact of multidimensional urbanization on carbon emissions in an ecological civilization experimental area of China. *Physics and Chemistry of the Earth Parts A/B/C*, *126*, 103120. doi:10.1016/j.pce.2022.103120

Magazzino, C. (2014). The relationship between CO2 emissions, energy consumption and economic growth in Italy. *International Journal of Sustainable Energy*, *35*(9), 844–857. doi:10.1080/14786451.2014.953160

Magazzino, C., Toma, P., Fusco, G., Valente, D., & Petrosillo, I. (2022). Renewable energy consumption, environmental degradation and economic growth: The greener the richer? *Ecological Indicators*, *139*, 1–12. doi:10.1016/j.ecolind.2022.108912

Mahaffey, J. (2015). *Atomic Accidents: A History of Nuclear Meltdowns and Disasters; From the Ozark Mountains to Fukushima*. Pegasus Books.

Mahmudova, A. I. (2010a). Varieties of network integration in industry. *Journal of Astrakhan State Technical University: Series: Economics*, *2010*(1), 211–218.

Majeed, M. T., & Tauqir, A. (2020). Effects of urbanization, industrialization, economic growth, energy consumption, financial development on carbon emissions: An extended STIRPAT model for heterogeneous income groups. *Pakistan Journal of Commerce and Social Sciences*, *14*(3), 652–681.

Makube, S. (2012). *South African Oil Dependency: Geo-political, Geo-economic and Geo-strategic Considerations*. University of Johannesburg. ujdigispace.uj.ac.za

Malhi, G. S., Kaur, M., & Kaushik, P. (2021). Impact of climate change on agriculture and its mitigation strategies: A review. *Sustainability (Basel)*, *13*(3), 1318. doi:10.3390u13031318

Maliszewski, P. J., & Perrings, C. (2012). Factors in the resilience of electrical power distribution infrastructures. *Applied Geography (Sevenoaks, England)*, *32*(2), 668–679. doi:10.1016/j.apgeog.2011.08.001

Mallapragada, D. S., Sepulveda, N. A., & Jenkins, J. D. (2020). Long-run system value of battery energy storage in future grids with increasing wind and solar generation. *Applied Energy*, *275*, 115390. doi:10.1016/j.apenergy.2020.115390

Malmodin, J., & Lundén, D. (2018). The Energy and Carbon Footprint of the Global ICT and E&M Sectors 2010–2015. *Sustainability (Basel)*, *10*(9), 3027. doi:10.3390u10093027

Manchev, B. (2010). Belene. NPP - Lectures Before the "Energetik" Club.

March, J. G. (1958). A Behavioral Theory of Decision Making. *The Personnel Administrator*, *21*(3), 8–10.

Marris, R. (1964). *The Economic Theory of 'Managerial' Capitalism*. Macmillan. doi:10.1007/978-1-349-81732-0

Marris, R. (1998). Managerial Theories of the Firm. In *Managerial Capitalism in Retrospect*. Palgrave Macmillan. doi:10.1057/9780230376168_5

Marshall, A. (1920). *Principal of Economics*. Macmillan.

Marzuki, S. Z., Zreik, M., Buyong, S. Z., Goyipnazarov, S., Mirzaliev, S., & Bakhramovna, I. A. (2023). An Importance Satisfaction Analysis of Hosting Events in Hangzhou, China: A Pilot Study. *Advances in Social Sciences Research Journal, 10*(6.2), 107–117. doi:10.14738/assrj.106.2.14996

Matveeva, L.G., & Aguzarov, Z.A. (2013). Institutional environment for the use of cluster strategies in the modernization of the economy of the South of Russia. *Terra Economicus*, *11*(2), 67-71.

Matveeva, L.G., Chernova, OA, & Klimuk, V.V. (2015). Evaluation of the effectiveness of import substitution policies in industry: methodological tools. *News of the Far Eastern Federal University. Economics and Management*, *3*(75), 3-14.

Mayneris-Perxachs, J., & Swann, J. R. (2019). Metabolic phenotyping of malnutrition during the first 1000 days of life. *European Journal of Nutrition*, *58*(3), 909–930. doi:10.100700394-018-1679-0 PMID:29644395

Mcdonald, N. (2012). Organisational resilience and industrial risk. Academic Press.

McKinsey. (2020). *COVID-19's impact on the global aviation sector*. https://www.mckinsey.com/industries/travel-logistics-and-infrastructure/our-insights/taking-stock-of-the-pandemics-impact-on-global-aviation

Mehmood, U. (2021). Transport energy consumption and carbon emissions: The role of urbanization towards environment in SAARC region. *Integrated Environmental Assessment and Management*, *17*(6), 1286–1292. doi:10.1002/ieam.4463 PMID:34009742

Mentel, U., Wolanin, E., Eshov, M., & Salahodjaev, R. (2022). Industrialization and CO2 emissions in Sub-Saharan Africa: The mitigating role of renewable electricity. *Energies*, *15*(3), 946. doi:10.3390/en15030946

Menyah, K., & Wolde-Rufael, Y. (2010). CO2 emissions, nuclear energy, renewable energy and economic growth in the US. *Energy Policy*, *38*(6), 2911–2915. doi:10.1016/j.enpol.2010.01.024

Mergel, I., Ganapati, S., & Whitford, A. B. (2020). Agile: A New Way of Governing. *Public Administration Review*, *81*(1), 161–165. doi:10.1111/puar.13202

MERN. (2023). *Başbakanlık Mevzuatı Geliştirme ve Yayın Genel Müdürlüğü*. https://www.resmigazete.gov.tr/eskiler/2012/02/20120225-7.htm

Miettinen, J., & Holttinen, H. (2019). Impacts of wind power forecast errors on the real-time balancing need: A Nordic case study. *IET Renewable Power Generation*, *13*(2), 227–233. doi:10.1049/iet-rpg.2018.5234

Milevska, T. S. (2012). Models of innovative development of economics. *Business Info*, *2012*(7), 40–46.

Mingaleva, Zh. A. (2011a). Theoretical and methodological approaches to the analysis of the dynamics of the sectoral structure of the economy. *Journal of Economic Theory*, *2011*(4), 126–136.

Ministry of Energy of the Republic of Bulgaria. (2023, May 18). https://www.me.government.bg/

Ministry of Foreign Affair of the People's Republic of China. (2023, May 16). *Providing New Opportunities to the World Through Chinese Modernization*. Retrieved from https://www.fmprc.gov.cn/eng/wjdt_665385/zyjh_665391/202305/t20230516_11078125.html

Ministry of Foreign Affairs of the People's Republic of China. (2015, June 27). *China's Role in the Global and Regional Order: Participant, Facilitator and Contributor*. Speech at the Luncheon of the Fourth World Peace Forum By H.E. Foreign Minister Wang Yi. Retrieved from https://www.fmprc.gov.cn/eng/wjb_663304/wjbz_663308/2461_663310/201506/t20150627_468568.html

Ministry of Foreign Affairs of the People's Republic of China. (2022, September 25). *Making Every Effort for Peace and Development and Shouldering the Responsibility for Solidarity and Progress*. The United Nations General Assembly. Retrieved from https://www.fmprc.gov.cn/eng/wjdt_665385/zyjh_665391/202209/t20220925_10771160.html#:~:text=China%20is%20a%20major%20trading,2030%20Agenda%20for%20Sustainable%20Development

Ministry of Foreign Affairs of the People's Republic of China. (2023). *Xi Jinping Attends and Addressed the Opening Ceremony of the Plenary Session of the Second Eurasian Economic Forum of the Eurasian Economic Union*. https://www.fmprc.gov.cn/mfa_eng/zxxx_662805/202305/t20230528_11084920.html

Ministry of Foreign Affairs of the People's Republic of China. (2023, February 21). *The Global Security Initiative Concept Paper*. Retrieved from https://www.fmprc.gov.cn/mfa_eng/wjbxw/202302/t20230221_11028348.html

Ministry of Foreign Affairs of the Republic of Türkiye. (2023). *Türkiye's International Energy Strategy*. https://www.mfa.gov.tr/turkiye_nin-enerji-stratejisi.tr.mfa

Ministry of Health (Bulgaria). (n.d.). http://www.mh.government.bg

Mintzberg, H. (1972). Research on strategy-making. *Proceedings - Academy of Management*, *1972*(1), 90–94. doi:10.5465/ambpp.1972.4981316

Miroshnychenko, I., Kravchenko, T., & Drobyna, Y. (2021). Forecasting electricity generation from renewable sources in developing countries (on the case of Ukraine). *Neuro-Fuzzy Modeling Techniques in Economics*, *10*(10), 164–198. doi:10.33111/nfmte.2021.164

MIT. (2022). *Study on the Future of Energy Storage*. MIT.

Mitali, J., Dhinakaran, S., & Mohamad, A. A. (2022). Energy storage systems: A review. *Energy Storage and Saving*.

Mitev, M. (2021). Aspects of radiation protection in licensing of nuclear facility. *Scientific conference "Radiation safety in the modern world", NSU "V. Levski"*, 88-93.

Mitter, R. (2013). *China's War with Japan, 1937–1945: The Struggle for Survival*. Allen Lane.

Moda, H. M., Filho, W. L., & Minhas, A. (2019). Impacts of climate change on outdoor workers and their safety: Some research priorities. *International Journal of Environmental Research and Public Health*, *16*(18), 3458. doi:10.3390/ijerph16183458 PMID:31533360

Mongird, K., Viswanathan, V. V., Balducci, P. J., Alam, M. J. E., Fotedar, V., Koritarov, V. S., & Hadjerioua, B. (2019). Energy storage technology and cost characterization report (No. PNNL-28866). Pacific Northwest National Lab.

Moody's Analytics. (2022). *Global Fiscal Policy in the Pandemic*. https://www.moodysanalytics.com/-/media/article/2022/global-fiscal-policy-in-the-pandemic.pdf

Moon, M. J. (2002). The evolution of e-government among municipalities: Rhetoric or reality? *Public Administration Review*, *62*(4), 424–433. doi:10.1111/0033-3352.00196

Moore, T., Horne, R., Gleeson, B. J., & de Haan, F. (2018). *Urban sustainability transitions*. Springer Nature Singapore. doi:10.1007/978-981-10-4792-3

Moran, D., & Russell, J. (2010). *Energy Security and Global Politics - The Militarization of Resource Management*. Routledge.

Morane, D. (Ed.). (2009). *Energy security and global politics: The militarization of resource management* (Vol. 1). Routledge.

Morelli, G., & Mele, M. (2020). Energy consumption, CO2 and economic growth nexus in Vietnam. *International Journal of Energy Economics and Policy*, *10*(2), 443–449. doi:10.32479/ijeep.8248

Mouli-Castillo, J., Wilkinson, M., Mignard, D., McDermott, C., Haszeldine, R. S., & Shipton, Z. K. (2019). Inter-seasonal compressed-air energy storage using saline aquifers. *Nature Energy*, *4*(2), 131–139. doi:10.103841560-018-0311-0

Mucuk, M., & Uysal, D. (2009). Türkiye ekonomisinde enerji tüketimi ve ekonomik büyüme [Energy consumption and economic growth in Turkish economy]. *Maliye Dergisi,* (157), 105-114.

Mudalal, M. W. (2021). Examining the Moderating Effect of Geopolitical Environment on Crisis Management and Strategic Planning. *International Journal of Academic Research in Business & Social Sciences*, *11*(9), 1025–1041. doi:10.6007/IJARBSS/v11-i9/10898

Mulder, M., & Scholtens, B. (2013). The impact of renewable energy on electricity prices in the Netherlands. *Renewable Energy*, *57*, 94–100. doi:10.1016/j.renene.2013.01.025

Munoz, N., Litchford, M., Cox, J., Nelson, J. L., Nie, A. M., & Delmore, B. (2022). Malnutrition and pressure ınjury risk in vulnerable populations: Application of the 2019 international clinical practice guideline. *Advances in Skin & Wound Care*, *35*(3), 156–165. doi:10.1097/01.ASW.0000816332.60024.05 PMID:35188483

Mwangi, L. (2023). Impact of Climate Change on Agricultural Food Production. *International Journal of Agriculture*, *8*(2), 1–10. doi:10.47604/ija.1994

Nabatov, N. (2015). Electric power of Bulgaria. TANGRA TanNakRa IC.

Nain, M. Z., Ahmad, W., & Kamaiah, B. (2015). Economic growth, energy consumption and CO2 emissions in India: A disaggregated causal analysis. *International Journal of Sustainable Energy*, *36*(8), 807–824. doi:10.1080/14786451.2015.1109512

Narayan, P., & Smyth, R. (2009). Multivariate granger causality between electricity consumption, exports and GDP: Evidence from a panel of Middle Eastern countries. *Energy Policy*, *37*(1), 229–236. doi:10.1016/j.enpol.2008.08.020

Nedopil, Ch. (2022). *China Belt and Road Initiative (BRI) Investment Report 2021*. Green Finance & Development Center. FISF Fudan University. https://greenfdc.org/brief-china-belt-and-road-initiative-bri-investment-report-2021/?cookie-state-change=1689081894767

Neeliah, H., & Shankar, B. (2008). Is nutritional improvement a cross or consequence of economicgrowth? Evidence from Mauritius. *Economic Bulletin*, *17*, 1–11.

Ng, M., Ng, K., Song, S., Emara, A., Ngo, J., Patel, A., & Piuzzi, N. (2020). U.S. Healthcare Insurance Market Concentration from 2001 to 2016: Increased Growth in Direct Written Premiums and Overall Decreased Market Consolidation. *Cureus*. Advance online publication. doi:10.7759/cureus.7491 PMID:32368423

Ninov, N., & Ninova, V. (2018). The Need for Insurance during Maternity in Bulgaria. *International E-Journal of Advances in Social Sciences*, 392-405. doi:10.18769/ijasos.455664

Ninov, N., & Ninova, V. (2021). Specifics and Features of Insurance Products with Coverage for COVID-19 Offered on the Bulgarian Insurance Market. In *Annual university scientific conference "Scientific management. Social, economic and legal sciences"* (pp. 322-328). Veliko Tarnovo.

Ninova, V. (2015). Health Insurance – a Tool for Achieving the Goals of the National Health Strategy (2014-2020). In *Jubilee International scientific conference on "European practices and national planning Reflections", Collection of reports - Svishtov 24-25 April 2015* (pp. 363-368). Svishtov: Tsenov Academic Publishing House.

Ninova, V. (2016). *Socio-Economic Characteristics of Health Insurance as the Second Pillar of the Social Health Insurance Model in Bulgaria*. Academic Press.

Ninova, V. (2021). Health Insurance Market in Bulgaria – State, Development and Trends. In Dedicated to the 85th anniversary since the establishment of D. A. Tsenov Academy of Economics (pp. 281-288). Svishtov: Tsenov Academic Publishing House.

Ninova, V. (2018). Bancassurance – Application and Advantages for the Insurance Market in Bulgaria. *Journal of Innovations and Sustainability*, *4*(2), 9–21. doi:10.51599/is.2018.04.02.09

Njoh, A. J. (2021). Renewable energy as a determinant of inter-country differentials in CO2 emissions in Africa. *Renewable Energy*, *172*, 1225–1232. doi:10.1016/j.renene.2021.03.096

Nonaka, I., & Takeuchi, H. (1995). *The Knowledge-Creating Company - How Japanese Companies Create the Dynamics of Innovation*. Oxford University Press.

Norris, D. F., & Moon, M. J. (2005). Advancing e-government at the grassroots: Tortoise or hare? *Public Administration Review*, *65*(1), 64–75. doi:10.1111/j.1540-6210.2005.00431.x

Novianto, D., Koerniawan, M. D., Munawir, M., & Sekartaji, D. (2022). Impact of lifestyle changes on home energy consumption during pandemic COVID-19 in Indonesia. *Sustainable Cities and Society*, *83*, 103930. doi:10.1016/j.scs.2022.103930 PMID:35581999

NRA. (2023, may 15). Nuclear Regulatory Agency. https://bnra.bg/bg/

Ntanos, S., Skordoulis, M., Kyriakopoulos, G., Arabatzis, G., Chalikias, M., Galatsidas, S., Batzios, A., & Katsarou, A. (2018). Renewable energy and economic growth: Evidence from European countries. *Sustainability (Basel)*, *10*(8), 2626. doi:10.3390u10082626

Nukusheva, A., Ilyassova, G., Rustembekova, D., Zhamiyeva, R., & Arenova, L. (2021). Global warming problem faced by the international community: International legal aspect. *International Environmental Agreement: Politics, Law and Economics*, *21*(2), 219–233. doi:10.100710784-020-09500-9

Nuttall, P. (2021, September). The power trap: Why the energy crisis is a crisis of politics. –. *New Statesman (London, England)*, *28*. https://www.newstatesman.com/international-politics/climate-international-politics/2021/09/the-power-trap-why-the-energy-crisis-is-a-crisis-of-politics

Nyuur, R. B., Brecic, R., & Debrah, Y. A. (2018). SME international innovation and strategic adaptiveness: The role of domestic network density, centrality and informality. *International Marketing Review*, *35*(2), 280–300. doi:10.1108/IMR-11-2015-0239

Ocal, O., & Aslan, A. (2013). Renewable energy consumption–economic growth nexus in Turkey. *Renewable & Sustainable Energy Reviews*, *28*, 494–499. doi:10.1016/j.rser.2013.08.036

OECD. (2018). *China's Belt and Road Initiative in the Global Trade, Investment and Finance Landscape*. Organisation for Economic Co-Operation and Development. Retrieved from https://www.oecd.org/finance/Chinas-Belt-and-Road-Initiative-in-the-global-trade-investment-and-finance-landscape.pdf

OECD. (2020). *COVID-19 and the aviation industry: Impact and policy responses*. https://www.oecd.org/coronavirus/policy-responses/covid-19-and-the-aviation-industry-impact-and-policy-responses-26d521c1/

OECD. (2023). *Aiming Better: Government Support for Households and Firms during the Energy Crisis*. OECD Economic Policy Paper No. 32. Available at: https://www.oecd-ilibrary.org/docserver/839e3ae1-en.pdf?expires=1692914306&id=id&accname=guest&checksum=0341DA666836280BAC460A99A84531BE

OECD. (2023a). *Gross domestic product (GDP) (indicator)*. doi:10.1787/dc2f7aec-en

OECD. (2023b). *Primary energy supply (indicator)*. doi:10.1787/1b33c15a-en

Ogundari, K., & Abdulai, A. (2013). Examining the heterogeneity in calorie-income elasticities: Ameta-analysis. *Food Policy*, *40*, 119–128. doi:10.1016/j.foodpol.2013.03.001

Ogundari, K., Ito, S., & Okoruwa, V. O. (2016). Estimating nutrition-income elasticities in sub-Saharan Africa: Implications on health. *Journal of Economic Studies (Glasgow, Scotland)*, *43*(1), 59–69. doi:10.1108/JES-07-2014-0125

Oil – Global Energy Review 2020 – Analysis. (n.d.). IEA. Retrieved July 12, 2023, from https://www.iea.org/reports/global-energy-review-2020/oil

Okun. (2021). Örgütsel Dayanıklılık. In *Örgütsel Davranış Üzerine Literatürel Analiz ve Ölçekler* (p. 760). Nobel Kitapevi.

Okur Dincsoy, M. (2008). A Statistical Analysis of lCT Developments and Regional GDP per capita Convergence in Major East Asian Countries. 岡山大学大学院社会文化科学研究科紀要, *26*(1), 125-143.

Okur Dincsoy, M. (2009). Can ICT Economically Catalyze a Regional GDP Per Capita Convergence? A Case Study of Major East Asian Countries. 北東アジア経済研究, *7*(1), 45-64.

Okur Dinçsoy, M. (2020). Sustainable Development and Industry Revolutions. In New Approaches to CSR, Sustainability and Accountability, Volume I. Accounting, Finance, Sustainability, Governance & Fraud: Theory and Application (pp. 61-79). Singapore: Springer. doi:10.1007/978-981-32-9588-9

Okur Dincsoy, M. (2016). A Comparative Study on Population and Employment Risks in Vulnerable Countries to Climate Change. *International Journal of Ecological Economics and Statistics*, *37*(2), 103–120.

Oliver Stoner, O., Lewis, J., Martínez, I. L., Gumy, S., Economou, T., & Adair-Rohani, H. (2021). Household cooking fuel estimates at global and country level for 1990 to 2030. *Nature Communications*, *12*(1), 5793. doi:10.103841467-021-26036-x PMID:34608147

Organisation for Economic Co-Operation and Development (OECD). (2023). *OECD Data*. Retrieved from https://data.oecd.org/

Ortar, N. (2014). Le quotidien peut-il être durable? Routines dans la baie de San Francisco. *Norois*, *231*(231), 13–25. doi:10.4000/norois.5066

Ortar, N. (2018). Dealing with energy crises: Working and living arrangements in peri-urban France. *Transport Policy*, *65*, 72–78. doi:10.1016/j.tranpol.2016.09.008

Overland, I. (2010). *The Resource Curse and Authoritarianism in the Caspian Petro-states. - Caspian Energy Politics. Azerbaijan, Kazakhstan and Turkmenistan*. Routledge. doi:10.4324/9780203865231

Özbakır, P. (2006). *Enerji yönetimi*. Academic Press.

Özbek, S., & Naimoğlu, M. (2021b). Enerji verimliliğinin dinamikleri: VAR analizi ile Türkiye üzerine ampirik bir tahmin. *19 Mayıs. Journal of Social Sciences*, *2*(2), 314–326. https://dergipark.org.tr/en/download/article-file/1569393

Ozturk, I., & Acaravcı, A. (2010). CO2 emissions, energy consumption and economic growth in Turkey. *Renewable & Sustainable Energy Reviews*, *14*(9), 3220–3225. doi:10.1016/j.rser.2010.07.005

Pachiyappan, D., Ansari, Y., Alam, M. S., Thoudam, P., Alagirisamy, K., & Manigandan, P. (2021). Short and Long-Run Causal Effects of CO2 Emissions, Energy Use, GDP and Population Growth: Evidence from India Using the ARDL and VECM Approaches. In Energies (Vol. 14, Issue 24). doi:10.3390/en14248333

Padarev, N. I. (2018). Analysis of the Relationship Between Climate Changes and Security Area. *International Conference Knowledge-Based Organization, Vol. XXIV. Conference proceedings 3, Applied technical Sciences and Military Technologies,* 169-173. https://www.iaea.org/sites/default/files/publications/reports/2018/gc63-5_rus.pdf

Pamir, A. N. (2003). Dünyada ve Türkiye'de enerji, Türkiye'nin enerji kaynakları ve enerji politikaları. *Metalurji Dergisi*, 1-39. Retrieved from https://metalurji.org.tr/dergi/dergi134/d134_73100.pdf

Pan, S.-Y., & Lo, J. T.-Y. (2017). Re-conceptualizing China's rise as a global power: A neo-tributary perspective. *The Pacific Review*, *30*(1), 1–25. doi:10.1080/09512748.2015.1075578

Pan, Zh. (2012). *Conceptual Gaps in China-EU Relations: Global Governance, Human Rights and Strategic Partnerships*. Palgrave Macmillan. doi:10.1057/9781137027443

Papaefthymiou, G., Grave, K., & Dragoon, K. (2014). *Flexibility options in electricity systems. Project number: POWDE14426*. Ecofys.

Paramati, S. R., Mo, D., & Gupta, R. (2017). The effects of stock market growth and renewable energy use on CO2 emissions: Evidence from G20 countries. *Energy Economics*, *66*, 360–371. doi:10.1016/j.eneco.2017.06.025

Paramati, S. R., Shahzad, U., & Doğan, B. (2022). The role of environmental technology for energy demand and energy efficiency: Evidence from OECD countries. *Renewable & Sustainable Energy Reviews*, *153*, 111735. doi:10.1016/j.rser.2021.111735

Pardesi, M. (2006). Energy and Security: The Geopolitics of Energy in the Asia-Pacific. Institute of Defence and Strategic Studies - Nanyang Technological University.

Park, Y., Meng, F., & Baloch, M. A. (2018). The effect of ICT, financial development, growth, and trade openness on CO2 emissions: An empirical analysis. *Environmental Science and Pollution Research International*, *25*(30), 30708–30719. doi:10.100711356-018-3108-6 PMID:30178410

Pascual, C. (2008). *The Geopolitics of Energy: From Security to Survival*. Brookings Institution. http://www.brookings.edu

Pascual, C., & Elkind, J. (Eds.). (2010). *Energy security: Economics, politics, strategies, and implications*. Brookings Institution Press.

Pedroni, P. (2004). *Panel Co-integration: Asymptotic and Finite Sample Properties of Pooled Time Series Tests with an Application to the PPP Hypothesis* (Department of Economics Working Papers, Issues 2004–15). Department of Economics, Williams College. https://econpapers.repec.org/RePEc:wil:wileco:2004-15

Pedroni, P. (1999). Critical Values for Co-integration Tests in Heterogeneous Panels with Multiple Regressors. *Oxford Bulletin of Economics and Statistics*, *61*(s1, S1), 653–670. doi:10.1111/1468-0084.61.s1.14

Peine, A., Faulkner, A., Jæger, B., & Moors, E. (2015). Science, technology and the 'grand challenge'of ageing—Understanding the socio-material constitution of later life. *Technological Forecasting and Social Change*, *93*, 1–9. doi:10.1016/j.techfore.2014.11.010

Pemunta, N. V., & Fubah, M. A. (2015). Socio-cultural determinants of infant malnutrition in Cameroon. *Journal of Biosocial Science*, *47*(4), 423–448. doi:10.1017/S0021932014000145 PMID:24717356

Peña, J. I., & Rodríguez, R. (2019). Are EU's Climate and Energy Package 20-20-20 targets achievable and compatible? Evidence from the impact of renewables on electricity prices. *Energy*, *183*, 477–486. doi:10.1016/j.energy.2019.06.138

Penrose, E. (1958). The Theory of the Growth of the Firm. Basil Blackwell.

Perera, F. (2018). Pollution from fossil-fuel combustion is the leading environmental threat to global pediatric health and equity: Solutions exist. *International Journal of Environmental Research and Public Health*, *15*(1), 16. doi:10.3390/ijerph15010016 PMID:29295510

Pesaran, M. H. (2004). General Diagnostic tests for Cross Section dependence in Panels:Cambridge working Paper in Economics. *IZA Discussion Paper, 1240.*

Pesaran, M., Shin, Y., & Smith, R. P. (1999). Pooled Mean Group Estimation of Dynamic Heterogeneous Panels. *Journal of the American Statistical Association*, *94*(446), 621–634. doi:10.1080/01621459.1999.10474156

Phillips, P. C. B., & Perron, P. (1988). Testing for a unit root in time series regression. *Biometrika*, *75*(2), 335–346. doi:10.1093/biomet/75.2.335

Picot, J., Hartwell, D., Harris, P., Mendes, D., Clegg, A. J., & Takeda, A. (2012). The effectiveness of interventions to treat severe acute malnutrition in young children: A systematic review. *Health Technology Assessment*, *16*(19), 1–316. doi:10.3310/hta16190 PMID:22480797

Porter, M. (1998, December). Clusters and the new economics of competitiveness. *Harvard Business Review*.

Postaljuk, M. P., & Gusarova, V. U. (2014). Mechanisms for ensuring innovation in economic development structures. *Problems of modernization and transition to an innovative economy*, *2014*, 27–30.

Prangishvili, I. V. (2000). System approach and system-wide patterns / I.V. *Prangishvili. M.: SINTEG*, *2000*, 22–23.

Praslov, A. V. (2007). Classification of innovations and their essence. *News from the Russian State Pedagogical University. A.I. Herzen*, *2007*, 156–162.

Pravana, N. K., Piryani, S., Chaurasiya, S. P., Kawan, R., Thapa, R. K., & Shrestha, S. (2017). Determinants of severe acute malnutrition among children under 5 years of age in Nepal: A community-based case-control study. *BMJ Open*, *7*(8), e017084. doi:10.1136/bmjopen-2017-017084 PMID:28851796

Prodanov, S. (2021). Competition and Concentration of the Bulgarian Non-life Insurance Market (2011-2020). Structural Analysis and Empirical Observations. In Dedicated to the 85th anniversary since the establishment of D. A. Tsenov Academy of Economics (pp. 116-125). Svishtov: Tsenov Academic Publishing House.

Prüss-Ustün, A., Wolf, J., Bartram, J., Clasen, T., Cumming, O., Freeman, M. C., Gordon, B., Hunter, P. R., Medlicott, K., & Johnston, R. (2019). Burden of disease from inadequate water, sanitation and hygiene for selected adverse health outcomes: An updated analysis with a focus on lowand middle-income countries. *International Journal of Hygiene and Environmental Health*, *222*(5), 765–777. doi:10.1016/j.ijheh.2019.05.004 PMID:31088724

Rabah, K. (2018). Convergence of AI, IoT, big data and blockchain: a review. *The Lake Institute Journal, 1*(1), 1-18.

Raghutla, C., & Chittedi, K. R. (2020). Financial development, energy consumption, technology, urbanization, economic output and carbon emissions nexus in BRICS countries: An empirical analysis. *Management of Environmental Quality, 32*(2), 290–307. doi:10.1108/MEQ-02-2020-0035

Raheem, I., Tiwari, A., & Balsalobre-Lorente, D. (2020). *The role of ICT and financial development in CO2 emissions and economic growth* (No. 105605). https:// mpra. ub. uni- muenc hen. de/ 105605/1/ MPRA_ paper_ 105605. Pdf

Raheem, I. D., Tiwari, A. K., & Balsalobre-Lorente, D. (2020). The role of ICT and financial development in CO2 emissions and economic growth. *Environmental Science and Pollution Research International, 27*(2), 1912–1922. doi:10.100711356-019-06590-0 PMID:31760620

Raihan, A. (2023). The dynamic nexus between economic growth, renewable energy use, urbanization, industrialization, tourism, agricultural productivity, forest area, and carbon dioxide emissions in the Philippines. *Energy Nexus, 9*, 100180. doi:10.1016/j.nexus.2023.100180

Raihan, A., Muhtasim, D. A., Farhana, S., Pavel, M. I., Faruk, O., Rahman, M., & Mahmood, A. (2022). Nexus between carbon emissions, economic growth, renewable energy use, urbanization, industrialization, technological innovation, and forest area towards achieving environmental sustainability in Bangladesh. *Energy and Climate Change, 3*, 100080. doi:10.1016/j.egycc.2022.100080

Ramo, J. C. (2004). *The Beijing Consensus*. The Foreign Policy Center.

Ranasinghe, R. (2021). Climate Change Information for Regional Impact and for Risk Assessment. In *Climate Change 2021: The Physical Science Basis. Contribution of Working Group I to the Sixth Assessment Report of the Intergovernmental Panel on Climate Change*. Cambridge University Press.

Rapley, J. (2004). Development studies and the post-development critique. *Progress in Development Studies, 4*(4), 350–354. doi:10.1191/1464993404ps095pr

Rasmussen, M. G., Andresen, G. B., & Greiner, M. (2012). Storage and balancing synergies in a fully or highly renewable pan-European power system. *Energy Policy, 51*, 642–651. doi:10.1016/j.enpol.2012.09.009

Rathmann, M. (2007). Do support systems for RES-E reduce EU-ETS-driven electricity prices? *Energy Policy, 35*(1), 342–349. doi:10.1016/j.enpol.2005.11.029

Reddy, M. V., Mauger, A., Julien, C. M., Paolella, A., & Zaghib, K. (2020). Brief history of early lithium-battery development. *Materials (Basel), 13*(8), 1884. doi:10.3390/ma13081884 PMID:32316390

Region in the new paradigm of the spatial organization of Russia. (2007a). *Economics*.

Republic of Türkiye Ministry of Foreign Affairs. (2023). https://www.mfa.gov.tr/yenilenebilir-enerji-kaynaklari.tr.mfa#:~:text=Yenilenebilir%20enerji%20kaynaklar%C4%B1n%C4%B1n%20en%20b%C3%BCy%C3%BCk,yayg%C4%B1n%20ve%20g%C3%BC%C3%A7l%C3%BC%20destek%20almalar-%C4%B1d%C4%B1r

Research and innovation in the Republic of Belarus. (2020c). *Statistical collection*. Minsk: National Statistical Committee of the Republic of Belarus.

Resolution of the Council of Ministers of the Republic of Belarus No. 149 dated 23 February 2016 "State programme for the development of small and medium-sized entrprises in the Republic of Belarus for 2016-2020". (2021k). http://www.economy.gov.by/uploads/files/gos-progr-2016-2020/Postanovlenie-149-v-red.-920.pdf

Reuters. (2023, March 16). *China Hopes Russia and Ukraine Will Hold Peace Talks, Says Senior Chinese Diplomat.* Retrieved from https://www.reuters.com/world/europe/china-hopes-ukraine-russia-will-not-close-door-political-solution-senior-chinese-2023-03-16/

Rexhäuser, S., & Löschel, A. (2015). Invention in energy technologies: Comparing energy efficiency and renewable energy inventions at the firm level. *Energy Policy*, *83*, 206–217. doi:10.1016/j.enpol.2015.02.003

Ribeiro, D., Mackres, E., Baatz, B., Cluett, R., Jarrett, M., Kelly, M., & Vaidyanathan, S. (n.d.). Enhancing Community Resilience through. *Energy Efficiency*.

Robinson, J., & Torvik, R. (2005, February). White Elephants. *Journal of Public Economics*, *89*(2–3), 197–210. doi:10.1016/j.jpubeco.2004.05.004

Rodríguez, S. (2014). Effects of Health Insurance Concentration Market on Insurance Coverage in Colombia. *Journal of Competitiveness*, *6*(3), 13–19. doi:10.7441/joc.2014.03.01

Roege, P. E., Collier, Z. A., Mancillas, J., McDonagh, J. A., & Linkov, I. (2014). Metrics for energy resilience. *Energy Policy*, *72*, 249–256. doi:10.1016/j.enpol.2014.04.012

Roidt, M., Chini, C. M., Stillwell, A. S., & Cominola, A. (2020). Unlocking the Impacts of COVID-19 Lockdowns: Changes in Thermal Electricity Generation Water Footprint and Virtual Water Trade in Europe. *Environmental Science & Technology Letters*, *7*(9), 683–689. doi:10.1021/acs.estlett.0c00381 PMID:37566299

Romano, A. A., & Scandurra, G. (2013). *Energy consumption–gross domestic product causal relationship in the Italian regions. In Classification and Data Mining*. Springer Berlin Heidelberg.

Romer, P. M. (1990). Endogenous Technological Change. *Journal of Political Economy*, *98*(5), S71–S102. doi:10.1086/261725

Ross, M. (2015). What Have We Learned About the Resource Curse? *Annual Review of Political Science*, *18*(1), 239–259. doi:10.1146/annurev-polisci-052213-040359

Rostow, W. W. (1959). The Stages of Economic Growth. *The Economic History Review, 12*(1), 1-16. https://www.ufjf.br/oliveira_junior/files/2009/06/rostow.pdf

Rothkopf, D. (2011, October). The Geopolitics of Energy in the 21st Century. *Foreign Policy, 5*. http://www.foreign-policy.com

Rudyak, M. (2019). *The Ins and Outs of China's International Development Agency*. Carnegie Endowment for International Peace. https://carnegieendowment.org/2019/09/02/ins-and-outs-of-china-s-international-development-agency-pub-79739

Rycroft, R. (2017). *The economics of inequality, discrimination, poverty, and mobility*. Routledge. doi:10.4324/9781315638867

Sadiq, M., Kannaiah, D., Khan, G. Y., Shabbir, M. S., Bilal, K., & Zamir, A. (2023). Does sustainable environmental agenda matter? The role of globalization toward energy consumption, economic growth, and carbon dioxide emissions in South Asian countries. *Environment, Development and Sustainability*, *25*(1), 76–95. doi:10.100710668-021-02043-2

Sadorsky, P. (2009). Renewable energy consumption and income in emerging economies. *Energy Policy*, *37*(10), 4021–4028. doi:10.1016/j.enpol.2009.05.003

Sahoo, M., & Sahoo, J. (2020). Effects of renewable and non-renewable energy consumption on CO2 emissions in India: Empirical evidence from disaggregated data analysis. *Journal of Public Affairs*, *22*(1), 1–12. https://onlinelibrary.wiley.com/doi/abs/10.1002/pa.2307

Saidi, K., Rahman, M. M., & Amamri, M. (2017). The causal nexus between economic growth and energy consumption: New evidence from global panel of 53 countries. *Sustainable Cities and Society*, *33*, 45–56. doi:10.1016/j.scs.2017.05.013

Salmuth, V., Brennan, E., Kerac, M., McGrath, M., Frison, S., & Lelijveld, N. (2021). Maternal-focused interventions to improve infant growth and nutritional status in low-middle income countries, A systematic review of reviews. *PLoS One*, *16*(8), e0256188. doi:10.1371/journal.pone.0256188 PMID:34407128

Salois, M. J., Tiffin, R., & Balcombe, K. G. (2012). Impact of income on nutrient intakes: Implications for undernourishment and obesity. *The Journal of Development Studies*, *48*(12), 1716–1730. doi:10.1080/00220388.2012.658376

Sampieva, L. D., & Tamashev, I. M. (2011). Principles and features of innovative development of enterprises of the agro-industrial complex. Terra Economicus, 9(4), 145-147.

Sari, R., Ewing, B. T., & Soytas, U. (2008). The relationship between disaggregate energy consumption and industrial production in the United States: An ARDL approach. *Energy Economics*, *30*(5), 2302–2313. doi:10.1016/j.eneco.2007.10.002

Sari, R., & Soytas, U. (2007). The growth of income and energy consumption in six developing countries. *Energy Policy*, *35*(2), 889–898. doi:10.1016/j.enpol.2006.01.021

Sarkodie, S. A., & Adams, S. (2018). Renewable energy, nuclear energy, and environmental pollution: Accounting for political institutional quality in South Africa. *The Science of the Total Environment*, *643*, 1590–1601. doi:10.1016/j.scitotenv.2018.06.320 PMID:30189575

Sarkodie, S. A., & Strezov, V. (2019). Effect of foreign direct investments, economic development and energy consumption on greenhouse gas emissions in developing countries. *The Science of the Total Environment*, *646*, 862–871. doi:10.1016/j.scitotenv.2018.07.365 PMID:30064112

Sarwar, S., & Alsaggaf, M. I. (2019). Role of urbanization and urban income in carbon emissions: Regional analysis of China. *Applied Ecology and Environmental Research*, *17*(10), 303–310. doi:10.15666/aeer/1705_1030310311

Sarwar, S., Chen, W., & Waheed, R. (2017). Electricity consumption, oil price and economic growth: Global perspective. *Renewable & Sustainable Energy Reviews*, *76*, 9–18. doi:10.1016/j.rser.2017.03.063

Satyam, A. (2017). *The Smart City transformations*. Bloomsbury Publishing India Pvt. Ltd.

Savage, R. (2023). China spent $240 billion bailing out 'Belt and Road' countries – study. *Reuters*. https://www.reuters.com/markets/china-spent-240-bln-bailing-out-belt-road-countries-study-2023-03-27/

Sawik, T. (2013). Selection of resilient supply portfolio under disruption risks. *Omega*, *41*(2), 259–269. doi:10.1016/j.omega.2012.05.003

Schill, W. P. (2020). Electricity storage and the renewable energy transition. *Joule*, *4*(10), 2059–2064. doi:10.1016/j.joule.2020.07.022

Schill, W. P., & Zerrahn, A. (2018). Long-run power storage requirements for high shares of renewables: Results and sensitivities. *Renewable & Sustainable Energy Reviews*, *83*, 156–171. doi:10.1016/j.rser.2017.05.205

Schobert, H. H. (2014). Energy and society: An introduction (2nd ed.). CRC Press, Taylor & Francis Group.

Schoppa, R. K. (2019). *Revolution and its past: Identities and change in modern Chinese history*. Routledge. doi:10.4324/9781315182025

Schuman, M., Fulton, J., & Gering, T. (2023, June 21). *How Beijing's newest global initiatives seek to remake the world order*. Atlantic Council. Retrieved from https://www.atlanticcouncil.org/in-depth-research-reports/issue-brief/how-beijings-newest-global-initiatives-seek-to-remake-the-world-order/

Schumpeter, J. A. (2008). The Theory of Economic Development: As Inquiry into Profits, Capital, Credit, Interest and the Business Cycle. Transaction Publishers. (Original publication 1934)

Schumpeter, J. A. (1939). *Business Cycles. A theoretical, Historical and Statistical Analysis of the Capitalist Process*. McGraw-Hill Book Company.

Schwab, K. (2017). *The Fourth Industrial Revolution*. Currency.

Sebri, M., & Ben-Salha, O. (2014). On the causal dynamics between economic growth, renewable energy consumption, CO2 emissions and trade openness: Fresh evidence from BRICS countries. *Renewable & Sustainable Energy Reviews*, *39*, 14–23. doi:10.1016/j.rser.2014.07.033

Senalp, U. E. (2021). Covid-19 Küresel Salgının Sanayi ve Hizmet Sektörlerinde Enerji Yoğunluğuna Etkisi. In H. Ö. Sarıdoğan & F. Çelebi (Eds.), İktisadi ve İdari Bilimlerde Özgün Çalışmalar (pp. 143–161). Academic Press.

Şenalp, U. E. (2021). In Ö. Sarıdoğan & D. Çelebi (Eds.), *Covid-19 Küresel Salgının Sanayi ve Hizmet Sektörlerinde Enerji Yoğunluğuna Etkisi* (pp. 143–161). İktisadi ve İdari Bilimlerde Özgün Çalışmalar.

Sensfuß, F. (2008). *Assessment of the impact of renewable electricity generation on the German electricity sector: An agent-based simulation approach* [Doctoral dissertation]. Karlsruhe, Univ.

Sensfuß, F., Ragwitz, M., & Genoese, M. (2008). The merit-order effect: A detailed analysis of the price effect of renewable electricity generation on spot market prices in Germany. *Energy Policy*, *36*(8), 3086–3094. doi:10.1016/j.enpol.2008.03.035

Sergeev, A. M. (2008b). Comparative advantages of clusters. *Panorama of competition*, *2008*(3), 83–88.

Seville, E., Brunsdon, D., Dantas, A., Le Masurier, J., Wilkinson, S., & Vargo, J. (2008). Organisational resilience: Researching the reality of New Zealand organisations. *Journal of Business Continuity & Emergency Planning*, *2*, 258–266. PMID:21339112

Sevüktekin, M., & Nargeleçekenler, M. (2010). *Ekonometrik Zaman Serileri Analizi*. Nobel Akademik Yayıncılık.

Shabani, D. Z., & Shahnazi, R. (2019). Energy consumption, carbon dioxide emissions, information and communications technology, and gross domestic product in Iranian economic sectors: A panel causality analysis. *Energy*, *169*, 1064–1078. doi:10.1016/j.energy.2018.11.062

Shahbaz, M. (2015). Electricity Consumption, Financial Development and Economic Growth Nexus in Pakistan: A Visit. *Bulletin of Energy Economics*, *3*(2), 48–65. https://EconPapers.repec.org/RePEc:ijr:beejor:v:3:y:2015:i:2:p:48-65

Shahbaz, M., Raghutla, C., Song, M., Zameer, H., & Jiao, Z. (2020). Public-private partnerships investment in energy as new determinant of CO2 emissions: The role of technological innovations in China. *Energy Economics*, *86*, 104664. doi:10.1016/j.eneco.2020.104664

Shahbaz, M., Sarwar, S., Chen, W., & Malik, M. N. (2017). Dynamics of electricity consumption, oil price and economic growth: Global perspective. *Energy Policy*, *108*, 256–270. doi:10.1016/j.enpol.2017.06.006

Share of energy consumption from renewable sources in Europe (8th EAP). (n.d.). Retrieved July 13, 2023, from https://www.eea.europa.eu/ims/share-of-energy-consumption-from

Sheraz, M., Deyi, X., Mumtaz, M. Z., & Ullah, A. (2022). Exploring the dynamic relationship between financial development, renewable energy, and carbon emissions: A new evidence from belt and road countries. *Environmental Science and Pollution Research International*, *29*(10), 14930–14947. doi:10.100711356-021-16641-0 PMID:34623587

Sheraz, M., Deyi, X., Sinha, A., Mumtaz, M. Z., & Fatima, N. (2022). The dynamic nexus among financial development, renewable energy and carbon emissions: Moderating roles of globalization and institutional quality across BRI countries. *Journal of Cleaner Production, 343*, 130995. doi:10.1016/j.jclepro.2022.130995

Shinkawa, N. (1998). An Outlook for Energy in Energy Conservation Point of View. Kyushu International Center, JICA & KITA,Kitakyushu, Japonya.

Shopov, D., & Atanasova, M. (2003a). Human resources management. *Trakia.*

Shtunder, I., Kushnir, S., Perevozova, I., Kalinina, S., Savchenko, E., & Nitsenko, V. (2022). Sustainable development of the economy in the conditions of the energy crisis. *Naukovyi Visnyk Natsionalnoho Hirnychoho Universytetu, 4*(4), 156–161. doi:10.33271/nvngu/2022-4/156

Shuman, M., Fulton, J., & Gering, T. (2023). *How Beijing's newest global initiatives seek to remake the world order.* Atlantic Council. https://www.atlanticcouncil.org/in-depth-research-reports/issue-brief/how-beijings-newest-global-initiatives-seek-to-remake-the-world-order/

Shuyan, L., & Fabuš, M. (2019). Study on the spatial distribution of China's Outward Foreign Direct Investment in EU and its influencing factors. *Entrepreneurship and Sustainability Issues, 6*(3), 1080–1096. doi:10.9770/jesi.2019.6.3(16)

Shuyan, L., & Fabus, M. (2019). The impact of OFDI reverse technology spillover on China's technological progress: Analysis of provincial panel data. *Journal of International Students, 12*(4), 325–336. doi:10.14254/2071-8330.2019/12-4/21

Silvius, R. (2021). China's Belt and Road Initiative as Nascent World Order Structure and Concept? Between Sino-Centering and Sino-Deflecting. *Journal of Contemporary China, 30*(128), 314–329. doi:10.1080/10670564.2020.1790905

Simon, H. A. (1947). *Administrative Behavior. A study of decision-making process in administrative organizations.* Macmillan.

Simon, H. A. (1957). *Models of Man.* John Wiley & Sons.

Simonova, N. E. (2012a). Evaluation of the effectiveness of integration projects. *Electronic Scientific Journal "Engineering Journal of Don".* https://cyberleninka.ru/article/n/otsenka-effektivnosti-integratsionnyh-proektov/viewer

Şimşek, T., & Yiğit, E. (2017). BRICT ülkelerinde yenilenebilir enerji tüketimi, petrol fiyatları, co2 emisyonu, kentleşme ve ekonomik büyüme üzerine nedensellik analizi. *Eskişehir Osmangazi Üniversitesi İktisadi ve İdari Bilimler Dergisi, 12*(3), 117-136. Retrieved from https://dergipark.org.tr/tr/pub/oguiibf/issue/30939/335630

Sinn, H. W. (2017). Buffering volatility: A study on the limits of Germany's energy revolution. *European Economic Review, 99*, 130–150. doi:10.1016/j.euroecorev.2017.05.007

Smil, V. (2010). *Energy transitions: History, requirements, prospects.* Praeger.

Smil, V. (2017). *Energy and civilization: A history.* The MIT Press. doi:10.7551/mitpress/9780262035774.001.0001

Smith, C. B., & Parmenter, K. E. (2016). *Energy management principles: Applications, benefits, savings* (2nd ed.). Elsevier. doi:10.1016/B978-0-12-802506-2.00003-3

Soe, R. M., & Drechsler, W. (2018). Agile local governments: Experimentation before implementation. *Government Information Quarterly, 35*(2), 323–335. doi:10.1016/j.giq.2017.11.010

Software programme IBM SPSS Statistics. (2021t). https://www.ibm.com/products/spss-statistics?lnk=hpmps_bupr

Sovacool, B. K. (2011). Evaluating energy security in the Asia pacific: Towards a more comprehensive approach. *Energy Policy, 39*(11), 7472–7479. doi:10.1016/j.enpol.2010.10.008

Spensberger, F. (2019). The digitalization of a social work theory: Experiences of a German child welfare social worker. *International Social Work*, *62*(6), 1575–1579. doi:10.1177/0020872819865018

Spuretling, D. (1970). *Zur Messung der wirtschafi chen Konzentration*. Academic Press.

Stange, G., Pagogna, R., Sterly, H., Sakdapolrak, P., Borderon, M., Schraven, B., & Serraglio, D. A. (2023). Impeded migration as adaptation: COVID-19 and its implications for translocal strategies of environmental risk management. *Advances in Southeast Asian Studies*, *16*(1), 157–169.

Stanway, D. (2021). *China starts Baihetan hydro project, biggest since Three Gorges*. Reuters. Available at: https://www.reuters.com/business/energy/chinas-giant-baihetan-hydro-plant-begins-generating-power-cctv-2021-06-28/

Statista. (2023). *Global gross domestic product (GDP) at current prices from 1985 to 2028*. https://www.statista.com/statistics/268750/global-gross-domestic-product-gdp

Stearns, P. (2021). *The Industrial Revolution in World History*. Routledge.

Stefanov, N., & Koleva, A. (2015). *Китай. Социално-икономическо развитие от древността до наши дни* [China. Social and Economic Development from Ancient Times to the Present Day]. East-West Publishing House.

Stern, D. I. (1993). Energy use and economic growth in the USA: A multivariate approach. *Energy Economics*, *15*(2), 137–150. doi:10.1016/0140-9883(93)90033-N

Stewart, J., & O'Donnell, M. (2007). Implementing change in a public agency: Leadership, learning and organisational resilience. *International Journal of Public Sector Management*, *20*(3), 239–251. doi:10.1108/09513550710740634

Stirling, A. (2010). Multicriteria diversity analysis: A novel heuristic framework for appraising energy portfolios. *Energy Policy*, *38*(4), 1622–1634. doi:10.1016/j.enpol.2009.02.023

Stratton, R. J., Green, C. J., & Elia, M. (2003). *Disease-related malnutrition: an evidence-based approach to treatment*. Cabi. doi:10.1079/9780851996486.0000

Sullivan de Estrada, K. (2023). India and order transition in the Indo-Pacific: Resisting the Quad as a 'security community.'. *The Pacific Review*, *36*(2), 378–405. doi:10.1080/09512748.2022.2160792

Su, M., Wang, Q., Li, R., & Wang, L. (2022). Per capita renewable energy consumption in 116 countries: The effects of urbanization, industrialization, GDP, aging, and trade openness. *Energy*, *254*, 1–18. doi:10.1016/j.energy.2022.124289

Sun, Y., Li, H., Andlib, Z., & Genie, M. G. (2022). How do renewable energy and urbanization cause carbon emissions? Evidence from advanced panel estimation techniques. *Renewable Energy*, *185*, 996–1005. doi:10.1016/j.renene.2021.12.112

Suszynski, C. (2013). *Business Enterprise. The Integration of Approaches*. Oficyna Wudawnicza Szkola Glowna Handlowa w Warszawie.

Sweet, W. (2012). *Energy Geopolitics: Quandaries Intensify*. Great Decisions, Foreign Policy Association. Available at: http://www.fpa.org

Swinand, G. P., & Godel, M. (2012, May). Estimating the impact of wind generation on balancing costs in the GB electricity markets. In *2012 9th International Conference on the European Energy Market* (pp. 1-8). IEEE. 10.1109/EEM.2012.6254790

Szymańska, E. J., Kubacka, M., & Polaszczyk, J. (2023). Households' Energy Transformation in the Face of the Energy Crisis. *Energies*, *16*(1), 466. doi:10.3390/en16010466

Tagliapietra, S., Zachmann, G., Edenhofer, O., Glachant, J. M., Linares, P., & Loeschel, A. (2019). The European union energy transition: Key priorities for the next five years. *Energy Policy*, *132*, 950–954. doi:10.1016/j.enpol.2019.06.060

Tan, F., Yang, S., & Niu, Z. (2022). The impact of urbanization on carbon emissions: Both from heterogeneity and mechanism test. *Environment, Development and Sustainability*, 1–17.

Tang, Y., Zhu, H., & Yang, J. (2022). The asymmetric effects of economic growth, urbanization and deindustrialization on carbon emissions: Evidence from China. *Energy Reports*, *8*, 513–521. doi:10.1016/j.egyr.2022.05.076

Tan, X., Choi, Y., Wang, B., & Huang, X. (2020). Does China's carbon regulatory policy improve total factor carbon efficiency? A fixed-effect panel stochastic frontier analysis. *Technological Forecasting and Social Change*, *160*, 120222. doi:10.1016/j.techfore.2020.120222

Taşdemir, F. D. (2021). Relationship Between Economic Growth and Construction Sector in Turkey. In Academic Research and Reviews in Social Sciences. Platanus Publishing House.

Temby, O., Kapsis, K., Berton, H., Rosenbloom, D., Gibson, G., Athienitis, A., & Meadowcroft, J. (2014). Building-Integrated Photovoltaics: Distributed Energy Development for Urban Sustainability. *Environment*, *56*(6), 4–17. doi:10.1080/00139157.2014.964092

Terziev, V. & Klimuk, V. (2021g). Designing a digital education ecosystem. *68 th International Scientific Conference on Economic and Social Development – Aveiro, 24-25 May, 2021*, 218-228.

Terziev, V. (2003). Noviyat sotsialen model, kato efektivna vazmozhnost za realizirane na aktivnata politika na pazara na truda v Balgariya. *Natsionalna nauchno-prakticheska konferentsiya „Gavkavata zaetost i problemi na neynata regulatsiya"*.

Terziev, V. (2005). A common analysis of the impact of the National program "From social support to employment" on the national labor market. *UNITECH'05*, 75-80.

Terziev, V. (2013). The active model of a social programme and its strategic advantage. *The 1st AARESOC International Conference On Business and Management*.

Terziev, V. (2013c). The active model of a social programme and its strategic advantage. // Spisanie za nauka "Novo znanie".

Terziev, V. (2013d). Social technology as a method for management of the social processes, VI *Mezhdunarodnaya nauchnaya konferentsiya "Innovatsii v tekhnologiyakh i obrazovanii" (KuzGTU)*.

Terziev, V. (2013f). *Programni metodi za regulirane na pazara na truda*. Natsionalen voenen universitet "Vasil Levski".

Terziev, V. (2013g). *Chuzhd opit za regulirane na sotsialnoto razvitie*. Natsionalen voenen universitet "Vasil Levski".

Terziev, V. (2013h). Politika v oblastta na zaetostta i bezrabotitsata v Balgariya v perioda na prehod kam pazarno stopanstvo. *Mezhdunarodna nauchna konferentsiya UNITEH, Gabrovo*.

Terziev, V. (2013i). *Politika v oblastta na zaetostta i bezrabotitsata v Balgariya- tseli i zadachi*. Mezhdunarodna nauchna konferentsiya UNITEH.

Terziev, V. (2013j). Osobenosti na trudovite otnosheniya v Balgariya v perioda na prehod ot planovo stopanstvo kam pazarna ikonomika. Mezhdunarodna nauchna konferentsiya "Iztochnoevropeyskiyat prehod i sotsialno-ikonomicheskoto razsloyavane".

Terziev, V. (2013k). Faktori, vliyaeshti varhu ravnovesieto i efektivnostta na fuktsioniraneto na pazara na truda v usloviyata na prehod. Mezhdunarodna nauchna konferentsiya, Kolezh po ikonomika i administratsiya.

Terziev, V. (2014a). Impact of labor market policies on employment. New Knowledge Journal of science, 3(3).

Terziev, V. (2014b). Sotsialnoto programirane v sistemata na sotsialnite kategorii. *VII Mezhdunarodnaya nauchnaya konferentsiya "Innovatsii v tehnologiyah i obrazovanii" (KuzGTU).*

Terziev, V. (2014c). Teoretichni osnovi za regulirane na pazara na truda. *VII Mezhdunarodnaya nauchnaya konferentsiya "Innovatsii v tehnologiyah i obrazovanii" (KuzGTU).*

Terziev, V. (2015a). Social programming in the system of sociological categories concerning market economy and labor market development in transition economy. Proceedings of "Culture, spirituality, society", 100-123.

Terziev, V. (2015d). An active model of a social program and its strategic advantage. Proceedings of "Value system of contemporary society", 113-131.

Terziev, V. (2015e). Social policy and labor market development in Bulgarian transition period. Proceedings of "Priority scirntific directions: from theory to practice", 139-154.

Terziev, V. (2015f). Social policy development in the Republic of Bulgaria during the transition period to a market economy. Scientific works "A new look" – International scientific papers 8, 230-265.

Terziev, V. (2015j). Criteria and indicators for social efficiency. Proceedings of "State and municipal governance in XXI century: theory, methodology and practice", 46-70.

Terziev, V. (2015k). Theoretical basis of development of labor market and social policy in the Republic of Bulgaria. Proceedings of "Science and modernity 2015", 233-251.

Terziev, V. (2015m). Methodological approach to research and evaluate main states and transitions on labor market. Konferentsiya „Problemay sovremennoy ekonomiki", TSRNS.

Terziev, V. (2015n). Flows of labor force and types of labor markets in transition economy. *Konferentsiya „Sotsialyno-ekonomicheskie nauki i gumanitarnaye issledovaniya", TSRNS.*

Terziev, V. (2020). Science as a tool for social development. *Review of Socio-Economic Perspectives, 5*(3), 117-134.

Terziev, V. (2020a). Science as a tool for social development. 18th RSEP International Economics, Finance & Business Conference – Virtual/Online 26-27 August 2020.

Terziev, V. (2020a). Social programming in the context of social economy development in Bulgaria. *51st International Scientific Conference on Economic and Social Development (Rabat, 26-27 March 2020)*, 387-396.

Terziev, V. (2020b). Programming as mechanism of managing, oriented towards results. *Economic and Social Development (Book of Proceedings), 50th International Scientific Conference on Economic and Social Development Development*, 92-98.

Terziev, V., & Arabska, E. (2014). Assessment of active social policies' impacts on labor market in the Republic of Bulgaria. *Collective monograph "Socio-economic and law bases of economic development"*. UFA.

Terziev, V., & Arabska, E. (2015h). Theoretical and methodological basis of social programming and social activity. Collective monograph "Socio-economic and law bases of economic development", 3-183.

Terziev, V., & Arabska, E. (2015o). Application of new instruments to increase effectiveness of implementation of social policies on labor market in Bulgaria. *Journal of Economic Development, Environment and People, 4*(3), 26-44.

Terziev, V., & Arabska, E. (2016). Social Policy Development and Implementation: Municipal level perspectives. *HAS-SACC 2016 - Human and Social Sciences at the Common Conference*, 19-24.

Terziev, V., & Georgiev, M. (2017). Active social programs development in Bulgaria: Contemporary challenges and social management instruments. *International Journal of Humanities and Social Science Invention*. www.ijhssi.org

Terziev, V., & Georgiev, M. (2017). Importance of human resources to social development. *International Journal of Management and Applied Science*, *3*(4), 37-39.

Terziev, V., & Georgiev, M. (2017a). The active model of a social programme and ITS strategic advantage. *Medical Teacher, 12*(2), 1418-1437.

Terziev, V., & Georgiev, M. (2017b). Impact of the labor market policies for ensuring employment. *International Journal of Management and Applied Science*, *3*(4), 29-36.

Terziev, V., & Georgiev, M. (2017c) Importance of human resources to social development. *International Journal of Management and Applied Science*, *3*(4), 37-39.

Terziev, V., & Klimuk, V. (2021). Factors and mechanisms affecting innovation development of industrial business organizations: cooperative resource model. *71st International Scientific Conference on Economic and Social Development – Online Conference*, 31-40.

Terziev, V., & Klimuk, V. (2021a). Methodological concepts for modernization of industrial enterprises in the concept of postindustrial development. *65th International Scientific Conference on Economic and Social Development – Online Conference*, 1-5.

Terziev, V., & Klimuk, V. (2021b). Mechanisms affecting innovation development of industrial business organizations. 21st RSEP International Economics, Finance & Business Conference – Virtual/Online 19-20 May 2021, HCC. St. Moritz Hotel, Barcelona, Spain, 132-141.

Terziev, V., & Klimuk, V. (2021c). Approaches to the application of the concepts of cooperative integration between organizations. *75th International Scientific Conference on Economic and Social Development – Belgrade, 02-03 December, 2021*, 383-387.

Terziev, V., & Klimuk, V. (2021d). Management of the innovation ecosystem development. *77th International Scientific Conference on Economic and Social Development – Online Conference, 27 January, 2022*, 24-28.

Terziev, V., & Klimuk, V. (2021e). Analysis of the procedures and sources of financing research and innovation. *70th International Scientific Conference on Economic and Social Development – Baku, 25-26 June, 2021*, 332-338.

Terziev, V., & Klimuk, V. (2021f). Modelling the forms of international scientific and educational cooperation. 20th RSEP International Economics, Finance & Business Conference – Virtual/Online 17-18 February 2021, Holiday Inn Vienna City, Vienna, Austria, 151-156.

Terziev, V., & Klimuk, V. (2021q). Directions for modernization of innovative youth startup design in Belarus. 20th RSEP International Economics, Finance & Business Conference – Virtual/Online 17-18 February 2021, Holiday Inn Vienna City, Vienna, Austria, 157-162.

Terziev, V., & Mladenov, Yu. (2012b). Aktivna sotsialna programa i neynoto strategichesko preimushtestvo. *Nauchni trudove. R: Rusenski universitet „Angel Kanchev"*.

Terziev, V. (2002). National program „From social support to employment. *The Labor Lawyer*, *2002*(11), 38–41.

Terziev, V. (2012). Social technology as a method for management of the social processes. *International Conference "Trends in economics and management for the 21st century"*, 79-80.

Terziev, V. (2012a). The active model of a social programme and its strategic advantage. *International Conference "Trends in economics and management for the 21st century"*, 77-78.

Terziev, V. (2012c). Kriterii i pokazateli za sotsialna efektivnost. *Mezhdunarodna nauchna konferentsiya.*

Terziev, V. (2013a). Social technology as a method for management of the social processes. *International Conference on Business and Economy (ICBE) Interdisciplinary studies on a new economy*, 258-265. 10.2139srn.3177801

Terziev, V. (2013b). The active model of a social programme and its strategic advantage. *International Scientific Conference: Management Horizons in Changing Economic Environment & Visions and Challenges*, 917-932.

Terziev, V. (2013l). *Impact of labor market policies on employment.* Dema press.

Terziev, V. (2015). *Impact of active social policies and programs in the period of active economic transformations in Bulgaria. In East West.* Association for Advances Studies and Higher Education GmbH.

Terziev, V. (2019b). The role and place of social programming in public governance. *Proceedings of SOCIOINT 2019- 6th International Conference on Education, Social Sciences and Humanities 24-26 June 2019- Istanbul, Turkey*, 354-362. 10.2139srn.3411580

Terziev, V., & Arabska, E. (2014e). *Assessment of active social policies' impacts on labor market in the Republic of Bulgaria. Collective monograph "Socio-economic and law basis of economy development"*. UFA-Aeterna.

Terziev, V., & Arabska, E. (2015b). Social policy and social programming: key implications concerning development of active labor market policies and employment. *Proceedings of 17th International Academic Conference*, 499-513.

Terziev, V., & Arabska, E. (2015i). *Assessment of the effectiveness of social programming* (Vol. 9). Knowledge International Journal, Scientific& Applicative Papers.

Terziev, V., & Arabska, E. (2015l). Development of social policies increasing employment opportunities on labor market in periods of transition. *2nd IBESRA Conference.* 10.2139srn.3166802

Terziev, V., & Arabska, E. (2015p). Bulgarian experience in labor market development. *18th International Academic Conference*, 710-733.

Terziev, V., & Arabska, E. (2016a). Monitoring active policies on labor market. *18th EBES Conference.*

Terziev, V., & Georgiev, M. (2020). The place of programming in the state's social policy. *Review of Behavioral Aspect in Organizations and Society*, *2*(1), 25–30. doi:10.32770/rbaos.vol225-30

Terziev, V., & Klimuk, V. (2022). *New incentives for development of the modern research and innovation ecosystem: a case study of Belarus.* doi:10.25313/978-611-01-2659-5

Terziev, V., & Stanchev, S. (2015c). Development of active social policies in Bulgaria. *First International Scientific Conference "Sustainability Challenges in Modern Organizations - Knowledge & Innovation in Management & Operation"*, 63-79.

Terziev, V., & Stanchev, S. (2015g). Challenges to labor market development in Bulgaria. *First International Scientific Conference "Sustainability Challenges in Modern Organizations - Knowledge & Innovation in Management & Operation"*, 41-62.

Teshome, F., & Tadele, A. (2022). Trends and determinants of minimum acceptable diet intake among infant and young children aged 6–23 months in Ethiopia: A multilevel analysis of Ethiopian demographic and health survey. *BMC Nutrition*, *8*(1), 44. doi:10.118640795-022-00533-8 PMID:35513888

The Geopolitics of Natural Gas. (2012). *Report of Scenarios Workshop of Harvard University's Belfer Center and Rice University's Baker Institute Energy Forum*. Available at: http://belfercenter.ksg.harvard.edu

The impact of coronavirus (COVID-19) and the global oil price shock on the fiscal position of oil-exporting developing countries. (n.d.). OECD. Retrieved July 12, 2023, from https://www.oecd.org/coronavirus/policy-responses/the-impact-of-coronavirus-covid-19-and-the-global-oil-price-shock-on-the-fiscal-position-of-oil-exporting-developing-countries-8bafbd95/

The State Council Information Office. (2017). *Jointly Shoulder Responsibility of Our Times, Promote Global Growth*. Keynote Speech by H.E. Xi Jinping, President of the People's Republic of China at the Opening Session of the World Economic Forum Annual Meeting. Davos. http://www.china.org.cn/node_7247529/content_40569136.htm

The State Council Information Office. (2021). *Xi declares China a moderately prosperous society in all respects*. http://english.scio.gov.cn/topnews/2021-07/01/content_77599525.htm

The State Council. (2021). *China's International Development Cooperation in the New Era*. The State Council Information Office of the People's Republic of China. https://english.www.gov.cn/archive/whitepaper/202101/10/content_WS5ffa6bbbc6d0f72576943922.html

The World Bank Data. (2023). *Worldbank Indicator*. Retrieved from https://data.worldbank.org/

Thomas, D. (2021). What did FOCAC 2021 deliver for Africa? *African Business*. https://african.business/2021/11/trade-investment/what-can-africa-expect-from-focac-2021

Thombs, R. P. (2017). The Paradoxical Relationship between Renewable Energy and Economic Growth: A Cross-National Panel Study, 1990-2013. *Journal of World-systems Research*, *23*(2), 540–564. doi:10.5195/jwsr.2017.711

Toda, H. Y., & Yamamoto, T. (1995). Statistical inference in vector autoregressions with possibly integrated processes. *Journal of Econometrics*, *66*(1-2), 225–250. doi:10.1016/0304-4076(94)01616-8

Todorov, A. (2015). Empirical Analysis of the Economic Concentration within the Largest Bulgarian Companies for the Period 2006-2013. *Dialogue*, 44–57.

Tomashevska, Yu. N., & Korchagina, N. A. (2010). International experience in identifying clusters: Prospects for use in the Russian Federation. *Scientific works of the Institute of National Economic Forecasting of the Russian Academy of Sciences*, *2010*, 727–742.

Tong, T., Ortiz, J., Xu, C., & Li, F. (2020). Economic growth, energy consumption, and carbon dioxide emissions in the E7 countries: A bootstrap ARDL bound test. *Energy, Sustainability and Society*, *10*(1), 20. doi:10.118613705-020-00253-6

Topallı, N., & Alagöz, M. (2014). Energy consumption and economic growth In Turkey: An empirical analysis. Selçuk Üniversitesi Sosyal Bilimler Enstitüsü Dergisi, (32), 151-159.

Tran, B.-L., Chen, C.-C., & Tseng, W.-C. (2022). Causality between energy consumption and economic growth in the presence of GDP threshold effect: Evidence from OECD countries. *Energy*, *251*, 1–12. doi:10.1016/j.energy.2022.123902

Trish, E., & Herring, B. (2015). How Do Health Insurer Market Concentration and Bargaining Power with Hospitals Affect Health Insurance Premiums? *Journal of Health Economics*, *42*, 104–114. doi:10.1016/j.jhealeco.2015.03.009 PMID:25910690

Tsani, S. Z. (2010). Energy consumption and economic growth: A causality analysis for Greece. *Energy Economics*, *32*(3), 582–590. doi:10.1016/j.eneco.2009.09.007

Tsaurai, K., & Ngcobo, L. (2020). Renewable Energy Consumption, Education and Economic Growth in Brazil, Russia, India, China, South Africa. *International Journal of Energy Economics and Policy*, *10*(2), 26–34. doi:10.32479/ijeep.8497

Tselishchev, I. S. (2012). *Восточная Азия: новая волна роста и структурная трансформация* [East Asia: A New Wave of Growth and Structural Transformation]. IMEMO RAS.

Tveten, Å. G., Bolkesjø, T. F., Martinsen, T., & Hvarnes, H. (2013). Solar feed-in tariffs and the merit order effect: A study of the German electricity market. *Energy Policy*, *61*, 761–770. doi:10.1016/j.enpol.2013.05.060

U.S. Department of State. (2009). *Closing Remarks for U.S.-China Strategic and Economic Dialogue*. https://2009-2017.state.gov/secretary/20092013clinton/rm/2009a/july/126599.htm

Udemba, E. N., Güngör, H., Bekun, F. V., & Kirikkaleli, D. (2021). Economic performance of India amidst high CO2 emissions. *Sustainable Production and Consumption*, *27*, 52–60. doi:10.1016/j.spc.2020.10.024

Ulucak, R., Danish, K., & Khan, S. (2020). Does information and communication technology affect CO2 mitigation under the pathway of sustainable development during the mode of globalization? *Sustainable Development (Bradford)*, *28*(4), 857–867. doi:10.1002d.2041

UNCTAD. (2023). *Investment Trends Monitor*. https://unctad.org/system/files/official-document/diaeiainf2023d1_en.pdf

UNCTAD. (n.d.). https://unctadstat.unctad.org/EN/Classifications.html

UNDP. (2015). *World Energy Assessment Overview: 2004 Update | United Nations Development Programme*. UNDP. https://www.undp.org/publications/world-energy-assessment-overview-2004-update

UNEP. (2021). *UN: %17 of all food available at consumer levels is wasted*. UN Enviroment Programme. Retrieved: https://www.unep.org/news-and-stories/press-release/un-17-all-food-available-consumer-levels-wasted

United Nations. (1992). *United Nations Framework Convention on Climate Change, 4 June 1992.*

United Nations. (1997). *Kyoto Protocol to the United Nations Framework Convention on Climate Change.*

United Nations. (2012). *Secretary-General to Global Development Center: 'Energy is the Golden Thread' Connecting Economic Growth, Social Equity, Environmental Sustainability*. Retrieved from https://www.un.org/press/en/2012/sgsm14242.doc.htm

United Nations. (2015). *Paris Agreement.*

Uribe-Quintero, R., Álvarez-Castaño-Castaño, L. S., Caicedo-Velásquez, B., & Ruiz-Buitrago, I. C. (2022). Trends in undernutrition mortality among children under five years of age and adults over 60. *Biomédica*, *42*(1), 41–53. doi:10.7705/biomedica.5937 PMID:35471169

Usman, A., Ozturk, I., Hassan, A., Zafar, S. M., & Ullah, S. (2021). The effect of ICT on energy consumption and economic growth in South Asian economies: An empirical analysis. *Telematics and Informatics*, *58*, 101537. doi:10.1016/j.tele.2020.101537

Usman, M., & Radulescu, M. (2022). Examining the role of nuclear and renewable energy in reducing carbon footprint: Does the role of technological innovation really create some difference? *The Science of the Total Environment*, *841*, 156662. doi:10.1016/j.scitotenv.2022.156662 PMID:35718170

Usman, M., Rahman, S. U., Shafique, M. R., Sadiq, A., & Idrees, S. (2023). Renewable Energy, Trade and Economic Growth on Nitrous Oxide Emission in G-7 Countries Using Panel ARDL Approach. *Journal of Social Sciences Review*, *3*(2), 131–143. doi:10.54183/jssr.v3i2.219

Usta, C. (2016). Türkiye'de enerji tüketimi ekonomik büyüme ilişkisinin bölgesel analizi [Regional analysis of relationship between energy consumption and economic growth in Turkey]. *Uluslararası Ekonomi ve Yenilik Dergisi, 2*(2), 181-201.

Vanderbruck, T. (2010). *Can the World Survive the Impending Oil Crisis?* Available at: http://www.oil-price.net

Vanderbruck, T. (2011). *Egypt Riots and Oil.* http://www.oil-price.net

Venn, F. (2002). *The Oil Crisis.* Routledge.

Verrastro, F. (2010). *The Geopolitics of Energy: Emerging Trends, Changing Landscapes, Uncertain Times.* Center for Strategic and International Studies. Available at: https://csis.org/

Vieira, V. C. (2019). From Third World Theory to Belt and Road Initiative. *Contexto Internacional, 41*(3), 529–551. doi:10.15900102-8529.2019410300003

Virtanen, I. (2011). Externalization of tacit knowledge implies a simplified theory of cognition. *Journal of Knowledge Management Practice, 12*(3), 139–145.

Walker, P. (2019). *The Theory of the Firm. An overview of the economic mainstream.* Routledge.

Wang, Y. (2022). *Global Security Initiative and Global Development Initiative: Two Wings for Building a Community with a Shared Future for Mankind.* Boym Institute. https://instytutboyma.org/en/global-security-initiative-and-global-development-initiative-two-wings-for-building-a-community-with-a-shared-future-for-mankind/

Wang, S., Li, Q., Fang, C., & Zhou, C. (2016). The relationship between economic growth, energy consumption, and CO2 emissions: Empirical evidence from China. *The Science of the Total Environment, 542*, 360–371. doi:10.1016/j.scitotenv.2015.10.027 PMID:26520261

Wang, W., Zhang, M., & Li, P. (2014). Exploring Temporal And Spatial Evolution Of Global Energy Production And Consumption. *Renewable & Sustainable Energy Reviews, 30*, 943–949. doi:10.1016/j.rser.2013.11.027

Wang, Y. Z., Zhou, S., & Ou, X. M. (2021). Development and application of a life cycle energy consumption and CO2 emissions analysis model for high-speed railway transport in China. *Advances in Climate Change Research, 12*(2), 270–280. doi:10.1016/j.accre.2021.02.001

Wang, Y., Zhang, D., Ji, Q., & Shi, X. (2020). Regional renewable energy development in China: A multidimensional assessment. *Renewable & Sustainable Energy Reviews, 124*, 109797. doi:10.1016/j.rser.2020.109797

Wanji, X., & Taniguch, K. (2002). *Does better nutrition cause economic growth? The efficiency cost ofHunger revisited.* FAO Working paper-ESA Working Paper No. 02-11.

Waterson, M. (2017). The characteristics of electricity storage, renewables and markets. *Energy Policy, 104*, 466–473. doi:10.1016/j.enpol.2017.01.025

Waterson, M., Trujillo-Baute, E., & Giulietti, M. (2022). Intermittency and the social role of storage. *Energy Policy, 165*, 112947. doi:10.1016/j.enpol.2022.112947

Weaver, M. (2022, December 8). Millions cannot afford to heat homes as UK faces Arctic snap. *The Guardian.* https://www.theguardian.com/society/2022/dec/08/uk-weather-millions-households-cannot-afford-heat-homes

Website of the European innovation scoreboard. (2021s), https://ec.europa.eu/growth/industry/policy/innovation/scoreboards_en

Website of the European Union. (2021h), https://ec.europa.eu/growth/industry/policy/innovation/scoreboards_en

Website of the European Union. (2021m), https://ec.europa.eu/growth/industry/policy/innovation/scoreboards_en

Website of the Global Innovation Index. (2021o), https://www.globalinnovationindex.org,

Website of the World Intellectual Property Organization (WIPO). (2021n). https://www.wipo.int

Wenling, C. (2022, April 12). *The Battlefield Is in Ukraine, but the Whole World Is a Front*. Academic Press.

Williamson, O. (1964). *The Economics of Discretionary Behavior: Managerial Objectives in a Theory of the Firm*. Prentice-Hall.

Williamson, O. (1970). *Corporate Control and Business Behavior*. Prentice-Hall.

Willis, K. (2011). *Theories and Practices of Development*. Taylor & Francis. doi:10.4324/9780203844182

Wolfers, A. (1952). "National Security" as an Ambiguous Symbol. *Political Science Quarterly*, *67*(4), 481–502. doi:10.2307/2145138

Wong, K. C. (2021). The Rise of China's Developmental Peace: Can an Economic Approach to Peacebuilding Create Sustainable Peace? *Global Society*, *35*(4), 522–540. doi:10.1080/13600826.2021.1942802

Wooldridge, J. M. (2010). *Econometric analysis of cross section and panel data* (2nd ed.). MIT Press.

Worlanyo, A. S., & Jiangfeng, L. (2021). Evaluating the environmental and economic impact of mining for post-mined land restoration and land-use: A review. *Journal of Environmental Management*, *279*, 111623. doi:10.1016/j.jenvman.2020.111623 PMID:33223352

World Bank. (2019). *Nigeria - North-West Geo-Political Zone: Energy Access Diagnostic Report Based on the Multi-Tier Framework*. World Bank.

World Bank. (2023). *GDP growth (annual %) – China*. https://data.worldbank.org/indicator/NY.GDP.MKTP.KD.ZG?end=2019&locations=CN&start=2010&view=chart

World Bank. (2023, April 20). *The World Bank in China*. Retrieved from https://www.worldbank.org/en/country/china/overview

World Energy Council. (2008). *Europe's Vulnerability to Energy Crises*. Author.

World Energy Investment 2020 – Analysis. (n.d.). IEA. Retrieved July 11, 2023, from https://www.iea.org/reports/world-energy-investment-2020

World Energy Trilemma 2013: Time to get real – the case for sustainable energy investment. (n.d.). World Energy Council. Retrieved July 12, 2023, from https://www.worldenergy.org/publications/entry/world-energy-trilemma-2013-time-to-get-real-a-the-case-for-sustainable-energy-investment

Worldscience. (2023). *Industrial Overcapacity and Duplicate Construction in China: Introduction*. https://www.worldscience.com/doi/pdf/10.1142/9789813277281_0001.pdf

Wright, J., & Conca, J. (2007). *The GeoPolitics of Energy: Achieving a Just and Sustainable Energy Distribution by 2040*. BookSurge Publishing.

Würzburg, K., Labandeira, X., & Linares, P. (2013). Renewable generation and electricity prices: Taking stock and new evidence for Germany and Austria. *Energy Economics*, *40*, S159–S171. doi:10.1016/j.eneco.2013.09.011

Xi, J. (2017, May). *Work Together to Build the Silk Road Economic Belt and The 21st Century Maritime Silk Road*. Opening Speech, The Belt and Road Forum for International Cooperation.

Xi, J. (2021). Understanding the new development stage, applying the new development philosophy, and creating a new development dynamic. *China Daily*. https://www.chinadaily.com.cn/a/202107/12/WS60ec3e56a310efa1bd6614fb.html

Xie, B., Yang, C., Song, W., Song, L., & Wang, H. (2023). The impact of environmental regulation on capacity utilization of China's manufacturing industry: An empirical research based on the sector level. *Ecological Indicators*, *148*, 110085. doi:10.1016/j.ecolind.2023.110085

Xi, J. (2014). *The Governance of China*. Foreign Languages Press.

Xinhua. (2022). *Xi hosts High-level Dialogue on Global Development.* https://english.news.cn/20220624/b373551325e8468c976463eb9e33b9e7/c.html

Xinhua. (2023). *Xi Focus: China pursues development for people's well-being*. https://english.news.cn/20230309/dbf2e73bf1724030ad7f4b435237a86b/c.html

Xinhua. (2023, March 19). *Global Civilization Initiative Injects Fresh Energy into Human Development*. The State Council Information Office. Retrieved from http://english.scio.gov.cn/topnews/2023-03/19/content_85177312.htm

Xu, S., Lu, Y. H. M., Mutailipu, M., Yan, K., Zhang, Y., & Qvist, S. (2022). Repowering Coal Power in China by Nuclear Energy—Implementation Strategy and Potential. *Energies*, *15*(3), 1072. doi:10.3390/en15031072

Yanar, R., & Kerimoğlu, G. (2011). Türkiye'de enerji tüketimi, ekonomik büyüme ve cari açık ilişkisi [Energy consumption, economic growth and current account deficit relations in Turkey]. *Ekonomi Bilimleri Dergisi, 3*(2), 191-201.

Yang, J., Yu, Y., Ma, T., Zhang, C., & Wang, Q. (2021). Evolution of energy and metal demand driven by industrial revolutions and its trend analysis. *Zhongguo Renkou Ziyuan Yu Huanjing*, *19*(3), 256–264. doi:10.1016/j.cjpre.2021.12.028

Yang, Z., & Zhao, Y. (2014). Energy consumption, carbon emissions, and economic growth in India: Evidence from directed acyclic graphs. *Economic Modelling*, *38*, 533–540. doi:10.1016/j.econmod.2014.01.030

Yao, Y. (2022, February 25). *Global Development Initiative Provides a Blueprint for Responding to World Changes* ["全球发展倡议"为因应世界变局擘画蓝图]". Interpret: China. Retrieved from https://interpret.csis.org/translations/global-development-initiative-provides-a-blueprint-for-responding-to-world-changes/

YaoS.YangX. (2008). *Airport Development and Regional Economic Growth in China.* Reseach Paper, The University of Nottingham. https://ssrn.com/abstract=1101574 doi:10.2139/ssrn.1101574

Yasheva, G.A. (2008). Cluster concept of innovative development of the economy: justification and implementation mechanism. *Journal of Russian University, 4,* 64-72.

Yergin, D. (2008). The prize: The epic quest for oil, money & power. Free Press.

Yergin, D. (2012). The quest: Energy, security and the remaking of the modern world. Penguin Books.

Yikun, Z., Gul, A., Saleem, S., Shabbir, M. S., Bilal, K., & Abbasi, H. M. (2021). The relationship between renewable energy sources and sustainable economic growth: Evidence from SAARC countries. *Environmental Science and Pollution Research International*, *28*(25), 33390–33399. doi:10.100711356-021-12795-z PMID:33641094

Yildiz, I. (2019). Review of climate change issues: A forcing function perspective in agricultural and energy innovation. *International Journal of Energy Research*, *43*(6), 2200–2215. doi:10.1002/er.4435

York, R., & Rosa, E. A. (2003). Key challenges to ecological modernization theory: Institutional efficacy, case study evidence, units of analysis, and the pace of eco-efficiency. *Organization & Environment*, *16*(3), 273–288. doi:10.1177/1086026603256299

Yuan, J., Su, F., & Ouyang, X. (2022). *China's Evolving Approach to Foreign Aid.* Stockholm International Peace Research Institute. doi:10.55163/WTNJ4163

Yu, S., Hu, X., Li, L., & Chen, H. (2020). Does the development of renewable energy promote carbon reduction? Evidence from Chinese provinces. *Journal of Environmental Management, 268*, 110634. doi:10.1016/j.jenvman.2020.110634 PMID:32389898

Zaghdoudi, T. (2017). Oil prices, renewable energy, CO2 emissions and economic growth in OECD countries. *Economic Bulletin, 37*(3), 1844–1850. http://accessecon.com/Pubs/EB/2017/Volume37/EB-17-V37-I3-P167.pdf

Zahariev, E., & Arabska, E. (2014d). Eclectic concepts for distribution and popularization of good management practices. *VII International scientific conference „Innovations in technology and education" - Belovo*, 149-153.

Zapariy, V. V. (2017). Formation and development of a territorial manufacturing complex for the production of heavy tanks in Chelyabinsk in 1940-1945. Economic History, 13(4), 48-58.

Zerrahn, A., & Schill, W. P. (2017). Long-run power storage requirements for high shares of renewables: Review and a new model. *Renewable & Sustainable Energy Reviews, 79*, 1518–1534. doi:10.1016/j.rser.2016.11.098

Zerrahn, A., Schill, W. P., & Kemfert, C. (2018). On the economics of electrical storage for variable renewable energy sources. *European Economic Review, 108*, 259–279. doi:10.1016/j.euroecorev.2018.07.004

Zhang, C., & Chen, P. (2021). Industrialization, urbanization, and carbon emission efficiency of Yangtze River Economic Belt—Empirical analysis based on stochastic frontier model. *Environmental Science and Pollution Research International, 28*(47), 66914–66929. doi:10.100711356-021-15309-z PMID:34236609

Zhang, C., & Liu, C. (2015). The impact of ICT industry on CO2 emissions: A regional analysis in China. *Renewable & Sustainable Energy Reviews, 44*, 12–19. doi:10.1016/j.rser.2014.12.011

Zhang, F., & Graham, D. J. (2020). Air transport and economic growth: A review of the impact mechanism and causal relationships. *Transport Reviews, 40*(4), 506–528. doi:10.1080/01441647.2020.1738587

Zhang, H., Xiong, P., Yang, S., & Yu, J. (2023). Renewable energy utilization, green finance and agricultural land expansion in China. *Resources Policy, 80*, 103163. doi:10.1016/j.resourpol.2022.103163

Zhang, N., Yu, K., & Chen, Z. (2017). How does urbanization affect carbon dioxide emissions? A cross-country panel data analysis. *Energy Policy, 107*, 678–687. doi:10.1016/j.enpol.2017.03.072

Zhao, Patwary, Qayyum, Alharthi, Bashir, Mohsin, Hanif, & Abbas. (2022). The determinants of renewable energy sources for the fueling of green and sustainable economy. *Energy, 238*(PC). doi:10.1016/j.energy.2021.122029

Zhao, K., Feng, J., & Feng, L. (2021). Analysis of the long-term impact of energy expenditure on economic growth: A case study of China. *Biophysical Economics and Sustainability, 6*(11), 2–16. doi:10.100741247-021-00094-7

Zhao, S. (2020). China's Belt-Road Initiative as the Signature of President Xi Jinping Diplomacy: Easier Said than Done. *Journal of Contemporary China, 29*(123), 319–335. doi:10.1080/10670564.2019.1645483

Zheng, H., Song, M., & Shen, Z. (2021). The evolution of renewable energy and its impact on carbon reduction in China. *Energy, 237*, 121639. doi:10.1016/j.energy.2021.121639

Zheng, S., Lam, C. M., Hsu, S. C., & Ren, J. (2018). Evaluating efficiency of energy conservation measures in energy service companies in China. *Energy Policy, 122*, 580–591. doi:10.1016/j.enpol.2018.08.011

Zi, L. (2019). *Online urbanization: Online services in China's rural transformation.* Springer. doi:10.1007/978-981-13-3603-4

Ziółkowska, M. J. (2021). Digital transformation and marketing activities in small and medium-sized enterprises. *Sustainability (Basel), 13*(5), 2512. doi:10.3390u13052512

Ziyadov, T. (2012). *Beyond the Resource Curse.* University of Pennsylvania Press.

Zohar, D., & Zohar, D. (2022). The Tao of Quantum Management. *Zero Distance: Management in the Quantum Age*, 71-80.

Zreik, M. (2020). The Dimensions of the US-China trade war. *Open Political Science, 3*(1), 47–55. doi:10.1515/openps-2020-0004

Zreik, M. (2022). Contemporary geopolitics of Eurasia and the Belt and Road Initiative. *Eurasian Research Journal, 4*(1), 7–26. doi:10.53277/2519-2442-2022.1-01

Zreik, M. (2023). The Integration of China's Belt and Road Initiative Into Global Supply Chains: New Pathways for Social and Environmental Responsibility. In *Government Impact on Sustainable and Responsible Supply Chain Management* (pp. 74–94). IGI Global. doi:10.4018/978-1-6684-9062-4.ch005

Zukowski, M. (2022). A Small Modular House as a Response to the Energy Crisis. *Energies, 15*(21), 21. Advance online publication. doi:10.3390/en15218058

About the Contributors

Meltem Okur Dinçsoy an Associate Professor in macroeconomics at Trakya University, Faculty of Economics and Administrative Sciences. She completed her undergraduate degree at Karadeniz Technical University/Türkiye, Faculty of Economics and Administrative Sciences, Department of Economics. She completed her masters and doctoral degree in Okayama University/Japan, Graduate School of Humanities and Social Sciences, Comparative Economics. In field of macroeconomics, she has many papers in journals, books, book chapters and conference papers in international meetings and experiences on book editing. She gives undergraduate and postgraduate lectures on her research subjects and proficiency. She is also an advisor of the student communities of Trakya Banking Research Society. In addition, she is a member of faculty board of directors.

Hamit Can studied for a BA in Computer Engineering, Nutrition and Dietetics, Business Admistration and MA in Economics and PhD in Computer Science, Economics. His research interests include artificial inteligence, machine learning, data science, energy economics, economic growth, sports nutrition, clinical nutrition, phytotherapy. His paper on "The relationship between renewable energy consumption and economic growth: The case of Bulgaria" won the "Outstanding Paper Award" through the Emerald Publishing for International Journal of Energy Sector Management (IJESM) in 2020. In addition to his research, He serves as a referee for numerous professional Web of Science, Scopus indexed journals, including Environmental Science and Pollution Research, International Journal of Energy Sector Management, International Journal of Social Economics, World Journal of Science, Technology and Sustainable Development, Sustainability Accounting, Management and Policy Journal, Environmental Science and Pollution Research. He serves at the editorial board of CSR and Socially Responsible Investing Strategies in Transitioning and Emerging Economies, Three Seas Economic Journal. He has been cited over 130 times in scientific literature(h-index = 4). He also has internationally accredited certificates in these fields, including The British Dietetic Association (BDA), The Academy of Nutrition and Dietetics, Harvard University, Cambridge University, University of Oxford, Stanford University, Yale University, John Hopkins University, Case Western Reverse University, University of Cophenagen, Universite de Lausanne, University of Sydney, Universita Commerciale Luigi Bocconi, University of Colorado and San Diego, McMaster University, University of Minnesota, Emory University, University of Pennsylvania, Ludwig Maximilian Universitat Munchen, University of Edinburg, Illinois University, University of Toronto, Korea Advanced Institute of Science and Technology, University of Michigan, John Hopkins University, University of Florida

* * *

Solomon Aboagye is interested in issues related to sustainable development. His research has focused heavily in the areas of energy conservation, economic growth and environmental economics. His recent articles has been published in OPEC Energy Review, International Journal of Energy Sector Management and African Development Review.

Sedat Akbiyik is a head of IT department in Tekirdag Metropolitian Municipality, Türkiye. He completed his undergraduate degree in System Engineering from Turkish Military Academy, Türkiye and his master's degree in Public Administration from Anadolu University, Türkiye. When he served as the longtime manager at the Turkish Military, he directed numerous public safety and security practices in operational areas across the country. He also worked as a senior manager in the Department of Press and Public Relations and the Department of Information Technologies in Tekirdag Metropolitian Municipality. He played a leading role in the execution of various European Union projects, especially the Black Sea Buildings Energy Efficiency Plan (BSBEEP) project. His research interests are in the areas of information technologies, strategic planning, organization management, economic growth and national security.

Adjera Alitoska Kazaz is a PhD student in field of economics at Trakya University, Institute of Social Sciences. She completed her undergraduate degree at Trakya University/Turkey, Faculty of Economics and Administrative Sciences, Department of Economics, she distinguished herself by achieving the third position in her department, which represents a significant accomplishment. She completed her master's degree at Istanbul Commerce University, Institute of Social Sciences. Adjera's PhD thesis is on the import dependency of Turkish Manufacturing firms, where she is working with very comprehensive firm-level data. She has published papers in both academic journals and book chapters. From 2021 to 2022, Adjera was engaged with comprehensive firm-level data as a research assistant for a project supported by the Turkish Research Council. Additionally, Adjera contributed as an assistant in two worldwide workshops, thereby acquiring valuable experience. She's a member of the Administrative Board of the Institute of Social Science at Trakya University as a student representative and also a member of the Unit Quality Commission of the Institute of Social Sciences as an international student representative.

Korhan Arun graduated from Hacettepe University. He received his PhD in Business Administration. Since 1998, he has worked in various positions in the Ministry of National Defense and NATO staff, and since 2014, he started to give lectures at Tekirdağ Namık Kemal University as a lecturer. There are numerous Social Science Scitation Index (SSCI), Sciences Citation Index (SCI), Sci-Expanded, Publications and Book Chapters in Scopus Scanned Journals.

Mukesh Shankar Bharti is a research scholar with a research background in foreign policy analysis and social science research. The author holds a PhD degree in International Relations with a specialization in East and Central Europe. His research area includes democracy, political institutions, European Union and South Asia.

Seher Can is a lecturer at the Department of Nutrition and Dietetics at Trakya University, Edirne, Turkey. She has many papers in journals, books, book chapters and conference papers in international meetings and experiences on book editing. She gives undergraduate and postgraduate lectures on her research subjects and proficiency.

Enver Erdinç Dinçsoy is an Associate Proffesor at the Faculty of Applied Sciences at Trakya University. He completed his undergraduate degree at Karadeniz Technical University, Faculty of Economics and Administrative Sciences, Department of Business Administration. He also completed his master's and doctoral degrees at the Okayama University/Japan, "Department of Natural Sciences and Technology". In the field of economics, he has studied some research topics which are 'development', 'banking and finance', 'income distribution', 'spatial analyzes, 'environmental economics and policies'. In this context, He has scientific articles published in various domestic and international scientific journals, books and book chapters, conferences and seminars. He gives undergraduate and postgraduate courses within the scope of his research subjects and proficiency.

Muhammet Atlas Doğan is a Credit Risk Consultant at Prometeia. He earned his B.A. in Finance and Banking from Trakya University, his M.A. in Economics from Istanbul University, and is currently pursuing his Ph.D. in Economics at Istanbul Technical University. His primary research interests include central bank digital currencies, development economics, environmental economics, and the economic impacts of ESG and climate risks. Doğan has published several papers on these subjects and also taught courses on Statistics and Corporate Finance at Istanbul Bilgi University.

Muhammet Doğan is a Consultant at Prometeia. He earned his B.A. in Finance and Banking from Trakya University, his M.A. in Economics from Istanbul University, and is currently pursuing his Ph.D. in Economics at Istanbul Technical University. His primary research interests include central bank digital currencies, development economics, environmental economics and the economic impacts of ESG and climate risks. Doğan has published several papers on these subjects and also taught courses on Statistics and Corporate Finance at Istanbul Bilgi University.

Nikolay Todorov Dolchinkov is a graduate of Kyiv Polytechnic Institute, Kyiv. He obtained a doctorate degree at the Vasil Levski National Military University. He works as a teacher at the National Military University - associate professor in the Department of "Protection of the Population and Infrastructure" of the Faculty of "Security and Defense". Since the beginning of his academic career, his scientific interests have been closely related to radiation safety, nuclear power, electromagnetic radiation, physics and space exploration. He participated in projects with academic and national funding, including being the head of 2 projects financed by the "Scientific Research" Fund in Bulgaria. He is an active member of the editorial board of 5 international scientific publications and the chairman of the organizing committees of 2 conferences "Radiation safety in the modern world" and "Near Space - a common goal". Member of the Management Board of the Union of Physicists in Bulgaria, the Expert Commission at the Nuclear Regulatory Agency for cooperation with JINR and others.

Sercan Edinsel completed his undergraduate education at the Military academy, and his master's and doctorate degrees at Süleyman Demirel University. His fields of study are Organizational Change and Development Human Resources Management Strategy, Management and Organizational Behavior Organization Organizational Behavior Management and Organization Education.

Michal Fabuš, PhD, is an associated professor of Management, obtained at Presov University and PhD. in International Economics Relations, obtained at University of Economics in Bratislava. Vice-rector for Foreign Affairs, Head of Department of Economics and Finance, Bratislava University of Economics and Management (BUEM). Special interest in International Economics Relations, International business, and Foreign Direct Investment.

Marin Georgiev is an Associate Professor from Georgi Rakovski Military Academy, Sofia, Bulgaria. Ph.D. in Organisation and Management at Vasil Levski National Military University, Veliko Tarnovo, Bulgaria. Assoc. Prof. Georgiev has over 200 scientific papers, articles, and reports in Bulgarian, Russian, and English published in scientific journals and proceedings of international conferences, 2 monographs in Bulgarian, and 1 textbook. There are more than 40 publications in the referenced systems of Web of Science and Scopus. His research interests are in the areas of Economics, Education, and National security. Assoc. Prof. Georgiev is the editor of a Scientific Journal Society and Health.

Antonina Habova is currently Associate Professor at the Department of International Relations, University of National and World Economy, Sofia. She holds a Ph.D. in Political Science and an M.A. in International Relations from Sofia University, Bulgaria. Dr. Habova has been a visiting fellow at the Robert Schuman Center for Advanced Studies at the European University Institute (Florence, Italy), Freedom House (USA), the Academy of International Business Officials, MOFCOM (China) and Georgetown Leadership Seminar alumna (Edmund A. Walsh School of Foreign Service, Georgetown University). Her research interests lie in the area of geopolitics and China's foreign policy and strategy. She published more than 25 publications in the last ten years, including two books: The European Union and China. Principles, Prospects, Challenges (2018); China: Strategy and Foreign Policy (2018). She was a chief expert at the Administration of the President of the Republic of Bulgaria (2007-2012). From 2000 until 2007 she was Program coordinator and then Program Director at the Institute for Regional and International Studies, Sofia.

Davut Kazaz is a PhD student in the field of economics at Trakya University, Institute of Social Sciences. He completed his undergraduate degree at Trakya University/Türkiye, Faculty of Economics and Administrative Sciences, Department of Economics. He completed his master's degree at Trakya University, Institute of Social Sciences. Davut's PhD thesis focuses on the energy intensity of Turkish manufacturing firms, utilizing comprehensive firm-level data to explore this exciting topic. Davut also worked as a research assistant on a project funded by the Turkish Research Council between 2021 and 2022 in which he was involved with detailed firm-level data. Furthermore, Davut gained experience as an assistant in two global workshops. Currently, he is engaged in a research study that focuses on analyzing the effects of CO2 emissions on FDI.

Paul Adjei Kwakwa is a senior lecturer in Economics with the University of Energy and Natural Resources, Sunyani, Ghana. He is interested in issues related to sustainable development. His research has focused heavily in the areas of energy conservation, water conservation, gender, and resource and environmental economics. His recent articles has been published in Journal of Energy and Development, OPEC Energy Review, Development in practice, International Journal of Energy Economics and Policy, Research in Globalization, Renewable and Sustainable Energy Review, and Journal of Environmental Management.

Nikolay Blagoev Ninov is a graduate of the D. A. Tsenov Academy of Economics, Svishtov, Bulgaria. He works as a lecturer at the Academy - Associate Professor in the Department of Insurance and Social Affairs, Faculty of Finance. In the period 2016-2019, he held the position of Deputy Rector "Student Policy and Institutional Communications". Since the beginning of his academic career, his research interests have been closely related to the study and analysis of problems of an organizational, administrative-management and strategic nature of the systems of social defense - health care, social services and social assistance. He has participated in projects with academic and national funding, including in the position of "leading functional expert". He is an active member of the editorial board of 3 national scientific publications.

Valentina Nikolaeva Ninova is Head Assistant Professor, PhD, in the Department of Insurance and social security at the D.A. Tsenov Academy of Economics, Svishtov, Bulgaria. In 2017 she acquired a PhD degree in the field of insurance at the D.A. Tsenov Academy of Economics. Since 2014 she has been an assistant professor at the Department of Insurance and Social Affairs at the D. A. Tsenov Academy of Economics, Svishtov, Bulgaria, and since 2018 she has been the head assistant professor at the same department. Valentina Ninova is a team member of the Research project „Artificial intelligence in the economic perspective" No. KP-06-M65/2 from 12.12.2022, funded by The Bulgarian National Science Fund at the Bulgarian Ministry of Education and Science. Research interests: insurance, health insurance, bancassurance, cyber insurance, and AI. Memberships of professional societies: Eastern European Risk and Insurance Association (EERIA) and Union of Scientists in Bulgaria. In 2022 Valentina Ninova received the First Special Award of the Industrial Capital Association of Bulgaria from the Eighteenth National Competition "Young Economist 2022", organized by the Union of Economists in Bulgaria.

Olcay Okun graduated from the National Defense University. He received his PhD in Business Administration. Since 1998, he has held various positions in the Ministry of National Defense and NATO staff. He is currently a lecturer at the National Defense University. He adopted positive social psychology and positive organizational behavior phenomena as communication and management style in his duties and worked in this direction. In his academic studies, he tries to produce results by trying to carry the phenomena of management and organization to daily life. Publications and Book Chapters are available in Social Science Scitation Index (SSCI), Sciences Citation Index (SCI), Sci-Expanded, Scopus Scanned Journals.

Umut Erksan Senalp is a lecturer at the Banking and Finance Department at Trakya University, Edirne, Turkey. He received his BA degree in Economics in Turkey. He worked in the finance sector for a short time, then moved to the UK and obtained his Master's degree in Economics at the University of Manchester. He then completed his PhD studies at the University of York and Loughborough University. His research is mainly about international trade, specifically firms' internationalisation strategies. He is also interested in the economics of the penetration of renewable energy and the Turkish electricity market. He has run several projects funded by prestigious institutions such as the British Academy and Turkish Research Council (TUBITAK).

Ninel Seniuk, holds PhD degree in economics. She works as Associate Professor in the Department of International Relations, Faculty of World Economy and International Affairs at National Research University Higher School of Economics (Moscow). For many years she is focusing on different aspects of Outward Foreign Direct investment of China and other Emerging markets (especially BRICS countries) and the role of the emerging markets governments in OFDI of emerging markets MNC's. For the last several years she has been focusing on foreign direct investment in Global Value Chains. She has been involved in many research projects, including collaboration with UNCTAD and UNIDO. Which resulted in more than 30 publications (books, chapters, research papers, articles). She developed her authors courses on "Emerging markets of BRICS countries and Russia" and research seminar on "Business and Entrepreneurship in Asia". She is a member of Financial Service Working Group of BRICS Business Council and honorable member of International Technology Transfer Network (China).

Fatma Dila Taşdemir completed two different undergraduate degrees at Anadolu University/Türkiye, Faculty of Economics, Department of Economics and at Eskişehir Osmangazi University/Türkiye, Faculty of Science, Department of Mathematics. She completed her master degree in Eskisehir Osmangazi University/Türkiye, Graduate School of Science, Applied Mathematics, and her doctoral degree in Trakya University/Türkiye, Graduate School of Social Sciences, Economics. She has some papers and book chapters in field of macroeconomics, especially unemployment and economic growth topics.

Venelin Terziev is the editor-in-chief of a Scientific Journal Society and Health. He is a Professor from Angel Kanchev Rousse University – Bulgaria, Vasil Levski National Military University, Veliko Tarnovo, Bulgaria, and University of Telecommunications and Post, Sofia, Bulgaria. D.Sc. in Economics – "Organization and management in the sphere of immaterial production (defence and national security)" at the Vasil Levski National Military University – Veliko Tarnovo, Bulgaria; D.Sc. in Economics – "Finance, currency, credit, and insurance (social security)" at Dimitar Tzenov Academy of Economics – Svishtov, Bulgaria; D.Sc. in Social Activities – "Organization and management of social activities" at Burgas Free University – Burgas, Bulgaria; Ph.D. in Political economy at Chernorisets Hrabar Varna Free University – Bulgaria. Full Member of the Russian Academy of Natural History, Moscow, Russia. Prof. Terziev has over 2000 scientific papers, articles, and reports in Bulgarian, Russian, English, and French published in scientific journals and proceedings of international conferences; 40 monographs in English and Russian; 4 monographs in Bulgarian and 4 textbooks and handbooks. There are more than 200 publications in the referenced systems of Web of Science and Scopus. His research interests are in the areas of Education, Health care, Economics, Social work, and National security.

Elizabeth Yoneva holds a Ph.D. degree in Political Science. She is Associate Professor in the International Relations Department and Vice-Dean in Scientific and Research Activity of the Faculty of International Economics and Politics, University of National and World Economy, Sofia (Bulgaria). Her teaching activity and research interests include energy security, European integration and regional cooperation in the Black Sea zone and Central Asia. Elizabeth Yoneva is author of over 50 research articles in national and international journals and conference proceedings. The topic of her PhD thesis was: "The Black Sea Region in EU Energy Security: Evolution of Strategies and Policies". She was involved in several research projects, financed by national and EU funds. Elizabeth Yoneva is a member of the Bulgarian European Studies Association and the Bulgarian Political Science Association. Additionally, she is a member of the editorial board of the "Bulgarian Journal of International Economics and Politics" and of the scientific board of "The Scientific Bulletin" of Fan S. Noli University, Albania.

Mohamad Zreik is a recognized scholar in International Relations. His extensive knowledge spans Middle Eastern Studies, China-Arab relations, East Asian and Asian Affairs, Eurasian geopolitics, and Political Economy, providing him a unique viewpoint in his field. Dr. Zreik is a proud recipient of a PhD from Central China Normal University (Wuhan). He's written numerous acclaimed papers, many focusing on China's Belt and Road Initiative and its Arab-region impact. His groundbreaking research has established him as a leading expert in his field. His significant contributions make him a crucial figure in understanding contemporary international relations.

Index

R

S

T

U

V

W

X

Recommended Reference Books

IGI Global's reference books are available in three unique pricing formats: Print Only, E-Book Only, or Print + E-Book.

Order direct through IGI Global's Online Bookstore at **www.igi-global.com** or through your preferred provider.

ISBN: 9781668445488
EISBN: 9781668445501
© 2022; 334 pp.
List Price: US$ **240**

ISBN: 9781668467503
EISBN: 9781668467527
© 2022; 296 pp.
List Price: US$ **240**

ISBN: 9781799889007
EISBN: 9781799889021
© 2022; 340 pp.
List Price: US$ **215**

ISBN: 9781799898511
EISBN: 9781799898535
© 2022; 276 pp.
List Price: US$ **250**

ISBN: 9781799896913
EISBN: 9781799896937
© 2022; 219 pp.
List Price: US$ **215**

ISBN: 9781668436868
EISBN: 9781668436875
© 2022; 2,064 pp.
List Price: US$ **2,085**

Do you want to stay current on the latest research trends, product announcements, news, and special offers?
Join IGI Global's mailing list to receive customized recommendations, exclusive discounts, and more.
Sign up at: **www.igi-global.com/newsletters.**

Publisher of Timely, Peer-Reviewed Inclusive Research Since 1988

IGI Global PUBLISHER of TIMELY KNOWLEDGE

www.igi-global.com | Sign up at www.igi-global.com/newsletters | facebook.com/igiglobal | twitter.com/igiglobal | linkedin.com/igiglobal

www.ingramcontent.com/pod-product-compliance
Lightning Source LLC
LaVergne TN
LVHW062114300926
849161LV00010B/2456